AF683125

CASENOTE® Legal Briefs®

CONTRACTS

Keyed to Courses Using

Farnsworth, Sanger, Cohen, Brooks, and Garvin's Contracts: Cases and Materials Tenth Edition

Authored by: Publisher's Editorial Staff

ASPEN PUBLISHING

To contact Customer Service, e-mail customer.service@aspenpublishing.com, call 1-800-950-5259, or mail correspondence to:

Aspen Publishing
Attn: Order Department
1 Wall Street
Burlington, MA 01803

Printed in the United States of America.

1 2 3 4 5 6 7 8 9 0

ISBN 979-8-8890-6554-8

About Aspen Publishing

Aspen Publishing is a leading provider of educational content and digital learning solutions to law schools in the U.S. and around the world. Aspen provides best-in-class solutions for legal education through authoritative textbooks, written by renowned authors, and breakthrough products such as Connected eBooks, Connected Quizzing, and PracticePerfect.

The Aspen Casebook Series (famously known among law faculty and students as the "red and black" casebooks) encompasses hundreds of highly regarded textbooks in more than eighty disciplines, from large enrollment courses such as Torts and Contracts to emerging electives such as Sustainability and the Law of Policing. Study aids such as the *Examples & Explanations* and the *Emanuel Law Outlines* series, both highly popular collections, help law students master complex subject matter.

Major products, programs, and initiatives include:

- **Connected eBooks** are enhanced digital textbooks and study aids that come with a suite of online content and learning tools designed to maximize student success. Designed in collaboration with hundreds of faculty and students, the Connected eBook is a significant leap forward in the legal education learning tools available to students.
- **Connected Quizzing** is an easy-to-use formative assessment tool that tests law students' understanding and provides timely feedback to improve learning outcomes. Delivered through CasebookConnect.com, the learning platform already used by students to access their Aspen casebooks, Connected Quizzing is simple to implement and integrates seamlessly with law school course curricula.
- **PracticePerfect** is a visually engaging, interactive study aid to explain commonly encountered legal doctrines through easy-to-understand animated videos, illustrative examples, and numerous practice questions. Developed by a team of experts, PracticePerfect is the ideal study companion for today's law students.
- The **Aspen Learning Library** enables law schools to provide their students with access to the most popular study aids on the market across all of their courses. Available through an annual subscription, the online library consists of study aids in e-book, audio, and video formats with full text search, note-taking, and highlighting capabilities.
- Aspen's **Digital Bookshelf** is an institutional-level online education bookshelf, consolidating everything students and professors need to ensure success. This program ensures that every student has access to affordable course materials from day one.
- **Leading Edge** is a community centered on thinking differently about legal education and putting those thoughts into actionable strategies. At the core of the program is the Leading Edge Conference, an annual gathering of legal education thought leaders looking to pool ideas and identify promising directions of exploration.

Format for the Casenote® Legal Brief

Nature of Case: This section identifies the form of action (e.g., breach of contract, negligence, battery), the type of proceeding (e.g., demurrer, appeal from trial court's jury instructions) or the relief sought (e.g., damages, injunction, criminal sanctions).

Party ID: Quick identification of the relationship between the parties.

Fact Summary: This is included to refresh your memory and can be used as a quick reminder of the facts.

Rule of Law: Summarizes the general principle of law that the case illustrates. It may be used for instant recall of the court's holding and for classroom discussion or home review.

Facts: This section contains all relevant facts of the case, including the contentions of the parties and the lower court holdings. It is written in a logical order to give you a clear understanding of the case. The plaintiff and defendant are identified by their proper names throughout and are always labeled with a (P) or (D).

Issue: The issue is a concise question that brings out the essence of the opinion as it relates to the section of the casebook in which the case appears. Both substantive and procedural issues are included if relevant to the decision.

Concurrence/Dissent: All concurrences and dissents are briefed whenever they are included by the casebook author.

Analysis: This last paragraph gives you a broad understanding of where the case "fits in" with other cases in the section of the book and with the entire course. It is a hornbook-style discussion indicating whether the case is a majority or minority opinion and comparing the principal case with other cases in the casebook. It may also provide analysis from restatements, uniform codes, and law review articles.

Holding and Decision: This section offers a clear and in-depth discussion of the rule of the case and the court's rationale. It is written in easy-to-understand language and answers the issue presented by applying the law to the facts of the case. When relevant, it includes a thorough discussion of the exceptions to the case as listed by the court, any major cites to the other cases on point, and the names of the judges who wrote the decisions.

Quicknotes: Conveniently defines legal terms found in the case.

Palsgraf v. Long Island R.R. Co.

Injured bystander (P) v. Railroad company (D)

N.Y. Ct. App., 248 N.Y. 339, 162 N.E. 99 (1928).

NATURE OF CASE: Appeal from judgment affirming verdict for plaintiff seeking damages for personal injury.

FACT SUMMARY: Helen Palsgraf (P) was injured on R.R.'s (D) train platform when R.R.'s (D) guard helped a passenger aboard a moving train, causing his package to fall on the tracks. The package contained fireworks which exploded, creating a shock that tipped a scale onto Palsgraf (P).

RULE OF LAW

The risk reasonably to be perceived defines the duty to be obeyed.

FACTS: Helen Palsgraf (P) purchased a ticket to Rockaway Beach from R.R. (D) and was waiting on the train platform. As she waited, two men ran to catch a train that was pulling out from the platform. The first man jumped aboard, but the second man, who appeared as if he might fall, was helped aboard by the guard on the train who had kept the door open so they could jump aboard. A guard on the platform also helped by pushing him onto the train. The man was carrying a package wrapped in newspaper. In the process, the man dropped his package, which fell on the tracks. The package contained fireworks and exploded. The shock of the explosion was apparently of great enough strength to tip over some scales at the other end of the platform, which fell on Palsgraf (P) and injured her. A jury awarded her damages, and R.R. (D) appealed.

ISSUE: Does the risk reasonably to be perceived define the duty to be obeyed?

HOLDING AND DECISION: (Cardozo, C.J.) Yes. The risk reasonably to be perceived defines the duty to be obeyed. If there is no foreseeable hazard to the injured party as the result of a seemingly innocent act, the act does not become a tort because it happened to be a wrong as to another. If the wrong was not willful, the plaintiff must show that the act as to her had such great and apparent possibilities of danger as to entitle her to protection. Negligence in the abstract is not enough upon which to base liability. Negligence is a relative concept, evolving out of the common law doctrine of trespass on the case. To establish liability, the defendant must owe a legal duty of reasonable care to the injured party. A cause of action in tort will lie where harm, though unintended, could have been averted or avoided by observance of such a duty. The scope of the duty is limited by the range of danger that a reasonable person could foresee. In this case, there was nothing to suggest from the appearance of the parcel or otherwise that the parcel contained fireworks. The guard could not reasonably have had any warning of a threat to Palsgraf (P), and R.R. (D) therefore cannot be held liable. Judgment is reversed in favor of R.R. (D).

DISSENT: (Andrews, J.) The concept that there is no negligence unless R.R. (D) owes a legal duty to take care as to Palsgraf (P) herself is too narrow. Everyone owes to the world at large the duty of refraining from those acts that may unreasonably threaten the safety of others. If the guard's action was negligent as to those nearby, it was also negligent as to those outside what might be termed the "danger zone." For Palsgraf (P) to recover, R.R.'s (D) negligence must have been the proximate cause of her injury, a question of fact for the jury.

ANALYSIS

The majority defined the limit of the defendant's liability in terms of the danger that a reasonable person in defendant's situation would have perceived. The dissent argued that the limitation should not be placed on liability, but rather on damages. Judge Andrews suggested that only injuries that would not have happened but for R.R.'s (D) negligence should be compensable. Both the majority and dissent recognized the policy-driven need to limit liability for negligent acts, seeking, in the words of Judge Andrews, to define a framework "that will be practical and in keeping with the general understanding of mankind." The Restatement (Second) of Torts has accepted Judge Cardozo's view.

Quicknotes

FORESEEABILITY A reasonable expectation that change is the probable result of certain acts or omissions.

NEGLIGENCE Conduct falling below the standard of care that a reasonable person would demonstrate under similar conditions.

PROXIMATE CAUSE The natural sequence of events without which an injury would not have been sustained.

Note to Students

Aspen Publishing is proud to offer *Casenote® Legal Briefs*—continuing thirty years of publishing America's best-selling legal briefs.

Casenote® Legal Briefs are designed to help you save time when briefing assigned cases. Organized under convenient headings, they show you how to abstract the basic facts and holdings from the text of the actual opinions handed down by the courts. Used as part of a rigorous study regimen, they can help you spend more time analyzing and critiquing points of law than on copying bits and pieces of judicial opinions into your notebook or outline.

Casenote® Legal Briefs should never be used as a substitute for assigned casebook readings. They work best when read as a follow-up to reviewing the underlying opinions themselves. Students who try to avoid reading and digesting the judicial opinions in their casebooks or online sources will end up shortchanging themselves in the long run. The ability to absorb, critique, and restate the dynamic and complex elements of case law decisions is crucial to your success in law school and beyond. It cannot be developed vicariously.

In addition to *Casenote® Legal Briefs*, Aspen Publishing offers the following study aids:

- *Casenote® Legal Briefs*
- *Emanuel® Law Outlines*
- Emanuel® *Law in a Flash* Flash Cards
- Emanuel® *CrunchTime®* Series

Each of these series is designed to provide you with easy-to-understand explanations of complex points of law. Each volume offers guidance on the principles of legal analysis and, consulted regularly, will hone your ability to spot relevant issues. We have titles that will help you prepare for class, prepare for your exams, and enhance your general comprehension of the law along the way.

To find out more about our law school tools for success, visit us at *www.AspenPublishing.com* or e-mail us at *customer.service@aspenpublishing.com*. We'll be happy to assist you.

How to Brief a Case

A. Decide on a Format and Stick to It

Structure is essential to a good brief. It enables you to arrange systematically the related parts that are scattered throughout most cases, thus making manageable and understandable what might otherwise seem to be an endless and unfathomable sea of information. There are, of course, an unlimited number of formats that can be utilized. However, it is best to find one that suits your needs and stick to it. Consistency breeds both efficiency and the security that when called upon you will know where to look in your brief for the information you are asked to give.

Any format, as long as it presents the essential elements of a case in an organized fashion, can be used. Experience, however, has led *Casenote® Legal Briefs* to develop and utilize the following format because of its logical flow and universal applicability.

NATURE OF CASE: This is a brief statement of the legal character and procedural status of the case (e.g., "Appeal of a burglary conviction").

There are many different alternatives open to a litigant dissatisfied with a court ruling. The key to determining which one has been used is to discover *who is asking this court for what.*

This first entry in the brief should be kept as *short as possible.* Use the court's terminology if you understand it. But since jurisdictions vary as to the titles of pleadings, the best entry is the one that addresses who wants what in this proceeding, not the one that sounds most like the court's language.

RULE OF LAW: A statement of the general principle of law that the case illustrates (e.g., "An acceptance that varies any term of the offer is considered a rejection and counteroffer").

Determining the rule of law of a case is a procedure similar to determining the issue of the case. Avoid being fooled by red herrings; there may be a few rules of law mentioned in the case excerpt, but usually only one is *the* rule with which the casebook editor is concerned. The techniques used to locate the issue, described below, may also be utilized to find the rule of law. Generally, your best guide is simply the chapter heading. It is a clue to the point the casebook editor seeks to make and should be kept in mind when reading every case in the respective section.

FACTS: A synopsis of only the essential facts of the case, i.e., those bearing upon or leading up to the issue.

The facts entry should be a short statement of the events and transactions that led one party to initiate legal proceedings against another in the first place. While some cases conveniently state the salient facts at the beginning of the decision, in other instances they will have to be culled from hiding places throughout the text, even from concurring and dissenting opinions. Some of the "facts" will often be in dispute and should be so noted. Conflicting evidence may be briefly pointed up. "Hard" facts must be included. Both must be *relevant* in order to be listed in the facts entry. It is impossible to tell what is relevant until the entire case is read, as the ultimate determination of the rights and liabilities of the parties may turn on something buried deep in the opinion.

Generally, the facts entry should not be longer than three to five *short* sentences.

It is often helpful to identify the role played by a party in a given context. For example, in a construction contract case the identification of a party as the "contractor" or "builder" alleviates the need to tell that that party was the one who was supposed to have built the house.

It is always helpful, and a good general practice, to identify the "plaintiff" and the "defendant." This may seem elementary and uncomplicated, but, especially in view of the creative editing practiced by some casebook editors, it is sometimes a difficult or even impossible task. Bear in mind that the *party presently* seeking something from this court may not be the plaintiff, and that sometimes only the cross-claim of a defendant is treated in the excerpt. Confusing or misaligning the parties can ruin your analysis and understanding of the case.

ISSUE: A statement of the general legal question answered by or illustrated in the case. For clarity, the issue is best put in the form of a question capable of a "yes" or "no" answer. In reality, the issue is simply the Rule of Law put in the form of a question (e.g., "May an offer be accepted by performance?").

The major problem presented in discerning what is *the* issue in the case is that an opinion usually purports to raise and answer several questions. However, except for rare cases, only one such question is really the issue in the case. Collateral issues not necessary to the resolution of the matter in controversy are handled by the court by language known as *"obiter dictum"* or merely *"dictum."* While dicta may be included later in the brief, they have no place under the issue heading.

To find the issue, ask *who wants what* and then go on to ask *why did that party succeed or fail in getting it.* Once this is determined, the "why" should be turned into a question.

The complexity of the issues in the cases will vary, but in all cases a single-sentence question should sum up the issue. *In a few cases,* there will be two, or even more rarely, three issues of equal importance to the resolution of the case. Each should be expressed in a single-sentence question.

Since many issues are resolved by a court in coming to a final disposition of a case, the casebook editor will reproduce the portion of the opinion containing the issue or issues most relevant to the area of law under scrutiny. A noted law professor gave this advice: "Close the book; look at the title on the cover." Chances are, if it is Property, you need not concern yourself with whether, for example, the federal government's treatment of the plaintiff's land really raises a federal question sufficient to support jurisdiction on this ground in federal court.

The same rule applies to chapter headings designating sub-areas within the subjects. They tip you off as to what the text is designed to teach. The cases are arranged in a casebook to show a progression or development of the law, so that the preceding cases may also help.

It is also most important to remember to *read the notes and questions* at the end of a case to determine what the editors wanted you to have gleaned from it.

HOLDING AND DECISION: This section should succinctly explain the rationale of the court in arriving at its decision. In capsulizing the "reasoning" of the court, it should always include an application of the general rule or rules of law to the specific facts of the case. Hidden justifications come to light in this entry: the reasons for the state of the law, the public policies, the biases and prejudices, those considerations that influence the justices' thinking and, ultimately, the outcome of the case. At the end, there should be a short indication of thedisposition or procedural resolution of the case (e.g., "Decision of the trial court for Mr. Smith (P) reversed").

The foregoing format is designed to help you "digest" the reams of case material with which you will be faced in your law school career. Once mastered by practice, it will place at your fingertips the information the authors of your casebooks have sought to impart to you in case-by-case illustration and analysis.

B. Be as Economical as Possible in Briefing Cases

Once armed with a format that encourages succinctness, it is as important to be economical with regard to the time spent on the actual reading of the case as it is to be economical in the writing of the brief itself. This does not mean "skimming" a case. Rather, it means reading the case with an "eye" trained to recognize into which "section" of your brief a particular passage or line fits and having a system for quickly and precisely marking the case so that the passages fitting any one particular part of the brief can be easily identified and brought together in a concise and accurate manner when the brief is actually written.

It is of no use to simply repeat everything in the opinion of the court; record only enough information to trigger your recollection of what the court said. Nevertheless, an accurate statement of the "law of the case," i.e., the legal principle applied to the facts, is absolutely essential to class preparation and to learning the law under the case method.

To that end, it is important to develop a "shorthand" that you can use to make marginal notations. These notations will tell you at a glance in which section of the brief you will be placing that particular passage or portion of the opinion.

Some students prefer to underline all the salient portions of the opinion (with a pencil or colored underliner marker), making marginal notations as they go along. Others prefer the color-coded method of underlining, utilizing different colors of markers to underline the salient portions of the case, each separate color being used to represent a different section of the brief. For example, blue underlining could be used for passages relating to the rule of law, yellow for those relating to the issue, and green for those relating to the holding and decision, etc. While it has its advocates, thecolor-coded method can be confusing and time-consuming (all that time spent on changing colored markers). Furthermore, it can interfere with the continuity and concentration many students deem essential to the reading of a case for maximum comprehension. In the end, however, it is a matter of personal preference and style. Just remember, whatever method you use, underlining must be used sparingly or its value is lost.

If you take the marginal notation route, an efficient and easy method is to go along underlining the key portions of the case and placing in the margin alongside them the following "markers" to indicate where a particular passage or line "belongs" in the brief you will write:

N	(NATURE OF CASE)
RL	(RULE OF LAW)
I	(ISSUE)
HL	(HOLDING AND DECISION, relates to the RULE OF LAW behind the decision)
HR	(HOLDING AND DECISION, gives the RATIONALE or reasoning behind the decision)
HA	(HOLDING AND DECISION, applies the general principle(s) of law to the facts of the case to arrive at the decision)

Remember that a particular passage may well contain information necessary to more than one part of your brief, in which case you simply note that in the margin. If you are using the color-coded underlining method instead of marginal notation, simply make asterisks or checks in the margin next to the passage in question in the colors that indicate the additional sections of the brief where it might be utilized.

The economy of utilizing "shorthand" in marking cases for briefing can be maintained in the actual brief writing process itself by utilizing "law student shorthand" within the brief. There are many commonly used words and phrases for which abbreviations can be substituted in your briefs (and in your class notes also). You can develop abbreviations that are personal to you and which will save you a lot of time. A reference list of briefing abbreviations can be found on page x of this book.

C. Use Both the Briefing Process and the Brief as a Learning Tool

Now that you have a format and the tools for briefing cases efficiently, the most important thing is to make the time spent in briefing profitable to you and to make the most advantageous use of the briefs you create. Of course, the briefs are invaluable for classroom reference when you are called upon to explain or analyze a particular case. However, they are also useful in reviewing for exams. A quick glance at the fact summary should bring the case to mind, and a rereading of the rule of law should enable you to go over the underlying legal concept in your mind, how it was applied in that particular case, and how it might apply in other factual settings.

As to the value to be derived from engaging in the briefing process itself, there is an immediate benefit that arises from being forced to sift through the essential facts and reasoning from the court's opinion and to succinctly express them in your own words in your brief. The process ensures that you understand the case and the point that it illustrates, and that means you will be ready to absorb further analysis and information brought forth in class. It also ensures you will have something to say when called upon in class. The briefing process helps develop a mental agility for getting to the *gist* of a case and for identifying, expounding on, and applying the legal concepts and issues found there. The briefing process is the mental process on which you must rely in taking law school examinations; it is also the mental process upon which lawyers rely in serving their clients and in making a living.

Abbreviations for Briefs

acceptance	acp
affirmed	aff
answer	ans
assumption of risk	a/r
attorney	atty
beyond a reasonable doubt	b/r/d
bona fide purchaser	BFP
breach of contract	br/k
cause of action	c/a
common law	c/l
Constitution	Con
constitutional	con
contract	K
contributory negligence	c/n
cross	x
cross-complaint	x/c
cross-examination	x/ex
cruel and unusual punishment	c/u/p
defendant	D
dismissed	dis
double jeopardy	d/j
due process	d/p
equal protection	e/p
equity	eq
evidence	ev
exclude	exc
exclusionary rule	exc/r
felony	f/n
freedom of speech	f/s
good faith	g/f
habeas corpus	h/c
hearsay	hr
husband	H
injunction	inj
in loco parentis	ILP
inter vivos	I/v
joint tenancy	j/t
judgment	judgt
jurisdiction	jur
last clear chance	LCC
long-arm statute	LAS
majority view	maj
meeting of minds	MOM
minority view	min
Miranda rule	Mir/r
Miranda warnings	Mir/w
negligence	neg
notice	ntc
nuisance	nus
obligation	ob
obscene	obs
offer	O
offeree	OE
offeror	OR
ordinance	ord
pain and suffering	p/s
parol evidence	p/e
plaintiff	P
prima facie	p/f
probable cause	p/c
proximate cause	px/c
real property	r/p
reasonable doubt	r/d
reasonable man	r/m
rebuttable presumption	rb/p
remanded	rem
res ipsa loquitur	RIL
respondeat superior	r/s
Restatement	RS
reversed	rev
Rule Against Perpetuities	RAP
search and seizure	s/s
search warrant	s/w
self-defense	s/d
specific performance	s/p
statute	S
statute of frauds	S/F
statute of limitations	S/L
summary judgment	s/j
tenancy at will	t/w
tenancy in common	t/c
tenant	t
third party	TP
third party beneficiary	TPB
transferred intent	TI
unconscionable	uncon
unconstitutional	unconst
undue influence	u/e
Uniform Commercial Code	UCC
unilateral	uni
vendee	VE
vendor	VR
versus	v
void for vagueness	VFV
weight of authority	w/a
weight of the evidence	w/e
wife	W
with	w/
within	w/i
without	w/o
without prejudice	w/o/p
wrongful death	wr/d

Table of Cases

A Alaska Packers' Assn. v. Domenico *106*
Algernon Blair, Inc., United States v. *240*
Austin Instrument, Inc. v. Loral Corporation *108*

B Baby M., In the Matter of *190*
Bains LLC v. Arco Prod. Co. *261*
Balla v. Gambro, Inc. *187*
Bartus v. Riccardi *201*
Bayliner Marine Corp. v. Crow *5*
Bayway Refining Co. v. Oxygenated Marketing & Trading A.G. *64*
Beaver v. Brumlow *95*
Bel-Ray Company v. Chemrite (Pty) Ltd. *301*
Black Industries, Inc. v. Bush *159*
Bloor v. Falstaff Brewing Corp. *177*
Blossom Farm Products Co. v. Kasson Cheese Co., Inc. *178*
Bollinger v. Central Pennsylvania Quarry Stripping and Construction Co. *125*
Britton v. Turner *210*
By-Lo Oil Co. v. ParTech, Inc. *218*

C C. Itoh & Co. (America) Inc., v. Jordan Intl. Co. *62*
C.R. Klewin, Inc. v. Flagship Properties, Inc. *88*
Callano v. Oakwood Park Homes Corp. *35*
Campbell Soup Co. v. Wentz *224*
Canadian Industrial Alcohol Co. v. Dunbar Molasses Co. *276*
Central Ceilings, Inc. v. National Amusements, Inc. *91*
Channel Home Centers, Division of Grace Retail Corp. v. Grossman *82*
Chase Precast Corp. v. John J. Paonessa Co. *280*
Cohen v. Cowles Media Company *31, 46*
Colfax Envelope Corp. v. Local No. 458-3M *141*
Columbia Nitrogen Corp. v. Royster Co. *138*
Corinthian Pharmaceutical Systems, Inc. v. Lederle Laboratories *55*
Cotnam v. Wisdom *34*
Crabtree v. Elizabeth Arden Sales Corp. *93*
Cundick v. Broadbent *104*
Cyberchron Corp. v. Calldata Systems Development, Inc. *81*

D D & G Stout, Inc. v. Bacardi Imports, Inc. *32*
Dalton v. Educational Testing Service *173*
Dave Gustafson & Co. v. State *257*
Delacy Investments, Inc. v. Thurman & Re/ Max Real Estate Guide, Inc. *302*
Delchi Carrier Spa v. Rotorex Corp. *250*
Dickinson v. Dodds *56*
Dixon v. Wells Fargo Bank, N.A. *78*
Doe v. Great Expectations *164*
Dorton v. Collins & Aikman Corp. *61*
Douglass v. Pflueger Hawaii, Inc. *100*
Drennan v. Star Paving Co. *57*
Dyer v. National By-Products, Inc. *13*

E Eastern Air Lines, Inc. v. Gulf Oil Corporation *277*
Ever-Tite Roofing Corporation v. Green *54*

F Fairchild Industries v. Maritime Air Service, Ltd. *149*
Fairmount Glass Works v. Crunden-Martin Woodenware Co. *48*
Feinberg v. Pfeiffer Co. *14, 28*
Fera v. Village Plaza, Inc. *252*
Figgie International, Inc. v. Destileria Serralles, Inc. *136, 255*
Frigaliment Importing Co. v. B.N.S. International Sales Corp. *132*

G Gibson v. Cranage *196*
Gill v. Johnstown Lumber Co. *209*
Graham v. Scissor-Tail, Inc. *162*
Greenfield v. Philles Records, Inc. *128*
Grigerik v. Sharpe *290*
Groves v. John Wunder Co. *236*

H Hadley v. Baxendale *248*
Hamer v. Sidway *12*
Harrington v. Taylor *17*
Hassler v. Circle C Resources *183*
Hawkins v. McGee *3, 7*
Hicks v. Bush *197*
Hill v. Gateway 2000, Inc. *68*
Hitz Restaurant Group, In re *283*
Hochster v. De La Tour *215*
Hoffman v. Red Owl Stores *76*
Hurst v. W.J. Lake & Co. *133*

I In re. *See name of party*
International Filter Co. v. Conroe Gin, Ice & Light Co. *52*
Internatio-Rotterdam, Inc. v. River Brand Rice Mills, Inc. *194*
In the Matter of. *See name of party*
Iron Trade Products Co. v. Wilkoff Co. *214*

J Jacob & Youngs v. Kent *204*
Jorgensen v. Pressnall *202*

K K & G Construction Co. v. Harris *206*
Kanavos v. Hancock Bank & Trust Co. *216*
Kannavos v. Annino *116*
Kauders v. Uber Technologies, Inc. *70*
Keith v. Buchanan *152*
Kenai Chrysler Center, Inc. v. Denison *105*

Kenford Co. v. County of Erie . . . 251
Kincaid v. Eaton . . . 50
Kingston v. Markward & Karafilis, Inc. . . . 299
Kingston v. Preston . . . 199
Kirksey v. Kirksey . . . 18
Klocek v. Gateway, Inc. . . . 69
Koken v. Black & Veatch Construction, Inc. . . . 143
Krell v. Henry . . . 278

L
Lake Land Employment Group of Akron, LLC v. Columber . . . 19
Lake River Corp. v. Carborundum Co. . . . 258
Lamps Plus, Inv. v. Varella . . . 130
Langman v. Alumni Association of the University of Virginia . . . 89
Laredo Hides Co., Inc. v. H & H Meat Products Co., Inc. . . . 233
Lawrence v. Fox . . . 286
Lefkowitz v. Great Minneapolis Surplus Store . . . 49
Lewis v. Mobil Oil Corporation . . . 145
Lucy v. Zehmer . . . 44
Luttinger v. Rosen . . . 193

M
Macedonia Church v. Lancaster Hotel Limited Partnership . . . 294
Market Street Associates Limited Partnership v. Frey . . . 176
Martinez-Gonzalez v. Elkhorn Packing Co. LLC . . . 109, 112
Masterson v. Sine . . . 123
Mattei v. Hopper . . . 22
McCloskey & Co. v. Minweld Steel Co. . . . 217
McKenna v. Vernon . . . 213
McKinnon v. Benedict . . . 157
Meyer v. Uber Technologies, Inc. . . . 73
Mills v. Wyman . . . 15
Mineral Park Land Co. v. Howard . . . 272
Mitchill v. Lath . . . 121
Monarco v. Lo Greco . . . 98
Mooers v. Middlebury College . . . 39
Morris v. Sparrow . . . 10
Murray v. ILG Technologies, LLC . . . 288

N
Nanakuli Paving & Rock Co. v. Shell Oil Co. . . . 135
Nelson v. Hazel . . . 211
New England Structures, Inc. v. Loranger . . . 208
Newsome v. Western Union Telegraph Co. . . . 253
Northern Indiana Public Service Co. v. Carbon County Coal Co. . . . 281
Northrop Corp. v. Litronic Industries . . . 66
Northwest, Inc. v. Ginsberg . . . 174
NY Drilling, Inc. v. TJM, Inc. . . . 147

O
O'Callaghan v. Waller & Beckwith Realty Co. . . . 161
Oglebay Norton Co. v. Armco, Inc. . . . 84
Ortelere v. Teachers' Retirement Bd. . . . 102
Owen v. Tunison . . . 47

P
Pacific Gas & Electric Co. v. G.W. Thomas Drayage & Rigging Co. . . . 126
Parker v. Twentieth Century-Fox Film Corp. . . . 246
Peacock Construction Co. v. Modern Air Conditioning, Inc. . . . 195
Peevyhouse v. Garland Coal & Mining Co. . . . 238
Plante v. Jacobs . . . 234
Prasad v. Pinnacle Property Management Services, LLC . . . 170
Pyeatte v. Pyeatte . . . 36

R
R.E. Davis Chemical Corp. v. Diasonics, Inc. . . . 239
Raffles v. Wichelhaus . . . 140
Renner v. Kehl . . . 268
Ricketts v. Scothorn . . . 27
Rockingham County v. Luten Bridge Co. . . . 241

S
Sally Beauty Co. v. Nexxus Products Co. . . . 297
Seaver v. Ransom . . . 287
Sedmak v. Charlie's Chevrolet, Inc. . . . 230
Shadis v. Beal . . . 181
Sheets v. Teddy's Frosted Foods . . . 186
Simeone v. Simeone . . . 189
Sisney v. Reisch . . . 293
Sisney v. State . . . 291
Snow Phipps Group, LLC v. KCAKE Acquisition, Inc. . . . 227
Speakers of Sport v. ProServ . . . 117
Specht v. Netscape Communications Corp. . . . 45
Stees v. Leonard . . . 267
Stewart v. Newbury . . . 200
Stoll v. Xiong . . . 168
Strong v. Sheffield . . . 21
Structural Polymer Group, Ltd. v. Zoltek Corp. . . . 23
Sullivan v. O'Connor . . . 8
Sumerel v. Goodyear Tire & Rubber Co. . . . 269
Sun Printing & Publishing Ass'n v. Remington Paper & Power Co. . . . 83
Swift Canadian Co. v. Banet . . . 279
Swinton v. Whitinsville Sav. Bank . . . 115

T
Taylor v. Caldwell . . . 273
Tolosa v. HSBC Bank USA, N.A. . . . 86
Tongish v. Thomas . . . 245
Transatlantic Financing Corporation v. United States . . . 274
Trident Center v. Connecticut General Life Ins. Co. . . . 129
Trinidad Bean & Elevator Co. v. Frosh . . . 242
Tuckwiller v. Tuckwiller . . . 158

U
United States Life Insurance Company v. Wilson . . . 59
United States Naval Institute v. Charter Communications, Inc. . . . 9
United States v. *See name of opposing party*

V
Van Wagner Advertising Corp. v. S & M Enterprises . . . 225
Vitex Manufacturing Corp. v. Caribtex Corp. . . . 232
Vokes v. Arthur Murray, Inc. . . . 118

W W.W.W. Associates, Inc. v. Giancontieri *127*
Walgreen Co. v. Sara Creek Property Co. *229*
Walker & Co. v. Harrison *205*
Wasserman's, Inc. v. Township of Middletown *260*
Watkins & Son v. Carrig *107*
Webb v. McGowin. *16*
White v. Benkowski. *11*
White v. Corlies & Tift *53*
Williams v. Walker-Thomas Furniture Co. *166*
Wood v. Lucy, Lady Duff-Gordon *26*
Wright v. Newman. *29*
Wucherpfenning v. Dooley. *51*

X X.L.O. Concrete Corp. v. Rivergate Corp. *180*

Y Young v. City of Chicopee *282*

CHAPTER 1

Legal Bases for Recognizing and Enforcing Promises

Quick Reference Rules of Law

PAGE

1. *Hawkins v. McGee.* A party's statement can form the basis of a contract where all the circumstances can be interpreted as indicating that the statement was intended to induce the other party's action. 3

2. *Bayliner Marine Corp. v. Crow.* In assessing the merchantability of goods, the Uniform Commercial Code 2-314(2)(a),(c) requirement that goods must be such as would "pass without objection in the trade" concerns whether a significant segment of the buying public would object to buying the goods, while the requirement that goods "are fit for the ordinary purposes for which such goods are used" concerns whether the goods are reasonably capable of performing their ordinary functions. 5

3. *Hawkins v. McGee.* The true measure of a buyer's damages is the difference between the value of the goods as they would have been if the warranty as to the quality had been true and the actual value at the time of sale, including any incidental consequences within the contemplation of the parties when they made their contract. 7

4. *Sullivan v. O'Connor.* Where there is clear proof, a patient can maintain an action for breach of a doctor's agreement or promise to cure or bring about a given result. 8

5. *United States Naval Institute v. Charter Communications, Inc.* Damages for breach of contract are generally measured by a plaintiff's actual loss. 9

6. *Morris v. Sparrow.* An action for specific performance for the delivery of personal property may be maintained in equity where the personal property is unique. 10

7. *White v. Benkowski.* (1) A jury may take inconvenience into account in awarding exemplary damages. (2) Punitive damages may not be awarded for breach of contract. 11

8. *Hamer v. Sidway.* Forbearance is valuable consideration. 12

9. *Dyer v. National By-Products, Inc.* Settlement of an unfounded claim asserted in good faith constitutes valuable consideration for settlement agreements. 13

10. *Feinberg v. Pfeiffer Co.* Past services are not a valid consideration for a promise. 14

11. *Mills v. Wyman.* A moral obligation is insufficient as consideration for a promise. 15

12. *Webb v. McGowin.* A moral obligation is a sufficient consideration to support a subsequent promise to pay where the promisor has received a material benefit. 16

13. *Harrington v. Taylor.* Gratitude for a gratuitous act is insufficient consideration to enforce a promise. 17

14. *Kirksey v. Kirksey.* To be legally enforceable, an executory promise must be supported by sufficient, bargained-for consideration. 18

15. *Lake Land Employment Group of Akron, LLC v. Columber.* Continued employment alone satisfies the contractual requirement of consideration in a covenant not to compete entered by an at-will employee who is already employed by the employer. 19

16. *Strong v. Sheffield.* A purported promise is illusory and not consideration if by its terms the performance of the promise is entirely optional with the promisor. 21

17. *Mattei v. Hopper.* "Satisfaction" clauses do not render a contract illusory or raise problems of mutuality of performance. 22

18. *Structural Polymer Group, Ltd. v. Zoltek Corp.* (1) As a matter of law, there is mutuality of obligations in a requirements contract, and, therefore, sufficient consideration to support the contract, where the purchaser's requirements are not entirely determinable by the purchaser's subjective preferences but are determinable by objective criteria outside of the purchaser's control. (2) Where a jury awards damages under a requirements contract for lost profits from two products, but the contract limits the quantity the purchaser may obtain of either product, but not both additively, a court does not abuse its discretion in limiting the award so it is not duplicative. 23

19. *Wood v. Lucy, Lady Duff-Gordon.* While an express promise may be lacking, the whole writing may be instinct with an obligation – an implied promise – imperfectly expressed so as to form a valid contract. 26

20. *Ricketts v. Scothorn.* A promise may be legally binding without consideration if it reasonably induced action or forbearance and if injustice can be avoided by its enforcement. 27

21. *Feinberg v. Pfeiffer Co.* Where one acts in reliance on a promise, there is an enforceable contract under the doctrine of promissory estoppel. 28

22. *Wright v. Newman.* An obligation to support a child may arise by contract through promissory estoppel where an individual who is not the child's biological parent lists himself on the child's birth certificate as the father, even though he knows he is not; holds himself out as the child's father and allows the child to believe that he is the child's natural father; and where the child's mother relies on the individual's conduct to her and the child's detriment by refraining from identifying and seeking support from the child's natural father. 29

23. *Cohen v. Cowles Media Co.* Under the doctrine of promissory estoppel, a court should consider all aspects of a transaction's substance in determining whether enforcement is necessary to prevent an injustice. 31

24. *D & G Stout, Inc. v. Bacardi Imports, Inc.* A promise that the promisor should reasonably expect to induce action or forbearance on the part of the promisee and a third person and that does induce such action or forbearance is binding if injustice can be avoided only by the enforcement of the promise. 32

25. *Cotnam v. Wisdom.* A physician may recover in quasi-contract a reasonable compensation for emergency services rendered on the spot to an unconscious accident victim. 34

26. *Callano v. Oakwood Park Homes Corp.* A party with no direct relationship to another is not necessarily obligated to pay for any benefit received from that latter party on the theory of quasi-contractual liability. 35

27. *Pyeatte v. Pyeatte.* (1) An agreement between two parties does not rise to the level of a binding contract where the agreement lacks essential terms upon which the liability of the parties may be precisely fixed. (2) An educational degree, a professional license, or the increased earning potential these represent is not community property subject to valuation and division upon marital dissolution. (3) A spouse who has supported the other spouse in obtaining education can be awarded in restitution, upon marital dissolution, for the other spouse's direct living and educational expenses where the spouse has expected compensation for such expenses and it would be unjust to allow the other spouse to retain the benefits conferred by the spouse. 36

28. *Mooers v. Middlebury College.* (1) Terms in a contract are not enforceable where they are merely aspirational and are not specific and concrete promises. (2) An unjust enrichment claim that is plausibly pled, not foreclosed as a matter of law, and pled in the alternative to a breach of contract claim, should not be dismissed at the pleading stage. 39

Hawkins v. McGee

Patient (P) v. Physician (D)

N.H. Sup. Ct., 84 N.H. 114, 146 A. 641 (1929)

NATURE OF CASE: Appeal from decision to set aside verdict against surgeon for breach of warranty of success of surgical operation.

FACT SUMMARY: McGee (D), a surgeon, before operating on Hawkins's (P) hand, said, "I will guarantee to make the hand a hundred percent perfect hand or a hundred percent good hand." Hawkins (P) sued McGee (D) in contract for failing to make his hand perfect; McGee (D) contended that no contract had been made.

RULE OF LAW

A party's statement can form the basis of a contract where all the circumstances can be interpreted as indicating that the statement was intended to induce the other party's action.

FACTS: McGee (D), a surgeon, was to remove scar tissue from Hawkins's (P) right palm and then graft skin from Hawkins's (P) chest and place it on his palm. Prior to the operation, McGee (D) allegedly said, "I will guarantee to make the hand a hundred percent perfect hand or a hundred percent good hand." After the operation, which did not result in a perfect, one hundred percent hand, Hawkins (P) sued McGee (D) in contract, claiming that McGee's (D) statement constituted a warranty of a successful operation. Hawkins (P) asserted that the statement was made as an inducement to permit the operation to proceed, so McGee (D) could experiment with skin grafting, with which he had little experience. Allegedly, McGee (D) also repeatedly solicited the opportunity to perform the operation for the purpose of gaining more experience with grafting. McGee (D) countered that even if he had in fact made this statement, no reasonable person would understand it as an intention to enter into a contractual relationship, so that, as a matter of law, no contract was entered. The trial court nevertheless allowed the jury to consider whether McGee's (D) statement, in light of all the circumstances, could form the basis of a contract when taken at face value. The jury concluded that McGee's (D) statement was a warranty. On appeal, McGee (D) argued that the trial court erroneously submitted the issue of contract formation to the jury. The state's highest court granted review.

ISSUE: Can a party's statement form the basis of a contract where all the circumstances can be interpreted as indicating that the statement was intended to induce the other party's action?

HOLDING AND DECISION: (Branch, J.) Yes. A party's statement can form the basis of a contract where all the circumstances can be interpreted as indicating that the statement was intended to induce the other party's action. Although, as McGee (D) correctly contends, there may be instances where a statement cannot, as a matter of law, have the meaning attributed to it by the party seeking to have the statement form the basis of a contract, that is not the case here, since there were circumstances raised by Hawkins (P) that tended to support the interpretation Hawkins (P) attributed to McGee's (D) statement. Specifically, there was evidence that McGee (D) repeatedly solicited the opportunity to perform the operation, on the theory that he would use the operation to gain knowledge of skin grafting. Thus, it was proper for the trial court to permit the jury to consider whether McGee's (D) statement constituted a warranty, notwithstanding McGee's (D) argument that no reasonable person would understand his statement to be a warranty given the common knowledge of the uncertainty that attends all surgical operations, and the improbability that a surgeon would ever contract to make a damaged part of the human body "one hundred percent" perfect. Under all the circumstances, the question of contract formation was properly placed before the jury. [The court also discussed the proper measure of damages; see the brief later in this chapter.]

ANALYSIS

Before the operation, McGee (D) had also stated that Hawkins (P) would be in the hospital three to four days, after which Hawkins (P) could go back home and back to work, in a few days, "with a good hand." The court found that this statement, unlike McGee's (D) "perfect," "hundred percent" hand statement, would not justify a finding that McGee (D) contracted to complete the hospital treatment in three or four days or that Hawkins (P) would be able to go back to work within a few days thereafter. Instead, the court determined (as a matter of law) that this statement could only be construed as an expression of opinion or a prediction as to the probable duration of the treatment and Hawkins's (P) resulting disability, so that if these estimates were exceeded, no contractual liability could be imposed on McGee (D) as a result of the statement. Arguably, the only meaningful difference between the statement regarding the length of the hospital stay and recovery period, and the statement regarding the "perfect" or "hundred percent" hand was that in the latter, McGee (D) used the word

Continued on next page.

"guarantee," whereas in the former he did not; otherwise, there seems not to have been a good reason for not letting the jury decide whether McGee's (D) statement regarding the length of stay and recovery was also to be taken at "face value."

Quicknotes

BREACH OF WARRANTY The breach of a promise made by one party to a contract on which the other party may rely, relieving that party from the obligation of determining whether the fact is true and indemnifying the other party from liability if that fact is shown to be false.

CONSEQUENTIAL DAMAGES Monetary compensation that may be recovered in order to compensate for injuries or losses sustained as a result of damages that are not the direct or foreseeable result of the act of a party, but that nevertheless are the consequence of such act and that must be specifically pled and demonstrated.

CURE In a commercial transaction, the seller has a right to correct a delivery of defective goods within the time originally provided for performance as specified in the contract.

Bayliner Marine Corp. v. Crow

Boat manufacturer (D) v. Boat purchaser (P)

Va. Sup. Ct., 257 Va. 121, 509 S.E.2d 499 (1999)

NATURE OF CASE: Boat manufacturer's appeal from a judgment against it in a breach of warranty suit.

FACT SUMMARY: In the summer of 1989, John Crow (P) was invited by a sales representative for Tidewater Yacht Agency, Inc. to ride on a new model sport fishing boat manufactured by Bayliner Marine Corp. (D). Crow (P) was most interested in the speed of the boat, and after being given copies of "prop matrixes" and other promotion material, Crow (P) entered into a written contract for the purchase of the 3486 Trophy Convertible in which he had ridden. He took delivery in September 1989, and in 1992 filed suit for breached express warranties, implied warranties of merchantability, and fitness for a particular purpose (alleging lack of attainment of maximum speed).

RULE OF LAW

In assessing the merchantability of goods, the Uniform Commercial Code § 2-314(2)(a),(c) requirement that goods must be such as would "pass without objection in the trade" concerns whether a significant segment of the buying public would object to buying the goods, while the requirement that goods "are fit for the ordinary purposes for which such goods are used" concerns whether the goods are reasonably capable of performing their ordinary functions.

FACTS: John Crow (P) sought to purchase a fishing boat. When he asked the manufacturer, Bayliner Marine Corp. (Bayliner) (D), about the maximum speed, Bayliner's (D) representative explained that he had no personal experience with the boat. Therefore, the representative consulted two documents described as "prop matrixes," which were included by Bayliner (D) in its dealer's manual. The representative gave Crow (P) copies of the "prop matrixes," which listed the boat models offered by Bayliner (D) and stated the recommended propeller sizes, gear ratios, and engine sizes for each model. The "prop matrixes" also listed the maximum speed for each model. The 3486 Trophy Convertible (the boat ultimately purchased) was listed as having a maximum speed of 30 miles per hour when equipped with a size "20 × 20" or "20 × 19" propeller. The boat Crow (P) purchased did not have either size propeller but, instead, had a size "20 × 17" propeller. At the bottom of one of the "prop matrixes" was the following disclaimer: "This data is intended for comparative purposes only and is available without reference to weather conditions or other variables. All testing was done at or near sea level, with full fuel and water tanks, and approximately 600 lb. passenger and gear weight." Crow (P) purchased the boat. During the next 12 to 14 months, Crow (P) made numerous repairs and adjustments to the boat in attempt to increase its speed capability. Despite these efforts, the boat consistently achieved a maximum speed of only 17 miles per hour, except for one brief period. Crow (P) sued the manufacturer Bayliner (D), arguing it had breached express warranties and implied warranties of merchantability and fitness for a particular purpose. Judgment was rendered for Crow (P), and Bayliner (D) appealed.

ISSUE: In assessing the merchantability of goods, does the UCC § 2-314(2)(a),(c) requirement that goods must be such as would "pass without objection in the trade" concern whether a significant segment of the buying public would object to buying the goods, while the requirement that goods "are fit for the ordinary purposes for which such goods are used" concerns whether the goods are reasonably capable of performing their ordinary functions?

HOLDING AND DECISION: (Keenan, J.) Yes. Uniform Commercial Code (UCC) § 2-314 provides that in all contracts for the sale of goods by a merchant, a warranty is implied that the goods will be merchantable. Under UCC § 2-314(2)(a),(c) to be merchantable, the goods must be such as would "pass without objection in the trade" and as "are fit for the ordinary purposes for which such goods are used." The first phrase concerns whether a "significant segment of the buying public" would object to buying the goods, while the second phrase concerns whether the goods are "reasonably capable of performing their ordinary functions." In order to prove that a product is not merchantable, the complaining party must first establish the standard of merchantability in the trade. Here, Bayliner Marine Corp. (Bayliner) (D) correctly noted that the record contained no evidence of the standard of merchantability in the offshore fishing boat trade. Nor did the record contain any evidence supporting a conclusion that a significant portion of the boat-buying public would object to purchasing an offshore fishing boat with the speed capability of the 3486 Trophy Convertible (the boat at issue). Crow (P) nevertheless relied on his own testimony that the boat's speed was inadequate for his intended use, and on another witness's opinion testimony that the boat took "a long time" to reach certain fishing grounds in the Gulf Stream off the coast of Virginia. However, this evidence

Continued on next page.

failed to address the standard of merchantability in the trade or whether Crow's (P) boat failed to meet that standard. Thus, Crow (P) failed to prove that the boat would not "pass without objection in the trade" as required by the UCC. As to whether the record supported a conclusion that Crow's (P) boat was not fit for its ordinary purpose as an offshore sport fishing boat, the evidence was uncontroverted that Crow (P) used the boat for offshore fishing, at least during the first few years after purchasing it, and that the boat's engines were used for 850 hours. While Crow (P) stated that many of those hours were incurred during various repair or modification attempts and that the boat was of little value to him, this testimony did not support a conclusion that a boat with this speed capability is generally unacceptable as an offshore fishing boat. Finally, the statement in the sales brochure that the model of boat bought by Crow (P) "delivers the kind of performance you need to get to the prime offshore fishing grounds" merely expressed Bayliner's (D) opinion concerning the quality of the boat's performance and did not create an express warranty that the boat was capable of attaining a speed of 30 miles per hour. Reversed.

ANALYSIS

In *Bayliner*, Crow (P) contended that the "particular purpose" for which the boat was intended was as an offshore fishing boat capable of traveling at a maximum speed of 30 miles per hour. However, to establish an implied warranty of fitness for a particular purpose, the buyer must prove as a threshold matter that he or she made known to the seller the particular purpose for which the goods were required. In this regard, the *Bayliner* court noted that the record did not support a conclusion that Crow (P) had informed the manufacturer or the seller of this precise requirement. Although Crow (P) had informed them that he intended to use the boat for offshore fishing and discussed the boat's speed in this context, these facts did not establish that the seller actually knew on the date of sale that a boat incapable of travelling at 30 miles per hour was unacceptable to Crow (P). Accordingly, the *Bayliner* court concluded that the evidence failed to support the trial court's ruling that Bayliner Marine Corp. (D) had breached an implied warranty of fitness for a particular purpose.

Quicknotes

EXPRESS WARRANTY An express promise made by one party to a contract that the other party may rely on a fact, relieving that party from the obligation of determining whether the fact is true and indemnifying the other party from liability if that fact is shown to be false.

Hawkins v. McGee

Patient (P) v. Physician (D)

N.H. Sup. Ct., 84 N.H. 114, 146 A. 641 (1929)

NATURE OF CASE: Appeal from decision to set aside verdict for breach of warranty of success of an operation.

FACT SUMMARY: Hawkins (P) sued McGee (D) for not making his hand perfect after McGee (D) operated on it.

RULE OF LAW

The true measure of a buyer's damages is the difference between the value of the goods as they would have been if the warranty as to the quality had been true and the actual value at the time of sale, including any incidental consequences within the contemplation of the parties when they made their contract.

FACTS: Dr. McGee (D) was to remove scar tissue from the right palm of Hawkins (P) and then graft skin from the chest of Hawkins (P) and place it on his palm. McGee (D) stated that the hospital stay should be three to four days, and a few days after that Hawkins (P) could return to work with a 100 percent perfect hand. At trial, McGee (D) argued that even if this statement was made, no reasonable man would understand this as an intention to enter a contractual relationship. The trial court allowed the jury to consider pain and suffering due to the surgery and the positive ill effects of the surgery. The verdict was in favor of Hawkins (P), but McGee (D) moved to set aside the verdict because the damages were excessive. The trial court found the damages to be excessive and set aside the verdict, unless Hawkins (P) remitted all sums over $500. When Hawkins (P) refused, the verdict was set aside. Hawkins (P) appealed.

ISSUE: Is the true measure of a buyer's damages the difference between the value of the goods as they would have been if the warranty as to the quality had been true and the actual value at the time of the sale?

HOLDING AND DECISION: (Branch, J.) Yes. The true measure of damage is the difference between the value of the goods as they would have been if the warranty as to the quality had been true and the actual value at the time of the sale, including any incidental consequences within the contemplation of the parties when they made their contract. Therefore, the true measure of damages in the present case is the difference between the value to Hawkins (P) of a perfect hand, such as promised by McGee (D), and the value of the hand in its present condition. Included are any incidental consequences fairly within the contemplation of the parties when they made the contract. Any other damages are not to be given. Suffering does not measure this difference in value. Pain is incident to a serious operation. Submitting to the jury as a separate element of damage any change for the worse in the condition of the hand was erroneous and misleading. Instead, damages might properly be determined for McGee's (D) failure to improve the condition of the hand. New trial ordered.

ANALYSIS

Prior to a third trial over damages, McGee (D) notified his malpractice insurer, United States Fidelity and Guaranty Co., that he wanted to pay $1,400 to Hawkins (P) to settle the case. He was going to look to them for payment. When the company refused, McGee (D) brought suit, but the court found in favor of the insurance company, having concluded that its policy did not cover special contracts to cure. *McGee v. United States Fidelity & Guaranty Co.*, 53 F.2d 953 (1st Cir. 1931). The insurance company denied coverage as the verdict was for breach of contract and not the tort of malpractice, and its defense was sustained.

Quicknotes

BREACH OF WARRANTY The breach of a promise made by one party to a contract on which the other party may rely, relieving that party from the obligation of determining whether the fact is true and indemnifying the other party from liability if that fact is shown to be false.

CONSEQUENTIAL DAMAGES Monetary compensation that may be recovered in order to compensate for injuries or losses sustained as a result of damages that are not the direct or foreseeable result of the act of a party, but that nevertheless are the consequence of such act and that must be specifically pled and demonstrated.

CURE In a commercial transaction, the seller has a right to correct a delivery of defective goods within the time originally provided for performance as specified in the contract.

Sullivan v. O'Connor

Patient (P) v. Plastic surgeon (D)

Mass. Sup. Jud. Ct., 363 Mass. 579, 296 N.E.2d 183 (1973)

NATURE OF CASE: Action for damages for breach of contract.

FACT SUMMARY: Sullivan (P) claimed that O'Connor (D), a surgeon, had failed to fulfill his promise to enhance her appearance by the plastic surgery he performed on her nose.

RULE OF LAW

Where there is clear proof, a patient can maintain an action for breach of a doctor's agreement or promise to cure or bring about a given result.

FACTS: Sullivan (P), an entertainer, was awarded $13,500 for the alleged breach of contract that occurred when the plastic surgery performed on her nose by O'Connor (D), a surgeon, failed to produce the desired result. Sullivan (P) maintained that O'Connor (D) had promised the surgery would improve her appearance and enhance her beauty, but the evidence showed that her appearance had actually been worsened. Although the jury did not find negligence, it found that O'Connor (D) had breached his contract by failing to provide the promised result. However, O'Connor (D) appealed, arguing that agreements by which a physician undertakes to affect a cure or bring about a given result should be declared unenforceable on grounds of public policy.

ISSUE: Where there is clear proof, can a patient maintain an action for breach of a doctor's agreement or promise to cure or bring about a given result?

HOLDING AND DECISION: (Kaplan, J.) Yes. Where there is clear proof that such an agreement existed, a patient can maintain an action for breach of a doctor's agreement or promise to cure or bring about a given result. Although some courts have held such agreements unenforceable on public policy grounds, many decisions take the better view that such agreements can be sued upon as long as they can be adequately proven. That has been done in this case. Therefore, recovery was proper. Affirmed.

ANALYSIS

The emphasis on proving that an actual agreement to cure or achieve a specific result arose reflects the general concern that patients who desire change will transform a doctor's optimistic opinion into firm promises in their own minds. Thus, the courts that will enforce this type of promise require clear proof of the presence of the assent necessary for an agreement to arise. So wary are some jurisdictions that they statutorily require such promises to be in writing and signed by the physician to be charged to be enforceable.

Quicknotes

BREACH OF CONTRACT Unlawful failure by a party to perform its obligations pursuant to contract.

United States Naval Institute v. Charter Communications, Inc.

Author's assignee (P) v. Publisher (D)

936 F.2d 692 (2d Cir. 1991)

NATURE OF CASE: Appeal and cross-appeal from a judgment on remand awarding damages and profits in an action for breach of contract.

FACT SUMMARY: When Charter Communications (Charter) (D), the exclusive licensee for a paperback edition of a book, for which the United States Naval Institution (Naval) (P) was the author's assignee, shipped the paperback edition to retail stores prior to the date set in the contract, Naval (P) filed suit for damages and Charter's (D) profits on the hardback edition of the book.

RULE OF LAW

Damages for breach of contract are generally measured by a plaintiff's actual loss.

FACTS: The United States Naval Institute (Naval) (P), as the assignee of the author's copyright in *The Hunt for Red October*, granted Charter Communications (D) and Berkley Publishing Group (collectively, Berkley) (D) an exclusive license to publish a paperback edition of the book "not sooner than October 1985." However, Berkley (D) shipped the paperbacks to retailers earlier than October, so that the paperback went on sale September 15, 1985. Naval (P) sued for breach of the licensing agreement. The court awarded damages to Naval (P), calculating actual damages as the profits Naval (P) would have earned from hardcover sales in September if the competing paperback edition had not been released. The court also awarded Berkley's (D) profit on the displacing copies to Naval (P). Naval (P) appealed as to the profits award, and Berkley (D) cross-appealed.

ISSUE: Are damages for breach of contract generally measured by a plaintiff's actual loss?

HOLDING AND DECISION: (Kearse, J.) Yes. Damages for breach of contract are generally measured by a plaintiff's actual loss. While on occasion a defendant's profits are used as the measure of damages, this generally occurs when those profits tend to define the plaintiff's loss. Here, Charter Communications (D) and Berkley Publishing Group (collectively, Berkley) (D) alleged profits did not define the United States Naval Institute's (Naval's) (P) loss because those who bought the paperback would not have bought the hardcover version in any event. However, the court correctly calculated Naval's (P) actual damages by relying on August sales rather than the lower September sales of the hardcover version. Although there was a declining trend of hardcover sales from March through August, Naval (P) continued to average sales of some 3,000 copies a month in the latter period. Nothing in the record foreclosed the possibility that, absent Berkley's (D) breach, sales of hardcover copies in the latter part of September would have outpaced sales of those copies in the early part of the month. Thus, it was within the prerogative of the court as finder of fact to look to Naval's (P) August sales to quantify Naval's (P) loss. Reversed as to the award of profits but affirmed in all other respects.

ANALYSIS

In its analysis, the court of appeals looked to § 347 and § 356 of the Restatement (Second) of Contracts. An award of a defendant's profits where they greatly exceed the plaintiff's loss and where there has been no tortious conduct on the part of the defendant would tend to be punitive, and punitive awards are not part of the law of contract damages. However, it is proper to lay the normal uncertainty in hypothesizing possible sales at the door of the wrongdoer who altered the proper course of events.

Quicknotes

BREACH OF CONTRACT Unlawful failure by a party to perform its obligations pursuant to contract.

Morris v. Sparrow

Ranch owner (D) v. Cowboy (P)

Ark. Sup. Ct., 225 Ark. 1019, 287 S.W.2d 583 (1956)

NATURE OF CASE: Appeal from order requiring delivery of personal property in action for specific performance.

FACT SUMMARY: Morris (D) contended that Sparrow (P) could not enforce through equity, by an action for specific performance, an agreement to deliver to Sparrow (P) a horse in exchange for work performed by Sparrow (P) on Morris's (D) ranch.

RULE OF LAW

An action for specific performance for the delivery of personal property may be maintained in equity where the personal property is unique.

FACTS: Morris (D) owned a ranch and participated in rodeos, as did Sparrow (P), a cowboy who was adept at training horses. The men met at a rodeo and then both went to Morris's (D) ranch. They agreed that while Morris (D) left the ranch for 16 weeks, Sparrow (P) would take care of it for $400. Sparrow (P) claimed that in addition to the money consideration, Morris (D) promised him a horse named Keno. At the time Sparrow (P) arrived at Morris's (D) ranch, Keno was unbroken, but during his spare time, Sparrow (P) trained the horse to the point where, with very little extra training, Keno would be a first-class roping horse. Although Morris (D) paid Sparrow (P) the money, he refused to give him Keno, contending that Sparrow (P) was to get Keno only if he did a good job, which Morris (D) contended Sparrow (P) failed to do. Sparrow (P) brought suit in equity for specific performance of the alleged agreement, and the trial court ordered that Morris (D) deliver Keno to him. The state's highest court granted review.

ISSUE: May an action for specific performance for the delivery of personal property be maintained in equity where the personal property is unique?

HOLDING AND DECISION: (Robinson, J.) Yes. An action for specific performance for the delivery of personal property may be maintained in equity where the personal property is unique. Ordinarily, equity will not enforce through specific performance a contract for the sale of chattels. However, it will do so where special and peculiar reasons exist that make it impossible for the injured party to obtain relief through a suit at law for damages. Here, Sparrow's (P) turning Keno from an unbroken horse into a roping horse would have a peculiar and unique value, so that if Sparrow (P) were otherwise entitled to prevail, he should get the horse and not its monetary market value. As to whether the contract was conditional (i.e., depending on how Sparrow (P) performed), that is a fact question that was determined by the trial court, and that court's determination was not against the preponderance of the evidence. Affirmed.

ANALYSIS

The court here assumes that Sparrow (P) could not have obtained sufficient relief from money damages, but theoretically, expectation damages may have made him whole. Expectation damages are based on the particular promisee (here, Sparrow (P)) and, as noted in Restatement (Second) of Contracts § 347, look to the loss in value to the promisee plus any other loss, including incidental or consequential loss, less any costs avoided by not having to perform. Here, the loss in value to Sparrow (P) through Morris's (D) breach could be measured by market value. The "other loss" potentially could have been measured by the value to Sparrow (P) of training an unbroken horse and turning it into a roping horse and of owning such a horse. While it is difficult to place a value on these "other losses" it is not impossible. Often when performance might provide a peculiar and unique value, courts express the view that money damages are too speculative or uncertain, but in essence are ruling that it might be too difficult, or a drain on court resources, to make such a determination.

Quicknotes

EQUITY Fairness; justice; the determination of a matter consistent with principles of fairness and not in strict compliance with rules of law.

EXPECTATION DAMAGES Damages awarded in actions for non-performance of a contract; they are calculated by subtracting the injured party's actual dollar position as a result of the breach from that party's expected dollar position had the breach not occurred.

PROMISEE The party to whom a promise is made.

SPECIFIC PERFORMANCE An equitable remedy whereby the court requires the parties to perform their obligations pursuant to a contract.

White v. Benkowski

Neighbor (P) v. Neighbor (D)

Wis. Sup. Ct., 37 Wis. 2d 285, 155 N.W.2d 74 (1967)

NATURE OF CASE: Action in damages for breach of contract.

FACT SUMMARY: The Whites (P) contracted with the Benkowskis (D) to supply water for their house.

RULE OF LAW

(1) A jury may take inconvenience into account in awarding exemplary damages.
(2) Punitive damages may not be awarded for breach of contract.

FACTS: The Whites (P) purchased a home that had no water supply. The Whites (P) entered into a 10-year contract with their next-door neighbors, the Benkowskis (D), to use the Benkowskis' well for water. After a few years, the relationship between the parties deteriorated. The Benkowskis (D) shut off the water several times allegedly to clear the pipes and to remind the Whites (P) that they were using too much water. The Whites (P), during these periods, had to bathe their children elsewhere and put up with bathroom odors. The Whites (P) filed suit for exemplary and punitive damages. The jury awarded the Whites (P) $10 in exemplary damages, no pecuniary loss being proved or pleaded, and $2,000 in punitive damages. The court reduced the exemplary damages to $1 since no pecuniary loss was proved and disallowed all punitive damages.

ISSUE:

(1) May a jury take into account inconvenience in awarding exemplary damages?
(2) May punitive damages be awarded for breach of contract?

HOLDING AND DECISION: (Wilkie, J.)

(1) Yes. A jury may take inconvenience into account in awarding exemplary damages.
(2) No. Punitive damages may not be awarded for breach of contract. A nominal award may be rendered for personal inconvenience due to a breach of contract. Ten dollars is such a nominal amount and is clearly sustainable under the evidence. Punitive damages are never authorized in breach of contract actions. It is immaterial whether the breach was either intentional and/or malicious. No moral penalties may be assessed for mere breach of contract. Reversed in part and affirmed in part.

ANALYSIS

Some breach of contract actions include tortious conduct for which punitive damages may be awarded. To recover such damages, a tort must be separately pleaded and proved. Every breach of contract is actionable. Trivial breaches or breaches that cause no pecuniary loss will normally result in an award of minimal damages as herein. Damages for breach of contract are meant only to place the injured party in the same position he or she would have been in if the breach had not occurred.

Quicknotes

BREACH OF CONTRACT Unlawful failure by a party to perform its obligations pursuant to contract.

EXEMPLARY DAMAGES Damages exceeding the actual injury suffered for the purposes of punishment, deterrence, and comfort to plaintiff.

PECUNIARY LOSS Loss of money or the loss of something of monetary value.

PUNITIVE DAMAGES Damages exceeding the actual injury suffered for the purposes of punishment, deterrence of the wrongful behavior, or comfort to the plaintiff. Also called "exemplary damages."

Hamer v. Sidway

Assignee (P) v. Estate executor (D)

N.Y. Ct. App., 124 N.Y. 538, 27 N.E. 256 (1891)

NATURE OF CASE: Action on appeal to recover upon a contract that is supported by forbearance of a right as consideration.

FACT SUMMARY: William E. Story, Sr., promised to pay $5,000 to William E. Story, 2d, if he would forbear in the use of liquor, tobacco, swearing, and playing cards or billiards for money until he became 21 years of age.

RULE OF LAW
Forbearance is valuable consideration.

FACTS: William E. Story, Sr., agreed with his nephew William E. Story, 2d, that if William E. Story, 2d, would refrain from drinking liquor, using tobacco, swearing, and playing cards or billiards for money until he became 21 years of age, he (William E. Story, Sr.) would pay him $5,000. Upon becoming 21 years of age, William E. Story, 2d, received a letter from his uncle stating he had earned the $5,000 and it would be kept at interest for him. Twelve years later William E. Story, Sr., died and this action was brought by the assignees of William E. Story, 2d, against the executor of the estate of William E. Story, Sr. Judgment was entered in favor of Hamer (P), the assignee, at the trial at Special Term and was reversed at General Term of the Supreme Court. Hamer (P) appealed.

ISSUE: Is forbearance on the part of a promisee sufficient consideration to support a contract?

HOLDING AND DECISION: (Parker, J.) Yes. Forbearance on the part of a promisee is sufficient consideration to support a contract. Valuable consideration may consist either of some right, interest, profit, or benefit accruing to the one party, or some forbearance, detriment, loss, or responsibility given, suffered, or undertaken by the other. The promise by William E. Story, Sr., is enforceable. Reversed.

ANALYSIS

The surrendering or forgoing of a legal right constitutes a sufficient consideration for a contract if the minds of the parties meet on the relinquishment of the right as a consideration. Consideration may be forbearance to sue on a claim, extension of time, or any other giving up of a legal right in consideration of a promise.

Quicknotes

CONSIDERATION Value given by one party in exchange for performance, or a promise to perform, by another party.

FORBEARANCE The act of refraining from doing something that one has the legal right to do.

PROMISEE The party to whom a promise is made.

Dyer v. National By-Products, Inc.

Employee (P) v. Employer (D)

Iowa. Sup. Ct., 380 N.W.2d 732 (1986)

NATURE OF CASE: Appeal for summary judgment dismissing a breach of contract action.

FACT SUMMARY: Dyer (P) sued National By-Products, Inc. (D) for breach of a settlement agreement regarding a job-related accident.

RULE OF LAW

Settlement of an unfounded claim asserted in good faith constitutes valuable consideration for settlement agreements.

FACTS: Dyer (P) was employed as a foreman for National By-Products, Inc. (National) (D). On October 29, 1981, Dyer (P) lost his right foot in a job-related accident. Dyer (P) returned to work as a foreman for National (D) on August 16, 1982, after a fully paid leave of absence. On March 11, 1983, National (D) indefinitely laid off Dyer (P). Dyer (P) sued National (D) for breach of a settlement agreement alleging that in exchange for Dyer (P) foregoing a lawsuit against National (D), National (D) agreed to employ Dyer (P) for life. National (D) denied making such a deal since Dyer (P) was barred from a civil lawsuit by Workers' Compensation. National (D) maintained that even if a settlement agreement existed, Dyer's (P) forbearance of an invalid claim did not constitute valuable consideration for the agreement. The trial court granted summary judgment, and Dyer (P) appealed.

ISSUE: Does settlement of an unfounded claim asserted in good faith constitute valuable consideration for a settlement agreement?

HOLDING AND DECISION: (Schultz, J.) Yes. Settlement of an unfounded claim asserted in good faith constitutes valuable consideration for a settlement agreement. It is in the best interests of the legal system to encourage settlement and negotiation. Thus, circumstances may arise where forbearance of an invalid claim can constitute sufficient consideration. So long as the forbearing party has a good-faith belief that he is forbearing the pursuit of a legitimate claim, such forbearance will be valid consideration. Summary judgment was inappropriate in the instant case because a material question of fact existed as to whether Dyer (P) had a good-faith belief that his civil claim was valid. Reversed and remanded.

ANALYSIS

This case highlights the significance of valuable consideration in the context of contractual obligations. Often, the issue of consideration can be manipulated to rectify social justice concerns. When one party has more power than another, valuable consideration in contractual obligations can be used to level the playing field.

Quicknotes

FORBEARANCE The act of refraining from doing something that one has the legal right to do.

GOOD FAITH An honest intention to abstain from taking advantage of another.

SUMMARY JUDGMENT Judgment rendered by a court in response to a motion made by one of the parties, claiming that the lack of a question of material fact in respect to an issue warrants disposition of the issue without consideration by the jury.

VALUABLE CONSIDERATION Value given by one party in exchange for performance, or a promise to perform, by another party.

Feinberg v. Pfeiffer Co.

Retired employee (P) v. Employer (D)

Mo. Ct. App., 322 S.W.2d 163 (1959)

NATURE OF CASE: Action on appeal by defendant to show failure of contract due to lack of consideration.

FACT SUMMARY: Anna Feinberg (P) was given a pension for life by Pfeiffer Co. (D) based upon her past service to Pfeiffer Co. (D). Pfeiffer Co. (D) subsequently refused to pay the pension claiming lack of consideration for its promise to do so.

RULE OF LAW

Past services are not a valid consideration for a promise.

FACTS: Anna Feinberg (P) had been a bookkeeper for Pfeiffer Co. (D) for 37 years. The board of Pfeiffer Co. (D) voted to give her a lifetime pension at any time she chose to retire. The pension was based upon Mrs. Feinberg's (P) past service to the company and not upon her continued service. A year and a half after learning of the pension, Mrs. Feinberg (P) retired and began receiving the pension. Six years after her retirement, Pfeiffer Co. (D) refused to continue paying Mrs. Feinberg (P) her pension upon the advice of its attorney and accountants that there existed no valid consideration for the promise to pay. Mrs. Feinberg (P) brought an action to compel payment of her pension by Pfeiffer Co. (D), and the lower court held for her. Pfeiffer Co. (D) appealed.

ISSUE: Are past services valid consideration for a promise?

HOLDING AND DECISION: (Doerner, Comm'r) No. Past services are not a valid consideration for a promise. Since Mrs. Feinberg (P) made no promise or agreement to continue in the employment of Pfeiffer Co. (D) in return for its promise to pay her a pension, there existed no mutuality of obligation, which is essential to the validity of a contract. Affirmed on other grounds.

ANALYSIS

Note that, in the present case, if Feinberg (P) were still healthy and able to work, the decision would have been different. In that situation, it would not be the case that injustice could be avoided only by enforcement of the promise. Note additionally that if Feinberg (P) had continued to work for Pfeiffer Co. (D) until she became physically unable to continue and was forced to retire, she probably could not recover on Pfeiffer Co.'s (D) promise. Her retirement would not have been in reliance on Pfeiffer's (D) promise as the doctrine of promissory estoppel requires.

Quicknotes

CONSIDERATION Value given by one party in exchange for performance, or a promise to perform, by another party.

MUTUALITY OF OBLIGATION Requires that both parties to a contract be bound or else neither is bound.

PROMISE The expression of an intention to act, or to forbear from acting, granting a right to the promisee to expect and enforce its performance.

PROMISEE The party to whom a promise is made.

PROMISOR The party who promises to render an obligation to another in the future.

PROMISSORY ESTOPPEL A promise that is enforceable if the promisor should reasonably expect that it will induce action or forbearance on the part of the promisee, that does in fact cause such action or forbearance, and that is the only means of avoiding injustice.

Mills v. Wyman

Nurse-caretaker (P) v. Parent (D)

Mass. Sup. Jud. Ct., 20 Mass. (3 Pick.) 207 (1825)

NATURE OF CASE: Action on appeal to recover on alleged promise.

FACT SUMMARY: Mills (P) took care of Wyman's (D) son without being requested to do so and for so doing was promised compensation by Wyman (D) for expenses arising out of the rendered care. Wyman (D) later refused to compensate Mills (P).

RULE OF LAW

A moral obligation is insufficient as consideration for a promise.

FACTS: Mills (P) nursed and cared for Levi Wyman, the son of Wyman (D). Upon learning of Mills's (P) acts of kindness toward his son, Wyman (D) promised to repay Mills (P) his expenses incurred in caring for Levi Wyman. Later, Wyman (D) refused to compensate Mills (P) for his expenses. Mills (P) filed an action in the Court of Common Pleas where Wyman (D) was successful in obtaining a nonsuit against Mills (P). Mills (P) appealed.

ISSUE: Is a moral obligation sufficient consideration for a promise?

HOLDING AND DECISION: (Parker, C.J.) No. A moral obligation is not sufficient consideration to support an express promise. However, the universality of the rule cannot be supported. Therefore, there must be some other preexisting obligation that will suffice as consideration. Affirmed.

ANALYSIS

In cases such as this one, the nearly universal holding is that the existing moral obligation is not a sufficient basis for the enforcement of an express promise to render the performance that it requires. The general statement is that it is not sufficient consideration for the express promise. The difficulties and differences of opinion involved in the determination of what is a moral obligation are probably much greater than those involved in determining the existence of a legal obligation. This tends to explain the attitude of the majority of courts on the subject and justifies the generally stated rule.

Quicknotes

CONSIDERATION Value given by one party in exchange for performance, or a promise to perform, by another party.

EXPRESS PROMISE The expression of an intention to act, or to forbear from acting, granting a right to the promisee to expect and enforce its performance.

MORAL OBLIGATION A duty that is not enforceable at law, but that is consistent with ethical notions of justice.

PROMISEE The party to whom a promise is made.

Webb v. McGowin

Conscientious worker (P) v. Grateful pedestrian (D)

Ala. Ct. App., 27 Ala. App. 82, 168 So. 196 (1935)

NATURE OF CASE: Action on appeal to collect on a promise.

FACT SUMMARY: Webb (P) saved the now deceased J. McGowin from grave bodily injury or death by placing himself in grave danger and subsequently suffering grave bodily harm. J. McGowin, in return, promised Webb (P) compensation. McGowin's executors (D) now refuse to pay the promised compensation.

RULE OF LAW

A moral obligation is a sufficient consideration to support a subsequent promise to pay where the promisor has received a material benefit.

FACTS: Webb (P), while in the scope of his duties for the W. T. Smith Lumber Co., was clearing the floor, which required him to drop a 75-lb. pine block from the upper floor of the mill to the ground. Just as Webb (P) was releasing the block, he noticed J. McGowin below and directly under where the block would have fallen. In order to divert the fall of the block, Webb (P) fell with it, breaking an arm and leg and ripping his heel off. The fall left Webb (P) a cripple and incapable of either mental or physical labor. In return for Webb's (P) act, J. McGowin promised to pay Webb (P) $15 every two weeks for the rest of Webb's (P) life. J. McGowin paid the promised payments until his death eight years later. Shortly after J. McGowin's death, the payments were stopped, and Webb (P) brought an action against N. McGowin (D) and J. F. McGowin (D) as executors of J. McGowin's estate for payments due him. The executors (D) of the estate were successful in obtaining a nonsuit against Webb (P) in the lower court. Webb (P) appeals.

ISSUE: Was the moral obligation to compensate as promised sufficient consideration?

HOLDING AND DECISION: (Bricken, P.J.) Yes. It is well settled that a moral obligation is a sufficient consideration to support a subsequent promise to pay where the promisor has received a material benefit, although there was no original duty or liability resting on the promisor. Reversed and remanded.

CONCURRENCE: (Samford, J.) If the benefit is material and substantial, and if it was to the person of the promisor rather than to his estate, it is within the class of material benefits which he has the privilege of recognizing and compensating either by an executed payment or an executed promise to pay.

PETITION FOR REHEARING: (Foster, J.) If the benefit was material and substantial, and if it was to the person of the promisor rather than to his estate, it is within the class of material benefits which he has the privilege of recognizing and compensating either by an executed payment or an executed promise to pay. When the compensation is not only for the benefits that the promisor received, but also for the injuries either to the property or person of the promisee by reason of the services rendered, it fits within the above general rule recognizing that more than a moral benefit is involved. The rehearing is denied.

ANALYSIS

In most cases where the moral obligation is asserted, the court feels that the promise ought not to be enforced; instead of going into the uncertain field of morality the court chooses to rely upon the rule that moral obligation is not a sufficient consideration. On the other hand, in cases where the promise is one that would have been kept by most citizens and the court feels that enforcement is just, a few courts will enforce the promise using the *Webb v. McGowin* rule. In general, the *Webb v. McGowin* rule is the minority rule and the *Mills v. Wyman* (Mass. 1825), the majority rule.

Quicknotes

EXECUTORY PROMISE A promise to perform an action that has not yet been performed.

MATERIAL BENEFIT An advantage gained by entering into a contract that is essential to the performance of the agreement and without which the contract would not have been entered into.

MORAL CONSIDERATION An inducement to enter a contract that is not enforceable at law, but is made based on a moral obligation, and may be enforceable in order to prevent unjust enrichment on the part of the promisor.

Harrington v. Taylor

Injured rescuer promisee (P) v. Rescued promisor (D)

N.C. Sup. Ct., 225 N.C. 690, 36 S.E.2d 227 (1945)

NATURE OF CASE: Appeal in action to enforce a contract.

FACT SUMMARY: In gratitude for Harrington's (P) efforts in saving his life, Taylor (D) promised to pay her for her injuries.

RULE OF LAW

Gratitude for a gratuitous act is insufficient consideration to enforce a promise.

FACTS: Harrington (P) prevented Taylor (D) from being killed by his wife. Harrington (P) was severely injured. The next day, Taylor (D) promised to pay Harrington (P) for her injuries. Taylor (D) paid a small amount and then refused to make further payments. Harrington (P) sued for breach of contract, and Taylor (D) alleged that the contract was unenforceable for lack of consideration. The trial court found for Taylor (D) and Harrington (P) appealed.

ISSUE: Is gratitude for a gratuitous act sufficient consideration to enforce a contract?

HOLDING AND DECISION: (Per curiam) No. Gratitude or moral obligations arising from a gratuitous, humanitarian act are not sufficient considerations to enforce a contract. No matter how much we personally find Taylor's (D) refusal to pay improper, as a matter of law the promise to pay for Harrington's (P) injuries is unenforceable. Affirmed.

ANALYSIS

If the original act was not intended to be gratuitous, an implied contract may be found. For example, if an unconscious person is brought to a hospital and is given care for his or her injuries, there is an implied promise to pay for these services. In cases of rescue, the act is gratuitous. The rescuer is not presumed to have expected payment for his or her actions. Therefore, there is no present consideration to support the subsequent promise to pay.

Quicknotes

CONSIDERATION Value given by one party in exchange for performance, or a promise to perform, by another party.

GRATUITOUS Something that is given without consideration received therefor.

IMPLIED CONTRACT An agreement between parties that may be inferred from their general course of conduct.

PROMISEE The party to whom a promise is made.

Kirksey v. Kirksey

Widow (P) v. Brother-in-law (D)

Ala. Sup. Ct., 8 Ala. 131 (1845)

NATURE OF CASE: Action to recover damages for breach of a promise.

FACT SUMMARY: Kirksey (D) promised "Sister Antillico" (P) a place to raise her family "if you will come down and see me."

RULE OF LAW

To be legally enforceable, an executory promise must be supported by sufficient, bargained-for consideration.

FACTS: Kirksey (D) wrote to his widowed sister-in-law, "Sister Antillico" (P), a letter containing the following clause: "If you will come down and see me, I will let you have a place to raise your family." "Sister Antillico" (P) moved 60 miles to Kirksey's (D) residence, where she remained for over two years. Kirksey (D) then required her to leave although her family was not yet "raised." "Sister Antillico" (P) contended that the loss that she sustained in moving was sufficient consideration to support Kirksey's (D) promise to furnish her with "a place" until she could raise her family. She was awarded $200, and Kirksey (D) appealed.

ISSUE: To be legally enforceable, must an executory promise be supported by sufficient, bargained-for consideration?

HOLDING AND DECISION: (Ormond, J.) Yes. To be legally enforceable, an executory promise must be supported by sufficient, bargained-for consideration. In this case, a promise on the condition "if you will come down and see me" is a promise to make a gift. Any expenses incurred by the promisee in "coming down and seeing" are merely conditions necessary to acceptance of the gift. In this case, Kirksey (D) did not appear to be bargaining either for "Sister Antillico's" (P) presence or for her 60-mile move. Instead, Kirksey (D) merely wished to assist her out of what he perceived as a grievous and difficult situation. Reversed.

ANALYSIS

This well-known case demonstrates the court's insistence on finding a bargained-for exchange before it will enforce an executory promise. A promise to make a gift is generally not legally binding until it is executed. Compare Williston's famous hypothetical in which a benevolent man says to a tramp: "If you go around the corner to the clothing shop there, you may purchase an overcoat on my credit." This hypothetical highlights the conceptual problem of the present case in that it is unreasonable to construe the walk around the corner as the price of the promise, yet it is a legal detriment to the tramp to make the walk. Perhaps a reasonable (though not conclusive) guideline is the extent to which the happening of the condition will benefit the promisor. The present case might be decided differently today under the doctrine of promissory estoppel, which had not yet been developed in 1845.

Quicknotes

BARGAINED-FOR EXCHANGE A requirement for adequate consideration; the promise made by the offeror induces the return promise or performance on the part of the offeree and that the promise or performance on the part of the offeree induces the promise made by the offeror.

BREACH OF CONTRACT Unlawful failure by a party to perform its obligations pursuant to contract.

CONSIDERATION Value given by one party in exchange for performance, or a promise to perform, by another party.

EXECUTORY PROMISE A promise to perform an action that has not yet been performed.

PROMISEE The party to whom a promise is made.

PROMISOR The party who promises to render an obligation to another in the future.

PROMISSORY ESTOPPEL A promise that is enforceable if the promisor should reasonably expect that it will induce action or forbearance on the part of the promisee, that does in fact cause such action or forbearance, and that is the only means of avoiding injustice.

Lake Land Employment Group of Akron, LLC v. Columber

Former employer (P) v. Former employee (D)

Ohio Sup. Ct., 101 Ohio St. 3d 242, 804 N.E.2d 27 (2004)

NATURE OF CASE: Suit for breach of covenant not to compete.

FACT SUMMARY: After Columber's (D) job ended, he started a company that competed with his former employer, Lake Land Employment Group of Akron, LLC (Lake Land) (P), in violation of his noncompetition agreement. Columber (D) resisted Lake Land's (P) suit by arguing that the agreement was void for lack of consideration.

RULE OF LAW

Continued employment alone satisfies the contractual requirement of consideration in a covenant not to compete entered by an at-will employee who is already employed by the employer.

FACTS: Columber (D) was an at-will employee of Lake Land Employment Group of Akron, LLC (Lake Land) (P) from 1988 to 2001. Lake Land (P) asked him to sign a covenant not to compete in 1991, and Columber (D) signed the agreement. The noncompetition agreement prohibited Columber (D) from being employed by a competitor of Lake Land (P) within a 50-mile radius of Akron, Ohio, for three years after his employment with Lake Land (P) ended. Columber (D) started a business similar to Lake Land's (P) after he stopped working for Lake Land (P). Lake Land (P) sued. Columber (D) answered by pleading that the noncompetition agreement was void for lack of consideration. The trial judge granted Columber's (D) motion for summary judgment, agreeing that no consideration supported the agreement because nothing material to Columber's (D) employment relationship changed after he signed the agreement. The court of appeals affirmed, but it also asked the Ohio Supreme Court to resolve a conflict between its rationale and the rationale used in a similar case by another of the state's intermediate appellate courts. The Ohio Supreme Court accepted jurisdiction over the case.

ISSUE: Does continued employment alone satisfy the contractual requirement of consideration in a covenant not to compete entered by an at-will employee who is already employed by the employer?

HOLDING AND DECISION: (Moyer, C.J.) Yes. Continued employment alone satisfies the contractual requirement of consideration in a covenant not to compete entered by an at-will employee who is already employed by the employer. Although disfavored, covenants not to compete are appropriate where they impose reasonable temporal and geographic limitations. States are split on the particular issue in this appeal, but, consistent with Ohio law, an at-will employer's forbearance from discharging an employee is sufficient consideration to support a noncompetition agreement. In Ohio, consideration can take either of two forms: a detriment to the promisee or a benefit to the promisor. Since at-will employment is an essentially contractual relationship, either side in the relationship can propose different terms for the relationship at any time. Viewed in this context, a request for an at-will employee to sign a noncompetition agreement is in effect a proposal to renegotiate the employment relationship. When the employee agrees to such different terms, the consideration lies in the employer's forbearance from ending the employer's employment. Reversed and remanded.

DISSENT: (Resnick, J.) No consideration supports the agreement here because, contrary to the majority's creative euphemisms, nothing changed in the underlying employment relationship in this case. Lake Land Employment Group of Akron, LLC (P) gave up nothing: after the agreement was executed, the company had the same right to fire Columber (D), for any reason or no reason at all, whenever it wanted. Likewise, Columber (D) received nothing, either. Any "forbearance" by the employer in such circumstances consists solely in not firing the employee until after he signs the agreement.

DISSENT: (Pfeifer, J.) What the majority finds to be consideration is instead coercion. Even so, the employee's execution of the noncompetition agreement and the employer's promise of continued employment alter the at-will employment relationship, because the employer must continue to employ the employee who executes the agreement for an unspecified period of time. It must be left to the courts to determine the reasonableness of that period.

ANALYSIS

Judge Resnick's dissent has much merit; compared to her arguments, the majority's rationale reads as an exercise in legal fiction. The potential weakness in Judge Resnick's own reasoning, though, appears in her statement: "[t]he only actual 'forbearance,' 'proposal,' or 'promise' made by the employer in this situation is declining to fire the employee until he executes the noncompetition agreement." Her reasonably reductive definition of "forbearance" focuses on the precise instant at which the employee signs the agreement. That

Continued on next page.

reductive sense of "forbearance" could be substantially more vital, though, if specific facts showed that an at-will employer was indeed ready to fire an employee unless he or she signed a noncompetition agreement.

Quicknotes

AT-WILL EMPLOYMENT The rule that an employment relationship is subject to termination at any time, or for any cause, by an employee or an employer in the absence of a specific agreement otherwise.

CONSIDERATION Value given by one party in exchange for performance, or a promise to perform, by another party.

FORBEARANCE The act of refraining from doing something that one has the legal right to do.

Strong v. Sheffield

Creditor (P) v. Endorser of note (D)

N.Y. Ct. App., 144 N.Y. 392, 39 N.E. 330 (1895)

NATURE OF CASE: Action to enforce payment on a promissory note.

FACT SUMMARY: Sheffield (D), payer, gave a note to Strong (P), payee, for an antecedent debt that was past due. The only consideration was that Strong (P) would forbear in his demand for payment, though no time period was set. Two years later, Strong (P) demanded payment and Sheffield (D) failed to pay.

RULE OF LAW

A purported promise is illusory and not consideration if by its terms the performance of the promise is entirely optional with the promisor.

FACTS: The demand note upon which the action was brought was made by the husband of Sheffield (D), endorsed by her at his request, and delivered to Strong (P), the payee, as security for an antecedent debt owing by the husband to Strong (P). The only consideration was Sheffield's (D) endorsement for Strong's (P) promise to forbear on demand for payment for an unspecified period of time. Strong (P) forbeared on demanding payment for a two-year period, at which time Sheffield (D) was unable to pay the note. The trial court found in favor of Strong (P), but the General Term reversed, and he appealed.

ISSUE: Is a promise illusory and not consideration if by its terms the performance of the promise is entirely optional with the promisor?

HOLDING AND DECISION: (Andrews, C.J.) Yes. A purported promise is illusory and not consideration if by its terms the performance of the promise is entirely optional with the promisor. A contract between the endorser of a promissory note and the payee is not an exception to the rule that a promise not supported by a consideration cannot support a contract. While an agreement to forbear the collection of a debt presently due is good consideration for an absolute or conditional promise of a third person to pay the debt without the creditor or payee binding himself at the time to forbear collection or to give time, his acquiescence in the request and actual forbearance is also good consideration. But here the note did not in law extend the payment of the debt for it was payable on demand. Strong (P) kept the note and held it personally till such time as he would make a demand. Had Strong (P) made a demand immediately upon receiving the note, his promise to forbear would have been satisfied. While Sheffield (D) may have hoped for a long period of forbearance, there was no agreement to forbear for a fixed or reasonable period of time, but for only as long as Strong (P) should elect. The consideration is to be tested by the agreement, and not by what was done under it. As there actually was no promise by Strong (P), there was no consideration, and, consequently, no enforceable contract. Affirmed.

ANALYSIS

Strong's (P) promise to hold the note only as long as he did not want the money did not commit him to anything. Because of this, he did not appear to have accepted the guarantor's (D) offer, nor was he supplied consideration for guarantor Sheffield's (D) promise to back the note. If a promise is entirely optional with the promisor, it is illusory. The modern trend is away from being overly literal as to whether the promise is illusory. The courts will tend more to consider the intent of the parties and the potential detriment to the party against whom cancellation of the contract is sought. Restatement (Second) of Contracts § 79 defines illusory promises as promises or apparent promises not being consideration if the terms allow the promisor to reserve a choice of alternate performances. Uniform Commercial Code § 3-408 has reversed the precise rule of this case. Under that section, no consideration is required to back an obligation guaranteeing an antecedent debt of any kind. Under Restatement (Second) of Contracts § 89(c), if it were shown than it should have reasonably been foreseen by Sheffield (D) that there would be forbearance of a substantial nature and the promise did induce such action or reliance, the case would have gone the other way.

Quicknotes

COMMERCIAL PAPER A negotiable instrument; a written promise, signed by the promisee, to pay a specified sum of money to the promisor either on demand or on a specified date.

ILLUSORY PROMISE A promise that is not legally enforceable because performance of the obligation by the promisor is completely within the promisor's discretion.

NUDUM PACTUM A promise that is unenforceable due to lack of consideration.

PROMISSORY NOTE A written promise to tender a stated amount of money at a designated time and to a designated person.

Mattei v. Hopper

Developer (P) v. Property owner (D)

Cal. Sup. Ct., 51 Cal. 2d 119, 330 P.2d 625 (1958)

NATURE OF CASE: Action for breach of contract.

FACT SUMMARY: Mattei (P) purchased property from Hopper (D)—the sale to be completed in 120 days if satisfactory leases could be obtained.

RULE OF LAW

"Satisfaction" clauses do not render a contract illusory or raise problems of mutuality of performance.

FACTS: After lengthy negotiations, Mattei (P) and Hopper (D) entered into a contract whereby Mattei (P) would purchase property owned by Hopper (D) to develop as a shopping center. Mattei (P) was to pay $1,000 down and the balance in 120 days, assuming satisfactory leases for the center could be obtained. A contract was signed, and the deposit was placed in escrow. Hopper (D) thereafter refused to perform even after being notified that satisfactory leases had been found and the balance of the purchase price had been tendered. Mattei (P) brought suit, and Hopper (D) alleged that the presence of the "obtaining satisfactory leases" clause rendered the contract illusory and was also void for lack of mutuality of performance since Mattei (P) could arbitrarily refuse to perform. The court agreed and dismissed the complaint. Mattei (P) appealed.

ISSUE: Does the presence of a "satisfaction" clause render a contract illusory or void it for lack of mutuality?

HOLDING AND DECISION: (Spence, J.) No. Depending on the nature of the "satisfaction," the court reads into the contract an obligation to act in good faith or as a reasonable man. Where satisfaction can be objectively ascertained (e.g., the performance of a product or equipment), the reasonable man standard is employed to determine the reasonableness of the rejection. Where, as here, no objective standards can be applied, it becomes a matter of taste, fancy, or judgment. In such cases, the rejecting party is subject to a requirement that he act in good faith. In either case, the mere presence of the "satisfaction" clause does not render the contract illusory or void for lack of mutuality since the validity of any rejection can be tested. Reversed.

ANALYSIS

An illusory contract is one under which the promises of one or more of the parties is not binding. It is totally discretionary on a party's part as to whether he or she will perform. Illusory contracts may, however, be enforced under quantum meruit for the reasonable value of services or materials actually rendered or under the doctrine of promissory estoppel, where a party relies to his or her detriment on the promises. These, however, are exceptions and, normally, neither party can enforce an illusory contract that is still executory.

Quicknotes

BREACH OF CONTRACT Unlawful failure by a party to perform its obligations pursuant to contract.

ILLUSORY CONTRACT A contract that is unenforceable for lack of consideration because a promise by one of the parties to perform is so insubstantial that no obligation is imposed.

MUTUALITY OF PERFORMANCE The requirement that for a contract to be valid the right to performance must be reciprocal.

PROMISSORY ESTOPPEL A promise that is enforceable if the promisor should reasonably expect that it will induce action or forbearance on the part of the promisee, that does in fact cause such action or forbearance, and that is the only means of avoiding injustice.

QUANTUM MERUIT Equitable doctrine allowing recovery for labor and materials provided by one party, even though no contract was entered into, in order to avoid unjust enrichment by the benefited party.

REASONABLE PERSON STANDARD The standard of care exercised by one who possesses the intelligence, education, knowledge, attention, and judgment required by society of its members when governing behavior; the standard applies to a person's judgment when determining breach of a duty under the theory of negligence.

Structural Polymer Group, Ltd. v. Zoltek Corp.

Buyer (P) v. Seller (D)

543 F.3d 987 (8th Cir. 2008)

NATURE OF CASE: Appeal by defendant from denial of motions for new trial and for judgment as a matter of law, and cross-appeal by plaintiff from the vacation of a damages award, in an action for breach of a requirements contract.

FACT SUMMARY: Structural Polymer Group and Structural Polymer Systems (together SP) (P) sued Zoltek Corp. (D) for breach of a requirements contract for carbon fiber, and a jury returned a verdict for SP (P), which the district court reduced. Zoltek (D) contended, inter alia, that the contract was void for lack of mutuality of obligation. SP (P) contended that the district court erred in reducing the award on the grounds that it was duplicative.

RULE OF LAW

(1) As a matter of law, there is mutuality of obligations in a requirements contract, and, therefore, sufficient consideration to support the contract, where the purchaser's requirements are not entirely determinable by the purchaser's subjective preferences but are determinable by objective criteria outside of the purchaser's control.

(2) Where a jury awards damages under a requirements contract for lost profits from two products, but the contract limits the quantity the purchaser may obtain of either product, but not both additively, a court does not abuse its discretion in limiting the award so it is not duplicative.

FACTS: Structural Polymer Group and Structural Polymer Systems (together SP) (P) and Zoltek Corp. (D) entered into a requirements-contract for large-tow (as opposed to small-tow) carbon fiber in 2000. Under the agreement, Zoltek (D) promised to manufacture and sell to SP (P) all of SP's (P) requirements between November 6, 2000, and December 31, 2010, for "Large Filament Count Carbon Fibers (Carbon Fibers) as defined by PANEX 33 specifications" at the "then-current market price." SP (P), in turn, promised to "obtain their total requirements for suitable quality, in the reasonable opinion of [SP], Carbon Fibers from [Zoltek]," the volume not to exceed "the amount actually purchased by [SP] in the preceding Contract Year plus one million . . . pounds." Around April 2002, Zoltek (D), which had produced a large-tow carbon fiber product called Panex 33, stopped Panex 33 production and began manufacturing a substitute product called Panex 35. SP (P) ordered no Panex 33 or 35 in 2003, and it ordered and received 548,935 pounds of Panex 35 in 2004. Two orders for Panex 35 that SP (P) placed with Zoltek (D) in 2005 and 2006 were never filled, and SP (P) sued Zoltek (D) for breach of contract alleging lost profits through December 31, 2006, and future lost profits through December 31, 2010. Because the parties disputed whether the agreement entitled SP (P) to both Panex 33 and Panex 35, SP's (P) damages expert made alternative lost profit calculations: $21,138,518 in then-current lost profits under Count I corresponding to 3,960,276 pounds of Panex 35, and $14,906,377 in then-current lost profits under Count II corresponding to 3,000,000 pounds of Panex 33. SP (P) argued that the contract was effectively modified to substitute Panex 35 for Panex 33. A jury awarded SP (P) lost profits under both counts through December 31, 2006, but it declined to award SP (P) future lost profits. The district court vacated the lesser award under Count II as duplicative, giving SP (P) a final sum of $21,138,518. Zoltek (D) moved for a new trial, and for judgment as a matter of law, but the district court denied both motions. Zoltek (D) appealed the district court's denial of those motions, contending, inter alia, that the district court erred by refusing to allow it to raise the argument to the jury that the agreement was void for lack of mutuality of obligation. SP (P) cross-appealed the district court's vacation of the jury's award under Count II of the complaint. The court of appeals granted review.

ISSUE:

(1) As a matter of law, is there mutuality of obligations in a requirements contract, and, therefore, sufficient consideration to support the contract, where the purchaser's requirements are not entirely determinable by the purchaser's subjective preferences but are determinable by objective criteria outside of the purchaser's control?

(2) Where a jury awards damages under a requirements-contract for lost profits from two products, but the contract limits the quantity the purchaser may obtain of either product, but not both additively, does a court abuse its discretion in limiting the award so it is not duplicative?

HOLDING AND DECISION: (Colloton, J.)

(1) Yes. As a matter of law, there is mutuality of obligations in a requirements contract, and, therefore, sufficient consideration to support the contract, where the purchaser's requirements are not entirely determinable by the purchaser's subjective preferences but

Continued on next page.

are determinable by objective criteria outside of the purchaser's control. Whether a contract is supported by sufficient consideration is determined by a court as a matter of law. Here, Zoltek Corp. (D) argues that Structural Polymer Group and Structural Polymer Systems (together SP) (P) could at all times order or not order Zoltek (D) fiber as it subjectively wanted because (1) SP had zero requirements for large-tow fiber when the contract was formed, (2) the price protection clause gave SP (P) the option to buy carbon fibers from other producers whenever SP (P) wanted to, and (3) SP (P) was free to buy small-tow fiber, which, according to Zoltek (D), was interchangeable with large-tow fiber, in place of large-tow whenever it pleased. All three of Zoletk's (D) arguments are rejected. As to its first argument, the duty of good faith that is implied into requirements contracts by state law renders SP's (P) obligation under the agreement non-illusory. Because of SP's (P) duty of good faith, if SP (P) failed to purchase anything from Zoltek (D) during the term of the agreement, Zoltek (D) could have claimed that SP (P) acted in bad faith by failing to make purchases, and that SP (P) had breached the agreement. As to Zoltek's (D) second argument, the price protection clause in the contract did not render SP's (P) obligation illusory. The price protection clause gave Zoltek (D) a right of first refusal to sell large-tow carbon fiber to SP (P) for the same price as offered by a third-party seller. If Zoltek (D) offered to match the price offered by another supplier, then SP (P) was obligated to purchase from Zoltek (D). Instead, only if SP (P) had an unfettered option to purchase from another supplier during the term of the contract, then this option would destroy the exclusivity of the arrangement and demonstrate lack of consideration. Here, Zoltek's (D) right of first refusal was sufficient to create mutuality of obligation and consideration. Finally, as to Zoltek's (D) third argument, even if small-tow and large-tow fibers are in fact interchangeable, as Zoltek (D) contends, this fact does not negate mutuality of obligation. Instead, when a buyer contracts to purchase its requirements for a product from a particular seller, but then, absent good faith, purchases an interchangeable product from a third party, the buyer may have breached the requirements contract. Thus, here, SP's (P) obligation to purchase in good faith all its requirements for large-tow fiber exclusively from Zoltek (D) was sufficient consideration to make the contract valid. For all these reasons, the district court did not err in concluding that there was mutuality of obligation and, therefore, consideration. Affirmed as to this issue.

(2) No. Where a jury awards damages under a requirements-contract for lost profits from two products, but the contract limits the quantity the purchaser may obtain of either product, but not both additively, a court does not abuse its discretion in limiting the award, so it is not duplicative. The verdict form submitted to the jury included alternative damages calculations corresponding to 3,000,000 pounds of Panex 33 and 3,960,276 pounds of Panex 35. The jury awarded SP (P) damages under both calculations. The district court concluded that the agreement entitled SP (P) to either Panex 33 or Panex 35, but not to both—which is why it vacated the lesser of the two awards as duplicative. Despite the alternative damages calculations presented to the jury by SP's (P) expert, the contract did not provide that SP (P) could order the maximum quantity of both Panex 33 and Panex 35. SP (P) instead was entitled to order the quantity of carbon fiber ordered in the immediately preceding year, plus one million pounds. Thus, between 2004 and 2005, it was entitled either to 3,960,276 pounds of Panex 35, or 3,000,000 pounds of Panex 33, but not both. The jury's award under both Count I and Count II gave SP (P) profit corresponding to 6,960,276 pounds of large-tow carbon fiber when at most SP (P) was entitled to 3,960,276 pounds. Accordingly, the district court did not abuse its discretion when it determined that the jury's award under both counts was duplicative and altered the judgment accordingly. Affirmed as to this issue.

ANALYSIS

Here, the district court concluded that Zoltek Corp.'s (D) claim of lack of mutuality was an affirmative defense that Zoltek (D) had failed to raise, and, therefore, had forfeited. The district court's ruling on Zoltek's (D) proposed defense, however, did not foreclose Zoltek (D) from arguing to the jury that Structural Polymer Group and Structural Polymer Systems (together SP) (P) breached the agreement. If Zoltek (D) had asserted that SP (P) acted in bad faith, that would be an argument that SP (P) had breached the agreement, not that the agreement lacked mutuality or consideration in the first place. Similarly, Zoltek (D) was free to argue that SP's (P) purchase of small-tow fiber from parties other than Zoltek (D) was a breach of the agreement to purchase large-tow fiber exclusively from Zoltek (D). In any event, even if Zoltek (D) had pursued such claims, the jury found that SP (P) performed its obligations under the contract, so that Zoltek (D) would not have prevailed on a breach of contract theory.

Continued on next page.

Quicknotes

BREACH The violation of an obligation imposed pursuant to contract or law, by acting or failing to act.

CONSIDERATION Value given by one party in exchange for performance, or a promise to perform, by another party.

MUTUALITY OF OBLIGATION Requires that both parties to a contract be bound or else neither is bound.

REQUIREMENTS CONTRACT An agreement pursuant to which one party agrees to purchase all its required goods or services from the other party exclusively for a specified time period.

Wood v. Lucy, Lady Duff-Gordon

Agent (P) v. Designer (D)

N.Y. Ct. App., 222 N.Y. 88, 118 N.E. 214 (1917)

NATURE OF CASE: Action for damages for breach of a contract for an exclusive right.

FACT SUMMARY: Wood (P), in a complicated agreement, received the exclusive right for one year, renewable on a year-to-year basis if not terminated by 90-day notice, to endorse designs with Lucy's (D) name and to market all her fashion designs for which she would receive one half the profits derived. Lucy (D) broke the contract by placing her endorsement on designs without Wood's (P) knowledge.

RULE OF LAW

While an express promise may be lacking, the whole writing may be instinct with an obligation—an implied promise—imperfectly expressed so as to form a valid contract.

FACTS: Lucy (D), a famous-name fashion designer, contracted with Wood (P) that for her granting to him an exclusive right to endorse designs with her name and to market and license all her designs, they were to split the profits derived by Wood (P) in half. The exclusive right was for a period of one year, renewable on a year-to-year basis, and terminable upon 90-day notice. Lucy (D) placed her endorsement on fabrics, dresses, and millinery without Wood's (P) knowledge and in violation of the contract. Lucy (D) claimed that the agreement lacked the elements of a contract as Wood (P) allegedly was not bound to do anything. The appellate division agreed and dismissed the complaint. Wood (P) appealed.

ISSUE: If a promise may be implied from the writing even though it is imperfectly expressed, is there a valid contract?

HOLDING AND DECISION: (Cardozo, J.) Yes. While the contract did not precisely state that Wood (P) had promised to use reasonable efforts to place Lucy's (D) endorsement and market her designs, such a promise can be implied. The implication arises from the circumstances. Lucy (D) gave an exclusive privilege, and the acceptance of the exclusive agency was an acceptance of its duties. Lucy's (D) sole compensation was to be one-half the profits resulting from Wood's (P) efforts. Unless he gave his efforts, she could never receive anything. Without an implied promise, the transaction could not have had such business efficacy as they must have intended it to have. Wood's (P) promise to make monthly accountings and to acquire patents and copyrights as necessary showed the intention of the parties that the promise had value by showing that Wood (P) had some duties. The promise to pay Lucy (D) half the profits and make monthly accountings was a promise to use reasonable efforts to bring profits and revenues into existence. Reversed.

ANALYSIS

A bilateral contract can be express, implied in fact, or a little of each. The finding of an implied promise for the purpose of finding sufficient consideration to support an express promise is an important technique of the courts in order to uphold agreements that seem to be illusory and to avoid problems of mutuality of obligation. This case is the leading case on the subject. It is codified in UCC § 2-306(2) where an agreement for exclusive dealing in goods imposes, unless otherwise agreed, an obligation to use best efforts by both parties. The broadest acceptance of the principle of this case has been in exclusive agency contracts but has been applied in many other contexts such as output contracts, contracts subject to obtaining a mortgage loan, and an implied promise to use best efforts in securing the loan. Basically, the court is interpreting the intentions and conduct of the parties.

Quicknotes

BILATERAL CONTRACT An agreement pursuant to which each party promises to undertake an obligation, or to forbear from acting, at some time in the future.

BREACH OF CONTRACT Unlawful failure by a party to perform its obligations pursuant to contract.

IMPLIED PROMISE A promise inferred by law from a document as a whole and the circumstances surrounding its implementation.

MUTUALITY OF OBLIGATION Requires that both parties to a contract are bound or else neither is bound.

Ricketts v. Scothorn

Executor (D) v. Promisee (P)

Neb. Sup. Ct., 57 Neb. 51, 77 N.W. 365 (1898)

NATURE OF CASE: Action to compel payment on a promissory note given without consideration.

FACT SUMMARY: In reliance on her grandfather's promise to pay money, Scothorn (P) quit her employment.

RULE OF LAW

A promise may be legally binding without consideration if it reasonably induced action or forbearance and if injustice can be avoided by its enforcement.

FACTS: J.C. Ricketts gave his granddaughter, Scothorn (P), a promissory note for $2,000 on demand. J.C. Ricketts indicated that the note was for the purpose of freeing Scothorn (P) from the necessity of working. Scothorn (P) immediately quit her employment. J.C. Ricketts thereafter died and Scothorn (P) then sued A.D. Ricketts (D), executor of the estate, for the amount due on the note and the District Court of Lancaster County rendered recovered judgment.

ISSUE: Is the abandonment, induced by a promise of a job, sufficient reliance to estop the promisor from refuting that promise on the ground that it was given without consideration?

HOLDING AND DECISION: (Sullivan, J.) Yes. When a promisee is induced by a promise to change his or her position in accordance with the real or apparent intention of the promisor, the doctrine of estoppel precludes the promisor from later claiming that the promise was not supported by consideration. This remedy is equitable in nature and is designed to prevent the gross injustice that would otherwise result. Affirmed.

ANALYSIS

In this leading case the court recognizes that Scothorn's (P) abandoning her job was not consideration for the note. Rather the note was a pure gift and thus, absent reliance, would ordinarily not be enforced because of lack of a bargained-for consideration. Traditionally, the estoppel doctrine had been limited to cases where one party had represented a fact to another party who then relied on the fact as represented. In the present case, the court for the first time extended the estoppel doctrine to promissory expressions (hence "promissory estoppel"). (Cf. Restatement (Second) § 90, which states the most recent version of the doctrine.) (Caveat: Courts have often confused and blended the doctrine of estoppel with the doctrine of consideration resulting in such statements as: "The reliance on the promise serves as the consideration for that promise." This is conceptually misleading since the promissory estoppel doctrine is basically a twentieth-century exception to the general rule that requires every enforceable promise to be supported by a bargained-for consideration.)

Quicknotes

CONSIDERATION Value given by one party in exchange for performance, or a promise to perform, by another party.

PROMISSORY ESTOPPEL A promise that is enforceable if the promisor should reasonably expect that it will induce action or forbearance on the part of the promisee, that does in fact cause such action or forbearance, and that is the only means of avoiding injustice.

PROMISSORY NOTE A written promise to tender a stated amount of money at a designated time and to a designated person.

RELIANCE Dependence on a fact that causes a party to act or refrain from acting.

Feinberg v. Pfeiffer Co.

Retired employee (P) v. Employer (D)

Mo. Ct. App., 322 S.W.2d 163 (1959)

NATURE OF CASE: Action on appeal by defendant to show failure of contract due to lack of consideration.

FACT SUMMARY: Anna Feinberg (P) was given a pension for life by Pfeiffer Co. (D) based upon her past service to Pfeiffer Co. (D). Pfeiffer Co. (D) subsequently refused to pay the pension claiming lack of consideration for its promise to do so.

RULE OF LAW

Where one acts in reliance on a promise, there is an enforceable contract under the doctrine of promissory estoppel.

FACTS: Anna Feinberg (P) had been a bookkeeper for Pfeiffer Co. (D) for 37 years. The board of Pfeiffer Co. (D) voted to give her a lifetime pension anytime she chose to retire. The pension was based upon Mrs. Feinberg's (P) past service to the company and not upon her continued service. A year and a half after learning of the pension, Mrs. Feinberg (P) retired and began receiving the pension. Six years after her retirement, Pfeiffer Co. (D) refused to continue paying Mrs. Feinberg (P) her pension upon the advice of its attorney and accountants that there existed no valid consideration for the promise to pay. Mrs. Feinberg (P) brought an action to compel payment of her pension by Pfeiffer Co. (D), and the lower court held for her. Pfeiffer Co. (D) appealed.

ISSUE: Where one acts in reliance on a promise, is there an enforceable contract under the doctrine of promissory estoppel?

HOLDING AND DECISION: (Doerner, Comm'r) Yes. Where one acts in reliance on a promise, there is an enforceable contract under the doctrine of promissory estoppel. Plaintiff retired from a lucrative position in reliance upon defendant's promise to pay her an annuity or pension. Judgment for plaintiff is affirmed per curiam.

ANALYSIS

Note that, in the present case, if Feinberg (P) were still healthy and able to work, the decision would have been different. In that situation, it would not be the case that injustice could be avoided only by enforcement of the promise. Note additionally that if Feinberg (P) had continued to work for Pfeiffer Co. (D) until she became physically unable to continue and was forced to retire, she could probably not recover on Pfeiffer's (D) promise. Her retirement would not have been in reliance on Pfeiffer's (D) promise as the doctrine of promissory estoppel requires.

Quicknotes

PROMISSORY ESTOPPEL A promise that is enforceable if the promisor should reasonably expect that it will induce action or forbearance on the part of the promisee, that does in fact cause such action or forbearance, and that is the only means of avoiding injustice.

Wright v. Newman

Child's non-biological father (D) v. Child's biological mother (P)

Ga. Sup. Ct., 266 Ga. 519, 467 S.E.2d 533 (1996)

NATURE OF CASE: Appeal from order of child support based on promissory estoppel.

FACT SUMMARY: Wright (D), who had had a relationship with Newman (P), contended that he should not be held liable for child support of Newman's (P) son because the son was not his biological child and he never formally contracted to provide such support. Wright (D) urged that, notwithstanding that for 10 years he had held himself out to others to be the son's father and allowed the child to consider him to be the natural father, such conduct was insufficient to require him to pay child support based on promissory estoppel.

RULE OF LAW

An obligation to support a child may arise by contract through promissory estoppel where an individual who is not the child's biological parent lists himself on the child's birth certificate as the father, even though he knows he is not; holds himself out as the child's father and allows the child to believe that he is the child's natural father; and where the child's mother relies on the individual's conduct to her and the child's detriment by refraining from identifying and seeking support from the child's natural father.

FACTS: When Newman's (P) son was born, Wright (D) listed himself as the father on the child's birth certificate and gave the child his last name, even though Wright (D) knew he was not the child's biological father. For ten years, Wright (D) held himself out to others as the child's father, and he allowed the child to consider him to be the natural father. Newman (P) severed the relationship and all ties with Wright (D) when the child was approximately three years old. For approximately the next five years, Newman (P) and Wright (D) did not communicate. Then over the following two years, Wright (D) visited with the child. However, Wright (D) did not support the child after the child was three. Newman (P) brought suit against Wright (D) for child support, asserting that his liability for such support could be based on promissory estoppel. She asserted that Wright (D) promised to support the child when he asserted that he was the child's parent, and that she and the child relied upon Wright's (D) promise to their detriment. Specifically, she refrained from identifying and seeking support from the child's natural father. The trial court ordered Wright (D) to pay child support for Newman's (P) son, and the state's highest court granted review.

ISSUE: May an obligation to support a child arise by contract through promissory estoppel where an individual who is not the child's biological parent lists himself on the child's birth certificate as the father, even though he knows he is not; holds himself out as the child's father and allows the child to believe that he is the child's natural father; and where the child's mother relies on the individual's conduct to her and the child's detriment by refraining from identifying and seeking support from the child's natural father?

HOLDING AND DECISION: (Carley, J.) Yes. An obligation to support a child may arise by contract through promissory estoppel where an individual who is not the child's biological parent lists himself on the child's birth certificate as the father, even though he knows he is not; holds himself out as the child's father and allows the child to believe that he is the child's natural father; and where the child's mother relies on the individual's conduct to her and the child's detriment by refraining from identifying and seeking support from the child's natural father. Notwithstanding that Wright (D) is neither the child's natural father nor an adoptive father, as a matter of law Wright (D) may still be liable for child support as a matter of contract. Here, there was no formal written contract, but Wright's (D) actions, when taken together, constitute a promise by Wright (D) to Newman (P) and her son that he would assume all the obligations and responsibilities of fatherhood, including that of providing support. He undertook his commitment knowingly and voluntarily, and he continued to do so for some 10 years. The facts can also support the inference that Newman (P) relied to her and her son's detriment by refraining from identifying and seeking support from the child's natural father. If she had not refrained from doing so, she might now have a source of financial support for the child and the child might now have a natural father to provide emotional, as well as financial, support. Thus, the elements of promissory estoppel are met. Those elements are: a promise that the promisor should reasonably expect to induce action or forbearance on the part of the promisee or a third person and that does induce such action or forbearance is binding if injustice can be avoided only by enforcement of the promise. Affirmed.

CONCURRENCE: (Sears, J.) It should be emphasized that Newman (P) did, in fact, rely upon Wright's (D) promise to her detriment. Wright (D) would have

Continued on next page.

known that Newman (P) refrained from seeking to identify and obtain support from the child's biological father while Wright (D) was fulfilling his commitment to her. Promissory estoppel requires only that the reliance by the injured party be reasonable, and it does not require the promisee to exhaust all other possible means of obtaining the benefit of the promise from any and all sources before being able to enforce the promise against the promisor. Contrary to the dissent's position, it would not be simple—if at all possible—for Newman (P) to identify the child's biological father and collect support from him. Because it likely will be impossible for Newman (P) to establish the identity of the child's biological father, bring a successful paternity action, and obtain support from that individual, an injustice will result if Wright (D) is allowed to renege on his obligation, since Newman (P) likely will not receive any support to assist in the cost of raising her son, despite having been promised the receipt of such by Wright (D). An even greater injustice will be inflicted upon the boy himself, because a child who has been told by any adult, regardless of the existence of a biological relationship, that he will always be able to depend upon the adult for parenting and sustenance, will suffer a great deal when that commitment is broken.

DISSENT: (Benham, C.J.) Here, Newman (P) cannot satisfy a key element of promissory estoppel, namely, that she suffered a detriment by relying on Wright's (D) actions. She has not alleged, nor does the record reveal, that she does not know the identity of the natural father, nor does she show that the natural father is dead or unable to be found. Consequently, she has failed to prove that she is unable to seek support from the natural father. Further, any prejudice incurred by Newman (P) because of the passage of ten years is not due to Wright's (D) actions, since, at least for the past seven years, Newman (P) has been in the same situation, i.e., receiving no support payments from Wright (D). Thus, Wright (D) is not legally obligated to support the child because Newman (P) has failed to show that she or the child incurred any detriment by Wright's (D) failure to fulfill his promise made ten years ago.

ANALYSIS

The doctrine of promissory estoppel prevents a promisor from reneging on a promise, when the promisor should have expected that the promisee would rely upon the promise, and the promisee does in fact rely upon the promise to her detriment. Sufficient consideration to enforce a contractual promise pursuant to promissory estoppel may be found in any benefit accruing to the promisor, or any reliance, loss, trouble, disadvantage, or charge imposed upon the promisee. Here, the majority focuses on the detriment to Newman (P) and her child, rather than on any benefit accruing to Wright (D).

Quicknotes

PROMISE The expression of an intention to act, or to forbear from acting, granting a right to the promisee to expect and enforce its performance.

PROMISEE The party to whom a promise is made.

PROMISOR The party who promises to render an obligation to another in the future.

PROMISSORY ESTOPPEL A promise that is enforceable if the promisor should reasonably expect that it will induce action or forbearance on the part of the promisee, that does in fact cause such action or forbearance, and that is the only means of avoiding injustice.

Cohen v. Cowles Media Co.

News source (P) v. Newspaper publisher (D)

Minn. Sup. Ct., 479 N.W.2d 387 (1992)

NATURE OF CASE: Remand from appeal of an award of damages for breach of contract and fraudulent misrepresentation.

FACT SUMMARY: Editors of two newspapers (D) broke their promises to Cohen (P), the source for a story, to keep his identity confidential.

RULE OF LAW

Under the doctrine of promissory estoppel, a court should consider all aspects of a transaction's substance in determining whether enforcement is necessary to prevent an injustice.

FACTS: Cohen (P) supplied the *Minneapolis Star Tribune* (*Tribune*), published by Cowles Media Co. (Cowles) (D), and the *St. Paul Pioneer Press Dispatch* (*Dispatch*) with disparaging information regarding a candidate for public office. The reporter for the *Tribune* and the *Dispatch* promised Cohen (P) that he would not be revealed as the source for the information. However, editors at the *Tribune* and the *Dispatch* later decided that it was important to reveal Cohen (P) as the source for the information because he was allied with an opposing candidate. After the story was published, Cohen (P) was fired from his job. Cohen (P) filed suit against Cowles (D) and the *Dispatch*'s publisher (D) for breach of contract and fraudulent misrepresentation. The jury awarded Cohen (P) $200,000 in compensatory damages and $250,000 in punitive damages. On appeal, the court set aside recovery on the basis of fraudulent misrepresentation but affirmed recovery of the compensatory damages on the basis of breach of contract. The Minnesota Supreme Court found that promissory estoppel could form the basis for recovery but held that First Amendment concerns precluded recovery of damages. The United States Supreme Court, concluding that the First Amendment was not implicated, overruled this decision and remanded the case to determine whether a retrial would be necessary.

ISSUE: Under the doctrine of promissory estoppel, should a court consider all aspects of a transaction's substance in determining whether enforcement is necessary to prevent an injustice?

HOLDING AND DECISION: (Simonett, J.) Yes. Under the doctrine of promissory estoppel, a court should consider all aspects of a transaction's substance in determining whether enforcement is necessary to prevent an injustice. A promise that is expected to, and does, induce definite action by the promisee is binding if injustice can be avoided only by enforcing the promise. The promise must be definite, clear, and intended to induce reliance. In the instant case, the record is clear that the *St. Paul Pioneer Press Dispatch*'s (*Dispatch*'s) and the *Minneapolis Star Tribune*'s (*Tribune*'s) reporters made unambiguous promises to treat Cohen (P) as an anonymous source, and Cohen (P) provided the information based on these promises. Thus, the only remaining issue is whether this promise must be enforced to prevent an injustice. Neither side in this case clearly holds the higher moral ground. However, even the *Tribune*'s witnesses acknowledged the importance of protecting the confidentiality of information sources. Additionally, it does not appear that there was a compelling need to break the promises in the present case. Therefore, it would be unjust to Cohen (P) unless the promises were enforced. Accordingly, the award of compensatory damages is affirmed but under a theory of promissory estoppel.

ANALYSIS

The court ruled that the damages instruction the trial court provided for breach of contract was also valid for promissory estoppel recovery. A study examining the effect of this decision on publishers revealed that there was no substantial change in policies regarding confidential sources. In fact, most publishers thought the result was just and proper.

Quicknotes

BREACH OF CONTRACT Unlawful failure by a party to perform its obligations pursuant to contract.

COMPENSATORY DAMAGES Measure of damages necessary to compensate victim for actual injuries suffered.

FRAUDULENT MISREPRESENTATION A statement or conduct by one party to another that constitutes a false representation of fact.

PROMISSORY ESTOPPEL A promise that is enforceable if the promisor should reasonably expect that it will induce action or forbearance on the part of the promisee, that does in fact cause such action or forbearance, and that is the only means of avoiding injustice.

PUNITIVE DAMAGES Damages exceeding the actual injury suffered for the purposes of punishment of the defendant, deterrence of the wrongful behavior, or comfort to the plaintiff. Also called "exemplary damages."

D & G Stout, Inc. v. Bacardi Imports, Inc.

Liquor distributor (P) v. Liquor company (D)

923 F.2d 566 (7th Cir. 1991)

NATURE OF CASE: Appeal from summary judgment dismissing a complaint for damages based on reliance on a promise.

FACT SUMMARY: When Bacardi Imports, Inc. (Bacardi) (D), after promising to retain General Liquors (General) (P) as its wholesale distributor in northern Indiana, withdrew its product line from General (P), General (P) was forced to sell itself at liquidation prices, after which it sought to recover damages from Bacardi (D).

RULE OF LAW

A promise that the promisor should reasonably expect to induce action or forbearance on the part of the promisee and a third person and that does induce such action or forbearance is binding if injustice can be avoided only by the enforcement of the promise.

FACTS: D & G Stout (P), operating as General Liquors, Inc. (General) (P), was Bacardi Import's (Bacardi) (D) wholesale liquor distributor in northern Indiana. After General (P) survived an industry shake-up and consolidation, it began negotiations with National Wine & Spirits (National) for a possible sale. Bacardi (D), knowing of the negotiations, promised that General (P) would remain its distributor for northern Indiana. Confident that it could continue operating, General (P) then rejected National's offer. But Bacardi (D) reneged on its promise and withdrew its line from General (P). Hiram Walker, General's (P) another major client, also withdrew. Its negotiating leverage destroyed, General (P) was forced to sell to National for $550,000 below the original offer. General (P) sued Bacardi (D) on promissory estoppel grounds for the $550,000 price differential. The district court granted Bacardi's (D) motion for summary judgment. General (P) appealed.

ISSUE: Is a promise that the promisor should reasonably expect to induce action or forbearance on the part of the promisee and a third person and that does induce such action or forbearance binding if injustice can be avoided only by the enforcement of the promise?

HOLDING AND DECISION: (Cudahy, J.) Yes. A promise that the promisor should reasonably expect to induce action or forbearance on the part of the promisee and a third person and that does induce such action or forbearance is binding if injustice can be avoided only by the enforcement of the promise. Through its repudiation, Bacardi Import's (Bacardi) (D) destroyed General Liquors, Inc.'s (General's) (P) negotiating leverage since General (P) no longer had the alternative of continuing as an independent concern. General (P) was left with one choice: sell at any price. Under these facts, General (P) had a reliance interest in Bacardi's (D) promise, given in full knowledge that General (P) planned to reject National's offer. While General's (P) allegations must still be proven at trial, Bacardi's (D) promise was of a sort on which General (P) might rely, with the possibility of damages for breach. Reversed and remanded.

ANALYSIS

Judge Cudahy emphasized that the lost future income expected from an at-will relationship, whether from wages or from profits, is not recoverable on a theory of promissory estoppel. Although an aspiring employee could not sue for lost wages on an employer's unfulfilled promise of at-will employment, he could sue for moving expenses because moving expenses are reliance costs resulting from a forgone opportunity. In summary, reliance costs are recoverable on a promissory estoppel theory, but expectancy damages are not. As a practical matter, the cost that General (P) incurred when it rejected National's offer was a reliance injury and therefore redressable.

Quicknotes

ANTICIPATORY REPUDIATION Breach of a contract subsequent to formation but prior to the time performance is due.

AT-WILL EMPLOYMENT The rule that an employment relationship is subject to termination at any time, or for any cause, by an employee or an employer in the absence of a specific agreement otherwise.

EXPECTANCY The expectation or contingency of obtaining possession of a right or interest in the future.

FORBEARANCE Refraining from doing something that one has the legal right to do.

PROMISSORY ESTOPPEL A promise that is enforceable if the promisor should reasonably expect that it will induce action or forbearance on the part of the promisee, that does in fact cause such action or forbearance, and that is the only means of avoiding injustice.

RELIANCE Dependence on a fact that causes a party to act or refrain from acting.

Continued on next page.

REPUDIATION The actions or statements of a party to a contract that evidence the party's intent not to perform, or to continue performance, the party's duties or obligations hereunder.

SUMMARY JUDGMENT Judgment rendered by a court in response to a motion by one of the parties, claiming that the lack of a question of material fact in respect to an issue warrants disposition of the issue without consideration by the jury.

Cotnam v. Wisdom

Estate administrator (D) v. Surgeon (P)

Ark. Sup. Ct., 83 Ark. 601, 104 S.W. 164 (1907)

NATURE OF CASE: Action to recover damages in quasi-contract for professional medical services.

FACT SUMMARY: Wisdom (P) rendered emergency professional medical services to Cotnam (D) after a streetcar accident.

RULE OF LAW

A physician may recover in quasi-contract a reasonable compensation for emergency services rendered on the spot to an unconscious accident victim.

FACTS: Harrison was rendered unconscious in a streetcar accident. Wisdom (P), a physician, was summoned to the scene by a passerby and thereafter performed a difficult and unsuccessful operation to save Harrison's life. Harrison died without regaining consciousness. Wisdom (P) sued Cotnam (D), administrator of Harrison's estate, in quasi-contract for the services rendered to Harrison. Judgment at trial was for Wisdom (P). Cotnam (D) appealed.

ISSUE: May a physician who renders necessary emergency medical services to an unconscious accident victim recover in quasi-contract even though the victim did not request the service, the victim clearly could not consent to the service, and the victim died a short time later?

HOLDING AND DECISION: (Hill, C.J.) Yes. One bereft of all sense and reason may be held liable for "necessaries" furnished to him in good faith. The fact that there was no request for, or consent to, the services is irrelevant since recovery rests on the legal fiction of quasi-contract, a mythical creation of the courts to do justice where there otherwise would be no remedy. Furthermore, the success or failure of an operation is not the measure of a physician's services. Although it is customary for physicians to graduate their charges according to a patient's ability to pay, this custom should not apply where a physician is summoned by a passerby to attend an unconscious and previously unknown victim. The quasi-contract fiction merely requires reasonable compensation and "the services are the same be the patient prince or pauper." The victim's marital status is not relevant to the case, and knowledge of his bachelorhood might well have affected the amount of recovery allowed by the jury. For these reasons, judgment must be reversed and the cause remanded.

CONCURRENCE: (Battle, J.) To allow the jury to consider that the estate would go to collateral heirs was a mistake.

ANALYSIS

This case should be compared with *Callano v. Oakwood Park Homes Corp.*, 219 A. 2d 332 (1966), where plaintiff, under contract to a third person, planted shrubbery on and enhanced the value of defendant's property, in which quasi-contractual recovery was not allowed. *Cotnam v. Wisdom* may be distinguished in several important ways: (1) Here the services rendered were "necessities" (i.e., a matter of life and death) and extremely emergent in nature. (2) Here the physician had no other remedy. And (3) here there was an obvious "direct relation" between doctor and patient. Underlying this decision is a fundamental public policy consideration. If the court does not allow recovery, doctors will be discouraged from acting in emergency situations (since they would be spending time and effort, not to mention risking malpractice suits, with no possibility of reward). Society, however, wishes to encourage professional action in such circumstances. The standard measure of damages in quasi-contract is the reasonable value of the benefit received. Since it is somewhat confusing to speak of "benefit received" by a patient who died without regaining consciousness (in fact Cotnam (D) tried to make an argument out of this), the court chooses to speak in terms of "reasonable compensation" for the service.

Quicknotes

PUBLIC POLICY Policy administered by the state with respect to the health, safety, and morals of its people in accordance with common notions of fairness and decency.

QUASI-CONTRACT An implied contract created by law to prevent unjust enrichment.

Callano v. Oakwood Park Homes Corp.

Plant nursery operators (P) v. Real estate developer (D)

N.J. Super. Ct., 91 N.J. Super. 105, 219 A.2d 332 (1966)

NATURE OF CASE: Action to recover damages in quasi-contract.

FACT SUMMARY: The Callanos (P), under contract to a third party, planted shrubbery on and enhanced the value of Oakwood Park Homes Corp.'s (D) property.

RULE OF LAW

A party with no direct relationship to another is not necessarily obligated to pay for any benefit received from that latter party on the theory of quasi-contractual liability.

FACTS: Pendergast contracted to buy a lot from Oakwood Park Homes Corp. (Oakwood Park) (D). Julia and Frank Callano (P), under separate contract with Pendergast, planted shrubbery on the lot. Thereafter Pendergast died without having paid the Callanos (P), and Pendergast's estate canceled the Oakwood Park (D) contract. Oakwood Park (D), not knowing of Pendergast's failure to pay the Callanos (P), then resold the property the value of which was enhanced by the presence of the shrubs. The Callanos (P) contended that Oakwood Park (D) was unjustly enriched and were awarded $475 at trial. Oakwood (D) appealed.

ISSUE: Is a party with no direct relationship to another necessarily obligated to pay for any benefit received from that latter party on the theory of quasi-contractual liability?

HOLDING AND DECISION: (Collester, J.) No. To recover in quasi-contract, a plaintiff must prove that the defendant was unjustly enriched. In the present case, both parties conceded that Oakwood Park Homes Corp. (Oakwood Park) (D) was enriched. However, that enrichment was not unjust since the Callanos (P) expected payment from Pendergast and there was no other direct relationship between the Callanos (P) and Oakwood Park (D). Nor did the Callanos (P) perform under any mistake. Recovery on a theory of quasi-contract was designed to provide a remedy where none existed. Here, a remedy exists; the Callanos (P) may sue Pendergast's estate. Reversed.

ANALYSIS

A quasi-contract is a contract "implied-in-law" (and should be carefully distinguished from an actual contract "implied-in-fact"). A quasi-contract is not a contract at all but is rather an obligation imposed by law to do justice (even though it is clear no promise was ever made, and no meeting of the minds was ever consummated). It is, in a sense, a noncontractual obligation treated procedurally as if it were a contract (a legal fiction). When allowed, a quasi-contractual recovery (for the reasonable value of benefit received by the defendant) is the court's way of protecting the plaintiff's restitution interest (by putting the defendant back in the position in which he or she would have been had the benefit never been recovered). Compare a protection of plaintiff's reliance interest (which would attempt to put plaintiff back in the position in which he or she would have been had he or she never conferred the benefit). Courts will look hard and long before granting this rather extraordinary remedy in light of the obvious problem of distinguishing between the "officious intermeddler" and the "deserving claimant." Note the court's emphasis in the present case on the Callanos' (P) remedy against Pendergast's estate.

Quicknotes

QUASI-CONTRACT An implied contract created by law to prevent unjust enrichment.

UNJUST ENRICHMENT The principle of retaining a benefit given to one by another, without compensating the giver, in situations where compensation is reasonably expected.

Pyeatte v. Pyeatte

Former spouse (P) v. Former spouse (D)

Ariz. Ct. App., 661 P.2d 196 (1982)

NATURE OF CASE: Appeal from award in a marital dissolution based on spouse's educational support of the other spouse.

FACT SUMMARY: Margrethe Pyeatte (Margrethe) (P) was awarded $23,000 in her marital dissolution action against her former husband, Charles Pyeatte (Charles) (D), on the grounds that the couple had an agreement that each would support the other while the other earned an advanced educational degree, and that Charles (D) had breached the agreement. Charles (D) contended that the agreement he had with Margrethe (P) did not rise to the level of a binding contract. Margrethe (P) countered that even if there had not been a contract, she was nonetheless entitled to restitution because Charles (D) had been unjustifiably enriched by her sacrifices.

RULE OF LAW

(1) An agreement between two parties does not rise to the level of a binding contract where the agreement lacks essential terms upon which the liability of the parties may be precisely fixed.

(2) An educational degree, a professional license, or the increased earning potential these represent is not community property subject to valuation and division upon marital dissolution.

(3) A spouse who has supported the other spouse in obtaining education can be awarded in restitution, upon marital dissolution, for the other spouse's direct living and educational expenses where the spouse has expected compensation for such expenses, and it would be unjust to allow the other spouse to retain the benefits conferred by the spouse.

FACTS: After Margrethe Pyeatte (Margrethe) (P) and Charles Pyeatte (Charles) (D) were married, they came to an oral agreement that each would support the other while the other earned an advanced educational degree. There was no contingency expressed or implied that this would not be carried out or enforced in the event of a divorce. Margrethe (P) carried out her part of the agreement in supporting Charles (D) while he obtained his law degree. Charles (D) was supposed to support Margrethe (P) while she obtained a masters degree. Soon after Charles (D) graduated from law school and was admitted to the Bar, the parties divorced. Margrethe (P) filed an action for marital dissolution, which was granted. The trial court, finding a contractual agreement between the parties, awarded Margrethe (P) $23,000 as damages for Charles's (D) breach of the contract, which represented the amount needed to pay for Margrethe (P) to obtain a masters degree. Charles (D), contended that the couple's agreement did not rise to the level of a binding contract because its terms were not definite and could not be legally enforced. Margrethe (P) countered that even though there was no legally binding contract, she was entitled to restitution for the benefits she conferred on Charles (D), on a quantum meruit basis, since Charles (D) received his legal education at her expense. She also argued that since Charles (D) had obtained his legal education through the exhaustion of community resources, her financing thereof was an extraordinary expenditure to which she was statutorily entitled to reimbursement. The state's intermediate appellate court granted review.

ISSUE:

(1) Does an agreement between two parties rise to the level of a binding contract where the agreement lacks essential terms upon which the liability of the parties may be precisely fixed?

(2) Is an educational degree, a professional license, or the increased earning potential these represent community property subject to valuation and division upon marital dissolution?

(3) Can a spouse who has supported the other spouse in obtaining education be awarded in restitution, upon marital dissolution, for the other spouse's direct living and educational expenses where the spouse has expected compensation for such expenses, and it would be unjust to allow the other spouse to retain the benefits conferred by the spouse?

HOLDING AND DECISION: (Corcoran, J.)

(1) No. An agreement between two parties does not rise to the level of a binding contract where the agreement lacks essential terms upon which the liability of the parties may be precisely fixed. Here, a sufficient mutual understanding regarding critical provisions of their agreement did not exist. For example, no agreement was made regarding the time when Margrethe (P) would attend graduate school and Charles (D) would be required to assume their full support. Other essential terms also were missing, including the place where Margrethe (P) would obtain her degree and the specific costs of the degree program. Although contracts should be interpreted, whenever reasonable, in such a way as to uphold the contract, especially where there has been performance by one party, the court's function cannot

Continued on next page.

be that of contract maker. Here, because the essential terms and requirements of this agreement were not sufficiently definite so that the obligations of the parties to the agreement could be determined, there can be no recovery for amounts necessary to further Margrethe's (P) education. [Reversed as to this issue.]

(2) No. An educational degree, a professional license, or the increased earning potential these represent is not community property subject to valuation and division upon marital dissolution. Margrethe (P) argues that she is entitled to reimbursement of her expenditures for Charles's (D) legal education under a statute that provides that a court, in disposing of property in a dissolution, may consider "excessive or abnormal expenditures . . . of community, joint tenancy and other property held in common." She contends that Charles's (D) education was an extraordinary expenditure that inured to his benefit and for which she paid and that she is entitled to equitable reimbursement in the form of a lien upon Charles's (D) separate estate. However, the statute concerns the disposition of property, and in this jurisdiction, it has been decided that a spouse's education, as well as a professional license and the increased earning potential of education or a license, cannot be characterized as community property that can be divided upon dissolution. [Judgment for Charles (D) as to this issue.]

(3) Yes. A spouse who has supported the other spouse in obtaining education can be awarded in restitution, upon marital dissolution, for the other spouse's direct living and educational expenses where the spouse has expected compensation for such expenses, and it would be unjust to allow the other spouse to retain the benefits conferred by the spouse. Margrethe (P) argues that Charles's (D) education, which she subsidized and which he obtained through the exhaustion of community assets, constitutes a benefit for which he must, in equity, make restitution. For the court to imply a contract under these circumstances, without regard to the parties' intentions, not only must Margrethe (P) have conferred a benefit upon Charles (D), she must have also expected to be compensated for conferring the benefit, and it also must be unjust for Charles (D) to retain the benefit. If these requirements are met, Margrethe (P) may be entitled to restitution under a theory of quasi-contract, which is an equitable doctrine designed to avoid an unjust result. Although the spousal agreement here failed to meet the requirements of an enforceable contract, the agreement still has importance in considering Margrethe's (P) claim for unjust enrichment because it evidences both her expectation of compensation and the circumstances that make it unjust to allow Charles (D) to retain the benefits of her extraordinary efforts. Based on all the circumstances, Margrethe (P) is entitled to equitable restitution. A variety of methods of computing unjust enrichment may be employed in ascertaining a working spouse's compensable interest in the attainment of a student spouse's education, degree, or license. Here, as a matter of equity, the restitution award should be limited to the financial contribution by Margrethe (P) for Charles's (D) living expenses and direct educational expenses. [Judgment for Margrethe (P) as to this issue.] Reversed and remanded.

ANALYSIS

Contracts implied-in-law or quasi-contracts, also called constructive contracts, are inferred by the law as a matter of reason and justice from the acts and conduct of the parties and circumstances surrounding the transactions, and are imposed for the purpose of bringing about justice without reference to the intentions of the parties. Restatement of Restitution § 1 provides that "A person who has been unjustly enriched at the expense of another is required to make restitution to the other." Comment (a) to that section notes that a person is enriched if he received a benefit and is unjustly enriched if retention of that benefit would be unjust. Comment (b) defines a benefit as being any form of advantage. Unjust enrichment does not depend upon the existence of a valid contract, nor is it necessary that a plaintiff suffer a loss corresponding to the defendant's gain for there to be valid claim for an unjust enrichment. A benefit may be any type of advantage, including that which saves the recipient from any loss or expense. Here, Margrethe's (P) support of Charles (D) during his period of schooling clearly constituted a benefit to him. Absent Margrethe's (P) support, Charles (D) may not have attended law school, may have been forced to prolong his education because of intermittent periods of gainful employment, or may have gone deeply into debt. Relieved of the necessity of supporting himself, he was able to devote full time and attention to his education. As this case makes clear, however, the mere fact that one party confers a benefit on another is not of itself sufficient to require the other to make restitution; retention of the benefit must be unjust. Here, the court concluded that Charles (D) had left the marriage with the only valuable asset acquired during the marriage—his legal education and qualification to practice law—and that it would be inequitable to allow him to retain this benefit without making restitution to Margrethe (P).

Continued on next page.

Quicknotes

BREACH OF CONTRACT Unlawful failure by a party to perform its obligations pursuant to contract.

CONTRACT An agreement pursuant to which a party agrees to act, or to forbear from acting, in exchange for performance on the part of the other party.

EQUITABLE Just; fair.

IMPLIED-AT-LAW CONTRACT Constructive conditions that set forth the order of performance of certain aspects of the agreement in the event that the express terms of the bargain have not specified such conditions.

QUANTUM MERUIT Equitable doctrine allowing recovery for labor and materials provided by one party, even though no contract was entered into, in order to avoid unjust enrichment by the benefited party.

QUASI-CONTRACT An implied contract created by law to prevent unjust enrichment.

UNJUST ENRICHMENT The principle of retaining a benefit given to one by another, without compensating the giver, in situations where compensation is reasonably expected.

Mooers v. Middlebury College

Student (P) v. College (D)

2021 WL 4225659 (D. Va. 2021)

NATURE OF CASE: Motion to dismiss putative class action asserting, inter alia, claims for breach of contract and, in the alternative, unjust enrichment.

FACT SUMMARY: Henry Mooers (P) and other students (P) at Middlebury College (Middlebury) (D) sought disgorgement of a prorated portion of tuition and fees for the time that Middlebury (D) switched to online learning in response to the COVID-19 pandemic, alleging, inter alia, claims of breach of contract and, in the alternative, unjust enrichment. Middlebury (D) moved to dismiss the action.

RULE OF LAW

(1) Terms in a contract are not enforceable where they are merely aspirational and are not specific and concrete promises.

(2) An unjust enrichment claim that is plausibly pled, not foreclosed as a matter of law, and pled in the alternative to a breach of contract claim, should not be dismissed at the pleading stage.

FACTS: Henry Mooers (P) and other undergraduate students (P) at Middlebury College (Middlebury) (D) paid Middlebury (D) around $28,940 for tuition and $218 in student activity fees to attend Middlebury (D) during the Spring 2020 semester, which started in February 2020 and ended in May 2020. In response to the global COVID-19 pandemic, Middlebury (D) did not hold any in-person classes for undergraduate students after March 13, 2020. Instead, Middlebury (D) offered all classes in a remote online format with no in-person instruction or interaction. Also, students were denied access to all on-campus facilities and activities. Mooers (P), representing a putative class of students, alleged in federal district court that he and the prospective class members were entitled to a prorated refund of the tuition and fees paid for the Spring 2020 semester for the period after March 13, 2020. Mooers (P) asserted, inter alia, claims of breach of contract and, in the alternative, unjust enrichment, alleging that he had entered into a contract with Middlebury (D) for on-campus, in-person education and other related services in exchange for tuition and fees. Mooers (P) further alleged that the terms of the agreement were set forth in various Middlebury (D) publications and marketing materials that were provided to prospective and enrolling students, including student handbooks, brochures, course offering bulletins, and similar documents. Middlebury (D) moved to dismiss. Although conceding the contractual nature of its relationship with its students, Middlebury (D) asserted that nowhere in its publications was there a "specific and concrete" promise to provide in-person instruction, so that Mooers (P) failed to plausibly plead a claim for breach of contract. The District Court considered the motion to dismiss.

ISSUE:

(1) Are terms in a contract enforceable where they are merely aspirational and are not specific and concrete promises?

(2) Should an unjust enrichment claim that is plausibly pled, not foreclosed as a matter of law, and pled in the alternative to a breach of contract claim be dismissed at the pleading stage?

HOLDING AND DECISION: (Reiss, J.)

(1) No. Terms in a contract are not enforceable where they are merely aspirational and are not specific and concrete promises. It is undisputed that the terms of a contract between a student and a college are found in the college's publications, including brochures, course offerings, bulletins, and the like. However, not all terms in such publications are enforceable contractual obligations, and courts will only enforce terms that are specific and concrete, and that can be found in the express text of the institution's publications. Language in a college's official publications or other statement that is merely aspirational in nature or that articulates a general statement of a school's ideals, goals, or mission is not enforceable. Thus, in the absence of a specific promise of an in-person education, aspirational or inspirational language about the value of a campus environment does not create an enforceable promise for in-person education. Here, none of the statements made by Middlebury College (Middlebury) (D) cited by Mooers (P) could reasonably be interpreted as a specific, concrete promise that Middlebury (D) would offer students in-person educational services even in the midst of a pandemic. Middlebury's (D) description of its on-campus facilities and its posts and pictures depicting campus life are informative rather than promissory, and its statements in its Handbook and on its website regarding an "inclusive" or "immersive" campus environment are aspirational in nature and neither specific, concrete, nor enforceable. Because breach of contract actions between a student and a school must be grounded in a text and because Mooers (P) has not identified a specific promise of an in-person

Continued on next page.

education, Middlebury's (D) motion to dismiss Mooers's (P) breach of contract claim is granted.

(2) No. An unjust enrichment claim that is plausibly pled, not foreclosed as a matter of law, and pled in the alternative to a breach of contract claim, should not be dismissed at the pleading stage. To establish unjust enrichment, a plaintiff must allege (1) that a benefit was conferred on defendant, (2) that defendant accepted the benefit, and (3) that it would be inequitable to allow defendant to retain the benefit. Unjust enrichment is a quasi-contractual theory of liability, by which the law implies a promise to pay when a party receives a benefit and retention of the benefit would be inequitable. As a quasi-contractual claim, unjust enrichment arises only in the absence of any agreement, and the existence of a valid and enforceable written contract governing a particular subject matter ordinarily precludes recovery for events arising out of the same subject matter. At the pleading stage, Mooers's (P) unjust enrichment claim is fairly characterized as a claim that he paid for in-person educational services and fee-related activities that he did not receive, thereby conferring a benefit on Middlebury (D) that it was not entitled to retain. Because an unjust enrichment claim does not require a contractual obligation or a specific promise, the claim remains available unless and until a factual record establishes that an enforceable contract forecloses it. Here, Mooers's (P) unjust enrichment claim is plausibly pled, not foreclosed as a matter of law, and pled in the alternative. Against this backdrop, it would be premature to dismiss it. Accordingly, Middlebury's (D) motion to dismiss Mooers's (P) unjust enrichment claim is denied.

ANALYSIS

The "general statements" in college publications that vaguely tout the benefits of an on-campus experience have been viewed by many courts as "merely aspirational in nature" and as not containing specific, concrete promises regarding in-person educational services, particularly in the midst of a pandemic. Such statements have been viewed by those courts as axiomatic of a failure to demonstrate language identifying a promise of in-person instruction. If a breach of contract claim were allowed to proceed on the basis of such statements, the aspirational nature of the language would prove unenforceable. For example, a plaintiff could not enforce a promise to offer a "vibrant campus culture" or a "hub of student activity from morning to night, with students pursuing the passions that drive them to know more," nor could a defendant defend against such claims. A jury, in turn, could not properly award damages for the failure to produce this type of educational environment. As one court has observed: "One of the most common types of promise that is too indefinite for legal enforcement is the promise where the promisor retains an unlimited right to decide later the nature or extent of his or her performance. In that situation, the promisor's unlimited choice in effect destroys the promise and makes it illusory. An illusory promise is one that is so indefinite that it cannot be enforced, or by its terms makes performance optional or entirely discretionary on the part of the promisor." *Acklie v. Greater Omaha Packing Co., Inc.*, 944 N.W.2d 297, 306 (Neb. 2020). For this very reason, a growing number of courts have rejected aspirational language as a basis for a tuition refund breach of contract claim.

Quicknotes

BREACH OF CONTRACT Unlawful failure by a party to perform its obligations pursuant to contract.

CLASS ACTION A suit commenced by a representative on behalf of an ascertainable group that is too large to appear in court, shares a commonality of interests, and will benefit from a successful result.

CONTRACTUAL OBLIGATION A duty that someone agrees to perform pursuant to a contract.

ILLUSORY PROMISE A promise that is not legally enforceable because performance of the obligation by the promisor is completely within the promisor's discretion.

PROMISE The expression of an intention to act, or to forbear from acting, granting a right to the promisee to expect and enforce its performance.

PROMISEE The party to whom a promise is made.

PROMISOR The party who promises to render an obligation to another in the future.

UNJUST ENRICHMENT The principle of retaining a benefit given to one by another, without compensating the giver, in situations where compensation is reasonably expected.

CHAPTER 2

Creating Contractual Obligations

Quick Reference Rules of Law

PAGE

1. *Lucy v. Zehmer.* If a person's words and acts, judged by a reasonable standard, manifest a certain intent, it is immaterial what may be the real but unexpressed state of that person's mind. 44

2. *Specht v. Netscape Communications Corp.* Where consumers are urged to download free software, mere reference to the existence of license terms on a submerged screen does not place consumers on inquiry notice or constructive notice of terms. 45

3. *Cohen v. Cowles Media Co.* The reporter's promise of anonymity is given as a moral commitment, but a moral obligation alone will not support a contract. 46

4. *Owen v. Tunison.* There can be no contract, no meeting of the minds, between the parties unless there is an offer. 47

5. *Fairmount Glass Works v. Crunden-Martin Woodenware Company.* Where prices are requested on an order and the vendor quotes those prices to the vendee, the vendor has offered to fill the order and is obligated to fill the order upon receipt within a reasonable time of vendee's acceptance. 48

6. *Lefkowitz v. Great Minneapolis Surplus Store.* A newspaper advertisement that is clear, definite, and explicit, and leaves nothing to negotiation is an offer, acceptance of which creates a binding contract. 49

7. *Kincaid v. Eaton.* The discovery of property voluntarily laid down by the property's owner within a bank, on a desk provided for the use of those having business at the bank, does not constitute "finding" of the property that would entitle the person discovering the property to a reward offered to "the finder." 50

8. *Wucherpfennig v. Dooley.* A contract cannot be formed where an alleged acceptance of an offer is not absolute, unequivocal, and unconditional, so that the offer and alleged acceptance do not express assent to the same thing. 51

9. *International Filter Co. v. Conroe Gin, Ice & Light Co.* As the offeror is in control of his offer, he may specify the type of acceptance that is required and can dispense with the requirement of its communication. 52

10. *White v. Corlies & Tift.* Acceptance of an offer must be manifested in such a way as to be communicated to the offeror. 53

11. *Ever-Tite Roofing Corp. v. Green.* Where a contract does not specify a time within which it may be accepted, a "reasonable time" will be implied. 54

12. *Corinthian Pharmaceutical Systems, Inc. v. Lederle Laboratories.* A seller's price list is not an offer to the buyer, and a subsequent partial shipment of the buyer's order is not an acceptance sufficient to form a contract. 55

13. *Dickinson v. Dodds.* An offeree may not bind an offeror by accepting a revoked offer, even if the revocation had not been communicated to him prior to acceptance. 56

CHAPTER 2

14. *Drennan v. Star Paving Co.* A promise that the promisor should reasonably expect to induce action or forbearance of a definite and substantial character on the part of a promisee and which does induce such action or forbearance is binding if injustice can be avoided only by enforcement of the promise. *57*

15. *United States Life Insurance Company v. Wilson.* The common-law mailbox rule for determining when an acceptance has been made applies to a paper check initiated electronically by the offeree and sent to the offeror by the offeree's agent in a manner permitted by the offer. *59*

16. *Dorton v. Collins & Aikman Corp.* An arbitration provision may be deemed a nonmaterial alteration of the contract in certain circumstances. *61*

17. *C. Itoh & Co. (America) Inc. v. Jordan Intl. Co.* Under the Uniform Commercial Code (UCC), where a merchant seller expressly conditions acceptance on the merchant buyer's assent to additional terms contained in the seller's standard sales acknowledgment form, but the buyer does not assent to those terms, and the parties nevertheless perform by delivery of goods and payment therefor, thus creating a contract by conduct under § 2-207(3), any "supplementary terms" in the contract thus formed are limited to the standardized "gap-filler" provisions of UCC Article Two. *62*

18. *Bayway Refining Co. v. Oxygenated Marketing & Trading A.G.* A merchant who asserts that a proposed additional term to a contract constitutes a material alteration under Uniform Commercial Code (UCC) § 2-207(2)(b) will not prevail on his claim where he fails to raise a factual issue as to whether the term results in surprise or hardship to him. *64*

19. *Northrop Corp. v. Litronic Industries.* Under the Uniform Commercial Code (UCC), where a seller's offer and a buyer's acceptance contain terms that are different from each other, the discrepant terms are knocked out and replaced by the UCC's default gap-filling terms. *66*

20. *Hill v. Gateway 2000, Inc.* Terms sent in the box with a product that state that they govern the sale unless the product is returned within 30 days are binding on a buyer who does not return the product. *68*

21. *Klocek v. Gateway.* A purchaser does not necessarily accept the standard terms and conditions agreement, which may include an arbitration clause, located in the package containing a mail order product. *69*

22. *Kauders v. Uber Technologies, Inc.* A putative online contract is not enforceable where there is no reasonable notice of its terms and no reasonable manifestation of assent to those terms. *70*

23. *Meyer v. Uber Technologies, Inc.* (1) For purposes of the enforceability of an arbitration agreement, the terms of which are provided on a smartphone application, the terms are reasonably conspicuous where, viewed from the perspective of a reasonable smartphone user, the design and interface of the application provide notice of the terms. (2) Where a smartphone user is on inquiry notice of an application's terms of service and the user is notified that by registering to use the application the user is agreeing to those terms, a user unambiguously assents to those terms by registering to use the application's service. *73*

24. *Hoffman v. Red Owl Stores.* It is not necessary for the promise needed to sustain a cause of action to embrace all essential details of a proposed transaction between promisor and promisee so as to be the equivalent of an offer that would result in a binding contract between the parties if the promisee were to accept the same. *76*

25. *Dixon v. Wells Fargo Bank, N.A.* A mortgagor states a claim for promissory estoppel where the mortgagor, in reliance on the mortgagee's oral promise to consider the mortgagor for a mortgage loan modification, has taken steps, including stopping payments on the loan, that render the mortgagor worse off by subjecting the mortgagor to foreclosure. *78*

26. *Cyberchron Corp. v. Calldata Systems Development, Inc.* Promissory estoppel has three elements: (1) a clear and unambiguous promise; (2) a reasonable and foreseeable reliance by the party to whom the promise is made; and (3) an injury sustained by the party asserting the estoppel by reason of the reliance. *81*

27. *Channel Home Centers, Division of Grace Retail Corp. v. Grossman.* A letter of intent to rent providing that the lessor will take the unit off the market is enforceable if the lessor uses the latter to help obtain financing. *82*

28. *Sun Printing & Publishing Ass'n v. Remington Paper & Power Co.* A contract will be deemed invalid due to incompleteness if the agreement does not establish the length of time the terms of the agreement, such as the price, shall apply. *83*

29. *Oglebay Norton Co. v. Armco, Inc.* If the parties intend to conclude a contract for the sale of goods where the price is not settled, the price is a reasonable price at the time of delivery if the price is to be fixed in terms of an agreed standard set by a third person or agency and is not so set. *84*

Lucy v. Zehmer

Farm purchaser (P) v. Joking seller (D)

Va. Sup. Ct. App., 196 Va. 493, 84 S.E.2d 516 (1954)

NATURE OF CASE: Appeal from dismissal of action for specific performance of a land sale contract.

FACT SUMMARY: Zehmer (D) claimed his offer to sell his farm to Lucy (P) was made in jest.

RULE OF LAW

If a person's words and acts, judged by a reasonable standard, manifest a certain intent, it is immaterial what may be the real but unexpressed state of that person's mind.

FACTS: Zehmer (D) and his wife (D) contracted to sell their 471-acre farm to Lucy (P) for $50,000. Zehmer (D) contends that his offer was made in jest while the three of them were drinking, and that Zehmer (D) only desired to bluff Lucy (P) into admitting he did not have $50,000. Lucy (P) appears to have taken the offer seriously by discussing its terms with Zehmer (D), by rewriting it to enable Mrs. Zehmer (D) to sign, by providing for title examination, and by taking possession of the agreement. Lucy (P) offered $5 to bind the deal and the next day sold a one-half interest to his brother (P) in order to raise money. When Zehmer (D) refused to perform the contract, Lucy (P) sued to enforce it, but the court dismissed the action. Lucy (P) appealed.

ISSUE: Does the law impute to a person an intention corresponding to the reasonable meaning of his words and acts?

HOLDING AND DECISION: (Buchanan, J.) Yes. The existence of an offer depends upon the reasonable meaning to be given the offeror's acts and words. For the formation of a contract, the mental assent of the parties is not required. If the words and acts of one of the parties have but one reasonable meaning, his undisclosed intention is immaterial except when an unreasonable meaning that he attaches to his manifestations is known to the other party. Accordingly, one cannot say he was merely jesting when his conduct and words would warrant reasonable belief that a real agreement was intended. Reversed and remanded.

ANALYSIS

Note that it is not what is said, but how it is heard and reasonably understood. Mutual assent of the parties is required for the formation of a contract, but mental assent is not. Where one party can reasonably believe from the other party's acts and words that a real agreement is intended, the other party's real but unexpressed intention is immaterial. Mutual assent is an objective determination based upon what a reasonable person would believe. An offer is an expression of will or intention creating a power of acceptance upon the offeree. If the offer to sell the farm had been for a price of $50, the court could judge the ridiculousness of the offer in determining whether a reasonable person would believe it to be serious.

Quicknotes

MUTUAL ASSENT A requirement of a valid contract that the parties possess a mutuality of assent as manifested by the terms of the agreement and not by a hidden intent.

SPECIFIC PERFORMANCE An equitable remedy whereby the court requires the parties to perform their obligations pursuant to a contract.

Specht v. Netscape Communications Corp.

User (P) v. Software program provider (D)

306 F.3d 17 (2d Cir. 2002)

NATURE OF CASE: Motion to compel arbitration.

FACT SUMMARY: Specht (P) downloaded from the Internet free software from Netscape Communications Corp. (Netscape) (D). When an issue arose as to Specht's (P) use of the software, Netscape (D) moved to compel arbitration.

RULE OF LAW

Where consumers are urged to download free software, mere reference to the existence of license terms on a submerged screen does not place consumers on inquiry notice or constructive notice of terms.

FACTS: Specht (P) downloaded from the Internet free software from Netscape Communications Corp. (Netscape) (D). Specht (P) then brought suit against Netscape (D), alleging that usage of the software transmitted to Netscape (D) private information about the user's file transfer activity on the Internet in violation of federal statute. Netscape (D) moved to compel arbitration, arguing that Specht's (P) downloading of the Netscape (D) software constituted acceptance of the compulsory arbitration provision contained in the online licensing agreement.

ISSUE: Where consumers are urged to download free software, does mere reference to the existence of license terms on a submerged screen place consumers on inquiry notice or constructive notice of terms?

HOLDING AND DECISION: (Sotomayor, J.) No. Mere reference to the existence of license terms on a submerged screen does not place consumers on inquiry notice or constructive notice of terms. The download webpage screen was printed in such a manner that it tended to conceal the fact that it was an express acceptance of Netscape Communications Corp.'s (Netscape's) (D) rules and regulations. There is no reason to assume that viewers will scroll down to subsequent screens simply because screens are there. Netscape (D) relies on cases that involve shrinkwrap licensing that placed consumers on inquiry notice. Those cases, *Hill v. Gateway 2000, Inc.*, 105 F.3d 1147 (7th Cir. 1997), and *ProCD, Inc. v. Zeidenberg*, 86 F.3d 1447 (7th Cir. 1996), do not help Netscape (D) because the licensing in those cases was conspicuous. Specht (P) was responding to an offer that did not carry an immediate visible notice of the existence of license terms or require unambiguous manifestations of assent to those terms. The uncontested evidence revealed that Specht (P) was unaware that Netscape (D) intended to attach license terms to the use of the downloaded software. The district court's denial of the motion to compel arbitration is affirmed.

ANALYSIS

As noted by the court in *Specht*, when products are "free" and users are invited to download them in the absence of reasonably conspicuous notice that they are about to bind themselves to contract terms, the transactional circumstances cannot be fully analogized to those "in the paper world" of arm's-length bargaining.

Quicknotes

CONSTRUCTIVE NOTICE Knowledge of a fact that is imputed to an individual who was under a duty to inquire and who could have learned of the fact through the exercise of reasonable prudence.

INQUIRY NOTICE The communication of information that would cause an ordinary person of average prudence to inquire as to its truth.

Cohen v. Cowles Media Co.

Political insider (P) v. Publishing company (D)

Minn. Sup. Ct., 457 N.W.2d 199 (1990)

NATURE OF CASE: Appeal from judgment awarding plaintiff damages for breach of contract.

FACT SUMMARY: Two newspapers broke promises their reporters had made to Cohen (P) by naming him as the source that had "leaked" unfavorable information to reporters during an electoral campaign.

RULE OF LAW

The reporter's promise of anonymity is given as a moral commitment, but a moral obligation alone will not support a contract.

FACTS: Cohen (P) was working for a candidate in a gubernatorial campaign and approached two reporters with an offer to disclose some newsworthy documents to them in return for their promise to preserve his anonymity. Both reporters agreed, but both published Cohen's (P) name as the source of the information about charges that had been filed against another candidate. Cohen (P) was subsequently fired and publicly attacked for his "sleazy" tactics. Cohen (P) sued Cowles Media Co. (D) and Northwest Publications (D), the newspapers' publishers, for fraudulent misrepresentation and breach of contract. A jury found liability on both claims and awarded compensatory and punitive damages. The court of appeals dismissed the claim based on fraudulent misrepresentation but allowed the breach of contract claim. Cowles Media (D) appealed.

ISSUE: Does a newspaper's promise to maintain a reporter's anonymity create a legal obligation?

HOLDING AND DECISION: (Simonett, J.) No. The reporter's promise of anonymity is given as a moral commitment, but a moral obligation alone will not support a contract. The reporters understand that only a moral, and not a legal, obligation is created when an arrangement is made for the exchange of information. No contract theory should be superimposed on a moral and ethical obligation. The law does not impose a contract where the parties did not intend one. Reversed.

ANALYSIS

The commercial media defendants in this case were held to be immune from breach of contract claims that would probably be enforced against nonmedia defendants. Cohen (P) did not file a defamation suit since the information he disclosed was true. This case was later reversed by the United States Supreme Court on First Amendment grounds.

Quicknotes

EXPECTATION DAMAGES Damages awarded in actions for nonperformance of a contract, which are calculated by subtracting the injured party's actual dollar position as a result of the breach from that party's expected dollar position had the breach not occurred.

PROMISSORY ESTOPPEL A promise that is enforceable if the promisor should reasonably expect that it will induce action or forbearance on the part of the promisee, that does in fact cause such action or forbearance, and that is the only means of avoiding injustice.

RELIANCE Dependence on a fact that causes a party to act or refrain from acting.

Owen v. Tunison

Would-be property buyer (P) v. Owner (D)

Me. Sup. Jud. Ct., 131 Me. 42, 158 A. 926 (1932)

NATURE OF CASE: Action for damages for breach of contract for sale of real property.

FACT SUMMARY: Tunison (D) replied by letter to Owen's (P) offer to buy Tunison's (D) lot and buildings thereon for $6,000, saying that he could not sell for less than $16,000.

RULE OF LAW

There can be no contract, no meeting of the minds, between the parties unless there is an offer.

FACTS: Owen (P) desired to purchase Tunison's (D) lot and buildings thereon in Bucksport, Maine. Owen (P) wrote Tunison (D) in this regard and offered a purchase price of $6,000. Several weeks later, Tunison (D) replied by letter that he could not sell "unless I was to receive $16,000 cash." Owen (P) replied that he accepted Tunison's (D) offer to sell for $16,000. Tunison (D) refused to go through with the sale, and Owen (P) sued for breach of contract.

ISSUE: Is the statement of a minimum sale price to be construed as an offer to sell at that price?

HOLDING AND DECISION: (Barnes, J.) No. It cannot be successfully argued that a potential seller's statement of the minimum price he would be willing to accept is an offer to sell at that price. Rather, it is to be construed as an invitation to the potential buyer to make further offers or to enter negotiations that might lead to a sale. Tunison's (D) letter was most likely written with the intent to open negotiations. It was not a proposal to sell. Judgment for Tunison (D).

ANALYSIS

When a potential seller states a price that would be the minimum price acceptable to him or her, the seller is not offering to sell at that price. Instead, the seller is indicating the level at which he or she may be willing to accept a new offer. The potential seller thereby invites new offers or indicates nothing more than a willingness to enter negotiations. In construing the potential seller's language, it may be helpful to redraft his or her response, i.e., "I will sell for $X," or "I will not consider an offer of less than $X," and then determine which response appears to come closer to the meaning of the actual language used.

Quicknotes

BREACH OF CONTRACT Unlawful failure by a party to perform its obligations pursuant to contract.

OFFER A proposed promise to undertake performance of an action, or to refrain from acting, that is to become binding upon acceptance by the offeree.

Fairmount Glass Works v. Crunden-Martin Woodenware Company

Glass company (D) v. Jar buyer (P)

Ky. Ct. App., 106 Ky. 659, 51 S.W. 196 (1899)

NATURE OF CASE: Appeal from judgment for plaintiff in action to recover damages for breach of contract for sale of goods.

FACT SUMMARY: Crunden-Martin Woodenware Company (Crunden) (P) requested by letter of Fairmount Glass Works (Fairmont) (D) the lowest price it could give on Crunden's (P) order for Mason jars, which prices Fairmount (D) gave to Crunden (P) but whose order Fairmount (D) then refused to fill.

RULE OF LAW

Where prices are requested on an order and the vendor quotes those prices to the vendee, the vendor has offered to fill the order and is obligated to fill the order upon receipt within a reasonable time of vendee's acceptance.

FACTS: Crunden-Martin Woodenware Company (Crunden) (P) requested of Fairmount Glass Works (Fairmont) (D) by letter dated April 20, 1895, the lowest price at which Fairmount (D) could fill Crunden's (P) order for ten carloads of Mason jars. Fairmount (D) answered by letter dated April 23, 1895, with its prices for different sizes of jars with terms and conditions "for immediate acceptance." Crunden (P) telegraphed a reply on April 24, 1895, to "enter order ten carloads as per your quotation. Specifications mailed." The same day, Fairmount (D) telegraphed back it could not fill the order, its output was sold out. Fairmount (D) then received by mail Crunden's (P) specifications calling for "strictly first-quality goods," which Fairmount (D) contends was not an acceptance of their offer (if the court finds an offer) as made. The lower court found for Crunden (P), and Fairmount (D) appealed.

ISSUE: Is the quotation of prices by the vendor upon vendee's request for such quotation as part of its order an offer by the vendor to the vendee for goods at the quoted prices, terms, and conditions for vendee to accept or reject?

HOLDING AND DECISION: (Hobson, J.) Yes. Where prices are requested on an order and the vendor quotes those prices to the vendee, the vendor has offered to fill the order and is obligated to fill the order upon receipt within a reasonable time of vendee's acceptance. In this case, the quotation of prices "for immediate acceptance" upon Crunden-Martin Woodenware Company's (Crunden's) (P) order was more than a simple quotation of prices; it was an offer. The true meaning of the correspondence is determined by reading it as a whole. After Crunden (P) had accepted the terms, Fairmount (D) could not withdraw its offer. Fairmount Glass Works' (Fairmount's) (D) use of the term "for immediate acceptance" when considered with previous communication indicates an intent to make an offer to Crunden (P), who could then accept or reject within a reasonable time. Fairmount's (D) claim that Crunden's (P) specifications which were received after Fairmount (D) withdrew its offer, were not within the terms of Crunden's (P) telegraphed acceptance fails as Fairmount (D) did not state this objection in its withdrawal of its offer. Affirmed.

ANALYSIS

Ordinarily, the mere quotation of prices is not an offer to sell at those prices but rather an invitation to make an offer. Where the evidence shows the intent of the parties to be otherwise, that is, an offer was intended, the general rule will not be followed. The existence of an offer is determined by considering what a reasonable person would believe from his or her consideration of the words and acts of the other party. It is also suggested that the court is holding the vendee's price inquiry upon an order as a strong basis for vendee's reliance on the vendor's price quotation. Where the price quotation is unsolicited or in response to the general question of what the vendor's lowest price would be, the vendee lacks the reliance seen in this case.

Quicknotes

ACCEPTANCE Assent to the specified terms of an offer, resulting in the formation of a binding agreement.

BREACH OF CONTRACT Unlawful failure by a party to perform its obligations pursuant to contract.

OFFER A proposed promise to undertake performance of an action, or to refrain from acting, that is to become binding upon acceptance by the offeree.

RELIANCE Dependence on a fact that causes a party to act or refrain from acting.

Lefkowitz v. Great Minneapolis Surplus Store

Customer (P) v. Advertiser (D)

Minn. Sup. Ct., 251 Minn. 188, 86 N.W.2d 689 (1957)

NATURE OF CASE: Action to recover damages for breach of contract.

FACT SUMMARY: Great Minneapolis Surplus Store (D) advertised one fur stole on a "first come first served" basis but would not sell the stole to Lefkowitz (P), who accepted the alleged offer.

RULE OF LAW

A newspaper advertisement that is clear, definite, and explicit, and leaves nothing to negotiation is an offer, acceptance of which creates a binding contract.

FACTS: Great Minneapolis Surplus Store (Surplus Store) (D) published the following advertisement in a Minneapolis newspaper:

> SATURDAY 9 A.M.
> 2 BRAND NEW PASTEL
> MINK 3-SKIN SCARFS
> Selling for $89.50
> Out they go
> Saturday. Each . . . $1.00
> 1 BLACK LAPIN STOLE BEAUTIFUL,
> worth $139.50 . . . $1.00
> FIRST COME FIRST SERVED

Lefkowitz (P) was the first to present himself on Saturday and demanded the Lapin Stole for one dollar. Surplus Store (D) refused to sell to him because of a "house rule "that the offer was intended for women only. Lefkowitz (P) sued Surplus Store (D) and was awarded $138.50 as damages. Surplus Store (D) appealed.

ISSUE: Is a newspaper advertisement that is clear, definite, and explicit, and leaves nothing to negotiation an offer, acceptance of which creates a binding contract?

HOLDING AND DECISION: (Murphy, J.) Yes. A newspaper advertisement that is clear, definite, and explicit, and leaves nothing to negotiation is an offer, acceptance of which creates a binding contract. The test of whether a binding obligation may originate in advertisements addressed to the public is whether the facts show that some performance was promised in positive terms in return for something requested. Whether an advertisement is an offer or merely an invitation for offers depends on the legal intention of the parties and the surrounding circumstances. Where an offer is clear, definite, and explicit, and leaves nothing open for negotiation, it constitutes an offer such that acceptance of it will create a contract. With respect to the Lapin fur, Surplus Store's (D) advertisement was such an offer. As to Surplus Store's (D) alleged "house rule," while an advertiser has the right at any time before acceptance to modify his offer, he does not have the right, after acceptance, to impose new or arbitrary conditions not contained in the published offer. Affirmed.

ANALYSIS

Although most advertisements for goods at a certain price are held not to be offers, the present case presents an interesting exception to that rule. Restatement (Second), § 25 (Illustration No. 1), indicates the basis of the court's decision is that the words "first come first served" create language of promise that is ordinarily lacking in an advertisement for the sale of goods. Probably it was this factor in conjunction with the statement of a quantity (to wit, one) that motivated the court. Caveat: The Uniform Commercial Code has dealt a blow to the present court's insistence that nothing be left open for negotiation [see Uniform Commercial Code § 2-204(3)].

Quicknotes

ACCEPTANCE Assent to the specified terms of an offer, resulting in the formation of a binding agreement.

BREACH OF CONTRACT Unlawful failure by a party to perform its obligations pursuant to contract.

DAMAGES Monetary compensation that may be awarded by the court to a party who has sustained injury or loss to his or her person, property, or rights due to another party's unlawful act, omission, or negligence.

OFFER A proposed promise to undertake performance of an action, or to refrain from acting, that is to become binding upon acceptance by the offeree.

OFFEREE A person or party to whom an offer to enter into a contractual agreement is made.

Kincaid v. Eaton

Reward claimant (P) v. Reward offeror(D)

Mass. Sup. Jud. Ct., 98 Mass. 139 (1867)

NATURE OF CASE: Appeal from judgment for plaintiff in action to collect on a reward for finding lost property.

FACT SUMMARY: Kincaid (P), who found Eaton's (D) pocketbook and its valuable contents while at a bank, contended that he was entitled to an advertised reward for the pocketbook upon returning the pocketbook and its contents to Eaton (D), because the reward had been offered to "the finder."

RULE OF LAW

The discovery of property voluntarily laid down by the property's owner within a bank, on a desk provided for the use of those having business at the bank, does not constitute "finding" of the property that would entitle the person discovering the property to a reward offered to "the finder."

FACTS: While at the bank, Kincaid (P) found a pocketbook, with valuable documents inside it, on a desk used by bank customers. Eaton (D), the pocketbook's owner, believing he had lost the pocketbook, advertised a $110 reward for its return, which Eaton (D) would pay to "the finder." Kincaid (P) had made efforts to find the pocketbook's owner, without success, but then learned of the advertised reward, and went to Eaton's (D) home to give Eaton (D) the pocketbook and claim the reward. When Eaton (D) refused to pay the reward, Kincaid (P) sued on the putative contract. A jury rendered judgment for Kincaid (P), and Eaton (D) appealed. The state's highest court granted review.

ISSUE: Does the discovery of property voluntarily laid down by the property's owner within a bank, on a desk provided for the use of those having business at the bank, constitute "finding" of the property that would entitle the person discovering the property to a reward offered to "the finder"?

HOLDING AND DECISION: (Wells, J.) No. The discovery of property voluntarily laid down by the property's owner within a bank, on a desk provided for the use of those having business at the bank, does not constitute "finding" of the property that would entitle the person discovering the property to a reward offered to "the finder." Kincaid (P) was not a "finder" of the pocketbook, because it had not truly been lost. Instead, the bank was the proper depositary of the pocketbook. Therefore, Kincaid (P) cannot establish a right to the reward according to the reward's terms because he was not a "finder" in the sense meant by the reward offer. Reversed.

ANALYSIS

The court in this case resolves the contractual issue presented by looking to property law for a definition of "finder." Common-law property principles provide that lost property is property that its owner unintentionally and unknowingly lost. Common law also provides that mislaid property is property that the owner intentionally placed in a given location and then left, either intentionally or unintentionally. Mislaid property belongs to the one who controls the *locus in quo* (the place where the mislaid property was left) until the true owner is located and the property is returned. Applying these principles here, the judge reasoned that Eaton's (D) pocketbook essentially was mislaid property, not lost property, and, hence, that it belonged to the bank until it was returned to Eaton (D). Not being "lost," the pocketbook could not have been "found" by Kincaid (P).

Wucherpfennig v. Dooley

Sibling (P) v. Sibling (D)

N.D. Sup. Ct., 351 N.W.2d 443 (1984)

NATURE OF CASE: Appeal from dismissal of claim for specific performance of alleged land sale contract.

FACT SUMMARY: Donald Wucherpfennig (Donald) (P) contended that he had a contract with his sister, Elizabeth Dooley (Elizabeth) (D), for the sale of her interest in their parents' farm, on the basis that Elizabeth (D) offered to sell the land to him, and that he accepted the offer, so that the contract could be enforced by specific performance.

RULE OF LAW
A contract cannot be formed where an alleged acceptance of an offer is not absolute, unequivocal, and unconditional, so that the offer and alleged acceptance do not express assent to the same thing.

FACTS: After their parents were deceased, Donald Wucherpfennig (Donald) (P), Elizabeth Dooley (Elizabeth) (D), and another sibling inherited different interests in their parents' farm. During probate, Elizabeth (D) expressed an interest in selling her share of the property to Donald (P). On January 4, 1979, she sent to Robert Case (Case), the attorney handling the probate of the estate, a letter that stated: "Now if Don wants to buy my share of the real estate, I will sell it to him for $200 an acre, provided it is a cash deal & handled promptly." Case responded by letter dated January 13, 1979, stating that Donald (P) was "interested" in such a transaction, and Case subsequently followed up with another letter, dated February 17, 1979, which stated: "Donald has made arrangements with the Federal Land Bank to secure funds to purchase your interest in the estate farmland and we are therefore ready to proceed with this transaction. Please let me know the exact dollar amount that you expect to receive for your interest in the land. . . ." Elizabeth (D) did not respond to this letter but revoked her offer to sell the land to Donald (P) for $200 per acre by a letter dated March 9, 1979. Donald (P) brought suit for specific enforcement of the alleged contract with Elizabeth (D), which Donald (P) claimed was formed by Elizabeth's (D) offer of January 4, and his acceptance as communicated by Case on February 17. The trial court, finding there had not been an acceptance of Elizabeth's (D) offer, dismissed. The state's highest court granted review.

ISSUE: Can a contract be formed where an alleged acceptance of an offer is not absolute, unequivocal, and unconditional, so that the offer and alleged acceptance do not express assent to the same thing?

HOLDING AND DECISION: (Sand, J.) No. A contract cannot be formed where an alleged acceptance of an offer is not absolute, unequivocal, and unconditional, so that the offer and alleged acceptance do not express assent to the same thing. Although Elizabeth Dooley (Elizabeth) (D) made an offer, Robert Case's (Case's) February 17 letter did not unequivocally accept that offer, since it merely stated that Donald Wucherpfennig (Donald) (P) had "made arrangements" and was "ready to proceed." The language of the February 17 letter does not embody an absolute, unequivocal, and unconditional acceptance of Elizabeth's (D) offer and is not expressive of an intent to create, without more, a contract. The terms of the letter appear to be more in the nature of negotiations with a view toward reaching an agreement in the future. Case also asks in the letter what amount Elizabeth (D) expects to receive for her interest in the property. Taken together, the words in the letter are not words of an unequivocal, unconditional acceptance of Elizabeth's (D) offer. This conclusion is supported by Donald's (P) testimony, which indicated that he believed Elizabeth (D) would not have accepted the amount he was prepared to pay. Thus, the parties can hardly be said to have mutually assented to the terms of a contract. Because there was no acceptance by Donald (P) of Elizabeth's (D) offer, there was no contract that could be specifically enforced. Affirmed.

ANALYSIS

The Restatement (Second) of Contracts defines acceptance of an offer by promise as the manifestation of assent to the terms of the offer made by the offeree in a manner invited or required by the offer. Acceptance by a promise requires that the offeree complete every act essential to the making of the promise. Under the Restatement, acceptance by performance requires that at least part of what the offer requests be performed or tendered and includes acceptance by a performance that operates as a return promise. Typically, transactions that involve significant economic value are based on an offer that seeks the offeree's promise in return for the offeror's promise.

Quicknotes

ACCEPTANCE Assent to the specified terms of an offer, resulting in the formation of a binding agreement.

SPECIFIC PERFORMANCE An equitable remedy whereby the court requires the parties to perform their obligations pursuant to a contract.

International Filter Co. v. Conroe Gin, Ice & Light Co.

Water purifier manufacturer (P) v. Ice manufacturer (D)

Tex. Comm. App., 277 S.W. 631 (1925)

NATURE OF CASE: Appeal from defense judgment in action for damages for breach of contract.

FACT SUMMARY: International Filter Co. (Filter) (P) offered a water purifier to Conroe Gin, Ice & Light Co. (Conroe) (D) by letter, stating that there would be a contract when Conroe's (D) acceptance was approved by Filter's (P) executive officer at its Chicago office. This was done, but Conroe (D) revoked its order claiming no contract existed.

RULE OF LAW

As the offeror is in control of his offer, he may specify the type of acceptance that is required and can dispense with the requirement of its communication.

FACTS: International Filter Co. (Filter) (P), through its traveling salesman, submitted to Conroe Gin, Ice & Light Co. (Conroe) (D) a letter offering a water purification system and stating that a contract for purchase would arise when Conroe's (D) order was received and approved by an executive officer of Filter (P) in its Chicago office. On the same day, Conroe (D) communicated its order, which was approved by Engel, Filter's (P) President and Vice President. Filter (P) then sent an acknowledgment of Conroe's (D) order and requested Conroe (D) send a water sample so the purifier could be properly adjusted before shipment. Two weeks later, Conroe (D) revoked its order, and Filter (P) sued, but the judge found in favor of Conroe (D). The appeals court affirmed, and Filter (P) appealed.

ISSUE: May an offeror specify the type of acceptance required?

HOLDING AND DECISION: (Nickels, J.) Yes. As the offeror is in control of his offer, he may specify the type of acceptance that is required and can dispense with the requirement of its communication. In this case, notice of acceptance of Conroe Gin, Ice & Light Co.'s (Conroe's) (D) order was not required to be communicated by International Filter Co. (Filter) (P) to Conroe (D). Engel's endorsement of the order was an approval by an executive officer at Filter's (P) Chicago office. The paper then became a contract as notice of acceptance was not required under the terms of the offer. A prompt order was required, and it was expressly stated that a contract would arise upon approval by Filter's (P) executive officer in Chicago. Even though notice of acceptance was not required, Filter's (P) letter of acknowledgment and request for a water sample sufficiently communicated acceptance anyway. The form of the notice of acceptance can be quite different from the acceptance itself. It was quite clear that Filter (P) intended to ship the system and would not have so intended unless it had accepted the order. Reversed and remanded by Cureton, C.J., as recommended.

ANALYSIS

Generally, when an offer looks to a bilateral contract, the offeree's promise must be communicated to the offeror. But as the offeror is the "master" of his or her offer, he or she can specify the type of acceptance required and can dispense with the requirement of a communication altogether. Restatement (Second) of Contracts, § 56 does not follow this case and requires that the offeree exercise "reasonable diligence to notify the offeror of acceptance or that the offeror will receive an acceptance seasonably." Usually, however, notification of acceptance does not explicitly have to be given if it is made clear by the course of events that it has been given implicitly.

Quicknotes

ACCEPTANCE Assent to the specified terms of an offer, resulting in the formation of a binding agreement.

BILATERAL CONTRACT An agreement pursuant to which each party promises to undertake an obligation, or to forbear from acting.

BREACH OF CONTRACT Unlawful failure by a party to perform its obligations pursuant to contract.

REVOCATION The cancellation or withdrawal of some authority conferred, or destruction or making void an instrument drafted.

White v. Corlies & Tift

Builder (P) v. Merchant (D)

N.Y. Ct. App., 46 N.Y. 467 (1871)

NATURE OF CASE: Appeal from plaintiff's verdict in action for damages for breach of contract.

FACT SUMMARY: White (P) attempted to accept an offer by Corlies & Tift (D) by beginning performance of "fitting up" a suite of offices, without indicating to Corlies & Tift (D) his intention to accept.

RULE OF LAW

Acceptance of an offer must be manifested in such a way as to be communicated to the offeror.

FACTS: Corlies & Tift (D) requested that White (P) make an estimate for the fitting up of a suite of offices. The day following White's (P) submission of his estimate, Corlies & Tift's (D) bookkeeper wrote to White (P): "Upon an agreement to finish the fitting up of offices at 57 Broadway in two weeks from date, you can begin at once. The writer will call again, probably between 5 and 6 this p.m." Without replying to the note, White (P) immediately commenced performance by purchasing lumber and beginning work thereon. The following day, Corlies & Tift (D) countermanded their offer. White (P) successfully brought this action for damages for breach of contract, and Corlies (D) appealed.

ISSUE: Can an offeree accept an offer by merely beginning performance without indicating his intention to accept to the offeror?

HOLDING AND DECISION: (Folger, J.) No. Acceptance of an offer must be manifested in such a way as to be communicated to the offeror. Where the offeree's act of beginning performance is no indication in itself that he intends to accept the offer, he must manifest his intent to accept by some appropriate act. The only overt act that White (P) claims as indicating his acceptance of the offer was the purchase of those materials necessary for the work and commencing work. Such action was as well referable to one state of facts as another, and such action did not, in itself, indicate acceptance of the offer. White (P), as offeree, had the duty to manifest his intention to accept in the proper way, to be in the usual course of events, in some reasonable time communicated to Corlies & Tift (D). It is not necessary that such manifestation actually reach the offeror before he is bound by the offeree's acceptance. It is enough that the offeree set in motion an indication of his acceptance of the offer, which would normally result in his communication to the offeror. Reversed; new trial ordered.

ANALYSIS

The problem in this case is the ambiguous meaning of the bookkeeper's note to White (P). Did the offer invite acceptance by return promise or by performance? Was the agreement yet to be accepted by White's (P) promise, or had a contract already been concluded, allowing immediate performance by White (P)? The lower court determined that White (P) had a right to act on the note that Corlies & Tift's (D) offer looked toward performance rather than toward a return promise, or a unilateral contract. However, this appraisal was reversed by the court of appeals which concluded the offer was not one that could be accepted by mere performance but looked toward and must be expressly assented to by a return promise or a bilateral contract.

Quicknotes

ACCEPTANCE Assent to the specified terms of an offer, resulting in the formation of a binding agreement.

BILATERAL CONTRACT An agreement pursuant to which each party promises to undertake an obligation, or to forbear from acting.

BREACH OF CONTRACT Unlawful failure by a party to perform its obligations pursuant to contract.

Ever-Tite Roofing Corp. v. Green

Roofing contractor (P) v. House owner (D)

La. Ct. App., 83 So. 2d 449 (1955)

NATURE OF CASE: Appeal from dismissal of action for damages for breach of contract.

FACT SUMMARY: The Greens (D) attempted to withdraw from a roofing contract after the Ever-Tite Roofing Corp. (P) workmen had arrived to perform the work.

RULE OF LAW

Where a contract does not specify a time within which it may be accepted, a "reasonable time" will be implied.

FACTS: The Greens (D) signed a document setting out work to be done and price to be paid to Ever-Tite Roofing Corp. (Ever-Tite) (P) for reroofing their residence. A provision in the agreement stated that it would become binding upon either written acceptance or commencement of performance by Ever-Tite (P), after credit approval was obtained. Nine days later, Ever-Tite (P) loaded its trucks and sent its workmen and material to the Greens' (D) residence, where they were not permitted to work, as other roofers had been retained in their stead. The Greens (D) contend they had given Ever-Tite (P) timely notice of their withdrawal from the contract, before Ever-Tite (P) commenced actual performance of the work. Ever-Tite (P) sued the Greens (D) for breach of contract.

ISSUE: Where a contract does not specify a time within which it may be accepted, will a "reasonable time" be implied?

HOLDING AND DECISION: (Ayres, J.) Yes. Where a contract does not specify a time within which it may be accepted, a "reasonable time" will be implied. Contrary to the lower court's ruling, Ever-Tite Roofing Corp. (Ever-Tite (P) commenced performance by the loading of its trucks and transporting of its materials and workmen to the Greens' (D) residence. Thus, Ever-Tite (P) did accept the offer before withdrawal of the Greens' (D) acceptance, even though actual work was not begun. Since the contract specified no time period within which it was to be accepted, "a reasonable time must be allowed therefor in accordance with the facts and circumstances and the evident intention of the parties." Since the Greens (D) knew a delay was necessary for credit approval, and since Ever-Tite (P) proceeded with due diligence, Ever-Tite (P) accepted by commencing performance within a reasonable time. Reversed.

ANALYSIS

The problem here is somewhat different from that of *White v. Corlies and Tift*, 46 N.Y. 467 (1871), where the manner of acceptance was simply omitted from the contract. The court there held with the original Restatement in its assumption that the offer looked toward a bilateral contract. The modern view, however, as stated in Uniform Commercial Code § 2-206, is that the offeree may choose either manner of acceptance when not explicitly restricted to a certain type of acceptance. Where an acceptance is contingent upon credit approval, as in this case, it is especially important that the manner of acceptance be clearly set out in the offer so that the parties will know exactly when the contract is formed. The provision of the offer requiring "written acceptance" or "commencing performance of the work" as alternate terms of acceptance could have been made more explicit by stating: (1) a specific time period allowed for acceptance and (2) what acts would constitute commencement of performance.

Quicknotes

ACCEPTANCE Assent to the specified terms of an offer, resulting in the formation of a binding agreement.

BILATERAL CONTRACT An agreement pursuant to which each party promises to undertake an obligation, or to forbear from acting.

BREACH OF CONTRACT Unlawful failure by a party to perform its obligations pursuant to contract.

DUE DILIGENCE The standard of care as would be taken by a reasonable person in accordance with the attendant facts and circumstances.

OFFEREE A person or party to whom an offer to enter into a contractual agreement is made.

Corinthian Pharmaceutical Systems, Inc. v. Lederle Laboratories

Distributor (P) v. Manufacturer (D)

724 F. Supp. 605 (S.D. Ind. 1989)

NATURE OF CASE: Motion for specific performance of sales contract.

FACT SUMMARY: Corinthian Pharmaceutical Systems, Inc. (Corinthian) (P), distributor of DTP vaccine, placed an order with Lederle Laboratories (Lederle) (D), manufacturer, for 1,000 vials of vaccine, but when only part of the order was delivered and the remainder was to be shipped later at a higher price, Corinthian (P) brought an action for breach of contract.

RULE OF LAW

A seller's price list is not an offer to the buyer, and a subsequent partial shipment of the buyer's order is not an acceptance sufficient to form a contract.

FACTS: Corinthian Pharmaceutical Systems, Inc. (Corinthian) (P) distributed DTP vaccines, which were purchased from Lederle Laboratories (Lederle) (D) on a regular basis. As a routine business practice, Lederle (D) issued price lists to its customers. The list stated that the prices were subject to change without notice and that any changes take effect at the time of shipment. In an internal memo to its representatives, Lederle (D) indicated that the price for the vaccine would be increased to $171 per vial due to the high cost of insurance and product liability lawsuits. The content of the memo was leaked to Corinthian (P) before the price increase was to be announced to the other customers. Corinthian (P) immediately placed an order for 1,000 vials through Lederle's (D) computer ordering system. The order stated that $64.32 would be the payable price for each vial. Lederle (D) made a partial shipment of 50 vials at the price indicated in Corinthian's (P) order, which was accepted. At the same time, Lederle (D) sent a letter to Corinthian (P) indicating that the partial shipment was to accommodate the buyer, and the remainder would be shipped for the price of $171 per vial. Subsequently, Corinthian (P) brought an action for breach of contract, seeking specific performance of the order. Lederle (D) moved for summary judgment.

ISSUE: Is a seller's price quote and a partial shipment of the buyer's order a valid offer and acceptance to form an enforceable contract?

HOLDING AND DECISION: (McKinney, J.) No. A contract is formed when the offer is properly accepted and supported by consideration. An offer is a manifestation of one's willingness to enter a bargain. Thus, price quotations are not offers but only invitations for the recipient to make an offer. As a result, Lederle Laboratories' (Lederle's) (D) price lists sent to Corinthian Pharmaceutical Systems, Inc. (Corinthian) (P) did not constitute an offer. The offer was actually made by Corinthian (P) when it placed an order via the computer ordering system. Since the parties were merchants and the offer was for sale of goods, Uniform Commercial Code § 2-206 governed the mode of acceptance. The Code allows for acceptance to be in any reasonable form and manner. In addition, it provides that shipment of nonconforming goods by the seller who gives notice that the shipment is merely an accommodation is not an acceptance but a counteroffer. Here, Lederle's (D) partial shipment, although nonconforming, was a counteroffer since it was followed by a notification that the shipment is only an accommodation. Thus, there was no contract formed between the parties. Motion for summary judgment granted.

ANALYSIS

This case involved the manner by which the offeree must indicate his or her commitment or promise. Uniform Commercial Code § 2-206 no longer requires that an acceptance be the mirror image of the offer, which was required by common law. Furthermore, the commitment may either be demonstrated by promissory language or a promissory act.

Quicknotes

BREACH OF CONTRACT Unlawful failure by a party to perform its obligations pursuant to contract.

CONSIDERATION Value given by one party in exchange for performance, or a promise to perform, by another party.

COUNTEROFFER An offer made by the offeree that has the effect of rejecting the offer deemed unsatisfactory and of proposing a new offer to the offeror.

OFFER A proposed promise to undertake performance of an action, or to refrain from acting, that is to become binding upon acceptance by the offeree.

SPECIFIC PERFORMANCE An equitable remedy whereby the court requires the parties to perform their obligations pursuant to a contract.

SUMMARY JUDGMENT Judgment rendered by a court in response to a motion by one of the parties, claiming that the lack of a question of material fact in respect to an issue warrants disposition of the issue without consideration by the jury.

Dickinson v. Dodds

Land buyer (P) v. Land seller (D)

C.A., Ch. D., L.R. 2 Ch. D. 463 (1876)

NATURE OF CASE: Appeal from decree of specific performance of a land sale contract.

FACT SUMMARY: Dodds (D) attempted to revoke an offer to sell land to Dickinson (P), but Dickinson (P) agreed to purchase prior to communication of the revocation to him.

RULE OF LAW

An offeree may not bind an offeror by accepting a revoked offer, even if the revocation had not been communicated to him prior to acceptance.

FACTS: Dodds (D) offered in writing to sell certain real estate to Dickinson (P). Dodds (D) later sought to revoke the offer, but the note of revocation was not delivered to Dickinson (P). Dickinson (P) communicated acceptance to Dodds (D), who informed him that he had sold the land to another. Dickinson (P) sued for specific performance. The chancellor issued a decree of specific performance, and Dodds (D) appealed.

ISSUE: Can an offeree bind an offeror by accepting a revoked offer, even if the revocation had not been communicated to him prior to acceptance?

HOLDING AND DECISION: (Lord James, J.) No. An offeree may not bind an offeror by accepting a revoked offer, even if the revocation had not been communicated to him prior to acceptance. A binding contract requires a "meeting of the minds." When an offeror withdraws his offer and the offeree accepts, no meeting has occurred. Even if the offer is still open to the knowledge of the offeree, the fact is that the offeror is no longer of a mind to form the contract, so acceptance does not bind him. Here, even though it was not communicated to Dickinson (P), Dodds (D) did revoke the offer, so no contract was formed. Reversed.

CONCURRENCE: (Lord Mellish, J.) If an offeror is no longer of a mind to offer for sale a property, he cannot be compelled to do so.

ANALYSIS

A traditional requirement for a contract was a "meeting of the minds," as described by the court here. The term used today is "mutual assent," as stated in § 17 of the Restatement (Second) of Contracts. The concept is the same.

Quicknotes

ACCEPTANCE Assent to the specified terms of an offer, resulting in the formation of a binding agreement.

MEETING OF THE MINDS A requirement of a valid contract that the parties possess a mutuality of assent as manifested by the terms of the agreement and not by a hidden intent; enforceability of the contract is limited to those terms to which the parties assented.

REVOCATION The cancellation or withdrawal of some authority conferred, or destruction or making void an instrument drafted.

SPECIFIC PERFORMANCE An equitable remedy whereby the court requires the parties to perform their obligations pursuant to a contract.

Drennan v. Star Paving Co.

General contractor (P) v. Paving subcontractor (D)

Cal. Sup. Ct., 51 Cal. 2d 409, 333 P.2d 757, *en banc* (1958)

NATURE OF CASE: Appeal from award of damages for failure to perform according to a bid.

FACT SUMMARY: Drennan (P), a contractor, in preparing his bid on a public construction project, used the bid for paving work by subcontractor Star Paving Co. (Star) (D), but after Drennan (P) was awarded the contract, Star (D) informed Drennan (P) that its paving bid was in error.

RULE OF LAW

A promise that the promisor should reasonably expect to induce action or forbearance of a definite and substantial character on the part of a promisee and that does induce such action or forbearance is binding if injustice can be avoided only by enforcement of the promise.

FACTS: Drennan (P) was preparing a bid on a public-school construction project. On the day the bid was to be submitted, Star Paving Co. (Star) (D) phoned in its bid of $7,131.60 for paving. That bid was recorded and posted on a master sheet by Drennan (P). It was customary in the area for bids to be phoned in on the day set for bidding and for general contractors to rely on them in computing their own bids. Star's (D) bid for paving was low and used by Drennan (P) in preparing his bid, which was low. The contract was awarded to Drennan (P) that same evening. The next day, Star (D) informed Drennan (P) of an error in its paving bid and refused to do the paving for less than $15,000. Drennan (P), after several months of searching, engaged another company to do the paving for $10,948.60 and sued for the cost difference. From adverse judgment in the lower courts, Star (D) appealed.

ISSUE: Is a promise that the promisor should reasonably expect to induce action or forbearance of a definite and substantial character on the part of a promisee and that does induce such action or forbearance binding if injustice can be avoided only by enforcement of the promise?

HOLDING AND DECISION: (Traynor, J.) Yes. A promise that the promisor should reasonably expect to induce action or forbearance of a definite and substantial character on the part of a promisee and that does induce such action or forbearance is binding if injustice can be avoided only by enforcement of the promise. Star Paving Co. (Star) (D) had reason to expect that if its bid was low it would be used by Drennan (P) and so induced "action . . . of a definite and substantial character on the part of the promisee." Star's (D) bid did not state or clearly imply revocability at any time before acceptance. Where there is an offer for a unilateral contract, the theory that the offer is revocable at any time before complete performance is obsolete. When any part of the consideration requested in the offer is given or tendered by the offeree, the offeror is bound. That is, the main offer includes a subsidiary promise, which is implied, that if part of the requested performance is given, the offeror will not revoke his offer, and if tender is made, it will be accepted. See Restatement § 45. In more extreme cases, merely acting in justifiable reliance of an offer may serve as sufficient reason to make the promise binding. See Restatement § 90. Section 90's purpose is to make a promise binding even though consideration is lacking; its absence is not fatal to the enforcement of the subsidiary promise. Reasonable reliance acts in lieu of ordinary consideration. Star (D) had a stake in Drennan's (P) reliance on its bid. This interest plus Drennan's (P) being bound by his own bid, make it only fair that Drennan (P) should have the chance to accept Star's (D) bid after the general contract was awarded to Drennan (P). While Star's (D) bid was the result of mistake, it was not such a mistake that Drennan (P) knew or should have known it was in error. A 160 percent variance in paving bids was not unusual in the area. Because the mistake misled Drennan (P) as to the paving cost under the circumstances, Star's (D) bid should be enforced. Affirmed.

ANALYSIS

The case greatly broadened the view of promissory estoppel, Restatement § 90, as interpreted by Judge Hand in *James Baird Co. v. Gimbel Bros.*, 64 F.2d 344 (2d Cir. 1933), to extend beyond the area of charitable or donative promises to general business use. This view was adopted in Restatement (Second) § 90, which was written after this case. Note that a subcontractor's bid must be more than a mere estimate, and, of course, if it reasonably appears to be based upon a mistake, reliance cannot be justified. The cases that apply promissory estoppel show the subcontractor to be bound by his bid, but the general contractor is not bound to accept the bid. Note that Judge Traynor works into Restatement § 90 through § 45 (the Brooklyn Bridge hypothetical), expanding the view that giving or tendering consideration will bind the promise to include justifiable reliance to have the same effect. In the *Drennan* case, circumstances and business practices peculiar to the

Continued on next page.

area were important. Telephoned bids were a common practice. Wide variances in paving costs were expected, thereby adding strength to Drennan's (P) position, as an error in a paving bid would not be reasonably noticed. Also see Restatement (Second) § 89B(2) for this viewpoint as extended to option contracts.

Quicknotes

PROMISSORY ESTOPPEL A promise that is enforceable if the promisor should reasonably expect that it will induce action or forbearance on the part of the promisee, that does in fact cause such action or forbearance, and that is the only means of avoiding injustice.

United States Life Insurance Company v. Wilson

Life insurer (D) v. Insured's beneficiary (P)

Md. Ct. Spec. App., 198 Md. App. 452, 18 A.3d 110 (2011)

NATURE OF CASE: Appeal from summary judgment for beneficiary of life insurance policy in breach of contract action against insurer.

FACT SUMMARY: United States Life Insurance Company (US Life) (D) and AMA Insurance Agency, Inc. (AMAIA) (D) contended that Dr. Griffith's life insurance policy, which had lapsed, had not been successfully reinstated prior to Dr. Griffith's accidental death on July 28, 2007, because a reinstatement payment he initiated on July 25, 2007 was not received by AMAIA (D)/US Life (D) until after his death on July 30, 2007.

RULE OF LAW

The common-law mailbox rule for determining when an acceptance has been made applies to a paper check initiated electronically by the offeree and sent to the offeror by the offeree's agent in a manner permitted by the offer.

FACTS: Dr. Griffith had a life insurance policy (Policy) with United States Life Insurance Company (US Life) (D), the insurance agency for which was AMA Insurance Agency, Inc. (AMAIA) (D). Dr. Griffith's wife, Ms. Wilson (P), was the beneficiary. After the Policy lapsed, Dr. Griffith was sent an "Application for Reinstatement of Coverage," which informed him that he could reinstate the Policy by simply paying the overdue premium within 31 days after the end of a "Grace Period," which ended on July 14, 2007. Thus, Dr. Griffith had until August 14, 2007, to reinstate the Policy. On July 25, 2007, he directed his bank, from his online account, to issue a check to AMAIA (D), the program administrator, for the overdue premium amount. The check was received on July 30, 2007. However, Dr. Griffith was killed in an accident on July 28, 2007. US Life (D) and AMAIA (D) took the position that the Policy had not been reinstated and denied Ms. Wilson (P) payment of the Policy's death benefits. Ms. Wilson (P) brought a breach of contract action against them, contending that the Policy had been reinstated. The trial court granted summary judgment to Ms. Wilson (P), and the state's intermediate appellate court granted review [applying Illinois law].

ISSUE: Does the common-law mailbox rule for determining when an acceptance has been made apply to a paper check initiated electronically by the offeree and sent to the offeror by the offeree's agent in a manner permitted by the offer?

HOLDING AND DECISION: (Eyler, J.) Yes. The common-law mailbox rule for determining when an acceptance has been made applies to a paper check initiated electronically by the offeree and sent to the offeror by the offeree's agent in a manner permitted by the offer. Insurance contracts initially are formed when an insurer unconditionally accepts an insured's application, which constitutes an offer, for coverage. Thereafter, the life insurance policy operates as a unilateral contract, i.e., one that is formed by performance. The periodic payment of premiums is the mechanism by which the insured keeps the insurance policy in force, so that the failure to pay the premiums will result in coverage lapsing. Life insurance policies have standard nonforfeiture clauses that allow for reinstatement after a lapse in coverage. Here, the "REINSTATEMENT" clause in the Policy was such a standard non-forfeiture clause. It provided that reinstatement would occur upon payment of an overdue premium within 31 days from the expiration of the "Grace Period." In contractual terms, the "REINSTATEMENT" clause is an offer of a unilateral contract to revive the Policy, with the insurer promising that revival will take place upon the insured's performing by paying the overdue premium. The issue thus becomes when Dr. Griffith's payment (and acceptance) occurred. At common law, what is often called the "mailbox rule," the "dispatch rule," or sometimes the "postal acceptance rule" is the widely adopted convention for pinpointing the time that an offer is accepted and a contract is formed. Under this rule, acceptance is effective when the offeree puts the signed contract in the mail. Similarly, under the Restatement (Second) of Contracts (Restatement), unless an offer states otherwise, an acceptance made in a manner and by a medium invited by the offer is operative and completes the manifestation of mutual assent as soon as it is put out of the offeree's possession, without regard to whether it ever reaches the offeror. The rationale for the rule is certainty and predictability, and it applies equally to bilateral and unilateral contracts. Additionally, the offeror must have authorized the use of the particular medium as a means of acceptance, and the acceptance must have been properly dispatched using that medium. However, an offeree's mere delivery of an acceptance to a third-party messenger with directions to mail or send it amounts to no acceptance until the messenger actually deposits it in the mail or initiates the sending of the acceptance if by a medium other than mail. The common-law "mailbox rule" is applicable here to determine when the Policy was revived, notwithstanding that Dr. Griffith's acceptance was initiated electronically. His electronic directive resulted in the

Continued on next page.

preparation of a paper check drawn on his bank account, which was physically received by AMA Insurance Agency, Inc. (AMAIA) (D). The check (a writing) complied with the requirements under the reinstatement offer and was sent via a permissible mode of acceptance to the proper recipient. Moreover, the nature of the transaction is not akin to those that have been determined to be outside the sphere of the dispatch rule, which has not been applied to substantially instantaneous two-way communication devices such as telephones or teletypes, since transactions effected by such devices do not resemble communication by mail. Application of the mailbox rule in this case produces the legal conclusion that the date of payment of the overdue premium was July 25, 2007. On July 23, 2007, Dr. Griffith electronically instructed his bank, as his agent, to make payment to AMAIA (D). The evidence viewed most favorably to United States Life Insurance Company (D) and AMAIA (D) supports a reasonable inference that Dr. Griffith could have reinstructed his bank not to make the payment; therefore, as of July 23, 2007, he had set in motion the means to accept the offer of reinstatement but still had the power to reverse course. On July 25, 2007, however, the bank remitted payment to AMAIA (D) by sending it a check for the premium amount. At that point, the permissible means for acceptance was in motion and, so far as is established by the common-law mailbox rule, was beyond Dr. Griffith's power to stop. This would be true whether the bank sent the check through the United States Postal Service, a courier service, or otherwise. Because the Policy was reinstated on July 25, 2007, it was in effect when Dr. Griffith died. Affirmed.

ANALYSIS

Majority of courts hold that the reinstatement of a life insurance policy does not involve the creation of a new contract but instead reinstates the original contract, under which the insured has the right to reinstatement on compliance with its requirements. Thus, under this majority rule, reinstatement does not involve the formation of a new life insurance policy. Instead, once the requirements for reinstatement are fulfilled, the original life insurance contract is revived, so there is no need for a new acceptance by the insurer. On the other hand, a minority of jurisdictions take the position that a reinstatement request by the insured is no different than an original insurance application and acts as an offer by the insured to enter into a new life insurance contract, which does not become effective until accepted by the insurer.

Quicknotes

ACCEPTANCE Assent to the specified terms of an offer, resulting in the formation of a binding agreement.

BREACH OF CONTRACT Unlawful failure by a party to perform its obligations pursuant to contract.

COMMON LAW A body of law developed through the judicial decisions of the courts as opposed to the legislative process.

MAILBOX RULE Common-law rule that acceptance of an offer is binding upon dispatch, at which time an enforceable contract is formed so long as it complies with the requirements for acceptance.

Dorton v. Collins & Aikman Corp.

Carpet retailer (P) v. Carpet manufacturer (D)

453 F.2d 1161 (6th Cir. 1972)

NATURE OF CASE: Action to compel arbitration.

FACT SUMMARY: Collins & Aikman's (D) acceptance form contained a compulsory arbitration clause, while Dorton's (P) order form did not.

RULE OF LAW

An arbitration provision may be deemed a nonmaterial alteration of the contract in certain circumstances.

FACTS: Dorton (P) orally ordered carpeting from Collins & Aikman (D). Collins & Aikman's (D) acceptance form contained a compulsory arbitration clause. Acceptance of an order, according to Collins & Aikman's (D) form, was subject to all terms and conditions of the form. Dorton (P) sued Collins & Aikman (D), and Collins & Aikman (D) attempted to obtain a stay of the proceedings pending arbitration as required under its form. The district court held that the language of the form did not make acceptance of all its provisions a condition precedent to the formation of a contract. It, therefore, found that the contract was controlled by Uniform Commercial Code § 2-207(3), where the conduct of the parties is such as to indicate that a contract has been formed. The court found, as a matter of law, that terms on an acceptance could not force arbitration on a party.

ISSUE: May an arbitration provision be deemed a nonmaterial alteration of the contract in certain circumstances?

HOLDING AND DECISION: (Celebreezze, J.) Yes. An arbitration provision may be deemed a nonmaterial alteration of the contract in certain circumstances. Uniform Commercial Code (UCC) § 2-207 was adopted to prevent the operation of the common-law mirror image rule. An acceptance and offer need not exactly match to find the existence of a valid contract. Traditionally, written offers and acceptances contain numerous provisions favorable to the drafter. In recognition of this fact, a contract is found where essential terms are present or inferable. Inconsistent terms do not become a part of the contract. If specific acceptance of the buyer's or seller's terms is made a condition precedent to the formation of the contract, no contract is formed absent an assent. Even in such cases, a contract may be formed by the actions if the parties and terms that materially alter the contract are deleted. We do not find that Collins & Aikman's (D) form requires acceptance of all terms as a condition precedent to formation of a contract. This must be specifically and unequivocally stated. Therefore, the question is whether the arbitration clause materially alters the contract as formed under UCC § 2-207(3). Arbitration clauses have gained wide acceptance, and we do not find that they constitute a per se material alteration. We remand for such a finding. Also, there was no evidence adduced to indicate that the oral offer did not contain an arbitration provision. This should also be determined on remand.

ANALYSIS

Under common law, silence is not deemed to be consent. The Uniform Commercial Code (UCC) alters this approach and would allow nonmaterial terms to become part of the contract unless they are objected to by the other party within 10 days of receipt. UCC § 2-207(2). Prior to *Dorton*, an arbitration provision was specifically found to constitute an unreasonable additional term that does not become a part of the contract unless specifically consented to by the other party. Thus, there is a split in the courts.

Quicknotes

ACCEPTANCE Assent to the specified terms of an offer, resulting in the formation of a binding agreement.

ARBITRATION CLAUSE Provision contained in a contract pursuant to which both parties agree that any disputes arising thereunder will be resolved through arbitration.

CONDITION PRECEDENT The happening of an uncertain occurrence that is necessary before a particular right or interest may be obtained or an action performed.

MIRROR-IMAGE RULE The common-law rule that for acceptance to be effective the offeree must accept each and every term of the offer.

OFFER A proposed promise to undertake performance of an action, or to refrain from acting, that is to become binding upon acceptance by the offeree.

C. Itoh & Co. (America) Inc. v. Jordan Intl. Co.

Merchant buyer (P) v. Merchant seller (D)

552 F.2d 1228 (7th Cir. 1977)

NATURE OF CASE: Appeal from denial of motion for stay pending arbitration in action for breach of contract.

FACT SUMMARY: C. Itoh & Co. (America) Inc. (Itoh) (P) sought to purchase steel coils from Jordan International Company (Jordan) (D). Although Jordan (D) expressly conditioned acceptance on Itoh's (P) assent to additional terms in Jordan's (D) standard sales acknowledgment form, which contained an arbitration provision, Itoh (P) did not manifest assent to those terms, and the parties nevertheless proceeded with the transaction by Jordan (D) delivering steel coils and Itoh (P) paying for them. Jordan (D) contended that the arbitration provision became a supplementary term to the contract created by the parties' conduct under Uniform Commercial Code § 2-207(3).

RULE OF LAW

Under the Uniform Commercial Code (UCC), where a merchant seller expressly conditions acceptance on the merchant buyer's assent to additional terms contained in the seller's standard sales acknowledgment form, but the buyer does not assent to those terms, and the parties nevertheless perform by delivery of goods and payment therefor, thus creating a contract by conduct under § 2-207(3), any "supplementary terms" in the contract thus formed are limited to the standardized "gap-filler" provisions of UCC Article Two.

FACTS: C. Itoh & Co. (America) Inc. (Itoh) (P) submitted a purchase order for steel coils to the Jordan International Company (Jordan) (D). In response, Jordan (D) sent its acknowledgment form, on the face of which appeared the statement: Seller's acceptance is, however, expressly conditional on Buyer's assent to the additional or different terms and conditions set forth below and printed on the reverse side. If these terms and conditions are not acceptable, Buyer should notify seller at once. One of the terms on the reverse side of Jordan's (D) form was a broad provision for arbitration. Itoh (P) neither expressly assented nor objected to the additional arbitration term. After the steel had been delivered by Jordan (D) and paid for by Itoh (P), Itoh (P) sued Jordan (D) in federal district court, claiming that the steel was defective and had been delivered late. Jordan (D) moved for a stay of the proceedings pending arbitration, and the district court denied the motion. Jordan (D) appealed, contending that the arbitration provision in its sales acknowledgment form became a supplementary term to the contract created by the parties' conduct under Uniform Commercial Code § 2-207(3). The court of appeals granted review.

ISSUE: Under the Uniform Commercial Code (UCC), where a merchant seller expressly conditions acceptance on the merchant buyer's assent to additional terms contained in the seller's standard sales acknowledgment form, but the buyer does not assent to those terms, and the parties nevertheless perform by delivery of goods and payment therefor, thus creating a contract by conduct under § 2-207(3), are any "supplementary terms" in the contract thus formed limited to the standardized "gap-filler" provisions of UCC Article Two?

HOLDING AND DECISION: (Sprecher, J.) Yes. Under the Uniform Commercial Code (UCC), where a merchant seller expressly conditions acceptance on the merchant buyer's assent to additional terms contained in the seller's standard sales acknowledgment form, but the buyer does not assent to those terms, and the parties nevertheless perform by delivery of goods and payment therefor, thus creating a contract by conduct under § 2-207(3), any "supplementary terms" in the contract thus formed are limited to the standardized "gap-filler" provisions of UCC Article Two. It is clear the statement contained in Jordan International Company's (Jordan's) (D) acknowledgment form comes within UCC § 2-207(1), so that the exchange of forms between Jordan (D) and C. Itoh & Co. (America) Inc. (Itoh) (P) did not result in the formation of a contract, and Jordan's (D) form became a counteroffer. The parties nevertheless performed, triggering § 2-207(3), which creates a contract on the basis of the parties' conduct that recognizes the existence of a contract. Under that section, where a contract has been consummated by the conduct of the parties, "the terms of the particular contract consist of those terms on which the writings of the parties agree, together with any supplementary terms incorporated under any other provisions of this Act." Since it is clear the Jordan (D) and Itoh (P) forms did not "agree" on arbitration, the only question that remains under the UCC is whether arbitration may be considered a supplementary term incorporated under some other provision of the UCC. Disputed additional terms, i.e., those terms on which the writings of the parties do not agree, that are necessarily excluded from a contract created by conduct under § 2-207(3), cannot be brought back into the contract under the guise of "supplementary terms." Thus, the "supplementary terms" contemplated by § 2-207(3) are limited to those supplied

Continued on next page.

by the standardized "gap-filler" provisions of UCC Article Two. A provision for arbitration is not such a "gap-filler" term. Accordingly, there was no arbitration term in the contract that was created by the parties' conduct under § 2-207(3). This result does not unfairly prejudice a seller that elects to insert in a standard sales acknowledgement form the statement that acceptance is expressly conditional on buyer's assent to additional terms contained therein. Such a seller obtains a substantial benefit under § 2-207(1) through the inclusion of an "expressly conditional" clause. If the seller decides after the exchange of forms that the particular transaction is not in its best interest, subsection (1) permits the seller to walk away from the transaction without incurring any liability so long as the buyer has not in the interim expressly assented to the additional terms. Moreover, whether a seller will be disadvantaged under subsection (3) as a consequence of inserting an "expressly conditional" clause in the seller's standard form is within the seller's control. If the seller does not intend to close a particular deal unless the additional terms are assented to, the seller can protect itself by not delivering the goods until such assent is forthcoming. If the seller does intend to close a deal irrespective of whether the buyer assents to the additional terms, the seller can hardly complain when the contract formed under subsection (3) as a result of the parties' conduct is held not to include those terms. The seller must accept the potential risk under subsection (3) of not getting the additional terms when it elects to proceed with performance without first obtaining buyer's assent to those terms. Since the seller injected ambiguity into the transaction by inserting the "expressly conditional" clause in the seller's standard form, the seller, and not the buyer, should bear the consequence of that ambiguity under subsection (3). Affirmed.

ANALYSIS

At common law, an acceptance that contained terms additional to those of the offer, constituted a rejection of the offer and thus became a counteroffer. Thus, the mere presence of the additional arbitration term in Jordan International Company's (Jordan's) (D) acknowledgment form would, at common law, have prevented the exchange of documents between Jordan (D) and C. Itoh & Co. (America) Inc. (P) from creating a contract, and Jordan's (D) form would have automatically become a counteroffer. Uniform Commercial Code § 2-207(1) was intended to alter this inflexible common-law approach to offer and acceptance, in recognition that in current commercial transactions, the terms of the offer and those of the acceptance will seldom be identical. Rather, under the current "battle of the forms," each party typically has a printed form drafted by its attorney that contains as many terms as could be envisioned to favor that party in the sales transactions. Whereas under common law the disparity between the fine-print terms in the parties' forms would have prevented the consummation of a contract when these forms are exchanged, § 2-207 recognizes that in many, but not all, cases the parties do not impart such significance to the terms on the printed forms. Thus, under subsection (1), a contract may be recognized notwithstanding that an acceptance contains terms additional to those of the offer. Concomitantly, it is well settled that the mere presence of an additional term, such as a provision for arbitration, in one of the parties' forms will not prevent the formation of a contract under § 2-207(1).

Quicknotes

ACCEPTANCE Assent to the specified terms of an offer, resulting in the formation of a binding agreement.

ARBITRATION An alternative resolution process where a dispute is heard and decided by a neutral third party, rather than through legal proceedings.

BREACH OF CONTRACT Unlawful failure by a party to perform its obligations pursuant to contract.

COUNTEROFFER An offer made by the offeree that has the effect of rejecting the offer deemed unsatisfactory and of proposing a new offer to the offeror.

OFFER A proposed promise to undertake performance of an action, or to refrain from acting, that is to become binding upon acceptance by the offeree.

Bayway Refining Co. v. Oxygenated Marketing & Trading A.G.

Seller (P) v. Buyer (D)

215 F.3d 219 (2d Cir. 2000)

NATURE OF CASE: Appeal from summary judgment for plaintiff in an action for breach of contract between merchants.

FACT SUMMARY: Oxygenated Marketing and Trading A.G. (OMT) (D), as a merchant buyer, contended that it had created a genuine issue of material fact that a contract term in a contract it had entered with Bayway Refining Co. (Bayway) (P), which allocated liability to the buyer for an excise tax, constituted a material alteration under Uniform Commercial Code § 2-207(2)(b), and, therefore, was presumed to have been rejected by OMT (D). Bayway (P) contended that the term constituted an additional term that was presumed to have been accepted under § 2-207(2)(b).

RULE OF LAW

A merchant who asserts that a proposed additional term to a contract constitutes a material alteration under Uniform Commercial Code (UCC) § 2-207(2)(b) will not prevail on his claim where he fails to raise a factual issue as to whether the term results in surprise or hardship to him.

FACTS: Oxygenated Marketing and Trading A.G. (OMT) (D), a merchant in the petroleum industry, made an offer to buy MTBE from Bayway Refining Co. (Bayway) (P), another merchant in the industry. Bayway's (P) response, which acted as an acceptance, contained a "Tax Clause," which provided that "Buyer shall pay seller the amount of any federal, state and local excise, gross receipts, import, motor fuel, superfund and spill taxes and all other federal, state and local taxes however designated, other than taxes on income, paid or incurred by seller directly or indirectly with respect to the oil or product sold hereunder and/or on the value thereof." OMT (D) did not object to the term, and accepted delivery of MTBE. The transaction created a tax liability, covered under the Tax Clause, of around $464,000. Bayway (P) paid the tax, and then demanded reimbursement from OMT (D), which refused to pay, contending it had never agreed to the Tax Clause. Bayway (P) sued OMT (D) for payment of the tax liability, and the district court held that the Tax Clause had properly been incorporated into the contract. The court of appeals granted review.

ISSUE: Will a merchant who asserts that a proposed additional term to a contract constitutes a material alteration under Uniform Commercial Code § 2-207(2)(b) prevail on his claim where he fails to raise a factual issue as to whether the term results in surprise or hardship to him?

HOLDING AND DECISION: (Jacobs, J.) No. A merchant who asserts that a proposed additional term to a contract constitutes a material alteration under Uniform Commercial Code § 2-207(2)(b) will not prevail on his claim where he fails to raise a factual issue as to whether the term results in surprise or hardship to him. Oxygenated Marketing and Trading A.G. (OMT) (D) bears the burden of proving that the Tax Clause constitutes a material alteration. Section 2-207(2)(b) is an exception to the general rule of § 2-207(2) that additional terms become part of a contract between merchants. This general rule is in the nature of presumption concerning the intent of the contracting parties. Thus, if neither party introduced any evidence, the Tax Clause would, by the plain language of § 2-207(2), become part of the contract. To implement that presumption, the burden of proving the materiality of the alteration must fall on the party that opposes inclusion—here, OMT (D). A material alteration is one that would "result in surprise or hardship if incorporated without express awareness by the other party." Some types of terms are per se material alterations, but the Tax Clause at issue is not one of them because, in part, it is limited, discrete and the subject of no special protection. Accordingly, OMT (D) must prove that in this case the Tax Clause resulted in surprise or hardship. Surprise, within the meaning of the material alteration exception, has both the subjective element of what a party actually knew and the objective element of what a party should have known. To carry the burden of showing surprise, a party must establish that, under the circumstances, it cannot be presumed that a reasonable merchant would have consented to the additional term. Although OMT (D) has adduced evidence that the term came as an amazement to its executives—and thus has shown that subjectively it was surprised—it has failed to show that, as a matter of objective surprise, a reasonable merchant in the industry would be surprised by the Tax Clause. On the other hand, Bayway (P) introduced evidence that the Tax Clause reflects custom and practice in the industry. The evidence was compelling that shifting tax liability to a buyer is the custom and practice in the petroleum industry. Moreover, common sense supports Bayway's (P) evidence of custom and practice, since the federal excise tax is imposed when taxable fuels are sold to any person who is not registered

Continued on next page.

under a specified federal statute. The buyer thereby controls whether any tax liability is incurred in a transaction. A trade practice that reflects a rational allocation of incentives would place the burden of the tax on the party that is in the position to obviate it—here, on OMT (D) as the buyer. Because shifting tax liability to a buyer is the custom and practice in the petroleum industry, OMT (D) could not have been objectively surprised by the Tax Clause. OMT (D) has also failed to raise a genuine issue as to hardship. It has only shown that it is a small business dependent on precarious profit margins, and that it would suffer a loss it cannot afford. That showing does not amount to hardship, which is typically found, if at all, when an additional term is one that creates or allocates an open-ended and prolonged liability. Here, the Tax Clause places on a buyer a contractual responsibility that bears on a specific sale of goods, that is not uncommon in the industry, and that the buyer could avoid by registration. Any loss that the Tax Clause imposed on OMT (D) is thus limited, routine and self-inflicted. For these reasons, the district court did not err in granting summary judgment to Bayway Refining Co. (P). Affirmed.

ANALYSIS

As the court notes, certain additional terms are deemed material as a matter of law. For example, an arbitration clause is per se a material alteration in those states that require an express agreement to commit disputes to arbitration, given that arbitration clauses waive a range of rights that are solicitously protected. Another example of additional terms that are deemed per se material alterations are waivers of warranties of merchantability or fitness for a particular purpose and clauses granting the seller the power to cancel upon the buyer's failure to meet any invoice.

Quicknotes

CUSTOM AND USAGE A customary practice that is so widespread that it has become mandatory and has the force of law.

PRESUMPTION A rule of law requiring the court to presume certain facts to be true based on the existence of other facts, thereby shifting the burden of proof to the party against whom the presumption is asserted to rebut.

Northrop Corp. v. Litronic Industries

Merchant buyer (P) v. Merchant seller (D)

29 F.3d 1173 (7th Cir. 1994)

NATURE OF CASE: Appeal from judgment for plaintiff in action for breach of warranty arising from allegedly defective goods.

FACT SUMMARY: Litronic Industries (D) contended that the 90-day warranty in its offer to sell wire boards to Northrop Corp. (P) was controlling in its transaction with Northrop (P), which bought the boards, rather than the unlimited warranty period contained in Northrop's (P) purchase order.

RULE OF LAW

Under the Uniform Commercial Code (UCC), where a seller's offer and a buyer's acceptance contain terms that are different from each other, the discrepant terms are knocked out and replaced by the UCC's default gap-filling terms.

FACTS: Litronic Industries (Litronic) (D) offered to sell to Northrop Corp. (P) wire boards. The offer contained a 90-day warranty stated to be in lieu of any other warranties, and provided that the terms of the offer would take precedence over any terms proposed by the buyer. Northrop (P) responded by sending a purchase order form. However, that form provided for a warranty without any time limit. Litronic (D) delivered the wire boards to Northrop (P), which, after 90 days, sought to return them as defective. Litronic (D) refused to accept the return of the boards, on the ground that its 90-day warranty had lapsed. Northrop (P) brought suit in federal district court against Litronic (D), contending that it had an unlimited warranty, as stated in the purchase order. The district court ruled that the parties' discrepant warranty terms knocked each other out and were replaced with the UCC's default gap-filling terms, which require rejection of nonconforming goods within a reasonable time. The district court, finding that Northrop's (P) rejection occurred within a reasonable time, entered judgment for Northrop (P). The court of appeals granted review.

ISSUE: Under the Uniform Commercial Code (UCC), where a seller's offer and a buyer's acceptance contain terms that are different from each other, are the discrepant terms knocked out and replaced by the UCC's default gap-filling terms?

HOLDING AND DECISION: (Posner, C.J.) Yes. Under the Uniform Commercial Code (UCC), where a seller's offer and a buyer's acceptance contain terms that are different from each other, the discrepant terms are knocked out and replaced by the UCC's default gap-filling terms. The UCC does not explain what happens if an offeree's response contains different terms, rather than additional ones, within the meaning of § 2-207(1), and there is no consensus on this issue. The majority view is that the discrepant terms in both the nonidentical offer and the acceptance drop out, and default terms found elsewhere in the UCC fill the resulting gap. Another view is that the offeree's discrepant terms drop out and the offeror's become part of the contract. A third view equates "different" with "additional" and makes the outcome turn on whether the new terms in the acceptance are materially different from the terms in the offer—in which event they operate as proposals, so that the offeror's terms prevail unless the offeror agrees to the variant terms in the acceptance—or not materially different from the terms in the offer, in which event they become part of the contract. The state [Illinois] whose law must be applied in the case at bar tends to follow majority rules in UCC cases. Thus, although the state has not ruled on this issue, it is presumed that it would adopt the majority rule in this case. This presumption has not been rebutted. The idea behind the majority view is that the presence of different terms in the acceptance suggests that the offeree didn't really accede to the offeror's terms, yet both parties wanted to contract, so why not find a neutral term to govern the dispute that has arisen between them? It may be that the offeree may not have had any serious objection to the terms in the offer at the time of contracting, and may have sent a boilerplate form in return, without giving any thought to its contents or to its suitability for the particular contract in question. However, it is just as likely that the discrepant terms in the offer itself were the product of a thoughtless use of a boilerplate form rather than a considered condition of contracting. If, on the other hand, the offeror doesn't want to do business other than on the terms in the offer, the offeror can protect itself by specifying that the offeree must accept all those terms for the parties to have a contract. Here, under the majority rule, Northrop Corp. (P) prevails. Affirmed.

ANALYSIS

As Judge Posner notes, under the prevailing minority view, whereby the offeree's discrepant terms drop out and the offeror's become part of the contract, an offeror may be tempted to spring a surprise on the offeree, hoping the latter won't read the fine print. Under the majority view, if the offeree tries to spring a surprise (under

Continued on next page.

this view, the offeror cannot spring a surprise, since its terms will not prevail if the acceptance contains different terms), the parties move to neutral ground, and the offeror can more easily protect itself against being surprised than the offeree can protect itself against being surprised by conditioning the contract on the offeree's acceptance of the offeror's terms. The third approach mentioned (and preferred) by Judge Posner, whereby "different" is equated with "additional" and makes the outcome turn on whether the new terms in the acceptance are materially different from the terms in the offer, dissolves such problems, but has not been widely adopted (at the time of this case, only California had adopted this approach). This third approach, which is bolstered by the drafting history of Uniform Commercial Code§ 2-207(1), which shows that the omission of "or different" from the section was a drafting error, in Judge Posner's view, substitutes a manageable inquiry into materiality for a "hair-splitting" inquiry into the difference between "different" and "additional."

Quicknotes

BREACH OF WARRANTY The breach of a promise made by one party to a contract on which the other party may rely, relieving that party from the obligation of determining whether the fact is true and indemnifying the other party from liability if that fact is shown to be false.

Hill v. Gateway 2000, Inc.

Consumer (P) v. Company (D)

105 F.3d 1147 (7th Cir. 1997)

NATURE OF CASE: Appeal of denial of a motion to compel arbitration.

FACT SUMMARY: Hill (P) brought a RICO suit against Gateway (D) after purchasing a mail order computer. Gateway (D) moved to compel arbitration. The request was denied, and Gateway (D) appealed.

RULE OF LAW

Terms sent in the box with a product that state that they govern the sale unless the product is returned within 30 days are binding on a buyer who does not return the product.

FACTS: Hill (P) purchased a computer from Gateway 2000, Inc. (Gateway) (D) through a telephone order and subsequently brought suit against Gateway (D), in which a civil Racketeer Influenced and Corrupt Organizations Act (RICO) claim and other claims were asserted. Gateway (D) thereupon sought enforcement of an arbitration clause that had been included in the terms sent to Hill (P) in the box in which the computer was shipped. The federal district court denied the arbitration request, and Gateway (D) appealed.

ISSUE: Are terms sent in the box with a product that state that they govern the sale unless the product is returned within 30 days binding on a buyer who does not return the product?

HOLDING AND DECISION: (Easterbrook, J.) Yes. Terms sent in the box with a product that state that they govern the sale unless the product is returned within 30 days are binding on a buyer who does not return the product. The Hills (P) conceded noticing the statement of terms but denied reading it closely enough to discover the agreement to arbitrate. An agreement to arbitrate must be enforced except upon such grounds as exist at law or in equity for the revocation of any contract. A contract need not be read to be effective. People who accept products take the risk that the unread terms may in retrospect prove unwelcome. Terms inside Gateway 2000, Inc.'s (Gateway's) (D) box stand or fall together. If they constitute the parties' contract because the Hills (P) had an opportunity to return the computer after reading them, then all must be enforced. The court rejects the Hills' (P) argument that the provision in the box should be limited to executory contracts and to licenses in particular. Both parties' performance of this contract was complete when the box arrived at their home. The case does not depend on the fact that the seller characterized the transaction as a license rather than as a contract, but rather treated it as a contract for the sale of goods and reserved the question whether for other purposes a "license" characterization might be preferable. All debates about characterization to one side, the transaction here was not executory. Vacated and remanded for arbitration.

ANALYSIS

While observing that the federal Magnuson-Moss Warranty Act requires firms to distribute their warranty terms on request, the court noted that the Hills (P) did not contend that Gateway 2000, Inc. (Gateway) (D) would have refused to enclose the remaining terms also. Concealment would be bad for business, scaring some customers away and leading to excessive returns from others. Second, said the court, shoppers can consult public sources (computer magazines, the websites of vendors) that may contain this information. Third, they may inspect the documents after the product's delivery. In this case, the Hills (P) took the third option. By keeping the computer beyond 30 days, the Hills (P) accepted Gateway's (D) offer, including the arbitration clause.

Quicknotes

ARBITRATION An alternative resolution process where a dispute is heard and decided by a neutral third party, rather than through legal proceedings.

ARBITRATION CLAUSE Provision contained in a contract pursuant to which both parties agree that any disputes arising thereunder will be resolved through arbitration.

RICO Racketeer Influenced and Corrupt Organization Act; federal and state statutes enacted for the purpose of prosecuting organized crime.

Klocek v. Gateway

Computer buyer (P) v. Computer company (D)

104 F. Supp. 2d 1332 (D. Kan. 2000)

NATURE OF CASE: Defense motion to dismiss fraud suit.

FACT SUMMARY: Klocek (P) sued Gateway (D) and a scanner manufacturer alleging that Gateway (D) induced him to purchase a computer by making false promises of technical support, and that the scanner manufacturer breached its duty to warn consumers that its product was incompatible with certain computers. Defendants moved to dismiss the suit.

RULE OF LAW

A purchaser does not necessarily accept the standard terms and conditions agreement, which may include an arbitration clause, located in the package containing a mail order product.

FACTS: Klocek (P), the purchaser of a computer and scanner, brought suit against Gateway (D) and the scanner manufacturer, alleging that Gateway (D) induced him to purchase the computer by making false promises of technical support and that the scanner manufacturer breached its duty to warn consumers that its product was incompatible with certain computers. Defendants moved to dismiss Klocek's (P) claims under the Federal Arbitration Act, which ensures that written arbitration agreements in maritime transactions and transactions involving interstate commerce are "valid, irrevocable, and enforceable," and that federal policy favors arbitration agreements and requires that they be rigorously enforced.

ISSUE: Does a purchaser necessarily accept the standard terms and conditions agreement, which may include an arbitration clause, located in the package containing the mail order computer?

HOLDING AND DECISION: (Vratil, J.) No. A purchaser does not necessarily accept the standard terms and conditions agreement, which may include an arbitration clause, located in the package containing the mail order computer. A seller's standard terms and conditions agreement that is included in a package containing a computer that is shipped to a buyer does not constitute a conditional acceptance or counter-offer, absent any evidence that, at the time of the sales transaction, the seller informed the buyer that the transaction was conditioned on the buyer's acceptance of its standard terms. The fact that here the computer buyer kept the computer more than five days after its delivery did not constitute acceptance of the standard terms and conditions agreement, which included an arbitration clause, located in the package containing the computer. Although the standard terms indicated that the buyer's retention of the computer amounted to the acceptance of its terms, the seller did not inform the buyer of a five-day review-and-return period as a condition of the sales transaction or that the parties contemplated additional terms to the sales agreement. Motion to dismiss denied.

ANALYSIS

The *Klocek* court noted that a party seeking to compel arbitration bears an initial summary judgment-like burden of establishing that it is entitled to arbitration and must present evidence sufficient to demonstrate the existence of an enforceable agreement to arbitrate.

Quicknotes

ARBITRATION AGREEMENT A mutual understanding entered into by parties wishing to submit to the decision-making authority of a neutral third party that is selected by the parties and charged with rendering a decision.

BATTLE OF THE FORMS The exchange of forms, pursuant to a contract for the sale of goods, between a buyer and seller.

MUTUAL ASSENT A requirement of a valid contract that the parties possess a mutuality of assent as manifested by the terms of the agreement and not by a hidden intent.

Kauders v. Uber Technologies, Inc.

User of online transportation-request service (P) v. Provider of online transportation-request service (D)

Mass. Sup. Jud. Ct., 486 Mass. 557, 159 N.E.3d 1033 (2021)

NATURE OF CASE: Appeal from reversal, on reconsideration, of grant of motion to compel arbitration of dispute between user of online transportation-request service and service provider.

FACT SUMMARY: The Kauders (P) registered to use Uber Technologies, Inc.'s (Uber's) (D) transportation-request service on their cellphones, using Uber's (D) application (app). When the Kauders (P) brought suit against Uber (D) in court, asserting claims arising from Uber's (D) service, Uber (D) sought to have the dispute settled by binding arbitration, pursuant to a provision in the terms and conditions on its app. The Kauders (P) contended that the terms and conditions did not constitute an enforceable arbitration agreement.

RULE OF LAW

A putative online contract is not enforceable where there is no reasonable notice of its terms and no reasonable manifestation of assent to those terms.

FACTS: Uber Technologies, Inc. (Uber) (D) provides a transportation-request service that can be used from a cellphone application (app). Christopher Kauders (P) and Hannah Kauders (P) (collectively, the Kauders (P)) each registered to use the Uber (D) service using their respective cellphones. The registration process required each user to first "create an account," then to "create a profile," and, finally, to "link payment." Each of these steps was presented on a separate cellphone screen. Once a user completed a step by filling in the required information, the user clicked on a "NEXT" button that took the user to the next step. At the bottom of the third screen there was text that stated, "By creating an Uber account, you agree to the Terms & Conditions and Privacy Policy." This text was oddly divided into two parts. The first part of the sentence, which informed the user "By creating an Uber account, you agree to the," was far less prominently displayed than the words "Terms & Conditions and Privacy Policy," which followed. The second part of the sentence—"Terms & Conditions and Privacy Policy"—was in a rectangular box and in boldface font. According to Uber (D), this presentation was used to indicate that the box was a clickable hyperlink. If a user clicked this box, the user would be taken to a screen that contained other clickable buttons, labeled "Terms & Conditions" and "Privacy Policy." Once at this linked screen, if the user clicked the "Terms & Conditions" button, the terms and conditions would appear on the screen. After a user filled in credit card information, a button labeled "DONE" became clickable in the top right corner. Once the user clicked "DONE," the user completed the account creation process. Uber's (D) terms and conditions were very favorable to Uber (D). Uber (D) could amend the terms and conditions whenever it wanted, without notice to the users that had already agreed to them, and any changes to the terms and conditions would be automatically binding. The terms and conditions contained an extensive "Limitation of Liability" section. The "Dispute Resolution" section appeared near the end of the terms and conditions. It provided that "any dispute, claim or controversy arising out of or relating to this Agreement . . . will be settled by binding arbitration." It also provided that an arbitrator's award damages had to be consistent with the terms of the "Limitation of Liability" section as to the types and the amounts of damages for which a party could be held liable. If Uber (D) made changes to the dispute resolution section, the user had 30 days in which to object to the changes. The Kauders (P) brought suit against Uber (D) in state court, alleging that several of its drivers violated state law by refusing to provide Christopher Kauders (P) with rides because he was blind and accompanied by a guide dog. Citing the "Dispute Resolution" section of its terms and conditions, Uber (D) moved to compel arbitration, which the court granted over the Kauders' (P) assertion that there was no enforceable arbitration agreement. The parties arbitrated their dispute, and the arbitrator ruled in favor of Uber (D) on all the Kauders' (P) claims. Three weeks later, the federal circuit court covering the state issued a decision in a different case involving Uber (D), holding that Uber's (D) registration process did not create a contract because it did not provide reasonable notice to users of the terms and conditions. Several months later, after Uber (D) moved to confirm the arbitration award, the judge who had granted the motion to compel arbitration allowed a motion for reconsideration and reversed his earlier decision, concluding that there was no enforceable contract requiring arbitration. Uber (D) appealed to the state's highest court, which granted review.

ISSUE: Is a putative online contract enforceable where there is no reasonable notice of its terms and no reasonable manifestation of assent to those terms?

HOLDING AND DECISION: (Kafkar, J.) No. A putative online contract is not enforceable where there is no reasonable notice of its terms and no reasonable manifestation of assent to those terms. Given that the online

Continued on next page.

contract at issue includes an arbitration agreement, it should be noted that although arbitration agreements are favored, ordinary contract-formation principles are applied to determine whether the parties agreed to arbitrate certain matters, as well as the terms of such agreements. In this court, the standard a court should use when considering issues of contract formation for online contracts is a matter of first impression. A framework for analyzing issues of online contract formation that has been used by a lower court in this jurisdiction uses a two-prong test that focuses on whether there has been reasonable notice of the terms and a reasonable manifestation of assent to those terms. This is the proper test to apply here. Regarding the first prong, an offeree has actual notice of the terms where the user has reviewed the terms, or where the user must somehow interact with the terms before agreeing to them. If a user has actual notice, the first prong is satisfied. Absent actual notice, the totality of the circumstances must be evaluated in determining whether reasonable notice has been given of the terms and conditions. This is a fact-intensive analysis that looks at various factors, including the interface and design involved. In examining the interface, the clarity and simplicity of the communication of the terms are evaluated. Ultimately, the offeror must reasonably notify the user that there are terms to which the user will be bound and give the user the opportunity to review those terms. Regarding the second prong, the court considers the specific actions required to manifest assent, such as by clicking or checking a box that states that the user agrees to the terms and conditions. Where such an action is required, the agreement is referred to as a "clickwrap" agreement and is ordinarily enforced. Requiring a user to expressly and affirmatively assent to the terms, such as by indicating "I Agree" or its equivalent, serves several important purposes. It puts the user on notice that the user is entering into a contractual arrangement. This is particularly important regarding online services, where services may be provided without requiring compensation or contractual agreements, and the users may not be sophisticated commercial actors. Requiring an expressly affirmative act, therefore, such as clicking a button that states "I Agree," can help alert users to the significance of their actions. Where they so act, they have reasonably manifested their assent. Where no such express agreement is required by the offeror, the totality of the circumstances must be considered, and assent may be inferred from other actions the users have taken. Where the connection between the action taken and the terms is unclear or where the action taken does not clearly signify assent, it will be difficult for the offeror to carry its burden to show that the user assented to the terms. Applying these principles here, the Kauders (P) did not have reasonable notice of the terms and conditions. Users of Uber Technologies, Inc.'s (Uber's) (D) app were registering for a service that connects drivers and riders for future short-term, small-money transactions. Reasonable users may not understand that by simply signing up for future ride services online they have entered into a contractual relationship. It is also by no means obvious that signing up via an app for ride services would be accompanied by the type of extensive terms and conditions present here. Given these circumstances, it must be carefully considered whether the app's interface reasonably focused the user on the terms and conditions. The Uber (D) app did not require the user to scroll through the conditions or even select them. The user could fully register for the service and click "done" without ever clicking the link to the terms and conditions. The connection between the creation of the account and the terms and conditions was also somewhat oddly displayed in the two-part format, with the significant information (i.e., that by creating the account, the user expresses his or her agreement) being displayed less prominently than other information. For these reasons, the notice of the terms was not reasonable. This is in striking contrast to the interface of the app provided to drivers by Uber (D), which required its drivers, before signing up, to review the terms and conditions by clicking a hyperlink. The contrast between the notice provided to drivers and that provided to users is telling. As Uber (D) is undoubtedly aware, most of those registering via mobile applications do not read the terms of use or terms of service included with the applications. Yet the design of the interface for the app here enables, if not encourages, users to ignore the terms and conditions. Further, the link to the terms and conditions was also at the very bottom of the "LINK PAYMENT" screen, the purpose of which primarily was for the user to enter payment information. Nothing about this third screen, therefore, conveyed to a user that the user should open a link that would reveal an extensive set of terms and conditions at the bottom of the screen to which the user was agreeing. In fact, most of the design elements of this screen seemed to have been designed to hide or minimize the prominence of the link to the terms, and a user could complete the "LINK PAYMENT" screen and the account creation process without ever focusing on the link or the notice on the screen. In sum, the notice provided by this interface was not reasonable. In such a transaction, a user may reasonably believe he or she is simply signing up for a service without understanding that he or she is entering into a significant contractual relationship governed by wide-ranging terms of use. Instead of requiring its users to review those terms and conditions as it appears to do with its drivers, Uber (D) designed an interface that allows the registration to be completed without reviewing or even acknowledging the terms and conditions. In these circumstances, Uber (D) has failed to show that it provided the plaintiffs with reasonable notice of the terms and conditions. Because there was not reasonable notice of the terms, a contract cannot have been formed here. Nonetheless, it should be observed that the interface here also obscured the

Continued on next page.

manifestation of assent to those terms. The interface did state in one sentence broken into two parts, one more prominent than the other, "By creating an Uber account, you agree to the Terms & Conditions and Privacy Policy." The words "Terms & Conditions and Privacy Policy" were more prominently displayed than what it meant to create the account. Uber (D) claims this highlights the terms and conditions. A reasonable alternative interpretation is that it downplays the legal significance of creating the account. What is clear is that a user could create an account without ever affirmatively stating that he or she agreed to the terms and conditions, or even opening those terms and conditions. Instead, the final step in the process was to input payment information and click "DONE." "DONE" is also different from, and less clear than, other affirmative language such as "I agree." Furthermore, there was nothing stating that "DONE" itself signified either creation of an account or acceptance of the terms. Again, Uber's (D) own registration process for its drivers stands in striking contrast. During that process, a driver was required to affirmatively manifest assent not only once, but twice. Clearly, Uber (D) knows how to obtain clear assent to its terms. Accordingly, there was no reasonable manifestation of assent here. In the absence of reasonable notice of the app's terms and conditions and reasonable manifestation of assent thereto, there was no enforceable agreement between Uber (D) and the Kauders (P), and, therefore, their dispute was not arbitrable. Affirmed and remanded.

ANALYSIS

The Massachusetts Supreme Judicial Court in this case required that for an online agreement to be enforceable, there would have to be only reasonable notice of, and assent to, the agreement's terms. The court did not require that the notice be "conspicuous," as required for certain types of contractual provisions or as required by other jurisdictions. For example, under California law, a user must have "[r]easonably conspicuous notice of the existence of contract terms."

Quicknotes

ARBITRATION An alternative resolution process where a dispute is heard and decided by a neutral third party, rather than through legal proceedings.

ARBITRATION AGREEMENT A mutual understanding entered into by parties wishing to submit to the decision-making authority of a neutral third party that is selected by the parties and charged with rendering a decision.

OFFEREE A person or party to whom an offer to enter into a contractual agreement is made.

OFFEROR Party who makes an offer.

Meyer v. Uber Technologies, Inc.

Accountholder of online ride-hailing service (P) v. Provider of online ride-hailing service (D)

868 F.3d 66 (2d Cir. 2017)

NATURE OF CASE: Appeal from denial of motion to compel arbitration in putative class action for illegal price fixing.

FACT SUMMARY: Spencer Meyer (P), who had registered to be an accountholder of Uber Technologies, Inc. (Uber) (D), which offered a ride-hailing service through its smartphone application ("Uber App"), brought a putative class action against Uber's (D) co-founder and former Chief Executive Officer, Travis Kalanick (D), alleging that the Uber application allows third-party drivers to illegally fix prices. Uber (D) and Kalanick (D) moved to compel arbitration pursuant to the Uber App's Terms of Service. Meyer (P) asserted he was not bound by those terms, claiming he did not have reasonably conspicuous notice of, and did not unambiguously manifest assent to, those terms.

RULE OF LAW

(1) For purposes of the enforceability of an arbitration agreement, the terms of which are provided on a smartphone application, the terms are reasonably conspicuous where, viewed from the perspective of a reasonable smartphone user, the design and interface of the application provide notice of the terms.

(2) Where a smartphone user is on inquiry notice of an application's terms of service and the user is notified that by registering to use the application the user is agreeing to those terms, a user unambiguously assents to those terms by registering to use the application's service.

FACTS: Spencer Meyer (P) registered to be an accountholder of Uber Technologies, Inc. (Uber) (D), which offers a ride-hailing service through its smartphone application ("Uber App"). After using the Uber App ten times, Meyer (P) brought a putative class action in federal district court against Uber's (D) co-founder and former Chief Executive Officer, Travis Kalanick (D), alleging that the Uber application allows third-party drivers to illegally fix prices. The district court joined Uber (D) as a defendant and denied motions by Kalanick (D) and Uber (D) to compel arbitration pursuant to a mandatory arbitration provision in the Uber App's Terms of Service. In doing so, the district court applied California law and concluded that Meyer (P) did not have reasonably conspicuous notice of and did not unambiguously manifest assent to Uber's (D) Terms of Service when he registered. When Meyer (P) registered, he was presented with a Registration Screen, where he manually entered his personal information. After completing the information on the Registration Screen and clicking "Next," Meyer (P) advanced to a second screen labeled "Payment" (the "Payment Screen"), on which he entered his credit card details. To complete the process, he had to click the button marked "REGISTER" in the middle of the Payment Screen. Below the input fields and buttons on the Payment Screen is black text advising users that "[b]y creating an Uber account, you agree to the TERMS OF SERVICE & PRIVACY POLICY." The capitalized phrase, which is bright blue and underlined, was a hyperlink that, when clicked, took the user to a third screen containing a button that, in turn, when clicked, would then display the current version of both Uber's (D) Terms of Service and Privacy Policy. Meyer (P) recalled entering his contact information and credit card details before registering but did not recall seeing or following the hyperlink to the Terms and Conditions. He declared that he did not read the Terms and Conditions, including the arbitration provision. Because the district court concluded that Meyer (P) did not have reasonably conspicuous notice of the Terms of Service and did not unambiguously manifest assent to the terms, the court held that Meyer (P) was not bound by the mandatory arbitration provision contained in the Terms of Service. It was undisputed that if Meyer (P) were bound by the arbitration provision, his claim would be covered by the provision. Kalanick (D) and Uber (D) appealed, and the Second Circuit Court of Appeals granted review.

ISSUE:

(1) For purposes of the enforceability of an arbitration agreement, the terms of which are provided on a smartphone application, are the terms reasonably conspicuous where, viewed from the perspective of a reasonable smartphone user, the design and interface of the application provide notice of the terms?

(2) Where a smartphone user is on inquiry notice of an application's terms of service and the user is notified that by registering to use the application the user is agreeing to those terms, does a user unambiguously assent to those terms by registering to use the application's service?

HOLDING AND DECISION: (Chin, J.)

(1) Yes. For purposes of the enforceability of an arbitration agreement, the terms of which are provided on a smartphone application, the terms are reasonably

Continued on next page.

conspicuous where, viewed from the perspective of a reasonable smartphone user, the design and interface of the application provide notice of the terms. State law principles of contract formation govern the arbitrability question. Here, California law applies. Under California law, an offeree, regardless of apparent manifestation of consent, is not bound by inconspicuous contractual provisions of which the offeree is unaware, contained in a document whose contractual nature is not obvious. Where there is no evidence that the offeree had actual notice of the terms of the agreement, the offeree will still be bound by the agreement if a reasonably prudent user would be on inquiry notice of the terms. Whether a reasonably prudent user would be on inquiry notice turns on the clarity and conspicuousness of arbitration terms; in the context of online contracts, clarity and conspicuousness are a function of the design and content of the relevant interface. In the interface at issue in this case, a putative user is not required to assent explicitly to the contract terms; instead, the user must click a button marked "Register," underneath which the screen states "By creating an Uber account, you agree to the TERMS OF SERVICE & PRIVACY POLICY," with hyperlinks to the Terms of Service and Privacy Policy. Courts considering similar agreements have found them valid where the existence of the terms was reasonably communicated to the user. Thus, it must be determined here whether Spencer Meyer (P) was on inquiry notice of the arbitration provision by virtue of the hyperlink to the Terms of Service on the Payment Screen. To resolve this issue, it must be viewed from the perspective of a reasonably prudent smartphone user. Given that smartphone use is ubiquitous and that smartphone users are familiar with how to use applications, when considering the perspective of a reasonable smartphone user, a court need not presume that the user has never before encountered an app or entered into a contract using a smartphone. Moreover, a reasonably prudent smartphone user knows that text that is highlighted in blue and underlined is hyperlinked to another webpage where additional information will be found. Here, the design of the screen interface and language used rendered the notice provided reasonable as a matter of California law. The screen was uncluttered, and the text warning that the user would be bound by the Terms of Service, appeared directly below the button for registration. The entire screen was visible at once, and the user did not need to scroll beyond what was immediately visible to find notice of the Terms of Service. Although the sentence was in a small font, the dark print contrasted with the bright white background, and the hyperlinks were in blue and underlined. Thus, notice of the Terms of Service was provided simultaneously to enrollment, thereby connecting the contractual terms to the services to which they applied. Therefore, a reasonably prudent smartphone user would understand that the terms were connected to the creation of a user account. Moreover, that the Terms of Service were available only by hyperlink does not preclude a determination of reasonable notice. As long as the hyperlinked text was itself reasonably conspicuous, a reasonably prudent smartphone user would have constructive notice of the terms. Though it may be the case that many users will not bother reading the additional terms, that is the choice the user makes; the user is still on inquiry notice. Finally, contrary to the district court's determination, the location of the arbitration clause within the Terms and Conditions was not a barrier to reasonable notice; once a user clicked through to the Terms of Service, the section heading "Dispute Resolution" and the sentence waiving the user's right to a jury trial on relevant claims were both bolded. For these reasons, the Uber App provided reasonably conspicuous notice of the Terms of Service as a matter of California law.

(2) Yes. Where a smartphone user is on inquiry notice of an application's terms of service and the user is notified that by registering to use the application the user is agreeing to those terms, a user unambiguously assents to those terms by registering to use the application's service. Although Meyer's (P) assent to arbitration was not express, it was unambiguous in light of the objectively reasonable notice of the terms. A reasonable user would know that by clicking the registration button, the user was agreeing to the terms and conditions accessible via the hyperlink, whether the user clicked on the hyperlink or not. Merely because the register button had two functions—creation of a user account and assent to the Terms of Service—does not render Meyer's (P) assent ambiguous. The registration process allowed Meyer (P) to review the Terms of Service prior to registration, unlike web platforms that provide notice of contract terms only after the user has manifested his or her assent. The transactional context of the parties' dealings reinforces this conclusion. Meyer (P) located and downloaded the Uber App, signed up for an account, and entered his credit card information with the intention of entering into a forward-looking relationship with Uber Technologies, Inc. (Uber) (D). The registration process clearly contemplated some sort of continuing relationship between the putative user and Uber (D), one that would require some terms and conditions, and the Payment Screen provided clear notice that there were terms that governed that relationship. For

Continued on next page.

these reasons, Meyer (P) unambiguously manifested his assent to Uber's (D) Terms of Service as a matter of California law. Accordingly, the district court's denial of the defendants' motions to compel arbitration is vacated.

ANALYSIS

With this decision, the Second Circuit upholds the legal fiction that ordinary consumers have knowingly and voluntarily waived their right to a trial by jury, because, as the district court in this case said, "they supposedly agreed to lengthy 'terms and conditions' that they had no realistic power to negotiate or contest and often were not even aware of." *Meyer v. Kalanick,* 200 F. Supp.3d 408 (S.D.N.Y 2016). As the district court also observed, this legal fiction is sometimes justified, at least where mandatory arbitration is concerned, by reference to the liberal federal policy favoring arbitration. Application of this policy to the Internet is said to inhere in the Federal Arbitration Act (FAA), but it is doubtful that the Congress that enacted that Act in 1925 remotely contemplated the vicissitudes of the Internet. Nevertheless, consumers are routinely forced to waive their constitutional right to a jury and their very access to courts and to submit instead to arbitration—as the Court of Appeal here forces Meyer (P) to do—on the theory that they have voluntarily agreed to do so in response to "endless, turgid, often impenetrable sets of terms and conditions, to which, by pressing a button, they have indicated their agreement." *Meyer v. Kalanick,* at 411.

Quicknotes

ARBITRATION An alternative resolution process where a dispute is heard and decided by a neutral third party, rather than through legal proceedings.

ARBITRATION CLAUSE Provision contained in a contract pursuant to which both parties agree that any disputes arising thereunder will be resolved through arbitration.

INQUIRY NOTICE The communication of information that would cause an ordinary person of average prudence to inquire as to its truth.

Hoffman v. Red Owl Stores

Would-be franchisee (P) v. Supermarket chain operator (D)

Wis. Sup. Ct., 26 Wis. 2d 683, 133 N.W.2d 267 (1965)

NATURE OF CASE: Action for damages grounded on promissory estoppel.

FACT SUMMARY: Hoffman (P), who desired to obtain a Red Owl Stores (Red Owl) (D) franchise, was assured that he had the necessary capital required. On the basis of the statements and conduct of Red Owl's (D) representative, Lukowitz, Hoffman (P) took certain steps including selling his bakery and moving to another city in order to acquire the franchise. Negotiations collapsed when it was clear Red Owl (D) had misrepresented the actual amount of capital required, which was nearly double the original figure.

RULE OF LAW

It is not necessary for the promise needed to sustain a cause of action to embrace all essential details of a proposed transaction between promisor and promisee so as to be the equivalent of an offer that would result in a binding contract between the parties if the promisee were to accept the same.

FACTS: In November 1959, Hoffman (P), owner and operator of a bakery, contacted Red Owl Stores (Red Owl) (D), which operated a supermarket chain, seeking to obtain a Red Owl Store (D) franchise. Having only $18,000 to invest, Hoffman (P) was assured by Red Owl (D) that was sufficient. In February 1961, upon Red Owl's (D) advice, Hoffman (P) acquired a grocery store that, three months later, Red Owl (D) told him to sell, assuring him they would find him a larger store. He was again assured that $18,000 was sufficient capital to invest. In September 1961, upon Red Owl's (D) advice, Hoffman (P) put $1,000 down on a lot in another town and was told, "Everything is ready to go. Get your money together and we are set." Red Owl (D) then told Hoffman (P) to sell his bakery, which he did for $10,000, a $2,000 loss. Hoffman (P) paid $125 rent on a house near the lot and spent $140 moving to another town to gain experience working in a grocery store, but that job never materialized, and he went to work on the nightshift at a bakery. Negotiations on the contract faltered as Red Owl (D) considered several arrangements when, by February 1962, $34,000 was required by Red Owl (D) for Hoffman (P) to acquire the franchise. Hoffman (P) then sued Red Owl (D) and was awarded the following damages: $2,000 for the sale of the bakery, $1,000 for the option on the lot, $140 moving expenses, and $125 rent. The trial court ordered a new trial on the jury's award of $16,735 for the sale of the grocery store.

ISSUE: Must the promise necessary to sustain an action for promissory estoppel embrace all essential details of a proposed transaction between promisor and promisee so as to be the equivalent of an offer that would result in a binding contract if accepted?

HOLDING AND DECISION: (Currie, C.J.) No. An action grounded upon promissory estoppel is not the equivalent of a breach of contract action. Originally, the doctrine of promissory estoppel was used as a substitute for consideration with the acts of detrimental reliance corresponding to consideration. To so limit the doctrine of promissory estoppel to the essentials of a contract—a promise supported by consideration—would be to expose any party who detrimentally relies during complicated negotiations to the grave risk of being taken advantage of without remedy. Restatement § 90 does not require the equivalent of a promise supported by consideration. To do so would be to hold a breach of contract action and an action grounded on promissory estoppel to be one and the same. All items of damage are sustained except on the sale of the grocery store, where damages should be limited to the difference between the sale price received and fair market value of the assets sold, giving consideration to any goodwill attaching. Affirmed.

ANALYSIS

This case, in broadening the doctrine of promissory estoppel, makes clear for the first time it is a separate action and not a breach of contract action. At the time Red Owl Stores (Red Owl) (D) could foresee Hoffman's (P) detrimental reliance, there arose the consideration sufficient to uphold Red Owl's (D) promise. The court's so finding enables it to utilize Restatement § 90. Promissory estoppel has become the basis of an action that is neither a contract, a quasi-contract, nor a tort. Note that loss of profit is not awarded because under the doctrine, damages to be awarded should only be in the amount the court deems necessary to prevent injustice, that is, to return the injured to the status quo. This is very similar to the theory of *culpa in contrahendo* (fault in negotiating), recognized by many European courts, which awards damages to the party injured when the other party at fault during negotiations prevents a contract's perfection by his or her conduct.

Continued on next page.

Quicknotes

CONTRACT An agreement pursuant to which a party agrees to act, or to forbear from acting, in exchange for performance on the part of the other party.

PROMISSORY ESTOPPEL A promise that is enforceable if the promisor should reasonably expect that it will induce action or forbearance on the part of the promisee, that does in fact cause such action or forbearance, and that is the only means of avoiding injustice.

QUASI-CONTRACT An implied contract created by law to prevent unjust enrichment.

TORT A legal wrong resulting in a breach of duty by the wrongdoer, causing damages as a result of the breach.

Dixon v. Wells Fargo Bank, N.A.

Mortgagor (P) v. Mortgagee (D)

798 F. Supp. 2d 336 (D. Mass. 2011)

NATURE OF CASE: Motion to dismiss in action for injunction; specific performance of an oral contract; and damages arising from a mortgagee's impending foreclosure on a mortgaged property.

FACT SUMMARY: The Dixons (P) contended that Wells Fargo Bank, N.A. (Wells Fargo) (D) was promissorily estopped from foreclosing on their house because Wells Fargo (D) had orally agreed to enter into a mortgage loan modification, and caused them, in reliance on its representations, to default on their payments.

RULE OF LAW

A mortgagor states a claim for promissory estoppel where the mortgagor, in reliance on the mortgagee's oral promise to consider the mortgagor for a mortgage loan modification, has taken steps, including stopping payments on the loan, that render the mortgagor worse off by subjecting the mortgagor to foreclosure.

FACTS: The Dixons (P) had a mortgage with Wells Fargo Bank, N.A. (Wells Fargo) (D). The Dixons (P) orally agreed with Wells Fargo (D) to take the steps necessary to be considered for a mortgage loan modification. As part of this agreement, Wells Fargo (D) instructed the Dixons (P) to stop making payments on their loan, i.e., to default, and it was contemplated that the unpaid payments would be added to the note as modified. In addition, Wells Fargo (D) requested certain financial information, which the Dixons (P) promptly supplied. Despite the Dixons' (P) compliance with Wells Fargo's (D) demands, Wells Fargo (D) refused to abide by the oral agreement to consider the Dixons (P) for a loan modification and instead sought to foreclose on the Dixon's (P) house, the fair market value of which exceeded the mortgage loan balance and any arrearage. The Dixons (P) filed suit against Wells Fargo (D), seeking (1) an injunction prohibiting Wells Fargo (D) from foreclosing on their home; (2) specific performance of the oral agreement to enter into a loan modification; and (3) damages. They argued that Wells Fargo (D) should have anticipated their compliance with the terms of its promise to consider them for a loan modification. They contended not only was it reasonable they would rely on the promise, but also that their reliance left them considerably worse off, for by entering default they became vulnerable to foreclosure. Wells Fargo (D), having removed the action from state court to federal district court, moved for dismissal of the Dixons' (P) complaint, arguing that the allegations were insufficient to invoke the doctrine of promissory estoppel.

ISSUE: Does a mortgagor state a claim for promissory estoppel where the mortgagor, in reliance on the mortgagee's oral promise to consider the mortgagor for a mortgage loan modification, has taken steps, including stopping payments on the loan, that render the mortgagor worse off by subjecting the mortgagor to foreclosure?

HOLDING AND DECISION: (Young, J.) Yes. A mortgagor states a claim for promissory estoppel where the mortgagor, in reliance on the mortgagee's oral promise to consider the mortgagor for a mortgage loan modification, has taken steps, including stopping payments on the loan, that render the mortgagor worse off by subjecting the mortgagor to foreclosure. This state (Massachusetts) has not used the term "promissory estoppel," but instead has used "detrimental reliance." An action based on reliance is equivalent to a contract action, and the party bringing such an action must prove all the necessary elements of a contract other than consideration, which is supplied by the detrimental reliance. However, even where detrimental reliance acts as a substitute for consideration, the promise on which a claim for promissory estoppel is based must be interchangeable with an offer, and must demonstrate an intention to act or refrain from acting in a specified way, so as to justify a promisee in understanding that a commitment has been made. The putative promise, like any offer, must be sufficiently definite and certain in its terms to be enforceable. Where an agreement to enter into a contract leaves the terms of that contract for future negotiation, it is too indefinite to be enforced, and the courts generally will not enforce such open-ended "agreements to agree." Moreover, it is believed that parties should be able to walk away from the transaction if they are unable to reach a deal. Because the complaint alleges that the parties had an "agreement to enter into a loan modification agreement," it appears that they had an unenforceable "agreement to agree," and that, therefore, Wells Fargo Bank, N.A. (Wells Fargo) (D) is correct that the complaint fails to state a claim. The Dixons (P) reply that they are not seeking specific performance of a promised loan modification, but that Wells Fargo (D) is held to its promise to consider them for a loan modification. Thus, if the court were to uphold the promissory estoppel claim, it would not be "trapping" Wells Fargo (D) into a vague, indefinite, and unintended loan modification masquerading as an agreement to agree. Furthermore, because the parties had not even begun to negotiate the terms of a

Continued on next page.

loan modification, Wells Fargo's (D) promise is more like an agreement to negotiate, rather than an agreement to agree, but even such agreements to negotiate tend not to be enforced, since judicial enforcement of vague agreements to negotiate would risk imposing on parties contractual obligations they had not taken on themselves. Nevertheless, Wells Fargo (D) made a specific promise to consider the Dixons' (P) eligibility for a loan modification if they defaulted on their payments and submitted certain financial information. This promise was not made in exchange for a bargained-for legal detriment, as there was no bargain between the parties; instead, the legal detriment that the Dixons (P) claim to have suffered was a direct consequence of their reliance on Wells Fargo's (D) promise. Promissory estoppel has evolved into an equitable remedy that seeks to avoid injustice worked by a negotiating party that has made a promise during negotiations on which the other party has relied to its detriment. It is no longer merely a consideration substitute. This is reflected in § 90 of the Restatement (Second) of Contracts, which Massachusetts has adopted. While the courts of Massachusetts have yet to formally embrace promissory estoppel as more than a consideration substitute, the state's continued insistence that a promise be definite is arguably in tension with its adoption of § 90. This tension is not irreconcilable, however, as the case law reveals a willingness on courts' part to enforce even an indefinite promise made during preliminary negotiations where the facts suggest that the promisor's words or conduct were designed to take advantage of the promisee, even where the promisor did not act fraudulently. Here, Wells Fargo (D) convinced the Dixons (P) that to be eligible for a loan modification they had to default on their payments, and it was only because they relied on this representation and stopped making their payments that Wells Fargo (D) was able to initiate foreclosure proceedings, thus gaining the upper hand by inducing the Dixons (P) to open themselves up to a foreclosure action. In specifically telling the Dixons (P) that stopping their payments and submitting financial information were the "steps necessary to enter into a mortgage modification," Wells Fargo (D) not only should have known that the Dixons (P) would take these steps believing their fulfillment would lead to a loan modification, but also must have intended that the Dixons (P) do so. Accordingly, as a matter of fair dealing, Wells Fargo (D) should not have attempted to foreclose on the Dixon's (P) home based on a situation created solely by Wells Fargo's (D) promise. Such conduct is what permits application of the promissory estoppel doctrine here. A remaining concern is that by imposing precontractual liability for specific promises made to induce reliance during preliminary negotiations, courts will restrict parties' freedom to negotiate by reading in a duty to bargain in good faith not recognized at common law. This concern can be minimized by limiting the promisee's recovery to reliance expenditures. Furthermore, the foreseeability and injustice requirements of § 90 render inquiry into whether the promisor acted in bad faith unnecessary, which, in turn, obviates any need to impose a precontractual duty to negotiate in good faith. Finally, contrary to the conventional wisdom that precontractual liability unduly restricts the freedom to negotiate, a default rule allowing recovery but limiting it to reliance expenditures may in fact promote more efficient bargaining. Thus, if the Dixons (P) can prove their allegations by a preponderance of the evidence, they will be entitled to the value of their expenditures in reliance on Wells Fargo's (D) promise. In sum, foreclosure is a powerful act with significant consequences, and where a bank has obtained the opportunity to foreclose by representing an intention to do the exact opposite—i.e., to negotiate a loan modification that would give the homeowner the right to stay in his or her home—the doctrine of promissory estoppel is properly invoked to provide at least reliance-based recovery. Motion to dismiss is denied.

ANALYSIS

As with this case, other cases reveal that where the promisor opportunistically has strung along the promisee, the imposition of liability despite the preliminary stage of the negotiations produces the most equitable result. This balancing of the harms is explicitly made an element of recovery under the doctrine of promissory estoppel by the last words of § 90 of the Restatement, which make the promise binding only if injustice can be avoided by its enforcement. Binding the promisor to a promise made to take advantage of the promisee is also the most efficient result, since, in cases of opportunism, the "willingness to impose a liability rule can be justified as efficient since such intervention may be the most cost-effective means of controlling opportunistic behavior, which both parties would seek to control ex ante as a means of maximizing joint gains. Because private control arrangements may be costly, the law-supplied rule may be the most effective means of controlling opportunism and maximizing joint gain." See Juliet P. Kostritsky, "The Rise and Fall of Promissory Estoppel or Is Promissory Estoppel Really as Unsuccessful as Scholars Say It Is: A New Look at the Data," 37 *Wake Forest L. Rev.* 531, 574 (2002).

Quicknotes

DETRIMENTAL RELIANCE Reliance by one party that is based on the conduct or promises of another, resulting in loss to the party.

Continued on next page.

FORECLOSURE An action to recover the amount due on a mortgage of real property where the owner has failed to meet the mortgage obligations, terminating the owner's interest in the property that must then be sold to satisfy the debt.

PROMISSORY ESTOPPEL A promise that is enforceable if the promisor should reasonably expect that it will induce action or forbearance on the part of the promisee, that does in fact cause such action or forbearance, and that is the only means of avoiding injustice.

SPECIFIC PERFORMANCE An equitable remedy whereby the court requires the parties to perform their obligations pursuant to a contract.

Cyberchron Corp. v. Calldata Systems Development, Inc.

Computer manufacturer (P) v. Contractor (D)

47 F.3d 39 (2d Cir. 1995)

NATURE OF CASE: Appeal from promissory estoppel award.

FACT SUMMARY: Grumman procured computer equipment from Cyberchron Corp. (P) in order to fill a government contract, but later purchased the equipment at a lower cost elsewhere.

RULE OF LAW

Promissory estoppel has three elements: (1) a clear and unambiguous promise; (2) a reasonable and foreseeable reliance by the party to whom the promise is made; and (3) an injury sustained by the party asserting the estoppel by reason of the reliance.

FACTS: Calldata Systems Development, Inc. (Calldata) (D), a subsidiary of Grumman, was under contract to provide customized computer equipment to the government. Cyberchron Corp. (P) attempted to produce some of this equipment, but none was ever delivered. A purchase order was delivered by Grumman to Cyberchron (P); however, Cyberchron (P) never agreed to its terms. The district court concluded no enforceable agreement existed, but it awarded reliance damages to Cyberchron (P) for materials and labor costs under a theory of promissory estoppel.

ISSUE: Does promissory estoppel have three elements: (1) a clear and unambiguous promise; (2) a reasonable and foreseeable reliance by the party to whom the promise is made; and (3) an injury sustained by the party asserting the estoppel by reason of the reliance?

HOLDING AND DECISION: (Mahoney, J.) Yes. Promissory estoppel has three elements: (1) a clear and unambiguous promise; (2) a reasonable and foreseeable reliance by the party to whom the promise is made; and (3) an injury sustained by the party asserting the estoppel by reason of the reliance. An unconscionable injury is sometimes required to satisfy the third element. Grumman's conduct by pressuring Cyberchron Corp. (P) to produce equipment at a great expense and then purchasing it cheaper elsewhere was unconscionable. Affirmed.

ANALYSIS

Though the court awarded reliance damages, it declined to award damages for administrative or engineering overhead because these were not specifically proven. The court states that the award of such damages is allowable where "there is a demonstrable past history of ongoing business operations, without requiring proof that a specific alternative project would have absorbed the overhead costs at issue." The case was remanded for a redetermination of damages on this issue.

Quicknotes

OVERHEAD The necessary costs associated with the operation of a business that are constant and are unrelated to the costs of production.

PROMISSORY ESTOPPEL A promise that is enforceable if the promisor should reasonably expect that it will induce action or forbearance on the part of the promisee, that does in fact cause such action or forbearance, and that is the only means of avoiding injustice.

RELIANCE Dependence on a fact that causes a party to act or refrain from acting.

UNCONSCIONABILITY Rule of law whereby a court may excuse performance of a contract, or of a particular contract term, if it determines that such term(s) are unduly oppressive or unfair to one party to the contract.

Channel Home Centers, Division of Grace Retail Corp. v. Grossman

Prospective tenant (P) v. Mall owner (D)

795 F.2d 291 (3d Cir. 1986)

NATURE OF CASE: Appeal of dismissal of action for damages for breach of contract.

FACT SUMMARY: Grossman (D) used a letter of intent to rent, executed by Channel Home Centers (P), to obtain financing, but then rented to a competitor.

RULE OF LAW

A letter of intent to rent providing that the lessor will take the unit off the market is enforceable if the lessor uses the latter to help obtain financing.

FACTS: Grossman (D) obtained a controlling interest in a retail mall and sought tenants. Grossman (D) intended to upgrade the facilities. Channel Home Centers (Channel Home) (P) expressed an interest in leasing space. Channel Home (P) executed a letter of intent to rent that provided Grossman (D) would take the space off the market. Grossman (D) used the letter in his efforts to obtain upgrade financing, which was consummated. Grossman (D) subsequently rented to a competitor of Channel Home (P). Channel Home (P) sued for breach. The district court found that no contract had been formed and dismissed. Channel Home (P) appealed.

ISSUE: Is a letter of intent to rent providing that the lessor will take the unit off the market enforceable if the lessor uses the letter to help obtain financing?

HOLDING AND DECISION: (Becker, J.) Yes. A letter of intent to rent providing that the lessor will take the unit off the market is enforceable if the lessor uses the letter to help obtain financing. Such a document may be seen as agreement to negotiate in good faith. This is more than an unenforceable "agreement to agree." It will be a binding contract if, like other contracts, both parties manifest an intention to be bound, the terms are sufficiently definite to be enforced, and consideration was exchanged. Here, the actions of the parties, both in terms of the agreement and subsequent activities, manifested such an intention. The terms were detailed, including the agreement that the space would be taken off the market. Finally, consideration was received by Grossman (D) in that the letter helped him obtain financing. The agreement had sufficient specificity to make it an enforceable contract if the parties so intended. Whether the parties intended to be bound must be determined at trial. Reversed and remanded.

ANALYSIS

Grossman (D) argued that no money was paid, and therefore no consideration was exchanged. This was an unduly narrow view of consideration. If a benefit is conferred upon a promisor, consideration is passed. Here, the value of the letter in obtaining financing was such a benefit.

Quicknotes

BREACH OF CONTRACT Unlawful failure by a party to perform its obligations pursuant to contract.

LETTER OF INTENT A written draft embodying the proposed intent of the parties and that is not enforceable or binding.

Sun Printing & Publishing Ass'n v. Remington Paper & Power Co.

Publishing company (P) v. Paper seller (D)

N.Y. Ct. App., 139 N.E. 470 (1923)

NATURE OF CASE: Appeal from appellate court reversal of judgment invalidating contract.

FACT SUMMARY: Sun Printing & Publishing Ass'n (Sun) (P) brought an action against Remington Paper & Power Co. (Remington) (D) to collect damages resulting from Remington's (D) refusal to deliver rolls of paper to Sun (P).

RULE OF LAW

A contract will be deemed invalid due to incompleteness if the agreement does not establish the length of time the terms of the agreement, such as the price, shall apply.

FACTS: Sun Printing & Publishing Ass'n (Sun) (P) and Remington Paper & Power Co. (Remington) (D) entered into an agreement for Remington (D) to sell Sun (P) 16,000 tons of paper between September 1919 and December 1920—1,000 tons per month. For the first four months of the agreement, which was drafted by Remington (D), the price and the length of time that price would apply were clearly established. The remaining time in the contract called for the price to be determined by the parties, but not to exceed the price charged by Canadian Export Paper Company. The length of time that price would apply was to be determined by the parties as well. Remington (D) delivered the paper to Sun (P) for the first four months, but then refused to deliver any more, claiming the contract was incomplete, as no price or length of time for a price had been established in the contract. Sun (P) demanded delivery for the remaining months and then sued Remington (D) for damages resulting from its failure to deliver. The trial court found in favor of Remington (D), stating that the contract was incomplete as it did not specify the length of time any agreed-upon price would be in effect. However, the appellate court reversed, noting that the parties intended to make a binding contract and that with the rule of reason, the court could fashion terms in the light of fair dealing. Remington (D) appealed.

ISSUE: Will a contract be deemed invalid due to incompleteness if the agreement does not establish the length of time the terms of the agreement, such as the price, shall apply?

HOLDING AND DECISION: (Cardozo, J.) Yes. A contract will be deemed invalid due to incompleteness if the agreement does not establish the length of time the terms of the agreement, such as the price, shall apply. Here, the contract, after the first four months, did not specify the price or the length of time that the price shall apply to the parties. Both elements are essential to the contract. If only the price were left open, it could be reasoned that Sun Printing & Publishing Ass'n (P) was the holder of an option. However, because the length of time that price would apply was left open, the contract was incomplete. Despite language regarding the maximum price charged by Canadian Export Paper Co., no one knew if that price would change, or when. Remington Paper & Power Co. (D) would be left on a day-to-day whim of the market, never assured of its position. Because of this, the agreement with respect to time is as essential as the agreement with respect to price. The court cannot take that active a role in determining what the parties intended when such terms are left out of the agreement. Therefore, while the time was undetermined, the agreement was invalid. Reversed.

DISSENT: (Crane, J.) Rules of reason and fair dealing should govern this case, and a fair contract should be fashioned. The parties intended for the sale of 16,000 tons of paper. Remington Paper & Power Co. (D) drew up the contract and was aware of the overall purpose of the agreement. As to the vagueness in price, the parties allowed for the maximum established by Canadian Export Paper Co. As for the vagueness in time, the court should fashion a fair interpretation of what the parties originally intended, from the facts available. This would not be an overinterpretation by the court, but rather an assertion of the principle of fair dealing.

ANALYSIS

This case highlights the issue of the formulation of contracts in the context of negotiations. Generally, when negotiations are in progress, agreements by the parties on specific points in the contract are not intended to have legal consequences until the whole contract takes effect.

Quicknotes

FAIR DEALING Implied warranty that the parties will deal honestly in the satisfaction of their obligations and without intent to defraud.

MATERIAL TERM OF CONTRACT A fact without the existence of which a contract would not have been entered.

Oglebay Norton Co. v. Armco, Inc.

Shipping company (P) v. Mining company (D)

Ohio Sup. Ct., 52 Ohio St. 3d 232, 556 N.E.2d 515 (1990)

NATURE OF CASE: Appeal from a judgment ordering specific performance of a long-term shipping contract.

FACT SUMMARY: When Oglebay Norton Co. (Oglebay) (P) and Armco, Inc. (D) could not agree on a shipping rate under their long-term contract, Oglebay (P) sought a declaratory judgment from the court that the contract rate was the correct rate, or, alternatively, that the court would set a reasonable rate.

RULE OF LAW

If the parties intend to conclude a contract for the sale of goods where the price is not settled, the price is a reasonable price at the time of delivery if the price is to be fixed in terms of an agreed standard set by a third person or agency and is not so set.

FACTS: Oglebay Norton Co. (Oglebay) (P) and Armco, Inc. (D) had a long-term contract for Oglebay (P) to ship iron ore for Armco (D). The price was established by reference to the regular rates as published in *Skillings Mining Review*. The contract was modified four times during the next 23 years, requiring substantial capital investment by Oglebay (P). When the parties were not able to agree on a rate because a new rate was no longer published, Oglebay (P) sought a declaratory judgment that the contract rate was the correct rate or, alternatively, for the court to declare a reasonable rate. The court set the rate for that season at $6.25 per gross ton, requiring notification of the court if the parties could not agree on a future rate. A court-appointed mediator would then help them reach a mutual agreement. The court of appeals affirmed. Armco (D) appealed.

ISSUE: If the parties intend to conclude a contract for the sale of goods and the price is not settled, is the price a reasonable price at the time of delivery if the price is to be fixed in terms of an agreed standard set by a third person or agency and is not so set?

HOLDING AND DECISION: (Per curiam) Yes. If the parties intend to conclude a contract for the sale of goods and the price is not settled, the price is a reasonable price at the time of delivery if the price is to be fixed in terms of an agreed standard set by a third person or agency and is not so set. In this case, the undisputed dramatic changes in the market prices of Great Lakes shipping rates and the length of the contract would make it impossible for a court to award Oglebay Norton Co. (P) accurate damages due to Armco, Inc.'s (D) breach. Thus, specific performance of the contract is necessary. Moreover, ordering the parties to mediate for the duration of the contract is proper, given their unique business relationship and their intent to be bound. Affirmed.

ANALYSIS

The fourth modification, in 1980, of the contract at issue here extended it to the year 2010. To meet Armco, Inc.'s (D) requirements, Oglebay Norton Co. (P) then began a $95 million capital improvement program. The parties were unable to agree on a rate after a serious downturn in the iron and steel industry in 1984. In the face of those changed circumstances, Armco (D) had argued that the complete breakdown of the primary and secondary contract pricing mechanisms rendered the 1957 contract unenforceable.

Quicknotes

DECLARATORY JUDGMENT A judgment of the court establishing the rights and other legal relations of the parties in a controversy.

SPECIFIC PERFORMANCE An equitable remedy whereby the court requires the parties to perform their obligations pursuant to a contract.

CHAPTER 3

Statutes of Frauds

Quick Reference Rules of Law

PAGE

1. *Tolosa v. HSBC Bank USA, N.A.* For promissory estoppel to be used to bar the application of the Statute of Frauds and allow the enforcement of an otherwise unenforceable agreement, the party asserting promissory estoppel must present evidence that the other party made an oral promise to sign a written agreement that satisfied the Statute of Frauds. *86*

2. *C.R. Klewin, Inc. v. Flagship Properties, Inc.* The Statute of Frauds, requiring a writing for an agreement that is not to be performed within one year from the making thereof, will not render unenforceable an oral contract that fails to specify explicitly the time for performance, even when performance will likely take more than one year. *88*

3. *Langman v. Alumni Association of the University of Virginia.* For purposes of a state Statute of Frauds that requires a "collateral" promise to answer for the debts of another to be in writing as a condition for holding the promisor liable for such debts, a grantee who assumes an existing mortgage is not a surety that has made such a collateral promise. *89*

4. *Central Ceilings, Inc. v. National Amusements, Inc.* Under the "leading object" or "main purpose" exception to the Statute of Frauds, an oral promise that is not a novation may be enforced where the promisor has made the promise to secure the promisee's performance and the satisfaction of any obligation of a third party that is made as a part of that promise is merely incidental to the promise. *91*

5. *Crabtree v. Elizabeth Arden Sales Corp.* To satisfy the Statute of Frauds, the memorandum expressing the contract may be pieced together out of separate writings, connected with one another either expressly or by the internal evidence of subject matter and occasion, rather than being contained in a single document. *93*

6. *Beaver v. Brumlow.* Specific performance of an oral contract for the sale of land is not barred by the Statute of Frauds where the terms of the contract other than the purchase price have been proved, there has been part performance by both parties to the agreement, the part performance refers unequivocally to the sale of land through possession and the making of improvements, and a remedy at law would be inadequate. *95*

7. *Monarco v. Lo Greco.* The doctrine of estoppel may be used to assert the Statute of Frauds to prevent fraud that would result from refusal to enforce oral contracts in certain circumstances. *98*

Tolosa v. HSBC Bank USA, N.A.

Mortgagor (P) v. Mortgagee (D)

2011 WL 13244704 (S.D. Tex. 2011)

NATURE OF CASE: Motion to dismiss post-foreclosure action asserting, inter alia, promissory estoppel.

FACT SUMMARY: The Tolosas (P), who had mortgaged their property to HSBC Bank USA, N.A. (HSBC) (D), alleged that HSBC (D) had verbally promised not to foreclose on their property during a loan modification review process. HSBC (D) moved to dismiss, on the ground that the Tolosas' (P) claim was barred by the Statute of Frauds.

RULE OF LAW

For promissory estoppel to be used to bar the application of the Statute of Frauds and allow the enforcement of an otherwise unenforceable agreement, the party asserting promissory estoppel must present evidence that the other party made an oral promise to sign a written agreement that satisfied the Statute of Frauds.

FACTS: The Tolosas (P) obtained a $276,000 loan from HSBC Bank USA, N.A. (HSBC) (D) to purchase their residence, evidencing the loan with a promissory note, and securing the loan with a deed of trust. They defaulted on the loan, and the property was sold in a foreclosure sale. The Tolosas (P) brought suit in state court seeking to delay post-foreclosure eviction proceedings. In addition to seeking injunctive relief, they asserted various claims, including promissory estoppel, alleging that HSBC (D) had verbally promised not to foreclose on their property during a loan modification review process. HSBC (D) removed the case to federal court and moved to dismiss, contending the Tolosas' (P) estoppel claim was barred by the Statute of Frauds. The federal district court considered the motion to dismiss.

ISSUE: For promissory estoppel to be used to bar the application of the Statute of Frauds and allow the enforcement of an otherwise unenforceable agreement, must the party asserting promissory estoppel present evidence that the other party made an oral promise to sign a written agreement that satisfied the Statute of Frauds?

HOLDING AND DECISION: (Atlas, J.) Yes. For promissory estoppel to be used to bar the application of the Statute of Frauds and allow the enforcement of an otherwise unenforceable agreement, the party asserting promissory estoppel must present evidence that the other party made an oral promise to sign a written agreement that satisfied the Statute of Frauds. Under state law, the Statute of Frauds requires all loan agreements involving more the $50,000.00 to be in writing and signed by the party to be bound in order to be enforceable. A "loan agreement" for purposes of the Statute of Frauds is defined to include promises by a financial institution to "delay repayment of money . . . or make a financial accommodation." Promissory estoppel, whether asserted as an affirmative claim or as a defense to the Statute of Frauds, requires that the promisor promised to sign a written document that would satisfy the Statute of Frauds. The Tolosas (P) have not alleged that Bank USA, N.A. (D) promised to sign a written document that would satisfy the Statute of Frauds as to the alleged promise not to foreclose. As a result, they have failed to state a claim of promissory estoppel, either as an affirmative claim or in opposition to the Statute of Frauds defense. Accordingly, HSBC Bank USA, N.A. (D) is entitled to dismissal of the promissory estoppel claim. The motion to dismiss is granted, and the case is dismissed.

ANALYSIS

Although the Statute of Frauds varies from state to state, a writing is generally required for contracts: (1) for the sale of an interest in land (which includes leases of one year or longer); (2) incapable of performance in less than one year (regardless of the subject matter of the contract); (3) for the sale of goods with a price of at least $500 (UCC § 2-201) (except specially manufactured goods, or where there is partial performance); (4) to guarantee satisfaction of another's debt or default (a collateral promise only, not a primary one); and (5) in consideration of marriage. In *Tolosa*, the state's Statute of Frauds, as codified by statute, also specified that, to be enforceable, loan agreements involving more than $50,000.00 had to be in writing and signed by the party to be charged. That Statute also provided that the rights and obligations of the parties to such an agreement would be determined solely from the written loan agreement, that any prior oral agreements between the parties would be superseded by and merged into the loan agreement, and that such a loan agreement could not be varied by any oral agreements or discussions that occurred before or contemporaneously with the execution of the agreement.

Continued on next page.

Quicknotes

DEED OF TRUST A legal document that acts as a mortgage, placing a security interest in the deeded property with a trustee to insure the payment of a debt.

FORECLOSURE An action to recover the amount due on a mortgage of real property where the owner has failed to meet the mortgage obligations, terminating the owner's interest in the property which must then be sold to satisfy the debt.

INJUNCTIVE RELIEF A court order issued as a remedy, requiring a person to do, or prohibiting that person from doing, a specific act.

PROMISSORY ESTOPPEL A promise that is enforceable if the promisor should reasonably expect that it will induce action or forbearance on the part of the promisee, does in fact cause such action or forbearance, and is the only means of avoiding injustice.

PROMISSORY NOTE A written promise to tender a stated amount of money at a designated time and to a designated person.

STATUTE OF FRAUDS A statute that requires specified types of contracts to be in writing in order to be binding.

C.R. Klewin, Inc. v. Flagship Properties, Inc.

Construction manager (P) v. Contractor (D)

Conn. Sup. Ct., 220 Conn. 569, 600 A.2d 772 (1991)

NATURE OF CASE: Certified appeal in action for breach of contract.

FACT SUMMARY: Flagship Properties, Inc. (D) orally agreed to use C.R. Klewin Properties, Inc. (Klewin) (P) as a construction manager on a project likely to take more than one year to complete, but it contracted with another contractor after becoming dissatisfied with Klewin's (P) work.

RULE OF LAW

The Statute of Frauds, requiring a writing for an agreement that is not to be performed within one year from the making thereof, will not render unenforceable an oral contract that fails to specify explicitly the time for performance, even when performance will likely take more than one year.

FACTS: Flagship Properties, Inc. (Flagship) (D) representatives held a dinner with C.R. Klewin, Inc. (Klewin) (P) representatives. During the meeting, Klewin (P) suggested what fee it would require to serve as a construction manager. At the end of the meeting, the Flagship (D) agent said that they had a deal and the agents from both parties shook hands. No other terms or conditions were conclusively established. The agreement was publicized, and a press conference was held. Construction began on May 4, 1987, on the first phase of the project. In March 1988, Flagship (D) retained another contractor for the next phase. Klewin (P) filed suit in district court for breach of an oral contract. Flagship's (D) motion for summary judgment was granted. Klewin (P) appealed. The Second Circuit Court of Appeals certified questions to the Connecticut Supreme Court on issues not addressed in Connecticut case law.

ISSUE: Will the Statute of Frauds, requiring a writing for an agreement that is not to be performed within one year from the making thereof, render unenforceable an oral contract that fails to specify explicitly the time for performance when performance of that contract within one year of its making is very unlikely?

HOLDING AND DECISION: (Peters, C.J.) No. The Statute of Frauds, requiring a writing for an agreement that is not to be performed within one year from the making thereof, will not render unenforceable an oral contract that fails to specify explicitly the time for performance, even when performance will likely take more than one year. The Statute of Frauds excludes contracts except those whose performance cannot possibly be completed within one year. Connecticut case law has narrowly construed the Statute of Frauds in this area. In this case, the oral agreement did not specify a time for completion. When an oral contract does not expressly dictate that performance will last beyond one year, the contract will be construed as a matter of law to be a contract of indefinite duration for purposes of the Statute of Frauds. Given this narrow interpretation of the Statute of Frauds, it is enough that the agreement left open the possibility of completion within one year. The contract is enforceable.

ANALYSIS

Historians are unclear as to the reason for including the one-year category in the Statute of Frauds. Commentators, however, agree the Statute does not accomplish any of its possible purposes very well. Most jurisdictions construe the one-year provision as narrowly as possible to minimize the number of contracts voided by its operation.

Quicknotes

STATUTE OF FRAUDS A statute that requires specified types of contracts to be in writing in order to be binding.

Langman v. Alumni Association of the University of Virginia

Grantor (P) v. Grantee (D)

Va. Sup. Ct., 442 S.E.2d 669 (1994)

NATURE OF CASE: Appeal in breach of contract action from judgment for grantee of gifted deed containing a debt-assumption clause.

FACT SUMMARY: Langman (P), who had made a gift of commercial property to the Alumni Association of the University of Virginia (Association) (D) via a deed containing a debt-assumption clause, contended that the Association (D) was liable to her for payments of the debt she had made after the Association (D) accepted the gift, on the grounds that the Association (D) was liable for the indebtedness. One of the Association's (D) arguments was that the state's Statute of Frauds barred its liability for the mortgage debt.

RULE OF LAW

For purposes of a state Statute of Frauds that requires a "collateral" promise to answer for the debts of another to be in writing as a condition for holding the promisor liable for such debts, a grantee who assumes an existing mortgage is not a surety that has made such a collateral promise.

FACTS: Langman (P) made a gift of commercial property to the Alumni Association of the University of Virginia (Association) (D) via a deed containing a mortgage debt-assumption clause that provided that the Association (D) would assume payments of the mortgage obligations on the property and would hold Langman (P) harmless from further liability on the obligation. The Association (D) accepted the gift and recorded the deed but did not sign a written agreement to assume the remaining mortgage debt. A few years later, when the loan charges and operating expenses exceeded the income from the property, Langman (P) was forced to pay the indebtedness that had accrued following the gift. Langman (P) brought suit against the Association (D) seeking reimbursement for the payments she made. The trial court rendered judgment for the Association (D), finding that it did not have a clear understanding of the deed's contents and that the parties did not have a meeting of the minds respecting the debt. The state's highest court granted review. One of the issues presented was whether the state's Statute of Frauds required the Association (D) to have signed a written assumption of the mortgage debt before it could be held liable therefor.

ISSUE: For purposes of a state Statute of Frauds that requires a "collateral" promise to answer for the debts of another to be in writing as a condition for holding the promisor liable for such debts, is a grantee who assumes an existing mortgage a surety that has made such a collateral promise?

HOLDING AND DECISION: (Milano Keenan, J.) No. For purposes of a state Statute of Frauds that requires a "collateral" promise to answer for the debts of another to be in writing as a condition for holding the promisor liable for such debts, a grantee who assumes an existing mortgage is not a surety that has made such a collateral promise. The Alumni Association of the University of Virginia (Association) (D) asserted that, because Langman (P) would remain secondarily liable on the mortgage debt even after an effective assumption of the debt, the Association's (D) agreement to assume the mortgage was a "collateral" promise falling within the scope of the state's Statute of Frauds. A grantee who assumes an existing mortgage is not a surety since the grantee makes no promise to the mortgagee to pay the debt of another but promises the grantor to pay to the mortgagee the debt the grantee owes to the grantor. Instead, such an assumption of mortgage debt is an original undertaking. A collateral undertaking to which the Statute of Frauds applies is one in which the promisor is merely a surety or guarantor, receives no direct benefit, and is liable only if the debtor defaults. Here, the Association (D) received a direct benefit and did not merely act as surety for the grantors. Therefore, the trial court did not err in ruling that the Statute of Frauds did not bar enforcement of the mortgage assumption clause. [Judgment for Langman (P) as to this issue.] [The disposition of the case is not presented in the casebook extract.]

ANALYSIS

The provision at issue in this case is known as the suretyship provision of the Statute of Frauds. The specific language of Virginia Code §11-2 at issue was: "Unless a promise, contract, agreement, representation, assurance, or ratification, or some memorandum or note thereof, is in writing and signed by the party to be charged or his agent, no action shall be brought in any of the following cases:. . .(4)To charge any person upon a promise to answer for the debt, default, or misdoings of another." The purposes served by this provision include an evidentiary function to prevent errors or even outright lies by an obligee and, also, a cautionary function to ensure as best as possible that the surety is committed to the obligations they are undertaking.

Continued on next page.

As this decision illustrates, however, not every promisor who agrees to assume another's debt is a surety, so the suretyship provision of the Statute of Frauds will not apply to every situation in which a party has agreed to take on another's obligations.

Quicknotes

BREACH OF CONTRACT Unlawful failure by a party to perform its obligations pursuant to contract.

COLLATERAL PROMISE A promise to pay another's debt without benefit to the party making the promise; must be in writing to be enforceable.

STATUTE OF FRAUDS A statute that requires specified types of contracts to be in writing in order to be binding.

SURETYSHIP A situation in which one party guarantees payment of the debt of another party to a creditor.

Central Ceilings, Inc. v. National Amusements, Inc.

Subcontractor (P) v. Property owner (D)

Mass. App. Ct., 70 Mass. App. Ct. 172, 873 N.E.2d 754 (2007)

NATURE OF CASE: Appeal from verdict and judgment against defendant in breach of contract action.

FACT SUMMARY: National Amusements, Inc. (National) (D) contended that its oral promise to pay Central Ceilings, Inc. (Central) (P), a subcontractor on the building of a theater complex owned by National (D), the sum that the general contractor, Old Colony Construction Corp. (Old Colony), owed to Central (P) was unenforceable under the Statute of Frauds and that the exception to the Statute of Frauds known as the "leading object" or "main purpose" exception was inapplicable because the alleged agreement did not constitute a novation.

RULE OF LAW

Under the "leading object" or "main purpose" exception to the Statute of Frauds, an oral promise that is not a novation may be enforced where the promisor has made the promise to secure the promisee's performance and the satisfaction of any obligation of a third party that is made as a part of that promise is merely incidental to the promise.

FACTS: Central Ceilings, Inc. (Central) (P), a carpentry subcontractor, was hired by Old Colony Construction Corp. (Old Colony) to do work on a theater complex owned by National Amusements, Inc. (National) (D). When the initial due date for completion had passed, and it became clear that Old Colony was having difficulty paying its bills, Central's (P) agent obtained an oral guaranty from National's (D) agent that National (D) would pay to Central (P) what Old Colony would owe to Central (P). National (D) was interested in completing the project on an expedited basis to outstrip its competitors. Based on National's (D) promise, Central (P) continued working on the project. Months later, when National (D) had finished its payments to Old Colony, it refused to pay Central (P), which sued for breach of contract and won a $600,000 verdict. National (D) appealed, claiming, inter alia, that the oral promise was, at best, a promise to pay for another's debt and therefore had to be in writing. It also argued that no exception to this requirement applied, since the promise did not constitute a novation. The state's intermediate appellate court granted review.

ISSUE: Under the "leading object" or "main purpose" exception to the Statute of Frauds, may an oral promise that is not a novation be enforced where the promisor has made the promise to secure the promisee's performance and the satisfaction of any obligation of a third party that is made as a part of that promise is merely incidental to the promise?

HOLDING AND DECISION: (Peretta, J.) Yes. Under the "leading object" or "main purpose" exception to the Statute of Frauds, an oral promise that is not a novation may be enforced where the promisor has made the promise to secure the promisee's performance and the satisfaction of any obligation of a third party that is made as a part of that promise is merely incidental to the promise. The "leading object" or "main purpose" exception to the Statute of Frauds provides that a promise does not have to be in writing where the fair inference is that the leading object (main purpose) of the promise is to obtain a benefit for the promisor from the promisee, so that the debt thus incurred may fairly be deemed to be that of the promisor. National Amusements, Inc. (National) (D) argues that the only way in which the oral agreement here could be excepted from the Statute of Frauds is if it were a novation, i.e., it released Old Colony Construction Corp. (Old Colony) from its obligation to Central Ceilings, Inc. (Central) (P) and substituted National (D) for Old Colony as the obligor. This argument is rejected because novation is only one way to remove an agreement from the Statute of Frauds. The "leading object" exception addresses a different situation, such as occurred here, whereby (1) a third party is indebted; (2) there is no novation; and (3) the third party's duty to the creditor will be terminated by the performance promised by the defendant. In such a situation, the "leading object" exception applies because the promise was given primarily or solely to serve the promisor's own interests. Case law recognizes that a property owner's promise to pay subcontractors or suppliers may, in appropriate circumstances, come within the "leading object" exception. Here, there was enough evidence to bring the agreement within this exception, because National (D) wanted the project completed by a certain date so it could profit thereby and beat out its competitors; Central (P) was a key subcontractor; and Central (P) was one of the few that could deliver the requested performance. Therefore, based on this evidence and under these circumstances, National's (D) promise was given to secure Central's (P) continued and expedited performance; any satisfaction of Old Colony's debt was merely incidental to this promise. Affirmed.

Continued on next page.

ANALYSIS

The issue of whether the promisor's "main purpose" or "leading object" is to secure a benefit for itself is typically a fact question for the jury. Thus, when asserting this exception, the plaintiff must plead sufficient facts from which such a "main purpose" can be inferred or ascertained. A few factors that could be probative include whether the third party has been in default or has repudiated its obligations, whether the value of the benefit is equal to the amount promised to be paid for it, and whether the promisor has initiated the agreement on its own without involving the third-party obligor.

Quicknotes

INTER ALIA Among other things.

NOVATION The substitution of one party for another in a contract with the approval of the remaining party and discharging the obligations of the released party.

PROMISEE The party to whom a promise is made.

PROMISOR The party who promises to render an obligation to another in the future.

STATUTE OF FRAUDS A statute that requires specified types of contracts to be in writing in order to be binding.

Crabtree v. Elizabeth Arden Sales Corp.

Employee (P) v. Employer (D)

N.Y. Ct. App., 305 N.Y. 48, 110 N.E.2d 551 (1953)

NATURE OF CASE: Appeal from affirmance of award of damages in action for breach of an employment contract.

FACT SUMMARY: Crabtree (P) was hired by Elizabeth Arden Sales Corp. (D) to be the latter's sales manager. No formal contract was signed, but separate writings pieced together showed Crabtree (P) to have been hired for a two-year term with pay raises after the first and second six months. When he did not receive his second pay raise, Crabtree (P) sued for damages for breach.

RULE OF LAW

To satisfy the Statute of Frauds, the memorandum expressing the contract may be pieced together out of separate writings, connected with one another either expressly or by the internal evidence of subject matter and occasion, rather than being contained in a single document.

FACTS: In September 1947, Crabtree (P) began negotiating with Elizabeth Arden Sales Corp. (Arden) (D) for the position of the latter's sales manager. Being unfamiliar with the cosmetics business and giving up a well-paying, secure job, Crabtree (P) insisted upon an agreement for a definite term. He asked for three years at $25,000 per year. But Arden (D) offered two years, with $20,000 per year the first six months, $25,000 per year the second six months, and $30,000 per year the second year. This was written down by Arden's (D) personal secretary with the notation "2 years to make good." A few days later, Crabtree (P) telephoned to Mr. Johns, Arden's (D) executive vice president, his acceptance. Crabtree (P) received a "welcome" wire from Miss Arden (D). When he reported for work, a "payroll change" card was made up and initialed by Mr. Johns showing the above pay arrangement with a salary increase noted "as per contractual agreement." Crabtree (P) received his first pay raise as scheduled but not his second one. Miss Arden (D) allegedly refused to approve the second increase, denying Crabtree (P) had been hired for any specific period. The trial court entered judgment for Crabtree (P), the state's intermediate appellate court affirmed, and the state's highest court granted review.

ISSUE: To satisfy the Statute of Frauds may the memorandum expressing the contract be pieced together out of separate writings, connected with one another either expressly or by the internal evidence of subject matter and occasion, rather than being contained in a single document?

HOLDING AND DECISION: (Fuld, J.) Yes. To satisfy the Statute of Frauds, the memorandum expressing the contract may be pieced together out of separate writings, connected with one another either expressly or by the internal evidence of subject matter and occasion, rather than being contained in a single document. First, as it is alleged that the contract is for a period of two years, there must be written evidence of its terms to be enforceable, as the two-year performance places it within the Statute of Frauds (the Statute). The payroll cards, one initialed by Elizabeth Arden Sales Corp.'s (Arden's) (D) executive vice president and the other by its controller, unquestionably constituted a memorandum under the Statute. It is enough that they were signed with the intent to authenticate the information contained therein and that such information evidences the terms of the contract. The cards had all essential terms except for duration. But as the memorandum can be pieced together from more than one document, all that is required between the papers is a connection established simply by reference to the same subject matter or transaction. Parol evidence is permissible in order to establish the connection. As the note prepared by Miss Arden's (D) personal secretary shows it was made in Miss Arden's (D) presence as well as that of Johns and of Crabtree (P), the dangers of parol evidence are at a minimum. All the terms must be set out in writing and cannot be shown by parol. That memo, the paper signed by Johns, and the paper signed by the controller all refer on their faces to the Crabtree (P) transaction. The controller's paper shows that it was prepared for the purpose of a "salary increase per contractual arrangements with Miss Arden" (D). That is a reference to more comprehensive evidence, and parol evidence can so explain. "2 years to make good" probably had no other purpose than to denote the duration of the arrangement, and parol evidence may explain its meaning. Affirmed.

ANALYSIS

When there is more than one writing and all are signed by the party to be charged, and it is clear by their contents that they relate to the same transaction, there is little problem. When not all the documents are signed, difficulties obviously crop up. It becomes difficult to say the memorandum has been authenticated to the party to be charged. When the unsigned document is

Continued on next page.

physically attached to the signed writing, the Statute of Frauds is satisfied. And, as illustrated by this case, this is true when the signed document by its terms expressly refers to the unsigned document. The cases conflict where the papers are not attached or fail to refer to the other. The minority holds that those circumstances constitute a failure to show sufficient authentication. The better view is that if the signed document does not expressly refer to the unsigned, it is sufficient if internal evidence refers to the same subject matter or transaction. If so, extrinsic evidence is admissible to help show the connection between the documents.

Quicknotes

BREACH OF CONTRACT Unlawful failure by a party to perform its obligations pursuant to contract.

EXTRINSIC EVIDENCE Evidence that is not contained within the text of a document or contract, but that is derived from the parties' statements or the circumstances under which the agreement was made.

PAROL EVIDENCE Evidence given verbally; extraneous evidence.

STATUTE OF FRAUDS A statute that requires specified types of contracts to be in writing in order to be binding.

Beaver v. Brumlow

Seller of land (P) v. Buyer of land (D)

N.M. Ct. App., 148 N.M. 172, 231 P.3d 628 (2010)

NATURE OF CASE: Appeal from judgment for defendants/counterclaim plaintiffs in action for ejectment.

FACT SUMMARY: The Beavers (P), who orally agreed to sell land to the Brumlows (D), but then reneged on the agreement, contended that the Statute of Frauds barred specific performance of the agreement because the Brumlows' (D) part performance was not "unequivocally referable" to the verbal agreement, and the verbal agreement was not certain as to the purchase price and time of performance.

RULE OF LAW

Specific performance of an oral contract for the sale of land is not barred by the Statute of Frauds where the terms of the contract other than the purchase price have been proved, there has been part performance by both parties to the agreement, the part performance refers unequivocally to the sale of land through possession and the making of improvements, and a remedy at law would be inadequate.

FACTS: The Beavers (P) agreed verbally to sell property to the Brumlows (D) on which the Brumlows (D) would site a house. Mr. Brumlow worked for the Beavers (P) at the time the agreement was made. In reliance on the Beavers' (P) promise, and with the Beavers' (P) permission, the Brumlows (D) cashed out their retirement plans and bought and installed a mobile home on the property and then added permanent improvements to it. The cost to the Brumlows (D) of purchasing the house and making improvements was around $85,000. The Beavers (P) supported the Brumlows' (D) efforts and helped them obtain necessary permits and applications. Throughout this time, the Brumlows (D) requested that the Beavers (P) formalize the parties' agreement, but the Beavers (P) never did, although they promised to and consulted an attorney about drafting the necessary documents. The parties also never agreed on a price or a date of closing. The Beavers (P) let the Brumlows (D) quietly enjoy possession of the land for several years. Then, all that changed. Mr. Brumlow (D) terminated his employment with the Beavers (P), as he was going to work for their competitor. Hurt and angry, the Beavers (P) decided not to sell the agreed upon tract of land to the Brumlows (D). Instead, they attempted to restructure the agreement as a "lease" by having the Brumlows (D) sign an agreement under which the Brumlows (D) would pay the Beavers (P) $400 per month, though the agreement used no language of a lease, so that the Brumlows (D) believed the agreement was for payment for the land. When the Brumlows (D) began writing "Land Payment" on the checks, the Beavers (P) stopped cashing the checks and alleged that the "agreement" was for rental. The Brumlows (D) attempted to amicably resolve the dispute by offering to pay cash in the amount of the fair market value for the property and to have the property surveyed at their expense. The Beavers (P) refused and then filed an ejectment action, alleging that the Brumlows (D) were in violation of their "rental" agreement. The Brumlows (D) denied the existence of a rental agreement and affirmatively alleged that their occupancy was pursuant to an agreement to purchase the property. The Brumlows (D) also filed counterclaims that included claims for breach of contract, fraud, and prima facie tort. The Beavers (P) pleaded the Statute of Frauds as a defense, arguing that the Brumlows' (D) part performance was not "unequivocally referable" to the verbal agreement, and the verbal agreement was not certain as to the purchase price and time of performance. The trial court held that the parties had entered into an agreement for the sale of land, and that by reneging on that agreement, the Beavers (P) injured the Brumlows (D), so that they committed a prima facie tort, which they knew would harm the Brumlows (D). The court rejected the Statute of Frauds defense on the grounds that part performance of the contract by both parties was sufficient to remove the contract from the Statute of Frauds. The court gave the Brumlows (D) a choice between money damages for the tort and specific performance of the contract, with the purchase price to be determined by an independent appraisal of the fair market value of the property, payable in cash within 30 days; the Brumlows (D) chose specific performance. The state's intermediate appellate court granted review.

ISSUE: Is specific performance of an oral contract for the sale of land barred by the Statute of Frauds where the terms of the contract other than the purchase price have been proved, there has been part performance by both parties to the agreement, the part performance refers unequivocally to the sale of land through possession and the making of improvements, and a remedy at law would be inadequate?

HOLDING AND DECISION: (Vigil, J.) No. Specific performance of an oral contract for the sale of land is not barred by the Statute of Frauds where the terms of the contract other than the purchase price have been proved, there has been part performance by both parties

Continued on next page.

to the agreement, the part performance refers unequivocally to the sale of land through possession and the making of improvements, and a remedy at law would be inadequate. The Statute of Frauds generally bars actions on contracts for the sale of land or interests in land where there has been no written agreement for the sale signed by the party to be charged or the party's representative. However, a judicially created exception to this rule known as the doctrine of part performance—effected to overcome the harshness and injustice that might result from a literal and mechanical application of the rule—provides that where an oral contract not enforceable under the Statute of Frauds has been performed to such extent as to make it inequitable to deny effect thereto, equity may consider the contract as removed from operation of the Statute of Frauds and decree specific performance. Here, it is uncontested that the agreement was made or even that the parties partially performed. The key objection by the Beavers (P) to application of the part performance doctrine is that the character of the Brumlows' (D) performance was not sufficiently indicative of an oral agreement to sell land to qualify as partial performance. To satisfy the part performance doctrine, part performance must be referrable to the contract. In other words, it must be shown that there was no other reason for the performance than performance under the contract. Here, the Beavers (P) argue that the Brumlows' (D) conduct was consistent with those taken by a person who needs a place to live and who is given an opportunity to reside on another person's property. The Beavers (P) argue that if there is an alternative explanation for the actions taken in reliance of the oral contract, those actions are not "unequivocally referable" to the contract, and application of the part performance doctrine is improper. This argument is rejected. First, the "unequivocally referable" concept does not mean that outside of the contract there can be no other plausible explanation for the part performance. Instead, it means that an outsider, knowing all of the circumstances of a case except for the claimed oral agreement, would naturally and reasonably conclude that a contract existed regarding the land, of the same general nature as that alleged by the claimant. In other words, the performance must lead an outsider to "naturally and reasonably" conclude that the contract alleged actually exists. Two indicators of such performance are taking possession of the property, and making valuable, permanent, and substantial improvements to the property. Here, the Brumlows (D) did both. In sum, the Brumlows' (D) reliance on the agreement and their part performance were sufficient to take the oral agreement outside of the Statute of Frauds. The Brumlows (D) also argue that the trial court impermissibly imposed on them a purchase price to which they had never agreed when the court ordered that the purchase price would be established by an appraisal and that the terms of the payment would be in cash payable within 30 days. Precedent provides that a claim for specific performance of a contract involving land will not fail for failure to specify a price where the contract is otherwise complete, and there has been part performance of the contract by a transfer of possession. In such situations, equity may imply a reasonable price to avoid inequity. Here, the contract was otherwise complete, and the Brumlows (D) relied on it to their detriment by taking possession and making improvements. Therefore, the trial court, in the exercise of its equitable powers, did not err in ordering that the purchase price be determined by an independent appraisal at fair market value. Significantly, the Beavers (P) do not challenge the fairness of the purchase price established by the trial court. Similarly, where a closing date has not been agreed to, equity may supply a reasonable time for performance. Finally, because it is well settled that land is unique and is assumed to have special value not replaceable in money, the Brumlows (D) did not have an adequate remedy at law. Affirmed.

ANALYSIS

As did the court in this case, the majority of courts, in deciding whether a promisee's performance is "unequivocally referable" to the contract, look for two key factors: (1) whether the party seeking enforcement has obtained possession of the property, and (2) whether that party has made valuable improvements to the property. If these two factors are present, a majority of courts will apply the part performance exception. For these courts, mere payment of money usually is not enough. The Restatement (Second) of Contracts does not use the "unequivocally referable" standard, but instead focuses on whether the party seeking enforcement has, in reliance on the contract, so changed his position that only specific performance can avoid injustice.

Quicknotes

BREACH OF CONTRACT Unlawful failure by a party to perform its obligations pursuant to contract.

COUNTERCLAIM An independent cause of action brought by a defendant to a lawsuit in order to oppose or deduct from the plaintiff's claim.

EJECTMENT An action to oust someone in unlawful possession of real property and to restore possession to the party lawfully entitled to it.

FAIR MARKET VALUE The price of particular property or goods that a buyer would offer and a seller would accept in the open market following full disclosure.

Continued on next page.

FRAUD A false representation of facts with the intent that another will rely on the misrepresentation to his or her detriment.

PART PERFORMANCE Partial performance of a contract, promise, or obligation.

PRIMA FACIE CASE An action where the plaintiff introduces sufficient evidence to submit the issue to the judge or jury for determination.

REMEDY AT LAW Compensation for violation of a right or injuries sustained that is available in a court of law, as opposed to a court of equity.

SPECIFIC PERFORMANCE An equitable remedy whereby the court requires the parties to perform their obligations pursuant to a contract.

STATUTE OF FRAUDS A statute that requires specified types of contracts to be in writing in order to be binding.

TORT DAMAGES Monetary compensation awarded by the court to a party injured as the result of the tortious act of another.

Monarco v. Lo Greco

Devisee (P) v. Stepson (D)

Cal. Sup. Ct., 35 Cal. 2d 621, 220 P.2d 737 (1950)

NATURE OF CASE: Action for partition of property and an accounting.

FACT SUMMARY: Christie (D) had been promised the family farm by his stepfather, Castiglia, now deceased, if he would abandon his plans to leave home and would, instead, work the farm. Christie (D) worked the farm for 20 years, increasing its value 25 times, but Castiglia secretly changed his will and left the farm to his grandson, Monarco (P).

RULE OF LAW

The doctrine of estoppel may be used to assert the Statute of Frauds to prevent fraud that would result from refusal to enforce oral contracts in certain circumstances.

FACTS: In 1926, Carmela and Natale Castiglia promised Christie Lo Greco (D), Carmela's son by a prior marriage, that if he would abandon his plans to leave home and work their farm instead, they would leave him the farm when they died. Christie (D) worked for room and board for twenty years, and the value of the farm rose from $4,000 to $100,000. Natale, shortly before his death, secretly changed his will to leave his interest in the farm to his grandson, Monarco (P). The will was probated, and the property was distributed to Monarco (P), who brought an action for partition of the properties and an accounting. Christie (D) cross-claimed to have Monarco (P) declared a constructive trustee of the property. The trial court found in his favor, and Monarco (P) appealed.

ISSUE: May the doctrine of estoppel be used to assert the Statute of Frauds to prevent fraud that would result from refusal to enforce oral contracts in certain circumstances?

HOLDING AND DECISION: (Traynor, J.) Yes. The use of the doctrine of estoppel to assert the Statute of Frauds (the Statute) to prevent fraud that would result from the refusal to enforce oral contracts under certain circumstances is permissible where an unconscionable injury would result from denying enforcement after one party has been induced by the other seriously to change his position in reliance on the contract or where unjust enrichment would result if a party who has received the benefits of the other party's performance were allowed to rely on the Statute. Both occurred here. Christie (D) relied on Natale's continued assurances, thus giving up the opportunity to accumulate property of his own, to make the family venture a success instead. Natale, meanwhile, reaped the benefits of the contract. He and his devisees would be unjustly enriched if the Statute could be invoked to relieve them of their contractual obligations. Where either unconscionable injury or unjust enrichment would result from refusal to enforce the contract, the doctrine of estoppel has been applied whether or not there was reliance upon representations going to the Statute requirements themselves. It is not the representation that the contract will be put into writing or that the Statute will not be induced, but the promise that the contract a party relies upon will be performed. Affirmed.

ANALYSIS

Cases that hold that part performance takes a case out of the Statute of Frauds can be explained on grounds of promissory estoppel in the sense that relief is granted because of detrimental reliance by a party on a promise. Note that the doctrine of part performance antedated the general concept of promissory estoppel and has its own particularized rules. Many jurisdictions have departed from the narrower path of part performance to base their decisions on grounds of estoppel whenever the equities are so great as to make a contrary decision unconscionable.

Quicknotes

CONSTRUCTIVE TRUST A trust that arises by operation of law whereby the court imposes a trust upon property lawfully held by one party for the benefit of another, as a result of some wrongdoing by the party in possession so as to avoid unjust enrichment.

DOCTRINE OF ESTOPPEL An equitable doctrine precluding a party from asserting a right to the detriment of another who justifiably relied on the conduct.

RELIANCE Dependence on a fact that causes a party to act or refrain from acting.

STATUTE OF FRAUDS A statute that requires specified types of contracts to be in writing in order to be binding.

CHAPTER 4

Policing the Bargaining Process

Quick Reference Rules of Law

		PAGE
1.	*Douglass v. Pflueger Hawaii, Inc.* A minor, who the legislature has determined may contract for employment, is not entitled to disaffirm his employment contract by reason of his minority status.	100
2.	*Ortelere v. Teachers' Retirement Bd.* A person incurs only voidable contractual duties by entering into a transaction if by reason of mental illness or defect (1) he is unable to understand in a reasonable manner the nature and consequences of the transaction, or (2) he is unable to act in a reasonable manner in relation to the transaction, and the other party has reason to know of his condition.	102
3.	*Cundick v. Broadbent.* Mental capacity to contract depends upon whether the allegedly disabled person possessed sufficient reason to enable him to understand the nature and effect of the act in issue.	104
4.	*Kenai Chrysler Center, Inc. v. Denison.* As a matter of law, a valid guardianship order voids an attempt by the guardianship's ward to create a binding contract.	105
5.	*Alaska Packers' Assn. v. Domenico.* A promise to pay a man for doing that which he is already under contract to do is without consideration.	106
6.	*Watkins & Son v. Carrig.* A modification made to meet the reasonable needs of standard and ethical practices of men in their business dealings with each other operates as a partial rescission of a prior contract and is thus enforceable since supported by consideration.	107
7.	*Austin Instrument, Inc. v. Loral Corporation.* A contract modification is voidable on the ground of duress when it is established that the party making the claim was forced to agree to it by means of a wrongful threat precluding the exercise of the party's free will.	108
8.	*Martinez-Gonzalez v. Elkhorn Packing Co. LLC.* An agreement is not the product of economic duress, and, therefore, rescindable, where, although the agreement may result from hard bargaining, no wrongful act has been committed against the party seeking rescission, and the party seeking rescission has reasonable alternatives to entering into a coerced agreement.	109
9.	*Martinez-Gonzalez v. Elkhorn Packing Co. LLC.* An agreement is not the product of undue influence and, therefore, rescindable where a dominating person or party has not applied excessive pressure on a servient person, who is particularly susceptible to such pressure, to take unfair advantage of the servient person to force his or her assent to the agreement.	112
10.	*Swinton v. Whitinsville Sav. Bank.* Where both parties to a contract of sale are dealing at arm's length, mere nondisclosure of latent defects in the goods will not render one party liable to the other party.	115
11.	*Kannavos v. Annino.* Where one party to a contract of sale goes beyond "bare nondisclosure" and knowingly misrepresents material facts by telling "half-truths," the other party may rescind the contract even though he could have ascertained the whole truth by checking public records.	116
12.	*Speakers of Sport v. ProServ.* A promise in the nature of puffing that is not part of a fraudulent scheme cannot be the basis of an action for fraudulent interference with a business relationship.	117
13.	*Vokes v. Arthur Murray, Inc.* Where one party has superior knowledge, statements made within the area of such knowledge may be treated as statements of fact.	118

Douglass v. Pflueger Hawaii, Inc.

Former employee (P) v. Former employer (D)

Hawaii Sup. Ct., 110 Haw. 520, 135 P.3d 129 (2006)

NATURE OF CASE: Appeal from grant of motion to stay action and to compel arbitration in an action for various employment-law claims.

FACT SUMMARY: Douglass (P), who was 17 when he went to work at Pflueger Hawaii, Inc. (Pflueger) (D), contended that he was not contractually bound by an arbitration provision set forth in Pflueger's (D) employee handbook because, at the time, he was a minor child who did not have the legal capacity to bind himself as a party to the arbitration agreement.

RULE OF LAW

A minor, who the legislature has determined may contract for employment, is not entitled to disaffirm his employment contract by reason of his minority status.

FACTS: Douglass (P) was 17 when he was hired by Pflueger Hawaii, Inc. (Pflueger) (D), a car dealership. Douglass (P) was given an employee handbook, which contained an arbitration provision that provided that any and all claims arising out of the employee's employment with the company would be settled by final binding arbitration. The handbook also included anti-harassment/discrimination policies. Douglass (P) signed an acknowledgment form that he had received the handbook. A few months later, Douglass (P) was seriously injured on the job when his supervisor sprayed him on the buttocks area with an air hose—Douglass's (P) anus, rectum and colon were instantaneously penetrated, inflated, and dilated by the force of the blast. Douglass (P) brought suit for several employment claims: (1) hostile, intimidating and/or offensive working environment; (2) unsafe working environment; (3) sexual assault and sexual discrimination; (4) negligent training (of its supervisor); and (5) negligent supervision. Pflueger (D) moved to stay the action and compel arbitration in accordance with the employee handbook's arbitration provision. The trial court granted the motion, and the state's highest court granted review.

ISSUE: Is a minor, who the legislature has determined may contract for employment, entitled to disaffirm his employment contract by reason of his minority status?

HOLDING AND DECISION: (Moon, C.J.) No. A minor, who the legislature has determined may contract for employment, is not entitled to disaffirm his employment contract by reason of his minority status. The threshold question is whether Douglass (P), as a minor, has an absolute right to disaffirm his employment contract with Pflueger Hawaii, Inc. (Pflueger) (D), including the arbitration provision. Under the common-law rule known as "the infancy doctrine" or "the infancy law doctrine" contracts entered by minors are voidable. Upon reaching the age of majority, the former minor may choose either to ratify or avoid contractual obligations entered during his or her minority. The underlying purpose of this doctrine is to protect minors from their inexperience and to protect them from unscrupulous adults who might take advantage of them. The rule that a minor's contracts are voidable, however, is not absolute. An exception to the rule is that a minor may not avoid a contract for goods or services necessary for his health and sustenance. The rationale for the exception is if minors were not able to contract for things absolutely necessary to their existence they would suffer. The state's legislature has codified this exception by providing statutorily that contracts relating to medical care, hospital care, and drug or alcohol abuse treatment are contracts for "necessaries" and that minors who enter into contracts for such services cannot later disaffirm them by reason of their minority status. Because Douglass's (P) employment was not a "necessary," his employment contract would not be covered by the "necessaries" exception to the infancy doctrine, so that if only the infancy doctrine applied, Douglass (P) would be able to avoid his employment contract. However, the state's child labor laws also must be looked to. Those laws incorporate the policy underpinning the infancy doctrine and provide that a minor who has attained the age of 16 years but not 18 years may be employed under certain circumstances. Thus, with respect to contracts of employment, it is apparent that, by relaxing the requirements for 16- and 17-year-olds to obtain employment, the legislature clearly viewed minors in this particular age group as capable and competent to contract for gainful employment and, therefore, should be bound by the terms of such contracts. Accordingly, the general rule that contracts entered by minors are voidable is not applicable in the employment context. While the statute requires a 16- or 17-year-old to obtain an age certificate from the state's department of labor, regardless of whether Douglass (P) obtained such a certificate before going to work at Pflueger's (D) is irrelevant to this issue. For these reasons, the trial court properly rejected Douglass's (P) argument that he was entitled to disaffirm his employment contract, including the arbitration provision, by reason of his minority status. The court went on to hold the arbitration provision was unenforceable as a consequence of its placement in the employment

Continued on next page.

handbook, which failed to alert Douglass (P) to its presence or scope, and therefore Douglass (P) could not assent to it. Accordingly, the court held that Douglass (P) could not be compelled to arbitrate his claims. Vacated and remanded.

ANALYSIS

It should be emphasized that contracts entered by minors generally are voidable under the infancy doctrine, but not void ab initio. However, the minor's right to disaffirm a contract may expressly be limited by statute, or it may be lost if the contract has received judicial approval at the time it was entered. In some states, the right may be lost through parental consent, and it may also be lost through ratification, where upon reaching majority, the former minor affirms the contract, as by continued performance under the contract. As this case demonstrates, it may also be lost through judicial interpretation of legislative intent.

Quicknotes

AB INITIO From its inception or beginning.

INFANCY Minority; refers to the state of not having achieved the age of legal majority.

Ortelere v. Teachers' Retirement Bd.

Decedent's husband (P) v. Public retirement system (D)

N.Y. Ct. App., 25 N.Y.2d 196, 250 N.E.2d 460 (1969)

NATURE OF CASE: Appeal from dismissal of action to avoid a contract entered into by a mentally infirm person.

FACT SUMMARY: Grace Ortelere, deceased, was a schoolteacher in New York City on leave from her work for mental illness after having suffered a mental breakdown. She had a $70,925 reserve in the public retirement system. While on leave, she borrowed the maximum amount possible from the system and made an irrevocable election for maximum retirement benefits of $450 during her lifetime, revoking an earlier election of $375 a month with the unexhausted reserve to be paid to her family. She did not tell her husband (P) of this change, which would leave him without her benefits upon her death that occurred two months later.

RULE OF LAW

A person incurs only voidable contractual duties by entering into a transaction if by reason of mental illness or defect (1) he is unable to understand in a reasonable manner the nature and consequences of the transaction, or (2) he is unable to act in a reasonable manner in relation to the transaction, and the other party has reason to know of his condition.

FACTS: Ortelere's (P) wife, Grace, who was a 60-year-old New York City schoolteacher on leave from work due to mental illness, had a retirement system reserve of $70,925. Her psychiatrist believed she also suffered from cerebral arteriosclerosis, and she had suffered a nervous breakdown. Ortelere (P) quit his job to care for his wife. Two months before her death, Grace, without telling her husband (P), made an irrevocable election to take maximum possible retirement benefits of $450 a month, thereby revoking a previous election of $325 per month that would have paid the balance of the $70,925 reserve to her family upon her death. She also borrowed the maximum amount possible from the system, $8,760. Her new plan would not pay the balance of her reserve to her family upon her death (two months later). Ortelere (P) sued to set aside Grace's election on the ground of mental incompetence. Her psychiatrist said in testimony that Grace was incapable of making any kind of rational decision. The appeals court dismissed the complaint, and Ortelere (P) appealed.

ISSUE: Does a person incur only voidable contractual duties by entering into a transaction if by reason of mental illness or defect he (1) is unable to understand in a reasonable manner the nature and consequences of the transaction, or (2) he is unable to act in a reasonable manner in relation to the transaction, and the other party has reason to know of his condition?

HOLDING AND DECISION: (Breitel, J.) Yes. A person incurs only voidable contractual duties by entering into a transaction if by reason of mental illness or defect (1) he is unable to understand in a reasonable manner the nature and consequences of the transaction, or (2) he is unable to act in a reasonable manner in relation to the transaction, and the other party has reason to know of his condition. Earlier, traditional legal standards of competency were developed when psychiatry was in its infancy; now those standards should be expanded in light of greater medical knowledge. The old test failed to account for one who by reason of mental illness is unable to control his conduct even though his cognitive ability seems unimpaired. Accordingly, when the other party knows or should know of the mentally ill person's condition, the contract should be voidable, in addition to the earlier rule where the contract is voidable by reason of mental illness or defect if he is unable to understand in a reasonable manner the nature and consequences of the transaction. See Restatement (Second) § 18(c). Forty years of contribution to a retirement system should not be allowed to be forfeited by a brief act by a known mentally ill person. As the trial court's findings were based on the traditional legal standard rather than on the broader, modern rule, the judgment is reversed, and a new trial is ordered.

DISSENT: (Jasen, J.) Because Grace sent a detailed letter to Teachers' Retirement Bd. (D) requesting various explanations as to the benefits of one retirement election over the other, it seems clear that if she had sufficient capacity to ask such questions, she had sufficient capacity to understand the answers. As her entire family income was retirement plan money, the extra $75 a month income was a necessity and a decision to change her retirement plan was rational and necessary. The traditional standard of mental competency, whether the mind was so affected as to render the ill person wholly and absolutely incompetent to comprehend and understand the nature of the transaction, has proved workable over the years and should be retained.

Continued on next page.

ANALYSIS

While older cases tend to hold contracts entered by the mentally incompetent as void, modern authority's overwhelming weight is to hold them voidable. Generally, insanity is considered to exist where a party does not understand the nature and consequences of his act at the time of the transaction. Courts will look to see if the transaction was entered during a "lucid interval" or a period of "insane delusion." While this has been criticized as being unscientific, the lack of psychiatric tests probably makes it easier for the court to reach just results. If the contract is fair and beneficial to the alleged incompetent, the tendency is to uphold it; if not, the tendency is to void the contract. This appears to be a consideration of the court in the instant case due to the loss of a great sum of money as a result of the alleged incompetent's decision.

Cundick v. Broadbent

Sheep rancher (P) v. Property purchaser (D)

383 F.2d 157 (10th Cir. 1967)

NATURE OF CASE: Appeal from dismissal of action to set aside an agreement to sell land.

FACT SUMMARY: Mrs. Cundick (P) claimed her husband did not have the mental capacity to enter into a contract to sell his land.

RULE OF LAW

Mental capacity to contract depends upon whether the allegedly disabled person possessed sufficient reason to enable him to understand the nature and effect of the act in issue.

FACTS: Cundick (P), a sheep rancher, entered into a contract with Broadbent (D) to sell his lands to Broadbent (D). The two men signed a handwritten agreement and later a long form document drafted by Cundick's (P) attorney. A month later the parties agreed to amend the agreement, again with the aid of Cundick's (P) attorney, in order to raise the purchase price. Under the agreement, Broadbent (D) would have purchased the land and Cundick's (P) interest in a development company for less than half of the assets' estimated value. Cundick's wife (P), after being appointed Cundick's (P) guardian ad litem, sought to rescind the contract, claiming that her husband was incompetent to make the contract. Two doctors and a psychologist testified at trial that Mr. Cundick (P) was confused and exhibited poor judgment. The trial court, however, dismissed the action. Mrs. Cundick (P) appealed.

ISSUE: Does mental capacity to contract depend upon whether the allegedly disabled person possessed sufficient reason to enable him to understand the nature and effect of the act in issue?

HOLDING AND DECISION: (Murrah, C.J.) Yes. Mental capacity to contract depends upon whether the allegedly disabled person possessed sufficient reason to enable him to understand the nature and effect of the act in issue. Weak-mindedness alone does not constitute incompetence requiring a contract to be voidable. Intelligence is not required to form a valid contract. The contracting parties must be able to understand the effect of the actions they are taking but not necessarily the wisdom of the action. Mr. Cundick (P) may be weak-minded, but he was not utterly incapable of transacting his business affairs at the time he made the contract. Furthermore, Broadbent (D) did not defraud Mr. Cundick (P) by taking advantage of his weakness. The initial price, although very low, was subsequently raised when the parties modified the contract. Mrs. Cundick (P) and her attorney both participated in making the deal and did not at that time raise questions as to Mr. Cundick's (P) capacity to make the deal. Affirmed.

DISSENT: (Hill, J.) The medical testimony clearly supports a finding of incompetence. No mentally competent rancher would dispose of his ranch interests for only half their value.

ANALYSIS

The early rule for incapacity stated that a contract was void if made by someone incompetent. The rule was subsequently relaxed to the point where an incompetent was allowed to contract, but the contract was voidable at his election. The decision to void the contract is subject to equitable considerations.

Quicknotes

GUARDIAN AD LITEM Person designated by the court to represent an infant or ward in a particular legal proceeding.

RESCISSION The canceling of an agreement and the return of the parties to their positions prior to the formation of the contract.

Kenai Chrysler Center, Inc. v. Denison

Car dealer (D) v. Guardian of developmentally disabled adult (P)

Alaska Sup. Ct., 167 P.3d 1240 (2007)

NATURE OF CASE: Appeal from summary judgment for plaintiffs in action for declaratory and injunctive relief from a contract entered by a guardianship's ward.

FACT SUMMARY: Kenai Chrysler Center, Inc., (Kenai Chrysler) (D) sold a car to David Denison, not knowing that David was developmentally disabled and subject to the legal guardianship of his parents (P). When the Denisons (P) tried to return the car and insisted that the contract was void, Kenai Chrysler (D) refused to take it back, contending that a valid guardianship order does not automatically void an attempt by the ward to create a binding contract, and that the party contracting with the ward, at the very least, is entitled to restitution.

RULE OF LAW

As a matter of law, a valid guardianship order voids an attempt by the guardianship's ward to create a binding contract.

FACTS: David Denison, a developmentally disabled young adult who lived independently, but was subject to the legal guardianship of his parents (P), used his debit card to buy a car from Kenai Chrysler Center, Inc. (Kenai Chrysler) (D). When the Denisons (P) tried to return the car and insisted that the contract was void, Kenai Chrysler (D) refused to take it back and demanded restitution to rescind the contract. The Denisons (P) sued Kenai Chrysler (D), seeking both a judgment declaring that the sales contract was void because of the guardianship and an injunction to prevent Kenai Chrysler (D) from enforcing the contract. The trial court granted summary judgment to the Denisons (P), and Kenai Chrysler (D) appealed. The state's highest court granted review.

ISSUE: As a matter of law, does a valid guardianship order void an attempt by the guardianship's ward to create a binding contract?

HOLDING AND DECISION: (Bryner, C.J.) Yes. As a matter of law, a valid guardianship order voids an attempt by the guardianship's ward to create a binding contract. Under the Restatement (Second) of Contracts § 13, the existence of a valid legal guardianship precludes the formation of a valid contract with the guardianship's ward. In keeping with this view, a party who attempts to enter into a contract with a ward is entitled to restitution only in the absence of actual or constructive knowledge of the ward's incompetence. Here, the guardianship order for David gave notice to the public of his incapacity. Thus, because Kenai Chrysler Center, Inc. (Kenai Chrysler) (D) had constructive notice of David's incapacity, it was not entitled to restitution. Also rejected is Kenai Chrysler's (D) argument that factual issues concerning David's state of mind at the time of the sale should have precluded summary judgment.

ANALYSIS

Comment a to Restatement (Second) of Contracts § 13 provides that guardianship proceedings are treated as giving public notice of the ward's incapacity and establish his status with respect to transactions during guardianship even though the other party to a particular transaction may have no knowledge or reason to know of the guardianship: the guardian is not required to give personal notice to all persons who may deal with the ward. Because the world is on constructive notice of the guardianship, the contract is void ab initio, rather than merely voidable.

Quicknotes

AB INITIO From its inception or beginning.

CONSTRUCTIVE NOTICE Knowledge of a fact that is imputed to an individual who was under a duty to inquire and who could have learned of the fact through the exercise of reasonable prudence.

GUARDIANSHIP A legal relationship whereby one party is responsible for the care and control over another and his or her property due to some legal incapacity on the part of the ward.

Alaska Packers' Assn. v. Domenico

Packing employer (D) v. Seamen (P)

117 F. 99 (9th Cir. 1902)

NATURE OF CASE: Action in admiralty for breach of contract.

FACT SUMMARY: Seamen (P), who had agreed to ship from San Francisco to Alaska at a fixed pay, refused to continue working once they reached Alaska, and demanded a new contract with more compensation.

RULE OF LAW

A promise to pay a man for doing that which he is already under contract to do is without consideration.

FACTS: A group of seamen (P) entered into a written contract with Alaska Packers' Association (Packers') (D) to go from San Francisco to Alaska on the Packers' (D) ships, and to work as sailors and fishermen. Compensation was fixed at $60 for the season, and two cents for each salmon caught. Once they had reached port in Alaska, the seamen (P) refused to continue work and demanded that compensation be increased to $100. A superintendent for Packers' (D), unable to hire a new crew, drew up a new contract, substituted in the sum of $100, and signed the contract although he expressed doubt at the time that he had the authority to do so. The seamen (P) resumed work, but upon the ship's return to San Francisco, Packers' (D) refused to honor the new contract. The seamen (P) filed an admiralty action for breach of contract.

ISSUE: Is a promise to pay a man for performing a duty he is already under contract to perform without consideration?

HOLDING AND DECISION: (Ross, J.) Yes. The performance of a pre-existing legal duty guaranteed by contract is not sufficient consideration to support a promise. No astute reasoning can change the plain fact that the party who refuses to perform, and thereby coerces a promise from the other party to pay him an increased compensation for doing that which he is legally bound to do, takes an unjustifiable advantage of the necessities of the other party. The parties in the present case have not voluntarily rescinded or modified their contract. Alaska Packers' Association's (D) second contract with the seamen is unenforceable although the seamen (P) completed their performance in reliance on it. Reversed.

ANALYSIS

A few cases have held that the promise to pay additional compensation is enforceable. Consideration is found in the promisee's giving up of his or her power to breach the first contract. In other words, by refusing to continue work, the promisee has invoked the option to pay money damages rather than to invest his labor in further performance. This view has been questioned on the ground that a promisee may have the power to breach a contract, but certainly not the legal right, and, in any event, he should not be encouraged to do so.

Quicknotes

ADMIRALTY That area of law pertaining to navigable waters.

CONSIDERATION Value given by one party in exchange for performance, or a promise to perform, by another party.

DETRIMENTAL RELIANCE Reliance by one party that is based on the conduct or promises of another, resulting in loss to the party.

PRE-EXISTING DUTY A common-law doctrine that renders unenforceable a promise to perform a duty that the promisor is already legally obligated to perform.

Watkins & Son v. Carrig

Excavator (P) v. Contractor (D)

N.H. Sup. Ct., 91 N.H. 459, 21 A.2d 591 (1941)

NATURE OF CASE: Action to recover damages for breach of an alleged contract.

FACT SUMMARY: After Watkins & Son (Watkins) (P) encountered solid rock in the course of excavation, Carrig (D) agreed to raise the price in the original excavation contract.

RULE OF LAW

A modification made to meet the reasonable needs of standard and ethical practices of men in their business dealings with each other operates as a partial rescission of a prior contract and is thus enforceable since supported by consideration.

FACTS: Watkins & Son (Watkins) (P) contracted to excavate "all material" from Carrig's (D) cellar for a stated price. After work commenced, solid rock was encountered and Carrig (D) orally agreed to pay a much greater price for the excavation. Watkins (P) successfully sought to recover the larger amount due under the later agreement. Carrig (D) appealed.

ISSUE: When two contracting parties enter a second agreement providing a higher price for the original work, may that second agreement be enforceable?

HOLDING AND DECISION: (Allen, C.J.) Yes. Although promise to pay more for work that is already owing under contract is without consideration, if the prior contract is first (or simultaneously) rescinded, the original work is consideration for the new promise in its entirety. But whether the contract was rescinded with a totally new one to take its place, or whether the old contract remained in force with a modification of its terms, is unimportant since a modification (or at least one which meets the reasonable needs of standard and ethical practices of men in their business dealings with each other) involves a partial rescission. Affirmed.

ANALYSIS

Note that the court expressly rejects Williston's suggestion to look at the "total effect" of the transaction (which has Carrig (D) paying "more for less") in favor of an examination of the "inherent makeup" of the transaction. Williston on Contracts, 2d Ed., § 130a. This may reflect the fact that the court had already made up its mind in light of "fundamental justice and reasonableness" and was searching for a way to justify its conclusions. A "gift" rationale, which is largely edited out in the casebook, is another example of how courts have stretched to get around the "preexisting duty" rule in their efforts to successfully distinguish coercive modifications from commercially useful ones. The present case anticipates Restatement (Second) of Contracts § 89(d). Note further that the court is not willing to come right out and say that a modification needs no consideration to be binding (see Uniform Commercial Code (UCC) § 2-209) but instead resorts to the old "rescission doctrine" of *Schwartzreich v. Bauman-Basch Inc.*, 231 N.Y. 196 (1921), by calling a modification a "partial rescission." Arguably, however, the court has arrived at the UCC position. (Caveat: Whereas the present case and Restatement (Second) of Contracts § 89(d) are involved with mutually executory contracts, UCC § 2-209 is not restricted to this category. But note the "good-faith" limitation in comment 2 therein.)

Quicknotes

ASSUMPSIT An oral or written promise by one party to perform or pay another.

CONSIDERATION Value given by one party in exchange for performance, or a promise to perform, by another party.

GOOD FAITH An honest intention to abstain from taking advantage of another.

MODIFICATION A change to the terms of a contract without altering its general purpose.

RESCISSION The canceling of an agreement and the return of the parties to their positions prior to the formation of the contract.

Austin Instrument, Inc. v. Loral Corporation

Components supplier (P) v. Radar manufacturer (D)

N.Y. Ct. App., 29 N.Y.2d 124, 272 N.E.2d 533 (1971)

NATURE OF CASE: Appeal from award of damages for price increases.

FACT SUMMARY: Austin Instrument, Inc. (P) threatened to withhold delivery of precision parts unless Loral Corporation (D) would raise the contract price.

RULE OF LAW

A contract modification is voidable on the ground of duress when it is established that the party making the claim was forced to agree to it by means of a wrongful threat precluding the exercise of the party's free will.

FACTS: Loral Corporation (D) was under contract to produce radar sets for the government. The contract contained a liquidated damage clause for late delivery and a cancellation clause in case of default by Loral (D). Loral (D), which did a substantial portion of its business with the government, awarded Austin Instrument, Inc. (Austin) (P) a subcontract to supply some of the precision parts. Subsequently, Austin (P) threatened to cease delivery of the parts unless Loral (D) consented to substantial increases in the subcontract price. After contacting 10 manufacturers of precision gears and finding none that could produce the parts in time to meet its commitment to the government, Loral (D) acceded to Austin's (P) demand, and then sued to recover payment. Austin (P) also sued, but its complaint was dismissed. It appealed an award of damages to Loral (D).

ISSUE: Is a contract modification acceded to by one party under circumstances amounting to economic duress enforceable against that party?

HOLDING AND DECISION: (Fuld, C.J.) No. A contract modification is voidable on the ground of duress when it is established that the party making the claim was forced to agree to it by means of a wrongful threat precluding the exercise of the party's free will. Loral Corporation (D) has made out a classic case of economic duress in that: (1) Austin Instrument, Inc. (Austin) (P) threatened to withhold delivery of "needful goods" unless Loral (D) agreed; (2) Loral (D) could not obtain the goods from another source of supply; and (3) the ordinary remedy of an action for breach of the original subcontract would not be adequate since so much was riding on Loral's (D) own general contract with the government. Thus, it is manifest that Austin's (P) threat deprived Loral (D) of its free will. Loral (D) actually had no choice. Affirmed as modified.

DISSENT: (Bergan, J.) The question of whether acts asserted as constituting economic duress produce the damaging effect attributed to them is a routine type of issue of fact. The fact was resolved at trial against Loral Corportion (D), and it was affirmed at the appellate division. The question should not have been reopened here.

ANALYSIS

Although it has generally been held that a threat to breach a contract does not constitute economic duress, courts have recently begun to hold that various kinds of unethical business compulsion do constitute duress. The present case is an example of this trend. Note that even under the Uniform Commercial Code (which recognizes modification without consideration – § 2-209), the requirement of good faith is ever present.

Quicknotes

DEFAULT Failure to carry out a legal obligation.

DURESS Unlawful threats or other coercive behavior by one person that causes another to commit acts that he or she would not otherwise do.

GOOD-FAITH REQUIREMENT An implied warranty that the parties will deal honestly in the satisfaction of their obligations and without an intent to defraud.

LIQUIDATION The reduction to cash of all assets for distribution to creditors.

MODIFICATION A change to the terms of a contract without altering its general purpose.

Martinez-Gonzalez v. Elkhorn Packing Co. LLC

Foreign farm laborer (P) v. Employer (D)

25 F.4th 613 (9th Cir. 2022)

NATURE OF CASE: Appeal from denial of motion to compel arbitration in action for labor and wage law violations.

FACT SUMMARY: Dario Martinez-Gonzalez (P), a Mexican citizen who had worked for Elkhorn Packing Co. LLC (Elkhorn) (D) as a farm laborer, on behalf of himself and others similarly situated, sued Elkhorn (D) for violations of federal and state labor and wage laws. Elkhorn (D) moved to compel arbitration on the basis of arbitration provisions in employment contracts that Martinez-Gonzalez (P) had signed. Martinez-Gonzalez (P) contended that the arbitration provisions were unenforceable because he had signed them under economic duress and undue influence.

RULE OF LAW

An agreement is not the product of economic duress, and, therefore, rescindable, where, although the agreement may result from hard bargaining, no wrongful act has been committed against the party seeking rescission, and the party seeking rescission has reasonable alternatives to entering into a coerced agreement.

FACTS: Elkhorn Packing Co. LLC (Elkhorn) (D), a U.S. farm labor contractor, hired Dario Martinez-Gonzalez (P), a Mexican citizen, to perform farm labor under an agricultural worker visa. Martinez-Gonzalez (P) had a secondary-school education and was the breadwinner for his family, for whom he provided housing and medical care. At the orientation for workers, which took place several days after the workers had already begun harvesting vegetables, Martinez-Gonzalez (P), along with approximately 150 other laborers, was asked to sign employment paperwork. To facilitate the signing of the paperwork, Elkhorn (D) representatives directed employees to form lines, where they stood—in at least one case for 40 minutes—and waited to sign the packages. Once at the front of the line, an Elkhorn (D) representative told each employee where to sign while flipping through the pages. Representatives urged employees to hurry so that others could have a chance to sign. The employment package included an arbitration agreement. The agreement required employees to resolve all disputes with Elkhorn (D) by arbitration. The agreement was written in Spanish, Martinez-Gonzalez's (P) native language. He signed the arbitration agreement without reading it. Elkhorn (D) representatives did not explain the contents of the arbitration agreement to him, did not give him a copy of the agreement, and did not tell him he could consult an attorney before signing it. On the other hand, Martinez-Gonzalez (P) did not ask for a copy of the agreement, attorney consultation, or time to read the agreement. Elkhorn (D) never expressly told Martinez-Gonzalez (P) that he had to sign the agreement to keep working for the company. After working for Elkhorn (D) that season, Martinez-Gonzalez (P) returned to Mexico. The following year, he returned to work for Elkhorn (D) and again signed paperwork that contained an arbitration agreement. However, he quit mid-season and returned to Mexico. He then sued Elkhorn (D) in state court on behalf of himself and other similarly situated workers, alleging a failure to pay federal minimum wages under the Fair Labor Standards Act, and state-law claims related to meals, wages, rest periods, and privacy. Elkhorn (D) removed the case to federal district court and moved to compel arbitration under the two arbitration agreements. The district court concluded that the agreements resulted from undue influence and economic duress and denied the motion to compel arbitration. Elkhorn (D) appealed, and the Ninth Circuit Court of Appeals granted review. [The casebook first presents the court's decision and the dissenting opinion regarding economic duress, and then separately presents the court's decision and dissenting opinion regarding undue influence. What follows is the treatment of the economic duress issue.]

ISSUE: Is an agreement the product of economic duress, and, therefore, rescindable, where, although the agreement may result from hard bargaining, no wrongful act has been committed against the party seeking rescission, and the party seeking rescission has reasonable alternatives to entering into a coerced agreement?

HOLDING AND DECISION: (Bumatay, J.) No. An agreement is not the product of economic duress, and, therefore, rescindable, where, although the agreement may result from hard bargaining, no wrongful act has been committed against the party seeking rescission, and the party seeking rescission has reasonable alternatives to entering into a coerced agreement. Under state law, a contract may be rescinded if it was signed under economic duress. Economic duress occurs when one party commits a (1) "wrongful act" and (2) that act is sufficiently coercive to cause a reasonably prudent person faced with no reasonable alternative to agree to an unfavorable contract. Here, Elkhorn Packing Co. LLC (Elkhorn) (D) did not commit a wrongful act against

Continued on next page.

Dario Martinez-Gonzalez (P), who had reasonable alternatives to entering into the contracts that contained arbitration agreements. Therefore, the doctrine of economic duress is inapplicable. "Wrongful acts" in this context need not be unlawful or tortious, but require more than merely hard bargaining and must be either coercive or taken in bad faith. Some examples of wrongful acts are the assertion of a false claim, a bad-faith threat to breach a contract, and a threat to withhold payment of an acknowledged debt. Martinez-Gonzalez (P) asserts that Elkhorn (D) committed a wrongful act by asking him to sign the arbitration agreement after he made the journey from Mexico to California, where he was dependent on Elkhorn (D) housing and had already started harvesting lettuce. This conduct, albeit not ideal, did not constitute a "wrongful act" under state law as it did not impinge on freedom of contract or undermine the proper functioning of the economic system. To the contrary, the orientation's location served a practical business function, as a convenient place to gather hundreds of farm workers in a single orientation. Here, too, Martinez-Gonzalez (P) had reasonable alternatives to entering into the arbitration agreements. Although being forced into bankruptcy, financial ruin, or selling one's home are not reasonable alternatives, the need for a job and money by itself is not grounds for a finding of economic duress. The district court's finding that Martinez-Gonzalez (P) lacked reasonable alternatives to signing the arbitration agreements because his challenging financial situation required him to keep his job with Elkhorn (D) was clearly erroneous. He could have asked whether signing the arbitration agreements was necessary for him to keep his job. Martinez-Gonzalez (P) conceded it was his "assumption" that the agreements were mandatory; a "reasonably prudent person" would not just assume an agreement is mandatory—at least not without someone saying so or without even asking. Moreover, the fear of termination, even if justified, cannot be used to prove the lack of reasonable alternatives. Martinez-Gonzalez (P) could have revoked the agreements, which by their terms were revokable within ten days, and nothing prevented him from quitting, in the same manner he did during the middle of the second season he worked for Elkhorn (D). Reversed and remanded.

DISSENT: (Rawlinson, J.) The majority gives short shrift to the clear-error standard of review. Credibility determinations made by the judge presiding over a trial must be afforded "special deference." The district court determined that Dario Martinez-Gonzalez (P) testified credibly regarding the signing of the arbitration agreements, and the majority should have deferred to the district court's factual finding unless such findings were illogical, implausible, or without support in the record. The majority should also have deferred to the district court's legal conclusions that were based on its detailed factual findings. Because the district court did not clearly err in concluding, after a bench trial, that the atmosphere surrounding the signing of the arbitration agreements rose to the level of a wrongful act, the majority was wrong to disagree with the district court's legal determination. State courts have increasingly recognized that the economic duress doctrine is equitable in nature, and that this doctrine should be applied to correct inequitable or unequal exchanges between parties of disproportionate bargaining power and a greater willingness not to enforce agreements that were entered into under coercive circumstances. In determining whether the party asserting economic duress had a reasonable alternative available, courts make a factual determination as to whether a reasonably prudent person would follow the alternative course, or whether a reasonably prudent person might submit. Based on the evidence presented during trial, the district court concluded that no reasonable migrant worker with Martinez-Gonzalez's (P) "significant financial obligations" and "without alternative employment prospects, an alternative place to live . . . and no practical way to return to Mexico," would have refused to sign the arbitration agreements. The majority opinion articulates no real issue with the findings of fact made by the district court but concludes, nevertheless, that Martinez-Gonzalez (P) was not subjected to economic duress. Contrary to the majority's conclusion, however, the case is a prime example of the inequitable or unequal exchanges between parties of disproportionate bargaining power that the economic duress doctrine aims to rectify. It is not difficult to contemplate the desperate circumstances that would compel Martinez-Gonzalez (P) to leave his family, travel twelve hours by bus to another country, and work in a field six days a week for nine-plus hours. What is difficult to understand is how the majority can consider a different case, which involved a contractor "only" obtaining 70% of what was owed, a "classic case of economic duress" while reducing the compelling facts of this case to the signing of a commonplace agreement. Another indication that the majority turned a blind eye to the district court's factual findings is that it questions whether extracting an arbitration agreement can ever constitute a "wrongful act." This, however, is a red herring. Martinez-Gonzalez (P) did not argue that making him sign an arbitration agreement in and of itself was improper. Rather, he sought to invalidate the arbitration agreement on the basis that he signed it under economic duress and as a result of undue influence. Additionally, the majority's conclusion that Martinez-Gonzalez (P) failed to demonstrate a lack of reasonable alternatives to signing the arbitration agreements is belied by the evidence adduced at trial that of the thousands of employees hired, no employee had ever refused to sign the arbitration agreement. The majority's diminishing

Continued on next page.

of Martinez-Gonzalez's (P) compelling situation as the need for "a job and . . . money," blatantly disregards the factual findings regarding Martinez-Gonzalez's (P) dire circumstances, as well as the realities of migrant workers. Moreover, each of the points the majority makes in support of its conclusion that Martinez-Gonzalez (P) had reasonable alternatives seems to conveniently ignore the rest of the story told by the district's court's factual findings. The majority's suggestion that "facts don't matter" to me or to the district court, is nothing short of gaslighting. The district court heard the testimony, weighed the conflicting evidence, and issued detailed factual findings, including credibility assessments. An appellate court may not disturb those detailed factual findings unless they are clearly erroneous. Because the district court's factual findings are anchored in the record developed during trial, the majority is actually the side ignoring the facts. For example, the majority notes that Martinez-Gonzalez (P) was not told that refusing to sign the agreement was grounds for termination. However, this is contradicted by evidence that the workers were not told that signing the documents was optional, and testimony that the signing of the agreement was not voluntary, and, in fact, was a condition of employment. In sum, the district court's finding of economic duress is amply supported by the evidence developed during trial, whereas the majority's contrary finding is not.

ANALYSIS

For purposes of determining whether a party to a contract engaged in economic duress, and, thus, whether the party engaged in any "wrongful act" under state law, the courts of the state (California) where this case was brought follow the Restatement (Second) of Contracts' definition of wrongful acts in § 176, which includes: bad faith threatened use of civil process; threats that are a breach of the duty of good faith and fair dealing under a contract with the recipient; threats that would harm the recipient without significantly benefitting the party making the threat; or threats where "what is threatened is otherwise a use of power for illegitimate ends." Based on this definition, and cases interpreting it, and noting that the district court did not find that Elkhorn Packing Co. LLC (Elkorn) (D) made any false claim, bad-faith threat, or refusal to repay its debt, the majority concluded that Elkhorn (D) had not engaged in wrongful acts, which, the majority concluded, requires more than hard bargaining or tough business tactics.

Quicknotes

ARBITRATION An alternative resolution process where a dispute is heard and decided by a neutral third party, rather than through legal proceedings.

ECONOMIC DURESS A defense to an action that a party was unlawfully coerced into the performance of an action by another due to fear of imminent economic loss and was not acting in accordance with his or her own free volition in performing the action.

FAIR LABOR STANDARDS ACT (FLSA) Enacted in 1938, the statute establishes a minimum wage, overtime pay, recordkeeping, and youth employment standards applicable to all employees in the private sector and in federal, state, and local governments. Executive, administrative, and professional employees paid on a salary basis are exempt from the minimum wage and overtime provisions of the FLSA.

FREEDOM OF CONTRACT A basic freedom that is guaranteed by Article I, § 10, cl. 1 of the U.S. Constitution and that may not be denied by the state.

UNDUE INFLUENCE Improper use of power that deprives an individual of freedom of choice and substitutes another's choice for the individual's own choice.

Martinez-Gonzalez v. Elkhorn Packing Co. LLC

Foreign farm laborer (P) v. Employer (D)

25 F.4th 613 (9th Cir. 2022)

NATURE OF CASE: Appeal from denial of motion to compel arbitration in action for labor and wage law violations.

FACT SUMMARY: Dario Martinez-Gonzalez (P), a Mexican citizen who had worked for Elkhorn Packing Co. LLC (Elkhorn) (D) as a farm laborer, on behalf of himself and others similarly situated, sued Elkhorn (D) for violations of federal and state labor and wage laws. Elkhorn (D) moved to compel arbitration on the basis of arbitration provisions in employment contracts that Martinez-Gonzalez (P) had signed. Martinez-Gonzalez (P) contended that the arbitration provisions were unenforceable because he had signed them under economic duress and undue influence.

RULE OF LAW

An agreement is not the product of undue influence and, therefore, rescindable where a dominating person or party has not applied excessive pressure on a servient person, who is particularly susceptible to such pressure, to take unfair advantage of the servient person to force his or her assent to the agreement.

FACTS: Elkhorn Packing Co. LLC (Elkhorn) (D), a U.S. farm labor contractor, hired Dario Martinez-Gonzalez (P), a Mexican citizen, to perform farm labor under an agricultural worker visa. Martinez-Gonzalez (P) had a secondary-school education and was the breadwinner for his family, for whom he provided housing and medical care. At the orientation for workers, which took place several days after the workers had already begun harvesting vegetables, Martinez-Gonzalez (P), along with approximately 150 other laborers, was asked to sign employment paperwork. To facilitate the signing of the paperwork, Elkhorn (D) representatives directed employees to form lines, where they stood—in at least one case for 40 minutes—and waited to sign the packages. Once at the front of the line, an Elkhorn (D) representative told each employee where to sign while flipping through the pages. Representatives urged employees to hurry so that others could have a chance to sign. The employment package included an arbitration agreement. The agreement required employees to resolve all disputes with Elkhorn (D) by arbitration. The agreement was written in Spanish, Martinez-Gonzalez's (P) native language. He signed the arbitration agreement without reading it. Elkhorn (D) representatives did not explain the contents of the arbitration agreement to him, did not give him a copy of the agreement, and did not tell him he could consult an attorney before signing it. On the other hand, Martinez-Gonzalez (P) did not ask for a copy of the agreement, attorney consultation, or time to read the agreement. Elkhorn (D) never expressly told him that he had to sign the agreement to keep working for the company. After working for Elkhorn (D) that season, Martinez-Gonzalez (P) returned to Mexico. The following year, he returned to work for Elkhorn (D), and again signed paperwork that contained an arbitration agreement. However, he quit mid-season and returned to Mexico. He then sued Elkhorn (D) in state court on behalf of himself and other similarly situated workers, alleging a failure to pay federal minimum wages under the Fair Labor Standards Act, and state-law claims related to meals, wages, rest periods, and privacy. Elkhorn (D) removed the case to federal district court and moved to compel arbitration under the two arbitration agreements. The district court concluded that the agreements resulted from undue influence and economic duress and denied the motion to compel arbitration. Elkhorn (D) appealed, and the Ninth Circuit Court of Appeals granted review. [The casebook first presents the court's decision and the dissenting opinion regarding economic duress, and then separately presents the court's decision and dissenting opinion regarding undue influence. What follows is the treatment of the undue influence issue.]

ISSUE: Is an agreement the product of undue influence and, therefore, rescindable where a dominating person or party has not applied excessive pressure on a servient person, who is particularly susceptible to such pressure, to take unfair advantage of the servient person to force his or her assent to the agreement?

HOLDING AND DECISION: (Bumatay, J.) No. An agreement is not the product of undue influence and, therefore, rescindable where a dominating person or party has not applied excessive pressure on a servient person, who is particularly susceptible to such pressure, to take unfair advantage of the servient person to force his or her assent to the agreement. By statute, undue influence results from three scenarios: (1) in the use, by one in whom a confidence is reposed by another, or who holds a real or apparent authority over the other, of such confidence or authority for the purpose of obtaining an unfair advantage over the other; (2) in taking an unfair advantage of another's weakness of mind; or (3) in taking a grossly oppressive and unfair advantage of another's

Continued on next page.

necessities or distress. Undue influence, however, cannot be used as a pretext to avoid bad bargains or escape from bargains that do not live up to expectations. In essence, undue influence involves the use of excessive pressure to persuade one vulnerable to such pressure. The doctrine consists of two elements: (1) undue susceptibility in the servient person, and (2) excessive pressure by the dominating person. The undue susceptibility element involves a lessened capacity of a party to make a free contract. It may be the result of mental incapacity, or it may be the consequence of a lack of full vigor owing to age, physical condition, emotional anguish, or a combination of such factors. The result is the inability to act with unencumbered volition. The district court did not make findings regarding this factor. However, the facts do not support a finding that Martinez-Gonzalez (P) was particularly susceptible to Elkhorn Packing Co. LLC's (Elkhorn's) (D) pressure. Notwithstanding his modest socioeconomic background, Martinez-Gonzalez (P) was able to support and take care of himself and his family, and his ability to quit his job when he became dissatisfied with it demonstrates he was not particularly susceptible to undue pressure. Given that Martinez-Gonzalez's (P) volition was not particularly encumbered, Elkhorn (D) would have had to have brought extraordinary force to bear against him for there to have been undue influence. That did not happen. Several factors tend to show that the dominant party exerted extraordinary force against the servient party. Here, for example, the district court found that (1) the time and place of the orientation was unusual—both because it was held after Martinez-Gonzalez (P) traveled to the United States and because it occurred in a hotel parking lot with no chairs; (2) there was a lack of time to read the agreement in advance or consult an attorney; (3) there was pressure to sign the agreements quickly after a long day's work; and (4) Elkhorn (D) supervisors made statements exhorting workers to follow the company's rules. However, given the totality of circumstances, the extraordinary force needed to establish undue influence is absent here, and the district court clearly erred in finding otherwise. Reversed and remanded.

DISSENT: (Rawlinson, J.) The district court's finding of undue influence was even stronger than its finding of economic duress. Under state law, undue influence exists when the weakness on one side, or strength on the other, or a combination of the two results in the overbearing of the will of the weaker side. State courts examine seven specific factors to determine the existence of excessive pressure resulting in the overbearing of one's will. The district court made specific factual findings directly corresponding to five of these in concluding that the force used by Elkhorn (D) to get the workers to sign the arbitration agreements was "excessive." The majority admits that the arbitration agreements were signed in an atypical place, but attempt to normalize that practice because Elkhorn (D) is a vegetable grower on remote farmlands. Regardless, as the district court found, a hotel parking lot is an unusual place to execute legally binding documents. Additionally, that workers had no place to sit down, no desks upon which they could review the documents prior to signing them, and no opportunity or privacy that would permit them to speak with an attorney or family member outside of the presence of their employer or co-workers added to the coercive effect of the unusual setting. The majority also elides the fact that workers signed the arbitration agreements after having worked a full day in the fields and while tired, hungry, and eager to get cleaned up before going to sleep. The majority concedes that Elkhorn (D) hurried workers to sign the new-hire documents, but the majority mischaracterizes that fact as an accommodation to other workers waiting in line to sign rather than "some bad-faith pressure tactic." In doing so, the majority blatantly ignores the district court's finding that Elkhorn (D) manufactured the coercive atmosphere by urging tired and hungry workers to execute an unexplained stack of documents at the end of a long workday, in a hotel parking lot. The bottom line is that the district court's determination that Martinez-Gonzalez (P) was subjected to economic duress and undue influence was firmly tethered to its review of the witness testimony and evidence presented during trial and was in no way clearly erroneous. The majority, instead of deferring to the district court's findings, substitutes its own assessment of the facts for the district courts, but the majority's conclusions, unlike those of the district court, are not supported by the evidence.

ANALYSIS

In California, where this case was brought, the seven factors that may show the presence of excessive pressure include: (1) discussion of the transaction at an unusual or inappropriate time, (2) consummation of the transaction in an unusual place, (3) insistent demand that the business be finished at once, (4) extreme emphasis on untoward consequences of delay, (5) the use of multiple persuaders by the dominant side against a single servient party, (6) absence of third-party advisers to the servient party, and (7) statements that there is no time to consult financial advisers or attorneys. Although excessive pressure usually involves several of these factors, there are no fixed definitions or inflexible formulas that determine whether a dominant party has exerted excessive pressure on a servient party. Instead, courts analyze the entire context in which an agreement was signed to determine whether the signer's will was overborne. In this regard, the majority indicated that it disagreed with the dissent that the inquiry regarding excessive pressure can be reduced to

Continued on next page.

a simple box-checking exercise of these seven factors, and that notwithstanding that the district court made findings on five of the seven factors, the appellate court still must determine whether the facts can support a finding of undue influence. The dissent responded by saying that contrary to the majority's characterization, neither the dissent nor the district court engaged in a "simple box-checking exercise," but, instead, the district court applied the seven factors, and the dissent gave appropriate deference to the district court's application of those factors to the evidence presented at trial. The dissent also accused the majority of erasing all the boxes (i.e., ignoring the factors altogether), discarding the district court's factual findings, and writing its own version of the facts based on a manufactured "totality of the circumstances" review.

Quicknotes

ARBITRATION An alternative resolution process where a dispute is heard and decided by a neutral third party, rather than through legal proceedings.

ARBITRATION AGREEMENT A mutual understanding entered into by parties wishing to submit to the decision-making authority of a neutral third party that is selected by the parties and charged with rendering a decision.

ECONOMIC DURESS A defense to an action that a party was unlawfully coerced into the performance of an action by another due to fear of imminent economic loss and was not acting in accordance with his or her own free volition in performing the action.

FAIR LABOR STANDARDS ACT (FLSA) Enacted in 1938, the statute establishes a minimum wage, overtime pay, recordkeeping, and youth employment standards applicable to all employees in the private sector and in federal, state, and local governments. Executive, administrative, and professional employees paid on a salary basis are exempt from the minimum wage and overtime provisions of the FLSA.

FREEDOM OF CONTRACT A basic freedom that is guaranteed by Article I, § 10, cl. 1 of the U.S. Constitution and that may not be denied by the state.

UNDUE INFLUENCE Improper use of power that deprives an individual of freedom of choice and substitutes another's choice for the individual's own choice.

Swinton v. Whitinsville Sav. Bank

House purchaser (P) v. Seller (D)

Mass. Sup. Jud. Ct., 311 Mass. 677, 42 N.E.2d 808 (1942)

NATURE OF CASE: Action in tort to recover damages for alleged fraudulent concealment of facts.

FACT SUMMARY: Whitinsville Sav. Bank (D) knowingly sold a termite-infested house to Swinton (P) but did not tell Swinton (P) of its condition.

RULE OF LAW

Where both parties to a contract of sale are dealing at arm's length, mere nondisclosure of latent defects in the goods will not render one party liable to the other party.

FACTS: Whitinsville Sav. Bank (Whitinsville) (D) sold a termite-infested house to Swinton (P). Although Whitinsville (D) knew the house was infested and Swinton (P) could not readily observe this condition upon inspection, Whitinsville (D) did not make known the true condition before the sale. Swinton (P) was subsequently put to unanticipated expense to control the termites.

ISSUE: Is one party to a contract liable to the second party for not revealing latent defects in the object of the contract?

HOLDING AND DECISION: (Qua, J.) No. Where there is (1) no false statement uttered, (2) no attempt by the concealor to affirmatively prevent the concealee from acquiring the true facts, and (3) no peculiar duty to speak (based on some unusual relationship between the parties), bare nondisclosure of truth will not render one party to a contract liable to the other. Otherwise, a seller would have to disclose every defect unknown to the buyer and presumably a buyer would have to disclose every defect unknown to the seller. The law has not yet reached the point of imposing upon the frailties of human nature a standard so idealistic as this. Judgment for Whitinsville Sav. Bank (D).

ANALYSIS

This well-known case is an example of the common-law doctrine of caveat emptor (let the buyer beware). The doctrine is founded on the theory that buyers and sellers of goods must look out for themselves and transact at their own risk. Although allowing parties to reap the benefit of superior knowledge admittedly has a certain appeal, a strict application of caveat emptor may lead to economic inefficiency. Consider, for example, that after the present case potential home buyers in Massachusetts will be forced to hire expensive inspection crews simply to discover what the seller already knows, and could reveal very cheaply, were he required to do so. In today's fast-paced society of adhesion contracts and big merchants, caveat emptor is not heard from too often since so many sales are not bargained at arm's length.

Quicknotes

ADHESION CONTRACT A contract, usually in standardized form, that is prepared by one party and offered to another, whose terms are so disproportionately in favor of the drafting party that courts tend to question the equality of bargaining power in reaching the agreement.

CAVEAT EMPTOR Let the buyer beware; doctrine that a buyer purchases something at his own risk.

Kannavos v. Annino

Apartment building buyer (P) v. Seller (D)

Mass. Sup. Jud. Ct, 356 Mass. 42, 247 N.E.2d 708 (1969)

NATURE OF CASE: Action to rescind a contract of sale for alleged fraudulent concealment of facts.

FACT SUMMARY: Annino (D) sold her multi-family dwelling to Kannavos (P) without telling him that the use of the house as a multi-family dwelling was illegal.

RULE OF LAW

Where one party to a contract of sale goes beyond "bare nondisclosure" and knowingly misrepresents material facts by telling "half-truths," the other party may rescind the contract even though he could have ascertained the whole truth by checking public records.

FACTS: Annino (D) converted her house into a multi-family dwelling in knowing violation of a city zoning ordinance. Kannavos (P) bought the house in response to an advertisement that indicated a buyer could make money by renting out the eight apartments in the house. Kannavos (P) did not check the zoning ordinances even though they were on public record; and Annino (D), knowing that Kannavos's (P) reason for buying was to rent out the apartments, did not inform him of the zoning regulations. Soon after the sale, the city started legal proceedings to abate the nonconforming use of the house; and then Kannavos (P) sought to rescind the sale.

ISSUE: May one party to a contract of sale rescind the contract if statements made by the other party go beyond the "bare nondisclosure" rule of *Swinton v. Whitinsville Sav. Bank*, 311 Mass. 677, (1942)?

HOLDING AND DECISION: (Cutter, J.) Yes. One party to a contract of sale may rescind the contract if statements made by the other party go beyond the "bare nondisclosure" rule of *Swinton v. Whitinsville Sav. Bank*, 311 Mass. 677, 42 N.E.2d 808 (1942). Where enough was said and done by the seller so that she was bound to disclose more to avoid deception of the buyer, and yet she did not disclose more, the buyer may rescind the contract for the seller's fraudulent deception. Although there may be no duty imposed upon one party to a transaction to speak for the information of the other if he does speak with reference to a given point of information, voluntarily or at the other's request, he is bound to speak honestly and to divulge all the material facts bearing upon the point that lies within his knowledge. Fragmentary information may be as misleading as active representation, and half-truths may be as actionable as whole lies. In this case, the original advertisement was the half-truth from which rose Annino's (D) duty to tell "all the material facts." The fact that Kannavos (P) could have checked the public record does not deprive him of his right to rescind. Affirmed in part and reversed in part.

ANALYSIS

This case demonstrates judicial reluctance to apply caveat emptor strictly. Perhaps the court was swayed by the fact that the misrepresented circumstance was itself an illegality. The present case, by not requiring the buyer to check through public records merely to discover what the seller already knew, is a step in the direction of economic efficiency.

Quicknotes

CAVEAT EMPTOR Let the buyer beware; doctrine that a buyer purchases something at his own risk.

FRAUD A false representation of facts with the intent that another will rely on the misrepresentation to his or her detriment.

RESCISSION The canceling of an agreement and the return of the parties to their positions prior to the formation of the contract.

Speakers of Sport v. ProServ

Sports agency (P) v. Sports agency (D)

178 F.3d 862 (7th Cir. 1999)

NATURE OF CASE: Appeal from summary judgment for defendant in action for tortious fraudulent interference with a business relationship

FACT SUMMARY: Speakers of Sport (Speakers) (P) contended that ProServ (D) tortiously interfered with the contract Speakers (P) had with Ivan Rodriguez, a professional baseball player, when ProServ (D) promised to get him between $2 and $4 million in endorsements if he signed with ProServ (D)—which he did—terminating his contract (which was terminable at will) with Speakers (P).

RULE OF LAW

A promise in the nature of puffing that is not part of a fraudulent scheme cannot be the basis of an action for fraudulent interference with a business relationship.

FACTS: Ivan Rodriguez, a highly successful catcher with the Texas Rangers baseball team, in 1991 signed the first of several one-year, terminable-at-will contracts making Speakers of Sport (Speakers) (P) his agent. ProServ (D) wanted to expand its representation of baseball players. In 1995 ProServ (D) invited Rodriguez to its office and there promised it would get him between $2 and $4 million in endorsements if he signed with ProServ (D). Rodriguez signed with ProServ, terminating his contract with Speakers (P). ProServ (D) failed to obtain significant endorsement for Rodriguez and after just one year Rodriguez switched to another agent who the following year landed him a five-year $42 million contract with the Rangers. Speakers (P) then brought suit against ProServ (D) charging that the promise of endorsements that ProServ had made to Rodriguez was fraudulent and had induced him to terminate his contract with Speakers (P). The district court granted ProServ's (D) motion for summary judgment. The court of appeals granted review.

ISSUE: Can a promise in the nature of puffing that is not part of a fraudulent scheme be the basis for an action of fraudulent interference with a business relationship?

HOLDING AND DECISION: (Posner, C.J.) No. A promise in the nature of puffing that is not part of a fraudulent scheme cannot be the basis of an action for fraudulent interference with a business relationship. What ProServ (D) did was in the nature of competition that is protected by the "competitor's privilege," which serves as a defense to the tort of improper interference. If it was a tort for one agent to promise a client to do better than the client's existing agent, not only would the competition that serves as the engine of our economy be stifled, but the agent making the promise would be running a grave legal risk. Of course, an agent cannot promise to do what he knows he cannot fulfill—that is fraud—but the kind of promise made by ProServ (D) here was puffing in the sense of a sales pitch that is intended, and that a reasonable person in the position of the "promisee" would understand, to be aspirational rather than enforceable. ProServ (D) did not guarantee or warranty Rodriguez a minimum amount of endorsements. The only reasonable meaning to attach to ProServ's (D) representations to Rodriguez is that it would try to get as many endorsements as possible for him and that it was optimistic that it could get him at least $2 million worth of them. Thus, ProServ's (D) representations were not a promise at all. However, even if they constituted a promise (or a warranty), they cannot be the basis for a finding of fraud because they were not part of a scheme to defraud evidenced by more than the allegedly fraudulent promise itself. Affirmed.

ANALYSIS

Speakers (P) could not sue Rodriguez for breach of contract because he had not broken their contract, which was terminable at will. Nor, therefore, could it accuse ProServ (D) of inducing a breach of contract. However, Speakers (P) was able to assert its claim against ProServ (D) because it did have a contract with Rodriguez, and inducing the termination of a contract, even when the termination is not a breach because the contract is terminable at will, can still be an actionable tort, either as an interference with prospective economic advantage, or as an interference with the contract at will itself. Here, however, Judge Posner found that ProServ's (D) actions were not actionable under either theory.

Quicknotes

PUFFING The communication of an opinion not intended as a representation of fact and upon which an action for fraud or misrepresentation cannot be based.

TERMINABLE AT WILL CONTRACT Contract for an employment relationship that the employer or employee may end at any time and for any cause.

Vokes v. Arthur Murray, Inc.

Dancer (P) v. Dance instructor (D)

Fla. Dist. Ct. App., 212 So. 2d 906 (1968)

NATURE OF CASE: Action for cancellation of contracts.

FACT SUMMARY: Vokes (P) was continually cajoled into purchasing thousands of hours of dancing lessons at Arthur Murray, Inc. (D).

RULE OF LAW

Where one party has superior knowledge, statements made within the area of such knowledge may be treated as statements of fact.

FACTS: Vokes (P), at age 51, decided she wished to become an accomplished dancer. Over a period of years, by flattery, cajolery, awards, etc., Vokes (P) was convinced to sign up, under a number of contracts, for $31,000 worth of dancing lessons from Arthur Murray, Inc. (D). Vokes (P) was repeatedly informed that she was a promising student who was quickly becoming sufficiently skilled to pursue a career as a professional dancer. Vokes (P) subsequently brought an action to cancel the unused portion of approximately 2,302 hours of lessons to which she had subscribed. Vokes (P) alleged that she had attained little or no skill as a dancer and obviously had no such aptitude. Vokes (P) alleged that Arthur Murray (D) employees had purposefully misrepresented her skills and had taken unconscionable advantage of her. Vokes (P) alleged that she had relied on Arthur Murray (D) employees' superior knowledge as to her ability and the skills necessary to become a professional dancer. The trial court dismissed the plaintiff's last amended complaint with prejudice.

ISSUE: May a party reasonably rely on opinions as assertions of fact when given by a party of superior knowledge on the subject?

HOLDING AND DECISION: (Pierce, J.) Yes. Normally, the party to a contract has no reasonable right to rely on opinions expressed by the other party to the contract. Misrepresentations of opinion are normally not actionable. However, a statement made by a party having superior knowledge may be regarded as a statement of fact even though it would be regarded as opinion if the parties were dealing on the basis of equal knowledge. Where a party undertakes to make representations based on its superior knowledge, it is under a duty to act honestly and to disclose the entire truth. Vokes (P) has stated a valid cause of action. Reversed.

ANALYSIS

Vokes is concerned with reliance and credibility. One has a right to rely on opinions of attorneys, doctors, etc. *Vokes* extends such reasonable reliance to experts or those highly knowledgeable in a field in which plaintiff is generally unfamiliar. *Ramel v. Chasebrook Construction Company*, 135 So. 2d 876 (1961). To be actionable, the misrepresentation must be material and there must be some overreaching in cases such as *Vokes*.

Quicknotes

MISREPRESENTATION A statement or conduct by one party to another that constitutes a false representation of fact.

RELIANCE Dependence on a fact that causes a party to act or refrain from acting.

CHAPTER 5

Determining the Parties' Obligations Under the Contract

Quick Reference Rules of Law

PAGE

1. *Mitchill v. Lath.* An oral agreement is permitted to vary a written contract only if it is collateral in form, does not contradict express or implied conditions of the written contract, and consists of terms that the parties could not reasonably have been expected to include in the written contract. *121*

2. *Masterson v. Sine.* Evidence of oral collateral agreements should be excluded only when the fact finder (the court) is likely to be misled. *123*

3. *Bollinger v. Central Pennsylvania Quarry Stripping and Construction Co.* A court of equity has the power to reform a writing and make it correspond to the understanding of the parties on the ground of mistake so long as that mistake is mutual. *125*

4. *Pacific Gas & Electric Co. v. G.W. Thomas Drayage & Rigging Co.* The test of admissibility of extrinsic evidence to explain the meaning of a written instrument is not whether it appears to the court to be plain and unambiguous on its face but whether the offered evidence is relevant to prove a meaning to which the language of the instrument is reasonably susceptible. *126*

5. *W.W.W. Associates, Inc. v Giancontieri.* When parties set down a writing in a clear, complete document, their writing should be enforced according to their terms, and extrinsic evidence is generally inadmissible to add to or vary the writing. *127*

6. *Greenfield v. Philles Records, Inc.* Extrinsic evidence can be admitted to explain the meaning of a general release even if the language of the contract is plain and unambiguous. *128*

7. *Trident Center v. Connecticut General Life Ins. Co.* Parol evidence is admissible to raise an ambiguity in a contract even where the writing itself contains no ambiguity. *129*

8. *Lamps Plus, Inc. v. Varela.* The Federal Arbitration Act preempts the *contra proferentem* doctrine, which provides that ambiguity in a contract should be construed against the drafter, since the doctrine is based on public policy considerations rather than the parties' intent. *130*

9. *Frigaliment Importing Co. v. B.N.S. International Sales Corp.* The party who seeks to interpret the terms of the contract in a sense narrower than their everyday use bears the burden of persuasion to so show. *132*

10. *Hurst v. W. J. Lake &Co.* Where a contract is made between members of the same trade group, notwithstanding that the contract is otherwise unambiguous on its face, evidence of special meanings that the trade gives to certain terms may be used to interpret the contract in conformity with trade usage. *133*

11. *Nanakuli Paving & Rock Co. v. Shell Oil Co.* Trade usage and course of performance will be read into contracts where such are so prevalent the parties would have to have meant to incorporate them in the terms of the contract. *135*

12. *Figgie International, Inc. v. Destileria Serralles, Inc.* Under the Uniform Commercial Code, usage of trade may supplement a commercial agreement with a remedy that is both limited and exclusive. *136*

CHAPTER 5

13. *Columbia Nitrogen Corp. v. Royster Co.* Under the Uniform Commercial Code, evidence of usage of trade and course of dealing may be used to explain or supplement the express terms of a written contract where the contract does not expressly preclude such evidence and where the terms to be explained or supplemented are set forth in only general terms. *138*

14. *Raffles v. Wichelhaus.* Where neither party knows or has reason to know of the ambiguity, or where both know or have reason to know, the ambiguity is given the meaning that each party intended it to have. *140*

15. *Colfax Envelope Corp. v. Local No. 458-3M.* A contract will not be rescinded merely because one or more of its terms is patently ambiguous and the parties have not attempted to clarify the patent ambiguity. *141*

16. *Koken v. Black & Veatch Construction, Inc.* A breach of the implied warranty of merchantability claim brought under the Uniform Commercial Code will not be sustained where the plaintiff has not adduced sufficient objective evidence that goods are not fit for the ordinary purposes for which they are used. *143*

17. *Lewis v. Mobil Oil Corporation.* Under the Uniform Commercial Code, an implied warranty of fitness for a particular use will be found to exist where there is evidence that the seller of goods has reason to know any particular purpose for which the goods are required and that the buyer is relying on the seller's skill or judgment to select or furnish suitable goods for that particular purpose. *145*

18. *NY Drilling, Inc. v. TJM, Inc.* For purposes of disclaiming the implied warranties of merchantability and fitness under the Uniform Commercial Code, an express disclaimer of those warranties is sufficiently conspicuous where it appears in a paragraph directly below a contract's signature block, is set off from the signature block, and is in all capital letters. *147*

19. *Fairchild Industries v. Maritime Air Service, Ltd.* The conspicuousness requirement set forth in Uniform Commercial Code (UCC) § 2-316(2) for the exclusion of the implied warranties of merchantability and fitness must be applied to provisions for the exclusion of warranties set forth in UCC § 2-316(3)(a), which is effected by terms like "as is" and "with all faults." *149*

20. *Keith v. Buchanan.* (1) Under Uniform Commercial Code § 2-313, an express warranty can be created by statements in a seller's advertising and sales literature and by statements made by the seller's representatives, where those statements have become part of the basis of the parties' bargain, notwithstanding that the buyer did not rely on these statements. (2) An implied warranty of fitness for a particular purpose is not created where a buyer relies on the buyer's own experts rather than on the seller's judgment or skill in choosing goods that conform to the purpose for which the buyer will use the goods. *152*

Mitchill v. Lath

Property purchaser (P) v. Property seller (D)

N.Y. Ct. App., 247 N.Y. 377, 160 N.E. 646 (1928)

NATURE OF CASE: Appeal from action for specific performance.

FACT SUMMARY: Mitchill (P) bought some property from Lath (D) pursuant to a full and complete written sales contract. She sought to compel Lath (D) to perform on his parol agreement to remove an icehouse on neighboring property.

RULE OF LAW

An oral agreement is permitted to vary a written contract only if it is collateral in form, does not contradict express or implied conditions of the written contract, and consists of terms that the parties could not reasonably have been expected to include in the written contract.

FACTS: Mitchill (P), through a contract executed by her husband, bought some property from Lath (D). The written contract of sale was completely integrated. Lath (D) then made an oral agreement with Mitchill (P) that in consideration of her purchase of the property, he would remove an icehouse that he maintained on neighboring property and that Mitchill (P) found objectionable. The trial court ruled for Mitchill (P) and the state's intermediate appellate court affirmed. The state's highest court granted review.

ISSUE: Is an oral agreement permitted to vary a written contract only if it is collateral in form, does not contradict express or implied conditions of the written contract, and consists of terms that the parties could not reasonably have been expected to include in the written contract?

HOLDING AND DECISION: (Andrews, J.) Yes. An oral agreement is permitted to vary a written contract only if it is collateral in form, does not contradict express or implied conditions of the written contract, and consists of terms that the parties could not reasonably have been expected to include in the written contract. Here, the parol agreement does not meet these requirements since it is closely related to the subject of the written contract. It could also be said to contradict the conditions of the written contract. The fact that the written contract was made with her husband while the oral agreement was made with Mitchill (P) herself is not determinative since the deed was given to her, and it is evident that she, and not her husband, was the principal in the transaction. Reversed.

DISSENT: (Lehman, J.) Although the general rule formulated by the majority is correct, the majority errs in its application to these facts because all the elements necessary to permit an oral agreement to vary a written one are present in this case. There is no question that the first condition was met, i.e., that the subject of the oral agreement is collateral to the written agreement. As to the second element, all the elements of the written contract were satisfied and the removal of the icehouse is not inconsistent with, and does not contradict, those terms. The dispute really boils down to whether the third element is satisfied. Here, the subject matter of the written contract was the conveyance of land. The question is whether the parties would have been expected to embody the agreement to remove the icehouse in the written contract. Proof of the oral agreement may be excluded only if it is shown that the written contract was intended to cover it. Here, on its face, the written contract was complete, and the parol agreement to remove the icehouse was not connected to the contract's subject. The only connection between the two agreements is that one would have not been made absent the other, but the overwhelming evidence establishes the oral agreement, which must be given effect.

ANALYSIS

Uniform Commercial Code § 2-202 provides, "Terms with respect to which the writings of the parties agree or which are set forth in a writing intended by the parties as a final expression of their agreement may not be contradicted by evidence of any prior agreement or of a contemporaneous oral agreement but may be explained or supplemented by course of dealing or usage of trade, or by course of performance, and by evidence of consistent additional terms unless the court finds the writing to have been intended as a complete and exclusive statement of the terms of the agreement." The section, according to the official commentator, conclusively rejects any assumption that, because a writing is final in some respects, it is to be interpreted as including all matters agreed upon by the parties.

Continued on next page.

Quicknotes

EXPRESS CONDITION A condition that is expressly stated in the terms of a written instrument.

IMPLIED CONDITION A condition that is not expressly stated in the terms of an agreement but that is inferred from the parties' conduct or the type of dealings involved.

PAROL AGREEMENT Evidence of prior or contemporaneous agreements, which are not contained within the text of a document or contract, usually offered for the purpose of repudiating or altering the terms of a written contract.

SPECIFIC PERFORMANCE An equitable remedy whereby the court requires the parties to perform their obligations pursuant to a contract.

Masterson v. Sine

Grantor (P) v. Grantees (D)

Cal. Sup. Ct., 68 Cal. 2d 222, 436 P.2d 561 (1968)

NATURE OF CASE: Action for declaratory relief to establish a right to enforce an option.

FACT SUMMARY: Dallas and Rebecca Masterson (P) owned a ranch as tenants in common and conveyed it to Medora and Lu Sine (D) by grant deed reserving an option to purchase the ranch back within 10 years—by February 25, 1968—for the same consideration as was paid for the ranch plus the depreciation value of any improvements the Sines (D) might have added. When Dallas went bankrupt, Rebecca (P) sought to establish her right to enforce the option.

RULE OF LAW

Evidence of oral collateral agreements should be excluded only when the fact finder (the court) is likely to be misled.

FACTS: Dallas Masterson and his wife, Rebecca Masterson (P), owned a ranch as tenants in common. On February 25, 1958, they conveyed by grant deed the ranch to his sister and her husband, Medora and Lu Sine (D), reserving an option to repurchase the ranch within 10 years from the date of conveyance for the consideration paid by the Sines (D) plus depreciation value of any improvements as allowed under U.S. income tax regulations. Dallas Masterson went bankrupt. Rebecca Masterson (P) and Dallas's trustee in bankruptcy (P) sought to establish their right to enforce the option. Parol evidence was admitted to clarify the meaning of the option.

ISSUE: Was the option provision too uncertain to be enforced so that parol evidence should not have been admitted as to clarify its meaning?

HOLDING AND DECISION: (Traynor, C.J.) No. Parol evidence was necessary to clarify the terms of the option, which expressly stated an intention to reserve an option. However, it was the error of the trial court to exclude extrinsic evidence that the option was personal to the grantors and therefore nonassignable. When a written contract is a complete and full embodiment of the agreement's terms, parol evidence cannot be used to add to or vary the terms. When only part of the agreement is complete, the same rule applies to that part, but parol evidence can be shown to prove elements as to the remainder not reduced to writing. It must be determined whether the parties intended the written agreement to be the complete and full embodiment of the terms. However, this rule has not been applied consistently. A parol evidence rule must take into consideration the problems of human memory being less accurate than a writing and the possibility of fraud. Accordingly, evidence of oral collateral agreements should be excluded only when the fact finder is likely to be misled. Under Restatement (First) of Contracts, § 240(1)(b), parol evidence of a collateral agreement is permitted if such an agreement is shown as might naturally be made as a separate agreement by parties situated as were parties to the written contract. Or from an opposite standpoint that is even more liberal: If the additional terms are such that if agreed upon they would certainly have been included, then parol evidence is not admissible (Uniform Commercial Code § 2-202). Here, the option clause did not explicitly provide that it contained the complete agreement. The deed does not speak to assignability. Nothing showed that the parties had any warnings as to the disadvantages of failing to put the whole agreement in the deed. Therefore, it appeared that collateral agreements might naturally be made as a separate agreement. The judgment must be reversed to permit parol evidence on the issue of assignability of the option.

DISSENT: (Burke, J.) Parol evidence should not be permitted to contradict the terms of this written agreement. To hold that parol evidence is admissible where the collateral oral agreement might naturally have been made as a separate agreement by the parties under the particular agreement is too uncertain and confusing. The holding permits a bankrupt to deceive his creditors by testifying to nonassignability, which he failed to state in the writing so as to keep the ranch out of the hands of the trustee. This appears to be evidence that would mislead the fact finder.

ANALYSIS

In this case, California opts for the more liberal approach to the parol evidence rule as supported by Corbin [3 Corbin, *Contracts* (1960) § 583]. Here, the California Court under Chief Justice Traynor found that when any rule of law is riddled with exceptions and decisions about it are difficult to reconcile, litigation is stimulated rather than reduced. The tendency toward liberalizing the admission of parol evidence is based upon the trial court judge's having control over the testimony and his determining when it would appear proffered testimony is perjured. The more liberal rule is supposed to remove the problems found in the restrictive rule favored by

Continued on next page.

Williston [Williston, 3d ed. (1961) § 638], which finds the intent of the parties in their writing only. In the extreme, this would disallow oral testimony as to intent whenever a writing exists thereby possibly defeating the true intent of the parties.

Quicknotes

COLLATERAL AGREEMENT An agreement that is made prior to or contemporaneous with a written agreement that is admissible in evidence so long as it is consistent with the written document.

PAROL EVIDENCE Evidence given verbally; extraneous evidence.

PAROL EVIDENCE RULE Doctrine precluding parties to an agreement from introducing evidence of prior or contemporaneous agreements in order to repudiate or alter the terms of a written contract.

Bollinger v. Central Pennsylvania Quarry Stripping and Construction Co.

Landowner (P) v. Construction firm (D)

Pa. Sup. Ct., 425 Pa. 430, 229 A.2d 741 (1967)

NATURE OF CASE: Action to reform and enforce as reformed a contract granting a right to the use of land.

FACT SUMMARY: The Bollingers (P) contracted to permit Central Pennsylvania Quarry Stripping and Construction Co. (Central) (D) to deposit its construction waste on the Bollingers' (P) property if Central (D) removed the topsoil and covered the waste with it. This oral condition was not included in the written agreement and was apparently omitted by mistake. Central (D) failed to remove the topsoil and cover the waste.

RULE OF LAW

A court of equity has the power to reform a writing and make it correspond to the understanding of the parties on the ground of mistake so long as that mistake is mutual.

FACTS: The Bollingers (P) contracted with Central Pennsylvania Quarry Stripping and Construction Co. (Central) (D) to permit the latter to deposit its construction waste from work on the Pennsylvania Turnpike on the Bollingers' (P) land. There was an oral understanding that Central (D) would remove the topsoil from the land, deposit the waste, and then cover the waste with the topsoil. The Bollingers (P) signed the agreement without reading it, assuming the provision was in the writing. Central (D) removed and replaced the topsoil at first but then ceased to continue the procedure and just dumped the waste. The Bollingers (P) filed an action asking that the contract be reformed to include the missing provision. The court granted the requested relief, and Central (D) appealed.

ISSUE: Does a court of equity have the power to reform a writing and make it correspond to the understanding of the parties on the ground of mistake so long as that mistake is mutual?

HOLDING AND DECISION: (Musmanno, J.) Yes. A court of equity has the power to reform a writing and make it correspond to the understanding of the parties on the ground of mistake so long as that mistake is mutual. One condition for reforming a contract is alleging and proving mutual mistake of the parties. Just because one party denies having made a mistake, it does not mean the court cannot find there was, in fact, a mutual mistake. When a mistake is real and actual, the court can correct the writing. Where a party simply has not understood what he was signing, the court will not touch the writing. The evidence showed that Central Pennsylvania Quarry Stripping and Construction Co. (Central) (D) had been fulfilling the oral agreement at first and that it followed the same topsoil procedure with the Bollingers' (P) neighbor. The court could conclude that Central (D) would not have done so if it had not so agreed. Affirmed.

ANALYSIS

Reformation of a writing will be decreed when its words do not express the meaning upon which the parties agreed. This must be proved convincingly. Various mistakes can be corrected such as omitting an agreed-upon provision and inserting an incorrect provision or a provision not assented to. A common error is an incorrect description of the subject matter of the writing. Should the legal effect of the words in which a contract or conveyance is expressed, if by reason or mistake of law, be different from the meaning upon which the parties agreed and intended, reformation is a proper remedy. It is improper if done to enforce terms to which a party never assented. Usually when a party fails to read the writing he or she has signed, he or she is considered negligent and bears the brunt of his error. Here, as it appeared, there was evidence of an agreement; the Bollingers (P) were permitted to attempt to show it.

Quicknotes

COURT OF EQUITY A court that determines matters before it consistent with principles of fairness and not in strict compliance with rules of law.

MUTUAL MISTAKE A mistake to a contract by both parties, who are in agreement as to what the contract terms should be, but the agreement as written fails to reflect that common intent; such contracts are voidable or subject to reformation.

REFORMATION A correction of a written instrument ordered by a court to cause the instrument to reflect the true intentions of the parties.

Pacific Gas & Electric Co. v. G.W. Thomas Drayage & Rigging Co.

Electric company (P) v. Turbine repairer (D)

Cal. Sup. Ct., 69 Cal. 2d 33, 442 P.2d 641 (1968)

NATURE OF CASE: Appeal from award of injury to property.

FACT SUMMARY: G.W. Thomas Drayage & Rigging Co. (Thomas) (D) contracted to repair Pacific Gas & Electric Co.'s (Pacific's) (P) steam turbine and to perform work at its own risk and expense and to indemnify Pacific (P) against all loss and damage. Thomas (D) also agreed not to procure less than $50,000 insurance to cover liability for injury to property. But when the turbine rotor was damaged, Pacific (P) claimed it was covered under that policy while Thomas (D) said it was only to cover injury to third persons.

RULE OF LAW

The test of admissibility of extrinsic evidence to explain the meaning of a written instrument is not whether it appears to the court to be plain and unambiguous on its face but whether the offered evidence is relevant to prove a meaning to which the language of the instrument is reasonably susceptible.

FACTS: G.W. Thomas Drayage & Rigging Co. (Thomas) (D) contracted to replace the upper metal cover on Pacific Gas & Electric Co.'s (Pacific's) (P) steam turbine and agreed to perform all work "at [its] own risk and expense" and to "indemnify" Pacific (P) against all loss, damage, expense, and liability resulting from injury to property arising out of or in any way connected with performance of the contract. Thomas (D) agreed to obtain not less than $50,000 insurance to cover liability for injury to property. Pacific (P) was to be an additional named insured, but the policy was to contain a cross-liability clause extending the coverage of Pacific's (P) property. During the work, the cover fell, damaging the exposed rotor in the amount of $25,144.51. Thomas (D) during trial offered to prove under similar contracts entered by Pacific (P) that the indemnity clause was meant to cover injury to third person's property only, not to Pacific's (P). Having determined that the contract had a plain meaning, the court refused to admit any contradictory evidence and ruled in favor of Pacific (P).

ISSUE: Was Thomas's (D) offered evidence relevant to proving a meaning to which the language of the instrument was susceptible?

HOLDING AND DECISION: (Traynor, C.J.) Yes. While the trial court admitted that the contract was "the classic language for a third-party indemnity provision," it held that the plain language of the contract would give a meaning covering Pacific Gas & Electric Co.'s (P) damage. However, this admission by the court clearly shows the ambiguous nature of the agreement and the need for extrinsic evidence in order to clarify the intentions of the parties. Extrinsic evidence for the purpose of showing the intent of the parties could be excluded only when it is feasible to determine the meaning of the words from the instrument alone. Rational interpretation requires at least an initial consideration of all credible evidence to prove the intention of the parties. Reversed.

ANALYSIS

This case strongly disapproves of the "plain meaning rule," which states that if a writing appears clear and unambiguous on its face, the meaning must be determined from "the four corners" of the writing without considering any extrinsic evidence at all. The trial court applied this rule. However, the rule, while generally accepted but widely condemned, would exclude evidence of trade usage, prior dealings of the parties, and even circumstances surrounding the creation of the agreement. Uniform Commercial Code § 2-202 expressly throws out the plain meaning rule. Instead, it allows use of evidence of a course of performance or dealing to explain the writing "unless carefully negated." Here, Chief Justice Traynor greatly expanded the admission of extrinsic evidence to show intent. When he says it should not be admitted only when it is feasible "to determine the meaning the parties gave to the words from the instrument alone," he is saying in all practicality that extrinsic evidence to show intent should be admissible in just about any case, that rarely will the instrument be so exact as to clearly show intent.

Quicknotes

EXTRINSIC EVIDENCE Evidence that is not contained within the text of a document or contract, but that is derived from the parties' statements or the circumstances under which the agreement was made.

W.W.W. Associates, Inc. v. Giancontieri

Developers (P) v. Sellers (D)

N.Y. Ct. App., 77 N.Y.2d 157, 566 N.E.2d 639 (1990)

NATURE OF CASE: Suit for specific performance of a contract to sell real property.

FACT SUMMARY: Developers (P) sought to compel specific performance of a contract to sell certain property.

RULE OF LAW

When parties set down a writing in a clear, complete document, their writing should be enforced according to their terms, and extrinsic evidence is generally inadmissible to add to or vary the writing.

FACTS: Owners (D) of two acres of property contracted to sell the property to developers (P). The parties signed a contract of sale containing a reciprocal cancellation provision and merger clause. In particular, paragraph 31 of the contract provided that if pending litigation were not concluded by June 1, 1987, then either party had the right to cancel the contract and the down payment was to be returned. The owners (D) moved for summary judgment and the court dismissed, holding that the agreement unambiguously conferred the right to cancel on both parties. The appellate division reversed, awarding specific performance of the contract to developers (P).

ISSUE: When parties set down a writing in a clear, complete document, should their writing be enforced according to their terms and is extrinsic evidence generally inadmissible to add to or vary the writing?

HOLDING AND DECISION: (Kaye, J.) Yes. When parties set down a writing in a clear, complete document, their writing should be enforced according to their terms and extrinsic evidence is generally inadmissible to add to or vary the writing. Here the contract plainly manifests the intent that all prior understandings be merged into the contract, which expresses the parties' full agreement. Furthermore, there is no ambiguity as to the cancellation clause, which confers a reciprocal right of cancellation on either party. Reversed and complaint dismissed.

ANALYSIS

The court also stated that extrinsic evidence should not be considered in order to create ambiguity in the agreement. The general rule is that if a document is clear on its face, extrinsic evidence is inadmissible to create an ambiguity where apparently there is none.

Quicknotes

EXTRINSIC EVIDENCE Evidence that is not contained within the text of a document or contract, but that is derived from the parties' statements or the circumstances under which the agreement was made.

MERGER CLAUSE A clause in a contract prohibiting modification of its terms by prior or oral agreements since all such agreements are assumed to have been merged into the document.

Greenfield v. Philles Records, Inc.

Singing group (P) v. Record producer (D)

N.Y. Ct. App., 98 N.Y.2d 562, 780 N.E.2d 166 (2002)

NATURE OF CASE: Appeal in contract dispute over redistribution rights.

FACT SUMMARY: Greenfield (P) brought suit for breach of contract, and Philles Records, Inc. (D) argued she was barred from receiving damages by virtue of a general release executed in her divorce decree.

RULE OF LAW

Extrinsic evidence can be admitted to explain the meaning of a general release even if the language of the contract is plain and unambiguous.

FACTS: Greenfield (P), formerly known as Veronica Bennett, was part of the 1960s singing group "The Ronettes." The Ronettes had entered into a recording contract with Philles Records, Inc. (Philles) (D), which was owned by Phil Spector. The contract provided that the artists transferred full ownership rights of their master recordings for redistribution in any technological format. The group disbanded in 1967, and Greenfield married Spector in 1968. Greenfield and Spector divorced in 1974, and as part of their divorce decree they executed a mutual general release agreement resolving all past and future claims and obligations between them. In the 1980s there was a resurgence of interest in 1960s music and Philles (D), by use of a new recording technology called "synchronization," began licensing master recordings of the Ronettes for use in movies and television. Philles (D) also licensed master recordings for domestic redistribution and sold compilation albums of the singing group's music. No royalties were paid to the members of the Ronettes, and the members of the singing group sued alleging breach of contract. Philles (D) initially denied the existence of any contract, but later stipulated to the use of an unexecuted copy of the original Ronettes contract to determine the party's rights. The trial court found that absolute ownership rights had not been conveyed to Philles (D) and awarded damages in favor of the plaintiffs. The court of appeals affirmed.

ISSUE: Can extrinsic evidence be admitted to explain the meaning of a general release even if the language of the contract is plain and unambiguous?

HOLDING AND DECISION: (Graffeo, J.) Yes. Extrinsic evidence can be admitted to explain the meaning of a general release even if the language of the contract is plain and unambiguous. The plain language of the recording contract provides: "Without limitation of the foregoing, [Philles] shall have the right to make phonographic records, tape recordings or other reproductions of the performances embodied in such recordings by any method now or hereafter known. . . ." Applying the "plain meaning rule," the court finds that absolute ownership rights, without royalties, were granted to Philles Records, Inc. (Philles) (D) in terms of the synchronization licensing—the new media form not in existence at the time of the contract. However, Philles (D) acknowledges that the royalty schedule in the contract encompasses the domestic redistribution of the compilation albums and that royalties are owed to plaintiffs on these sales. Philles (D) argues that as to Greenfield (P), the one member of the singing group who married and divorced its owner Phil Spector, all damages are barred as a result of the general release agreement executed in conjunction with their divorce. However, in contrast to New York's "four corners rule" to contract interpretation that applies to the recording contract, the divorce decree was issued in accordance with California law, and California's rules of construction apply. In California, extrinsic evidence is admissible if it is relevant to prove a meaning "to which the language of the instrument is reasonably susceptible." The trial court, applying this rule, determined that the general release in the divorce decree did not apply to the rights of compensation governed under the recording contract. Affirmed as modified.

ANALYSIS

Conflict of laws issues predominate in contract cases and winning a dispute over which forum's laws of construction apply is frequently determinant of the issues in the case. This case illustrates both the strict application of the plain meaning rule in New York, and the application of California's rule to allow extrinsic evidence for interpreting a contract in conformity with a "reasonably susceptible" meaning of the language employed.

Quicknotes

EXTRINSIC EVIDENCE Evidence that is not contained within the text of a document or contract, but that is derived from the parties' statements or the circumstances under which the agreement was made.

Trident Center v. Connecticut General Life Ins. Co.

Commercial group (P) v. Lender (D)

847 F.2d 564 (9th Cir. 1988)

NATURE OF CASE: Appeal from a dismissal of contract action.

FACT SUMMARY: The district court dismissed Trident Center's (Trident) (P) declaratory relief action, ruling that the contract was clear and did not allow for prepayment of a loan, which Trident (P) sought to establish by parol evidence.

RULE OF LAW

Parol evidence is admissible to raise an ambiguity in a contract even where the writing itself contains no ambiguity.

FACTS: Trident Center (Trident) (P), an enterprise consisting of an insurance company and two large, sophisticated law firms, entered into a loan agreement with Connecticut General Life Ins. Co. (Connecticut) (D). The written agreement provided Trident (P) would borrow $56 million to construct an office building. The loan was to be paid off over a period of time; however, the contract precluded full repayment within the first 12 years. Because of a drop of interest rates, Trident (P) sought to repay the loan in full after four years. It claimed, despite the clear language of the contract, that the parties intended to allow prepayment at any time if a penalty was paid. Trident (P) brought a declaratory relief action requesting a court interpretation of the contract. Trident (P) unsuccessfully sought to present parol evidence of the meaning of the contract while admitting the language was unambiguous. The court dismissed the action, and Trident (P) appealed.

ISSUE: Is parol evidence admissible to show an ambiguity in an otherwise unambiguous contract?

HOLDING AND DECISION: (Kozinski, J.) Yes. Parol evidence is admissible to show an ambiguity in an otherwise unambiguous contract. Because language cannot infallibly communicate the true meaning or intent of parties to a contract, parol evidence must be allowed where such intent is in issue. Thus, it was error to deny use of such evidence and to dismiss the action. Reversed and remanded.

ANALYSIS

This case does not represent the traditional common-law view of the parol evidence rule. The opinion is very critical of the outcome, which is mandated by the law of California, where the case arose. The opinion foresees considerable litigation invited by this decision and a breakdown in the finality of a written agreement.

Quicknotes

AMBIGUITY Language that is capable of more than one interpretation.

PAROL EVIDENCE RULE Doctrine precluding parties to an agreement from introducing evidence of prior or contemporaneous agreements in order to repudiate or alter the terms of a written contract.

Lamps Plus, Inc. v. Varela

Employer (D) v. Employee (P)

587 U.S. ___, 139 S. Ct. 1407 (2019)

NATURE OF CASE: Appeal from affirmance of judgment ordering classwide arbitration pursuant to an employer's arbitration agreement.

FACT SUMMARY: Lamps Plus, Inc. (D) contended, inter alia, that under the Federal Arbitration Act (FAA), the ambiguity of the arbitration agreement it had with its employees as to class arbitration could not be construed according to the state contract-law principle of *contra proferentem*, since that principle is based on public policy considerations, rather than the parties' intent, and is therefore preempted by the FAA.

RULE OF LAW

The Federal Arbitration Act preempts the *contra proferentem* doctrine, which provides that ambiguity in a contract should be construed against the drafter, since the doctrine is based on public policy considerations rather than the parties' intent.

FACTS: Varela (P), a Lamps Plus, Inc. (D) employee, filed a putative class action against Lamps Plus (D) in federal district court on behalf of employees whose private information had been compromised, allegedly as a consequence of Lamps Plus's (D) negligence. Pursuant to an arbitration agreement it had with its employees, Lamps Plus (D) sought to compel arbitration—on an individual rather than a class-wide basis—and to dismiss the suit. The district court rejected the individual arbitration request but authorized class arbitration and dismissed Varela's (P) claims. Lamps Plus (D) appealed, arguing that the district court erred by compelling class arbitration. The court of appeals affirmed, concluding the United States Supreme Court's holding in *Stolt-Nielsen S.A. v. Animal Feeds Intl. Corp.*, 559 U.S. 662 (2010), that a court may not compel class-wide arbitration when an agreement is silent on the availability of such arbitration, was not controlling because the agreement in this case was ambiguous rather than silent on the issue of class arbitration. The court of appeals based its decision on the state law *contra proferentem* doctrine, which counsels that contractual ambiguities should be construed against the drafter. The United States Supreme Court granted certiorari.

ISSUE: Does the Federal Arbitration Act preempt the *contra proferentem* doctrine, which provides that ambiguity in a contract should be construed against the drafter, since the doctrine is based on public policy considerations rather than the parties' intent?

HOLDING AND DECISION: (Roberts, C.J.) Yes. The Federal Arbitration Act (FAA) preempts the *contra proferentem* doctrine, which provides that ambiguity in a contract should be construed against the drafter, since the doctrine is based on public policy considerations rather than the parties' intent. The *contra proferentem* doctrine applies only as a last resort when the meaning of a provision remains ambiguous after exhausting the ordinary methods of interpretation. At that point, *contra proferentem* resolves the ambiguity against the drafter based on public policy factors, primarily equitable considerations about the parties' relative bargaining strength. Thus, the doctrine is not designed to ferret out the parties' intent—which is crucial under the FAA since arbitration is strictly a matter of consent. Reversed.

DISSENT: (Kagan, J.) The majority's holding is not based in the Federal Arbitration Act (FAA), or well-established contract interpretation principles, but springs from the majority's policy belief that class arbitration undermines the central benefits of arbitration itself. That policy view cannot justify displacing generally applicable state law about how to interpret ambiguous contracts. Under the FAA, courts must enforce arbitration agreements according to their terms, which are to be interpreted according to state law, except when state contract law discriminates against arbitration agreements. That happens when any state rule treats arbitration agreements worse than other types of contracts, in which event the state rule is preempted. However, if a state rule treats arbitration agreements the same as all other types of contracts, the FAA does not intervene. Here, California's anti-drafter rule is as even-handed as contract rules come, since, as even the majority admits, it applies to every conceivable type of contract—and treats each identically to all others. It is an entirely neutral rule that favors no particular outcome, as, for example, between class and individualized dispute resolution; it only asks about who wrote the contract. Accordingly, Varela (P) should prevail even if the Lamps Plus, Inc. (D) agreement is ambiguous. A court's policy views should not enter the equation, since nothing in the FAA shields a contracting party, operating against the backdrop of impartial state law, from the consequences of its own drafting decisions. If the majority means to claim—as it must to prove its point—that the anti-drafter rule has no concern with what the parties agreed to, then the majority is flat-out wrong. From an

Continued on next page.

ex ante perspective, the rule encourages the drafter to set out its intent in clear contractual language, for the other party then to see and agree to, and from an *ex post* perspective, the rule enables an interpreter to resolve any remaining uncertainty in line with the parties' likely expectations. The upshot is that the rule protects against "unintended" consequences. In any event, nothing in the FAA's text requires the displacement of state contract rules. The idea that the FAA blocks a neutral state rule because (a court finds) the rule has too much "public policy" in it comes only from the majority's collective mind—not from precedent or well-established legal principles. Thus, the majority's approach disrespects the preeminent role of the states in designing and enforcing contract rules. It discards a universally accepted principle of contract interpretation in favor of unsupported assertions about what the parties must have (or could not possibly have) consented to, and it subordinates authoritative state law to (at most) the impalpable emanations of federal policy, impossible to see except in just the right light. The only reason this case has reached this Court is because it involves class proceedings, which are anathema to the majority. That is clear because the heart of the majority's opinion lies in its cataloging of class arbitration's many sins and is of a piece with the majority's efforts to pare back class litigation. The majority's holding is a product merely of its desire to prohibit class arbitration, regardless of the parties' agreement, or neutral and commonplace default rules of contract interpretation. Instead, the Court should have left the parties' agreement, as construed by state law, alone.

ANALYSIS

Although all the justices agreed that the Federal Arbitration Act requires courts to enforce arbitration agreements in accordance with their terms, they did not agree as to whether the agreement at bar was ambiguous or silent as to class arbitration. Chief Justice Roberts, writing for the Court, noted that the Court deferred to the Ninth Circuit's conclusion that the agreement was ambiguous as to class arbitration for purposes of the Court's analysis, but also intimated that the agreement could be viewed as being silent on that issue. Justice Thomas, concurring, was of the opinion that the agreement was silent as to class arbitration and provided no contractual basis for concluding that the parties agreed to class arbitration; he would have reversed the Ninth Circuit on that basis alone, without the need to displace state law at all. Justice Sotomayor, dissenting, found the agreement ambiguous as to class arbitration, but pointed out that although the Court normally acts with great solicitude when it comes to the possible preemption of state law, the majority invaded California contract law without pausing to address whether its incursion was necessary. She concluded that such haste was ill-advised.

Quicknotes

AMBIGUITY Language that is capable of being understood to have more than one interpretation.

EX ANTE Based on assumption and prediction, rather than actual results.

EX PARTE A proceeding commenced by one party without providing any opposing parties with notice or that is uncontested by an adverse party.

Frigaliment Importing Co. v. B.N.S. International Sales Corp.

Chicken purchaser (P) v. Seller (D)

190 F. Supp. 116 (S.D.N.Y. 1960)

NATURE OF CASE: Action for breach of warranty of a contract for the sale of goods.

FACT SUMMARY: Frigaliment Importing Co. (Frigaliment) (P) ordered a large quantity of "chicken" from B.N.S. International Sales Corp. (B.N.S.) (D), intending to buy young chicken suitable for broiling and frying, but B.N.S. (D) believed, in considering the weights ordered at the prices fixed by the parties, that the order could be filled with older chicken suitable for stewing only and termed "fowl" by Frigaliment (P).

RULE OF LAW

The party who seeks to interpret the terms of the contract in a sense narrower than their everyday use bears the burden of persuasion to so show.

FACTS: Frigaliment Importing Co. (Frigaliment) (P), a Swiss corporation, and B.N.S. International Sales Corp. (B.N.S.) (D), a New York corporation, made two almost identical contracts for the sale of chicken by the latter to the former as follows: U.S. fresh frozen chicken, Grade A, government inspected, eviscerated, all wrapped and boxed suitably for export, 75,000 lbs. 2½–3 lbs. at $33 per 100 lbs. [and] 25,000 lbs. 1½–2 lbs. at $36.50 per 100 lbs. The second contract was the same except for 25,000 lbs. less of the heavier chicken and a price of $37 per 100 lbs. for the lighter birds. B.N.S. (D), being new to the poultry business, believed any kind of chicken could be used to fill the order, including stewing chicken. Most of the order for heavier birds was filled with stewing chicken as that was the only way B.N.S. (D) could make a profit on the contract. Frigaliment (P) sued for breach of warranty.

ISSUE: Does the party who seeks a narrow interpretation of the terms of a contract bear the burden of persuasion to so show?

HOLDING AND DECISION: (Friendly, J.) Yes. The party who seeks to interpret the terms of the contract in a narrower sense than their everyday usage bears the burden of persuasion to so show. Frigaliment Importing Co. (Frigaliment) (P) failed to support its burden. While cables leading up to negotiations were predominantly in German, the use of the English word "chicken" as meaning "young chicken" rather than the German word "Huhn" meaning broilers and stewers lost its force when B.N.S. International Sales Corp. (B.N.S.) (D) asked if any kind of chickens were wanted to which an affirmative answer meaning "Huhn" was given. Because B.N.S. (D) was new to the chicken trade, the other party must show the other's acceptance of the trade use of a term. Frigaliment (P) failed to offer such proof. There was conflicting evidence anyway as to the trade use of the word "chicken." B.N.S.'s (D) price of $33 per 100 lbs. for the larger birds was $2 to $4 less than for broilers. Frigaliment (P) could not say that the price appeared reasonable because it was closer to the $35 broiler price than the $30 stewer price. B.N.S. (D) could not be expected to sell at a loss. While the evidence is generally conflicting, overall, it appeared that B.N.S. (D) believed it could comply by supplying stewing chicken. This did conform to one dictionary meaning, to the definition in the department of animal regulations to which at least there was a contractual reference, and to some trade usage. This evidence must be relied upon as the contract language itself could not settle the question here. Judgment shall be entered dismissing the complaint with costs.

ANALYSIS

In determining the intent of the parties, the court will turn first to the language of the contract to see whether the meaning of the ambiguous term can be raised. If this is unsuccessful, the court must look to other evidence. Under Restatement (First), § 235, certain guidelines aid in determining meaning. First, the ordinary meaning of language throughout the country is given to words unless circumstances show that a different meaning is applicable. Also, all circumstances surrounding the transaction may be taken into consideration. Also, if after consideration of all factors, it is still uncertain what meaning should be given, a reasonable, lawful, and effective meaning to all manifestations of intention is preferred to an interpretation that leaves a part of such unreasonable, unlawful, or ineffective, Restatement (First), § 236(a). Even so, the principal apparent purpose of the parties should be given greater weight in determining the meaning to be given.

Quicknotes

AMBIGUOUS Vague; unclear; capable of being understood to have more than one meaning.

BREACH OF WARRANTY The breach of a promise made by one party to a contract on which the other party may rely, relieving that party from the obligation of determining whether the fact is true and indemnifying the other party from liability if that fact is shown to be false.

Hurst v. W.J. Lake & Co.

Meat supplier (P) v. Meat scraps buyer (D)

Or. Sup. Ct., 16 P.2d 627 (1932)

NATURE OF CASE: Appeal from judgment on the pleadings for defendant in action for recovery on a contract.

FACT SUMMARY: Hurst (P), who had contracted to provide W.J. Lake & Co. (Lake) (D) with horse meat scraps at $50 per ton, contended that, as a matter of trade usage, terms in the contract referring to "minimum 50 percent protein" and "less than 50 percent protein" meant not less than 49.5 percent protein, so that Lake (D) could not take a discount for meat that contained between 49.5 percent protein and 50 percent protein.

RULE OF LAW

Where a contract is made between members of the same trade group, notwithstanding that the contract is otherwise unambiguous on its face, evidence of special meanings that the trade gives to certain terms may be used to interpret the contract in conformity with trade usage.

FACTS: Hurst (P) entered into a contract with W.J. Lake & Co. (Lake) (D) to provide Lake (D) with horse meat scraps at $50 per ton. The contract specified that the meat was to contain "minimum 50 percent protein," and also provided a $5 per ton discount for meat that analyzed at "less than 50 percent protein." Lake (D) took the discount on 140 tons of meat that analyzed at between 49.53 percent and 49.96 percent protein, paying only $45 per ton. Hurst (P) brought suit to recover the $5 per ton on the 140 tons, contending that, as a matter of trade usage, terms in the contract referring to "minimum 50 percent protein" and "less than 50 percent protein" meant not less than 49.5 percent protein, so that Lake (D) could not rightfully take a discount for meat that contained between 49.5 percent protein and 50 percent protein. Hurst (P) also asserted that he and Lake (D) were members of a group that traded in horse meat, and that this usage was well known to Lake (D). The trial court, taking the contracts words and terms at their common meanings, rendered judgment on the pleadings for Lake (D). The state's highest court granted review.

ISSUE: Where a contract is made between members of the same trade group, notwithstanding that the contract is otherwise unambiguous on its face, may evidence of special meanings that the trade gives to certain terms be used to interpret the contract in conformity with trade usage?

HOLDING AND DECISION: (Rossman, J.) Yes. Where a contract is made between members of the same trade group, notwithstanding that the contract is otherwise unambiguous on its face, evidence of special meanings that the trade gives to certain terms may be used to interpret the contract in conformity with trade usage. There are many examples of terms used in different trades that have special meanings that differ from their ordinary meanings. For example, in the bricklaying trade, a contract that fixes the bricklayer's compensation at "$5.25 a thousand" does not contemplate that the bricklayer need lay 1,000 bricks and no less to earn $5.25, but that the bricklayer must build a wall of a certain size. Numerous other instances could readily be cited showing the manner in which the meaning of words has been contracted, expanded, or otherwise altered by local usage, trade custom, dialect influence, code agreement, etc. Although, as W.J. Lake & Co. (D) points out, many courts will not permit evidence of trade usage when interpreting contracts, but will place upon the contract's terms and words only their common meanings, such an inflexible approach risks a court's failing to give to those words and terms the special meanings given them by the parties. Such a rigid rule has the advantage of simplicity, but that alone cannot justify excluding evidence of custom or usage in a particular context, even if such context cannot be gleaned from the contract alone. Reversed.

ANALYSIS

The Uniform Commercial Code (UCC) addresses trade usage in section 1-303. Section 1-303(c) indicates that "A 'usage of trade' is any practice or method of dealing having such regularity of observance in a place, vocation, or trade as to justify an expectation that it will be observed with respect to the transaction in question. The existence and scope of such a usage must be proved as facts. If it is established that such a usage is embodied in a trade code or similar record, the interpretation of the record is a question of law." The UCC goes on to provide, in section 1-303(d), that "usage of trade in the vocation or trade in which the parties are engaged or of which they are or should be aware is relevant in ascertaining the meaning of the parties' agreement, may give particular meaning to specific terms of the agreement, and may supplement or qualify the terms of the agreement. A usage of trade applicable in the place in which part of the performance under the agreement is to occur may be so utilized as to that part

Continued on next page.

of the performance." Thus, the UCC codifies the *Hurst* court's holding.

Quicknotes

CONFORMING GOODS Goods tendered pursuant to a contract for sale that conform with the contract's requirements.

TRADE USAGE A course of dealing or practice commonly used in a particular trade.

Nanakuli Paving & Rock Co. v. Shell Oil Co.

Paving contractor (P) v. Asphalt supplier (D)

664 F.2d 772 (9th Cir. 1981)

NATURE OF CASE: Appeal from order setting aside award of damages for breach of contract.

FACT SUMMARY: Shell Oil Co. (D) contended it was not obligated to price protect Nanakuli Paving & Rock Co. (P), and its conduct in the past did not constitute a course of conduct governing the contract.

RULE OF LAW

Trade usage and course of performance will be read into contracts where such are so prevalent the parties would have to have meant to incorporate them in the terms of the contract.

FACTS: Nanakuli Paving & Rock Co. (Nanakuli) (P) contracted with Shell Oil Co. (Shell) (D) to purchase its requirements of asphalt under two long-term contracts. The contract contained specific prices for the asphalt. Between 1969 and 1974, Shell (D) kept the price static to Nanakuli (P), while raising it to others. Thereafter, the price steadily increased. Nanakuli (P) sued, contending that an implied element of the contract was Shell's (D) duty to price protect. It argued the duty was such a clearly understood policy in the trade that it was assumed to be a part of the contract. This was strengthened, it argued, by Shell's (D) past performance of the contract. Shell (D) contended such was not part of the trade in which it dealt, and its past performance was a waiver of the price terms for that time. Finally, it argued the specific price terms controlled. The court set aside a jury verdict for Nanakuli (P), and Nanakuli (P) appealed.

ISSUE: Will trade usage and course of performance be read into contracts?

HOLDING AND DECISION: (Hoffman, J.) Yes. Trade usage and course of conduct will be read into contracts where such are so prevalent that the parties would have to have meant to incorporate them in the contract terms. Evidence was presented showing the prevalence of price protection in the asphalt trade. This, along with Shell Oil Co.'s (D) past performance, was sufficient to allow the jury to find that the terms were incorporated in the contract. As a result, the verdict should have been upheld. Reversed.

CONCURRENCE: (Kennedy, J.) This opinion should not be interpreted to permit juries to import price protection from a concept of good faith not based on well-established custom or usage.

ANALYSIS

Custom and course of performance are important tools in the interpretation of contracts. Often they are used to define words that take on a specific meaning within the confines of an industry or trade in which the contract is executed. Often, as in this case, they are used as a general guide to interpret the contract as a whole and to fill gaps created by unexpected contingencies.

Quicknotes

JUDGMENT N.O.V. A judgment entered by the trial judge reversing a jury verdict if the jury's determination has no basis in law or fact.

TRADE USAGE A course of dealing or practice commonly used in a particular trade.

Figgie International, Inc. v. Destileria Serralles, Inc.

Equipment manufacturer/seller (P) v. Equipment buyer (D)

190 F.3d 252 (4th Cir. 1999)

NATURE OF CASE: Appeal from grant of summary judgment to plaintiff, and from denial of partial summary judgment to defendant, in declaratory action seeking determination of appropriate remedies for breach of contract.

FACT SUMMARY: Destileria Serralles, Inc. (Serralles) (D), a rum bottler, contended that usage of trade in the bottle-labeling industry was inapplicable to limit its remedies against Figgie International, Inc. (Figgie) (P), a manufacturer and seller of bottle-labeling equipment, arising from the parties' agreement under which Figgie (P) provided Serralles (D) with bottle-labeling equipment that turned out to not work properly.

RULE OF LAW

Under the Uniform Commercial Code, usage of trade may supplement a commercial agreement with a remedy that is both limited and exclusive.

FACTS: Destileria Serralles, Inc. (Serralles) (D), a rum bottler, and Figgie International, Inc. (Figgie) (P), a manufacturer and seller of bottle-labeling equipment, entered into an agreement whereby Figgie (P) supplied bottle-labeling equipment to Serralles (D) for creating and placing labels on Serralles's (D) rum bottles. Problems arose with the equipment as soon as it was installed, and Figgie (P) spent several months trying to repair it, without success. Accordingly, Figgie (P) refunded the purchase price, and Serralles (D) returned the equipment. However, Serralles (D) also asked Figgie (P) to pay for damages arising out of the equipment's failure to perform as expected and the delay in obtaining alternative equipment. After the parties failed to come to agreement as to proper remedies, Figgie (P) instituted a declaratory judgment action in federal district court, asserting that it owed no further obligations to Serralles (D) under the agreement because Serralles's (D) remedy for breach was limited to repair, replacement, or refund—both under the written terms and conditions of the sales agreement and pursuant to usage of trade in the bottle-labeling industry. Figgie (P), which had lost its copy of the agreement, pointed to standard terms and conditions of its sales agreements, which limited a buyer's remedies to repair, replacement, or refund. Figgie (P) also presented affidavits of persons with extensive experience in the bottle-labeling and packaging industry, attesting that sellers in the industry always limit the available remedies in the event of a breach to repair, replacement, or return, and specifically exclude consequential damages. Serralles (D) presented its copy of the sales agreement, the last page of which stated that it was subject to additional general terms and conditions of sale printed on the reverse, but the reverse side of the page was blank. Figgie (P) asserted that the absence of the general terms and conditions on Serralles's (D) copy was most certainly a copying mistake, whereas Serralles (D) asserted that they were never part of the agreement. Although conceding that a factual dispute existed as to whether the written standards and conditions accompanied the original sales agreement, Figgie (P) asserted that it is nevertheless entitled to summary judgment because, under the Uniform Commercial Code (UCC), usage of trade in the bottle-labeling industry would supplement the sales agreement with the identical limited remedy of repair, replacement, or refund. Serralles (D) disputed that usage of trade imposed this limitation and, alternatively, asserted that because the limited remedy had failed of its essential purpose, it was entitled to the full array of remedies provided by the UCC. The district court granted summary judgment to Figgie (P) and denied partial summary judgment to Serralles (D). The court of appeals granted review.

ISSUE: Under the Uniform Commercial Code, may usage of trade supplement a commercial agreement with a remedy that is both limited and exclusive?

HOLDING AND DECISION: (Traxler, J.) Yes. Under the Uniform Commercial Code (UCC), usage of trade may supplement a commercial agreement with a remedy that is both limited and exclusive. UCC § 2-719 allows parties to a commercial sales agreement to provide for remedies in addition to those provided by the UCC, or to limit themselves to specified remedies in lieu of those provided by the UCC. The UCC in § 1-201(3) provides that an "agreement" is "the bargain of the parties in fact, as found in their language or by implication from other circumstances including course of dealing or usage of trade." The UCC also provides, in § 1-205(3), that a course of dealing between parties and any usage of trade in the vocation or trade in which they are engaged or of which they are or should be aware, give particular meaning to and supplement or qualify terms of an agreement. In turn, the UCC defines "usage of trade" in § 1-205(2) as "any practice or method of dealing having such regularity of observance in a place, vocation or trade as to justify an expectation that it will be observed with respect to the transaction in question." Moreover, under UCC § 1-205(4), where possible and reasonable, usage of trade is to be construed as consistent with an agreement's

Continued on next page.

express terms. Under the UCC, therefore, and because Destileria Serralles, Inc. (Serralles) (D) did not present any evidence contradicting Figgie International, Inc.'s (Figgie's) (P) evidence of trade usage, the district court did not err in granting summary judgment to Figgie (P) limiting Serralles (D) to the exclusive remedy of repair, replacement, or return. Affirmed.

ANALYSIS

Destileria Serralles, Inc. (D) argued that it could not be limited to the remedy of repair, replacement, or return because the written agreement did not "explicitly" state that this remedy was exclusive, and also argued that a limited remedy imposed or implied by trade usage cannot be an exclusive remedy because it is neither "expressly agreed to" nor "explicit." The court rejected these arguments, instead agreeing with other circuit courts that have rejected similar contentions that a limited remedy cannot be exclusive if imposed by usage of trade, see, e.g., *Western Indus. Inc. v. Newcor Canada Ltd.*, 739 F.2d 1198 (7th Cir. 1984) (rejecting contention that trade custom cannot limit liability because § 2-719(1)(b) of the UCC provides that resort to a remedy is optional unless expressly agreed to be exclusive); *Transamerica Oil Corp. v. Lynes, Inc.*, 723 F.2d 758 (10th Cir. 1983) (holding that, under the UCC, "[u]sage of trade may add an exclusive remedy to an agreement"); and *Posttape Assoc. v. Eastman Kodak Co.*, 537 F.2d 751 (3d Cir. 1976) (holding that "[t]he totality of the agreement. . . must include a provision, present in the trade usage, or otherwise expressed, that the limited remedy is an exclusive one").

Quicknotes

COURSE OF DEALING Previous conduct between two parties to a contract that may be relied upon to interpret their actions.

TRADE USAGE A course of dealing or practice commonly used in a particular trade.

Columbia Nitrogen Corp. v. Royster Co.

Phosphate purchaser (D) v. Phosphate producer (P)

451 F.2d 3 (4th Cir. 1971)

NATURE OF CASE: Appeal from judgment for plaintiff in breach of contract action.

FACT SUMMARY: Columbia Nitrogen Corp. (D) contended that under the Uniform Commercial Code usage of trade and course of dealing could properly be used to explain or supplement the express terms of a written contract it had entered with Royster Co. (P) for the purchase of phosphate where the contract did not expressly preclude such evidence and where default and damages terms were set forth in only general terms.

RULE OF LAW

Under the Uniform Commercial Code, evidence of usage of trade and course of dealing may be used to explain or supplement the express terms of a written contract where the contract does not expressly preclude such evidence and where the terms to be explained or supplemented are set forth in only general terms.

FACTS: Columbia Nitrogen Corp. (Columbia) (D) and Royster Co. (P) were both in the fertilizer business, and for years Royster (P) had purchased nitrogen from Columbia (D). Then Royster (P) began producing phosphate and Columbia (D) agreed to purchase a minimum of 31,000 tons of phosphate a year for three years. After the agreement was entered, phosphate prices plunged and Columbia (D) was unable to resell at competitive prices, so it purchased only one-tenth of the agreed-to tonnage during the first year. Royster (P) sold the remaining phosphate at market price and sued Columbia (D) for the difference between that price and the contract price. Columbia (D) adduced evidence that trade practice was that express price and quantity terms in the mixed fertilizer industry were mere projections to be adjusted according to market forces. It also attempted to show that in its dealings with Royster (P) over the years, there was repeated and substantial deviation from stated amount or price. The trial court excluded this evidence on the ground that "custom and usage or course of dealing are not admissible to contradict the express, plain, unambiguous language of a valid written contract, which by virtue of its detail negates the proposition that the contract is open to variances in its terms." The court of appeals granted review.

ISSUE: Under the Uniform Commercial Code, may evidence of usage of trade and course of dealing be used to explain or supplement the express terms of a written contract where the contract does not expressly preclude such evidence and where the terms to be explained or supplemented are set forth in only general terms?

HOLDING AND DECISION: (Butzner, J.) Yes. Under the Uniform Commercial Code (UCC), evidence of usage of trade and course of dealing may be used to explain or supplement the express terms of a written contract where the contract does not expressly preclude such evidence and where the terms to be explained or supplemented are set forth in only general terms. Although the UCC provides that evidence of usage of trade and course of dealing should be excluded whenever it cannot be reasonably construed as consistent with the terms of the contract, such evidence, as here, may be admitted even where a contract on its face appears complete, provided the explanatory or supplemental terms are consistent with the contract. Here, the evidence adduced by Columbia Nitrogen Corp. (D) is consistent with the written contract. First, the contract does not expressly exclude the use of such evidence. Second, the contract is silent about adjusting prices and quantities to reflect market fluctuations, neither permitting nor prohibiting such adjustments. This silence is a "fitting occasion" for using evidence of trade usage and course of dealing to supplement and explain the contract. Similarly, the contract's use of "Products Supplied Under Contract" in reference to minimum tonnages and additional quantities is a description that permits the use of this extrinsic evidence. Finally, the contract neither specifies what constitutes default nor what damages will be, and, again, extrinsic evidence may be used to supplement and explain terms that would cover these situations. It is insufficient, as Royster Co. (P) urges, to merely fill in these gaps by applying general common-law contract principles, since the policy underlying the UCC is to reflect market realities and avoid overly legalistic interpretations. Also rejected is Royster's (P) argument that the contract's merger clause, which provides that "no verbal understanding will be recognized by either party hereto . . . ," also should preclude the evidence. Verbal understanding is not synonymous with trade usage and course of dealing. The outcome would have been different had the merger clause explicitly provided evidence of trade usage and course of dealing would be excluded in any dispute over the contract's meaning. The UCC supports this position, as its official comment notes that course of dealing

Continued on next page.

and trade usage are admissible unless expressly negated. Vacated and remanded.

ANALYSIS

Under the Uniform Commercial Code, it is assumed that the parties to a contract take course of dealing and usage of trade into account when the contract is negotiated and drafted, and thus these become an element of the meaning of the words used. As this case illustrates, only when the contract itself expressly negates the use of course of dealing and usage of trade is this assumption also negated. In any event, the course of actual performance by the parties is considered the best indication of what they intended the contract to mean.

Quicknotes

BREACH OF CONTRACT Unlawful failure by a party to perform its obligations pursuant to contract.

COURSE OF DEALING Previous conduct between two parties to a contract that may be relied upon to interpret their actions.

USAGE OF TRADE A course of dealing or practice commonly used in a particular trade.

Raffles v. Wichelhaus

Cotton seller (P) v. Cotton buyer (D)

Ct. of Exchequer, 2 H. & C. 906, 159 Eng. Rep. 375 (1864)

NATURE OF CASE: Action for damages for breach of contract for the sale of goods.

FACT SUMMARY: Raffles (P) contracted to sell cotton to Wichelhaus (D) to be delivered from Bombay at Liverpool on the ship "Peerless." Unknown to the parties was the existence of two different ships carrying cotton, each named "Peerless," arriving at Liverpool from Bombay, but at different times.

RULE OF LAW

Where neither party knows or has reason to know of the ambiguity, or where both know or have reason to know, the ambiguity is given the meaning that each party intended it to have.

FACTS: Raffles (P) contracted to sell Wichelhaus (D) 125 bales of Surat cotton to arrive from Bombay at Liverpool on the ship "Peerless." Wichelhaus (D) was to pay 17 pence per pound of cotton within an agreed-upon time after the arrival of the goods in England. Unknown to the parties, there were two ships called "Peerless," each of which was carrying cotton from Bombay to Liverpool. Wichelhaus expected the cotton to be shipped on the "Peerless" that was to sail in October, while Raffles (P) had expected the cotton to be shipped on the "Peerless" set to sail in December. As Wichelhaus (D) could not have the delivery he expected, he refused to accept the later delivery.

ISSUE: Did a latent ambiguity arise showing that there had been no meeting of the minds, hence, no contract?

HOLDING AND DECISION: (Per curiam) Yes. While the contract did not show which particular "Peerless" was intended, the moment it appeared two ships called "Peerless" were sailing from Bombay to Liverpool with a load of cotton, a latent ambiguity arose, and parol evidence was admissible for the purpose of determining that both parties had intended a different "Peerless" to be subject in the contract. When there is an ambiguity, it is given the meaning that each party intended it to have. However, if different meanings were intended, there is no contract if the ambiguity relates to a material term. Consequently, there was no meeting of the minds, and no binding contract. Judgment for the defendants.

ANALYSIS

When there is no integration of the contract, the standard for its interpretation is the meaning that the party making the manifestation should reasonably expect the other party to give it, i.e., a standard of reasonable expectation. This case illustrates an exception to this rule. Where there is an ambiguity, if both parties give the same meaning to it, there is a contract. If the parties each give a different meaning to the ambiguity, then there is no contract as occurred here. The ambiguity struck at a material term, as payment was to be made within an agreed upon time after delivery. The parties could not even agree on the time of delivery. The other exception occurs when one party has reason to know of the ambiguity and the other does not, so it will bear the meaning given to it by the latter, that is, the party who is without fault. Note that under Uniform Commercial Code § 2-322, delivery "exship," it would make no difference which ship would be carrier of the goods and the case would have gone the other way. However, Restatement (First) § 71 would appear to follow the general rule of the present case.

Quicknotes

AMBIGUITY Language that is capable of more than one interpretation.

MATERIAL TERM OF CONTRACT A fact without the existence of which a contract would not have been entered.

MUTUAL ASSENT A requirement of a valid contract that the parties possess a mutuality of assent as manifested by the terms of the agreement and not by a hidden intent.

Colfax Envelope Corp. v. Local No. 458-3M

Manufacturer (P) v. Labor union (D)

20 F.3d 750 (7th Cir. 1994)

NATURE OF CASE: Appeal from summary judgment for defendant in declaratory judgment action brought under the Taft-Hartley Act, 29 U.S.C. § 185.

FACT SUMMARY: Colfax Envelope Corp. (Colfax) (P) contended that an essential term in a collective bargaining agreement was so ambiguous that there was no meeting of the minds between Colfax (P) and Local No. 458-3M (D), and that, therefore, the entire agreement had to be rescinded.

RULE OF LAW

A contract will not be rescinded merely because one or more of its terms is patently ambiguous and the parties have not attempted to clarify the patent ambiguity.

FACTS: Colfax Envelope Corp. (Colfax) (P) manufactured envelopes, and a few of its employees, who printed the envelopes, were unionized, belonging to Local No. 458-3M (the "union") (D). Ordinarily, Colfax (P) did not participate in the collective bargaining negotiations between the association of printing companies that it was part of and the union (D). Instead, when a collective bargaining agreement was reached between the association and the union (D), the union (D) would send a copy to Colfax (P), and, at its option, it could subscribe to the agreement or bargain on its own with the union (D) for different terms. When the latest agreement was negotiated between the association and the union (D), the union (D) sent a summary to Colfax (P), which, based on interpretations of its union members familiar with the negotiations, accepted the terms in the summary. A key term, relating to the number of people needed to operate different kinds of printing presses, listed "4C 60 Press-3 Men" and "5C 78 Press-4 Men." Colfax (P) believed this meant that all presses operated as four-color presses would require only three individuals to man them. A copy of the actual agreement contained a typo that supported this interpretation. However, when the corrected agreement was sent to Colfax (P), the manning requirements were different from what Colfax (P) had understood them to be. The agreement provided that four-color presses between 45 and 60 inches required three individuals (the prior agreement was less generous, requiring three individuals for presses between 45 and 50 inches), but that all four-color presses over 60 inches required four. Colfax (P) refused to sign the agreement, but the union (D) claimed that it was bound by its acceptance of the summary. Colfax (P) brought suit under section 301 of the Taft-Hartley Act, 29 U.S.C. § 185, for a declaration that it had no collective bargaining contract with the union (D) because the parties never agreed on an essential term—the manning requirements for Colfax's (P) printing presses. The union (D) counterclaimed for an order to arbitrate, since the agreement required arbitration of disputes. The district court granted summary judgment for the union (D), and the court of appeals granted review.

ISSUE: Will a contract be rescinded merely because one or more of its terms is patently ambiguous and the parties have not attempted to clarify the patent ambiguity?

HOLDING AND DECISION: (Posner, C.J.) No. A contract will not be rescinded merely because one or more of its terms is patently ambiguous and the parties have not attempted to clarify the patent ambiguity. The term in dispute is "4C 60 Press-3 Men." Colfax Envelope Corp. (Colfax) (P) believes it refers to four-color presses 60 inches and over, whereas the union maintains that it refers to four-color presses between 45 and 60 inches. If the disagreement over this term is so deep as to support the conclusion that no agreement was ever entered, then the contract must be rescinded. One way this has been previously expressed is that there has been no "meeting of the minds." This premise, that there must be a meeting of the minds to have a binding contract, is strained, however. Most contract disputes arise because the parties did not foresee and provide for some contingency that has subsequently materialized, over which it can be said there was no meeting of minds. Nonetheless, in most cases, such disputes are treated as disputes over contractual meaning, not as grounds for rescinding the contract. Thus, a literal meeting of the minds is not required to have a binding contract. A better rule is that a contract may be rescinded without liability when there is "no sensible basis for choosing between conflicting understandings" of the contractual language and where neither party is responsible (or both are equally responsible) for the ambiguity. The clearest cases for rescission on the ground that there was "no meeting of the minds" (or, better, that there was a "latent ambiguity" in the sense that neither party knew that the contract was ambiguous) are ones in which an offer is garbled in transmission, which is defined broadly. While the case at bar is superficially similar to such case, the difference is that here, Colfax (P) should have known that the term 4C 60 Press was unclear and susceptible of different interpretations. Thus, Colfax (P) merely

Continued on next page.

gambled that its interpretation would be the one accepted by a court in the event of a dispute. This case does not present a term that reasonably seems unequivocal to the parties but in reality is not; it is only in those cases of true latent ambiguity that rescission is permitted, but not in cases such as the one here where the parties should have realized that the term was ambiguous and could have, but chose not to, clarify the ambiguous term. Having failed to clarify the patently ambiguous term, Colfax (P) must have the meaning of the term arbitrated, and the arbitrator must decide if in fact there was no meeting of the minds. Affirmed.

ANALYSIS

In subsequent analysis, Judge Posner indicated that even where neither party may be blamed for the ambiguity, or where both parties are equally to blame, rescission should not be ordered where doing so will provide a windfall to one of the parties.

Quicknotes

AMBIGUOUS Vague; unclear; capable of being understood to have more than one meaning

CONTRACT An agreement pursuant to which a party agrees to act, or to forbear from acting, in exchange for performance on the part of the other party.

LATENT AMBIGUITY Language capable of more than one interpretation that seems clear on its face, but the introduction of extrinsic evidence proves it to have a different meaning.

MEETING OF THE MINDS A requirement of a valid contract that the parties possess a mutuality of assent as manifested by the terms of the agreement and not by a hidden intent; enforceability of the contract is limited to those terms to which the parties assented.

Koken v. Black & Veatch Construction, Inc.

Manufacturer or distributor (D) v. General contractor (P)

426 F.3d 39 (1st Cir. 2005)

NATURE OF CASE: Appeal from summary judgment for defendant in breach of warranty action.

FACT SUMMARY: Black & Veatch Construction, Inc. (P) contended that a fire blanket used to protect a welding area was unfit for its ordinary purpose because it failed to protect against fire during a torch-cutting operation, and, therefore, the implied warranty of merchantability was breached.

RULE OF LAW

A breach of the implied warranty of merchantability claim brought under the Uniform Commercial Code will not be sustained where the plaintiff has not adduced sufficient objective evidence that goods are not fit for the ordinary purposes for which they are used.

FACTS: Black & Veatch Construction, Inc. (B&V) (P) was the general contractor on a project during which a fire occurred during a torch-cutting operation. A fire blanket had been used to protect the area where the welding occurred, and although the fire was quickly extinguished, a generator was damaged by the chemicals in the fire extinguisher and $9 million in delay and repair damages occurred as a result. B&V (P) sued the fire blanket's manufacturer (D) and distributor (D) under the theory that under the Uniform Commercial Code the blanket was unfit for its ordinary purpose and therefore that the implied warranty of merchantability had been breached. B&V (P) presented no evidence of an ordinary user's reasonable expectations of how the fire blanket should have performed. The district court held that as a matter of law there was no breach of the implied warranty of merchantability since the blanket performed as expected, and the court accordingly granted summary judgment to the manufacturer (D) and distributor (D). The court of appeals granted review.

ISSUE: Will a breach of the implied warranty of merchantability claim brought under the Uniform Commercial Code be sustained where the plaintiff has not adduced sufficient objective evidence that goods are not fit for the ordinary purposes for which they are used?

HOLDING AND DECISION: (Dyk, J.) No. A breach of the implied warranty of merchantability claim brought under the Uniform Commercial Code (UCC) will not be sustained where the plaintiff has not adduced sufficient objective evidence that goods are not fit for the ordinary purposes for which they are used. It is not disputed here that the manufacturer (D) and distributor (D) are merchants for UCC purposes, and, therefore, the UCC's implied warranty of merchantability applies to the blanket. To be merchantable, a good must be "fit for the ordinary purposes for which such goods are used." The issue of whether the blanket was being used for its ordinary purpose was waived below, so the only remaining issue is whether the blanket was "unfit" for this purpose. Where a good performs as expected, it is fit for its intended purpose. The question, therefore, is whether the blanket performed as expected. This question is not a subjective one, but rather must be based on the reasonable expectations of an ordinary user, i.e., the standard is an objective one. Black & Veatch Construction, Inc. (P) bears the burden of proving that the blanket was unfit for its intended purpose, but it did not adduce evidence as to the reasonable expectations of consumers of the fire blanket. It did not, for example, present expert testimony on trade customs or industry standards, or any evidence of consumers' reasonable expectations. It was not enough to present only the testimony of the single user of the fire blanket who believed it did not perform as expected, as this was merely evidence of the subjective expectations of a particular user. Therefore, summary judgment was appropriate. Affirmed.

ANALYSIS

As this case demonstrates, the implied warranty of merchantability applies to the ordinary use to which goods are put, and not to every particular, non-ordinary use that a purchaser may put them to. To cover instances where a purchaser intends to put goods to a non-ordinary use, the Uniform Commercial Code provides, in § 2-315, the implied warranty of fitness for a particular purpose. Whether this implied warranty arises is a fact question determined by the circumstances as to whether a seller of goods has reason to know of such particular purpose and that the buyer is relying on the seller to provide goods that will be fit for such a purpose.

Quicknotes

BREACH OF WARRANTY The breach of a promise made by one party to a contract on which the other party may rely, relieving that party from the obligation of determining whether the fact is true and indemnifying the other party from liability if that fact is shown to be false.

Continued on next page.

IMPLIED WARRANTY An implied promise made by one party to a contract that the other party may rely on a fact, relieving that party from the obligation of determining whether the fact is true and indemnifying the other party from liability if that fact is shown to be false.

IMPLIED WARRANTY OF MERCHANTABILITY An implied promise made by a merchant in a contract for the sale of goods that such goods will function as they should when used for the ordinary purposes for which such goods are originally or regularly intended to be used.

Lewis v. Mobil Oil Corporation

Sawmill operator (P) v. Oil company (D)

438 F.2d 500 (8th Cir. 1971)

NATURE OF CASE: Appeal from jury verdict for plaintiff in breach of warranty action.

FACT SUMMARY: Mobil Oil Corporation (Mobil) (D) contended that there was no implied warranty of fitness for a particular use when it supplied oil for Lewis's (P) hydraulic equipment, even though Lewis (P) had indicated that he needed the lubricant for a hydraulic system for his sawmill operations and that he himself did not know the appropriate type of oil, and, after problems arose, Lewis (P) requested that Mobil (D) ascertain that the oil was the correct type for his operations.

RULE OF LAW

Under the Uniform Commercial Code, an implied warranty of fitness for a particular use will be found to exist where there is evidence that the seller of goods has reason to know any particular purpose for which the goods are required and that the buyer is relying on the seller's skill or judgment to select or furnish suitable goods for that particular purpose.

FACTS: Lewis (P), a sawmill operator, converted his equipment to a hydraulic system. He had done business for a long time with Mobil Oil Corporation (Mobil) (D) through its local dealer, Rowe. Lewis (P) asked Rowe to determine and supply the correct oil for the new hydraulic system. Rowe, too, did not know what the proper lubricant for Lewis's (P) machinery was but told Lewis (P) he would find out. The only information given to Rowe by Lewis (P) was that the machinery was operated by a gear-type pump; Rowe did not request any further information. Rowe then sold Lewis (P) a type of oil with no chemical additives. Within days, the equipment began experiencing problems, and in six months the system broke down and had to be replaced. The cause of the breakdown was undetermined, but the oil was suspected, and Lewis (P) asked Rowe to be sure he was supplying the right kind of oil. Rowe continued to supply the same oil. For the next two years, Lewis (P) continued experiencing trouble with the system, and numerous pumps were replaced. Finally, a Mobil (D) representative inspected the equipment and recommended a different type of oil that contained certain anti-foaming additives. Following this change, the system worked satisfactorily. Lewis (P) sued for damages caused by Mobil's (D) oil on the theory that the implied warranty of fitness for a particular purpose had been breached, since the oil was not suitable for such use, and that the improper oil caused the mechanical breakdowns, with consequent damages to his business. A jury returned a verdict and damages for Lewis (P), and the court of appeals granted review.

ISSUE: Under the Uniform Commercial Code, will an implied warranty of fitness for a particular use be found to exist where there is evidence that the seller of goods has reason to know any particular purpose for which the goods are required and that the buyer is relying on the seller's skill or judgment to select or furnish suitable goods for that particular purpose?

HOLDING AND DECISION: (Gibson, J.) Yes. Under the Uniform Commercial Code (UCC), an implied warranty of fitness for a particular use will be found to exist where there is evidence that the seller of goods has reason to know any particular purpose for which the goods are required and that the buyer is relying on the seller's skill or judgment to select or furnish suitable goods for that particular purpose. Mobil Oil Corporation (Mobil) (D) contends that there was no warranty of fitness in this case and that the equipment problems were attributable to improper filtration. It also contends that at most there was a warranty of merchantability, and since the oil provided to Lewis (P) was not unfit for use in hydraulic systems generally, this warranty was not breached. Because there was a warranty of fitness, it is unnecessary to determine whether the warranty of merchantability was breached. Under the UCC, there are two requirements for an implied warranty of fitness: (1) that the seller has "reason to know" of the use for which the goods are purchased, and (2) that the buyer relies on the seller's expertise in supplying the proper product. Both requirements were met here. The evidence shows that Rowe (and therefore Mobil (D)) knew that Lewis (P) was purchasing the oil for his particular hydraulic system and not for just a hydraulic system in general. It is also clear that Lewis (P) was relying on Mobil (D) to supply him with the proper oil for the system. Whether there is a warranty of fitness is a question of fact to be determined by all the circumstances. A buyer does not need to provide the seller actual knowledge of the particular purpose for which the goods are intended or of his reliance on the seller's skill and judgment, if the circumstances are such that the seller has reason to realize the purpose intended or that the reliance exists. Here, Lewis (P) made it clear he did not know what kind of oil was necessary and that he was relying on Mobil's (D) expertise to provide the correct oil. If Mobil (D) needed more information to make a proper determination, it was incumbent on Mobil (D) to

Continued on next page.

get the additional information before making its recommendation. As the evidence shows, this could have easily been done in the first place by sending an engineer to the sawmill to inspect the equipment. Mobil (D) argues that even if there was a warranty of fitness, the damages were caused by abnormalities in Lewis's (P) system. First, this argument goes to causation, not to the existence of the warranty. Second, even if the system had certain peculiarities, the whole point of an implied warranty of fitness is that a product be suitable for a specific purpose and that a seller should not supply a product that is not so suited. In any event, there was no evidence here that the system was abnormal, since it functioned properly when the correct oil was used. Affirmed.

ANALYSIS

As to damages, the Uniform Commercial Code (UCC) provides in § 2-714(2) that the "measure of damages for breach of warranty is the difference at the time and place of acceptance between the value of the goods accepted and the value they would have had if they had been as warranted, unless special circumstances show proximate damages of a different amount." In UCC §§ 2-714(3) and 2-715, incidental and consequential damages are permitted, and § 2-715(2)(a) permits consequential damages including "any loss resulting from general or particular requirements and needs of which the seller at the time of contracting had reason to know and which could not reasonably be prevented by cover or otherwise." Thus, in this case, the ordinary measure of damages for breach of warranty was not applicable, since Lewis (P) did not pay a price exceeding the value of the oil delivered. Rather, since the breach was of an implied warranty of fitness for a particular purpose, the "special circumstances" exception was applicable.

Quicknotes

IMPLIED WARRANTY An implied promise made by one party to a contract that the other party may rely on a fact, relieving that party from the obligation of determining whether the fact is true and indemnifying the other party from liability if that fact is shown to be false.

MEASURE OF DAMAGES Monetary compensation that may be awarded by the court to a party who has sustained injury or loss to his or her person, property, or rights due to another party's unlawful act, omission, or negligence.

WARRANTY OF FITNESS An implied promise made by a merchant in a contract for the sale of goods that such goods are suitable for the purpose for which they are purchased.

WARRANTY OF MERCHANTABILITY An implied promise made by a merchant in a contract for the sale of goods that such goods are suitable for the purpose for which they are purchased.

NY Drilling, Inc. v. TJM, Inc.

Equipment purchaser (P) v. Equipment seller (D)

573 F. Supp.3d 854 (E.D.N.Y. 2021)

NATURE OF CASE: Action for breach of the implied warranties of merchantability and fitness.

FACT SUMMARY: N.Y. Drilling, Inc. (P), which purchased two "hydraulic crawler drilling rigs" from TJM, Inc. (D) pursuant to a written contract, alleged that the rigs malfunctioned multiple times, so that TJM (D) breached the implied warranties of merchantability and fitness by its sale of the defective rigs. TJM (D) moved to dismiss, on the basis that the parties' written contract expressly disclaimed those warranties.

RULE OF LAW

For purposes of disclaiming the implied warranties of merchantability and fitness under the Uniform Commercial Code, an express disclaimer of those warranties is sufficiently conspicuous where it appears in a paragraph directly below a contract's signature block, is set off from the signature block, and is in all capital letters.

FACTS: N.Y. Drilling, Inc. (P) purchased two "hydraulic crawler drilling rigs" from TJM, Inc. (D) pursuant to written contract. The first rig, Model HD110-4T, cost around $482,000. A N.Y. Drilling (P) representative executed the purchase contract, which contained a warranty disclaimer underneath the representative's signature. The disclaimer expressly disclaimed the implied warranties of merchantability and fitness. The disclaimer was set off from the signature block and other boilerplate terms in the contract by a few lines of blank space. Its text was in all capital letters, and it appeared to be of the same size font as the majority of the contract, except that certain shipment and payment terms were larger and in bold, as were certain headings. Also, the contract contained no language preceding the signature block that directed the reader to the disclaimer. The HD110-4T rig malfunctioned shortly after delivery. TJM (D) delivered replacement parts and repaired the machine. The rig then failed again a few months later, as which point TJM (D) replaced the HD110-46 with another rig, this time a model HD200A. The parties executed a separate contract for the HD200A. This contract included an identical warranty disclaimer in the same location and in the same manner as the first contract. The HD200A also malfunctioned on a number of occasions, and TJM (D) made at least two repairs. After NY Drilling (P) notified TJM (D) that the rig was having structural failings, TJM (D) retrieved the rig, but neither repaired nor returned the machine. N.Y. Drilling (P) brought suit in federal district court, asserting that TJM (D) breached the implied warranties of merchantability and fitness, and that the disclaimers were unenforceable. TJM (D) defended on the basis of the disclaimers and moved to dismiss. The district court considered the motion.

ISSUE: For purposes of disclaiming the implied warranties of merchantability and fitness under the Uniform Commercial Code, is an express disclaimer of those warranties sufficiently conspicuous where it appears in a paragraph directly below a contract's signature block, is set off from the signature block, and is in all capital letters?

HOLDING AND DECISION: (Komitee, J.) Yes. For purposes of disclaiming the implied warranties of merchantability and fitness under the Uniform Commercial Code (UCC), an express disclaimer of those warranties is sufficiently conspicuous where it appears in a paragraph directly below a contract's signature block, is set off from the signature block, and is in all capital letters. Although the contracts for the rigs contained express implied warranty disclaimers, the parties dispute whether the disclaimers suffice to exclude the implied warranties at issue. Under the state's version of the UCC, to exclude an implied warranty of merchantability, a contract's disclaimer must mention merchantability, and, in the case of a writing, must be "conspicuous." Similarly, an exclusion of the implied warranty of fitness must be by a writing and conspicuous. The statute defines "conspicuous" in a common-sense way: it means "so written, displayed, or presented that a reasonable person against which it is to operate ought to have noticed it." UCC § 1-201(b)(10). Whether a term is conspicuous or not is a decision for the court. The state's case law is relatively quiet on the subject of whether a disclaimer must precede the signature blocks to be conspicuous. Courts in other states, applying essentially the same definition of "conspicuous" as used in this state, however, have frequently found disclaimers appearing below a signature line to be conspicuous. Taking these factors into consideration, the disclaimers at issue bear characteristics that are sufficiently conspicuous to overcome their suboptimal placement. The text is in all capital letters and it clearly and explicitly disclaims the warranties of fitness and merchantability. Each disclaimer is also set off in its own discrete paragraph, in a font and type size that differs from the text surrounding it. Taken together, these characteristics are sufficient in light of the weight of persuasive (if not binding) authority. Because, when viewed holistically, the disclaimers conspicuously

Continued on next page.

excluded the implied warranties of fitness and merchantability from the contracts at issue, the claims predicated on those implied warranties must be dismissed.

ANALYSIS

Some courts have found even less prominent disclaimers than the ones at issue in this case to be conspicuous. For example, in *Ireland v. J.L.'s Auto Sales, Inc.*, 156 Misc. 2d 845 at 848 (1992), the disclaimer was held to be conspicuous even though it not only came after the signature blocks, but also appeared on the reverse side of that last page—it was enough, in that case, that a notation below the signature line directed the reader to turn the page. The *Ireland* contract directed the reader to "see other side for additional terms" in capital letters and "large, dark print" appearing one inch below the plaintiff's signature. The "other side," in turn, included a disclaimer that the court found conspicuous.

Quicknotes

IMPLIED WARRANTY OF FITNESS When a merchant knows or has reason to know of a particular purpose for which goods are being purchased by the buyer, an implied promise made by the merchant in a contract for the sale of the goods that such goods are suitable, or "fit," for the purpose for which they are purchased.

IMPLIED WARRANTY OF MERCHANTABILITY An implied promise made by a merchant in a contract for the sale of goods that such goods will function as they should when used for the ordinary purposes for which such goods are originally or regularly intended to be used.

Fairchild Industries v. Maritime Air Service, Ltd.

Helicopter seller (D) v. Helicopter buyer (P)

Md. Ct. App., 333 A.2d 313 (1975)

NATURE OF CASE: Questions certified by federal court to state's highest court in action for breach of warranties.

FACT SUMMARY: Fairchild Industries (Fairchild) (D) sold a helicopter to Maritime Air Service, Ltd. (Maritime) (P) pursuant to a purchase agreement that indicated the helicopter was sold "as is" and that Fairchild (D) made no warranties of any kind, except for the warranty of title. Maritime (P) sued Fairchild (D), alleging breaches of express and implied warranties arising from the sale. Fairchild (D) defended on the ground that the purchase agreement disclaimed any warranties asserted by Merchant (P). The question arose as to whether the requirement found in Uniform Commercial Code (UCC) § 2-316(2)—that to exclude or modify the implied warranty of merchantability or any part of it, the language must mention merchantability, and in the case of a writing, the language must be conspicuous, and to exclude or modify any implied warranty of fitness, the exclusion must be by a writing and conspicuous—applied to the provisions for the exclusion of warranties set forth in UCC § 2-316(3)(a).

RULE OF LAW

The conspicuousness requirement set forth in Uniform Commercial Code (UCC) § 2-316(2) for the exclusion of the implied warranties of merchantability and fitness must be applied to provisions for the exclusion of warranties set forth in UCC § 2-316(3)(a), which is effected by terms like "as is" and "with all faults."

FACTS: After Maritime Air Service, Ltd. (Maritime) (P) leased a helicopter from Fairchild Industries (Fairchild) (D) for almost a year, Maritime (P) purchased the helicopter from Fairchild (D) pursuant to a printed purchase form on which relevant provisions were inserted by typewriter. Among those typewritten provisions was the following: "It is specifically understood and agreed by the parties that the Aircraft is sold in an 'As is' condition. Seller makes no representation or warranties express or implied whatsoever except Warranty of Title. Buyer acknowledges that before entering into this Agreement he has examined the Aircraft as fully as he desires." After the sale, Maritime (P) brought suit in state court for alleged breaches of express and implied warranties. The action was removed to federal district court. Fairchild (D) moved to dismiss, on the grounds that it had disclaimed all warranties. The federal district court then certified two questions to the state's highest court, the first of which effectively was: "Does the requirement found in Uniform Commercial Code (UCC) § 2-316(2), that 'to exclude or modify the implied warranty of merchantability or any part of it the language must mention merchantability and in case of a writing must be conspicuous, and to exclude or modify any implied warranty of fitness the exclusion must be by a writing and conspicuous' apply to the provisions for exclusion of warranties set forth in UCC § 2-316(3)(a)?" UCC § 2-316(3)(a) provides that "[u]nless the circumstances indicate otherwise, all implied warranties are excluded by expressions like 'as is,' 'with all faults' or other language which in common understanding calls the buyer's attention to the exclusion of warranties and makes plain that there is no implied warranty." The state's highest court answered this first question, determining that its answer obviated the need to answer the second.

ISSUE: Must the conspicuousness requirement set forth in Uniform Commercial Code (UCC) § 2-316(2) for the exclusion of the implied warranties of merchantability and fitness be applied to provisions for the exclusion of warranties set forth in UCC § 2-316(3)(a), which is effected by terms like "as is" and "with all faults"?

HOLDING AND DECISION: (Levine, J.) Yes. The conspicuousness requirement set forth in Uniform Commercial Code (UCC) § 2-316(2) for the exclusion of the implied warranties of merchantability and fitness must be applied to provisions for the exclusion of warranties set forth in UCC § 2-316(3)(a), which is effected by terms like "as is" and "with all faults." Fairchild Industries (Fairchild) (D) urges that the conspicuousness requirement need not be applied to (3)(a), contending that the two subsections were intended to be mutually exclusive. It argues this intent of the drafters that the two subsections be independent of each other is expressed by these phrases that preface the subsections: "Subject to subsection (3)" at the outset of subsection (2) and "Notwithstanding subsection (2)" at the beginning of subsection (3). Thus, Fairchild (D) maintains, these subsections, taken together, provide two alternative methods of disclaiming implied warranties: The first, under subsection (2), by language mentioning "merchantability" where an implied warranty of merchantability is excluded, which, if in writing, must be conspicuous, and by a conspicuous writing where an implied warranty of fitness is excluded; and the second, under (3)(a), by the use of language like "as is" or "with all faults." Thus,

Continued on next page.

according to Fairchild (D), the conspicuousness requirement does not apply to the second method. However, contrary to Fairchild's (D) argument, it is not clear from (3)(a) which of the requirements in subsection (2) is dispensed with by the use of an "as-is" type of disclaimer. Given this ambiguity in the statute's language, the court must ascertain the legislative intent in light not only of the statute's text and literal meaning, but also in light of the setting, the objectives and purposes of the enactment, and the consequences that may result from one meaning rather than another, with the real legislative intent prevailing over the literal intent. Moreover, as a principle of statutory construction, the court's interpretation should not lead to absurd results. According to Official Comment 1 to UCC § 2-316, the purpose of the section is to deal with those frequent clauses in sales contracts that seek to exclude "all warranties, express or implied." It seeks to protect a buyer from unexpected and unbargained language of disclaimer by denying effect to such language when inconsistent with language of express warranty and permitting the exclusion of implied warranties only by conspicuous language or other circumstances that protect the buyer from surprise. It is also clear that subsection (3) aims at maintaining this protection for the buyer. In light of the legislative purpose of UCC § 2-316 to ensure that exclusions of warranties are brought to a buyer's attention, although expressions like "as is" put the buyer on notice of the disclaimer, they do so only when brought to the buyer's attention. This means that in the case of a written disclaimer, the writing must be conspicuous. To hold otherwise could result in all warranties being disclaimed even where the term "as is," or a similar term, is buried in the fine print of a lengthy document. Such an anomalous result would not further the avowed purpose of § 2-316 "to protect a buyer from unexpected and unbargained language of disclaimer." Therefore, the words "as is" (or the like) are sufficient to put the buyer on notice that there are no implied warranties, but only when they are brought to the buyer's attention. Also rejected is Fairchild's (D) argument that had the drafters intended the expression "as is" to be conspicuous, they would have employed the capital case "AS IS" rather than the lower case, but the same lower case is also used in the exclusions mentioned in subsection (2), where conspicuousness is not contested. Finally, as a case from another jurisdiction dealing with this issue explained, the use of expressions like "as is" in (3)(a) was intended merely to give effect to common terms in addition to those specified in subsection (2) as a means for disclaiming certain warranties, but there is no evidence of a legislative purpose to require conspicuous language in one case and not when expressions like "as is" are used. The court in that case also persuasively reasoned that it serves no intelligible design to protect buyers by conspicuous language when the term "merchantability" is used, but to allow an effective disclaimer when the term "as is" is buried in fine print, because the buyer's expectations need as much protection in the former case as in the latter. To not require disclaimers such as "as is" to be conspicuous to be effective would bring about an absurd result that would be contrary to the UCC's spirit, and to the policy disfavoring exclusion of warranties and construing such disclaimers against the seller. Question answered.

DISSENT: (Singley, J.) Contrary to the majority's conclusion, the separate Uniform Commercial Code (UCC) sections at issue can be read independently of one another, and there is no ambiguity presented in the statute regarding these sections. Subsection (3) does not explicitly provide for a conspicuousness requirement for an "as is" disclaimer to be effective; if the UCC's drafters had intended that there be such a requirement, they could have easily said so. Therefore, the first certified question should be answered in the negative.

ANALYSIS

As this case illustrates, although under a literal application of Uniform Commercial Code (UCC) § 2-316(3)(a), the requirement of "conspicuousness" does not apply to an "as is" clause, most courts, like the *Fairchild* court, have read into the UCC a requirement that an "as is" clause be conspicuous. In addition to the reasons given by the *Fairchild* court for requiring conspicuousness for "as is" disclaimers, another reason is that, in the absence of conspicuousness, there is no basis for concluding that the "as is" clause had, in fact, been agreed to by the parties or formed a part of the basis of their bargain. "As is" language in a contract was held not to be sufficiently "conspicuous" to disclaim implied warranties where, although the paragraph that contained the "as is" language was separately numbered, that paragraph appeared in the same size font as the rest of the contract's printed terms, the "as is" phrasing within that paragraph was not in larger or contrasting type or color, and the paragraph made no mention of any exclusion, disclaimer, or limitation on remedies or warranties. *Bailey v. Tucker Equipment Sales, Inc.*, 236 Ga. App. 289, 510 S.E.2d 904 (1999).

Quicknotes

BREACH OF EXPRESS WARRANTY The breach of an express promise made by one party to a contract on which the other party may rely, relieving that party from the obligation of determining whether the fact is true and indemnifying the other party from liability if that fact is shown to be false.

Continued on next page.

EXPRESS WARRANTY A promise made by one party to a contract that the other party may rely on a fact, relieving that party from the obligation of determining whether the fact is true and indemnifying the other party from liability if that fact is shown to be false.

IMPLIED WARRANTY OF FITNESS When a merchant knows or has reason to know of a particular purpose for which goods are being purchased by the buyer, an implied promise made by the merchant in a contract for the sale of the goods that such goods are suitable, or "fit," for the purpose for which they are purchased.

IMPLIED WARRANTY OF MERCHANTABILITY An implied promise made by a merchant in a contract for the sale of goods that such goods will function as they should when used for the ordinary purposes for which such goods are originally or regularly intended to be used.

WARRANTY OF TITLE The implied promise in a contract for the sale of goods that the seller has title to the goods that are the subject of the contract.

Keith v. Buchanan

Sailboat purchaser (P) v. Sailboat seller (D)

Cal. Ct. App., 173 Cal. App. 3d 13, 220 Cal. Rptr. 392 (1985)

NATURE OF CASE: Appeal from judgment for defendant sellers in action for breach of warranty.

FACT SUMMARY: Keith (P), who purchased a sailboat yacht, contended that the sellers (D) created an express warranty for the vessel's seaworthiness through their advertising and sales brochures and materials, and that he was not required to prove reliance on the warranty thus created to prevail on a breach of express warranty claim. Keith (P) also contended that an implied warranty of fitness had been created, notwithstanding evidence that he did not rely on the sellers' (D) judgment or skill in selecting the vessel.

RULE OF LAW

(1) Under Uniform Commercial Code § 2-313, an express warranty can be created by statements in a seller's advertising and sales literature and by statements made by the seller's representatives, where those statements have become part of the basis of the parties' bargain, notwithstanding that the buyer did not rely on these statements.

(2) An implied warranty of fitness for a particular purpose is not created where a buyer relies on the buyer's own experts rather than on the seller's judgment or skill in choosing goods that conform to the purpose for which the buyer will use the goods.

FACTS: Keith (P), who had extensive experience with sailboats and yachts, but had never owned one, sought to purchase a sailboat yacht that conformed to his precise specifications and needs, including that the vessel would be ocean-going and would cruise long distances. After going to boat shows, looking at numerous boats, speaking to sales representatives, and reading advertising and sales literature, Keith (P) became interested in buying a vessel called an "Island Trader 41." In the literature, this sailboat was described as a seaworthy vessel. In one sales brochure, the vessel was described as "a picture of sure-footed seaworthiness." In another, it was called "a carefully well-equipped, and very seaworthy live-aboard vessel." Keith (P) testified he relied on representations in the sales brochures in regard to the purchase. Keith (P) also had one of his friends, Ebsen, who was involved in a boat building enterprise, inspect the boat. Ebsen and one of his associates—both of whom had extensive experience with sailboats—observed the boat and advised Keith (P) that the vessel would suit his stated needs. After Keith (P) purchased the vessel and it was delivered, a dispute arose in regard to its seaworthiness. Keith (P) brought suit for breach of express and implied warranties. The trial court rendered judgment for the sellers (D), concluding that no express warranty was established by the evidence because none of the sellers (D) had undertaken in writing to preserve or maintain the utility or performance of the vessel or to provide compensation for any failure in utility or performance. The trial court further found that no implied warranty of fitness was created because Keith (P) did not rely on the skill and judgment of the sellers (D) to select and furnish a suitable vessel but had rather relied on his own experts in selecting the vessel. The state's intermediate appellate court granted review.

ISSUE:

(1) Under Uniform Commercial Code § 2-313, can an express warranty be created by statements in a seller's advertising and sales literature and by statements made by the seller's representatives, where those statements have become part of the basis of the parties' bargain, notwithstanding that the buyer did not rely on these statements?

(2) Is an implied warranty of fitness for a particular purpose created where a buyer relies on the buyer's own experts rather than on the seller's judgment or skill in choosing goods that conform to the purpose for which the buyer will use the goods?

HOLDING AND DECISION: (Ochoa, J.)

(1) Yes. Under Uniform Commercial Code (UCC) § 2-313, an express warranty can be created by statements in a seller's advertising and sales literature and by statements made by the seller's representatives, where those statements have become part of the basis of the parties' bargain, notwithstanding that the buyer did not rely on these statements. Under § 2-313, to ascertain if an express warranty has been created, it must be determined whether the seller's statement constitutes an "affirmation of fact or promise" or "description of the goods," or whether it is rather "merely the seller's opinion or commendation of the goods." Second, assuming the language used by the seller is susceptible to creation of a warranty, it must then be determined whether the statement was "part of the basis of the bargain." The determination as to whether a particular statement is an expression of opinion or an affirmation of fact is often difficult and frequently depends on the context in which the statement was made. Courts have liberally construed

Continued on next page.

affirmations of quality made by sellers in favor of injured consumers, and statements made by a seller during the course of negotiation over a contract are presumptively affirmations of fact unless it can be demonstrated that the buyer could only have reasonably considered the statement as a statement of the seller's opinion. Factors that tend to indicate an opinion statement include (1) a lack of specificity in the statement made, (2) a statement that is made in an equivocal manner, or (3) a statement that reveals that the goods are experimental in nature. Applying these principles here, it becomes clear that the sellers' (D) statements were affirmations of fact. The vessel purchased was described in sales brochures as "a picture of sure-footed seaworthiness" and "a carefully well-equipped and very seaworthy vessel." The sellers' (D) representative was aware that Keith (P) was looking for a vessel sufficient for long-distance ocean-going cruises. The statements in the brochure were specific and unequivocal in asserting that the vessel was seaworthy, and nothing in the negotiation indicated that the vessel is experimental in nature. In fact, one sales brochure assured prospective buyers that production of the vessel was commenced "after years of careful testing." The next question, therefore, is whether those affirmations of fact became a part of the bargain. To show that they have, a buyer need not show that he would not have entered into the agreement absent the warranty or even that it was a dominant factor inducing the agreement. A warranty statement is deemed to be part of the basis of the bargain and to have been relied upon as one of the inducements for the purchase of the product. Under the UCC, affirmations of fact made by the seller about the goods during a bargain are regarded as part of the description of those good, so that no particular reliance on such statements need be shown to weave them into the fabric of the agreement; in other words, the representation need only be part of the basis of the bargain, or merely a factor or consideration inducing the buyer to enter into the bargain, and such a warranty statement made by a seller presumptively becomes part of the basis of the bargain, and the burden is on the seller to prove that the resulting bargain does not rest at all on the representation. Although a buyer's actual knowledge of the true condition of the goods prior to the making of the contract may make it plain that the seller's statement was not relied upon as one of the inducements for the purchase, the burden is on the seller to demonstrate such knowledge on the part of the buyer. Where the buyer inspects the goods before purchase, he may be deemed to have waived the seller's express warranties, but such an inspection does not necessarily discharge the seller from an express warranty if the defect was not actually discovered and waived. Here, Keith's (P) having his friends inspect the boat did not constitute a waiver of the express warranty of seaworthiness, since there was no ability to test the vessel in the water, and seaworthiness necessarily can only be assessed once a vessel has been put to sea. Therefore, the sellers (D) have not overcome the presumption that the representations regarding seaworthiness were part of the basis of this bargain. The sellers' (D) statements created an express warranty about the vessel's seaworthiness and the case must remanded for the trial court to determine if that warranty was breached. Judgment for Keith (P) as to this issue. Reversed and remanded as to this issue.

(2) No. An implied warranty of fitness for a particular purpose is not created where a buyer relies on the buyer's own experts rather than on the seller's judgment or skill in choosing goods that conform to the purpose for which the buyer will use the goods. The key question in determining the existence of an implied warranty of fitness for a particular purpose is the reliance by the buyer upon the skill and judgment of the seller to select an article suitable for the buyer's needs. If a seller has no reason to know that the buyer is relying on the seller, the seller's conduct in providing goods cannot fairly be deemed a tacit representation of their suitability for a particular purpose. If the buyer did not in fact rely on the seller, then the principal justification for imposing a fitness warranty disappears. Here, the trial court determined that Keith (P) did not rely on the sellers (D) to furnish him with a vessel that met his stated needs, but instead relied on his own experts. If this finding is supported by substantial evidence, it must be affirmed. The record reveals ample evidence that Keith (P) did not rely on the sellers (D), but instead relied on his own knowledge and experience and that of his expert friends. Thus, the trial court's finding is supported by substantial evidence. Judgment for sellers (D). Affirmed as to this issue.

ANALYSIS

Although evidence was presented of examination or inspection of the boat after the making of the contract of sale and prior to delivery and acceptance of the vessel, such an inspection would be irrelevant to any issue of express warranty. Although it deals with implied warranties as opposed to express warranties, Uniform Commercial Code comment 8 to § 2-316 is instructive, providing that warranties may be excluded or modified by the circumstances where the buyer examines the goods or a sample or model of them before entering into the contract. Examination, however, is not synonymous

Continued on next page.

with inspection before acceptance or at any other time after the contract has been made and goes to the nature of the responsibility assumed by the seller at the time of the making of the contract. Moreover, as was determined in this case, an examination or inspection by the buyer of goods does not necessarily discharge the seller from an express warranty if the defect covered by the warranty was not actually discovered and waived.

Quicknotes

BASIS OF THE BARGAIN The promise made by the offeror that induces the return promise or performance on the part of the offeree, and the promise or performance on the part of the offeree that induces the promise made by the offeror.

BREACH OF EXPRESS WARRANTY The breach of an express promise made by one party to a contract on which the other party may rely, relieving that party from the obligation of determining whether the fact is true and indemnifying the other party from liability if that fact is shown to be false.

BREACH OF WARRANTY The breach of a promise made by one party to a contract on which the other party may rely, relieving that party from the obligation of determining whether the fact is true and indemnifying the other party from liability if that fact is shown to be false.

IMPLIED WARRANTY OF FITNESS When a merchant knows or has reason to know of a particular purpose for which goods are being purchased by the buyer, an implied promise made by the merchant in a contract for the sale of the goods that such goods are suitable, or "fit," for the purpose for which they are purchased.

CHAPTER 6

Limits on the Bargain and Its Performance

Quick Reference Rules of Law

PAGE

1. *McKinnon v. Benedict.* Contracts that are oppressive, i.e., that fail to meet the test of reasonableness, will not be enforced in equity. *157*

2. *Tuckwiller v. Tuckwiller.* Whenever a contract concerning real property is in its nature and incidents entirely unobjectionable, it is as much a matter of course for a court of equity to decree specific performance of it, as it is for a court of law to give damages for the breach of it. *158*

3. *Black Industries, Inc. v. Bush.* Differences in the relative values of the consideration in a contract between businessmen dealing at arm's length without fraud will not affect the validity of the contract. *159*

4. *O'Callaghan v. Waller & Beckwith Realty Co.* A lease clause exculpating a landlord from liability for his own negligence should be upheld and is not void as against public policy. *161*

5. *Graham v. Scissor-Tail, Inc.* A contract of adhesion is enforceable against the adhering party where the contract falls within the reasonable expectations of that party. *162*

6. *Doe v. Great Expectations.* Where a consumer form contract violates state law that provides for actual damages or a set amount, whichever is greater, a consumer is entitled to a full refund of the contract price paid as restitutionary damages. *164*

7. *Williams v. Walker-Thomas Furniture Co.* The defense of unconscionability to action on a contract is judicially recognized. *166*

8. *Stoll v. Xiong.* A contract is unconscionable where, if enforced, it would render the actual price of the contract so gross as to shock the conscience and would be onerous to one side of the contracting parties while solely benefitting the other, so that no fair and honest person would propose, and no rational person would enter into, such a contract. *168*

9. *Prasad v. Pinnacle Property Management Services, LLC.* Where an employment arbitration agreement contains unconscionable provisions that are collateral to the agreement's main purpose, the agreement may be enforced after severing the unconscionable provisions. *170*

10. *Dalton v. Educational Testing Service.* Implicit in all contracts is a covenant of good faith and fair dealing. *173*

11. *Northwest, Inc. v. Ginsberg.* The Airline Deregulation Act of 1978 preempts a state-law claim for breach of the implied covenant of good faith and fair dealing if it seeks to enlarge the contractual obligations that the parties voluntarily adopt. *174*

12. *Market Street Associates v. Frey.* A party to a contract may not intentionally exploit the other party's oversight of an important fact. *176*

13. *Bloor v. Falstaff Brewing Corp.* A contractual provision obligating one to use its "best efforts" to promote and maintain a high volume of sales of a certain product is breached by a policy that emphasizes profit without fair consideration of the effect on sales volume. *177*

14. *Blossom Farm Products Co. v. Kasson Cheese Co., Inc.* Where there is evidence that a contract's promisee has knowingly acted under the contract to further the promisor's improper conduct, the contract is unenforceable on grounds of public policy, so the promisee cannot recover on the contract. *178*

15. *X.L.O. Concrete Corp. v. Rivergate Corp.* Antitrust defenses to a contract will be upheld where enforcement of the contract would compel the precise conduct made unlawful by the antitrust laws. 180

16. *Shadis v. Beal.* Where a case presents a question of federal law, a contract provision that conflicts with federal public policy underpinning a federal statute may be found to be void and unenforceable. 181

17. *Hassler v. Circle C Resources.* (1) The liberal blue-pencil rule, pursuant to which a court may narrow the terms of a noncompete agreement to make it reasonable, must be overruled where that rule is contrary to traditional contract law, has worked an injustice on employees, and has contributed to uncertainty in business relationships by encouraging employers to draft overly broad, unreasonable restraints on trade. (2) A noncompete agreement that is unreasonable on its face is void as violating public policy. 183

18. *Sheets v. Teddy's Frosted Foods.* An employee hired at-will may maintain an action for wrongful discharge if he can prove that the discharge violates public policy. 186

19. *Balla v. Gambro, Inc.* In-house counsel may not sue his former employer for the tort action of retaliatory discharge. 187

20. *Simeone v. Simeone.* Contracting parties are normally bound by their agreements without regard to whether the terms thereof were read and fully understood and whether the agreements embodied reasonable or good bargains. 189

21. *In the Matter of Baby M.* Surrogate contracts violate public policy and are unenforceable. 190

McKinnon v. Benedict

Homeowner (P) v. Resort owner (D)

Wis. Sup. Ct., 38 Wis. 2d 607, 157 N.W.2d 665 (1968)

NATURE OF CASE: Action brought in equity to enjoin property owner from violating contractual restrictions on the use of land.

FACT SUMMARY: The Benedicts (D), in order to buy a summer resort, borrowed $5,000 from adjoining property owner, McKinnon (P), who promised to help the Benedicts (D) attract tourists if the Benedicts (D) would not cut trees between the resort and his property nor make certain other improvements for a period of 25 years. When the resort did not prosper and the Benedicts (D) began to add a trailer park and tent camp, McKinnon (P) brought suit to enjoin further improvements.

RULE OF LAW

Contracts that are oppressive, i.e., that fail to meet the test of reasonableness, will not be enforced in equity.

FACTS: Mr. Benedict (D), a retail jeweler, and his wife (D), in order to purchase a summer resort consisting of a lodge and some cabins on about 80 acres of land adjoining McKinnon's (P) 1,000 acres of land, borrowed $5,000 interest-free from McKinnon (P) who promised also to help attract business. The Benedicts (D), in return, promised not to cut trees between the camp and McKinnon's (P) land and to make no improvements closer to his land than the present buildings. The restrictions were for a term of 25 years. They did not affect all the resort but did affect all the most desirable part. When the resort did not prosper, the Benedicts (D), who had repaid the $5,000 loan in seven months, spent $9,000 bulldozing and installing utilities for a trailer park and tent camp. When McKinnon (P), who wintered in Arizona, returned, he filed suit and obtained an injunction enjoining the improvements.

ISSUE: Was the restrictive contract reasonable so as to be enforced in action in equity?

HOLDING AND DECISION: (Heffernan, J.) No. The contract, being oppressive, cannot be enforced in equity. Coupled with the general equitable principle is the policy that restrictions on the use of land are not favored in the law. The Benedicts (D) are under great hardship. The only monetary consideration was a loan that they repaid on time. The loan was not unsecured as McKinnon (P) took a mortgage on their cottage property. McKinnon's (P) aid in generating business was booking one group, which stayed a week. The Benedicts' (D) great need for the loan placed them in an untenable bargaining position that made it impossible for them to deal at arm's length with McKinnon (P). Accordingly, the inadequacy of consideration was so gross as to be unconscionable. The contract, therefore, being unreasonable, will not be enforced by a court of equity. As the improvements to the land are barely visible during summer, the only time McKinnon (P) is on the land, the damage to him is minimal, while the damage of enforcing the restrictions against the Benedicts (D) would be major, it is within the discretion of the court to protect persons from equitable remedies that would cause them harshness or oppression. Reversed.

ANALYSIS

This case was brought in equity, this is to say, there was no remedy available to the plaintiff at law. Instead, the Benedicts (D) sought specific performance of the contract, abeyance of the restriction through injunction enjoining any violation of the contract. Cases in equity are decided by the judge sitting without a jury and such cases are decided on a basis of fair play and common decency. Often the phrase "balancing the equities" is used to describe the weighing of the rights of the parties against each other. The court did not give the Benedicts (D) carte blanche to bulldoze and cut trees as they please. But permission to make improvements that would not harm McKinnon (P), though outside the bounds of this agreement, was given. The contract was oppressive, as the Benedicts (D), being of very weak bargaining power next to McKinnon (P), received inadequate consideration for the severe restriction he promised to uphold.

Quicknotes

EQUITABLE Just; fair.

INJUNCTION A court order requiring a person to do, or prohibiting that person from doing, a specific act.

OPPRESSION The abuse of one's authority resulting in the infliction of injury on another.

SPECIFIC PERFORMANCE An equitable remedy whereby the court requires the parties to perform their obligations pursuant to a contract.

UNCONSCIONABILITY Rule of law whereby a court may excuse performance of a contract, or of a particular contract term, if it determines that such terms are unduly oppressive or unfair to one party to the contract as a result of disparity in bargaining power during the formation of the contract.

Tuckwiller v. Tuckwiller

Caretaker (P) v. Estate executor (D)

Mo. Sup. Ct., 413 S.W.2d 274 (1967)

NATURE OF CASE: Action for specific performance of a contract for the transfer of real property.

FACT SUMMARY: Mr. and Mrs. Tuckwiller (P) lived on the Hudson family farm as renters; about half the farm was owned by Mrs. Metta Hudson Morrison, who returned to live on the farm after contracting Parkinson's disease. She asked Mrs. Tuckwiller (P) to care for her during her remaining lifetime and signed a paper promising to give Mrs. Tuckwiller (P) her farm, which was willed for sale, the proceeds of which were to go to the creation of a student loan fund at Davidson College. Mrs. Morrison died before she could change the will.

RULE OF LAW

Whenever a contract concerning real property is in its nature and incidents entirely unobjectionable, it is as much a matter of course for a court of equity to decree specific performance of it, as it is for a court of law to give damages for the breach of it.

FACTS: John and Ruby Tuckwiller (P) were renters on the Hudson family farm, half of which was owned by Metta Hudson Morrison who returned to the farm after contracting Parkinson's disease. Having no immediate relatives and not wanting to live in an impersonal nursing home, she asked Ruby Tuckwiller (P) to care for her during her life and she signed a paper promising her farm to Ruby Tuckwiller (P) in return for care. Ruby Tuckwiller (P) quit her job to provide Mrs. Morrison with three meals a day, "a good bed," and "any possible act of nursing, and . . . her every possible pleasure." The farm was willed to Davidson College for sale, the proceeds of which were to create a student loan fund. Mrs. Morrison made an appointment with her lawyer to change the will; however, she fainted and fell. In the ambulance, she had the attendants witness the paper. She died the next month without having changed the will. The college and Mrs. Morrison's executor (Marion Tuckwiller) (D) resisted giving the farm to the Tuckwillers (P).

ISSUE: Is there the requisite essential fairness and adequate consideration necessary for the enforcement in equity of the contract for real estate?

HOLDING AND DECISION: (Welborn, Commr.) Yes. While prior services cannot provide the consideration essential to a binding contract, such prior services and the past relations of the parties may properly be considered in connection with the fairness of the contract and adequacy of the consideration. Having no immediate family and not desiring to stay in an impersonal nursing home, Mrs. Morrison felt freer to dispose of the farm without an exact quid pro quo. Her insistence that the contract be witnessed and her unsuccessful attempt to change her will are clear evidence of her satisfaction with the bargain. While Mrs. Tuckwiller's (P) services were but for a short duration with a monetary value unquestionably far less in value to that of the farm, it is not necessary with a contract for real estate to award the monetary value of Mrs. Tuckwiller's (P) services to her. Once essential fairness and adequate consideration are found, the fact that the contract is one for real estate determines the question of the adequacy of the legal remedy of monetary damages. Whenever a contract for real property is entirely unobjectional so that it possesses no features appealing to the discretion of the court, a court of equity (as in this case) will decree specific performance, while a court of law will give damages for breach. Affirmed.

ANALYSIS

An action for specific performance is inherently an equitable remedy. It is not a legal remedy. An action in equity cannot be brought if there is an available remedy in law. Courts of equity, which sit without juries, have great discretion in determining the issue. Here, the contract was aleatory, that is, involving risk or hazard. The surrounding circumstances in equity actions become important in guiding the court to its decision. Because of the lack of relatives of Mrs. Morrison, her satisfaction expressed by her actions, and in some respects the fact Mrs. Tuckwiller (P) quit her job to fulfill her side of the bargain, the court can determine the good intent of the parties and enforce the contract.

Quicknotes

ALEATORY Dependent upon the occurrence of an uncertain or fortuitous event.

EQUITABLE REMEDY A remedy that is based upon principles of fairness as opposed to rules of law; a remedy involving specific performance rather than money damages.

QUID PRO QUO Something for something; in contract law, the consideration, something of value, passed between the parties to render the contract binding.

SPECIFIC PERFORMANCE An equitable remedy whereby the court requires the parties to perform their obligations pursuant to a contract.

Black Industries, Inc. v. Bush

Middleman (P) v. Manufacturer (D)

110 F. Supp. 801 (D. N.J. 1953)

NATURE OF CASE: Action for damages for breach of contract for the sale of goods.

FACT SUMMARY: Bush (D), who was to produce mechanical parts for Black Industries, Inc. (Black) (P), which was reselling them to another company that was selling the equipment to the United States, failed to deliver the parts, claiming Black (P) was receiving excessive profits in violation of public policy when the government was involved in the Korean War. Bush (D) moved for summary judgment.

RULE OF LAW

Differences in the relative values of the consideration in a contract between businessmen dealing at arm's length without fraud will not affect the validity of the contract.

FACTS: Black Industries, Inc. (Black) (P) contracted with Bush (D) for the latter to produce and sell to Black (P) 1.3 million anvils at $4.40 per thousand; 750,000 holder primers at $11.50 per thousand; and 700,000 plunger supports at $12 per thousand, all to be made to government specifications. Black (P) was to resell the items to two other companies that were using the parts to satisfy contracts they had with the government. Black (P) was to make a profit of 84.09 percent on anvils, 39.13 percent on holder primers, and 68.33 percent on plunger supports. Bush (D) was to deliver directly to the companies to which Black (P) was reselling the parts. Black (P) was to handle all the billing and be responsible for differences between Bush's (D) quotations and the ultimate price. Bush (D), alleging Black (P) was receiving excessive profits against public policy during time of [the Korean] war because the price was eventually passed on to the U.S. government, failed to deliver. Black (P) alleged it lost about $19,000 on its two resale contracts. Bush (D) moved for summary judgment.

ISSUE: Will differences in the relative values of the consideration in a contract between businessmen dealing at arm's length without fraud affect the validity of the contract?

HOLDING AND DECISION: (Forman, C.J.) No. Differences in the relative values of the consideration in a contract between businessmen dealing at arm's length without fraud will not affect the validity of the contract. To be void as against public policy without evidence of fraud, the contract must fall into at least one of three categories. It must be a contract by which the defendant pays the plaintiff to induce a public official to act in a certain manner; it must be a contract to do an illegal act; or it must be a contract contemplating collusive bidding on a public contract. The first and third categories are those directly impinging on governmental activities and the ones upon which Bush (D) most heavily relied. But the contract's only effect upon the government was indirect in that the government was to buy machines made by component parts manufactured by Bush (D) and resold by Black Industries, Inc. (Black) (P) to manufacturers who would sell the finished product to the government. Even if it were shown that Black (P) was to have received a far greater profit than Bush (D) for a much smaller contribution, Bush (D) nevertheless would be bound by the familiar rule that relative values of the consideration in a contract between businessmen dealing at arm's length without fraud will not affect the validity of the contract. The court does not believe that it should determine the validity of a contract between ordinary businessmen on the basis of its beliefs as to the adequacy of the consideration. This would lead the court to having to determine the fairness of profits taken by all middlemen. Motion for summary judgment denied.

ANALYSIS

First, this is a case brought for damages. Such an action is an action in law. In an action in law, the court will not look to the adequacy of consideration as it will do in an action for specific performance, which is an action in equity. The court's discretion is not as wide in an action in law as in an action in equity. This case appears to be guided by the somewhat old, but strict, rule that the court would be making an unwarranted interference if it were to relieve an adult party from a bad bargain. But also, courts do not want to prescribe prices because it is thought the administration of the law of contracts would become inefficient. Additionally, the test of enforceability would become clouded by vague rules of "fairness" and "reasonableness." Notice, too, that the middleman generally performs an important function in contracting by bringing together sellers and buyers who would otherwise be ignorant of the business needs of each other. Also, here, Black Industries, Inc. (P), as middleman, took the risk of the difference in the ultimate price from that of the quoted price, which is perhaps a justification for the high profit.

Continued on next page.

Quicknotes

ACTION IN EQUITY Lawsuit in which a plaintiff seeks equitable remedies.

ADEQUACY OF CONSIDERATION Value given by one party in exchange for performance or a promise to perform by another party that is fair and reasonable in proportion to the value of what is received.

SUMMARY JUDGMENT Judgment rendered by a court in response to a motion by one of the parties, claiming that the lack of a question of material fact in respect to an issue warrants disposition of the issue without consideration by the jury.

O'Callaghan v. Waller & Beckwith Realty Co.

Injured tenant (P) v. Landlord (D)

Ill. Sup. Ct., 15 Ill. 2d 436, 155 N.E.2d 545 (1958)

NATURE OF CASE: Action to recover damages for negligence.

FACT SUMMARY: O'Callaghan (P) was injured by her landlord's negligence under a lease that exculpated the landlord from liability for negligence.

RULE OF LAW

A lease clause exculpating a landlord from liability for his own negligence should be upheld and is not void as against public policy.

FACTS: O'Callaghan (P), a tenant in an apartment building maintained and operated by Waller & Beckwith Realty Co. (Waller) (D), was injured in the apartment's courtyard on defective pavement attributed to Waller's (D) alleged negligence. O'Callaghan's (P) lease contained an exculpatory clause that clearly purported to relieve Waller (D) from liability for negligence. O'Callaghan's (P) jury verdict was reversed by the appeals court, and she appealed.

ISSUE: In a residential lease, is an exculpatory clause releasing the landlord from liability for his own negligence void as against public policy?

HOLDING AND DECISION: (Schaefer, J.) No. Exculpatory clauses in the landlord-tenant forum (whether business or residential) should be enforced for the following reasons: (1) the lessor-lessee relationship has been considered a matter of private, not public, concern; (2) exculpatory clauses for landlords benefit tenants as well; (3) the landlord-tenant relationship is not possessed of the monopolistic characteristics that have characterized some other relations with respect to which exculpatory clauses have been held invalid; and (4) the subject is appropriate for legislative, rather than judicial, action. Furthermore, any disparity in bargaining power caused by a housing shortage, which may or may not have existed when the lease was drawn, was a sporadic and transitory sort of condition. Judicial determination should rest upon a durable moral basis. Affirmed.

DISSENT: (Bristow, J.) In the pervasive arena of the landlord-tenant relationship, the important negligence standard that has been developed to protect members of society from one another has been effectively destroyed by the majority opinion. The landlord-tenant relationship is not significantly distinguishable from the employer-employee relationship in which exculpatory clauses have been declared void as against public policy.

ANALYSIS

The present case was decided before the landmark case of *Henningsenv. Bloomfield Motors*, 32 N.J. 358 (1960), which finally recognized in judicial opinion the doctrine of "contracts of adhesion." Although today the boundaries of "public policy" are in a state of confusion, the trend is away from the majority's decision in the present case. Many courts have made a distinction (in deciding whether to allow exculpatory clauses) between commercial and residential leases on grounds of the relative bargaining power of the parties involved. Even where exculpatory clauses are not struck down, they are usually strictly construed.

Quicknotes

ADHESION CONTRACT A contract, usually in standardized form, that is prepared by one party and offered to another, whose terms are so disproportionately in favor of the drafting party that courts tend to question the equality of bargaining power in reaching the agreement.

EXCULPATORY CLAUSE A clause in a contract relieving one party from liability for certain unlawful conduct.

NEGLIGENCE Conduct falling below the standard of care that a reasonable person would demonstrate under similar conditions.

PUBLIC POLICY Policy administered by the state with respect to the health, safety, and morals of its people in accordance with common notions of fairness and decency.

Graham v. Scissor-Tail, Inc.

Concert promoter (P) v. Agent (D)

Cal. Sup. Ct., 171 Cal. Rptr. 604, *en banc* (1981)

NATURE OF CASE: Appeal from judgment confirming an arbitration award, on grounds that contract requiring arbitration was an unenforceable contract of adhesion and that the arbitration clause therein was unconscionable.

FACT SUMMARY: Graham (P), an experienced and sophisticated concert promoter, contended that a union-provided form contract he entered into was an unenforceable contract of adhesion, notwithstanding that the contract fell within his reasonable expectations, and that an arbitration clause in the contract was unconscionable.

RULE OF LAW

A contract of adhesion is enforceable against the adhering party where the contract falls within the reasonable expectations of that party.

FACTS: Bill Graham (P), an experienced and sophisticated contract promoter, entered into several identical contracts with Scissor-Tail, Inc. (D), which represented the well-known recording artist Leon Russell, for a multicity concert tour. Each contract was a form contract, known in the industry as an American Federation of Musicians (AFM) Form B Contract. All AFM members were prohibited from entering contracts other than those provided by the union, so that Graham (P) was unable to negotiate a separate contract with Russell. The contracts provided that any disputes arising from the contracts would be arbitrated before the AFM's international executive board. Graham (P), who had entered into thousands of AFM contracts, had previously appeared before the AFM's international executive board to resolve disputes arising from other contracts. When a dispute arose regarding the Russell concert tour, Graham (P) brought suit for breach of contract. Scissor-Tail (D) moved successfully to compel arbitration. After the union's international executive board ruled in Scissor-Tail's (D) favor, Graham (P) appealed the confirmation of the arbitration award, contending that the Form B Contract was an unenforceable contract of adhesion and that the arbitration clause therein was unconscionable. The state's highest court granted review.

ISSUE: Is a contract of adhesion enforceable against the adhering party where the contract falls within the reasonable expectations of that party?

HOLDING AND DECISION: [Judge not listed in casebook excerpt.] Yes. A contract of adhesion is enforceable against the adhering party where the contract falls within the reasonable expectations of that party. The term "contract of adhesion" signifies "a standardized contract, which, imposed and drafted by the party of superior bargaining strength, relegates to the subscribing party only the opportunity to adhere to the contract or reject it." *Neal v. State Farm Ins. Cos.*, 199 Cal. App. 2d 690, 694 (1961). Here, notwithstanding Graham's (P) stature in the music business, he was forced to enter into the Form B contract, so that he was an "adherent" of the contract, and the contract was a contract of adhesion. Characterizing a contract as one of adhesion, however, does not indicate its legal effect per se. Such contracts are fully enforceable unless other factors are present that make them unenforceable. Generally, there are two judicially imposed limitations on the enforcement of adhesion contracts or provisions thereof. First, if a contract of adhesion or one of its provisions does not fall within the reasonable expectations of the weaker or "adhering" party, the contract or provision will not be enforced against him. Second, a contract or provision, even if consistent with the reasonable expectations of the parties, will be denied enforcement if, considered in its context, it is unduly oppressive or unconscionable. Here, it cannot be said that the contract at issue was in any way contrary to Graham's (P) reasonable expectations, given that he had been a party to thousands of American Federation of Musicians (AFM) contracts containing a similar arbitration provision. He had been involved in prior proceedings before the AFM regarding disputes with other musical groups arising under prior contracts, and he even indicated he would go before the AFM if the dispute was not settled to his satisfaction. These facts indicate that he was well aware that all disputes arising under the contracts were to be resolved by arbitration before the AFM. For all of these reasons it must be concluded that the provisions requiring such arbitration were wholly consistent with Graham's (P) reasonable expectations upon entering into the contract, and the contract is enforceable unless the arbitration provision was unconscionable. [The court went on to conclude that the arbitration provision was unconscionable because it designated as the arbitrator the AFM's international executive board, which the court concluded was presumptively biased in favor of its members.] Reversed.

Continued on next page.

ANALYSIS

Although the court in this decision concluded that the arbitration provision in the contract at issue was unconscionable, because it designated a biased arbitrator, this conclusion would not necessarily preclude the parties from arbitrating their dispute, especially given the strong public policy favoring arbitration. On remand, the parties could be afforded a reasonable opportunity to agree on a suitable, non-biased arbitrator and, failing such agreement, the trial court, on petition of either party, could appoint the arbitrator. Only in the absence of an agreement or petition to appoint would the court proceed to a judicial determination of the controversy.

Quicknotes

ADHESION CONTRACT A contract, usually in standardized form, that is prepared by one party and offered to another, whose terms are so disproportionately in favor of the drafting party that courts tend to question the equality of bargaining power in reaching the agreement.

ARBITRATION CLAUSE Provision contained in a contract pursuant to which both parties agree that any disputes arising thereunder will be resolved through arbitration.

UNCONSCIONABILITY Rule of law whereby a court may excuse performance of a contract, or of a particular contract term, if it determines that such terms are unduly oppressive or unfair to one party to the contract as a result of disparity in bargaining power during the formation of the contract.

Doe v. Great Expectations

Unnamed individuals (P) v. Dating service (D)

N.Y. Civ. Ct., 809 N.Y.S.2d 819 (2005)

NATURE OF CASE: Consolidated actions to recover amounts paid under social referral services contracts.

FACT SUMMARY: Doe (P) and Roe (P) contended that they were entitled to recover amounts paid under a social referral services contract they had each entered separately with Great Expectations (D) on the grounds that the contract and service violated the state's Dating Service Law.

RULE OF LAW

Where a consumer form contract violates state law that provides for actual damages or a set amount, whichever is greater, a consumer is entitled to a full refund of the contract price paid as restitutionary damages.

FACTS: Doe (P) and Roe (P) each separately entered into social referral services contracts with Great Expectations (D), which with some minor variations were identical, boilerplate form contracts. Doe (P) paid $1,000 for six months and Roe (P) paid $3,790 for 36 months, which was later extended to 54 months. Roe (P) was given oral assurances of 12 introductions to be provided over the course of 36 months. Under the form contract, Great Expectations (D) offered to expand a client's social horizons primarily by posting a client's video and profile on an Internet site on which other clients could review them and, thereafter, as desired, approach a selected client for actual social interaction. Great Expectations (D) did not guarantee a match. Under the state's Dating Service Law, where the dating service did not assure it would furnish a client with a specified number of social referrals per month, the service was permitted to charge no more than $25. The service was also required to provide notice of a three-day "cooling off" right to cancel, and to provide each client with a "Dating Service Consumer Bill of Rights." The service was also required to provide each client with several other rights. The law also provided that damages would be actual damages or $50, whichever was greater. Doe (P) and Roe (P) brought suit to recover the amounts they had paid under their respective contracts on the grounds that the contracts violated the state's Dating Service Law.

ISSUE: Where a consumer form contract violates state law that provides for actual damages or a set amount, whichever is greater, is a consumer entitled to a full refund of the contract price paid as restitutionary damages?

HOLDING AND DECISION: (Lebedeff, J.) Yes. Where a consumer form contract violates state law that provides for actual damages or a set amount, whichever is greater, a consumer is entitled to a full refund of the contract price paid as restitutionary damages. Here, the contracts fall within the purview of the Dating Service Law, which covers services that match members by creating a location and mechanism for members to assess each other by reviewing another member's video, photograph, and profile. It does not matter whether the service actually matches members; it is sufficient if the service makes available the matching of members or supplies the means for matching the members. The service here is not taken out of the law's scope merely because the matching was to be done over the Internet, since the law specifically includes services that utilize computers. Given that the service was subject to the Dating Service Law, there were numerous violations here. The most glaring was massive overcharging, since where the dating service does not ensure it will furnish a client with a specified number of social referrals per month, the service may charge no more than $25—so here the amounts charged were much greater than that (even though Roe (P) was orally assured of 12 introductions to be provided over the course of 36 months, the service failed to commit to any number of introductions in any given month, so it still violated the law in this regard). The form contract also violated every mandate of the Dating Service Law, with the single exception that each contract did contain notice of a three-day "cooling off" right to cancel. The service failed to provide to the clients written notice of a mandatory "Dating Service Consumer Bill of Rights," which also had to be provided to them and was not. Other provisions that were not provided in the contract included various cancellation rights, the right to put the membership on hold, return of a client's private information and materials, and other rights. As to damages, the Dating Service Law states that "[a]ny person who has been injured by reason of a violation of this section may bring . . . an action to recover his or her actual damages or fifty dollars whichever is greater." Here, "actual damages" includes the difference between each contract price and the $25 fee, which is the maximum fee permitted under the Dating Service Law for these contracts. Both Roe (P) and Doe (P) seek a return of the full balance paid, which raises the question of whether they establish damages justifying a return of the additional $25 each. Because (based on the credibility of the claimants) neither of them would have entered into these contracts if they had properly been informed of their rights and the contracts contained

Continued on next page.

the appropriate provisions, each claimant is entitled to a refund of the final $25 balance at issue, plus interest from the contract date. That is, they are each entitled to a full refund as restitutionary damages. This is supported by the statute's legislative history, which added "actual damages" in addition to authorizing the state's attorney general to bring enforcement actions. This "evened the playing field" by offering a single remedy of restitution to a consumer, which could be achieved by the alternate routes of commencing an individual suit or filing a complaint with the attorney general. It follows, logically, that the legislature, by adding the "actual damage" language to the statute did not intend to erode the state's commitment to protect consumers from price gouging by dating services, so that "actual damage" may include the maximum fee that may be charged by such services.

In addition, Great Expectations (D) should return personal material to each claimant, even though the contracts as written do not require it to do so, so that it will be in compliance with the law. Finally, the court has the judicial discretion to report Great Expectations (D) to the appropriate government authorities. It may do so considering all the circumstances, such as the nature of the offense, the effect of such report on the administration of justice, and, in particular, on the court's truth determining function. Also to be considered is whether a report could be "undesirable" if it "would dissuade witnesses on trial from telling the whole truth or encourage the threat of possible criminal proceedings as a means of pressure, for settlement purposes or otherwise, by one litigant against another," and whether the report is in the public interest. Weighing all these factors, it is determined that Great Expectations (D) should be reported, because, among other things, doing so is in the public interest, given that its acts violated rules governing a regulated industry and appear to reflect a continuing pattern and practice as indicated by, among other things, the use of a printed boiler plate form found not to be in accordance with applicable laws. Also, the court's past and future truth-determining function has not been, and will not be, affected by a report since the proceeding is concluded, and a question touching upon the administration of justice and the integrity of a court order may be posed in that a similar course of conduct by Great Expectations (D) or a related entity was previously litigated. Actual damages for the plaintiffs awarded.

ANALYSIS

As this case illustrates, courts may police the use of standard form contracts not only by giving effect to protective legislation by determining whether the contracts adhere to statutory law, but also by reporting violations to various government authorities, such as a state's attorney general or consumer protection agency.

Quicknotes

RESTITUTION The return or restoration to rightful owner to prevent unjust enrichment.

Williams v. Walker-Thomas Furniture Co.

Furniture buyer (D) v. Retailer (P)

350 F.2d 445 (D.C. Cir. 1965)

NATURE OF CASE: Action to replevy goods for breach of contract.

FACT SUMMARY: Walker-Thomas Furniture Co. (P) sold to Williams (D) furniture burdened by a cross-collateral clause and, subsequent to Williams's (D) default, sought to replevy all goods previously purchased by Williams (D).

RULE OF LAW

The defense of unconscionability to action on a contract is judicially recognized.

FACTS: Walker-Thomas Furniture Co. (Walker-Thomas) (P) sold furniture to Williams (D) under a printed form contract containing a cross-collateral clause, the effect of which was to keep a balance due on every item purchased until the balance due on all items, whenever purchased, was liquidated. As a result, Walker-Thomas (P) retained by the terms of the contract the right to repossess all items previously purchased in the event of any default. At the time Williams (D) made her last purchase, she had a balance of $164 still owing from her prior purchases, although she had already paid $1,400 toward clearing her account. Subsequently, Williams (D) defaulted on payment and Walker-Thomas (P) sought to replevy all goods previously sold to Williams (D). This case involves Williams's (D) defense of that action.

ISSUE: Does the court have the power to refuse enforcement of contracts found to be unconscionable?

HOLDING AND DECISION: (Wright, J.) Yes. "Where the element of unconscionability is present at the time a contract is made, the contract should not be enforced. Unconscionability has generally been recognized to include an absence of meaningful choice on the part of one of the parties together with contract terms that are unreasonably favorable to the other party." Meaningfulness of choice is to be determined in light of all the circumstances—for example, gross disparity of bargaining power. The case should be remanded to the lower court for findings on the issue of unconscionability.

DISSENT: (Danaher, J.) Congress should consider corrective legislation to protect the public from exploitative contracts.

ANALYSIS

The majority opinion, written by J. Skelly Wright, relies heavily on Uniform Commercial Code (UCC) § 2-302 to support its position. But the meaning and effect of UCC § 2-302 has been hotly debated. Comment I to that provision defines "unconscionability" in terms of itself and says its principle is to prevent "oppression and unfair surprise," not to disturb the "allocation of risks because of superior bargaining power." It is not clear whether the present case involves procedural unconscionability (i.e., some sort of "bargaining nastiness" like deliberately concealing the cross-collateral clause in a maze of fine print) or substantive unconscionability (in which case the concern is with the allegedly "unfair" terms themselves, regardless of how they were presented). It is equally unclear whether the ambiguous UCC § 2-302 is intended to apply to both kinds of unconscionability. If Judge Wright was concerned with procedural unconscionability (i.e., Walker-Thomas [P], through bargaining nastiness created Williams's [D] "lack of meaningful choice"), there is little about which to quarrel. But if he had substantive unconscionability on his mind many analytical problems arise. For example, UCC § 2-302 (2) allows the court to take "commercial setting, purpose, and effect" into account. But isn't it a business person's "commercial purpose" to make money? And if the cross-collateral clause has that "effect," why should the court strike it down (absent bargaining nastiness)? Consider further what will happen if Walker-Thomas (P) is not allowed to use its clause: either (1) furniture prices will rise correspondingly and more poor people will be unable to afford furniture at all or perhaps (2) Walker-Thomas (P) will be forced to refuse sale outright to risky clients. Unless a less onerous alternative is found, the cross-collateral clause is probably better left as is. This decision is not untypical of other Skelly Wright opinions, which are full of good intentions, but which contain potentially deeper evils with the opposite effect. (See, for example, *Javins v. First Nat. Realty Corp.*, 428 F. 2d 1071 (D.C. Cir. 1970) in the field of landlord-tenant law.) Note, finally, that any court that declares a contract "substantively" unconscionable is dealing in the dangerous and tenuous business of substituting its own valuation of the contract goods for that of the parties involved. This kind of paternalism should be approached with caution.

Quicknotes

CROSS-COLLATERAL CLAUSE Provision contained in a contract pursuant to which both parties provide security

Continued on next page.

that performance will be rendered or that payment will be made.

REPLEVIN An action to recover personal property wrongfully taken.

UNCONSCIONABILITY Rule of law whereby a court may excuse performance of a contract, or of a particular contract term, if it determines that such terms are unduly oppressive or unfair to one party to the contract as a result of disparity in bargaining power during the formation of the contract.

Stoll v. Xiong

Real estate seller (P) v. Real estate buyer (D)

Okla. Ct. Civ. App., 241 P.3d 301 (2010)

NATURE OF CASE: Appeal from summary judgment for defendants in breach of contract action, on the grounds that a clause in the contract was unconscionable as a matter of law.

FACT SUMMARY: Stoll (P), who sold farmland to Xiong (D) and his wife, Yang (D) (collectively, the Buyers) (D), contended that a provision in the land sale contract, which required the Buyers (D) to provide Stoll (P) for 30 years with all the chicken litter their poultry generated for no extra consideration, was not unconscionable.

RULE OF LAW

A contract is unconscionable where, if enforced, it would render the actual price of the contract so gross as to shock the conscience and would be onerous to one side of the contracting parties while solely benefitting the other, so that no fair and honest person would propose, and no rational person would enter into, such a contract.

FACTS: In January 2005, Stoll (P) sold 60 acres of farmland to Xiong (D) and Yang (D) (collectively, the Buyers) (D), for $2,000 per acre plus $10,000 for an access road. Xiong (D) and Yang (D), a married couple, were immigrants from Laos and were relatively uneducated and illiterate. Xiong's (D) sister and her husband (the Lees), who had purchased adjacent land from Stoll (P), and who likewise were immigrants who did not know English well, assisted Xiong (D) and Yang (D) with the transaction (in fact, the Lees were the subject of a companion action brought by Stoll (P) that raised the same issues as those in this case). Stoll (P), on his own initiative, had included a clause in the land sale contract that provided that the Buyers (D) would build a chicken litter shed into which they would place all the litter from their chickens every year, and that Stoll (P) would be entitled to take that litter each year for 30 years. The provision did not provide for any compensation to the Buyers (D) for their efforts and costs in generating and gathering the litter, or for the litter itself. (An identical provision was at issue in the companion case against the Lees). In February 2009, Xiong (D) traded the chicken litter from the first complete clean out of their six poultry houses for shavings. At the time, the annual value of the litter from de-caking alone (i.e., which did not include additional volumes of litter from a complete clean out) ranged from roughly $7,200 to $15,000. For 30 years, the estimated value of the de-caked chicken litter using the lower value of the range would be $216,000, or roughly an additional $3,325.12 more per acre just from de-caked chicken litter sales than the $2,000 per acre purchase price stated on the first page of the contract. In late March 2009, after Stoll (P) discovered the Buyers (D) were selling the litter to others, and that the chicken shed on their property was empty, he brought suit for breach of contract, seeking specific performance and a temporary injunction to prevent the Buyers (D) from selling their chicken litter to third-parties. The Buyers (D), who answered and stated various affirmative defenses and counterclaims, moved for summary judgment on the grounds that the contract was unconscionable as a matter of law. Stoll (P) likewise moved for summary judgment, alleging, inter alia, that the Buyers (D) had a prior draft of their agreement that contained the same paragraph in dispute but did not attempt to have it translated or explained to them, and that they should not benefit by failing to take such steps or from their failure to read the agreement. At the hearing on the opposing motions for summary judgment, Stoll (P) argued the contract was not unconscionable and it was simply a matter of buyer's remorse. The Buyers (D) responded, arguing their illiteracy forced them to rely upon representations made to them and the interpreter available to them, Xiong's (D) sister, explained the land purchase price but did not herself understand the meaning of the chicken litter paragraph. The trial court, finding that the chicken litter clause was unconscionable as a matter of law, granted summary judgment to the Buyers (D) and entered judgment accordingly. The state's intermediate appellate court granted review.

ISSUE: Is a contract unconscionable where, if enforced, it would render the actual price of the contract so gross as to shock the conscience and would be onerous to one side of the contracting parties while solely benefitting the other, so that no fair and honest person would propose, and no rational person would enter into, such a contract?

HOLDING AND DECISION: (Hetherington, Jr., J.) Yes. A contract is unconscionable where, if enforced, it would render the actual price of the contract so gross as to shock the conscience and would be onerous to one side of the contracting parties while solely benefitting the other, so that no fair and honest person would propose, and no rational person would enter into, such a contract. The question of unconscionability is one of law for a court to decide. Here, if the clause at issue were given effect, Stoll (P) would effectively become a partner in Xiong (D) and Yang's (D) (collectively, the Buyers') business for no consideration, or he would receive almost double to much

Continued on next page.

more than double the purchase price for his land over 30 years. Such an arrangement shocks the conscience. The consideration actually to be paid under the contract would far exceed that stated, and the contract would be onerous to one side of the contracting parties while solely benefitting the other. Here, the parties to be surcharged with the extra expense were, due to language and education, unable to understand the nature of the contract. In essence, the actual price the Buyers (D) would pay under the paragraph Stoll (P) included in the land sale contract is so gross as to shock the conscience. As the Buyers (D) argued, no fair and honest person would propose, and no rational person would enter into, a contract containing a clause imposing a premium for land and that, without any consideration to them, imposes additional costs in the hundreds of thousands over a 30-year period that both are unrelated to the land itself and far exceed the value of the land. Affirmed.

ANALYSIS

As this case illustrates, the equitable concept of unconscionability is meaningful only within the context of otherwise defined factors of onerous inequality, deception, and oppression. The determination of unconscionability thus must be made in light of all circumstances existing at the time of the contract's making. Additionally, unconscionability has generally been recognized to include an absence of meaningful choice on the part of one of the parties, together with contractual terms that are unreasonably favorable to the other party. In this case, therefore, it was significant to the court's determination that Xiong (D) and Yang (D), because of their lack of education and their language skills, truly did not understand the ramifications of the chicken litter clause, so they could not assent to it.

Quicknotes

BREACH OF CONTRACT Unlawful failure by a party to perform its obligations pursuant to contract.

SHOCK THE CONSCIENCE This phrase is used to express judicial disapproval of some type of outrageous conduct or outcome.

UNCONSCIONABILITY Rule of law whereby a court may excuse performance of a contract, or of a particular contract term, if it determines that such terms are unduly oppressive or unfair to one party to the contract as a result of disparity in bargaining power during the formation of the contract.

Prasad v. Pinnacle Property Management Services, LLC

Employee (P) v. Employer (D)

2018 WL 4599645 (N.D. Cal. 2018)

NATURE OF CASE: Motion to compel arbitration pursuant to an employment arbitration agreement.

FACT SUMMARY: Prasad (P), an employee of Pinnacle Property Management Services, LLC (Pinnacle) (D), contended that Pinnacle's (D) Issue Resolution Agreement (IRA), which contained an arbitration provision for resolution of disputes arising out of an employee's employment, was unconscionable, and, therefore, should not be enforced. Pinnacle (D) countered that the IRA was not unconscionable, that if any provisions of the IRA were found to be unconscionable, those provisions could be severed from the IRA, and the remainder could properly be enforced. Accordingly, Pinnacle (D) moved to compel arbitration in an action brought against it in federal district court by Prasad (P).

RULE OF LAW

Where an employment arbitration agreement contains unconscionable provisions that are collateral to the agreement's main purpose, the agreement may be enforced after severing the unconscionable provisions.

FACTS: Prasad (P) was an employee of Pinnacle Property Management Services, LLC (Pinnacle) (D). She (P) brought a putative class action in federal district court against Pinnacle (D), asserting numerous claims arising from Pinnacle's (D) employment of her and others. Additionally, she (P) asserted several individual claims. Pinnacle (D) moved to compel arbitration pursuant to an Issue Resolution Agreement (IRA) it claimed Prasad (P) assented to and signed when she applied for employment with the company. The IRA provided, in relevant part, that all claims arising out of or relating to employment with Pinnacle (D) would be exclusively resolved by binding arbitration. The IRA also contained a class action waiver. Prasad (P) opposed Pinnacle's (D) motion on the grounds that the IRA was unconscionable and, therefore, unenforceable. Based on an intervening United States Supreme Court case, *Epic Sys. Corp. v. Lewis*, 138 S. Ct. 1612 (2018), Prasad (P) conceded that her challenge to the class arbitration waiver was foreclosed, so that she could no longer maintain her class claims, but she nevertheless maintained that *Epic* did not affect her unconscionability argument. Pinnacle (D) maintained that the IRA was neither procedurally nor substantively unconscionable, and that, to the extent there were any improper provisions, those could be severed from the IRA and the remainder of the IRA could properly be enforced. The district court considered the motion to compel.

ISSUE: Where an employment arbitration agreement contains unconscionable provisions that are collateral to the agreement's main purpose, may the agreement be enforced after severing the unconscionable provisions?

HOLDING AND DECISION: (Demarchi, J.) Yes. Where an employment arbitration agreement contains unconscionable provisions that are collateral to the agreement's main purpose, the agreement may be enforced after severing the unconscionable provisions. Although the Federal Arbitration Act (FAA) governs the enforceability and scope of an arbitration agreement, in determining whether grounds exist to invalidate an arbitration agreement or its provisions, such as unconscionability, a court will apply state-law principles that govern the formation of contracts. Under state [California] law, unconscionability has both a procedural and a substantive element, the former focusing on oppression or surprise due to unequal bargaining power, the latter on overly harsh or one-sided results. A court will first determine if an agreement is procedurally unconscionable. Hence, the unconscionability analysis begins with an inquiry into whether the contract is one of adhesion, i.e., a standardized contract, which, imposed and drafted by the party of superior bargaining strength, relegates to the subscribing party only the opportunity to adhere to the contract or reject it. If the contract is adhesive, the court must then determine whether other factors are present that operate to render it unenforceable. The specter of unconscionability is particularly strong in the employment setting, where economic pressure exerted by employers on all but the most sought-after employees may be particularly acute. Here, Prasad (P) satisfies the oppression aspect of procedural unconscionability. She contends that the Issue Resolution Agreement (IRA) is a non-negotiable contract of adhesion, offered on a take-it-or-leave-it basis, and Pinnacle Property Management Services, LLC (Pinnacle) (D) concedes that it had superior bargaining power. Although she does not satisfy the surprise element of procedural unconscionability, Prasad (P) nonetheless contends that she did not make an informed decision with respect to the IRA because the IRA (1) contained a number of unfavorable terms, which were scattered throughout the IRA, and (2) failed to disclose the disadvantages imposed upon her by those terms. Although Pinnacle (D) asserts that the IRA clearly stated that it was an arbitration agreement, courts have held that a one-sided explanation of benefits, without a corresponding explanation of disadvantages of arbitration, render an arbitration

Continued on next page.

agreement procedurally unconscionable. For these reasons, Prasad (P) has established some procedural unconscionability, given that the IRA was a contract of adhesion with no meaningful opt-out, and that her agreement to the IRA was not an informed decision to the extent that the IRA does not explain the potential pitfalls and drawbacks of proceeding with arbitration versus litigation. However, a finding of procedural unconscionability does not mean that a contract will not be enforced, but rather that courts will conduct a substantive unconscionability analysis that will scrutinize the substantive terms of the contract to ensure they are not manifestly unfair or one-sided as of the time the contract was made. Prasad (P) argues that the IRA is substantively unconscionable for six reasons. The first reason is that the class arbitration waiver provision was unconscionable, but given the Supreme Court's decision in *Epic*, Prasad (P) concedes this waiver no longer is a basis for finding unconscionability. Accordingly, the waiver provision is not unconscionable. The second reason is that the IRA imposes a one-sided, one-year limitations period only on employees. Prasad (P) argues that this provision is unconscionable because the statutes on which her claims are based have limitations periods of more than one year, i.e., up to four years. She (P) also argues that in this regard the IRA is doubly unfair because it only shortens the limitations period for employees, not for Pinnacle (D). Pinnacle (D) acknowledges some unfairness inherent in this provision but says the level of unconscionability relative to the IRA as a whole is slim. It argues that this is so because the IRA does not affect tolling doctrines under applicable state laws or an employee's ability to arbitrate continuing violations. On balance, this provision is substantively unconscionable because it shortens the limitations period only for employees, and Pinnacle (D) has not presented a reason why a unilateral reduction in the statute of limitations is required. The third reason is that the IRA requires employees to pay a $50.00 filing fee to Pinnacle (D) to initiate arbitration. Prasad (P) argues this is unconscionable because it essentially requires employees to pay Pinnacle (D) for the privilege of bringing a claim. Pinnacle (D) responds that the fee goes toward the cost of arbitration and is not retained by Pinnacle (D); that the fee is much smaller than the fee to initiate a court action ($400); and that Prasad (P) never claimed an inability to pay the court filing fee. All these arguments are unavailing. The state's highest court has ruled that when an employer imposes mandatory arbitration as a condition of employment, the arbitration agreement or arbitration process cannot generally require the employee to bear any type of expense that the employee would not be required to bear if he or she were free to bring the action in court. Here, because the fee essentially requires employees to pay the fee to the very entity against which they seek redress, and therefore would not be a type of expense that the employee would be required to bear in court, the IRA's filing fee is substantively unconscionable. The fourth reason pressed by Prasad (P) is that the IRA requires the parties to split the costs of arbitration, no matter what the result, except that the employee's share is limited to $100. The court of appeals has held that the fact that an employee potentially could be held responsible for the defendant employer's arbitration costs if her claim fails is sufficient to find the cost-sharing provision unconscionable, and that such a cost-sharing provision is especially unfair because it would require even a successful employee to bear her share of the arbitration costs. Based on a strict interpretation of this precedent, the IRA's cost-sharing provision is unconscionable, but only to a very small degree. Prasad's (P) fifth reason is that the IRA is unconscionable because it gives Pinnacle (D) the unilateral right to modify or terminate the IRA's terms. Pinnacle (D) argues that any measure of unconscionability is minimal because the IRA clearly requires advance notice to employees and also prohibits retroactive modifications. However, the court of appeals has held that such advance notice is trivial when there is no meaningful opportunity to negotiate the terms of the agreement, so that by granting itself the sole authority to amend or terminate the arbitration agreement, an employer proscribes an employee's ability to consider and negotiate the terms of her contract. Based on this controlling precedent, the IRA's unilateral modification provision is unconscionable because it withholds bargaining power from employees and because the IRA is a contract of adhesion in the first instance. The sixth and final reason is that the IRA provides that the arbitration will be confidential, except in a narrow set of circumstances. Prasad (P) argues that such provisions favor companies over employees because they essentially operate as "gag orders" and make it difficult for a plaintiff to mitigate the effects of bad behavior by a "repeat offender" employer. Pinnacle (D) contends that the confidentiality provision is not unconscionable because it provides that the parties can agree otherwise and also provides that arbitration will not be confidential if confidentiality is disallowed by statute. Although the court of appeals in other cases held that confidentiality provisions that are so broad as to prevent an employee from investigating and preparing her case are unconscionable, the IRA provision here is not nearly as broad as those held unconscionable by the court of appeals. Moreover, the court of appeals endorsed a state court's ruling on a confidentiality provision much like the one in the IRA, that there is nothing unreasonable or prejudicial about "a secrecy provision with respect to the parties themselves." Therefore, the IRA's confidentiality provision is not substantively unconscionable.

Pinnacle (D) argues that any unconscionable terms may be severed from the IRA, and that the remaining terms properly may be enforced. Prasad (P) contends that any agreement that contains more than one unconscionable term necessarily is permeated with unlawfulness

Continued on next page.

and must be held unenforceable. Under state law, courts have discretion whether to sever unconscionable clauses and enforce the remainder of a contract, but refuse to enforce the entire agreement, only when it is permeated by unconscionability and its central purpose is tainted thereby. If, however, unconscionable provisions are collateral to the agreement's main purpose and can be severed or restricted, then such severance and restriction are appropriate. Here, claims of both Pinnacle (D) and its employees are subject to arbitration, and there is no limitation on the relief available to employees. Although several provisions of the IRA are unconscionable, each of those provisions is collateral to the IRA's central purpose, which is to provide an alternate forum for the resolution of disputes between Pinnacle (D) and its employees. Thus, the IRA is not so tainted with illegality that there is no lawful object of the contract to enforce, nor would extirpating the unconscionable provisions from the IRA render the contract a nullity. Accordingly, the IRA's unconscionable provisions are severed, and Pinnacle's (D) motion to compel arbitration of Prasad's (P) individual claims is granted pursuant to the severed IRA. Motion to compel granted; judgment for Pinnacle (D).

ANALYSIS

In contrast to the court's holding in this decision, courts have refused to enforce an agreement where unconscionable provisions are too numerous and too important to be severed from the whole. For example, two defects in an employment arbitration agreement that rendered the agreement as a whole unconscionable were (1) a provision that purported to limit an employee's damages allowed by statute; and (2) provisions that made arbitration unilateral, i.e., employees were required to arbitrate their claims against the employer, but the employer was free to litigate its claims against employees in court. Although the unlawful damages provision by itself would not have justified a court's refusal to enforce the agreement, the lack of a bilateral arbitration requirement as between the employer and its employees was not a defect that could be fixed by severance or restriction, but only by the addition of terms. Because such reformation of the contract was not authorized, the entire agreement was found unenforceable, especially when combined with other terms that stacked the deck unconscionably in favor of the employer. See, e.g., *Armendariz v. Foundation Health Psychcare Servs., Inc.*, 24 Cal. 4th 83 (2000); *Ingle v. Circuit City Stores, Inc.*, 328 F.3d 1165 (9th Cir. 2003).

Quicknotes

ADHESION CONTRACT A contract, usually in standardized form, that is prepared by one party and offered to another, whose terms are so disproportionately in favor of the drafting party that courts tend to question the equality of bargaining power in reaching the agreement.

ARBITRATION CLAUSE Provision contained in a contract pursuant to which both parties agree that any disputes arising thereunder will be resolved through arbitration.

CLASS ACTION A suit commenced by a representative on behalf of an ascertainable group that is too large to appear in court, who share a commonality of interests and who will benefit from a successful result.

PROCEDURAL RULE Rule relating to the process of carrying out a lawsuit.

SUBSTANTIVE UNCONSCIONABILITY Rule of law whereby a court may excuse performance of a contract, or of a particular contract term, if it determines that such terms are unduly oppressive or unfair to one party to the contract and violate the subordinate party's reasonable expectations.

Dalton v. Educational Testing Service

Test taker (P) v. Testing service (D)

N.Y. Ct. App., 87 N.Y.2d 384, 663 N.E.2d 289 (1995)

NATURE OF CASE: Breach of contract suit.

FACT SUMMARY: Dalton (P) sued Education Testing Service (ETS) (D) after ETS (D) informed him that they were canceling his second SAT score on the basis that it was taken by another individual.

RULE OF LAW

Implicit in all contracts is a covenant of good faith and fair dealing.

FACTS: Dalton (P) took the Scholastic Aptitude Test (SAT) two times, the second time increasing his score more than 410 points. The members of Education Testing Service (ETS) (D) reviewed his exams and, upon concluding there was disparate handwriting, submitted the exams to a handwriting specialist who opined they were taken by two different people. Dalton's (P) later score was subsequently canceled. Dalton (P) commenced suit to prevent ETS (D) from canceling the score. The trial court found that ETS (D) breached its contract to act in good faith and ordered the immediate release of the score. The appellate division affirmed.

ISSUE: Is a covenant of good faith and fair dealing implicit in all contracts?

HOLDING AND DECISION: (Kaye, C.J.) Yes. Implicit in all contracts is a covenant of good faith and fair dealing. Encompassed within that implied obligation is a pledge that neither party will interfere with the right of the other to "receive the fruits of the contract." Where the contract is discretionary, this includes a pledge not to act arbitrarily or irrationally in exercising that discretion. However, no obligation may be implied that is inconsistent with the terms of the contract. ETS (D) failed to meet its obligation in not considering relevant material provided by Dalton (P) and thus did not meet its covenant of good faith. Affirmed as modified.

ANALYSIS

Note that the court states that once the relevant material information is considered by Education Testing Service (D), then it fulfills its contractual obligation and becomes the "final arbiter" of the appropriate weight to accord such information and the validity of Dalton's (P) score. Such determination is considered discretionary and is subject to the arbitrary or irrational standard.

Quicknotes

SPECIFIC PERFORMANCE An equitable remedy whereby the court requires the parties to perform their obligations pursuant to a contract.

Northwest, Inc. v. Ginsberg

Airline (D) v. Frequent flyer (P)

572 U.S. 273 (2014)

NATURE OF CASE: Appeal in putative class action asserting breach of the implied covenant of good faith and fair dealing.

FACT SUMMARY: Ginsberg (P), a former member of Northwest, Inc.'s (D) frequent flyer program, brought a putative class action against Northwest (D) claiming, inter alia, that the airline had terminated his membership in the program in violation of the implied duty of good faith and fair dealing. Northwest (D) contended that the Airline Deregulation Act of 1978 (ADA) preempted his claim.

RULE OF LAW

The Airline Deregulation Act of 1978 preempts a state-law claim for breach of the implied covenant of good faith and fair dealing if it seeks to enlarge the contractual obligations that the parties voluntarily adopt.

FACTS: Ginsberg (P) had been a member of Northwest, Inc.'s (D) airline frequent flyer program, WorldPerks, and, as a result of extensive travel achieved "Platinum Elite" status (the highest level available). The WorldPerks agreement permitted Northwest (D), in its sole discretion, to terminate a member's account for abusing the program or improper conduct, as determined by Northwest (D). Relying on this provision of the agreement, Northwest (D) terminated Ginsberg's (P) Platinum Elite status on the grounds that he had abused the program—by complaining about late-arriving luggage and other travel problems and by requesting compensation therefor. Alleging that Northwest (D) had ended his membership as a cost-cutting measure tied to Northwest's (D) merger with another airline, Ginsberg (P) filed a class action in federal district court on behalf of himself and all other similarly situated WorldPerks members. One of his claims was that Northwest (D) had violated the duty of good faith and fair dealing because it terminated his membership in a way that contravened his reasonable expectations with respect to the manner in which Northwest (D) would exercise its discretion. The district court held that this claim was preempted by the Airline Deregulation Act of 1978. The United States Supreme Court granted certiorari in the case.

ISSUE: Does the Airline Deregulation Act of 1978 (ADA) preempt a state-law claim for breach of the implied covenant of good faith and fair dealing if it seeks to enlarge the contractual obligations that the parties voluntarily adopt?

HOLDING AND DECISION: (Alito, J.) Yes. The Airline Deregulation Act of 1978 (ADA) preempts a state-law claim for breach of the implied covenant of good faith and fair dealing if it seeks to enlarge the contractual obligations that the parties voluntarily adopt. Terms and obligations of an agreement that is privately negotiated are not subject to preemption, but those imposed by a state are preempted. Here, it is clear Ginsberg's (P) implied covenant claim is based on a state-imposed obligation under the applicable state law [Minnesota]. Under that law, parties cannot contract out of the covenant, which shows that the obligation cannot be implied, but is law imposed. When a state law does not authorize parties to free themselves from the covenant, a breach of covenant claim is pre-empted under the ADA. This conclusion is supported by the fact that state law applicable here holds that the implied covenant applies to "every contract," with the notable exception of employment contracts. The exception for employment contracts is based, in significant part, on policy reasons, and, therefore, the decision not to exempt other types of contracts must be based on a policy determination, namely, that the policy reasons that support the rule for employment contracts do not apply (at least with the same force) in other contexts. When the application of the implied covenant depends on state policy, a breach of implied covenant claim cannot be viewed as simply an attempt to vindicate the parties' implicit understanding of the contract. For these reasons, Ginsberg's (P) implied covenant of good faith and fair dealing is preempted and must be dismissed.

ANALYSIS

Based on this decision, whether an airline's frequent flyer program, or any other customer program, is preempted by the Airline Deregulation Act of 1978 will depend on state law, thus potentially presenting the airlines with a patchwork of rules they would have to follow. However, in those instances where a state's laws govern the airline's customer agreements, and the state's implied covenant rules permit an airline to contract around such rules, the airline could specify that the agreement does not incorporate the covenant. Although the inclusion of such a provision could potentially impose transaction costs, and presumably would not enhance the attractiveness of the program,

Continued on next page.

an airline can decide whether the benefits of such a provision are worth the potential costs.

Quicknotes

IMPLIED COVENANT OF GOOD FAITH AND FAIR DEALING An implied warranty that the parties will deal honestly in the satisfaction of their obligations and without an intent to defraud.

Market Street Associates v. Frey

Lessee's assignee (P) v. Lessor (D)

941 F.2d 588 (7th Cir. 1991)

NATURE OF CASE: Appeal from summary judgment dismissing action seeking specific performance.

FACT SUMMARY: A principal of Market Street Associates (P) allegedly deliberately failed to notify General Electric Pension Trust (General Electric) (D) of a particular paragraph in a contract that could result in forfeiture of General Electric's (D) property.

RULE OF LAW

A party to a contract may not intentionally exploit the other party's oversight of an important fact.

FACTS: J.C. Penney entered into a sale-leaseback arrangement with General Electric Pension Trust (General Electric) (D) on a property. Paragraph 34 in the lease provided if General Electric (D) failed to negotiate with the lessee regarding future financing, the property could be purchased at less than market value. Years later Market Street Associates (Market Street) (P)—J.C. Penney's assignee—attempted to negotiate financing with General Electric (D). General Electric (D), no longer being aware of the clause, refused to negotiate. Market Street (P) then sought to exercise its option and sued for specific performance. At his deposition, the principal of Market Street (P) primarily responsible for the property testified his counterpart at General Electric (D) might not be aware of the clause and that he had realized it during negotiations. Based on this, the district court entered summary judgment dismissing the action, holding Market Street (P) to have acted in bad faith. Market Street (P) appealed.

ISSUE: May a party to a contract intentionally exploit the other party's oversight of an important fact?

HOLDING AND DECISION: (Posner, J.) No. A party to a contract may not intentionally exploit the other party's oversight of an important fact. That parties to a contract must act in good faith does not mean, as some courts seem to believe, that the parties must act in an altruistic or fiduciary manner toward each other; they need not do so. Furthermore, it is quite legitimate for a party to use his superior knowledge to drive an advantageous bargain. However, it is one thing to have superior knowledge, but it is quite another to know that the other party is unaware of a crucial fact and take advantage of this ignorance. This constitutes sharp practice, which departs from good faith. Here, the district court held that Market Street Associates's (P) principal had engaged in such conduct. This may be true, but it is a factual issue, addressable only at trial, not at the summary judgment level. Reversed and remanded.

ANALYSIS

A mutual mistake is grounds for nullifying a contract or a term thereof. Unilateral mistake may or may not be. As the court stated here, unilateral mistake combined with an opponent's overreaching may be grounds for rescission.

Quicknotes

GOOD FAITH An honest intention to abstain from taking advantage of another.

MUTUAL MISTAKE A mistake to a contract by both parties, who are in agreement as to what the contract terms should be, but the agreement as written fails to reflect that common intent; such contracts are voidable or subject to reformation.

RESCISSION The canceling of an agreement and the return of the parties to their positions prior to the formation of the contract.

SPECIFIC PERFORMANCE An equitable remedy whereby the court requires the parties to perform their obligations pursuant to a contract.

SUMMARY JUDGMENT Judgment rendered by a court in response to a motion made by one of the parties, claiming that the lack of a question of material fact in respect to an issue warrants disposition of the issue without consideration by the jury.

Bloor v. Falstaff Brewing Corp.

Trustee (P) v. Brewery (D)

601 F.2d 609 (2d Cir. 1979)

NATURE OF CASE: Action for damages for breach of contract.

FACT SUMMARY: Bloor (P), Reorganization Trustee of the once-successful Ballantine Brewery, brought suit alleging that Falstaff Brewing Corp. (D) had breached its contractual obligation to use its "best efforts to promote and maintain a high volume of sales" of the Ballantine brands.

RULE OF LAW

A contractual provision obligating one to use its "best efforts" to promote and maintain a high volume of sales of a certain product is breached by a policy that emphasizes profit without fair consideration of the effect on sales volume.

FACTS: Falstaff Brewing Corp. (Falstaff) (D) contracted to purchase Ballantine's brewing labels, trademarks, etc., for $4 million plus a fifty-cent royalty on each barrel of Ballantine brands sold between 1972 and 1978. The contract provided Falstaff (D) would use its best efforts to promote and maintain a high volume of sales of Ballantine products and contained a liquidated damages clause operative if Falstaff (D) ever substantially discontinued distribution of beer under the brand name "Ballantine." With policies based on profit to Falstaff (D), there was a continual decline in sales volume, and Bloor (P)—the Reorganization Trustee of the company that had been Ballantine & Sons—sued to recover damages for breach of contract. The trial court found Falstaff (D) had breached the best efforts clause, for which damages were to be awarded, but that such did not trigger the liquidated damages clause.

ISSUE: Does one breach a contract obligating one to use best efforts to maintain a high volume of sales of an item if one makes policy based primarily on considerations of profit?

HOLDING AND DECISION: (Friendly, J.) Yes. Where, as in this case, a party contractually obligates itself to use its best efforts to promote and maintain a high volume of sales of a particular item, its action in making policies and decisions based primarily on considerations of profit and without fair consideration of the effect on sales volume constitutes a breach of that contractual provision, and damages may be sought. Even accounting for Falstaff Brewing Corp.'s (D) right to give reasonable consideration to its own interest, including the profit interest, it breached its duty to use best efforts to maintain and promote a high sales volume with regard to Ballantine brands. It must therefore pay damages based on a reasonable estimate of the royalties that would have been paid had such breach not occurred. That was the standard used by the lower court. Affirmed.

ANALYSIS

Uniform Commercial Code § 2-306(2) provides for the imposition of an obligation on the part of both parties to an agreement for exclusive dealing in goods to use their "best efforts." It is a codification of the judicially made rule that was formed over the years, i.e., that certain contracts carried an implied obligation to use "best efforts" because they would otherwise lack mutuality of obligation.

Quicknotes

BEST EFFORTS In order to enforce an agreement pursuant to which only one party appears to be furnishing consideration, the court will imply a promise on the part of the other party to use its best efforts.

LIQUIDATED DAMAGES An amount of money specified in a contract representing the damages owed in the event of breach.

Blossom Farm Products Co. v. Kasson Cheese Co., Inc.

Supplier of cheese additive (P) v. Buyer of cheese additive (D)

Wis. Ct. App., 133 Wis.2d 386, 395 N.W.2d 619 (1986)

NATURE OF CASE: Appeal from judgment dismissing an action to recover money owed on a contract.

FACT SUMMARY: Blossom Farm Products Co. (Blossom) (P) contended that its open-account contract with Kasson Cheese Co., Inc. (Kasson) (D) for the cheese additive Isokappacase was not illegal and could be enforced, so that it could recover monies owed by Kasson (D) to Blossom (P).

RULE OF LAW

Where there is evidence that a contract's promisee has knowingly acted under the contract to further the promisor's improper conduct, the contract is unenforceable on grounds of public policy, so the promisee cannot recover on the contract.

FACTS: Blossom Farm Products Co. (Blossom) (P) sold the cheese additive Isokappacase to Kasson Cheese Co., Inc. (Kasson) (D), a cheese manufacturer, under an open-account contract. Isokappacase could be used both as a "starter" medium for cheese and as a "yield enhancer." Under federal rules, if it was used as a yield enhancer, the resulting product had to be labeled as imitation cheese, rather than as real cheese. The state adopted those federal standards. Kasson (D) used the Isokappacase as a yield enhancer but failed to comply with the federal and state standards, by failing to label its products as imitation cheese. Blossom (P) had to have been aware that Kasson's (D) extremely large volume purchases of the product could only be accounted for by Kasson's (D) use of Isokappacase as a yield enhancer, and both parties benefited economically from this volume purchase and use. In fact, Kasson (D) purchased about 100 times as much Isokappacase as it would have needed if it was using it only as a starter medium. Moreover, because imitation cheese commanded only half the price of real cheese, those in the industry who worked with Isokappacase knew that Kasson could not possibly have survived economically if its end product had been sold as an imitation cheese. When Blossom (P) brought suit for payment of over $138,000 owed to it by Kasson (D) for Kasson's (D) last purchase of Isokappacase, the trial court, finding the contract between the parties to be illegal and therefore unenforceable, dismissed Blossom's (P) action. The state's intermediate appellate court granted review.

ISSUE: Where there is evidence that a contract's promisee has knowingly acted under the contract to further the promisor's improper conduct, is the contract unenforceable on grounds of public policy, so the promisee cannot recover on the contract?

HOLDING AND DECISION: (Scott, C.J.) Yes. Where there is evidence that a contract's promisee has knowingly acted under the contract to further the promisor's improper conduct, the contract is unenforceable on grounds of public policy, so the promisee cannot recover on the contract. Generally, if a promisee has substantially performed its part of the contract, enforcement of a promise is not precluded on grounds of public policy because of some improper use that the promisor intends to make of what the promisor obtains. However, if the promisee acts for the purpose of furthering the promisor's improper use, the promisee is barred from recovering, and whether the promisee has acted for such purpose is a question of fact. Here, sufficient evidence supported the trial court's findings that Kasson Cheese Co., Inc. (Kasson) (D) had acted improperly and that notwithstanding Blossom Farm Products Co.'s (Blossom's) (P) knowledge of the improper conduct it continued to do business with Kasson (D). Blossom's (P) contract to sell Isokappacase to Kasson (D) was legal, since the use of a yield enhancer is legal as long as the end product is properly labeled. Even with Kasson's (D) intended purpose of improperly labeling its end product, enforcement of Kasson's (D) promise to pay Blossom (P) for the Isokappacase would not be precluded on grounds of public policy without knowledgeable involvement by Blossom (P). Testimony from several parties involved in the production of Isokappacase and the cheese industry provided sufficient evidence of Blossom's (P) knowledgeable involvement in Kasson's (D) improper conduct. Thus, despite Blossom's (P) direct knowledge of Kasson's (D) use of Isokappacase as a yield enhancer and its tacit knowledge of Kasson's (D) misbranding of its end product as real cheese, it still continued to ship volume orders of Isokappacase to Kasson (D), thereby facilitating Kasson's (D) improper conduct. Whether a contract term is rendered unenforceable on public policy grounds requires careful balancing, in light of all the circumstances, of (1) the strength of that policy as manifested by legislation or judicial decisions; (2) the likelihood that a refusal to enforce the term will further that policy; (3) the seriousness of any misconduct involved and the extent to which it was deliberate; and (4) the directness of the connection between that misconduct and the term. If the conduct

Continued on next page.

to be engaged in by the promisor is deemed improper conduct because it is against public policy, the promisee's doing of specific acts to facilitate the improper use is a bar to recovery. Here, the state legislature's adoption of federal standards enforces the public policy of accurately distinguishing imitation or analog cheese from real cheese and labeling it accordingly. Despite being aware of Kasson's (D) improper conduct, Blossom (P) chose to overlook it and continued to supply volume shipments to Kasson (D), thereby engaging in a course of dealing that facilitated Kasson (D) in its improper conduct while benefitting both Blossom (P) and Kasson (D). Because mislabeling cheese involves conduct offensive to public policy, the trial court correctly concluded that the transaction that anticipated such improper conduct is unenforceable. Affirmed.

ANALYSIS

The appellate court in this case took pains to distinguish between an illegal contract and a contract that is unenforceable on public policy grounds. Although the trial court had held that the contract was "illegal," the appellate court expressly restricted its holding to whether the contract was unenforceable. Because state cases relied on by the parties had not distinguished between illegal contracts that are unenforceable and legal contracts that contravene public policy and are thus unenforceable, the appellate court relied on the Restatement (Second) of Contracts (1981), which makes such a distinction. Thus, although the contract between Blossom Farm Products Co. (Blossom) (P) and Kasson Cheese Co., Inc. (D) was legal, it was unenforceable on public policy grounds.

Quicknotes

PROMISEE The party to whom a promise is made.

PROMISOR The party who promises to render an obligation to another in the future.

PUBLIC POLICY Policy administered by the state with respect to the health, safety, and morals of its people in accordance with common notions of fairness and decency.

X.L.O. Concrete Corp. v. Rivergate Corp.

Concrete subcontractor (P) v. General contractor (D)

N.Y. Ct. App. 83 N.Y.2d 513, 634 N.E.2d 158 (1994)

NATURE OF CASE: Certified question in action for breach of contract, account stated, and unjust enrichment.

FACT SUMMARY: When X.L.O. Concrete Corp. (P) completed a project allocated to it by the Mafia, Rivergate Corp. (D) refused to pay the balance due on the contract on the ground that it was part of an extortion and labor bribery operation.

RULE OF LAW

Antitrust defenses to a contract will be upheld where enforcement of the contract would compel the precise conduct made unlawful by the antitrust laws.

FACTS: The "Club" was made up of the heads of several Mafia families who controlled the subcontracting of concrete contractors in the city of New York. X.L.O. Concrete Corp. (X.L.O.) (P) was awarded a project through the Club. Rivergate Corp. (D), the general contractor, negotiated the contract in full awareness of the involvement of the Club. X.L.O. (P) fully performed the contract, but Rivergate (D) refused to pay the outstanding balance, contending that the contract violated the New York antitrust laws and was therefore per se illegal. X.L.O. (P) brought suit for breach of contract.

ISSUE: Will antitrust defenses to a contract be upheld if enforcement of the contract would compel the precise conduct made unlawful by the antitrust laws?

HOLDING AND DECISION: (Ciparick, J.) Yes. Antitrust defenses to a contract will be upheld where enforcement of the contract would compel the precise conduct made unlawful by the antitrust laws. Allowing the use of antitrust defenses often has the effect of enriching the party who has reaped the benefit of a contract and then tries to avoid paying for those benefits. Therefore, the defense should only be allowed when not enforcing the contract would prevent the activity the antitrust laws were intended to prevent. In deciding whether to permit the interposition of an antitrust defense, the court must consider whether the contract was an indivisible, effectuating component of an illegal arrangement, whether the contract price was excessive, and whether sustaining the illegality defense would render the contract void. The relative culpability, bargaining power, and knowledge of the parties should also be considered in assessing the possibility of unjust enrichment. These are all questions that require further development at trial. Affirmed and the certified question answered in the affirmative.

ANALYSIS

The court also noted that public policy favored frustrating or discouraging the sorts of schemes perpetuated by the Club. However, other remedies were available to the state attorney general, including injunctions and prosecutions, that would attack the alleged antitrust violations in a more direct fashion. In addition, state law provided that the injured party could recover treble damages and other relief for antitrust violations.

Quicknotes

BREACH OF CONTRACT Unlawful failure by a party to perform its obligations pursuant to contract.

BRIBERY The offering, giving, receiving, or soliciting of something of value for the purpose of influencing the action of an official in the discharge of his or her public or legal duties.

EXTORTION The unlawful taking of property of another by threats of force.

PUBLIC POLICY Policy administered by the state with respect to the health, safety, and morals of its people in accordance with common notions of fairness and decency.

UNJUST ENRICHMENT The principle of retaining a benefit given to one by another, without compensating the giver, in situations where compensation is reasonably expected.

Shadis v. Beal

Prevailing party in class action (P) v. State official (D)

685 F.2d 824 (3d Cir. 1982)

NATURE OF CASE: Appeal from judgment holding that a contact provision between a state and a legal services corporation that denied attorney's fees in cases brought against the state or its employees was void as against federal public policy.

FACT SUMMARY: The Commonwealth of Pennsylvania (Commonwealth) (D) contended that contracts it had with Community Legal Services (CLS), a legal services corporation serving indigents (P), that prohibited CLS from requesting or accepting attorneys' fees in suits against the Commonwealth (D) or its employees were not void as contrary to public policy.

RULE OF LAW

Where a case presents a question of federal law, a contract provision that conflicts with federal public policy underpinning a federal statute may be found to be void and unenforceable.

FACTS: Community Legal Services (CLS), a legal services corporation that served indigents (P) in the Commonwealth of Pennsylvania (Commonwealth) (D), had a series of annual funding contracts with the state that contained "no fees" provisions that prohibited CLS from requesting or accepting attorneys' fees in suits against the Commonwealth (D) or its employees. After CLS helped indigent clients (P) prevail in a class action civil rights suit against the Commonwealth (D) brought under federal law, the clients, as prevailing plaintiffs (P), sought attorneys' fees for CLS pursuant to the federal Fees Awards Act, 42 U.S.C. § 1988 (the Act). The district, finding that the case presented an issue of federal law, rather than state contract law, held that the no fees provisions were unenforceable because they counteracted the federal public policy underlying the Act. Congress enacted the Act to encourage private citizens to enforce fundamental rights under the civil rights laws, and the policy behind the Act is to encourage compliance with and enforcement of those laws. Based on the Act and its legislative history, the district court concluded that the federal policy underpinning the Act is important and vital, and that Congress considered fee awards as an integral part of the remedies necessary to obtain compliance with the civil rights laws. The Commonwealth (D) countered that there were public policy factors that favored enforcement of the no fees provisions—such as a public benefit in funding legal services programs with fixed and known budgets. The district court, applying a balancing approach found in the Restatement (Second) of Contracts, concluded that any countervailing state policy considerations were outweighed by federal policy. The court of appeals granted review.

ISSUE: Where a case presents a question of federal law, may a contract provision that conflicts with federal public policy underpinning a federal statute be found to be void and unenforceable?

HOLDING AND DECISION: (Hunter, III, J.) Yes. Where a case presents a question of federal law, a contract provision that conflicts with federal public policy underpinning a federal statute may be found to be void and unenforceable. As a threshold matter, the district court correctly concluded that the case presents a question of federal law, and not one of Commonwealth of Pennsylvania (Commonwealth) (D) contract law. The underlying claim in this case was not based on contracts but was a federal civil rights claim. Part of that claim was a request for attorneys' fees, made under a federal statute, to which a contract provision was raised as a defense. Therefore, the district court was correct in concluding that federal law provided the rules of decision for the case. The district court was also correct in the approach it used in determining whether the no fees provisions were contrary to public policy, by considering and balancing the factors in favor of enforcement of the contracts against the public policies weighing against enforcement. The district court did not err in concluding that fee awards are an important and vital aspect of the scheme Congress designed to promote compliance with the civil rights laws. It is clear Congress contemplated that states and state officials would often be the targets of civil rights actions, and an important aspect of the enforcement scheme designed by Congress is the collection of attorneys' fees from the states when states are losing defendants. It is also clear that Congress intended legal services programs to receive fees under the Fees Awards Act, 42 U.S.C. § 1988 (the Act), since allowing them to recover fees enhances their capabilities to assist in the enforcement of congressionally favored individual rights and encourages potential defendants to comply with civil rights statutes. To great extent, legal services organizations must allocate limited resources among various possible clients, and the potential for fee recovery will be one of the factors considered in the allocation and use of resources for the maximum benefit of the poor. By enacting the Act, Congress gave the judiciary the discretion to grant attorneys' fees in civil rights cases. Here, the Commonwealth (D) has attempted to vitiate, by contract, a significant portion of the power

Continued on next page.

and duty that Congress granted to the judiciary as an essential tool in the scheme of civil rights enforcement. It is axiomatic to our federal system that neither private parties nor the states can avoid the equitable powers of the federal courts. Thus, the existence of a contrary private agreement cannot successfully be asserted as a defense to the district court's statutorily mandated supervisory power over attorneys' fees. Like any private lawyer, Community Legal Services (CLS) must remain within a budget and only do the legal work that it can afford to do. What the Commonwealth (D) has attempted to do here is to buy immunity from CLS lawyers. In return for a steady partial subsidy, the Commonwealth (D) has demanded that CLS not seek attorneys' fees in cases brought against the Commonwealth (D). The obvious effect of this, if the agreement is enforced, is to cause CLS not to bring actions against the Commonwealth (D). The result of enforcing the no fees provisions would be that an important member of the plaintiffs' civil rights bar would be removed from the scene, and the vigorous enforcement of the laws would be materially quelled. The Commonwealth (D) asserts that there are countervailing public policy considerations that outweigh the federal public policy considerations. First, the Commonwealth (D) argues that there is a public benefit in funding legal services programs with a fixed and known budget. This is true; but it misses the mark. Attorneys' fees-awards to prevailing parties in civil rights litigation are not part of public funding to legal services programs. They are distinct payments of the cost of litigation in accordance with rights and responsibilities determined by Congress. The Commonwealth (D) would have had the burden of paying fees under the Act for violations of civil rights had the litigants' counsel been private. The fact that the taxpayer may be the ultimate payor is not a reason for supporting the no fees restraints. In any event, it is equally plausible to argue that the taxpayer ultimately gains from the payment of attorneys' fees because civil rights litigation is generally recognized as benefiting the public as a whole. The Commonwealth (D) next argues that its funding of legal service programs is an effective substitute for the Act's provisions, contending that the state's funding scheme promotes civil rights litigation more effectively than does the statute, thereby rendering the Act all but superfluous. However, the Commonwealth's (D) argument that its grant to CLS of the minimum amount of money required of it in order to obtain federal funding benefits the poor more than the potential of attorneys' fees awards is disingenuous. The case at bar proves the contrary. Advanced funding does not serve as an inducement to a state to comply with civil rights laws, but the prospect of having to pay attorneys' fees does provide such an incentive. Indeed, the state may also have an incentive to settle a case early. In balancing the policy considerations in connection with the contractual fee restraints, the district court used the approach presented in Sections 178 and 179 of the Restatement (Second) of Contracts. The Commonwealth (D) argues that the district court's application of the Restatement's formulation was incorrect because it failed to require that the legislation in question either "expressly prohibit(s) the contract or . . . require(s) a performance or a result that directly contradicts what the contract requires." Neither federal nor Commonwealth (D) law requires such a direct, explicit conflict. Such a requirement would require that a contract be "illegal" in a literal sense before it could be invalid. However, the scope of the public policy doctrine is broader and more encompassing than the concept of illegality. Nor does the Restatement itself require that the legislation in question expressly prohibit or require an act inconsistent with the contract; it is sufficient if the legislature makes an adequate declaration of public policy that is inconsistent with the contract's terms. For these reasons, the no fees provisions at issue are void as contrary to public policy. Affirmed.

ANALYSIS

Sections 178 and 179 of the Restatement (Second) of Contracts represent an accurate reflection of the law regarding the public policy contractual defense, and the Pennsylvania Supreme Court, among many other courts in other jurisdictions, has endorsed the Restatement's approach. That court has indicated that a contract that is injurious to the public interest may be held void even in the absence of express legislative mandates contrary to the provisions of the agreement.

Quicknotes

PUBLIC POLICY Policy administered by the state with respect to the health, safety, and morals of its people in accordance with common notions of fairness and decency.

Hassler v. Circle C Resources

Employee (D) v. Employer (P)

Wyo. Sup. Ct., 505 P.3d 169 (2022)

NATURE OF CASE: Appeal from grant of summary judgment for employer in action asserting breach of noncompete agreement.

FACT SUMMARY: Circle C Resources (Circle C) (P) sued its former employee, Charlene Hassler (D), for breach of a noncompete agreement. Hassler (D) claimed the agreement was unenforceable and void as against public policy.

RULE OF LAW

(1) The liberal blue-pencil rule, pursuant to which a court may narrow the terms of a noncompete agreement to make it reasonable, must be overruled where that rule is contrary to traditional contract law, has worked an injustice on employees, and has contributed to uncertainty in business relationships by encouraging employers to draft overly broad, unreasonable restraints on trade.

(2) A noncompete agreement that is unreasonable on its face is void as violating public policy.

FACTS: Circle C Resources (Circle C) (P), which provided day and residential habilitation services to disabled clients, hired Charlene Hassler (D) to provide residential habilitation care in her home for one of its clients (Client). At the time of hire, Hassler (D) signed a noncompete agreement that provided that during her term of employment and two years after her employment, Hassler (D) would not be affiliated in any way with any business that competed with Circle C (P), would not herself compete with Circle C (P) in any way, and would not solicit Circle C's clients. The noncompete specified geographic areas to which it applied. Circle C (P) trained Hassler (D) for a month before Client moved into her home. Circle C (P) was paid $121,142.10 per year through Medicaid, and Circle C, in turn, paid Hassler (D) approximately $26,400 per year, resulting in an annual net profit to Circle C of $94,742.10. Almost two years after Hassler (D) was hired, Client changed providers and Hassler (D) left Circle C's (P) employ, though she continued to provide the same services to Client, being paid by the new provider. Hassler (D) worked to obtain her own Medicaid number so she could be a provider, but in the meantime, she was paid significantly more by the new provider than she was by Circle C (P). A few months later, Circle C (P) notified Hassler (D) that she was in violation of the noncompete agreement. Notwithstanding that Hassler (D) received her Medicaid number two months later, she stopped providing paid service for the Client, although Client continued to live in her home and she occasionally helped with Client's care. Instead, Hassler's (D) husband and daughter cared for Client most of the time and were paid through Medicaid for their services. Two years later, Circle C filed suit against Hassler (D), seeking damages for breach of the noncompete agreement. Hassler (D) defended by asserting, among other things, that the noncompete agreement was unenforceable and void as against public policy. Both parties moved for summary judgment, and the trial court ruled in favor of Circle C (P). It decided the noncompete agreement was reasonable and enforceable if the geographical area subject to restriction was narrowed and the duration of the restriction was changed from 24 to 12 months. Applying the liberal blue-pencil rule, pursuant to which a court may narrow the terms of a noncompete agreement to make it reasonable, the trial court narrowed the restrictions accordingly and awarded Circle C (P) $94,742.10, which represented its lost profits for 12 months. Hassler (D) appealed, and the state's highest court granted review.

ISSUE:

(1) Must the liberal blue-pencil rule, pursuant to which a court may narrow the terms of a noncompete agreement to make it reasonable, be overruled where that rule is contrary to traditional contract law, has worked an injustice on employees, and has contributed to uncertainty in business relationships by encouraging employers to draft overly broad, unreasonable restraints on trade?

(2) Is a noncompete agreement that is unreasonable on its face void as violating public policy?

HOLDING AND DECISION: (Kautz, J.)

(1) Yes. The liberal blue-pencil rule, pursuant to which a court may narrow the terms of a noncompete agreement to make it reasonable, must be overruled where that rule is contrary to traditional contract law, has worked an injustice on employees, and has contributed to uncertainty in business relationships by encouraging employers to draft overly broad, unreasonable restraints on trade. As a matter of traditional contract law, although competent parties have the right to freely contract, contracts that are contrary to public policy are void. Ordinarily, instead of revising agreements to make them consistent with public policy, courts simply declare contracts that violate public policy to be void. When considering the enforceability of noncompete agreements, courts

Continued on next page.

must balance competing principles: the public's interest in free competition and trade, the parties' freedom to contract, and the employee's freedom to work. Because public policy encourages employees to seek better jobs from other employers or to go into business for themselves, contracts that hinder them from doing so are strictly construed and rigidly scanned and are declared void unless necessary for the reasonable protection of the employer. Although an employer may use a noncompete agreement to protect itself from improper and unfair competition by a former employee, it is not entitled to protection from ordinary competition. Thus, to be enforceable, a noncompete agreement must be (1) in writing; (2) part of a contract of employment; (3) based on reasonable consideration; (4) reasonable in duration and geographical limitations; and (5) not against public policy. Because a noncompete agreement is a restraint on trade, it is prima facie invalid as a violation of public policy. Prior to the adoption by the state's courts of the liberal blue-pencil rule, noncompete agreements with unreasonable terms were unenforceable in the state. The liberal blue-pencil rule was adopted in the belief that it would efficiently promote public policy, notwithstanding that it departed from black-letter law that prohibits courts from enforcing contracts in violation of public policy or reforming parties' poorly drafted contracts, especially in situations where employers had provided employees with valuable information and training. At heart, the liberal blue-pencil rule was intended to be a tool to prevent former employees from unfairly competing with employers who had provided them valuable information and training and to promote certainty in the business environment. However, in practice, the rule places an unfair burden on employees and creates uncertainty in business relationships. At the time of hire and execution of a noncompete agreement, the scales generally weigh in favor of the employer who holds a superior bargaining position and is the drafter of the noncompete agreement. In practice, the liberal blue-pencil rule further tips the scales toward employers by encouraging them to draft noncompete agreements with overly broad and unreasonable trade restraints. When challenged, the employer gets the benefit of the court redrafting the agreement to make it reasonable. In fact, in this case, Circle C Resources (Circle C) (P) included a paragraph in the noncompete agreement that specifically contemplated court intervention to redraft the agreement if its terms overstepped the bounds of reasonable trade restrictions. That is not a proper use of judicial resources or a próper role for judges, as it is not the function of a court to write or rewrite contracts for parties to enable enforcement of a contract that, as written, violates the public policy of the state. Furthermore, the liberal blue-pencil rule, with its specter of eventual court intervention, means neither employers nor employees can rely, with any assurance, on the specific terms of the agreements they execute. Because future litigation may result in the enforcement of a noncompete agreement with terms different from those agreed to by the parties, the rule creates uncertainty in the business environment, undermining the very policy the rule was intended to serve. The doctrine of stare decisis does not obligate an appellate court to follow precedent that is unjust, clearly contrary to plain and obvious principles of law, or has proven unworkable. The liberal blue-pencil rule has had all those effects, and, therefore, its use must be overruled. The law's general distaste for agreements in restraint of trade and assignment to the employer of the duty to show any restraint is reasonable should extend to all terms of the agreement; it is hoped that a rejection of the liberal blue-pencil rule will encourage employers to incorporate only reasonable trade restraints into their employment contracts and to assure such restraints are reasonably tied to legitimate interests requiring protection. Accordingly, a noncompete agreement that includes unreasonable restrictions on trade violates public policy and is invalid, and the courts of this state will no longer exceed the scope of their traditional authority in contract interpretation by redrafting noncompete agreements to bring them within the bounds of reason. [Reversed as to this issue.]

(2) Yes. A noncompete agreement that is unreasonable on its face is void as violating public policy. There is no dispute that the original terms of the noncompete agreement between Hassler (D) and Circle C (P) were unreasonable. Circle C (P) did not attempt to justify the geographical restriction that covered many counties outside the area where it actively engaged in its trade, and it sought enforcement of the agreement only in two counties. Also, the trial court ruled Circle C (P) had not met its burden of showing the 24-month term of the agreement was reasonable. Circle C (P) does not challenge that ruling on appeal. Because there is no dispute that the duration and geographical terms of the noncompete agreement are unreasonable, and because the blue-pencil rule is no longer available to make noncompete agreements reasonable, the entire agreement is void in violation of public policy. Accordingly, Hassler (D) is entitled to judgment in her favor. Reversed and remanded.

ANALYSIS

Another reason given by the court in *Hassler* for abandoning the use of the liberal blue-pencil rule, which the

Continued on next page.

court found encourages employers to draft overly broad restrictive covenants, is that the tendency of employers to draft overly broad covenants has an *in terrorem* effect on employees who respect their contractual obligations and on competitors who fear legal complications if they employ a covenantor, thereby interfering with the mobility of employees. Because an overly broad non-compete agreement typically dissuades employees from leaving a job for a better opportunity out of fear of being sued by the employer, it is contrary to the public policy of encouraging employees to seek better jobs from other employers or to go into business for themselves. Additionally, employers draft overly broad non-compete agreements in the belief that most employees will not challenge them, and this belief is borne out by the fact that for every agreement that makes its way to court, many more do not, again unjustifiably inhibiting employee mobility and unreasonably restraining trade.

Quicknotes

BLUE-PENCIL RULE Allows parts of a contract deemed unenforceable by a court to be deleted or revised by the court, so that the contract as modified will be enforceable.

COVENANTOR The party who makes a promise by convenant.

IN TERROREM By way of intimidation or threat.

NONCOMPETE CLAUSE A provision, typically contained in an employment contract or a contract for the sale of a business, pursuant to which the promisor agrees not to compete with the promisee for a specified time period and/or within a particular geographic area.

STARE DECISIS Doctrine whereby courts follow legal precedent unless there is good cause for departure.

Sheets v. Teddy's Frosted Foods

Fired employee (P) v. Employer (D)

Conn. Sup. Ct., 179 Conn. 471, 427 A.2d 385 (1980)

NATURE OF CASE: Appeal from dismissal of wrongful discharge lawsuit.

FACT SUMMARY: Sheets (P) contended that he had been terminated in violation of public policy.

RULE OF LAW

An employee hired at-will may maintain an action for wrongful discharge if he can prove that the discharge violates public policy.

FACTS: Sheets (P) was hired for an indefinite term as quality control director by Teddy's Frosted Foods (Teddy's) (D). After Sheets (P) attempted to apprise management of repeated mislabeling in violation of the state food and drug law, he was terminated by Teddy's (D). He filed suit for wrongful discharge. Teddy's (D) motion to strike the complaint was granted on the grounds that there can be no liability in tort for termination of an at-will employment contract. Sheets (P) appealed.

ISSUE: May an employee hired at will maintain an action for wrongful discharge?

HOLDING AND DECISION: (Peters, J.) Yes. An employee hired at-will may maintain an action for wrongful discharge. It remains generally true that, unless the parties have provided otherwise, employment is at-will and terminable by either party. However, an employer cannot, without liability, terminate an employee for exercising some right available to him at law or from refraining to do something in violation of the law; an employee should not have to choose between a living and illegal conduct. Here, Teddy's Frosted Foods (D) was selling mislabeled food in violation of state law; moreover, as one involved in the manufacturing process and aware of the nonconformity of the products, Sheets (P) himself would have been in violation of the law had he ignored the problem. Since Sheets (P) has stated a cause of action for intentionally tortious conduct, the motion to strike should not have been granted. Reversed and remanded.

DISSENT: (Cotter, C.J.) The court has created an overly broad cause of action that is sure to lead to a large number of nuisance suits by disgruntled ex-employees.

ANALYSIS

Many states, either by decision or statute, follow the rule here. Others have stopped short of a public policy exception to at-will termination but have created a general "good cause" requirement for discharge. The leading case that first established a restriction on the employer's power to terminate involved an employee fired for refusing to submit to sexual overtures by her foreman. See *Monge v. Beebe Rubber Co.*, 316 A.2d 549 (N.H. 1974).

Quicknotes

AT-WILL EMPLOYMENT The rule that an employment relationship is subject to termination at any time, or for any cause, by an employee or an employer in the absence of a specific agreement otherwise.

PUBLIC POLICY Policy administered by the state with respect to the health, safety, and morals of its people in accordance with common notions of fairness and decency.

Balla v. Gambro, Inc.

Former in-house counsel (P) v. Former employer (D)

Ill. Sup. Ct., 145 Ill. 2d 492, 584 N.E.2d 104 (1991)

NATURE OF CASE: Appeal from reversal of summary judgment for defendant employer in action for retaliatory discharge.

FACT SUMMARY: After Balla (P) was discharged as Gambro, Inc.'s (D) in-house counsel because he informed his employer he would stop the sale by Gambro (D) of defective dialysis equipment, Balla (P) contended that he was entitled to recover under the tort of retaliatory discharge.

RULE OF LAW

In-house counsel may not sue his former employer for the tort action of retaliatory discharge.

FACTS: Balla (P) served as Gambro, Inc.'s (D) in-house counsel and as its manager of regulatory affairs. Gambro (D) was in the business of selling kidney dialysis equipment. When Balla (P) told Gambro's (D) president to reject a shipment of equipment because it did not comply with United States Food and Drug Administration (FDA) regulations, the president ignored him and sought a buyer. Upon learning this, Balla (P) told the president he would do whatever he could to stop the sale. Thereafter, Gambro (D) discharged Balla (P). Balla (P) informed the FDA of the shipment. The FDA determined the shipment was adulterated. Balla (P) sued Gambro (D) for the tort of retaliatory discharge, seeking $22 million in damages. The trial court granted summary judgment to Gambro (D), but the state's intermediate appellate court reversed and remanded. The state's highest court granted review.

ISSUE: May in-house counsel sue his former employer for the tort action of retaliatory discharge?

HOLDING AND DECISION: (Clark, J.) No. In-house counsel may not sue his former employer for the tort action of retaliatory discharge. The tort of retaliatory discharge is a limited and narrow exception to the general rule of at-will employment. Because in-house counsel is already bound by the state's rules of professional conduct, the public policy protected by the tort of retaliatory discharge—in this case, the protection of citizens' lives and property—is adequately safeguarded without extending the tort of retaliatory discharge to in-house counsel. The rules of professional conduct require an attorney, including in-house counsel, to reveal information about a client to the extent it appears necessary to prevent the client from committing an act that would result in death or serious bodily injury. Here, the adulterated equipment potentially could have caused death or bodily injury, so Balla (P) was under a duty to report the sale of the equipment. Contrary to Balla's (P) argument, he was not faced with the choice of complying with his duties and losing his job, or not complying with his duties and keeping his job. Balla (P) had no choice in the matter: he was required to comply with his obligations as an attorney. Attorneys know or should know that at certain times in their professional career they will have to forgo economic gains in order to protect the integrity of the legal profession. Further, extending the tort of retaliatory discharge to in-house counsel would have an undesirable effect on the attorney-client relationship that exists between employers and their in-house counsel, and might have a chilling effect on attorney-client communications. Employers have the right to terminate their attorneys at any time, with or without cause. If in-house counsel were granted the right to sue their employers for retaliatory discharge, employers might be less willing to be forthright and candid with their in-house counsel and might be hesitant to turn to their in-house counsel for advice regarding potentially questionable corporate conduct, knowing that their in-house counsel could use this information in a retaliatory discharge suit. It would also be inappropriate to extend the retaliatory discharge tort to in-house counsel because doing so would force the employer to bear the cost of the attorney's compliance with the rules of professional conduct. Instead, the attorney must bear that economic burden. Finally, Balla's (P) argument that he learned of the defective equipment in his role of manager of regulatory of affairs is not supported by the evidence, since his discharge resulted from information he learned as in-house counsel and from conduct he performed as an attorney. Reversed. The decision of the trial court is affirmed.

ANALYSIS

Critics of the reasoning in *Balla* have observed that it appears to reflect not only an unspoken adherence to an anachronistic model of the attorney's place and role in contemporary society, but also an inverted view of the consequences of the in-house attorney's essential professional role. Some critics have also commented that it seems bizarre that a lawyer employee, who has affirmative duties concerning the administration of justice, should be denied redress for discharge resulting from trying to carry out those very duties. While these critics agree with the court in *Balla* that a good beginning point for analysis may well be the employer's right to

Continued on next page.

discharge the lawyer-employee, they find that that cannot be the ending point as well, given that the lawyer-client relationship exists in the context of employment law as well as law regulating the lawyer's duties to third persons, the courts, and the government. Some courts have also rejected the reasoning of the court in *Balla*. For example, the California Supreme Court in *General Dynamics Corporation v. The Superior Court of San Bernardino County,* 876 P.2d 487 (Cal. 1994), reasoned that precisely because of in-house counsels' uniquely influential position, they should be accorded a retaliatory discharge remedy in those instances in which mandatory ethical norms embodied in the rules of professional conduct collide with illegitimate demands of the employer and the attorney insists on adhering to his or her clear professional duty. Because it is the purpose of the retaliatory discharge tort to vindicate fundamental public policies by encouraging employees to act in ways that advance them, by providing the employee with a remedy in tort damages for resisting socially damaging organizational conduct, the courts mitigate the otherwise considerable economic and cultural pressures on the individual employee to silently conform.

Quicknotes

AT-WILL EMPLOYMENT The rule that an employment relationship is subject to termination at any time, or for any cause, by an employee or an employer in the absence of a specific agreement otherwise.

RETALIATORY DISCHARGE The firing of an employee in retaliation for an act committed against the employer's interests.

Simeone v. Simeone

Wife (P) v. Husband (D)

Pa. Sup. Ct., 525 Pa. 392, 581 A.2d 162 (1990)

NATURE OF CASE: Divorce proceedings.

FACT SUMMARY: Catherine (P) signed a prenuptial agreement without the advice of counsel, limiting her potential recovery upon divorce to $25,000.

RULE OF LAW

Contracting parties are normally bound by their agreements without regard to whether the terms thereof were read and fully understood and whether the agreements embodied reasonable or good bargains.

FACTS: Catherine (P) and Frederick (D) entered into a prenuptial agreement on the eve of their wedding. Frederick's (D) attorney presented Catherine (P) with the document limiting her recovery upon divorce to $25,000. She signed the agreement without counsel. The couple later divorced, and Catherine (P) applied for alimony. The prenuptial agreement was upheld, and Catherine (P) appealed.

ISSUE: Are contracting parties normally bound by their agreements without regard to whether the terms thereof were read and fully understood and whether the agreements embodied reasonable or good bargains?

HOLDING AND DECISION: (Flaherty, J.) Yes. Contracting parties are normally bound by their agreements without regard to whether the terms thereof were read and fully understood and whether the agreements embodied reasonable or good bargains. Prenuptial agreements are subject to the same standards as other contracts. There is no merit in the contention that the agreement should be declared void because Catherine (P) failed to consult with independent counsel. Affirmed.

CONCURRENCE: (Papadakos, J.) I view prenuptial contracts as being in the nature of contracts of adhesion with one party generally being in a position of greater authority than the other.

DISSENT: (McDermott, J.) Upon divorce, a spouse should be able to avoid the operation of a prenuptial agreement with clear and convincing evidence that despite full and fair disclosure at the time of the agreement's execution it was nevertheless so inequitable and unfair that it should not be enforced.

ANALYSIS

This decision expressly overruled the prior rule of *Estate of Geyer*, 533 A.2d 423 (1987), which held a prenuptial agreement valid "if it either made a reasonable provision for the spouse or was entered after a fair and full disclosure of the general financial positions of the parties." The court's rationale was that such a rule was based on outdated, paternalistic notions of the relationships between the sexes. The rule set forth here was intended to reflect the equal status of men and women in modern society.

Quicknotes

ADHESION CONTRACT A contract, usually in standardized form, that is prepared by one party and offered to another, whose terms are so disproportionately in favor of the drafting party that courts tend to question the equality of bargaining power in reaching the agreement.

PRENUPTIAL AGREEMENT An agreement entered into by two individuals, in contemplation of their impending marriage, in order to determine their rights and interests in property upon dissolution or death.

In the Matter of Baby M

Surrogate parents (P) v. Birth mother (D)

N.J. Sup. Ct., 109 N.J. 396, 537 A.2d 1227 (1988)

NATURE OF CASE: Appeal from judgment in an action regarding a surrogacy contract.

FACT SUMMARY: Stern (P) sued Whitehead (D), the birth mother, to enforce a surrogacy contract and to obtain custody of Baby M.

RULE OF LAW

Surrogate contracts violate public policy and are unenforceable.

FACTS: Stern (P) and Whitehead (D) entered into a contract whereby Whitehead (D) agreed to be artificially inseminated by Stern (P) for $10,000 and to give up all parental rights to the child. Whitehead (D) carried and gave birth to Baby M. However, Whitehead (D) refused to give up Baby M, and Stern (P) sued to enforce the surrogate contract. The trial court affirmed the contract and awarded custody of Baby M to Stern (P) because that was in the best interest of the child. Whitehead (D) appealed.

ISSUE: Are surrogate contracts enforceable?

HOLDING AND DECISION: (Wilentz, C.J.) No. Surrogate contracts violate public policy and are unenforceable. The state has a strong interest in protecting children. Thus, there are laws against buying and selling children. Natural parents must not be coerced into surrendering their rights. Additionally, surrogate contracts violate a state policy that the rights of the natural parents are equal, in that the mother's right has already been contracted away. While Whitehead (D) agreed to the contract, she was not counseled as to the ramifications, nor did anyone take into consideration the rights of the child. Furthermore, the best interests of a child must remain paramount over the freedom to contract. Taking into account the best interests of Baby M, custody should still go to Stern (P), and Whitehead's (D) visitation rights should be restored. Reversed in part, affirmed in part, and remanded.

ANALYSIS

This case highlights the evolution of the courts' involvement in the freedom to contract. Before the Great Depression, courts were highly reluctant to limit anyone's right to contract as such actions were viewed as anathema to individual liberty. More recently, courts have recognized that they have constitutional authority to regulate contracts in many ways.

Quicknotes

ARTIFICIAL INSEMINATION The impregnation of a woman by the injection of semen into the uterus.

SURROGACY CONTRACT An agreement between parties that sets forth the parental rights and responsibilities of each party according to the role it has played in the life of the child.

CHAPTER 7

Performance and Breach

Quick Reference Rules of Law

PAGE

1. *Luttinger v. Rosen.* A condition precedent is a fact or an event that the parties intend must exist or take place before there is a right to performance, and if the condition precedent is not fulfilled the contract is not enforceable. *193*

2. *Internatio-Rotterdam, Inc. v. River Brand Rice Mills, Inc.* A condition, which is an act or event, other than a lapse of time, must be literally complied with. *194*

3. *Peacock Construction Co. v. Modern Air Conditioning, Inc.* Ambiguous provisions in subcontracts, which do not expressly shift the risk of payment failure by the owner to the subcontractor, will be interpreted as constituting absolute promises to pay and not as setting payment by the owner as a condition precedent to payment. *195*

4. *Gibson v. Cranage.* Where two parties agree that one of them must be "personally satisfied" before liability will arise, that party may insist on his right to personal satisfaction. *196*

5. *Hicks v. Bush.* Parol evidence is admissible to prove an oral condition precedent to the legal effectiveness of a written agreement if the condition does not contradict the express terms of such written agreement. *197*

6. *Kingston v. Preston.* Breach of a covenant by one party to a contract relieves the other party's obligation to perform another covenant that is dependent thereon, the performance of the first covenant being an implied condition precedent to the duty to perform the second covenant. *199*

7. *Stewart v. Newbury.* Where a contract is made to perform work and no agreement is made as to payment, the work must be substantially performed before payment can be demanded. *200*

8. *Bartus v. Riccardi.* A seller may offer to cure a nonconforming tender even though the buyer has previously revoked his acceptance and it is beyond the contract time if there are reasonable grounds to believe that the nonconforming goods would be accepted and there is reasonable notice of intent to cure. *201*

9. *Jorgensen v. Pressnall.* Under the Uniform Commercial Code, a buyer may revoke acceptance of goods after discovering nonconformities and timely notifying the seller thereof, where the seller fails to cure the nonconformities in a reasonably timely manner and the nonconformities substantially impair the value to the buyer. *202*

10. *Jacob & Youngs v. Kent.* An omission, both trivial and innocent, will sometimes be atoned for by allowance of the remitting damage and will not always be the breach of a condition to be followed by forfeiture. For damages in construction contracts, the owner is entitled merely to the difference between the value of the structure if built to specifications and the value it has as constructed. *204*

11. *Walker & Co. v. Harrison.* A party attempting to repudiate a contract must convince the court that the other party has materially breached the contract. *205*

12. *K & G Construction Co. v. Harris.* (1) Where a subcontractor materially breaches a contract, the contractor may justifiably withhold a progress payment to account for the damages caused by the subcontractor's breach. (2) Where a contractor justifiably withholds a progress payment to a subcontractor to account for damages caused by the subcontractor's material breach, the subcontractor's continued performance under the contract is not excused by the contractor's withholding of the progress payment. *206*

13.	*New England Structures, Inc. v. Loranger.* In stating his reasons for rejecting performance or his objections to a performance that he has accepted, a promisee has not excused other grounds upon which he may have rejected the defective performance unless the promisor shows that it has relied to its detriment upon the particular ground stated.	*208*
14.	*Gill v. Johnstown Lumber Co.* When consideration for work done is apportionable or apportioned in the contract, that contract will be interpreted as divisible (severable) in case of part performance.	*209*
15.	*Britton v. Turner.* A defaulting party, although unable to recover on his contract, may recover under a quasi-contractual theory the reasonable value of his services less any damages to the other party arising out of the default.	*210*
16.	*Nelson v. Hazel.* Where a building contractor fails to substantially perform under a building contract, the contractor nevertheless is entitled to recover the value of the contractor's work offset by the building owner's damages.	*211*
17.	*McKenna v. Vernon.* A contract condition will be waived where it has previously and repeatedly been waived in the course of performance.	*213*
18.	*Iron Trade Products Co. v. Wilkoff Co.* Mere difficulty of performance will not excuse a breach of contract even though the difficulty was created by the other contracting party.	*214*
19.	*Hochster v. De La Tour.* A party to a contract who renounces his intention to perform may not complain if the other party, instead of waiting until performance is due, elects to sue immediately for breach of contract.	*215*
20.	*Kanavos v. Hancock Bank & Trust Co.* A party's ability to recover for breach of a contract giving a right of first refusal depends on his having had the financial resources to exercise the option.	*216*
21.	*McCloskey & Co. v. Minweld Steel Co.* In order to give rise to a renunciation amounting to a breach of contract, there must be an absolute and unequivocal refusal to perform or a distinct and positive statement of an inability to do so.	*217*
22.	*By-Lo Oil Co. v. ParTech, Inc.* Under the Uniform Commercial Code, a court may determine, as a matter of law, whether a party to a contract has reasonable grounds for insecurity and whether a party has given adequate assurance.	*218*

Luttinger v. Rosen

Sellers (D) v. Purchasers (P)

Conn. Sup. Ct., 164 Conn. 45, 316 A.2d 757 (1972)

NATURE OF CASE: Action to recover a deposit on real property.

FACT SUMMARY: The Rosens (P) signed a contract to purchase the Luttingers' (D) premises and put down a deposit "subject to and conditional upon" their obtaining specified mortgage financing.

RULE OF LAW

A condition precedent is a fact or an event that the parties intend must exist or take place before there is a right to performance, and if the condition precedent is not fulfilled the contract is not enforceable.

FACTS: The contract by which the Rosens (P) agreed to purchase the Luttingers' (D) premises for $85,000 was "subject to and conditional upon" their obtaining "first mortgage financing on said premises from a bank or other lending institution" of $45,000 for no less than 20 years at an interest rate not exceeding 8 percent per annum. They agreed to use due diligence in seeking such financing but put in only one application because only one bank was then lending as much as $45,000 on single-family dwellings. It would not commit to an interest rate any lower than 8 percent. However, the Luttingers' (D) attorney offered to make up the difference between the interest rate offered by the bank and the 8 percent rate provided in the contract. The Rosens (P) refused and sued for a refund of their deposit. The trial court rendered judgment in their favor, and the Luttingers (D) appealed.

ISSUE: Is a contract enforceable if a condition precedent is not fulfilled?

HOLDING AND DECISION: (Loiselle, J.) No. If a condition precedent is not fulfilled, a contract is unenforceable. A condition precedent is a fact or an event that the parties intend must exist or take place before there is a right to performance. Looking at the contract in this case, it is clear the parties conditioned the purchase by the Rosens (P) on their obtaining a mortgage as specified therein. Since this condition precedent was not fulfilled, the contract is unenforceable. Affirmed.

ANALYSIS

The use of "subject to financing" clauses is widespread, although many similar clauses are not as specific as this one and speak of the buyer obtaining "reasonable financing" or "proper financing." Since the plaintiff attempting to enforce the agreement has the burden of proof as to conditions precedent, failure to clearly delineate what will constitute satisfaction of the financing condition can prove treacherous.

Quicknotes

CONDITION PRECEDENT The happening of an uncertain occurrence that is necessary before a particular right or interest may be obtained or an action performed.

Internatio-Rotterdam, Inc. v. River Brand Rice Mills, Inc.

Exporter (P) v. Rice processor (D)

259 F.2d 137 (2d Cir. 1958)

NATURE OF CASE: Action for damages for breach of contract for sale of goods.

FACT SUMMARY: Internatio-Rotterdam, Inc. (Internatio) (P) ordered 95,600 pockets of rice from River Brand Rice Mills, Inc. (River Brand) (D) under a contract requiring at least two weeks' notice for December delivery at either Houston or Lake Charles. When Internatio (P) did not give notice by December 17—the last day an order could be placed for delivery within December—River Brand (D) rescinded the contract.

RULE OF LAW

A condition, which is an act or event, other than a lapse of time, must be literally complied with.

FACTS: Internatio-Rotterdam, Inc. (Internatio) (P), a rice exporter, contracted to buy 95,600 pockets of rice from River Brand Rice Mills, Inc. (River Brand) (D), a rice processor, at $8.25 to be delivered alongside ship at Lake Charles or Houston, Texas. Shipment was to be made in December 1952, with two weeks' notice from Internatio (P). Internatio (P) elected to have 50,000 pockets delivered at Lake Charles and so notified River Brand (D) on December 10. River Brand (D) made delivery. By December 17, the last day an order could be made for delivery within the month, River Brand (D) had not received instructions for delivery of the other 45,600 pockets. Internatio (P) was having difficulty finding a ship and dock space at Houston. On December 18, River Brand (D) rescinded the contract for the remaining rice. Internatio (P) sued for breach. The trial court dismissed the complaint.

ISSUE: Must a condition, which is an act or event, other than a lapse of time, be literally complied with?

HOLDING AND DECISION: (Hincks, J.) Yes. A condition, which is an act or event, other than a lapse of time, must be literally complied with. Notice was a condition precedent to shipment. Shipment could not be made until the ship and location to which River Brand Rice Mills, Inc. (River Brand) (D) was to deliver was identified. If shipment within December was of the essence of the contract, then failure to notify by December 17 was a breach as that was the last day notice could be given in order to allow River Brand (D) two weeks to ship by December 31. December delivery went to the essence of the contract as December was the peak rice month and both sides wanted the protection of a specified delivery period. A postponement of notice could damage River Brand (D) in light of fluctuating rice prices. The letter of credit guaranteed payment only for December deliveries. The mere establishment of the letter of credit was not an act of performance but was made in preparation thereof and was of no benefit to River Brand (D). As there was an option on delivery sites, the contract was divisible, and by continuing Lake Charles deliveries, River Brand (D) did not waive its right to cancel the Houston deliveries. Duties of the parties to the Lake Charles shipment were in no way dependent on the Houston deliveries. Affirmed.

ANALYSIS

A condition precedent is an act or event, other than a lapse of time, which must exist or occur before a duty of immediate performance of a promise arises. However, the term "condition" ordinarily describes acts or events that must occur before a duty of performance under an existing contract becomes absolute. Here, the court looked for intent. By starting with a promise to sell for a promise to buy, the promise to sell was contingent upon notice by December 17, that is, timely instruction. In this way, time was of the essence. Unless the condition is met, the promise to perform will be excused. Note that the buyer, Internatio-Rotterdam, Inc. (Internatio) (P), took the risk that the price after contracting would go down, and the seller, River Brand Rice Mills, Inc. (River Brand) (D), took the risk that prices would go up. The price did, in fact, go up. But after December 17, River Brand (D) assumed the risk both ways. Hence, Internatio (P) could not wait to give notice up to the end of December for January delivery.

Quicknotes

CONDITION PRECEDENT The happening of an uncertain occurrence that is necessary before a particular right or interest may be obtained or an action performed.

LETTER OF CREDIT An agreement by a bank or other party that it will honor a customer's demand for payment upon the satisfaction of specified conditions.

RESCISSION The canceling of an agreement and the return of the parties to their positions prior to the formation of the contract.

Peacock Construction Co. v. Modern Air Conditioning, Inc.

Builder (D) v. Subcontractor (P)

Fla. Sup. Ct., 353 So. 2d 840 (1977)

NATURE OF CASE: Consolidation on appeal of action for breaches of identical contractual provisions.

FACT SUMMARY: Modern Air Conditioning, Inc. (P) had subcontracted to do work for Peacock Construction Co. (D) under a contract calling for final payment of subcontractors "within 30 days after the completion of the work. . .and full payment therefore by the Owner."

RULE OF LAW

Ambiguous provisions in subcontracts, which do not expressly shift the risk of payment failure by the owner to the subcontractor, will be interpreted as constituting absolute promises to pay and not as setting payment by the owner as a condition precedent to payment.

FACTS: As builder of a condominium project, Peacock Construction Co. (Peacock) (D) subcontracted the heating and air conditioning work to Modern Air Conditioning, Inc. (Modern Air) (P) and the "rooftop swimming pool" work to Overly Manufacturing (Overly) (P). Both subcontractors signed agreements providing that they would receive final payment "within 30 days after the completion of the work included in this subcontract, written acceptance by the Architect and full payment therefore by the Owner." When the work was completed, both subcontractors requested final payment, which Peacock (D) withheld because it had not received full payment from the owner. Although Peacock (D) urged that payment by the owner was a condition precedent to its duty to pay the subcontractors, the trial court disagreed and granted summary judgments to the subcontractors (P) when they sued for damages for breach of contract. The decisions were affirmed on appeal.

ISSUE: Will a subcontract be interpreted as making the owner's payment a condition precedent to payment of the subcontractors only if such is unambiguously provided for in the contract?

HOLDING AND DECISION: (Boyd, C.J.) Yes. This case will be decided under the rule adopted in a majority of jurisdictions, that a subcontract will not be interpreted as making the owner's payment a condition precedent to payment of the subcontractors unless such is unambiguously provided for in the contract. In the typical subcontracting situation, it is not intended that the subcontractor will assume the risk of the owner's failure to pay the general contractor. That is the reason for this majority rule. Of course, the parties can, by express and unambiguous contractual language, shift the risk of payment failure by the owner to the subcontractor. In this case, there was no such express provision. Thus, payment by the owner is not a condition precedent to paying the subcontractors. Affirmed.

ANALYSIS

Restatement (Second) § 224 defines a "condition" as "an event, not certain to occur, which must occur, unless its nonoccurrence is excused, before performance under a contract becomes due." Conditions can be express, implied in fact (inferred from the contract's express provisions), or "constructive" (created by operation of law).

Quicknotes

CONDITION PRECEDENT The happening of an uncertain occurrence that is necessary before a particular right or interest may be obtained or an action performed.

SUMMARY JUDGMENT Judgment rendered by a court in response to a motion made by one of the parties, claiming that the lack of a question of material fact in respect to an issue warrants disposition of the issue without consideration by the jury.

Gibson v. Cranage

Artist (P) v. Client (D)

Mich. Sup. Ct., 39 Mich. 49 (1878)

NATURE OF CASE: Appeal from defense verdict in action to recover damages for breach of contract.

FACT SUMMARY: Cranage's (D) liability to Gibson (P) was conditioned on Cranage's (D) personal satisfaction with a portrait.

RULE OF LAW

Where two parties agree that one of them must be "personally satisfied" before liability will arise, that party may insist on his right to personal satisfaction.

FACTS: Gibson (P) contracted to make a portrait for Cranage (D). It was further agreed that if the portrait failed to satisfy Cranage (D), Cranage (D) need not accept or pay for it. The portrait failed to satisfy Cranage (D), and Gibson (P) sued for the contract price. The trial court ruled in favor of Cranage (D), and Gibson (P) appealed.

ISSUE: May two parties make a contract wherein personal satisfaction of one of the parties is necessary for contractual liability to arise?

HOLDING AND DECISION: (Marston, J.) Yes. Where two parties agree that one of them must be "personally satisfied" before liability will arise, that party may insist on his right to personal satisfaction. That which is an excellent portrait in the eyes of one party may certainly prove very unsatisfactory to another. Affirmed.

ANALYSIS

Note that the condition precedent to liability in this well-known case was a completely subjective test of personal satisfaction. The parties might have made the test objective by including such a clause as: "and acceptance and payment shall not be unreasonably withheld." However, they did not do so, and since a subjective test does not violate public policy in this situation, the court decided in favor of freedom of contract. Note further that the court expresses some doubt as to whether there was even a contract at all (since the subjective test may render Cranage's (D) promise illusory and therefore not consideration for a return promise) but does not pursue the matter. It would seem, however, that where personal satisfaction is called for, a minimum "good-faith" requirement must be imposed to remove such a "contract" from the class of illusory agreements. Often where satisfaction is a matter of "mechanical fitness, utility, or marketability," an objective "reasonable person" test is presumed by the courts.

Quicknotes

ASSUMPSIT An oral or written promise by one party to perform or pay another.

CONDITION PRECEDENT The happening of an uncertain occurrence that is necessary before a particular right or interest may be obtained or an action performed.

ILLUSORY AGREEMENT An agreement that is not legally enforceable because performance of the obligation by the promisor is completely within his or her discretion.

PLAINTIFF IN ERROR Appellant; a party that appeals from a lower court judgment.

Hicks v. Bush

Shareholder in corporation (P) v. Shareholder in a different corporation (D)

N.Y. Ct. App., 180 N.E.2d 425 (1962)

NATURE OF CASE: Appeal in action for specific performance of a merger agreement.

FACT SUMMARY: Hicks (P) contended that parol evidence of a purported oral understanding he had with shareholders (D) in the Clinton G. Bush Company, that a fully integrated written merger agreement was subject to the raising of certain equity expansion funds, was inadmissible.

RULE OF LAW

Parol evidence is admissible to prove an oral condition precedent to the legal effectiveness of a written agreement if the condition does not contradict the express terms of such written agreement.

FACTS: Hicks (P), an owner of certain corporate interests, entered into a completely integrated agreement with the shareholders (D) of the Clinton G. Bush Company (Bush Company), whereby the parties were to merge their various corporate interests into a single holding company, to be known as Bush-Hick Enterprises. Each party was to subscribe to a certain number of shares in the new entity, and the consideration was to be each party's exiting shares in the parties' respective existing corporate entities. Hicks (P) transferred his shares, but the shareholders (D) of the Bush Company did not, and the merger fell through. Hicks (P) brought suit for specific performance. As a defense, the Bush Company shareholders (D) asserted that an oral condition to the contract was that certain equity expansion funds be raised and that such funds were not raised. The trial court determined that these funds were essential to the successful operation of the new venture and that the parties had an oral understanding that the entire merger was subject to the condition that these funds be secured. Hicks (P) denied the oral condition, claiming no such condition had been placed on the written agreement. The trial court rendered judgment for the Bush Company shareholders (D), and the state's highest court granted review.

ISSUE: Is parol evidence admissible to prove an oral condition precedent to the legal effectiveness of a written agreement if the condition does not contradict the express terms of such written agreement?

HOLDING AND DECISION: (Fuld, J.) Yes. Parol evidence is admissible to prove an oral condition precedent to the legal effectiveness of a written agreement if the condition does not contradict the express terms of such written agreement. This parol evidence rule does not bar proof of every orally established condition precedent but only of those that in a real sense contradict the terms of the written agreement. Here, there is no such contradiction. The merger agreement was silent as to the equity expansion funding and, although the contract contained another condition precedent to the merger, the condition requiring the equity expansion funding did not contradict that other condition. The two conditions can stand side by side, and the equity funding condition is a condition in addition to the other. Moreover, evidence of an oral condition is not to be excluded as contradictory or inconsistent merely because the written agreement contains other conditions precedent. Accordingly, the trial court could properly conclude that the parties intended and understood that the merger was to be one of proposal only and that, even though the formal preliminary steps were to be taken, the writing was not to become operative as a contract or the merger effective until the equity expansion funding was raised, especially given that such a condition was not unreasonable under the circumstances. Therefore, the trial court did not err in admitting the parol evidence, and in holding that there was no operative merger contract that could be enforced. [Affirmed.]

ANALYSIS

The Uniform Commercial Code (UCC) provides in § 2-202 that terms with respect to which the confirmatory memoranda of the parties agree or which are otherwise set forth in a writing intended by the parties as a final expression of their agreement with respect to such terms as are included therein may not be contradicted by evidence of any prior agreement or of a contemporaneous oral agreement but may be explained or supplemented by course of dealing or usage of trade, or by course of performance, and by evidence of consistent additional terms unless the court finds the writing to have been intended also as a complete and exclusive statement of the terms of the agreement. As with the result reached in this case, the UCC provides that consistent additional terms, not reduced to writing, may be proved. However, under the UCC approach, the additional terms may not be proved if the court finds that the writing was intended by both parties as a complete and exclusive statement of all the terms. If the additional terms are such that, if agreed upon, they would

Continued on next page.

certainly have been included in the document in the view of the court, then evidence of their alleged making must be kept from the trier of fact.

Quicknotes

PAROL EVIDENCE Evidence given verbally; extraneous evidence.

PAROL EVIDENCE RULE Doctrine precluding parties to an agreement from introducing evidence of prior or contemporaneous agreements in order to repudiate or alter the terms of a written contract.

SPECIFIC PERFORMANCE An equitable remedy whereby the court requires the parties to perform their obligations pursuant to a contract.

Kingston v. Preston

Business owner (P) v. Purchaser (D)

K.B., Lofft 194, 2 Doug. 689, 99 Eng. Rep. 437 (1773)

NATURE OF CASE: Action to recover damages for breach of contract.

FACT SUMMARY: Preston (D) agreed to sell his business to Kingston (P), and Kingston (P) agreed to, but did not, give security for the payments.

RULE OF LAW

Breach of a covenant by one party to a contract relieves the other party's obligation to perform another covenant that is dependent thereon, the performance of the first covenant being an implied condition precedent to the duty to perform the second covenant.

FACTS: Preston (D) agreed (among other things) to sell his business to Kingston (P). Kingston (P) agreed (among other things) to give sufficient security for his payments. Kingston's (P) personal worth was negligible. Kingston (P) failed to provide sufficient security, and thereafter Preston (D) refused to sell.

ISSUE: When one party agrees to sell and a second party agrees to give sufficient security for his payments, are those covenants mutual and independent so that it is no excuse for nonperformance by the first party for him to allege breach of covenant by the second party?

HOLDING AND DECISION: (Lord Mansfield, J.) No. When one party covenants to sell and a second party covenants in return to give sufficient security for his payments, those covenants are dependent. Therefore, Kingston (P) must show that he has provided or is ready and willing to provide sufficient security as a condition precedent to Preston's (D) duty to sell. The dependence or independence of covenants is to be determined from the intention of the parties, which in turn will normally be determined by the "order of time in which the intent of the transaction requires their performance." Here, the security was to be given "at and before the sealing and delivery of the deeds" conveying the business. Thus, according to the "temporal sequence" test, Preston's (D) duty to convey his business was dependent on Kingston's (P) giving of sufficient security. Furthermore, it would be the greatest injustice if Kingston (P) should prevail. The giving of sufficient security was the essence of this agreement and therefore must necessarily be a condition precedent. Judgment for the defendant.

ANALYSIS

Although Lord Mansfield in this famous decision focused on the time sequence of the contract provisions (e.g., a provision to be performed after another provision is dependent on that other provision), he was very likely reacting primarily to the personal poverty of Kingston (P) and the "injustice" that would be done by making Preston (D) go through with his performance and then sue poor Kingston (P) for damages. (Kingston (P), presumably, might run the business into the ground very quickly, leaving Preston's (D) court victory a purely theoretical one.) Note that Lord Mansfield, in determining the time sequence (which he felt was so important), apparently looked not only to the contract itself but also to what he thought must have been the reasonable intentions of the parties.

Quicknotes

CONDITION PRECEDENT The happening of an uncertain occurrence that is necessary before a particular right or interest may be obtained or an action performed.

Stewart v. Newbury

Builder (P) v. Foundry owner (D)

N.Y. Ct. App., 220 N.Y. 379, 115 N.E. 984 (1917)

NATURE OF CASE: Appeal from award of damages for breach of a construction contract.

FACT SUMMARY: Stewart (P), who was contracted to do excavating for Newbury (D), alleged that he was to be paid in the "usual manner," i.e., 85 percent every 30 days, 15 percent being retained until work was completed, even though this was not written into the contract. When Newbury (D) failed to pay, Stewart (P) stopped work.

RULE OF LAW

Where a contract is made to perform work and no agreement is made as to payment, the work must be substantially performed before payment can be demanded.

FACTS: Stewart (P) was contracted by Newbury (D) to do excavating work and claimed that over the telephone Newbury (D) promised to pay in the "usual manner." This is to say, 85 percent each 30 days or end of the month, 15 percent being retained until completion of the work. Newbury (D) denied so promising. Excavation began in July and continued until the end of September when Newbury (D) refused to pay the first bill. Stewart (P) claimed that Newbury (D) would not permit him to continue work because there were alleged variations from specifications. The trial judge charged the jury that if no agreement for payment was made, the builder could expect payment at reasonable intervals, if it were not understood that payments were due monthly, and if payments were not made, builder could abandon the work. The jury found for Stewart (P), and Newbury (D) appealed.

ISSUE: Where a contract is made to perform work and no agreement is made as to payment, must the work be substantially performed before payment can be demanded?

HOLDING AND DECISION: (Crane, J.) Yes. Where a contract is made to perform work and no agreement is made as to payment, the work must be substantially performed before payment can be demanded. It is settled that where a contract is made to perform work and no agreement is made as to payment, the work must be substantially performed before payment can be demanded. As the case was submitted also upon the ground that variation from specifications may have constituted breach, and since it is impossible to tell under which theory the jury arrived at its conclusion, the judgment must be reversed, and a new trial ordered.

ANALYSIS

It is not unusual in a bilateral contract that the parties will neglect to state in what order their promises will be performed. First, a party must perform before he or she is entitled to payment. This is to say, performance is a constructive condition precedent to payment. Periodic payments, as herein illustrated, are not implied. If periodic payments are agreed to, performance is a constructive condition precedent to the first payment, which is a constructive condition precedent to the next stage of performance, etc. These rules are ordinary business practice and have been said to be the "practice of centuries."

Quicknotes

CONDITION PRECEDENT The happening of an uncertain occurrence that is necessary before a particular right or interest may be obtained or an action performed.

CONSTRUCTIVE CONDITION A condition that is not expressly stated in or implied by the terms of an agreement but is imposed by law.

Bartus v. Riccardi

Hearing aid seller (P) v. Buyer (D)

N.Y. City Ct., 284 N.Y.S.2d 222, 55 Misc. 2d 3 (1967)

NATURE OF CASE: Action for breach of contract.

FACT SUMMARY: Bartus (P) sold Riccardi (D) an Acousticon hearing aid, Model A-665, which was supposedly the improved model of the A-660 hearing aid ordered by Riccardi (D).

RULE OF LAW

A seller may offer to cure a nonconforming tender even though the buyer has previously revoked his acceptance and it is beyond the contract time if there are reasonable grounds to believe that the nonconforming goods would be accepted and there is reasonable notice of intent to cure.

FACTS: Riccardi (D) was informed by a hearing clinic that he needed a hearing aid. The Model A-660 Acousticon was recommended for his needs. Riccardi (D) was informed by Bartus (P), who sold hearing aids, that the A-660 had been improved, and Riccardi (D) purchased the improved model, the A-665. After using the model for several days, Riccardi (D) returned it. Bartus (P) subsequently informed Riccardi (D) that he would get him the A-660 or any other model he wished. Riccardi (D) refused to accept a replacement, and Bartus (P) brought suit on the unpaid balance of the contract price of the A-665. Bartus (P) alleged that he had the right to cure even after the rejection of the model as nonconforming.

ISSUE: Does the failure to tender strict performance and the subsequent rejection and revocation by the buyer prevent the seller from attempting a cure?

HOLDING AND DECISION: (Hymes, J.) No. Uniform Commercial Code (UCC) § 2-508 has altered the concept of strict performance. A seller is permitted to cure a nonconforming delivery before the expiration of the contract time by notifying the buyer of his intention and by delivery before the contract has expired. UCC § 2-508(2) would allow a cure beyond the contract time even if acceptance has been revoked if the seller had reasonable grounds to believe the nonconforming goods would be accepted and he reasonably notifies the buyer of his intent to promptly deliver conforming goods. Bartus (P) had reason to believe that the A-665 would be accepted, and he reasonably notified Riccardi (D) of his offer to cure. Riccardi (D) had not altered his position at that time by purchasing a hearing aid elsewhere. Judgment for Bartus (P).

ANALYSIS

If the buyer, after rejecting the nonconforming goods, alters his or her position before notice of an attempted cure, and this was commercially reasonable under the circumstances, the buyer will not be liable where the seller subsequently attempts to cure. Whether the action is commercially reasonable depends on whether the contract has expired, the buyer's needs for prompt delivery, the seller's apparent ability to perform, prior conduct of the parties, etc.

Quicknotes

CURE In a commercial transaction, the seller has a right to correct a delivery of defective goods within the time originally provided for performance as specified in the contract.

MATERIAL BREACH Breach of a contract's terms by one party that is so substantial as to relieve the other party from its obligations pursuant thereto.

SUBSTANTIAL PERFORMANCE Performance of all the essential obligations pursuant to an agreement.

Jorgensen v. Pressnall

Mobile home purchaser (P) v. Mobile home seller (D)

Or. Sup. Ct., 274 Or. 285, 545 P.2d 1382 (1976)

NATURE OF CASE: Appeal from judgment for plaintiffs in action to rescind a purchase contract and to recover a down payment and damages, and from judgment for counterclaimant financing company for breach of warranty.

FACT SUMMARY: The Jorgensens (P) bought a mobile home from Pressnall (D) and financed the transaction through Commercial Credit Company (Commercial Credit) (D). After discovering numerous defects, which Pressnall (D) did not timely repair, they brought suit against Pressnall (D) and Commercial Credit (D) for rescission of the contract, the return of their down payment, and damages. Commercial Credit (D) counterclaimed against Pressnall (D) for breach of warranty. Pressnall (D) contended that rescission was not justified, asserting that (1) there was no evidence of a material misrepresentation inducing the purchase, (2) there was no evidence that the uncorrected defects were material or that they rendered the unit unfit for use as a dwelling, (3) rescission was not a proper remedy because the Jorgensens (P) refused to allow reasonable efforts to repair, and (4) the Jorgensens' (P) continued possession and use of the mobile home constituted an assertion and exercise of the right of ownership inconsistent with their attempted revocation of acceptance.

RULE OF LAW

Under the Uniform Commercial Code, a buyer may revoke acceptance of goods after discovering nonconformities and timely notifying the seller thereof, where the seller fails to cure the nonconformities in a reasonably timely manner and the nonconformities substantially impair the value to the buyer.

FACTS: The Jorgensens (P) bought a new mobile home from Pressnall (D), using their old mobile home as a down payment and financing the balance through Commercial Credit Company (D). Pressnall (D) assigned the financing contract to Commercial Credit (D), warranting the enforceability of the assigned contract. Soon after the Jorgensens (P) moved in, they discovered numerous defects, including water and air leaks, gaps in a hinged section, and defective doors, cabinets, vents, and walls. They promptly gave Pressnall (D) a list of these defects and were assured by Pressnall (D) that the problems would be corrected. After a series of requests for repairs, first to Pressnall (D) and then to the manufacturer, that did not result in the problems being remedied, or that resulted in new problems being created, the Jorgensens (P) rejected Pressnall's (D) further efforts to make repairs and sought rescission of the contract. They tendered back the mobile home, subject to their security interest, and demanded return of the down payment as well as consequential damages. On advice of counsel, they continued to occupy the mobile home until approximately three weeks before the trial. A couple of months later, Commercial Credit (D) repossessed the mobile home and resold it at a loss. Pressnall (D) contended that rescission was not justified, asserting that (1) there was no evidence of a material misrepresentation inducing the purchase, (2) there was no evidence that the uncorrected defects were material or that they rendered the unit unfit for use as a dwelling, (3) rescission was not a proper remedy because the Jorgensens (P) refused to allow reasonable efforts to repair, and (4) the Jorgensens' (P) continued possession and use of the mobile home constituted an assertion and exercise of the right of ownership inconsistent with their attempted revocation of acceptance. Commercial Credit (D) counterclaimed for losses incurred in repossession of the mobile home and if rescission was granted, sought recovery of damages from Pressnall (D) for breach of warranty. The trial court found for the Jorgensens (P) against Pressnall (D) and for Commercial Credit (D) on its cross-complaint against Pressnall (D). The state's highest court granted review.

ISSUE: Under the Uniform Commercial Code, may a buyer revoke acceptance of goods after discovering nonconformities and timely notifying the seller thereof, where the seller fails to cure the nonconformities in a reasonably timely manner and the nonconformities substantially impair the value to the buyer?

HOLDING AND DECISION: (O'Connell, C.J.) Yes. Under the Uniform Commercial Code (UCC), a buyer may revoke acceptance of goods after discovering nonconformities and timely notifying the seller thereof, where the seller fails to cure the nonconformities in a reasonably timely manner and the nonconformities substantially impair the value to the buyer. The contract at bar is governed by the UCC and its provisions on a buyer's right to revoke acceptance. Here, the Jorgensens' (P) rescission letter constituted a revocation of acceptance under the UCC. Pressnall's (D) contentions are that there is no proof of nonconformities substantially impairing the value of the goods and that there has been no failure to seasonably cure the nonconformities, as required by

Continued on next page.

the UCC. The UCC provides that the buyer may revoke acceptance of goods "whose nonconformity substantially impairs its value to him." Determining the value to the buyer is a subjective question that looks at the buyer's particular needs and circumstances, not those of an average buyer. Conversely, determining whether the nonconformities have substantially impaired that value is an objective question that calls for evidence from which it can be inferred that the buyer's needs were not met because of the nonconformity. The existence of substantial impairment depends upon the facts and circumstances in each case. Here, the Jorgensens (P) purchased the mobile home for the purpose of using it as their residence. Because of the defects they discovered and Pressnall's (D) failure to cure them, the value of the mobile home to the Jorgensens (P) as a residence was substantially impaired. Pressnall (D) argues that since the Jorgensens (P) did not produce any evidence showing that the cost of repairs was substantial in relation to the purchase price, there was no proof of substantial impairment of value. This argument would have some force if the test for a substantial impairment of value were an objective one. However, since the test is a subjective one, permitting revocation of acceptance if it is shown that the value to the purchaser is impaired, the relatively small amount of money needed to repair the defect is not necessarily relevant because the impairment of the value to the purchaser may be substantial even though the cost of curing the defect may be relatively small. Thus, in the present case, although the defects in the mobile home probably could have been repaired at a relatively small cost, the Jorgensens (P) were deprived of the benefits of a comfortable home for a substantial period of time as a result of Pressnall's (D) failure to make timely repairs. Pressnall (D) also argues that impairment of value is not shown unless the goods are useless for the purchaser's purposes. This is not true; revocation of acceptance is permissible not only where there is complete impairment but also where the impairment is substantial but not complete. Pressnall (D) further argues that any failure to cure the nonconformities was excused because the Jorgensens (P) unreasonably refused to allow further attempts to repair the unit. This argument is unpersuasive because Pressnall (D) failed to act within a reasonable amount of time. Pressnall's (D) final argument is likewise unavailing. Pressnall (D) contends that the Jorgensens' (P) continued possession and use of the mobile home constituted an assertion and exercise of the right of ownership inconsistent with their attempted revocation of acceptance and created a new acceptance. However, the Jorgensens (P) retained a security interest in the mobile home after the revocation of acceptance, which entitled them to continue in possession to preserve their collateral. They acted properly, and Pressnall (D) was not prejudiced thereby since the trial court awarded an offset to Pressnall (D) for the rental value of the mobile home during their occupancy. Affirmed.

ANALYSIS

In analyzing the substantial impairment issue under Uniform Commercial Code § 2-608, the test does not ask what the seller had reason to know at the time of contracting. Instead, as illustrated by this case, the question is whether the nonconformity is such as will in fact cause a substantial impairment of value to the buyer though the seller had no advance knowledge as to the buyer's particular circumstances or needs. That is because it cannot be known ahead of time what will cause substantial impairment of value to a buyer, since what may cause one person great inconvenience or financial loss may not adversely affect another.

Quicknotes

BREACH OF WARRANTY The breach of a promise made by one party to a contract on which the other party may rely, relieving that party from the obligation of determining whether the fact is true and indemnifying the other party from liability if that fact is shown to be false.

MATERIALITY Importance; the degree of relevance or necessity to the particular matter.

MISREPRESENTATION A statement or conduct by one party to another that constitutes a false representation of fact.

OBJECTIVE STANDARD A standard that is not personal to an individual but is dependent on some external source.

REVOCATION The cancellation or withdrawal of some authority conferred, or destruction or making void an instrument drafted.

SECURITY INTEREST An interest in property to secure the performance of an obligation (especially repayment of a debt). In bankruptcy, it is a lien created by an agreement.

SUBJECTIVE STANDARD A standard that is based on the personal belief of an individual.

Jacob & Youngs v. Kent

Contractor (P) v. Customer (D)

N.Y. Ct. App., 230 N.Y. 239, 129 N.E. 889 (1921)

NATURE OF CASE: Appeal from grant of new trial in action for damages for breach of a construction contract.

FACT SUMMARY: Jacob & Youngs (P) was hired to build a $77,000 country home for Kent (D). When the dwelling was completed, it was discovered that through an oversight, pipe, not of Reading manufacture (though of comparable quality and price) that had been specified in the contract, was used. Kent (D) refused to make final payment of $3,483.46 upon learning of this.

RULE OF LAW

For damages in construction contracts, the owner is entitled merely to the difference between the value of the structure if built to specifications and the value it has as constructed.

FACTS: Jacob & Youngs (Jacob) (P) built a country home for $77,000 for Kent (D) and sued for $3,483.46, which remained unpaid. Almost a year after completion, Kent (D) discovered that not all pipe in the home was of Reading manufacture as specified in the contract. Kent (D) ordered the plumbing replaced, but as it was encased in the walls, except in those spots where it must necessarily remain exposed, Jacob (P) refused to replace the pipe, stating that the pipe used was of comparable price and quality. It appears that the omission was neither fraudulent nor willful and was due to oversight. Kent (D) refused to pay the balance of the construction cost still due. The trial court directed a verdict for Kent (D), but the appellate division reversed, and granted a new trial.

ISSUE: For damages in construction contracts, is the owner entitled merely to the difference in the value of the structure if built to specifications and the value it has as constructed?

HOLDING AND DECISION: (Cardozo, J.) Yes. For damages in construction contracts, the owner is entitled merely to the difference between the value of the structure if built to specifications and the value it has as constructed. Where the significance of the default or omission is grievously out of proportion to the oppression of the forfeiture, the breach is considered trivial and innocent. A change will not be tolerated if it is so dominant and pervasive as to frustrate the purpose of the contract. The contractor cannot install anything he believes to be just as good. It is a matter of degree judged by the purpose to be served, the desire to be gratified, the excuse for deviation from the letter, and the cruelty of enforced adherence. Under the circumstances, the measure of damages should not be the cost of replacing the pipe, which would be great. Instead, the difference in value between the dwelling as specified and the dwelling as constructed should be the measure, even though it may be nominal or nothing. Usually, the owner is entitled to the cost of completion, but not where it is grossly unfair and out of proportion to the good to be obtained. This simply is a rule to promote justice when there is substantial performance with trivial deviation. Affirmed.

DISSENT: (McLaughlin, J.) Jacob (P) failed to perform as specified. It makes no difference why Kent (D) wanted a particular kind of pipe. Failure to use the kind of pipe specified was either intentional or due to gross neglect, which amounted to the same thing. Therefore, the majority's reliance on the rule of substantial performance, with damages for unsubstantial omissions, is inapplicable under the facts of the case.

ANALYSIS

Substantial performance cannot occur where the breach is intentional, as it is the antithesis of material breach. The part unperformed must not destroy the purpose or value of the contract. Because here, there is a dissatisfied landowner who stands to retain the defective structure built on his land, there arises the problem of unjust enrichment. Usually, it would appear the owner would pocket the damages he collected rather than remedying the defect by tearing out the wrong pipe and replacing it with the specified pipe. The owner would have a home substantially in compliance and a sum of money greatly in excess of the harm suffered by him. Note that under the doctrine of *de minimis non curat lex*, trivial defects, even if willful, will be ignored. The party who claims substantial performance has still breached the contract and is liable for damages but in a lesser amount than for a willful breach.

Quicknotes

DE MINIMIS NON CURAT LEX Not of sufficient significance to invoke legal action. Shortened to "de minimis."

SUBSTANTIAL PERFORMANCE Performance of all the essential obligations pursuant to an agreement.

Walker & Co. v. Harrison

Sign servicer (P) v. Dry cleaner (D)

Mich. Sup. Ct., 347 Mich. 630, 81 N.W.2d 352 (1957)

NATURE OF CASE: Appeal from award of damages for breach of contract.

FACT SUMMARY: Harrison (D) rented a neon sign and sought to repudiate the rental agreement when Walker & Co. (P) delayed in repairing the sign.

RULE OF LAW

A party attempting to repudiate a contract must convince the court that the other party has materially breached the contract.

FACTS: Walker & Co. (Walker) (P) contracted to rent a neon sign to Harrison (D). The rental agreement included repair service "as deemed necessary by [Walker (P)] to keep sign in first class advertising condition." Shortly after the sign was installed, someone hit it with a tomato. Rust was allegedly visible on the chrome and cobwebs had collected in the corners. Harrison (D) made several calls to Walker (P) complaining of the sign's condition, but maintenance was not forthcoming. Harrison (D) repudiated the contract and Walker (P) sued for the rent. [Walker (P) subsequently repaired the sign.] From a judgment for Walker (P), Harrison (D) appealed.

ISSUE: Must a party attempting to repudiate a contract convince the court that the other party has materially breached the contract?

HOLDING AND DECISION: (Smith, J.) Yes. A party attempting to repudiate a contract must convince the court that the other party has materially breached the contract. It is essential to one party's repudiation of a contract that he demonstrates a "material breach" by the other party. As to the criterion for "materiality," there is no single touchstone. Here, Harrison (D) claims that Walker's (P) repeated failures to repair or maintain the sign constituted material breach. Although Walker's (P) delay in rendering service was certainly irritating, it cannot be said as a matter of law that the delay was a material breach. There was no valid ground for Harrison's (D) repudiation and failure to comply with the terms of the contract was itself a material breach, entitling Walker (P) to judgment. Affirmed.

ANALYSIS

The primary advantage in alleging "material breach" is that the alleging party, if successful, may rescind the whole contract. If a breach is not material, the breachee may recover damages flowing therefrom but may not cancel the contract. In the present case, for example, it would not be surprising to find that Harrison (D) wanted out of his contract for reasons other than the breach and alleged "materiality" as a means to this end. As the court indicates, there is no simple test for materiality, which is unfortunate since so much can hinge on the characterization. Among the factors often considered are: (1) To what extent was the contract performed prior to the breach? (2) Was the breach willful? (3) Was the breach "quantitatively" serious? and (4) What will be the consequences of the determination, e.g., will it work extreme hardship on one of the parties? Some of the above factors should undoubtedly be given more weight than others and arguably some of them overlap. Perhaps the most important factor is the last one that openly acknowledges "materiality" as a conclusory label to be applied insofar as a sense of "justice" requires it.

Quicknotes

ASSUMPSIT An oral or written promise by one party to perform or pay another.

MATERIALITY Importance; the degree of relevance or necessity to the particular matter.

RECOUPMENT The right of a defendant to have the plaintiff's award of damages reduced because of either prior payment tendered or some unlawful action on the part of the plaintiff.

REPUDIATION The actions or statements of a party to a contract that evidence the party's intent not to perform, or to continue performance of, the party's duties or obligations thereunder.

K & G Construction Co. v. Harris

General contractor (P) v. Subcontractor (D)

Md. Ct. App., 223 Md. 305, 164 A.2d 451 (1960)

NATURE OF CASE: Appeal from judgment for defendant in action to recover damages for breach of contract.

FACT SUMMARY: Harris (D), a subcontractor, caused damage to K & G Construction Co. (K&G) (P), the contractor. K&G (P) withheld a progress installment payment to account for the damage. Harris (D) then ceased work entirely under the contract on the basis of the withheld progress payment, and K&G (P) was forced to hire another subcontractor to complete the work at greater cost. K&G (P) contended that Harris (D) was liable for the damage, as well as for the additional cost K&G (P) incurred to have the work completed and that K&G (P) had justifiably withheld the progress payment. Harris (D) contended that K&G (P) was liable for the profit Harris (D) would have made had Harris (D) completed the job, as well as for the amount of the installment payment.

RULE OF LAW

(1) Where a subcontractor materially breaches a contract, the contractor may justifiably withhold a progress payment to account for the damages caused by the subcontractor's breach.
(2) Where a contractor justifiably withholds a progress payment to a subcontractor to account for damages caused by the subcontractor's material breach, the subcontractor's continued performance under the contract is not excused by the contractor's withholding of the progress payment.

FACTS: Harris (D), a subcontractor, was hired by K & G Construction Co. (K&G) (P), a general contractor, to perform excavation and earth-moving work. The contract stipulated that the work was to be performed in a "workmanlike manner." Harris (D) was to be paid each month after submission of a requisition of the prior month's work. After one of Harris's (D) employees caused $3,400 damage to a house with a bulldozer, Harris (D) refused to repair the house or compensate K&G (P) for the damage, claiming Harris (D) was not liable for the damage. K&G (P) in turn did not pay Harris's (D) requisition for the month in which the accident occurred. Soon after, Harris (D) ceased working on the project, at which point the value of the work done for which Harris (D) had not been paid was $1484.50. If Harris (D) had completed the remaining work to be done under the contract, Harris (D) would have made a profit of $1,340.00 on the remaining uncompleted portion of the contract. It cost K&G (P) $450 above the contract price to have another excavating contractor complete the remaining work required under the contract. K&G (P) sued Harris (D) (1) for the bulldozer damage and (2) for the $450.00 costs above the contract price in having another excavating subcontractor complete the uncompleted work in the contract. Harris (D) counterclaimed for $1,484.50, the value of the work for which Harris (D) had not received payment, and for the loss of the anticipated profits on the uncompleted portion of work in the amount of $1,340.00. The first count was submitted to a jury, which found for K&G (P) as to the bulldozer damage in the amount of $3,400.00. Harris (D) subsequently paid K&G (P) this amount. The second count and the counterclaim were submitted to the judge for determination, without a jury, and the judge found for Harris (D) in the amount of $2,824.50, from which K&G (P) appealed. The state's highest court granted review.

ISSUE:

(1) Where a subcontractor materially breaches a contract, may the contractor justifiably withhold a progress payment to account for the damages caused by the subcontractor's breach?
(2) Where a contractor justifiably withholds a progress payment to a subcontractor to account for damages caused by the subcontractor's material breach, is the subcontractor's continued performance under the contract excused by the contractor's withholding of the progress payment?

HOLDING AND DECISION: (Prescott, J.)

(1) Yes. Where a subcontractor materially breaches a contract, the contractor may justifiably withhold a progress payment to account for the damages caused by the subcontractor's breach. Stated succinctly, the question presented regarding this issue is whether K & G Construction Co. (K&G) (P) had the right, under the circumstances, to refuse to make the progress payment due on Harris's (D) requisition. It would be anomalous to hold that a building contractor, who has obtained a subcontractor to do work on a project and has agreed to pay each month for the work performed in the previous month, must continue the monthly payments, irrespective of the degree of skill and care displayed in the performance of work, and that the contractor's only recourse is to sue for breach. If this were the law, it is likely that many contractors would become insolvent before

Continued on next page.

they were able to complete their contracts. Covenants are to be construed as dependent or independent according to the intention of the parties and the circumstances of the case. Here, Harris (D) materially breached the contract when Harris's (D) employee negligently caused damage to K&G (P), as this was a breach of Harris's (D) promise to perform work in a "workmanlike manner." Moreover, there is no doubt that the breach was material, as the damage was more than double the payment due under the requisition. Because Harris (D) failed to substantially perform, K&G (P) was justified in withholding the progress payment. Although Harris (D) was required under the contract to obtain liability insurance, merely because Harris (D) did so would not by itself require K&G (P) to have made the installment payment. Harris (D) and the insurance company denied liability, and the mere furnishing by Harris (D) of the insurance did not constitute a license to perform work in a careless, negligent, or unworkmanlike manner. Also, the acceptance by K&G (P) of the insurance did not preclude K&G (P) from asserting a claim for unworkmanlike performance directly against Harris (D).

(2) No. Where a contractor justifiably withholds a progress payment to a subcontractor to account for damages caused by the subcontractor's material breach, the subcontractor's continued performance under the contract is not excused by the contractor's withholding of the progress payment. Harris's (D) abandonment of work after K&G (P) justifiably withheld the progress payment was a wrongful repudiation of the contract. The promises in the contract were mutually dependent, and Harris (D) materially breached the contract when Harris's (D) employee negligently caused damage with the bulldozer, thus failing to perform in a workmanlike manner. This justified K&G (P) in refusing to make the installment payment; hence, because K&G (P) was not in default, Harris (D) again breached the contract when Harris (D) discontinued work on the project, which rendered Harris (D) liable (by the express terms of the contract) to K&G (P) for the increased cost in having the excavating done in the amount of $450. Accordingly, the judgment against K&G (P) is reversed, and judgment for $450 is entered against Harris (D).

ANALYSIS

The present case demonstrates the basic modern rule that a party who is to perform work must perform (according to the contract) before that party is entitled to payment. In other words, performance of work is a constructive condition precedent to payment. The present case, which concerns periodic payments, involves a series of alternating constructive conditions precedent (e.g., performance by Harris (D) is a constructive condition precedent to K & G Construction Co.'s (K&G's) (P) duty to make the first payment, which is in turn a constructive condition precedent to Harris's (D) duty to perform the next stage of work, etc.). Thus, K&G's (P) refusal to pay was justified and not a "breach," since the payment was conditioned on the prior "workmanlike" performance by Harris (D) that was not forthcoming.

Quicknotes

CONDITION PRECEDENT The happening of an uncertain occurrence that is necessary before a particular right or interest may be obtained or an action performed.

MATERIAL BREACH Breach of a contract's terms by one party that is so substantial as to relieve the other party from its obligations pursuant thereto.

REPUDIATION The actions or statements of a party to a contract that evidence the party's intent not to perform, or to continue performance of, the party's duties or obligations thereunder.

New England Structures, Inc. v. Loranger

Subcontractor (D) v. General contractor (P)

Mass. Sup. Jud. Ct., 354 Mass. 62, 234 N.E.2d 888 (1968)

NATURE OF CASE: Action for damages for breach of a construction contract.

FACT SUMMARY: Loranger (P), which contracted with New England Structures, Inc. (Structures) (D) for the latter to construct a gypsum roof on a school, terminated the deal, contending that Structures (D) failed to provide enough skilled workmen as required by the contract.

RULE OF LAW

In stating his reasons for rejecting performance or his objections to a performance that he has accepted, a promisee has not excused other grounds upon which he may have rejected the defective performance unless the promisor shows that it has relied to its detriment upon the particular ground stated.

FACTS: Loranger (P), general contractor on a school project, contracted on July 11, 1961, with New England Structures, Inc. (Structures) (D), a subcontractor, to install a gypsum roof deck in the school. Structures (D) began work on November 24, 1961. On December 18, 1961, Loranger (P) sent a telegram to Structures (D) terminating the agreement on the ground that Structures (D) had failed to provide a sufficient number of skilled workmen as required by article 5 of the contracts. Loranger (P) stated its intention of obtaining other workers and charging any higher costs to Structures (D). As five days' notice was required, Structures (D) was told to remove itself from the project by December 26, 1961. Loranger (P) claimed that all the work was not properly done, while Structures (D) claimed it was not allowed to complete its five days and had it been, it could have completed the work. The trial judge ruled as a matter of law that Loranger's (P) justification of termination as being Structures' (D) failure to supply enough skilled workers confined Loranger (P) to that ground only, which, if so found, would have been sufficient for the jury to find Structures (D) in breach. The judge also instructed that Structures (D) could not be found in breach if it had supplied a sufficient number of skilled workers even though it may have done improper work as Loranger (P) limited grounds for breach by its telegram. But if Structures (D) was found to have breached, these other allegations could be considered for the purposes of setting damages.

ISSUE: In stating his reasons for rejecting performance or his objections to a performance that he has accepted, has a promisee excused other grounds upon which he may have rejected the defective performance unless the promisor shows that it has relied to its detriment upon the particular ground stated?

HOLDING AND DECISION: (Cutter, J.) No. In stating his reasons for rejecting performance or his objections to a performance that he has accepted, a promisee has not excused other grounds upon which he may have rejected the defective performance unless the promisor shows that it has relied to its detriment upon the particular ground stated. The grounds for breach would not be limited unless New England Structures, Inc. (Structures) (D) showed it has detrimentally relied on the justification given. When one has several reasons for acting the way he did, he is not prevented from relying upon them simply because he put forth only one originally, unless the other party has been misled to its harm, or he is estopped on some other ground. When a period of notice is required, the contract remains in force and must continue to be performed during the established period set after notice of termination, here, five days. "Strong practical considerations" make it appear that a five-day period was intended to permit the subcontractor to remove his workers and equipment rather than give time to permit an attempt to cure the defect in performance. Nothing suggests that had Structures (D) cured the defect within five days, Loranger (P) would have had to withdraw termination. But if Loranger (P) was not justified in terminating, it would be liable for breach. Accordingly, exceptions are sustained.

ANALYSIS

The view of this case is a more modern view and is typical of a growing trend away from cases that had limited termination to the stated grounds rather than the general grounds of the contract. Basically, one can change one's defense unless the other party has relied on it. In Restatement (First) § 305, this is dealt with where performance of the condition or promise requires the tender of money. If the tender is not made with tender legal for that purpose, but it is rejected without reason, the party making tender cannot have a defense on the ground no reason was given.

Quicknotes

DETRIMENTAL RELIANCE Reliance by one party that is based on the conduct or promises of another, resulting in loss to the party.

Gill v. Johnstown Lumber Co.

Log driver (P) v. Sawmill (D)

Pa. Sup. Ct., 151 Pa. 534, 25 A. 120 (1892)

NATURE OF CASE: Appeal from directed verdict for the defense action to recover damages for breach of contract.

FACT SUMMARY: Gill (P) contracted to drive and deliver four million feet of logs but had delivered only a part of that amount when a flood swept away the rest of the logs.

RULE OF LAW

When consideration for work done is apportionable or apportioned in the contract, that contract will be interpreted as divisible (severable) in case of part performance.

FACTS: Gill (P) contracted to drive four million feet of logs to Johnstown Lumber Co.'s (Johnstown's) (D) boom. The work undertaken by Gill (P) consisted of driving logs of oak and other kinds of timber and also driving cross-ties. Gill (P) was to be paid $1 per thousand feet for the oak logs, $0.75 per thousand feet for all other logs, and $0.03 each for cross ties. Gill (P) did deliver some of the logs as promised, but a flood swept other logs past Johnstown's (D) boom after Gill (P) had driven them part of the way. Gill (P) sued for payment, but the court directed a verdict for Johnstown (D) based on Gill's (P) default. Gill (P) appealed.

ISSUE: When consideration for work done is apportionable or apportioned in the contract, will that contract be interpreted as divisible (severable) in case of part performance?

HOLDING AND DECISION: (Heydrick, J.) Yes. If the part to be performed by one party consists of several and distinct items, and the price to be paid by the other is (1) apportioned to each item to be performed or (2) left to be implied by law, such a contract will generally be held to be severable. The consideration to be paid for Gill's (P) work was not an entire sum but was apportioned among the several items at the rate of $1 per thousand feet for the oak logs, $0.75 per thousand feet for all other logs, $0.03 each for cross ties, etc. Applying the test of an apportionable or apportioned consideration to the contract in question, it will be seen at once that it is severable. Thus, Gill (P) may recover at the contract rate for the logs delivered as promised. If the consideration to be paid is single and entire, the contract must be held to be entire. With respect to each log (or bunch of logs), the consideration to be paid is an entire sum for the whole distance and is not apportionable to parts of the drive. The contract in this respect is like a contract of common carriage that is dependent upon the delivery of the goods at the designated place. Thus, Gill (P) may not recover for any part-way shipment that took place before the flood. Reversed.

ANALYSIS

A more general test of divisibility is whether, had the parties thought of it, they would have been willing to exchange the part performances irrespective of what transpired subsequently. It is rare that the parties express an intention on this question so that whether a contract is "divisible" (separable) or "entire" is usually a matter of interpretation. Thus, the "apportionable consideration" test, which the court uses in the present case, is a bit facile and cannot always be counted on as the appropriate manifestation of the parties' intention to enter a divisible contract.

Quicknotes

BREACH OF CONTRACT Unlawful failure by a party to perform its obligations pursuant to contract.

CONSIDERATION Value given by one party in exchange for performance, or a promise to perform, by another party.

PART PERFORMANCE Partial performance of a contract, promise, or obligation.

Britton v. Turner

Laborer (P) v. Employer (D)

N.H. Sup. Ct., 6 N.H. 481 (1834)

NATURE OF CASE: Appeal from recovery in quantum meruit for work done.

FACT SUMMARY: Britton (P) contracted to work for Turner (D) for an entire year but left without cause before the year was up.

RULE OF LAW

A defaulting party, although unable to recover on his contract, may recover under a quasi-contractual theory the reasonable value of his services less any damages to the other party arising out of the default.

FACTS: Britton (P) was under contract to labor for Turner (D) for one year and was to be paid $120 for the work. Britton (P), without cause, left Turner's (D) employ after nine and one-half months and sought to recover the reasonable value of his labor. A jury awarded Britton (P) a verdict for $95. Turner (D) appealed.

ISSUE: May a defaulting party, although unable to recover on his contract, recover under a quasi-contractual theory the reasonable value of his services less any damages to the other party arising out of the default?

HOLDING AND DECISION: (Parker, J.) Yes. A defaulting party, although unable to recover on his contract, may recover under a quasi-contractual theory the reasonable value of his services less any damages to the other party arising out of the default. Although it is clear one who has labored for only a portion of the contract term may not recover on the contract, he may recover in quantum meruit the reasonable value of his services to the extent that the other party has received a benefit in excess of damages arising from the breach. A contrary result would be unjust and unequal in its operation. By that result, the party who attempts performance may be placed in a much worse situation than he who wholly disregards his contract, and the other party may receive much more, by the breach of the contract, than the injury, which he sustained by such breach, and more than he could be entitled to if he was seeking to recover damages by an action. In the present case, Turner (D) has been receiving benefit from day to day that he cannot now reject, and the circumstance is not distinguishable from those circumstances surrounding contracts to build houses where quantum meruit recoveries have been allowed despite deviations from the building contracts. Since Turner (D) has alleged no damages arising from Britton's (P) breach, the jury's verdict should be affirmed.

ANALYSIS

The court here acknowledges the contrary rule that will not allow a breaching party any recovery after only part performance (subject to the doctrine of substantial performance). Even today the present case still represents the minority view although the trend is in its direction. The court emphasizes the injustice of the prevailing role that one who attempts performance is in a worse position than one who totally ignores the contract. Although there is a temptation to respond "So what?," courts following Britton's (P) lead have pointed to the arbitrary forfeitures that breachers would suffer and the pure windfalls to the breachees. Further, the current trend in contract law is not to treat a breach as an inherently evil thing; the effect of allowing an unabashed forfeiture would be to sanction a kind of punitive damage.

Quicknotes

ASSUMPSIT An oral or written promise by one party to perform or pay another.

QUANTUM MERUIT Equitable doctrine allowing recovery for labor and materials provided by one party, even though no contract was entered into, in order to avoid unjust enrichment by the benefited party.

QUASI-CONTRACT An implied contract created by law to prevent unjust enrichment.

Nelson v. Hazel

Contractor (P) v. Homeowner (D)

Idaho Sup. Ct., 91 Idaho 850, 433 P.2d 120 (1967)

NATURE OF CASE: Appeal from judgment, rendered on remand, for plaintiff in action to foreclose a mechanic's and materialman's lien.

FACT SUMMARY: The Hazels (D), who had hired Nelson (P), a contractor, to remodel their house, contended that because Nelson (P) had failed to substantially perform under the parties' contract, Nelson (P) was not entitled to any damages as a defaulting party, and challenged an award to Nelson (P) of labor and materials offset by the amounts the Hazels (D) had already paid Nelson (P), plus the amount of the Hazels' (D) damages for the cost of repairing Nelson's (P) defective construction.

RULE OF LAW

Where a building contractor fails to substantially perform under a building contract, the contractor nevertheless is entitled to recover the value of the contractor's work offset by the building owner's damages.

FACTS: The Hazels (D) hired Nelson (P), a contractor, to remodel their house. Nelson (D), who had failed to perform the remodeling work in a workmanlike manner, nevertheless sued the Hazels (D) to foreclose on Nelson's (P) mechanic's and materialman's lien. The Hazels (D) contended that Nelson (P) could not foreclose on the lien because Nelson (P) had failed to substantially perform under the parties' contract. The state's highest court agreed with the Hazels (D), ruled that Nelson (P) was not entitled to damages for breach of contract or to enforce the lien, and remanded the case for a determination of the Hazels' (D) damages. On remand, the trial court determined that Nelson (P) was entitled to recover $5,090.86 for labor and materials, less $1,997.51, which the Hazels (D) had already paid on the contract. The trial court then awarded the Hazels (D) damages for the cost of repairing Nelson's (P) defective construction in the amount of $2,494.50, and offset that amount against the amount to which Nelson (P) was entitled. Accordingly, the trial court entered judgment in favor of Nelson (P) for $598.85. The Hazels (D) appealed, contending that because Nelson (P) defaulted on the contract by failing to substantially perform, Nelson (P) was entitled to nothing under the damages calculation. The state's highest court granted review.

ISSUE: Where a building contractor fails to substantially perform under a building contract, is the contractor nevertheless entitled to recover the value of the contractor's work offset by the building owner's damages?

HOLDING AND DECISION: (Smith, J.) Yes. Where a building contractor fails to substantially perform under a building contract, the contractor nevertheless is entitled to recover the value of the contractor's work offset by the building owner's damages. Building contracts constitute an exception to the usual contract rule that a defaulting party in a contract action cannot recover damages. This exception is based on the reasoning that unjust enrichment would result were the building owner to retain the value of improvements in excess of that caused by the contractor's breach. Even where the contract cannot be said to be substantially performed, as in this case, the weight of authority allows a negligent contractor to recover for the benefits actually conferred, to avoid a forfeiture. If the defective performance, though less than substantial, has conferred benefits on the owner in excess of the owner's injury, the owner is under a quasi-contractual duty to pay that excess. Accordingly, the trial court did not err in determining the cost of labor and materials that Nelson (P) had incurred in the work already done for the Hazels (D), and offsetting that amount by the Hazels' (D) anticipated cost of remedying Nelson's (P) defective work and the payments they had already made. Affirmed.

ANALYSIS

In the context of construction contracts, if a contractor's negligent or defective performance is remediable, the owner's recovery will be based on the market price of completing or correcting the performance, and that market price will normally be shown by the cost of completing the work by another person. Thus, for example, in this case, two expert witnesses testified as to the cost or remedying Nelson's (P) defective work, and, in calculating the Hazels' (D) damages, the trial court used the higher of those two estimates.

Quicknotes

BREACH OF CONTRACT Unlawful failure by a party to perform its obligations pursuant to contract.

DAMAGES Monetary compensation that may be awarded by the court to a party who has sustained injury or loss to his or her person, property, or rights due to another party's unlawful act, omission, or negligence.

Continued on next page.

LIEN A claim against the property of another in order to secure the payment of a debt.

MATERIALMAN'S LIEN A lien enforceable pursuant to statute in structures and/or improvements constructed in order to secure payment for the value of materials furnished.

MECHANIC'S LIEN A lien enforceable pursuant to statute in structures and/or improvements constructed in order to secure payment for the value of labor performed or materials furnished.

SUBSTANTIAL PERFORMANCE Performance of all the essential obligations pursuant to an agreement.

UNJUST ENRICHMENT The principle of retaining a benefit given to one by another, without compensating the giver, in situations where compensation is reasonably expected.

McKenna v. Vernon

Contractor (P) v. Property owner (D)

Penn. Sup. Ct., 258 Pa. 18, 101 A. 919 (1917)

NATURE OF CASE: Appeal from judgment for plaintiff in action for payment of balance due on a construction contract.

FACT SUMMARY: Vernon (D) contended that McKenna (P) was not entitled to payment of the balance due on a construction contract because the contract specified that an architect's certificate of work done was a condition of payment, and no such certificate was secured. McKenna (P) argued that this condition was waived because prior payments had been made in the absence of the architect's certificate.

RULE OF LAW

A contract condition will be waived where it has previously and repeatedly been waived in the course of performance.

FACTS: McKenna (P), a general contractor, entered into an agreement with Vernon (D) to build a movie theater. The contract provided that the contract price of $8,750 was to be paid in installments and that the work was to be done under the direction of an architect, whose certificate of work done was a condition of each installment payment by Vernon (D). With one exception, Vernon (D) paid seven of the installments, amounting to $6,000, without having secured the architect's certificate. McKenna (P) brought suit for the remainder owing after Vernon (D) failed to pay him the balance, claiming the work was defective. The architect testified that the work complied with the building specifications, and judgment was rendered for McKenna (P). Vernon (D) appealed, claiming there was no right of action absent the architect's certificate of completion. McKenna (P) asserted this condition had been waived. The state's highest court granted review.

ISSUE: Will a contract condition be waived where it has previously and repeatedly been waived in the course of performance?

HOLDING AND DECISION: (Stewart, J.) Yes. A contract condition will be waived where it has previously and repeatedly been waived in the course of performance. Having consistently and repeatedly waived the condition before, it is too late now for Vernon (D) to assert the condition as a bar to McKenna's (P) recovery. Given that Vernon (D) waived the condition during the progress of the work, which was shown to have been satisfactorily completed, there are no grounds for him to assert that he did not also waive the final payment. [Affirmed.]

ANALYSIS

"Waiver" is often inexactly defined as "the voluntary relinquishment of a known right." When the waiver is reinforced by reliance, enforcement is often said to rest on "estoppel." Since the more common definition of estoppel is limited to reliance on a misrepresentation of an existing fact, reliance on a waiver or promise as to the future is sometimes said to create a "promissory estoppel." The common definition of waiver may lead to the incorrect inference that the promisor must know his or her legal rights and must intend the legal effect of the promise, but at least under the approach in Restatement § 93, it is sufficient if he or she has reason to know the essential facts. That section provides that a waiver is not binding unless the promisor knew or had reason to know the essential facts of the previous transaction to which the promise relates, but his or her knowledge of the legal effect of the facts is immaterial.

Quicknotes

PROMISSORY ESTOPPEL A promise that is enforceable if the promisor should reasonably expect that it will induce action or forbearance on the part of the promisee, that does in fact cause such action or forbearance, and that is the only means of avoiding injustice.

WAIVER The intentional or voluntary forfeiture of a recognized right.

Iron Trade Products Co. v. Wilkoff Co.

Rail purchaser (P) v. Supplier (D)

Pa. Sup. Ct., 272 Pa. 172, 116 A. 150 (1922)

NATURE OF CASE: Action to recover damages for breach of contract.

FACT SUMMARY: Wilkoff Co. (D) contracted to deliver rails to Iron Trade Products Co. (Iron Trade) (P) but refused to do so after Iron Trade (P) reduced the available supply and made Wilkoff's (D) performance more difficult.

RULE OF LAW

Mere difficulty of performance will not excuse a breach of contract even though the difficulty was created by the other contracting party.

FACTS: Iron Trade Products Co. (Iron Trade) (P) contracted to purchase 2,600 tons of rails from Wilkoff Co. (D) at the rate of $41 per ton. Iron Trade (P) thereafter purchased additional rails from one of the very few rail suppliers, thereby reducing the overall rail supply and driving up the market price. Because of the reduced supply and increased price of rails, it became difficult and unprofitable for Wilkoff (D) to procure rails for Iron Trade (P). Wilkoff (D) failed to deliver. Iron Trade (P) subsequently covered at a higher price and sued for damages. The trial court entered judgment for Iron Trade (P), and Wilkoff (D) appealed.

ISSUE: Does one party's conduct, which renders performance by the second party more difficult, excuse that second party's refusal to perform?

HOLDING AND DECISION: (Walling, J.) No. If a party seeking to secure all the merchandise that he could entered into a contract for a quantity of the required goods, and subsequently made performance of the contract by the seller more difficult by making other purchases that increased the scarcity of the available supply, his conduct would furnish no excuse for refusal to perform the prior contract. Here, Iron Trade Products Co.'s (Iron Trade's) (P) conduct did not render performance by Wilkoff Co. (D) impossible but only more difficult. Mere difficulty of performance will not excuse a breach of contract. The case of *U.S. v. Peck*, 102 U.S. 64 (1880), in which one party cut off the other party's only available source of supply, thus rendering performance impossible, is not parallel. Finally, there was no restriction in the contract on subsequent purchases by Iron Trade (P). Affirmed.

ANALYSIS

Although there is no straightforward rule that explains the result in all the cases similar to the present one, perhaps the connecting thread is an assumption-of-risk notion. The court here undoubtedly felt that a deflated supply (and the resulting inflated market price) was a foreseeable commercial risk that Wilkoff Co. (D) undertook when it entered the contract. However, if Iron Trade Products Co. (Iron Trade) (P) had interfered with what it knew to be Wilkoff's (D) only source of supply, Wilkoff's (D) duty might have been discharged since Wilkoff (D) would not be held to have assumed the risk of Iron Trade's (P) knowing interference. See *Patterson v. Meyerhofer*, 204 N.Y. 96 (1912). A court will use its instinct for "justice" in each case.

Quicknotes

BREACH OF CONTRACT Unlawful failure by a party to perform its obligations pursuant to contract.

Hochster v. De La Tour

Prospective employee (P) v. Employer (D)

Q.B., 2 E. & B. 678, 118 Eng. Rep. 922 (1853)

NATURE OF CASE: Action to recover damages for breach of contract.

FACT SUMMARY: Before Hochster (P) was due to perform his contract of employment for De La Tour (D), De La Tour (D) announced his intention to repudiate the contract, whereupon Hochster (P) immediately commenced an action for breach of contract.

RULE OF LAW

A party to a contract who renounces his intention to perform may not complain if the other party, instead of waiting until performance is due, elects to sue immediately for breach of contract.

FACTS: In April, Hochster (P) contracted to serve as De La Tour's (D) employee beginning on June 1. On May 11, De La Tour (D) wrote to Hochster (P) that he had changed his mind and declined Hochster's (P) services. On May 22, Hochster (P) brought this action for breach of contract.

ISSUE: When the time for performance has not arrived, but one party nevertheless indicates his intention not to perform, must the other party wait until the performance should have occurred before bringing action for breach of contract?

HOLDING AND DECISION: (Lord Campbell, C.J.) No. The man who wrongfully renounces a contract into which he has deliberately entered cannot justly complain if he is immediately sued for a compensation in damages by the man whom he has injured; and it seems reasonable to allow an option to the injured party, either to sue immediately, or to wait till the time when the act was to be done. If Hochster (P) had to wait until June 1 to sue, he would not be able to enter any employment that would interfere with his promise to begin work at that time. But it is surely more rational that after renunciation by De La Tour (D), Hochster (P) should be at liberty to consider himself absolved from any future performance. Thus, he would be free to seek other employment in mitigation of damages. De La Tour's (D) renunciation may be treated as a breach of contract. Judgment for Hochster (P).

ANALYSIS

This is the leading case on the so-called doctrine of "anticipatory breach." The court's reasoning is erroneous insofar as it felt that Hochster (P) would otherwise be caught in a dilemma: to remain idle and hope for a favorable future judgment or to obtain other employment and thereby forfeit his rights against De La Tour (D). The court overlooked the rule that where a party manifests prospective unwillingness to perform the other party may suspend his performance and change his position without surrendering his right to sue after the breach occurs. In other words, the court could have considered the repudiation as (1) a defense to an action brought by De La Tour (D) and (2) an excuse of the constructive condition that Hochster (P) be ready, willing, and able to perform on June 1. The fact that the leading case is based on erroneous premises has caused hostility by some commentators toward the doctrine of "anticipatory breach." The doctrine, however, has been widely accepted both in England and the United States. There is much, from a practical viewpoint, to support the doctrine, and it could perhaps rest more cleanly on a constructive duty not to repudiate. Compare other constructive conditions and duties of cooperation imposed on contracting parties.

Quicknotes

ACTION IN ASSUMPSIT Action to recover damages for breach of an oral or written promise to perform or pay pursuant to a contract.

ANTICIPATORY BREACH Breach of a contract subsequent to formation but prior to the time performance is due.

REPUDIATION The actions or statements of a party to a contract that evidence the party's intent not to perform, or to continue performance of, the party's duties or obligations thereunder.

Kanavos v. Hancock Bank & Trust Co.

Option holder (P) v. Stockholder (D)

Mass. Sup. Jud. Ct., 395 Mass. 199, 479 N.E.2d 168 (1985)

NATURE OF CASE: Appeal of reversal of directed verdict in action for damages for breach of contract.

FACT SUMMARY: Hancock Bank & Trust Co. (D) sold certain stock to which Kanavos (P) had earlier been given a contractual right of first refusal.

RULE OF LAW

A party's ability to recover for breach of a contract giving a right of first refusal depends on his having had the financial resources to exercise the option.

FACTS: Kanavos (P) contracted with Hancock Bank & Trust Co. (the Bank) (D) for the right of first refusal in the purchase of a limited partnership controlling certain real estate. The Bank (D) eventually sold the shares without notifying Kanavos (P), who sued for breach. At trial, the Bank (D) was granted a nonsuit. This was reversed by the court of appeals. On remand, the trial court held that Kanavos's (P) right to recover was not dependent on his ability to have exercised the right at the time of sale.

ISSUE: Does a party's ability to recover for breach of a contract giving a right of first refusal depend on his having had the financial resources to exercise the option?

HOLDING AND DECISION: (Wilkins, J.) Yes. A party's ability to recover for breach of a contract giving a right of first refusal depends on his having had the financial resources to exercise the option. It is the general rule that when performance under a contract is concurrent, one party cannot put another in default unless he is able to perform his obligation. From this general rule it has been held that the financial ability of a prospective buyer of property is a material issue in his action for damages against a repudiating seller. The situation here falls squarely within this rule, and the trial court therefore erred. Remanded for retrial.

ANALYSIS

A sub-issue here was who had the burden of proof regarding Kanavos's (P) ability to pay. The court held that Kanavos (P) had to prove he was able to pay. The court admitted that the rulings on this issue vary from state to state but believed Kanavos (P) was in a better position to give evidence on this issue.

Quicknotes

DIRECTED VERDICT A verdict ordered by the trial judge in a jury trial.

NONSUIT Judgment against a party who fails to make out a case.

McCloskey & Co. v. Minweld Steel Co.

Contractor (P) v. Subcontractor (D)

220 F.2d 101 (3d Cir. 1955)

NATURE OF CASE: Appeal from dismissal of action for damages for breach of a construction contract.

FACT SUMMARY: Minweld Steel Co. (Minweld) (D), a subcontractor, had contracted to supply and erect certain steel portions for McCloskey & Co. (McCloskey) (P), the general contractor, on a state hospital project for Pennsylvania. When, because of the outbreak of the Korean War, Minweld (D) had difficulty procuring steel and requested, by letter, McCloskey's (P) aid, McCloskey (P) treated Minweld's (D) letter as an admission of breach and terminated the agreement.

RULE OF LAW

In order to give rise to a renunciation amounting to a breach of contract, there must be an absolute and unequivocal refusal to perform or a distinct and positive statement of an inability to do so.

FACTS: McCloskey & Co. (McCloskey) (P), a contractor on a Pennsylvania state hospital project, made three contracts with Minweld Steel Co. (Minweld) (D) for the latter to furnish and erect all structural steel for two of the hospital buildings. If Minweld (D) failed or refused to supply sufficient materials of proper quality, McCloskey (P) would have the right to terminate on two days' notice. When Minweld (D) had difficulty procuring steel due to the outbreak of the Korean War, it wrote McCloskey (P), requesting its help or the state's help in finding steel. McCloskey (P) treated this letter as notice of Minweld's (D) alleged positive intention not to perform the contracts, hence, a breach. At trial, Minweld's (D) motion for judgment on the ground McCloskey (P) had failed to state a cause of action was granted.

ISSUE: In order to give rise to a renunciation amounting to a breach of contract, must there be an absolute and unequivocal refusal to perform or a distinct and positive statement of an inability to do so?

HOLDING AND DECISION: (McLaughlin, J.) Yes. In order to give rise to a renunciation amounting to a breach of contract, there must be an absolute and unequivocal refusal to perform or a distinct and positive statement of an inability to do so. The letter conveyed no idea of contract repudiation by Minweld Steel Co. (Minweld) (D). While it was in a desperate situation, Minweld (D) realistically faced its problem and did not indicate definite abandonment or loss of all hope of finishing the project. Minweld (D) did not absolutely or unequivocally refuse to perform. Moreover, failure to take preparatory action before the time when any performance is promised is not anticipatory breach, even though such failure made it impossible for performance to take place, though the promisor at the time of failure does not intend to perform his promise. Minweld (D) was no more than unable to give assurances as to preparatory arrangements. Affirmed.

ANALYSIS

A statement such as "I will not perform" is an anticipatory breach if it is made before performance is due. Under the doctrine of prospective unwillingness to perform, the other party may suspend his performance and change his position. As the repudiation was an anticipatory breach, the other party may sue immediately. But if the statement is basically "I doubt that I will be able to perform," as occurred in this case, there is no repudiation. Accordingly, suit cannot be brought immediately under the doctrine of anticipatory repudiation. However, under the doctrine of prospective unwillingness to perform, the other party could suspend his performance and demand assurances and take any other steps allowable under the doctrine. This is the same for the circumstance where a party says, "I will not perform unless X occurs." It is very possible that the unforeseen circumstance, the tightening up of the steel industry resulting from the outbreak of the Korean War and subsequent presidential directive, moved the court to excuse Minweld Steel Co.'s (D) words, which basically did have the effect of a repudiation.

Quicknotes

ANTICIPATORY BREACH Breach of a contract subsequent to formation but prior to the time performance is due.

RENUNCIATION The abandonment of a right or interest.

REPUDIATION The actions or statements of a party to a contract that evidence the party's intent not to perform, or to continue performance of, the party's duties or obligations thereunder.

By-Lo Oil Co. v. ParTech, Inc.

Software consumer (P) v. Software company (D)

11 Fed. Appx. 538 (6th Cir. 2001)

NATURE OF CASE: Appeal from grant of summary judgment to defendant in action for anticipatory breach of contract.

FACT SUMMARY: By-Lo Oil Co. (By-Lo) (P) claimed that it had reasonable grounds for insecurity in early 1998 based on the software support contract it had with ParTech, Inc. (D) where ParTech (D) informed By-Lo (P) that it had not at that point made a decision how to ensure that its software would be Y2K-compliant, and By-Lo (P) further claimed that ParTech's (D) assurance that it would let By-Lo (P) know its decision in time to avert Y2K-related software problems was inadequate. By-Lo (P) also contended that these were factual issues that should not have been decided judicially as a matter of law.

RULE OF LAW

Under the Uniform Commercial Code, a court may determine, as a matter of law, whether a party to a contract has reasonable grounds for insecurity and whether a party has given adequate assurance.

FACTS: ParTech, Inc. (D) supplied By-Lo Oil Co. (By-Lo) (P) software for By-Lo's (P) operations. Their contract provided that ParTech (D) would provide continuing support to By-Lo (P) for a fixed monthly fee. This included making the software Y2K-compliant. By-Lo (P) wrote to ParTech (D) in 1997 expressing its concern the software would continue to function properly after December 31, 1999. By-Lo (P) again wrote to ParTech (D) in early 1998, this time requesting a response and assurance that the software would be Y2K-compliant. The letter also threatened a lawsuit if no response was forthcoming and warned that By-Lo (P) would replace the software and seek the replacement cost from ParTech (D). A few weeks later, ParTech (D) responded, stating that ParTech (D) had not as of that time made a decision as to how to deal with the Y2K problem, and that it would notify By-Lo (P) as soon as the decision was made. After By-Lo's (P) representative travelled to ParTech's (D) headquarters and received essentially the same response—i.e., that By-Lo (P) would be notified once a decision had been made—By-Lo (P) filed suit against a different ParTech entity on May 1, 1998, but later realized that it was not the entity with which it had the software contract. Then, in June 1998, By-Lo (P) purchased new software and hardware from a different computer systems supplier for over $175,000. Unaware of these events, ParTech (D), on November 20, 1998, gave By-Lo (P) the definitive answer for which it had been looking. ParTech (D) stated it would supply the needed software at no cost and that the software needed to be installed prior to January 1, 1999. On December 18, 1998, ParTech (D), as promised, sent By-Lo (P) the necessary software with detailed instructions for loading it. Because By-Lo (P) was now operating on a different system, it did not install the software. Instead, By-Lo (P) sued ParTech (D) in May 1999 in state court, and the action was removed to federal district court. By-Lo (P) claimed it had a right to obtain new computer equipment because of ParTech's (D) actions, which it characterized as an anticipatory breach under the state's UCC §§ 2-609 and 2-610. ParTech (D) moved for summary judgment on the grounds that (1) it had not made an overt communication of intent to repudiate the contract and therefore there was not a breach under § 2-610; and (2) By-Lo (P) did not have the reasonable grounds for insecurity necessary to seek assurance, and the assurance ParTech (D) gave was adequate, and therefore there was no basis to find a breach under § 2-609. The district court granted ParTech's (D) motion. The court of appeals granted review.

ISSUE: Under the Uniform Commercial Code, may a court determine, as a matter of law, whether a party to a contract has reasonable grounds for insecurity and whether a party has given adequate assurance?

HOLDING AND DECISION: (Kennedy, J.) Yes. Under the Uniform Commercial Code, a court may determine, as a matter of law, whether a party to a contract has reasonable grounds for insecurity and whether a party has given adequate assurance. The district court did not improperly decide questions of fact in analyzing the anticipatory repudiation claim. Generally, the question of whether a party has reasonable grounds for insecurity, and whether a party has given adequate assurance, are factual questions left to the trier of fact. However, in certain cases—this being one of them—the court has the power to determine these issues as a matter of law. As to the reasonableness of By-Lo Oil Co.'s (By-Lo's) (P's) insecurity, that is to be determined by commercial standards. The issue thus becomes whether it was commercially reasonable for By-Lo (P) to be insecure two years before the Y2K fix (if any) was necessary. In other words, would a reasonable merchant in By-Lo's (P) position feel that his expectation of receiving full performance was threatened? The fact that performance was to come due at some point is not sufficient under § 2-609. Merely

Continued on next page.

becoming aware of the Y2K problem (of which the parties were not aware when they entered the contract) also is by itself an insufficient ground for insecurity. ParTech, Inc.'s (D) failure to return calls might have given rise to reasonable grounds for insecurity at some point before Y2K, but not in January 1998. That is because By-Lo (P) did not complain about ParTech's (D) previous service, nor was there any indication that it was under a time constraint to obtain a new system if ParTech (D) did not respond quickly. There also was no indication that By-Lo (P) had reason to believe it would take a lengthy period of time to make any corrections ParTech (D) required. Further, evidence presented by By-Lo (P) attempting to show that as of May 1998 it had little time to obtain new software and implement it or to install any software sent by ParTech (D) is unconvincing. For all these reasons, there was little reason for By-Lo (P) to be concerned at such an early date—so little that no reasonable jury could have found for By-Lo (P). A similar analysis applies to the issue of adequate assurance. The question is: What are the minimum kinds of promises or acts on the part of the promisor that would satisfy a reasonable merchant in the position of the promisee that his expectation of receiving due performance will be fulfilled? In evaluating the assurance, the court should keep in mind the reputation of the promisor, the grounds for insecurity, and the kinds of assurance available. As already determined By-Lo (P) did not have reasonable grounds for insecurity in January 1998, given that the Y2K problem was almost two years away. There was no indication that ParTech (D) had failed to fulfill its obligations in the past, nor was there any evidence that ParTech's (D) reputation should have given By-Lo (P) cause for concern. Because it is not clear what else ParTech (D) could have done, other than what it did, the district court was correct to hold that, as a matter of law, ParTech's (D) assurance that it was evaluating the matter was adequate despite the fact that it was less than requested. Affirmed.

ANALYSIS

Uniform Commercial Code § 2-609 provides that when reasonable grounds for insecurity arise with respect to the performance of either party, the other may in writing demand adequate assurance of due performance, and, until it receives such assurance, may, if commercially reasonable, suspend any performance for which it has not already received the agreed return. While this section imposes a written demand requirement, some courts have held that an oral demand for assurance may suffice provided as it communicates a clear understanding of the insecure party's intent to suspend performance until receipt of adequate assurance from the other party.

Quicknotes

ANTICIPATORY BREACH Breach of a contract subsequent to formation but prior to the time performance is due.

ANTICIPATORY REPUDIATION Breach of a contract subsequent to formation but prior to the time performance is due.

CHAPTER 8

Remedies for Breach

Quick Reference Rules of Law

PAGE

1. *Campbell Soup Co. v. Wentz.* Where a purchaser has contracted in advance for goods of a special type that are unavailable on the open market and that support the purchaser's good reputation, specific performance should be granted where the seller has breached the contract. *224*

2. *Van Wagner Advertising Corp. v. S & M Enterprises.* Where there is substantial, reliable information as to the monetary value of the subject matter of a breached contract and where specific performance would create harm to the defendant disproportionate to its aid to the plaintiff, specific performance is not available. *225*

3. *Snow Phipps Group, LLC v. KCAKE Acquisition, Inc.* Under the prevention doctrine, where a party's breach by nonperformance contributes materially to the nonoccurrence of a condition of one of the breaching party's duties, the condition will be deemed to have been met and the nonoccurrence of the condition excused. *227*

4. *Walgreen Co. v. Sara Creek Property Co.* Where the costs of injunctive relief are less than the costs of a damages remedy, injunctive relief is an appropriate remedy, even when the damages remedy is not shown to be inadequate. *229*

5. *Sedmak v. Charlie's Chevrolet, Inc.* Under Uniform Commercial Code § 2-716(1), a court may decree specific performance as a buyer's remedy for breach of contract to sell goods where the goods are unique or in other proper circumstances, such as where the goods are in limited supply and cannot be obtained other than from the buyer except at considerable expense, trouble, or loss. *230*

6. *Vitex Manufacturing Corp. v. Caribtex Corp.* In a claim for lost profits, overhead should be treated as part of the gross profits and recoverable as damages and should not be considered as part of the seller's (or processor's) costs. *232*

7. *Laredo Hides Co., Inc. v. H & H Meat Products Co., Inc.* When a seller wrongfully repudiates a contract or fails to make delivery of the goods thereunder, the buyer may "cover" by obtaining such goods elsewhere and sue the seller for the difference between the cost of cover and the contract price plus any incidental or consequential damages. *233*

8. *Plante v. Jacobs.* There can be no recovery on a contract as distinguished from quantum meruit unless there is substantial performance, which is defined as where the performance meets the essential purpose of the contract. *234*

9. *Groves v. John Wunder Co.* Value of the land as distinguished from the value of the intended product of the contract, which ordinarily will be equivalent to its reasonable cost, is no proper part of any measure of damages for willful breach of a building contract. *236*

10. *Peevyhouse v. Garland Coal & Mining Co.* Where a contract provision breached is merely incidental to the main purpose, and where the economic benefit that would result to lessor by full performance of the work is grossly disproportionate to the cost of performance, the damages that lessor may recover are limited to the diminution in value resulting to the premises because of the nonperformance. *238*

11. *R.E. Davis Chemical Corp. v. Diasonics, Inc.* An aggrieved seller may recover, after resale, lost profits from the original sale if he can show that the subsequent sale would have occurred absent the breach and would have been profitable. *239*

12. *United States v. Algernon Blair, Inc.* A promisee is allowed to recover in quantum meruit the value of services he gave to a defendant who breached the contract irrespective of whether he would have lost money had the contract been fully performed and would thus be precluded from recovering in a suit on the contract. *240*

13. *Rockingham County v. Luten Bridge Co.* After an absolute repudiation or refusal to perform by one party to a contract, the other party cannot continue to perform and recover damages based on full performance. *241*

14. *Trinidad Bean & Elevator Co. v. Frosh.* Under Uniform Commercial Code § 2-713(1), the measure of damages for a buyer upon anticipatory repudiation by the seller is the difference between the contract price and the price of the goods on the date of repudiation, so long as it would be commercially reasonable for the buyer to cover on the date of repudiation. *242*

15. *Tongish v. Thomas.* When a seller breaches, market damages should be awarded even though in excess of the buyer's actual loss. *245*

16. *Parker v. Twentieth Century-Fox Film Corp.* The general measure of recovery by a wrongfully discharged employee is the amount of salary agreed upon for the period of service, less the amount that the employer affirmatively proves the employee has earned or with reasonable effort might have earned from other employment. *246*

17. *Hadley v. Baxendale.* The injured party (1) may recover those damages as may reasonably be considered arising naturally from the breach itself and (2) may recover those damages as may reasonably be supposed to have been in contemplation of the parties, at the time they made the contract, as the probable result of a breach of it. *248*

18. *Delchi Carrier SpA v. Rotorex Corp.* A contract plaintiff may collect damages to compensate for the full loss, which includes, but is not limited to, foreseeable lost profits. *250*

19. *Kenford Co. v. County of Erie.* In order to impose extraordinary damages on a breaching party, such damages must have been brought within the contemplation of the parties as the probable result of a breach at or prior to the time of contracting. *251*

20. *Fera v. Village Plaza, Inc.* A new business may recover lost profit damages for breach of a lease if the profits are not excessively speculative. *252*

21. *Newsome v. Western Union Telegraph Co.* Consequential damages may not be awarded for breach of a telecommunications contract by a public service corporation where the damages resulting from the breach are remote and speculative. *253*

22. *Figgie International, Inc. v. Destileria Serralles, Inc.* Under Section 2-719 of the Uniform Commercial Code, where the parties' exclusive remedy under a contract is repair, replacement, or return of defective goods, this remedy does not fail of its essential purpose where the seller has first unsuccessfully attempted repair, on the theory that the seller has thereby forgone its remedy of return and refund of the purchase price. *255*

23. *Dave Gustafson & Co. v. State.* A provision for payment of a stipulated sum as a liquidation of damages will ordinarily be sustained if it appears that: at the time the contract was made the damages in the event of a breach will be incapable or very difficult of accurate estimation; there was a reasonable attempt by the parties to fix fair compensation; and the amount stipulated bears a reasonable relation to probable damages and is not disproportionate to any damages reasonably to be anticipated. *257*

24. *Lake River Corp. v. Carborundum Co.* A minimum-guarantee provision is an unenforceable penalty, rather than an enforceable liquidated damages clause, where it is designed always to assure the promisee more than its actual damages. *258*

25. *Wasserman's, Inc. v. Township of Middletown.* Provisions for liquidated damages are enforceable only if they are a reasonable forecast of just compensation for the harm caused by the breach. *260*

26. *Bains LLC v. Arco Prod. Co.* (1) A jury award of punitive damages can be predicated on a jury award of nominal damages to a corporation arising from racial discrimination in violation of 42 U.S.C.A. § 1981 where the awards are not inconsistent and can be harmonized. (2) In a case of highly reprehensible conduct such as racial discrimination, though not threatening to life or limb, that causes economic harm to a corporation, to be constitutional, the amount of a punitive damages award should be in the range of a single-digit ratio between punitive and compensatory damages, as well as in line with punitive damages awarded in comparable cases. *261*

Campbell Soup Co. v. Wentz

Soup manufacturer (P) v. Carrot farmer (D)

172 F.2d 80 (3d Cir. 1948)

NATURE OF CASE: Appeal from denial of equitable relief in action for specific performance.

FACT SUMMARY: Campbell Soup Co. (P) contended that its contract with the Wentzes (D) for delivery of a certain kind of carrot that was otherwise unavailable on the market should have been enforced through specific performance.

RULE OF LAW

Where a purchaser has contracted in advance for goods of a special type that are unavailable on the open market and that support the purchaser's good reputation, specific performance should be granted where the seller has breached the contract.

FACTS: Campbell Soup Co. (Campbell) (P) entered into a contract with the Wentzes (D) for delivery of all Chantenay red cored carrots to be grown on 15 acres of the Wentzes' (D) farm, with Campbell (P) providing the seed for the carrots. The price ranged from $23 to $30 per ton, depending on time of delivery. Campbell (P) used this particular kind of carrot in 15 of the 21 soups it manufactured, as its shape made it easy to process and its bright color made it unique looking. The Wentzes (D) harvested around 100 tons of the carrots from the acreage covered by the contract, but they refused to deliver the carrots at the contract price because the market price had increased to $90 per ton. They sold around 62 tons to their neighbor farmer (neighbor) (D), who then sold these on the open market, with about half going to Campbell (P). The carrots were otherwise virtually unobtainable on the open market. Campbell (P), suspecting that the neighbor (D) was selling "contract" carrots, brought suit to enjoin further sales of the contract carrots to anyone other than Campbell (P) and for specific performance. The district court denied the requested equitable relief, and the court of appeals granted review.

ISSUE: Where a purchaser has contracted in advance for goods of a special type that are unavailable on the open market and that support the purchaser's good reputation, should specific performance be granted where the seller has breached the contract?

HOLDING AND DECISION: (Goodrich, J.) Yes. Where a purchaser has contracted in advance for goods of a special type that are unavailable on the open market and that support the purchaser's good reputation, specific performance should be granted where the seller has breached the contract. The general rule, that specific performance of a contract for the sale of chattels is appropriate where the legal remedies would be inadequate, applies here. Based on the particular facts of this case, legal remedies would be inadequate since it was virtually impossible to obtain Chantenay red cored carrots on the open market, the carrots' blunt shape makes them easier to process, and its color, being brighter than that of other carrots, makes their appearance uniform in Campbell Soup's (Campbell's) (P) products. This uniformity of appearance in a food article marketed throughout the country and sold under the manufacturer's name is of considerable commercial significance and one that should be considered in determining whether a substitute ingredient is just as good as the original. The district court concluded that Campbell (P) had failed to objectively establish that the carrots are not unique goods, but since that is not purely a factual conclusion but rather a legal one, and since the appropriateness of specific performance may be judged by a subjective standard, that issue must be revisited. Given the general standards applicable to determining the adequacy of a legal remedy, specific performance should have been granted because a legal remedy here would have been inadequate given that the carrots were of a special type, were unavailable on the open market, had been contracted for in advance in anticipation of Campbell's (P) needs, and were part of the uniformity of appearance on which Campbell (P) had built its good reputation. Affirmed.

ANALYSIS

The court in this case ultimately affirmed the district court's denial of equitable relief because it found that the contract was too one-sided in favor of Campbell Soup (Campbell) (P). The court's determination that legal remedies would be inadequate is questionable. It seems that Campbell's (P) damages could have been ascertained by calculating the difference between what it had to pay the neighbor farmer (D), $90, and the contract prices. The court's conclusion that Campbell (P) could not have obtained the carrots is also questionable since Campbell (P) was in fact able to obtain them from the farmer (D), albeit at a price higher than specified in the contract.

Quicknotes

BREACH OF CONTRACT Unlawful failure by a party to perform its obligations pursuant to contract.

Van Wagner Advertising Corp. v. S & M Enterprises

Billboard space lessee (P) v. Building owner (D)

N.Y. Ct. App., 67 N.Y.2d 186, 492 N.E.2d 756 (1986)

NATURE OF CASE: Appeal by defendant from award to defendant for breach of contract and appeal by plaintiff from denial of specific performance.

FACT SUMMARY: When S & M Enterprises (S & M) (D) purchased a building and wrongfully attempted to terminate a lease of billboard space that S & M's (D) predecessor had made with Van Wagner Advertising (Van Wagner) (P), Van Wagner (P) abandoned the space under protest and sued for specific performance to reinstate the lease.

RULE OF LAW

Where there is substantial, reliable information as to the monetary value of the subject matter of a breached contract and where specific performance would create harm to the defendant disproportionate to its aid to the plaintiff, specific performance is not available.

FACTS: Michaels leased for ten years space on a side of its Manhattan building to Van Wagner Advertising Corp. (Van Wagner) (P), and Van Wagner (P) erected a billboard. One month later, S & M Enterprises (S & M) (D) purchased the building from Michaels and purported to exercise a termination clause in the lease. Van Wagner (P) abandoned the space under protest and sued S & M (D) for specific performance to reinstate the lease. The trial court determined that S & M (D) had wrongfully terminated the lease but denied Van Wagner (P) specific performance, instead awarding it monetary damages for the period through trial and allowing it to sue for damages in the future if S & M (D) would not reinstate the lease. Both parties appealed, Van Wagner (P) arguing that the property was unique, making monetary damages an inadequate remedy requiring specific performance, S & M (D) arguing that future damages were too speculative and uncertain. The appellate division affirmed, and both parties appealed to the New York court of appeals.

ISSUE: Where there is substantial, reliable information as to the monetary value of the subject matter of a breached contract and where specific performance would create harm to the defendant disproportionate to its aid to the plaintiff, is specific performance available?

HOLDING AND DECISION: (Kaye, J.) No. Where there is substantial, reliable information as to the monetary value of the subject matter of a breached contract and where specific performance would create harm to the defendant disproportionate to its aid to the plaintiff, specific performance is not available. To obtain specific performance, the plaintiff must show that monetary damages are inadequate because the subject matter of the contract is unique or because damages are too speculative to be awarded. The subject matter of a contract is unique where there is little reliable information as to its economic value, creating a high risk that monetary damages will over- or undercompensate the plaintiff. In this case, however, there is an abundance of reliable information on the value of the contract since leases of Manhattan building space for billboard use are very common. Thus, the leased space is not unique, and both parties are wrong in asserting that an estimate of future losses would be too speculative. Furthermore, specific performance is not available since the trial court found that specific performance would inequitably burden S & M Enterprises (D) by imposing hardship disproportionate to Van Wagner Advertising Corp.'s (Van Wagner's) (P) benefit. Affirmed after modified. [The case was remitted to the trial court to adjust the amount of damages previously awarded and to allow Van Wagner (P) to establish all future damages at once.]

ANALYSIS

The comment to the Restatement (Second) of Contracts § 360 explains that specific performance of contracts for the sale of land has historically been given special treatment. Land is traditionally considered unique, and monetary damages are considered inadequate compensation for a piece of land that the buyer is said to have chosen for its subjective value to him or her. Where the buyer has already sold the property to a third party, the "uniqueness" argument does not apply, but courts still find monetary damages inadequate since the buyer may be subject to a lawsuit by the third party unless the buyer can convey the property. Even an aggrieved seller is usually granted specific performance of a land sale contract because the value of land may be too speculative to allow for proof of lost profits, and finding a new buyer for the property may take a long time, especially where there is a dispute over a prior land sale contract.

Continued on next page.

Quicknotes

LOST PROFITS The potential value of income earned or the potential value of goods that are the subject of the contract; may be used in calculating damages where the contract has been breached.

MONETARY DAMAGES Monetary compensation sought by or awarded to a party who incurred loss as a result of a breach of contract or tortious conduct on behalf of another party.

SPECIFIC PERFORMANCE An equitable remedy whereby the court requires the parties to perform their obligations pursuant to a contract.

Snow Phipps Group, LLC v. KCAKE Acquisition, Inc.

Seller of company (P) v. Potential buyer of company (D)

Del. Ch. Ct., 2021 WL 1714202 (2021)

NATURE OF CASE: Action for breach of contract seeking specific performance as a remedy.

FACT SUMMARY: Snow Phipps Group, LLC (Snow Phipps) (P), which owned DecoPac Holdings Inc. (DecoPac) (P), entered into a Stock Purchase Agreement (SPA) with Kohlberg & Company, LLC, (Kohlberg) (D) for Kohlberg (D) to acquire DecoPac (P). With the development of the COVID-19 pandemic, Kohlberg (D) sought to exit the transaction. Snow Phipps (P) and DecoPac (P) (collectively, the Plaintiffs) (P) sued Kohlberg (D) for breach of contract, and, as a remedy, asked the court to order specific performance. In doing so, Plaintiffs (P) alleged, inter alia, that Kohlberg (D) had breached its obligation to use reasonable best efforts to obtain financing. Although the SPA provided that specific performance would be available only if certain debt financing was funded by the time of closing, the Plaintiffs (P) contended that because Kohlberg (D) breached its obligation to obtain such financing, under the prevention doctrine, Kohlberg (D) could not assert the nonoccurrence of the debt-financing condition to prevent specific performance.

RULE OF LAW

Under the prevention doctrine, where a party's breach by nonperformance contributes materially to the nonoccurrence of a condition of one of the breaching party's duties, the condition will be deemed to have been met and the nonoccurrence of the condition excused.

FACTS: Snow Phipps Group, LLC (Snow Phipps) (P), a private equity firm, owned DecoPac Holdings Inc. (DecoPac) (P), which sold cake decorations and technology to supermarkets for use in their in-store bakeries. In December 2019, Snow Phipps (P) decided to sell DecoPac (P), and the following month approached Kohlberg & Company, LLC, (Kohlberg) (D), another private equity firm, for that purpose. In February 2020, Kohlberg (D) expressed interest, and, after conducting due diligence, made a bid of $600 million for DecoPac (P). Snow Phipps (P) accepted, and the parties proceeded to complete diligence and to negotiate a formal purchase and sale agreement. In early March 2020, the COVID-19 global pandemic began. Though Snow Phipps (P) requested on March 4 that "pandemics" and "epidemics" be added to the material adverse event (MAE) definition in the purchase agreement, Kohlberg (D) rejected that language. That same day, Kohlberg (D) demanded a price reduction, to which Snow Phipps (P) agreed. On March 6, the parties signed a purchase agreement and related documents. As part of the transaction, under the Stock Purchase Agreement (SPA), Kohlberg (D) committed to use its reasonable best efforts to obtain debt financing, and, failing that, to obtain alternative financing. The parties also agreed that a $33 million termination fee would be Snow Phipps' (P) "sole and exclusive" monetary remedy, and that in no event would Snow Phipps (P) be entitled to both specific performance and the termination fee. In the background, the COVID-19 pandemic was escalating, and, as the pandemic started, DecoPac's (P) weekly sales declined precipitously. Although DecoPac's (P) highly experienced management team predicted that sales would recover rapidly, Kohlberg (D) was less confident, and sought to exit the deal. Rather than use reasonable best efforts to work toward a definitive credit agreement, Kohlberg (D) called their litigation counsel and began evaluating ways to get out of the deal. Without input from DecoPac (D) management, they prepared a draconian reforecast of DecoPac's (D) projected sales based on uninformed (and largely unexplained) assumptions that were inconsistent with real-time sales data. Kohlberg (D) sent this reforecast to its lenders with demands for more favorable debt financing terms. When the lenders refused those demands, Kohlberg (D) informed Snow Phipps (P) that debt funding was no longer available. Kohlberg (D) then conducted a perfunctory and unsuccessful four-day search for alternative debt financing at Snow Phipps' (P) insistence. On April 8, 2020, Kohlberg (D) informed Snow Phipps (P) that it would not close because debt financing remained unavailable, and for other reasons. Snow Phipps (P) and DecoPac (P) (collectively, the Plaintiffs) (P) sued Kohlberg (D) in Delaware Chancery Court for breach of contract, and, as a remedy, asked the court to order specific performance. Kohlberg (D) counterclaimed. Although the SPA provided that specific performance would be available only if certain debt financing was funded by the time of closing, the Plaintiffs (P) contended that because Kohlberg (D) breached its obligation to obtain such financing using its reasonable best efforts, under the prevention doctrine, Kohlberg (D) could not assert the nonoccurrence of the debt-financing condition to prevent specific performance. The Delaware Chancery Court considered the case.

ISSUE: Under the prevention doctrine, where a party's breach by nonperformance contributes materially to the nonoccurrence of a condition of one of the breaching

Continued on next page.

party's duties, will the condition be deemed to have been met and the nonoccurrence of the condition excused?

HOLDING AND DECISION: (McCormick, J.) Yes. Under the prevention doctrine, where a party's breach by nonperformance contributes materially to the nonoccurrence of a condition of one of the breaching party's duties, the condition will be deemed to have been met and the nonoccurrence of the condition excused. The court's task is to interpret the Stock Purchase Agreement (SPA) in a way that effectuates the parties' intent. Here, Snow Phipps Group, LLC (Snow Phipps) and DecoPac Holdings Inc. (DecoPac) (collectively, the Plaintiffs) (P) ask the court to order specific performance and force Kohlberg (D) to close on the SPA. Alternatively, they ask the court to order Kohlberg & Company, LLC, (Kohlberg) (D) to use reasonable best efforts to obtain alternative debt financing. A party seeking specific performance must establish that (1) a valid contract exists, (2) the party is ready, willing, and able to perform, and (3) the balance of equities tips in favor of the party seeking performance. Here, the parties stipulated to the remedy of specific performance, but that stipulation applies "if and only if . . . the full proceeds of the Debt Financing have been funded to Buyer . . . at Closing. . . ." (the "debt-funding condition"). Plaintiffs' (P) post-trial entitlement to specific performance therefore depends on whether the prevention doctrine applies. An extensive review of the facts established at trial shows that Kohlberg (D) improperly terminated the SPA. The evidence also shows that Kohlberg (D) breached its obligations under the SPA by failing to use its reasonable best efforts to obtain the committed debt financing and then failing to obtain alternative financing. Accordingly, under the prevention doctrine, Kohlberg (D) is barred from asserting the absence of debt financing as a basis to avoid specific performance under the SPA (Section 11.14(b)), and that condition is deemed to have been met. Plaintiffs (P) have provided clear and convincing evidence that the balance of equities tips in their favor. Kohlberg (D) is therefore ordered to close on the SPA.

ANALYSIS

As this case illustrates, the prevention doctrine provides that non-occurrence is excused when "where a party's breach by nonperformance contributes materially to the non-occurrence of a condition of one of his duties, the non-occurrence is excused." Restatement (Second) of Contracts § 245 (1981). To establish that a party's breach contributed materially to the nonoccurrence of a condition, it is not necessary to show that the condition would have occurred but for the lack of cooperation. It is required only that the breach has contributed materially to the nonoccurrence. A breach contributes materially to the nonoccurrence of a condition if the conduct made satisfaction of the condition less likely. However, if it can be shown that the condition would not have occurred regardless of the lack of cooperation, the failure of performance would not have contributed materially to the condition's nonoccurrence, and the rule does not apply. The burden of making such a showing is on the breaching party.

Quicknotes

BEST EFFORTS In order to enforce an agreement pursuant to which only one party appears to be furnishing consideration, the court will imply a promise on the part of the other party to use its best efforts.

BREACH OF CONTRACT Unlawful failure by a party to perform its obligations pursuant to contract.

SPECIFIC PERFORMANCE An equitable remedy whereby the court requires the parties to perform their obligations pursuant to a contract.

Walgreen Co. v. Sara Creek Property Co.

Tenant (P) v. Landlord (D)

966 F.2d 273 (7th Cir. 1992)

NATURE OF CASE: Appeal from a grant of permanent injunctive relief in suit for breach of contract.

FACT SUMMARY: Walgreen Co. (P) filed suit to enforce a clause contained in its lease agreement that provided that no space in the mall would be rented to a competing pharmacy.

RULE OF LAW

Where the costs of injunctive relief are less than the costs of a damages remedy, injunctive relief is an appropriate remedy, even when the damages remedy is not shown to be inadequate.

FACTS: Walgreen Co. (P) operated a pharmacy in a mall under a lease that provided that the landlord, Sara Creek Property Co. (Sara Creek) (D), would not lease space to anyone else who wanted to operate a pharmacy or store containing a pharmacy in the mall. After losing its primary tenant, Sara Creek (D) informed Walgreen (P) that it intended to lease space to Phar-Mor, a "deep discount" chain. The Phar-Mor store would include a pharmacy. Walgreen (P) filed a diversity suit for breach of contract and asked for injunctive relief mandating compliance with the nonrental clause. Evidence was offered by Sara Creek (D) that Walgreen's (P) damages were readily ascertainable. The injunction was granted, and Sara Creek (D) appealed.

ISSUE: Where the costs of injunctive relief are less than the costs of a damages remedy, is injunctive relief an appropriate remedy even when the damages remedy is not shown to be inadequate?

HOLDING AND DECISION: (Posner, J.) Yes. Where the costs of injunctive relief are less than the costs of a damages remedy, injunctive relief is an appropriate remedy, even when the damages remedy is not shown to be inadequate. Generally, the plaintiff seeking an injunction has the burden of persuasion. In the case of a permanent injunction, it must be shown that damages are inadequate. If it is likely that the costs of the damages remedy would exceed the costs of the injunction, then for the sake of efficiency, the injunction is the proper remedy. In this case, despite testimony by Sara Creek Property Co. (Sara Creek) (D) to the contrary, the damages remedy would have been difficult to compute. It would have required calculation of lost profits for at least ten years into the future. An injunction, on the other hand, removes the evidentiary issue from the court. And since supervision of the injunction would rest with Walgreen Co. (P), the future cost to the court is likewise minimal. By imposing the injunction on Sara Creek (D), the issue becomes one of private bargaining. The parties are free to negotiate a fee for the removal of the injunction. The trial court properly weighed the costs and benefits of injunctive relief. Affirmed.

ANALYSIS

Certain categories of contracts will regularly win equitable remedies. When subject matter is unique, such as with real estate, specific performance will usually be granted. The rationale is that money damages cannot adequately compensate for the loss of a unique item. This is, however, something of a fallacy since most individuals would be willing to bargain away rights to a specific item for some price. The problem, however, rests with the trier of fact, as it is next to impossible to determine the appropriate premium to pay for the loss of a unique item.

Quicknotes

BURDEN OF PERSUASION The duty of a party to introduce evidence to support a fact that is in dispute in an action.

INJUNCTIVE RELIEF A court order issued as a remedy, requiring a person to do, or prohibiting that person from doing, a specific act.

PERMANENT INJUNCTION A remedy imposed by the court ordering a party to cease the conduct of a specific activity until the final disposition of the cause of action.

Sedmak v. Charlie's Chevrolet, Inc.

Prospective car purchaser (P) v. Prospective car seller (D)

Mo. Ct. App., 622 S.W.2d 694 (1981)

NATURE OF CASE: Appeal from order of specific performance in action for breach of contract.

FACT SUMMARY: The Sedmaks (P) contended they had a contract with Charlie's Chevrolet, Inc. (Charlie's) (D), a car dealership, for the purchase of a limited-edition Corvette automobile at the manufacturer's retail price plus the cost of custom changes. When the car arrived at Charlie's (D), the Sedmaks (P) were informed they instead would have to bid on the car. The Sedmaks (P) contended that Charlie's (D) breached their contract, and they sought specific performance as a remedy.

RULE OF LAW

Under Uniform Commercial Code § 2-716(1), a court may decree specific performance as a buyer's remedy for breach of contract to sell goods where the goods are unique or in other proper circumstances, such as where the goods are in limited supply and cannot be obtained other than from the buyer except at considerable expense, trouble, or loss.

FACTS: The Sedmaks (P), who were car enthusiasts and collected Corvette automobiles, learned that Chevrolet, the manufacturer of Corvettes, had plans to manufacture a limited edition of the Corvette to commemorate the selection of the Corvette as the Indianapolis 500 Pace Car. They contacted a Chevrolet dealership, Charlie's Chevrolet, Inc. (Charlie's) (D), and asked Tom Kells, the sales manager, if they could purchase a "Pace Car" if Charlie's (D) were to receive one. Kells told them they could purchase such a car if Charlie's (D) acquired one. A few months later, the Sedmaks (P) called again to see if a Pace Car could be ordered. Kells indicated he would require a deposit, so Mrs. Sedmak (P) went to the dealership to deliver a check for the deposit amount of $500. Prior to tendering the deposit, Mrs. Sedmak (P) asked Kells if the Sedmaks (P) were "definitely going to be the owners." Kells replied, "yes." After the deposit had been paid, Mrs. Sedmak (P) stated they wanted some changes made to the stock model. Kells was able to make the changes, and, when the car arrived, it was equipped as requested. Kells had informed Mrs. Sedmak (P) that the price of the Pace Car would be the manufacturer's retail price, approximately $15,000.00. The dollar figure could not be quoted more precisely because Kells was not sure what the ordered changes would cost, nor was he sure what the "appearance package," which comprised decals and a special paint job, would cost. Kells also told Mrs. Sedmak (P) that, after the changes had been made, a "contract"—a retail dealer's order form—would be mailed to them. However, no form or written contract was ever mailed. A few months later, Kells notified the Sedmaks (P) that the car had arrived, but also told them that they would not be able to purchase the car for the manufacturer's retail price because demand for the car had inflated its value beyond the suggested price. Kells also told the Sedmaks (P) they could bid on the car. The Sedmaks (P) then filed suit for breach of contract and sought specific performance as the remedy. The trial court ruled for the Sedmaks (P) and ordered specific performance, finding that the parties had entered into an oral contract, that the contract was excepted from the Statute of Frauds, and that the Sedmaks (P) had no adequate remedy at law because they could not go to the open market and purchase an automobile of this kind with the same mileage, condition, ownership and appearance as the Pace Car, except, if at all, with considerable expense, trouble, loss, great delay, and inconvenience. Charlie's (D) appealed, and the state's intermediate appellate court granted review.

ISSUE: Under Uniform Commercial Code § 2-716(1), may a court decree specific performance as a buyer's remedy for breach of contract to sell goods where the goods are unique or in other proper circumstances, such as where the goods are in limited supply and cannot be obtained other than from the buyer except at considerable expense, trouble, or loss?

HOLDING AND DECISION: (Satz, J.) Yes. Under Uniform Commercial Code (UCC) § 2-716(1), a court may decree specific performance as a buyer's remedy for breach of contract to sell goods where the goods are unique or in other proper circumstances, such as where the goods are in limited supply and cannot be obtained other than from the buyer except at considerable expense, trouble, or loss. Under the UCC, a court may decree specific performance as a buyer's remedy for breach of contract to sell goods where the goods are unique or in other proper circumstances. The general term "in other proper circumstances" expresses the drafters' intent to "further a more liberal attitude than some courts have shown in connection with the specific performance of contracts of sale." UCC § 2-716(1), cmt. 1. However, even before passage of the UCC, courts in this state took a practical approach in determining whether specific performance

Continued on next page.

would lie for the breach of contract for the sale of goods and did not limit this relief only to the sale of "unique" goods. In one prior case, *Boeving v. Vandover*, 240 Mo. App. 117, 218 S.W.2d 175 (1949), which had facts very similar to the case at bar, specific performance was granted for the sale of a car that, although not "unique" in the traditional legal sense, was "unique" because at the time all cars were difficult to obtain because of war-time shortages. The court held specific performance was the proper remedy for the plaintiff because a new car "could not be obtained elsewhere except at considerable expense, trouble or loss, which cannot be estimated in advance and under such circumstances (plaintiff) did not have an adequate remedy at law." Thus, *Boeving* presaged the broad and liberalized language of UCC § 2-716(1) and exemplifies one of the "other proper circumstances" contemplated by that subsection for ordering specific performance. [Affirmed.]

ANALYSIS

In *Sedmak,* the Pace Car ordered by the Sedmaks (P) was not unique in the traditional legal sense. It was not an heirloom or, arguably, one of a kind. However, its "mileage, condition, ownership, and appearance" did make it difficult, if not impossible, to obtain its replication without considerable expense, delay, and inconvenience. Although Chevrolet produced 6,000 Pace Cars, this number of cars was a limited production. In addition, only one of these cars was available to each dealer, and only a limited number of these were equipped with the specific options ordered by the Sedmaks (P). Charlie's Chevrolet, Inc. (Charlie's) (D) had not received a car like the Pace Car in the previous two years. Notwithstanding that the sticker price for the car was $14,284.21, Charlie's (D) (located in Missouri) received offers from individuals in Hawaii and Florida to buy the Pace Car for $24,000.00 and $28,000.00, respectively. As inferred by the trial court, the location and size of these offers demonstrated that this limited-edition automobile was in short supply and in great demand, which, the appellate court agreed, constituted a "proper circumstance" for ordering specific performance.

Quicknotes

BREACH OF CONTRACT Unlawful failure by a party to perform its obligations pursuant to contract.

ORAL CONTRACT A contract that is not reduced to written form.

REMEDY Compensation for violation of a right or for injuries sustained.

SPECIFIC PERFORMANCE An equitable remedy whereby the court requires the parties to perform their obligations pursuant to a contract.

STATUTE OF FRAUDS A statute that requires specified types of contracts to be in writing in order to be binding.

Vitex Manufacturing Corp. v. Caribtex Corp.

Cloth processor (P) v. Importer (D)

377 F.2d 795 (3d Cir. 1967)

NATURE OF CASE: Appeal from award of damages for breach of a contract for services.

FACT SUMMARY: Caribtex Corp. (D) contracted with Vitex Manufacturing Corp. (Vitex) (P) for the latter to process a large quantity of wool in its factory. Vitex (P) reopened a factory in order to fulfill its side of the bargain, but Caribtex (D) never sent the wool to be processed.

RULE OF LAW

In a claim for lost profits, overhead should be treated as part of the gross profits and recoverable as damages and should not be considered as part of the seller's (or processor's) costs.

FACTS: At the time of this suit, there were high tariffs on imported woolens, but if such goods were imported into the Virgin Islands and were processed so that their finished value exceeded importation value by at least 50 percent, then high tariffs to importation into the continental United States could be avoided. This enabled Virgin Island–processed wool to enjoy a price advantage. So that Congress would not be moved to change the situation, the island government imposed quotas on processors, limiting their output. Vitex Manufacturing Corp. (Vitex) (P) had not yet fulfilled its quota and so contracted to process 125,000 yards of woolen material at $0.26 a yard with Caribtex Corp. (D). Vitex (P) reopened a closed plant to begin processing, but because Caribtex (D) was unsure as to whether the wool could enter duty-free after processing, it did not send any wool to Vitex (P) for processing. Vitex (P) received an award of $21,114 for lost profits, and Caribtex (D) appealed, arguing that overhead should have been included in the calculation.

ISSUE: In a claim for lost profits, should overhead be treated as part of the gross profits and recoverable as damages, and should it not be considered as part of the seller's (or processor's) costs?

HOLDING AND DECISION: (Staley, C.J.) Yes. In a claim for lost profits, overhead should be treated as part of the gross profits and recoverable as damages and should not be considered as part of the seller's (or processor's) costs. Because of the uncertainty in exactly setting Vitex Manufacturing Corp.'s (Vitex's) (P) costs due to Caribtex Corp.'s (D) wrongful conduct in repudiating its contract before Vitex (P) could perform, Caribtex (D) was not permitted to benefit by the uncertainty it caused. Overhead includes the continuous expenses of the business irrespective of the outlay on a particular contract. While Vitex (P) did not expressly seek recovery for overhead, if a portion of that expense was allocated as costs to the Caribtex (D) contract, the damages should be reduced accordingly. However, the court believed it was the better rule to treat overhead as part of the gross profits rather than as part of the seller's costs in a claim for lost profits. If Vitex (P) had not entered into any contracts including the Caribtex (D) contract for the rest of the year, Vitex's (P) profits would have been found by deducting its production costs and overhead from gross receipts yielded in previous transactions. Its overhead would have remained constant whether or not it entered into the Caribtex (D) contract. Its additional expenses were incurred in reopening the plant, recalling employees, buying fuel oil, and buying chemicals. Since overhead remained constant, it could not be attributable to or affected by the Caribtex (D) contract and cannot be considered as a cost of Vitex's (P) performance deductible from the gross proceeds from the Caribtex (D) contract. Affirmed.

ANALYSIS

First, the breach here was straightforward and complete. Vitex Manufacturing Corp. (Vitex) (P) relied on the contract by reopening its plant, recalling employees, and taking other necessary steps to begin processing. For this, Vitex (P) received reliance damages. Generally, most damages prayed for are awarded upon a willful breach. The general formula "damages = loss in value cost avoided + other loss" came into play here. Vitex's (P) loss on the bargain was the difference between loss in value and cost avoided. The loss in value to the injured party is the difference in the value of what the other party was to have done and of what that party did. The cost avoided arises when the breach is total, which is the money saved by being excused from completing performance. Therefore, the loss on the bargain plus any other loss resulting from the breach equals the damages. Other loss may be any physical harm to the injured party's property or person and any expenses incurred by the injured party in an attempt to salvage the transaction after the breach.

Quicknotes

BREACH OF CONTRACT Unlawful failure by a party to perform its obligations pursuant to contract.

OVERHEAD The necessary costs associated with the operation of a business that are constant and are unrelated to the costs of production.

Laredo Hides Co., Inc. v. H & H Meat Products Co., Inc.

Leather purchaser (P) v. Seller (D)

Tex. Civ. App. Ct., 513 S.W.2d 210 (1974)

NATURE OF CASE: Action for damages for breach of contract.

FACT SUMMARY: When H & H Meat Products Co., Inc. (D) refused to continue to deliver hides under its contract with Laredo Hides Co. (Laredo) (P), Laredo (P) purchased them from other sources and sued to recover the price difference.

RULE OF LAW

When a seller wrongfully repudiates a contract or fails to make delivery of the goods thereunder, the buyer may "cover" by obtaining such goods elsewhere and sue the seller for the difference between the cost of cover and the contract price plus any incidental or consequential damages.

FACTS: Laredo Hides Co., Inc. (Laredo) (P) contracted with H & H Meat Products Co., Inc. (H&H) (D) to buy its entire production of hides during the period March through December 1972. When a check Laredo (P) sent was delayed in the mail, H&H (D) issued an ultimatum for immediate payment and stated it considered the contract breached and canceled when such was not forthcoming. Thus, H&H (D) stopped delivering hides to Laredo (P), which had already contracted with a tannery for sale of all the hides it expected to receive under its contract with H&H (D). Laredo (P) then proceeded to purchase substitute hides from other dealers and sued H&H (D) for damages. It had to pay $142,254.48 more for the hides than it would have under the contract with H&H (D) and incurred additional transportation and handling costs of $3,448.95. The trial court rendered judgment for H&H (D), and Laredo (P) appealed.

ISSUE: Upon wrongful repudiation by the seller, can the buyer "cover" by buying substitute goods elsewhere and sue the seller for the difference between the cost of cover and the contract price plus any incidental or consequential damages?

HOLDING AND DECISION: (Bissett, J.) Yes. The Texas Business and Commerce Code, like the Uniform Commercial Code, allows a buyer faced with a seller's wrongful repudiation of a contract or his failure to make delivery of the goods thereunder to "cover" by making a good-faith reasonable purchase of substitute goods elsewhere without unreasonable delay. The buyer can then recover from the seller as damages the difference between the cost of "cover" and the contract price together with any incidental or consequential damages, or he can have damages measured by the difference between the market price at the time when the buyer learned of the breach and the contract price together with any incidental and consequential damages. In this case, H & H Meat Products Co., Inc. (D) wrongfully repudiated the contract. Laredo Hides Co., Inc. (P) acted properly to "cover" and is thus entitled to recover the difference between the "cover" price and the contract price plus the additional expenses thus engendered. Reversed.

ANALYSIS

The rule on "cover" is found in Uniform Commercial Code § 2-712, in that article of the Code that covers contracts for the sale of goods only. Under this very innovative rule, when a buyer complies with the requirements of § 2-712, the buyer's purchase of substitute goods is presumed proper, and the seller has the burden of proving that "cover" was not properly obtained.

Quicknotes

BREACH OF CONTRACT Unlawful failure by a party to perform its obligations pursuant to contract.

COVER The purchase of an alternate supply of goods by a buyer, after a seller has breached a contract for sale, for which the buyer may recover the difference between the cost of the substituted goods and the price of the original goods pursuant to the contract, so long as the buyer purchases the alternate goods in good faith and without unreasonable delay.

REPUDIATION The actions or statements of a party to a contract that evidence the party's intent not to perform, or to continue performance of, the party's duties or obligations thereunder.

Plante v. Jacobs

Contractor (P) v. Customer (D)

Wis. Sup. Ct., 10 Wis. 2d 567, 103 N.W.2d 296 (1960)

NATURE OF CASE: Action to establish a lien upon property for breach of a construction contract.

FACT SUMMARY: When the Jacobses (D) believed that Plante (P), whom they had contracted to build a home on their lot for $26,765, used faulty workmanship and incomplete construction, they stopped further payments to him after having paid $20,000. Plante (P) then refused to complete and sued to establish a lien on the property.

RULE OF LAW

There can be no recovery on a contract as distinguished from quantum meruit unless there is substantial performance, which is defined as where the performance meets the essential purpose of the contract.

FACTS: Plante (P) contracted with Frank and Carol Jacobs (D) to furnish materials and construct a house on their lot in accordance with plans and specifications for $26,765. Plante (P) received $20,000 during the course of construction when a dispute arose between the parties as to faulty workmanship and incomplete construction. The Jacobses (D) refused to continue payments, and Plante (P) refused to complete construction. Plante (P) then sued to establish a lien on the property to recover the unpaid balance plus extras. The Jacobses (D) alleged that faulty workmanship on at least 20 items plus decreasing the width of the living room by one foot did not amount to substantial performance. The trial court found no legal damage suffered by the defendants.

ISSUE: Can there be recovery on a contract without there having been substantial performance?

HOLDING AND DECISION: (Hallows, J.) No. There can be no recovery on a contract as distinguished from quantum meruit unless there is substantial performance, which is defined as where the performance meets the essential purpose of the contract. When applied to house construction, this does not mean that every detail must be in strict compliance with specifications and plans. Here, the specifications were standard printed forms and the plan was a "stock floor plan." While the Jacobses (D) received a house with which they were dissatisfied, the contract was substantially performed. The misplacing of a wall by one foot so to narrow the living room did not affect the value of the home. Gutters and rainspouts, kitchen cabinets, and clothes closet poles were omitted. As the measure of damages for substantial but incomplete performance, Plante (P) should receive the contract price less the damages caused the Jacobses (D) by incomplete performance. For faulty construction, the "diminished value" rule pertains, which is the difference between the value of the house as it would stand complete and as it stands faulty but substantially complete. The trial court applied the "cost of repair" rule, which allows the cost to repair a number of small defects and omissions. If the separation of defects would lead to confusion, the diminished value rule can be applied to all defects. There was no confusion here in separating the defects. Whether a defect comes under the diminished value or cost of repair rule depends upon the magnitude of defect. However, the trial court was not in error in applying the cost of repair rule (usually applied to small items) to repairing a patio floor, plaster cracks in the ceiling, and repair of a nonstructural patio wall. The misplaced wall in the living room was of a magnitude sufficient as to place it under the diminished value rule, but as misplacing the wall was of no effect to the value of the house and as it would have been economical waste to move it, no legal damage was suffered. Affirmed.

ANALYSIS

The doctrine of substantial performance is applied when the unperformed portion does not destroy the purpose or value of the contract. Of course, this is like saying that the breach must not be material. Here, when the Jacobses (D) occupied the house, they showed that it served its purpose and thereby they assumed the burden to show performance was not substantial to the terms of the contract. The primary application of the doctrine of substantial performance is with building contracts where fairly large defaults have been treated as immaterial, while a small default is often sufficient to breach a sales contract due to practical considerations. The unhappy buyer can return the goods or refuse delivery. The unhappy landowner keeps the incomplete structure; hence, greater are the possibilities for unjust enrichment.

Quicknotes

COST OF REPAIR RULE A measure of computing damages pursuant to a breach of contract, representing the cost

Continued on next page.

to the non-breaching party to place him- or herself in the same position he or she would have been in had the contract not been breached.

DIMINISHED VALUE RULE A measure of computing damages pursuant to a breach of contract, representing the decrease in the value of the subject matter of the contract as a result of the breach, as measured by the difference in the value of the realty before and after the breach.

LIEN A claim against the property of another in order to secure the payment of a debt.

QUANTUM MERUIT Equitable doctrine allowing recovery for labor and materials provided by one party, even though no contract was entered into, in order to avoid unjust enrichment by the benefited party.

SUBSTANTIAL PERFORMANCE Performance of all the essential obligations pursuant to an agreement.

Groves v. John Wunder Co.

Gravel pit lessor (P) v. Lessee (D)

Minn. Sup. Ct., 205 Minn. 163, 286 N.W. 235 (1939)

NATURE OF CASE: Appeal from award of damages for breach of a contract for the lease of land.

FACT SUMMARY: When John Wunder Co. (Wunder) (D) surrendered the gravel pit it leased from S. J. Groves & Sons Co. (P), John Wunder Co. (D) was found to have deliberately breached the contract by removing the best and richest gravel without having restored the land to its existing grade.

RULE OF LAW

Value of the land as distinguished from the value of the intended product of the contract, which ordinarily will be equivalent to its reasonable cost, is no proper part of any measure of damages for willful breach of a building contract.

FACTS: In August 1927, S. J. Groves & Sons Co. (Groves) (P) and John Wunder Co. (Wonder) (D) contracted for the latter to lease from the former Groves's (P) gravel pit and gravel screening plant (besides getting rid of Groves [P] as a competitor) for a period of seven years for $105,000. A condition of the contract was that Wunder (D) agreed to remove sand and gravel while leaving the land "at a uniform grade, substantially the same as the grade now existing." Wunder (D) deliberately breached by removing the best and richest gravel without having restored the grade and leaving the land broken and uneven. The trial court found that 288,495 cubic yards of soil would need to be excavated and deposited elsewhere at a cost of $60,000 in order to restore the grade, but if Wunder (D) had left the land at the end of the lease at the correct grade, the land's value would have been $12,160, and gave judgment in that lesser amount. Groves (P) appealed the amount of damages awarded him as too low.

ISSUE: Is value of the land as distinguished from the value of the intended product of the contract, which will ordinarily be equivalent to its reasonable cost, a proper part of any measure of damages for willful breach of a building contract?

HOLDING AND DECISION: (Stone, J.) No. Value of the land as distinguished from the value of the intended product of the contract, which ordinarily will be equivalent to its reasonable cost, is no proper part of any measure of damages for willful breach of a building contract. Where a contractor willfully and fraudulently breaches a construction contract, he cannot sue upon it nor can he have the benefit of the doctrine of substantial performance. As a willful transgressor, John Wunder Co. (D) must accept the penalty of his transgression. Nowhere will change be tolerated if it is so dominant or pervasive as in any real or substantial measure to frustrate the purpose of the contract. Damages for a breach of a construction contract should give the injured party, as far as money is concerned, what he was promised. Therefore, S. J. Groves & Sons Co. (P) was entitled to recover what it would cost to complete the grading as contemplated by the contract. No past decision has suggested that lack of value in the land furnished to the contractor who has bound himself to improve it is any escape from the ordinary consequences of a breach of contract. The level from which to figure damages is the hypothetical point of accomplishment rather than value that would have been reached had the work been done as contracted. An owner's right to improve his property is not limited by its small value. To lessen damages recoverable by the low value landholder would be to favor the faithless contractor. Reversed and a new trial ordered.

DISSENT: (Olson, J.) The diminished value rule should be applied in absence of evidence showing that the completed product was to satisfy the personal taste of the promisee. The willfulness of the breach should not affect the measure of damages.

ANALYSIS

Where on the surface the contract appears to be for the lease of land, the provision for improvement brings it within the rules governing construction contracts. If the court in determining damages considered the low value of the land, the owner would be greatly limited in what he or she could do with the land. It has been said that a landowner can submit to any caprice or folly in the control of his or her own land, but if in dealing with contractors in amounts greater than the value of the land, it would be unfair to limit recovery to the value of the land only should the contractor breach. This would place the low value landowner at the mercy of unethical contractors. As has been seen, if there would be economic waste in approving a large amount of damages, such as in tearing out one manufacture of plumbing for the same quality but originally specified plumbing, such an order would not be declared. But if it is shown that the owner's purpose was to satisfy some personal taste or fancy, damages equal to the cost of completion will be awarded even if it involves economic waste.

Continued on next page.

Quicknotes

BREACH OF CONTRACT Unlawful failure by a party to perform its obligations pursuant to contract.

MEASURE OF DAMAGES Monetary compensation that may be awarded by the court to a party who has sustained injury or loss to his or her person, property, or rights due to another party's unlawful act, omission, or negligence.

Peevyhouse v. Garland Coal & Mining Co.

Farm owner (P) v. Coal mining lessee (D)

Okla. Sup. Ct., 1962 Okla. 267, 382 P.2d 109 (1963)

NATURE OF CASE: Cross-appeals from award of damages for breach of contract.

FACT SUMMARY: Garland Coal Mining & Mining Co. (D) promised it would perform restorative and remedial work on the Peevyhouses' (P) farm at the end of the lease period, but then argued that the cost of the repair work would far exceed the total value of the farm.

RULE OF LAW

Where a contract provision breached is merely incidental to the main purpose, and where the economic benefit which would result to lessor by full performance of the work is grossly disproportionate to the cost of performance, the damages which lessor may recover are limited to the diminution in value resulting to the premises because of the nonperformance.

FACTS: The Peevyhouses (P) owned a farm with coal deposits on it. This land was leased in November 1954 to Garland Coal & Mining Co. (Garland) (D) for five years for coal mining purposes. Garland (D) also agreed to perform restorative and remedial work at the end of the lease period at a cost estimated at about $29,000. After Garland (D) failed to restore the land, the Peevyhouses (P) sued for $25,000. Garland (D) introduced testimony at trial as to the diminution of value of the farm due to Garland's (D) failure to perform under the contract. The jury awarded the Peevyhouses (P) $5,000, which was more than the total value of the farm even after the remedial work was done, but only a fraction of the cost of performance. The Peevyhouses (P) appealed, arguing that damages should be the cost to obtain performance of the work not done due to Garland's (D) default.

ISSUE: Where a contract provision breached was merely incidental to the main purpose, and where the economic benefit that would result to lessor by full performance of the work is grossly disproportionate to the cost of performance, are the damages that lessor may recover limited to the diminution in value resulting to the premises because of the nonperformance?

HOLDING AND DECISION: (Jackson, J.) Yes. Where a contract provision breached was merely incidental to the main purpose, and where the economic benefit that would result to lessor by full performance of the work is grossly disproportionate to the cost of performance, the damages that lessor may recover are limited to the diminution in value resulting to the premises because of the nonperformance. The damages recoverable are to be a reasonable amount that is not contrary to substantial justice and that prevents the Peevyhouses (P) from recovering a greater amount for breach of an obligation than would have been gained by full performance. The judgment was excessive and should be reduced to $300. Affirmed as modified.

DISSENT: (Irwin, J.) Garland Coal & Mining Co. (D) knew that the cost of performance would be disproportionate to the value or benefits received by the Peevyhouses (P) when it entered into the contract. The function of a court is to enforce a contract as it is written. The Peevyhouses (P) were entitled to specific performance or, failing that, the cost of that performance.

ANALYSIS

The Restatement (Second) of Contracts § 348 reflects this court's decision. Section 348(2)(a) states that "if a breach results in defective or unfinished construction and the loss in value to the injured party is not proved with sufficient certainty, the injured party may recover damages based on the diminution in the market price of the property caused by the breach." Under § 348(2)(b), the injured party may, in the alternative, recover damages based on "the reasonable cost of completing performance or of remedying the defects if that cost is not clearly disproportionate to the probable loss of value."

Quicknotes

BREACH OF CONTRACT Unlawful failure by a party to perform its obligations pursuant to contract.

DIMINUTION IN VALUE A measure of computing damages pursuant to a breach of contract representing the decrease in the value of the subject matter of the contract as a result of the breach.

NONPERFORMANCE Failure to perform a duty.

R.E. Davis Chemical Corp. v. Diasonics, Inc.

Medical facility operator (P) v. Equipment manufacturer (D)

826 F.2d 678 (7th Cir. 1987)

NATURE OF CASE: Appeal of summary judgment awarding damages as restitution.

FACT SUMMARY: Diasonics, Inc. (D) claimed it lost a "volume sale" when R.E. Davis Chemical Corp. (P) breached a contract of sale.

RULE OF LAW

An aggrieved seller may recover, after resale, lost profits from the original sale if he can show that the subsequent sale would have occurred absent the breach and would have been profitable.

FACTS: R.E. Davis Chemical Corp. (Davis) (P) contracted to purchase certain diagnostic equipment from Diasonics, Inc. (D). Davis (P) placed a $300,000 deposit. Davis (P) later reneged, and Diasonics (D) resold the equipment at a comparable price. Diasonics (D) contended it was entitled to keep the deposit as lost profits from the sale. Davis (P) sued for restitution. The district court granted summary judgment in favor of Davis (P), and Diasonics (D) appealed.

ISSUE: May an aggrieved seller recover, after resale, lost profits from the original sale if he can show that the subsequent sale would have occurred absent the breach and would have been profitable?

HOLDING AND DECISION: (Cudahy, J.) Yes. An aggrieved seller may recover, after resale, lost profits from the original sale if he can show that the subsequent sale would have occurred absent the breach and would have been profitable. Uniform Commercial Code (UCC) § 2-708 concerns itself with damages from lost profits. Section 2-706 measures damages in the traditional contract price less market price manner. The UCC does not give much guidance as to when any particular measure is applicable. The district court apparently concluded that when § 2-706 is available, § 2-708 should not be used. This approach is supported neither by law nor by good reasoning. Simply because a seller has availed himself of the chance to resell an item is no reason to deny him lost profits so long as he can show the subsequent sale would have occurred anyway, as in the case of a volume seller. The seller must show, however, that the subsequent sale would have occurred even if the original breach had not and would have generated a profit. This matter must be resolved at trial. Reversed and remanded.

ANALYSIS

"Lost volume" sales are as legitimate as more traditional types. However, courts vary as to the level of proof required. Some have required proof involving economic/market condition analysis, such as the existence of a "seller's market." Others have been more lenient.

Quicknotes

LOST PROFITS The potential value of income earned or the potential value of goods that are the subject of the contract; may be used in calculating damages where the contract has been breached.

LOST-VOLUME SELLER A seller who can accommodate more than one buyer and for whom a buyer's breach does not release the goods for sale to another customer; in such a case, the appropriate measure of damages is the net profit the seller would have earned pursuant to the sale.

RESTITUTION The return or restoration of some thing to its rightful owner to prevent unjust enrichment.

SUMMARY JUDGMENT Judgment rendered by a court in response to a motion made by one of the parties, claiming that the lack of a question of material fact in respect to an issue warrants disposition of the issue without consideration by the jury.

UCC § 2-706 Provides that where resale by the seller is made in good faith and in a commercially reasonable manner, the seller may recover the difference between the resale price and the contract price.

UCC § 2-708 The measure of damages for nonacceptance or repudiation by the buyer is the difference between the market price at the time and place for tender and the unpaid contract price, plus incidental damages, minus expenses saved due to the breach.

United States v. Algernon Blair, Inc.

Federal government (P) v. Prime contractor (D)

479 F.2d 638 (4th Cir. 1973)

NATURE OF CASE: Action to recover in quantum meruit the value of labor and equipment furnished.

FACT SUMMARY: Coastal Steel Erectors, a subcontractor, brought suit in the name of the United States (P) against Algernon Blair, Inc. (D), the prime contractor on a government project, to recover in quantum meruit the value of the labor and materials it had furnished up to the point at which it justifiably ceased work.

RULE OF LAW

A promisee is allowed to recover in quantum meruit the value of services he gave to a defendant who breached the contract irrespective of whether he would have lost money had the contract been fully performed and would thus be precluded from recovering in a suit on the contract.

FACTS: Algernon Blair, Inc. (Algernon) (D) was the prime contractor on a U.S. government project. Coastal Steel Erectors (Coastal), a subcontractor on the project, furnished materials and labor up to the point that Algernon (D) breached its contract with Coastal. At that point, Coastal ceased work and brought an action under the Miller Act, in the name of the United States (P), to recover in quantum meruit the value of the equipment and labor it had theretofore supplied. The district court found Algernon (D) had breached the contract but held that Coastal would have lost money on the contract had it been fully performed. For this reason, it denied recovery, and Coastal appealed.

ISSUE: Even if a promisee would have lost money had he completed the contract, can he nonetheless recover in quantum meruit the value of services he gave to a defendant who breached the contract?

HOLDING AND DECISION: (Craven, J.) Yes. Regardless of whether the promisee would have lost money had he completed the contract, he can recover in quantum meruit the value of the services he gave to a defendant who breached the contract. It is an accepted principle of contract law, often applied in the case of construction contracts, that the promisee upon breach has the option to forgo any suit on the contract and claim only the reasonable value of his performance. Thus, Coastal Steel Erectors (Coastal) can recover for the equipment and labor it supplied despite the fact it would have lost money on the contract and would thus have been unable to recover in a suit on the contract. Recovery in quantum meruit is measured by the reasonable value of the performance and is undiminished by any loss which would have been incurred by complete performance. Reversed and remanded for findings as to the reasonable value of the equipment and labor supplied by Coastal.

ANALYSIS

The applicable standard in determining the "reasonable value" of services rendered is the amount for which such services could have been purchased from one in the plaintiff's position at the time and place the services were rendered. Some courts have held that the contract price is not only evidence of the reasonable value but is a ceiling on recovery; others disagree. The rationale is that one should not recover more for part performance than he or she would have upon full performance.

Quicknotes

QUANTUM MERUIT Equitable doctrine allowing recovery for labor and materials provided by one party, even though no contract was entered into, in order to avoid unjust enrichment by the benefited party.

Rockingham County v. Luten Bridge Co.

County commissioners (D) v. Bridge builder (P)

35 F.2d 301 (4th Cir. 1929)

NATURE OF CASE: Appeal from award damages for breach of a construction contract.

FACT SUMMARY: Rockingham County (the County) (D) had contracted to have Luten Bridge Co. (Luten) (P) build a bridge upon which the latter began construction. Due to public opposition to the bridge, the County (D) notified Luten (P) to stop work under the contract, but Luten (P) refused, having already expended $1,900, and completed the bridge for $18,000.

RULE OF LAW

After an absolute repudiation or refusal to perform by one party to a contract, the other party cannot continue to perform and recover damages based on full performance.

FACTS: On January 7, 1924, the Board of Commissioners of Rockingham County (the County) (D) contracted to have Luten Bridge Co. (Luten) (P) build a bridge. After Luten (P) had expended $1,900 for labor and material, the County (D) decided not to go ahead with the contract due to great public opposition to the proposed bridge. The County (D) so notified Luten (P), which refused to stop the project and built the bridge in accordance with the contract. Luten (P) sued successfully for $18,301.07 due on the construction cost, and the County (D) appealed.

ISSUE: After an absolute repudiation or refusal to perform by one party to a contract, can the other party continue to perform and recover damages based on full performance?

HOLDING AND DECISION: (Parker, J.) No. After an absolute repudiation or refusal to perform by one party to a contract, the other party cannot continue to perform and recover damages based on full performance. Even though Rockingham County (D) had no right to rescind the contract, and notice of such amounted to a breach, after receiving notice, Luten Bridge Co. (Luten) (P) had the duty not to increase the amount of damages flowing from the breach. Luten's (P) remedy was to treat the contract as broken when it received notice and sue to recover such damages as it may have sustained from the breach, including any profit it may have realized upon performance, as well as any other losses that it may have suffered. The completed bridge, standing alone in the forest without connecting roads, is now without value. As Luten (P) was obviously interested only in its profit, it would have been wiser to sue for that and use the time spent on bridge construction in a more worthwhile manner. Reversed.

ANALYSIS

The rule of mitigation of damages basically states that one cannot sue for a loss he could have avoided. Obviously then, Luten Bridge Co. (Luten) (P) should not have increased the damages by going ahead with the project. On the other hand, if Luten (P) had repudiated the contract, Rockingham County (the County) (D) would have had to mitigate damages by securing another contractor. In line with this is Uniform Commercial Code (UCC) § 2-610(a), but remember that the UCC does not apply to construction contracts. Only reasonable efforts to mitigate damages are required; there is no penalty for failing to mitigate successfully. In cases where the defendant who repudiates still receives a benefit from the plaintiff who fails to mitigate, the defendant may then have to pay for the completed work. In this case, the bridge, lacking connecting roads, was useless. The County (D) clearly received no benefit and did not have to pay damages, which could have been mitigated.

Quicknotes

MITIGATION Reduction in penalty.

REPUDIATION The actions or statements of a party to a contract that evidence the party's intent not to perform, or to continue performance of, the party's duties or obligations thereunder.

RESCISSION The canceling of an agreement and the return of the parties to their positions prior to the formation of the contract.

Trinidad Bean & Elevator Co. v. Frosh

Bean buyer (P) v. Bean seller (D)

Neb. Ct. App., 494 N.W.2d 347 (1992)

NATURE OF CASE: Appeal from jury verdict for defendant in action for breach of contract.

FACT SUMMARY: Soon after Trinidad Bean & Elevator Co. (Trinidad) (P) entered into a contract to purchase beans from Elmo Frosh (D), Frosh (D) anticipatorily repudiated the contract. Trinidad (P) contended that under Uniform Commercial Code § 2-713, which provides for damages as the difference between the contract price and market price, it was entitled to damages as of the date of performance due under the contract, rather than when it first learned of the repudiation.

RULE OF LAW

Under Uniform Commercial Code § 2-713(1), the measure of damages for a buyer upon anticipatory repudiation by the seller is the difference between the contract price and the price of the goods on the date of repudiation, so long as it would be commercially reasonable for the buyer to cover on the date of repudiation.

FACTS: On April 26, 1988, Trinidad Bean & Elevator Co. (Trinidad) (P) entered into a contract to purchase 1,875 hundredweight of dried, edible navy beans from Elmo Frosh (D), a bean farmer. One option under the contract provided for payment of $16.25 per hundredweight on January 15, 1989, and a second option provided for a 50 percent payment at $16 per hundredweight upon the completion of the harvest and for the other 50 percent payment at $16 per hundredweight on December 1, 1988. According to Frosh (D), on May 1, 1988, he asked a Trinidad (P) agent to tear up the contract, but the agent disputed that Frosh (D) ever made such a request. At that time, the contract and market prices for the beans were the same. On August 31, 1988, Frosh visited Trinidad's (P) local operations and asked if the contract had been torn up. On September 8, he sent a letter to Trinidad's (P) corporate headquarters stating he felt the contract was void. Harvest was completed in mid-October, and no beans were delivered as promised in the contract. Because of drought conditions, the price of navy beans rose during the 1988 growing season from $16 per hundredweight in April, to $32 per hundredweight in late August to early September, and to $36 per hundredweight in late September, when Trinidad (P) purchased beans from other sources. Trinidad (P) sued Frosh (D) for breach of contract. A jury returned a general verdict for Frosh (D), and Trinidad (D) appealed on various grounds. One assignment of error was that the jury was wrongly instructed, in Instruction No. 7, that it should apply the defense of mitigation of damages to reduce Trinidad's (P) recovery. Also at issue was Instruction No. 6, which indicated that the language "at the time the plaintiff learned of the breach" referred to the time in which performance by the seller was required under the contract, which, in this case, was at the time of harvesting the bean crop. Trinidad (P) also appealed the denial by the trial court of its motions for judgment notwithstanding the verdict, for a directed verdict, and for a new trial. The state's intermediate appellate court granted review.

ISSUE: Under Uniform Commercial Code § 2-713(1), is the measure of damages for a buyer upon anticipatory repudiation by the seller the difference between the contract price and the price of the goods on the date of repudiation, so long as it would be commercially reasonable for the buyer to cover on the date of repudiation?

HOLDING AND DECISION: (Connolly, J.) Yes. Under Uniform Commercial Code (UCC) § 2-713(1), the measure of damages for a buyer upon anticipatory repudiation by the seller is the difference between the contract price and the price of the goods on the date of repudiation, so long as it would be commercially reasonable for the buyer to cover on the date of repudiation. Trinidad Bean & Elevator Co.'s (Trinidad's) (P) assignments of error require the court to determine the measure of a buyer's damages under UCC § 2-713(1) upon anticipatory repudiation. Specifically, the question is whether the language "at the time when the buyer learned of the breach," § 2–713(1), refers to the time when the seller repudiated or the time when the performance came due. UCC § 2-610(b) provides a remedy for breach of contract before the time of performance has arrived. If a buyer chooses to treat the repudiation as a breach, the buyer may proceed under UCC § 2-711, which provides that the buyer may cancel and recover any amount paid to the seller, as well as seek damages for cover under § 2-712, or the contract-market differential, under § 2-713. Here, Trinidad (P) chose not to cover and instead sought damages for the contract-market differential under § 2-713, which states, "... the measure of damages for nondelivery or repudiation by the seller is the difference between the market price at the time when the buyer learned of the breach and the contract price. . . ." Because the term "breach" as used in § 2-713 is ambiguous, it must be interpreted within its statutory setting. The most common interpretation, accepted by a majority of courts, is that § 2-713(1) refers to time of repudiation. Those commentators and courts

Continued on next page.

that have preferred the time-of-performance interpretation have noted that the UCC drafters used the express language "learned of the repudiation" in § 2-713(1), and have reasoned that when the drafters intended to base damages on the date a party "learned of the repudiation," they did so by explicit language. Thus, using the performance-date interpretation would achieve consistency between the various UCC sections. On the other hand, a shortcoming of the performance-date interpretation is that it fails to explain § 2-610(a), which appears to allow an aggrieved party to await performance only "for a commercially reasonable time." Thus, if a buyer is entitled to market-contract damages measured at the time of performance, it is difficult to explain why the anticipatory repudiation section limits the buyer to a commercially reasonable time to await performance. Another shortcoming of the performance-date interpretation is that when a performance measure is applied, an aggrieved buyer in a rising market will speculate that prices will continue to rise. If the market falls after repudiation, the buyer will obtain the same goods at a price lower than under the contract. The effect is to overcompensate the buyer and penalize the seller. Accordingly, the date of repudiation is the better alternative. This conclusion is bolstered by § 2-712, under which a buyer may cover by making in good faith any reasonable purchase of substitute goods, so long as the buyer does not delay unreasonably. If the performance measure is correct, then in a rising market no reason would exist for requiring the buyer to act without unreasonable delay when seeking to cover following an anticipatory repudiation. For these reasons, the best interpretation of "learned of the breach" is that it refers to the time the buyer learned of the seller's repudiation. Therefore, the measure of damages for a buyer upon anticipatory repudiation by the seller is the difference between the contract price and the price of the goods on the date of repudiation, so long as it would be commercially reasonable for the buyer to cover on the date of repudiation. Conditioning the repudiation date measurement on commercial reasonableness is required by § 2-712(3), which provides that the "Failure of the buyer to effect cover within this section does not bar him from any other remedy." However, an aggrieved buyer ought to bear the burden of showing that it was commercially unreasonable for him to cover on the repudiation date. Turning to the facts of this case, it must be determined when repudiation occurred. According to Elmo Frosh (D), this occurred in May 1988. The gist of Trinidad's (P) argument for directed verdict and judgment notwithstanding the verdict is that it was insignificant that Frosh (D) repudiated because, even if he did, Trinidad (P) was entitled to await performance under the performance-date interpretation of § 2-713. Further, under that interpretation, damages were to be calculated at the time Trinidad (P) learned of the breach—when performance was due—so that Trinidad (P) thereafter had a reasonable time to cover. Because the factual issues of the time of Frosh's (D) repudiation and the reasonableness of Trinidad's (P) delay could not be decided as a matter of law, a directed verdict was not warranted. Moreover, since on a motion for judgment notwithstanding the verdict, the moving party is deemed as having admitted as true all relevant evidence favorable to the nonmoving party and the nonmoving party must be given the benefit of every favorable inference, Frosh's (D) repudiation occurred in early May, when the contract and market price were identical. The jury's finding in favor of Frosh (D), therefore, was not clearly wrong. Finally, the gravamen of Trinidad's (P) assignment of error based on the trial court's overruling its motion for new trial is that the court erred by instructing on mitigation. Although Trinidad (P) is correct that the trial court erred in instructing on mitigation, Trinidad (P) was not prejudiced by the error, because the jury could have found for Frosh (D) even in the absence of the erroneous instruction, since it could have found that Trinidad (P) should either have mitigated or effected cover on the date of repudiation. Affirmed.

ANALYSIS

Trinidad Bean & Elevator Co. (Trinidad) (P) also argued that even if the jury had found that repudiation occurred in early May 1988, as asserted by Elmo Frosh (D), it was commercially reasonable for Trinidad (P) to have waited four months, because the futures market for edible beans was fluctuating daily. In this regard, Trinidad (P) argued that "[b]ecause of the nature of forward contracting any commodity, the reasonableness of purchasing commodities to cover the amount of a commodity in a repudiated contract will always be questionable." The court, however, was not persuaded by this argument. The court explained that if an aggrieved buyer claims it was reasonable to delay after repudiation, the buyer has the burden of showing that it was commercially unreasonable to cover on the date of repudiation, and that the Uniform Commercial Code's policy is to make an aggrieved buyer whole, not to encourage or reward speculative behavior. Thus, the court reasoned, that as long as a well-ordered market is accessible, cover would be commercially reasonable at the earliest time following repudiation. Since Trinidad (P) had not shown that it could not gain access to the futures market for edible beans in early May, the court concluded that Trinidad (P) failed to show that it was commercially unreasonable to cover on the date of repudiation.

Continued on next page.

Quicknotes

COVER The purchase of an alternate supply of goods by a buyer, after a seller has breached a contract for sale, for which the buyer may recover the difference between the cost of the substituted goods and the price of the original goods pursuant to the contract, so long as the buyer purchases the alternate goods in good faith and without unreasonable delay.

DAMAGES Monetary compensation that may be awarded by the court to a party who has sustained injury or loss to his or her person, property, or rights due to another party's unlawful act, omission, or negligence.

DIRECTED VERDICT A verdict ordered by the court in a jury trial.

GRAVAMEN The material part of a cause of action setting forth the injury that is sought to be redressed.

JUDGMENT NOTWITHSTANDING THE VERDICT (JNOV) A judgment entered by the trial judge reversing a jury verdict if the jury's determination has no basis in law or fact.

REPUDIATION The actions or statements of a party to a contract that evidence the party's intent not to perform, or to continue performance of, the party's duties or obligations thereunder.

Tongish v. Thomas

Farmer (D) v. Sunflower seed purchaser (P)

Kan. Sup. Ct., 251 Kan. 728, 840 P.2d 471 (1992)

NATURE OF CASE: Review of order awarding damages for breach of contract.

FACT SUMMARY: After the Decatur Coop Association (P) lost money on a resale contract due to Tongish's (D) breach, it contended that the market price measure of damages should be used instead of its actual loss.

RULE OF LAW

When a seller breaches, market damages should be awarded even though in excess of the buyer's actual loss.

FACTS: Tongish (D), a farmer, agreed to sell sunflower seeds to the Decatur Coop Association (Coop) (P) at a specified price. Coop (P) planned to resell the seeds for the same price it paid Tongish (D) and pocket a small handling fee. The price of sunflower seeds increased substantially prior to delivery. Tongish (D) refused to honor the contract and sold to another at a higher price. Coop (P) sued Tongish (D). The trial court awarded $455 in handling charges based on Coop's (P) actual loss. The court of appeals reversed, holding that the proper measure of damages was market price under Uniform Commercial Code (UCC) § 2-713. Tongish (D) appealed.

ISSUE: When a seller breaches, should market damages be awarded?

HOLDING AND DECISION: (McFarland, J.) Yes. When a seller breaches, market damages should be awarded. Tongish (D) contends that market price damages in the situation of a seller's failing to honor a sales contract conflict with the general principle embodied in Uniform Commercial Code (UCC) § 1-106, i.e., that contract remedies are designed to put parties in the position they would have attained absent the breach. Damages awarded under UCC § 2-713 often, as in this case, greatly exceed actual damages, resulting in a windfall for the nonbreaching party. However, § 2-713 encourages parties to honor contracts by preventing a breaching party from being able to take advantage of market fluctuations. Therefore, more contracts are honored, resulting in a more efficient and stable market. Affirmed.

ANALYSIS

Uniform Commercial Code (UCC) § 1-106 is a general, axiom-like statute. UCC § 2-713 deals with a specific situation. The usual role of statutory construction is that a specific rule will prevail over a general rule. This, in fact, was the result here.

Quicknotes

BREACH OF CONTRACT Unlawful failure by a party to perform its obligations pursuant to contract.

UCC § 2-713 Provides that the measure of damages for non-delivery by the seller is the difference between the market price at the time the buyer learned of the breach and the contract price.

Parker v. Twentieth Century-Fox Film Corp.

Actress (P) v. Film studio (D)

Cal. Sup. Ct., 3 Cal. 3d 176, 474 P.2d 689 (1970)

NATURE OF CASE: Appeal from award of damages for breach of a contract for employment.

FACT SUMMARY: Parker (P), an actress, was to have the lead role in the motion picture "Bloomer Girl," but Twentieth Century-Fox Film Corp. (D) decided not to make the movie and offered her the leading role in a film, "Big Country, Big Man," instead.

RULE OF LAW

The general measure of recovery by a wrongfully discharged employee is the amount of salary agreed upon for the period of service, less the amount that the employer affirmatively proves the employee has earned or with reasonable effort might have earned from other employment.

FACTS: Parker (P), an actress professionally known as Shirley MacLaine, was hired for the lead role in the film "Bloomer Girl," to be produced by Twentieth Century-Fox Film Corp. (Fox) (D). She was to receive a salary of $750,000 for 14 weeks. Under the contract, Parker (P) was to have approval over the director or any substitute, the dance director, and the screenplay. Fox (D) decided not to make the film and offered Parker (P) the lead in "Big Country, Big Man," which, unlike the other film, was not a musical but a western. Also, Fox (D) did not offer Parker (P) approval of the director or screenplay (and there was no need for a dance director). "Bloomer Girl" was to have been filmed in Los Angeles; "Big Country, Big Man" was to be made in Australia. Parker (P) rejected the second film offer and successfully sued for her salary and resulting damages.

ISSUE: Is the general measure of recovery by a wrongfully discharged employee the amount of salary agreed upon for the period of service, less the amount that the employer affirmatively proves the employee has earned or with reasonable effort might have earned from other employment?

HOLDING AND DECISION: (Burke, J.) Yes. The general measure of recovery by a wrongfully discharged employee is the amount of salary agreed upon for the period of service, less the amount that the employer affirmatively proves the employee has earned or with reasonable effort might have earned from other employment. Twentieth Century-Fox Film Corp. (D), in claiming that Parker (P) unreasonably refused the second film offer, must show that the other employment was comparable to the first or, at least, substantially similar to that which their employee has been deprived. The employee's rejection of or failure to seek other available employment of a different or inferior kind may not be used to mitigate damages. If the western film offer were found different or inferior to the musical film offer, it makes no difference whether Parker (P) reasonably or unreasonably refused the second offer. The western was a different and inferior film where Parker (P) could not use her singing and dancing talents as in the musical. The western required travel to Australia for extensive outdoor filming rather than the use of sound stages in Los Angeles. The "Big Country" offer impaired or eliminated several rights of approval. Accordingly, as the second offer was different and inferior to the first, Parker (P) is awarded $750,000. Affirmed.

DISSENT: (Sullivan, C.J.) Employment that is different in kind should not be required to be accepted by the employee, but the mere existence of differences between two jobs in the same field should not be sufficient to release the employee and would effectively eliminate any obligation to attempt to minimize damage arising from a wrongful discharge.

ANALYSIS

The court points out that if the other offer of employment is of a different or inferior kind, it does not matter whether the employee acts reasonably or unreasonably in rejecting the offer. The person with the duty to mitigate need not expose him- or herself to undue risk, expense, or humiliation. It may be possible that, considering the kinds of movies Parker (P) had made in the past, which included no westerns, in the management of an actress's career, such a film may have been considered a risk or, even possibly, a humiliation. Also, many cases have held that the employee is not required to accept employment unreasonably distant from the original location. The court apparently thought that Australia was unreasonably distant when Parker (P) was regularly working in Los Angeles and had intended to work on "Bloomer Girl" there. Note that in mitigating, the employee also does not have to accept a position of lesser rank or at a lower salary. Also, Parker (P) asked for damages in addition to her salary, but such special damages are rarely awarded in cases of wrongful discharge. Damages for injury to the reputation of the employee are considered too remote and not within the contemplation of the parties. There is authority for damages when the denied employment would have

Continued on next page.

enhanced the employee's reputation, such as a motion picture credit, but this has been applied only once in the United States, although it is common in England. The dissent would apparently foist an unacceptable film role upon an actress. Due to the nature of the industry and its regularly accepted business practices, the majority probably kept in mind the actor's need "to feel right" about a role and script before accepting it.

Quicknotes

WRONGFUL DISCHARGE Unlawful termination of an individual's employment.

Hadley v. Baxendale

Mill operator (P) v. Shipping company (D)

Ct. of Exchequer, 9 Ex. 341, 156 Eng. Rep. 145 (1854)

NATURE OF CASE: Action for damages for breach of a carrier contract.

FACT SUMMARY: Hadley (P), a mill operator in Gloucester, arranged to have Baxendale's (D) company, a carrier, ship his broken mill shaft to the engineer in Greenwich for a copy to be made. Hadley (P) suffered a £300 loss when Baxendale (D) unreasonably delayed shipping the mill shaft, causing the mill to be shut down longer than anticipated.

RULE OF LAW

The injured party (1) may recover those damages as may reasonably be considered arising naturally from the breach itself and (2) may recover those damages as may reasonably be supposed to have been in contemplation of the parties, at the time they made the contract, as the probable result of a breach of it.

FACTS: Hadley (P), a mill operator in Gloucester, arranged to have Baxendale's (D) shipping company return his broken mill shaft to the engineer in Greenwich who was to make a duplicate. Hadley (P) delivered the broken shaft to Baxendale (D) who, in consideration for his fee, promised to deliver the shaft to Greenwich in a reasonable time. Baxendale (D) did not know that the mill was shut down while awaiting the new shaft. Baxendale (D) was negligent in delivering the shaft within a reasonable time. Reopening of the mill was delayed five days, costing Hadley (P) lost profits and paid-out wages of £300. Hadley (P) had paid Baxendale (D) 2£ 4s to ship the mill shaft. Baxendale (D) paid into court £25 in satisfaction of Hadley's (P) claim. The judge left the case to the jury, which awarded an additional £25, for a total £50 award. [Note: The headnote taken from the English reporter and reprinted in the casebook is in error when it states that Hadley's (P) servant told Baxendale (D) the mill was stopped, and the shaft must be sent immediately.]

ISSUE: Shall damages to be awarded be left to the discretion of the jury?

HOLDING AND DECISION: (Baron Alderson, J.) No. Damages to be awarded shall not be left to the discretion of the jury. The jury requires a rule for its guidance in awarding damages justly. When a party breaches his contract, the damages he pays ought to be those arising naturally from the breach itself and, in addition, those as may reasonably be supposed to have been in contemplation of the parties, at the time they made the contract, as the probable result of the breach of it. Therefore, if the special circumstances under which the contract was made were known to both parties, the resulting damages upon breach would be those reasonably contemplated as arising under those communicated and known circumstances. But if the special circumstances were unknown, then damages can only be those expected to arise generally from the breach. Hadley's (P) telling Baxendale (D) that he ran a mill and that the mill shaft he wanted shipped was broken did not notify Baxendale (D) that the mill was shut down. Baxendale (D) could have believed reasonably that Hadley (P) had a spare shaft or that the shaft to be shipped was not the only defective machinery at the mill. Here, it does not follow that a loss of profits could fairly or reasonably have been contemplated by both parties in case of breach. Such a loss would not have flowed naturally from the breach without the special circumstances having been communicated to Baxendale (D). New trial ordered.

ANALYSIS

This case lays down two rules guiding damages. First, only those damages as may fairly and reasonably be considered arising from the breach itself may be awarded. Second, those damages that may reasonably be supposed to have been in contemplation of the parties at the time they made the contract as the probable result of a breach of it may be awarded. The second is distinguished from the first because with the latter, both parties are aware of the special circumstances under which the contract is made. Usually, those special circumstances are communicated by the plaintiff to the defendant before the making of the contract. But that is not an absolute condition. If the consequences of the breach are foreseeable, the party that breaches will be liable for the lost profits or expectation damages. Foreseeability and assumption of the risk are ways of describing the bargain. If there is an assumption of the risk, the seller or carrier must necessarily be aware of the consequences. A later English case held that there would be a lesser foreseeability for a common carrier than for a seller as a seller would tend to know the purpose and use of the item sold while the common carrier probably would not know the use of all items it carried. If all loss went on to the seller, this would obviously be an incentive not to enter into contracts. Courts balance what has become a "seller beware" attitude by placing limitations on full recovery. The loss

Continued on next page.

must be foreseeable when the contract is entered into. It cannot be overly speculative. The seller's breach must be judged by willingness, negligence, bad faith, and availability of replacement items. Restatement (First) § 331(2) would allow recovery in the situation in this case under an alternative theory. If the breach were one preventing the use and operation of property from which profits would have been made, damages can be measured by the rental value of the property or by interest on the value of the property. Uniform Commercial Code § 2-715(2) allows the buyer consequential damages for any loss that results from general or particular needs that the seller had reason to know.

Quicknotes

ASSUMPTION OF RISK DOCTRINE An affirmative defense to a negligence suit contending that the plaintiff knowingly and voluntarily subjected him- or herself to a hazardous condition, wholly absolving the defendant of liability for injuries incurred.

NOLLE PROSEQUI A formal entry on the record by either a prosecutor or a plaintiff that he or she will discontinue prosecution of an action.

RULE NISI Motion by one party to make a final ruling against the opponent, unless the opponent can show cause as to why such ruling should not be ordered.

Delchi Carrier SpA v. Rotorex Corp.

Buyer (P) v. Seller (D)

71 F.3d 1024 (2d Cir. 1995)

NATURE OF CASE: Appeal from judgment for plaintiff for contract damages.

FACT SUMMARY: Delchi Carrier SpA (P) was awarded damages for lost profits and other consequential damages when Rotorex Corp. (D) shipped nonconforming compressors for air conditioners.

RULE OF LAW

A contract plaintiff may collect damages to compensate for the full loss, which includes, but is not limited to, foreseeable lost profits.

FACTS: Rotorex Corp. (D), a New York corporation, contracted to sell compressors to Delchi Carrier SpA (Delchi) (P), an Italian manufacturer of air conditioners. Prior to execution of the contract, Rotorex (D) sent a sample compressor and written performance specifications. When the compressors arrived in Italy, they were rejected in quality control checks because they had lower cooling capacity and consumed more power than the sample model and specifications. Rotorex (D) refused to supply new, conforming compressors, claiming the performance specifications were inadvertently communicated to Delchi (P). Delchi (P) then cancelled the contract and suffered a loss in its sales volume because it could not obtain substitute compressors in time. Delchi (P) filed suit under the United Nations Convention on Contracts for the International Sale of Goods (CISG) for breach of contract and failure to deliver conforming goods. The court granted Delchi's (P) motion for summary judgment and awarded damages that included lost profits. Delchi (P) appealed, claiming the judge erroneously denied damages for various consequential and incidental damages because they would allegedly constitute a double recovery.

ISSUE: May a contract plaintiff collect damages to compensate for the full loss, which includes, but is not limited to, foreseeable lost profits?

HOLDING AND DECISION: (Winter, J.) Yes. A contract plaintiff may collect damages to compensate for the full loss, which includes, but is not limited to, foreseeable lost profits. The award for lost profits did not compensate Delchi Carrier SpA (P) for costs actually incurred that led to no sales. Awarding damages for costs actually incurred in no way creates a double recovery. Affirmed in part, reversed in part and remanded.

ANALYSIS

The United Nations Convention on Contracts for the International Sale of Goods (CISG) did not expressly provide for calculating lost profits. The district court applied the standard formula most American courts use and deducted only variable costs from sales revenue. On appeal, the district court's decision in that regard was upheld as correct.

Quicknotes

BREACH OF CONTRACT Unlawful failure by a party to perform its obligations pursuant to contract.

CONSEQUENTIAL DAMAGES Monetary compensation that may be recovered in order to compensate for injuries or losses sustained as a result of damages that are not the direct or foreseeable result of the act of a party, but that nevertheless are the consequence of such act and that must be specifically pled and demonstrated.

LOST PROFITS The potential value of income earned or goods that are the subject of the contract; may be used in calculating damages where the contract has been breached.

Kenford Co. v. County of Erie

Landowner (P) v. County (D)

N.Y. Ct. App., 73 N.Y.2d 312, 537 N.E.2d 176 (1989)

NATURE OF CASE: Breach of contract suit.

FACT SUMMARY: Kenford Co. (P) sued Erie County (the County) (D) for loss of anticipated increase in value of peripheral lands as a result of the County's (D) breach of a contract to build a stadium on such property.

RULE OF LAW

In order to impose extraordinary damages on a breaching party, such damages must have been brought within the contemplation of the parties as the probable result of a breach at or prior to the time of contracting.

FACTS: The County of Erie (the County) (D) adopted enabling legislation authorizing it to finance and contract a domed sports stadium. When the County (D) learned that the project would cost $22 million in excess of its bond resolution it terminated the contract. Kenford Co. (P), owner of the proposed site, brought suit for breach of contract and specific enforcement of the agreement, or for damages of $90 million. The jury awarded $18 million in lost appreciation, $6 million in out-of-pocket, and $25.6 million in lost profits. The appellate division reversed the breach of contract claim and DSI, the management company, sought review. On retrial the jury awarded $6.5 million for loss of anticipated land appreciation. The appellate division affirmed and the County (D) appealed.

ISSUE: In order to impose extraordinary damages on a breaching party, must such damages have been brought within the contemplation of the parties as the probable result of a breach at or prior to the time of contracting?

HOLDING AND DECISION: (Mollen, J.) Yes. In order to impose extraordinary damages on a breaching party, such damages must have been brought within the contemplation of the parties as the probable result of a breach at or prior to the time of contracting. In the absence of a provision regarding entitlement to recover damages for lost anticipated appreciation in the value of peripheral lands, the applicable rule is to consider what the parties would have concluded had they considered the subject. Here there was no provision in the contract, nor evidence in the record, to demonstrate that the parties reasonably contemplated that the County of Erie (D) would be liable for lack of appreciation in the value of Kenford's (P) peripheral lands in the event the stadium was not built. Kenford Co. (P) is not entitled to recovery for lost appreciation in the value of peripheral lands cause by the breach. Reversed.

ANALYSIS

The general rule is that a nonbreaching party may recover damages for the natural and probable consequences of a breach. Anything more must be within the "reasonable contemplation" of the parties taking into account the circumstances surrounding the contract. The court must also consider "what liability the defendant fairly may be supposed to have assumed consciously, or to have warranted the plaintiff reasonably to suppose that it assumed, when the contract was made." *Globe Ref. Co. v. Landa Cotton Oil Co.*, 190 U.S. 540, 544.

Quicknotes

ANTICIPATORY REPUDIATION Breach of a contract subsequent to formation but prior to the time performance is due.

BREACH OF CONTRACT Unlawful failure by a party to perform its obligations pursuant to contract.

COVER The purchase of an alternate supply of goods by a buyer, after a seller has breached a contract for sale, for which the buyer may recover the difference between the cost of the substituted goods and the price of the original goods pursuant to the contract, so long as the buyer purchases the alternate goods in good faith and without unreasonable delay.

SPECIFIC PERFORMANCE An equitable remedy whereby the court requires the parties to perform their obligations pursuant to a contract.

Fera v. Village Plaza, Inc.

Prospective lessee (P) v. Lessor (D)

Mich. Sup. Ct., 396 Mich. 639, 242 N.W.2d 372 (1976)

NATURE OF CASE: Appeal from reversal of award of damages for breach of contract.

FACT SUMMARY: A portion of damages awarded to Fera (P) involving a new business consisted of lost profits.

RULE OF LAW

A new business may recover lost profit damages for breach of a lease if the profits are not excessively speculative.

FACTS: Fera (P), intending to open a liquor-related business in a shopping center operated by Village Plaza, Inc. (D), leased retail space. However, Village Plaza (D) misplaced its copy of the lease and subsequently let to another. Fera (P) brought an action to recover his deposit and lost profits. At trial, extensive evidence regarding Fera's (P) qualifications and the market conditions was presented. The jury awarded $200,000. The court of appeals reversed, holding that new business lost profit damages were inherently speculative. Fera (P) appealed.

ISSUE: May a new business recover lost profit damages for breach of a lease if the profits are not excessively speculative?

HOLDING AND DECISION: (Kavanagh, C.J.) Yes. A new business may recover lost profit damages for breach of a lease if the profits are not excessively speculative. It is the general rule that lost profit damages may be awarded, provided they can be proven. From this axiom had developed a dichotomy allowing lost profits to be awarded to an ongoing business but denied to a new business. New businesses were denied lost profit damages not because they were new but because it was thought that the damages could not be proven. If such damages could be proven, it was not per se improper to allow such damages. Here, a good deal of testimony was presented at trial concerning market conditions and other economic factors, and the trial court was satisfied that this was sufficient to allow the issue to go to a jury. The trial court was within its rights in doing this and the reversal was improper. Reversed.

CONCURRENCE AND DISSENT: (Coleman, J.) While agreeing with the principle enunciated here, the plaintiff in this case did not meet his burden of proof.

ANALYSIS

Lost profit damages were once universally frowned upon. This was due to the inherent uncertainty surrounding them. However, as time passed, advances in economics and related social sciences have increased the predictability of lost profits sufficiently to convince a majority of jurisdictions that they are proper.

Quicknotes

LOST PROFITS The potential value of income earned or goods that are the subject of the contract; may be used in calculating damages where the contract has been breached.

Newsome v. Western Union Telegraph Co.

Telegram sender (P) v. Telegraph company (D)

N.C. Sup. Ct., 153 N.C. 153, 69 S.E. 10 (1910)

NATURE OF CASE: Appeal from award of damages for negligent performance of telegraph transmission contract.

FACT SUMMARY: Western Union Telegraph Co. (Western Union) (D) contended that the negligence of its agent in transmitting Newsome's (P) telegram, which resulted in whiskey not being sent to Newsome's (P) raft hands, could support an award only of nominal damages, rather than consequential damage, which Western Union (D) claimed were too speculative and remote, notwithstanding that the agent had been informed of Newsome's (P) purpose in sending the telegram.

RULE OF LAW

Consequential damages may not be awarded for breach of a telecommunications contract by a public service corporation where the damages resulting from the breach are remote and speculative.

FACTS: Newsome (P) sent a telegram via Western Union Telegraph Co. (Western Union) (D), a public agency regulated by the state, which set its prices. He informed the Western Union (D) agent that the purpose of the telegram was to order whiskey for Newsome's (P) raft hands, who were to construct rafts and transport his timber and rosin during the rise of a river through melting snow (a freshet), and that if they did not receive the whiskey, the raft hands would not do the work, in which case he would lose the benefit of the freshet. The agent incorrectly transcribed the signature on the telegram, which, according to Newsome (P), resulted in the whiskey not being delivered. Newsome (P) brought suit for damages under the telegram transmission contract, and the trial court awarded consequential damages to Newsome (P). Western Union (D) contended that damages should have been limited to nominal damages, and the state's highest court granted review.

ISSUE: May consequential damages be awarded for breach of a telecommunications contract by a public service corporation where the damages resulting from the breach are remote and speculative?

HOLDING AND DECISION: (Brown, J.) No. Consequential damages may not be awarded for breach of a telecommunications contract by a public service corporation where the damages resulting from the breach are remote and speculative. Here, because Western Union Telegraph Co. (Western Union) (D) is a public service corporation and must accept telegrams from the public at fixed prices, it cannot be said that Newsome (P) contracted for consequential damages, notwithstanding that Newsome (P) informed Western Union's (D) agent of the telegram's purpose. Moreover, the damages asserted by Newsome (P) are too remote and speculative to be covered by a telegram transmission contract. To be entitled to such damages, Newsome (P) would have to show that the damages were certain and flowed directly and naturally from the breach. Damages that are uncertain and speculative, or that are not the natural and probable result of the breach, are too remote to be recoverable; something more than a possible result must be proved. Here, there are too many conceivable possible causes for Newsome's (P) damages. Although the whiskey's not being delivered to the raft hands may have caused them not to construct the rafts, it is a far cry between having the rafts constructed and the timber and rosin reaching its final destination. The raft may have been constructed and loaded, and still never have reached the final destination. It requires quite a stretch of the imagination to conceive that, had the whiskey been delivered, the raft would have been properly constructed, loaded, and safely conducted over a heavy freshet, and the merchandize duly and profitably marketed. Accordingly, Newsome (P) is entitled to recover nominal damages only. Reversed.

ANALYSIS

Although telegrams and telegraph companies are long gone, the rationale behind the *Newsome* opinion remains part of the law of damages, insofar as consequential damages must be proved with greater certainty than direct damages and compensation may not be based on a mere conjectural probability of future loss.

Quicknotes

CONSEQUENTIAL DAMAGES Monetary compensation that may be recovered in order to compensate for injuries or losses sustained as a result of damages that are not the direct or foreseeable result of the act of a party, but that nevertheless are the consequence of such act and that must be specifically pled and demonstrated.

NEGLIGENCE Conduct falling below the standard of care that a reasonable person would demonstrate under similar conditions.

Continued on next page.

NOMINAL DAMAGES A small sum awarded to a plaintiff in order to recognize that he or she sustained an injury that is either slight or incapable of being established.

REMOTE DAMAGES Damages that are unexpected and unforeseeable, and over which the negligent party has no control.

Figgie International, Inc. v. Destileria Serralles, Inc.

Equipment manufacturer/seller (P) v. Equipment buyer (D)

190 F.3d 252 (4th Cir.1999)

NATURE OF CASE: Appeal from grant of summary judgment to plaintiff, and from denial of partial summary judgment to defendant, in declaratory action seeking determination of appropriate remedies for breach of a contract.

FACT SUMMARY: Destileria Serralles, Inc. (Serralles) (D), a rum bottler, entered into a contract with Figgie International, Inc. (Figgie) (P), a manufacturer and seller of bottle-labeling equipment, for bottle-labeling equipment that turned out to not work properly. Although the parties' exclusive remedy for the defective equipment was repair, replacement, or return of the equipment and a refund of the purchase price, Serralles (D) contended that once Figgie (P) elected to attempt repair, it forwent replacement or return as a remedy, so that under Uniform Commercial Code (UCC) § 2-719(2) the remedy failed of its essential purpose, thus entitling Serralles (D) to pursue the full array of remedies provided under the UCC.

RULE OF LAW

Under § 2-719 of the Uniform Commercial Code, where the parties' exclusive remedy under a contract is repair, replacement, or return of defective goods, this remedy does not fail of its essential purpose where the seller has first unsuccessfully attempted repair, on the theory that the seller has thereby forgone its remedy of return and refund of the purchase price.

FACTS: Destileria Serralles, Inc. (Serralles) (D), a rum bottler, and Figgie International, Inc. (Figgie) (P), a manufacturer and seller of bottle-labeling equipment, entered into an agreement whereby Figgie (P) supplied bottle-labeling equipment to Serralles (D) for creating and placing labels on Serralles's (D) rum bottles. Problems arose with the equipment as soon as it was installed, and Figgie (P) spent several months trying to repair it, without success. Accordingly, Figgie (P) refunded the purchase price, and Serralles (D) returned the equipment. However, Serralles (D) also asked Figgie (P) to pay for damages arising out of the equipment's failure to perform as expected and the delay in obtaining alternative equipment. After the parties failed to come to agreement as to proper remedies, Figgie (P) instituted a declaratory judgment action in federal district court, asserting that it owed no further obligations to Serralles (D) under the agreement because Serralles's (D) remedy for breach was limited to repair, replacement, or refund—both under the written terms and conditions of the sales agreement and pursuant to usage of trade in the bottle-labeling industry. After the trial court ruled that the parties' exclusive remedy was repair, replacement, or return and refund, Serralles (D) asserted that this remedy failed of its essential purpose under Uniform Commercial Code (UCC) § 2-719(2), on the theory that once Figgie (P) attempted repair, it forwent replacement or return and refund as a remedy, and, because Figgie's (P) repair efforts were unsuccessful, the remedy failed of its purpose, thus entitling Serralles (D) to pursue the full array of remedies provided under the UCC. The court of appeals granted review.

ISSUE: Under § 2-719 of the Uniform Commercial Code, where the parties' exclusive remedy under a contract is repair, replacement, or return of defective goods, does this remedy fail of its essential purpose where the seller has first unsuccessfully attempted repair, on the theory that the seller has thereby forgone its remedy of return and refund of the purchase price?

HOLDING AND DECISION: (Traxler, J.) No. Under § 2-719 of the Uniform Commercial Code (UCC), where the parties' exclusive remedy under a contract is repair, replacement, or return of defective goods, this remedy does not fail of its essential purpose where the seller has first unsuccessfully attempted repair, on the theory that the seller has thereby forgone its remedy of return and refund of the purchase price. Section 2-719(1)(a) specifically contemplates that parties to an agreement may, as they did in this case, limit available remedies in the event of a breach to "return of the goods and repayment of the price or to repair and replacement of nonconforming goods or parts." Section 2-719(2), however, provides that the general remedies of the UCC will apply, notwithstanding an agreed-upon exclusive remedy, if the "circumstances cause [the remedy] . . . to fail of its essential purpose." Here, however, there is no evidence that the limited remedy of repair, replacement, or return has failed of its essential purpose or that the contracting parties have been deprived of the substantial value of the bargain. Destileria Serralles, Inc. (Serralles) (D) argued that Figgie International, Inc. (Figgie) (P), by first attempting to repair the equipment, elected to pursue repair as the exclusive remedy and, thereby, forgo enforcement of the remedy of return and reimbursement. From this premise, Serralles (D) contended that Figgie's (P) failure to repair the machines resulted in the remedy failing of its essential purpose. There is no support in the language of the UCC or in the cases interpreting it for this novel argument and

Continued on next page.

no evidence that this contemplated remedy of return and refund, once invoked, failed of its essential purpose. Although Serralles (D) correctly noted that a limited remedy of repair or replacement can fail of its essential purpose where the seller's repair or replacement is unsuccessful, here, Serralles's (D) remedies were not limited to repair or replacement but also included return. When attempts to repair failed, the equipment was returned and the purchase price refunded. Hence, the remedies invoked were exactly those envisioned by § 2-719(1)(a) and contemplated by the agreement. Accordingly, the limited remedy of repair, replacement, or return did not fail of its essential purpose. Affirmed.

ANALYSIS

As the court in this case observes, it does not make commercial sense for a seller to eliminate the remedy of return and refund of the purchase price by merely attempting repair or replacement first. On the contrary, one would expect a manufacturer or seller to first attempt to repair or replace equipment in order to meet its contractual obligations to the purchaser, and resort to a return and refund only if unsuccessful in doing so—particularly in the context of an agreement between two commercial entities for the purchase of sophisticated equipment.

Quicknotes

BREACH OF CONTRACT Unlawful failure by a party to perform its obligations pursuant to contract.

DECLARATORY JUDGMENT A judgment of the court establishing the rights and other legal relations of the parties in a controversy.

Dave Gustafson & Co. v. State

General contractor (P) v. State (D)

S.D. Sup. Ct., 156 N.W.2d 185 (1968)

NATURE OF CASE: Appeal from judgment for defendant in action for payment on a construction contract.

FACT SUMMARY: When the State (D) withheld a portion of the contract payment for Dave Gustafson & Co.'s (Gustafson's) (P) highway paving work, pursuant to a contract provision that provided for "liquidated damages" arising from delays, Gustafson (P) brought suit, contending the amount withheld was in the nature of an unenforceable penalty.

RULE OF LAW

A provision for payment of a stipulated sum as a liquidation of damages will ordinarily be sustained if it appears that: at the time the contract was made the damages in the event of a breach will be incapable or very difficult of accurate estimation; there was a reasonable attempt by the parties to fix fair compensation; and the amount stipulated bears a reasonable relation to probable damages and is not disproportionate to any damages reasonably to be anticipated.

FACTS: Dave Gustafson & Co. (Gustafson) (P) entered into a contract with the State (D) for paving a highway. The contract provided a graduated scale of per diem liquidated damages that depended on the size of the contract. For Gustafson's (P) contract, the per diem amount was $210 for every day's delay. Based on a delay of 67 days, the State (D) withheld $14,070 from what it paid Gustafson (P). Gustafson (P) brought suit, claiming that the amount withheld was an unenforceable penalty. The trial court held that the amount was valid liquidated damages, and the state's highest court granted review.

ISSUE: Will a provision for payment of a stipulated sum as a liquidation of damages ordinarily be sustained if it appears that: at the time the contract was made the damages in the event of a breach will be incapable or very difficult of accurate estimation; there was a reasonable attempt by the parties to fix fair compensation; and the amount stipulated bears a reasonable relation to probable damages and is not disproportionate to any damages reasonably to be anticipated?

HOLDING AND DECISION: (Hanson, P.J.) Yes. A provision for payment of a stipulated sum as a liquidation of damages will ordinarily be sustained if it appears that: at the time the contract was made the damages in the event of a breach will be incapable or very difficult of accurate estimation; there was a reasonable attempt by the parties to fix fair compensation; and the amount stipulated bears a reasonable relation to probable damages and is not disproportionate to any damages reasonably to be anticipated. Judged by this standard, the provision at issue is one for liquidated damages rather than a penalty. First, damages for delay in constructing a new highway are impossible of measurement. Second, the amount stated in the contract as liquidated damages indicates an effort by the parties to fix fair compensation for the loss, inconvenience, added costs, and deprivation of use caused by delay. Daily damage is graduated according to total amount of work to be performed, and it may properly be assumed that a large project involves more loss than a small one, and that each day of delay adds to the loss, inconvenience, cost, and deprivation of use. Third, for these reasons, the amount stipulated in the contract bears a reasonable relation to probable damages and is not, as a matter of law, disproportionate to any and all damage reasonably to be anticipated from the unexcused delay in performance. Affirmed.

ANALYSIS

This case reflects the modern tendency not to look with disfavor on liquidated damages provisions in contracts. When they are fair and reasonable attempts to fix just compensation for anticipated loss caused by breach of contract, liquidated damages provisions are enforced because they serve a particularly useful function when damages are uncertain in nature or amount or are unmeasurable, as is the case in many government contracts. Provisions requiring liquidated damages for delay are not against public policy and are an appropriate means of inducing due performance, or of giving compensation in case of failure to perform.

Quicknotes

LIQUIDATED DAMAGES An amount of money specified in a contract representing the damages owed in the event of breach.

Lake River Corp. v. Carborundum Co.

Distributor (P) v. Powder manufacturer (D)

769 F.2d 1284 (7th Cir. 1985)

NATURE OF CASE: Appeal from judgments in diversity suit for liquidated damages and counterclaim for conversion.

FACT SUMMARY: Lake River Corp. (P) sued Carborundum Co. (D) for liquidated damages resulting from breach of a distributorship agreement. Carborundum Co. (D) counterclaimed under the theory of conversion. The district judge entered judgment for both parties. Both parties appealed.

RULE OF LAW

A minimum-guarantee provision is an unenforceable penalty, rather than an enforceable liquidated damages clause, where it is designed always to assure the promisee more than its actual damages.

FACTS: Carborundum Co. (D) manufactures "Ferro Carbo," an abrasive powder used in making steel. Carborundum (D) entered into a distributorship contract with Lake River Corp. (P) to better serve its midwestern clients. Lake River (P) had a warehouse in Illinois and agreed to receive Ferro Carbo in bulk from Carborundum (D), "bag" it, and ship the bagged product to Carborundum's (D) customers. To honor this agreement, Carborundum (D) insisted that Lake River (P) install a new bagging system. Lake River (P) sought to ensure that it would be able to recover the cost of this new system ($89,000) and make a profit of 20 percent. Thus, Lake River (P) insisted on a minimum-quantity guarantee that in consideration of the new bagging system, Carborundum (D) would ship to Lake River (P) for bagging a minimum of 22,500 tons of Ferro Carbo. If this minimum was not met, Lake River (P) would invoice Carborundum at the then-prevailing rates for the difference between the quantity bagged and the minimum guaranteed. Shortly after the contract between Carborundum (D) and Lake River (P) was signed, the demand for domestic steel fell dramatically and Carborundum (D) failed to ship the guaranteed amount. Lake River (P) demanded payment for the difference and Carborundum (D) refused. At this time, Lake River (P) had 500 tons of bagged Ferro Carbo in its warehouse, having a market value of $269,000, which it refused to release unless Carborundum (D) paid the $241,000 difference due under the formula. Carborundum (D) trucked in bagged Ferro Carbo from the East to serve its customers in Illinois at an additional cost of $31,000. Lake River (P) brought suit for $241,000 and Carborundum (D) counterclaimed for the value of the bagged Ferro Carbo that Lake River (P) had impounded. The district judge entered judgment for both parties. Both parties appealed, and the court of appeals granted review. [The court affirmed the district court's ruling that Lake River (P) did not have a valid lien on the bagged powder.]

ISSUE: Is a minimum-guarantee provision an unenforceable penalty, rather than an enforceable liquidated damages clause, where it is designed always to assure the promisee more than its actual damages?

HOLDING AND DECISION: (Posner, C.J.) Yes. A minimum-guarantee provision is an unenforceable penalty, rather than an enforceable liquidated damages clause, where it is designed always to assure the promisee more than its actual damages. Leaving aside the theoretical question of whether courts should (paternalistically) refuse to enforce a contract provision that acts as a penalty against a large, sophisticated company—given that it can be argued on the one hand that there are some benefits to having penalties in contracts, but on the other hand that penalties also may discourage efficient as well as inefficient breaches of contract—the court must apply state law. Here, applicable state law requires that a liquidated damages clause, in order to be enforceable, must be a reasonable estimation at the time of contracting of the probable damages from breach, and the need for estimation must be based on the likely difficulty of assessing the actual damages suffered in the event of breach; otherwise, such clause is void as a penalty. Here, the damage formula is a penalty because it is designed always to assure Lake River Corp. (P) more than its actual damages. The formula—full contract price minus the amount already invoiced to Carborundum Co. (D)—is invariant to the gravity of the breach. It also indicates a failure to reasonably estimate actual damages. Regardless of when a breach occurs, Lake River (P) will recover more than its expected profit at that point. If the breach occurs early, Lake River (P) will receive a windfall; if it occurs late, Lake River (P) still would get more than the profits it could reasonably anticipate if there had not been a breach. Despite the fact that the damage formula is invalid, Lake River (P) is still entitled to its common-law damages (the unpaid contract price of $241,000) minus the costs that Lake River (P) saved by not having to complete the contract (the variable costs on the other 45 percent of the Ferro Carbo that it never had to bag). Remanded to the district court to fix these damages.

Continued on next page.

ANALYSIS

Although the court here sustains the distinction between penalty clauses and liquidated damages provisions, Judge Posner expressly states his disagreement with such a distinction. While he admits that penalty clauses impute a sense of exigency into the contract's terms, this advantage is heavily outweighed by countervailing concerns. First, the presence of the penalty clause increases the costs of contracting. Second, penalty clauses may discourage efficient breaches of contract. Nevertheless, he concludes that such a distinction is to be determined by the state courts in accordance with the common law and may not be dictated by federal judges.

Quicknotes

LIQUIDATED DAMAGES An amount of money specified in a contract representing the damages owed in the event of breach.

PENALTY CLAUSE A provision in a contract that imposes penalties for failure to comply with the terms of the contract; the clause is usually unenforceable.

Wasserman's, Inc. v. Township of Middletown

Lessee (P) v. Municipality lessor (D)

N.J. Sup. Ct., 137 N.J. 238, 645 A.2d 100 (1994)

NATURE OF CASE: Appeal from judgment awarding stipulated damages in breach of contract action.

FACT SUMMARY: A lease between Wasserman's, Inc. (P) and the Township of Middletown (D) contained a stipulated damages provision based on Wasserman's (P) gross receipts.

RULE OF LAW

Provisions for liquidated damages are enforceable only if they are a reasonable forecast of just compensation for the harm caused by the breach.

FACTS: The Township of Middletown, N.J. (the Township) (D) leased a commercial property to Wasserman's, Inc. (P). The lease contained a provision fixing damages in the event of a breach by the Township (D) as follows: a pro rata reimbursement of any improvement costs plus 25 percent of Wasserman's (P) gross receipts for one year. Wasserman's (P) subsequently sublet the premises to Jo-Ro, Inc. (P). Years later, the Township (D) canceled the lease and sold the property. Wasserman's (P) and Jo-Ro (P) sued to enforce the stipulated damages provision. The trial court upheld the clause and, applying it, awarded $346,058.45. The appellate division affirmed, and the New Jersey Supreme Court granted review.

ISSUE: Are provisions for liquidated damages enforceable only if they are a reasonable forecast of just compensation for the breach?

HOLDING AND DECISION: (Pollock, J.) Yes. Provisions for liquidated damages are enforceable only if they are a reasonable forecast of just compensation for the breach. At common law, courts generally looked with suspicion on such clauses. This was because such provisions often constituted a penalty and were more or less forced upon the party having lesser bargaining power. Also, they often did not reflect actual loss, as contractual remedies are designed to do. Finally, courts felt that allowing parties to set their own measure of damages usurped a judicial function. Today, this early unfavorable attitude has relaxed somewhat. Stipulated damage provisions that constitute a legitimate attempt to predict actual damages are valid liquidated damages provisions; those that do not are considered penalty provisions that do not advance the aims of contract law and thus are not enforceable. In general, gross receipts do not reflect actual losses incurred when a lease is canceled. It is not possible to determine from the record here whether the stipulated damages are arbitrary or would be likely to flow from the breach. The court should consider the parties' reasoning behind the damages calculation, the duty to mitigate, and the market value of replacement space. Therefore, this matter must be remanded to the trial court for a determination of whether the stipulated damages clause based on gross receipts is a valid liquidated damages clause. Affirmed in part and remanded.

ANALYSIS

A subissue that can arise when the reasonableness of a damages provision is challenged is that of timing. Some courts set the time for considering damages as of the time the contract is executed. Others look to the time of the breach. The modern trend is to assess reasonableness at either time. The Uniform Commercial Code reflects this trend in § 2-718 with a reference to "anticipated or actual harm."

Quicknotes

LIQUIDATED DAMAGES An amount of money specified in a contract representing the damages owed in the event of breach.

STIPULATION An agreement by the parties regarding an issue before the court so as to avoid unnecessary expense and delay.

Bains LLC v. Arco Prod. Co.

Gas station and hauling company (P) v. Oil refining company (D)

405 F.3d 764 (9th Cir. 2005)

NATURE OF CASE: Appeal from award of punitive damages to company for racial discrimination under 42 U.S.C.A. § 1981.

FACT SUMMARY: Bains LLC (P), doing business as Flying B (P), a Sikh-owned gas station and gas hauling company, was awarded nominal compensatory damages and $5 million in punitive damages against Arco Prod. Co. (ARCO) (D), based on racially discriminatory treatment of Bains (P) and its employees by ARCO's (D) employees that allegedly caused ARCO (D) to terminate a contract it had with Bains (P). ARCO (D) contended, inter alia, that the punitive damages award was excessive.

RULE OF LAW

(1) A jury award of punitive damages can be predicated on a jury award of nominal damages to a corporation arising from racial discrimination in violation of 42 U.S.C.A. § 1981 where the awards are not inconsistent and can be harmonized.

(2) In a case of highly reprehensible conduct such as racial discrimination, though not threatening to life or limb, that causes economic harm to a corporation, to be constitutional, the amount of a punitive damages award should be in the range of a single-digit ratio between punitive and compensatory damages, as well as in line with punitive damages awarded in comparable cases.

FACTS: After a petroleum pipeline ruptured in the state of Washington, Arco Prod. Co. (ARCO) (D) hired companies to truck the fuel from its refinery to its distribution center. One company ARCO (D) hired was Bains LLC (P) d/b/a as Flying B (P), a gas station and hauling company owned by three brothers who were originally from India and had become American citizens. The Bains brothers were religiously observant Sikhs who wore turbans and had long beards. After signing a fuel hauling contract with ARCO (D), Flying B (P) added three fuel tanker trucks to its fleet and hired more drivers, most of whom were also observant Sikhs. During the period that Flying B (P) transported fuel for ARCO (D), the Bains brothers and their drivers had to endure a considerable measure of abuse from Davis, the lead man at ARCO's (D) terminal where the drivers dropped off their fuel. Davis did not like the Flying B (P) drivers and purposely made their unloading work at the terminal difficult. He made a point of delaying the Flying B (P) drivers by ignoring their presence when they needed their papers signed after a delivery. Because ARCO (D) paid by the load, the delays meant that Flying B's (P) drivers could haul fewer loads and make less money. Davis made them stand out in the rain while other drivers were allowed to stay in their trucks or seek shelter. Davis also falsely accused Flying B (P) drivers of various safety violations and made them clean up spills left by other drivers instead of making those responsible clean up their own spills. Davis's rudeness included—and by inference arose from—his ethnic animus against Sikhs. For example, Davis called one of the Bains brothers a "diaperhead" to his face despite the brother's protest that his turban was an important religious symbol, and also called him "raghead." One of Flying B's (P) hired drivers said Davis commonly called him "stupid Indian," "motherfucking Indian," and similar sobriquets, and when he asked for a rag after Davis had told him to clean up a spill, Davis refused and told him to take the "fucking rag from your head and clean it." Davis also asked Flying B's (P) only two Caucasian drivers, "How did you get hooked up with these fuckers?" There were other instances of abuse committed by Davis. Although the Bains reported this abuse to Davis's supervisor, Lawrence, the problems continued, as did Davis's abuse. Then, after about four months, without any notice as required by the contract, ARCO (D) terminated Flying B (P). Flying B (P) was forced to lay off a number of employees and to sell their now superfluous trucks. Flying B (P) brought suit in federal district court against ARCO (D), asserting state-law claims for breach of contract, and claims that it had been subject to racial discrimination while performing under the contract and that the contract had been terminated in violation of 42 U.S.C. § 1981. An economist testified that Flying B (P) suffered a $576,000 loss on account of the termination, based solely on the profits the company would have made from November 1, 2000, when Flying B (P) was terminated, to June 30, 2001, when the pipeline was fixed and ARCO (D) no longer needed drivers to move the fuel. A jury found for Flying B (P) on all counts and awarded $1.00 in nominal damages on the § 1981 claim, $5,000,000.00 in punitive damages on the § 1981 claim, and $50,000.00 on the breach of contract claim. ARCO (D) moved for judgment as a matter of law or a new trial or, alternatively, to set aside or remit the punitive damages. The district court denied the motions. The court of appeals granted review.

Continued on next page.

ISSUE:

(1) Can a jury award of punitive damages be predicated on a jury award of nominal damages to a corporation arising from racial discrimination in violation of 42 U.S.C.A. § 1981 where the awards are not inconsistent and can be harmonized?

(2) In a case of highly reprehensible conduct such as racial discrimination, though not threatening to life or limb, that causes economic harm to a corporation, to be constitutional, should the amount of a punitive damages award be in the range of a single-digit ratio between punitive and compensatory damages, as well as in line with punitive damages awarded in comparable cases?

HOLDING AND DECISION: (Kleinfeld, J.)

(1) Yes. A jury award of punitive damages can be predicated on a jury award of nominal damages to a corporation arising from racial discrimination in violation of 42 U.S.C.A. § 1981 where the awards are not inconsistent and can be harmonized. Arco Prod. Co. (ARCO) (D) argues that the jury verdict awarding one dollar in nominal damages for the § 1981 violation establishes that the ethnic discrimination caused no economic harm to Bains LLC (P) d/b/a as Flying B (P), and that there can be no injury to a corporation without economic damages. Here, the jury had been instructed that it could award damages for harm to the corporation, and its award of nominal damages was not its entire verdict. The jury also found that ARCO (D) had in fact discriminated against Flying B (P) because of race, that it caused a $50,000 loss by breaking its contract with Flying B (P), and that ARCO (D) deserved to be punished for its racial discrimination to the extent of $5 million. Although these verdicts could be viewed as inconsistent, the district court was able to read them in light of the evidence in a manner that rendered them consistent, and the district court correctly concluded that the verdicts did not establish the absence of economic harm. The district court correctly held that the jury could have found on the evidence that (1) racial discrimination had caused lost profits by delaying Flying B's (P) drivers and thereby reducing the number of loads Flying B (P) hauled; but (2) the jury did not have testimony that would enable it to put a number on how many loads were lost; so (3) even though lost profits were proved, the "amount" of lost profits could not be established "with reasonable certainty," as the jury was instructed to find. Moreover, the damages to Flying B (P), as a predicate for punitive damages, did not have to be from the contract's termination. Section 1981 extends its prohibition against racial discrimination in the making and enforcement of contracts to cover all phases and incidents of the contractual relationship, not just the termination of a contract. The testimony established that ARCO (D) employees made Flying B's (P) drivers wait longer to fill their trucks and to use slower pumps than other drivers, and that Flying B (P) drivers suffered damaged morale. The jury could have concluded that Flying B (P) suffered economic harm during the contractual relationship from the intentional delays and its drivers' damaged morale, which resulted in a reduced number of loads—and therefore less money under a contract that paid by the load—and that all of this was caused by Davis's racial harassment. Although Flying B's (P) economics expert testified that Flying B (P) would have made $576,000 if it had continued to haul the same number of loads it did until the broken pipeline was fixed, he did not offer testimony on how much money Flying B (P) lost because of the slowdowns caused by Davis's racial harassment. Thus, the jury could reasonably have concluded that Flying B (P) had made less money while it was hauling because of Davis's racial harassment, yet reasonably have found no number that it could attach to the harm, and therefore awarded nominal damages. Accordingly, the district court was able to reconcile the verdicts and did not err in doing so. Judgment for Flying B (P) as to this issue.

(2) Yes. In a case of highly reprehensible conduct such as racial discrimination, though not threatening to life or limb, that causes economic harm to a corporation, to be constitutional, the amount of a punitive damages award should be in the range of a single-digit ratio between punitive and compensatory damages, as well as in line with punitive damages awarded in comparable cases. Based on Supreme Court precedent, to determine whether a punitive damages award meets due process concerns, a court looks to three guideposts: (1) the degree of reprehensibility, (2) the disparity between the harm suffered and the punitive damages award, and (3) the difference between this remedy and the civil penalties authorized or imposed in comparable cases. As to reprehensibility, the harm to Flying B (P) was economic and did not evince reckless disregard of health or safety, and there was no threat of physical harm. That reduces reprehensibility. On the other hand, the conduct was not an isolated incident but repeated, the target was highly vulnerable financially, and the harm resulted from intentional malicious conduct. There can be no excuse for intentional, repeated ethnic harassment, so the reprehensibility here is worse than conduct that might have some legitimate purpose. Also, given ARCO's (D) clear failure to remedy or even address the discriminatory effects of its employee's conduct, the jury could properly have concluded that punitive damages were necessary to prevent such

Continued on next page.

discrimination from occurring in the future. As to the second guidepost, the jury could properly consider not only the one dollar in nominal damages awarded for discrimination under § 1981 but also the $50,000 in compensatory damages awarded for breach of contract. Relying on precedent, Flying B (P) argued that "potential harm" could also be considered to produce a much higher punitive damages award, but such potential harm addresses additional harm if additional wrongful conduct occurs and if there is possible harm to other victims. Here, wrongful conduct succeeded—Flying B's (P) contract was terminated—and there was no potential additional harm. Also, as for the harm to the individual drivers, the award to Flying B (P) did not impair their own rights to sue for whatever common law or state statutory torts that might lie, such as intentional infliction of mental distress. Thus, $50,000 may be considered the amount of harm suffered. The United States Supreme Court has held that few awards exceeding a single-digit ratio between punitive and compensatory damages, to a significant degree, will satisfy due process. The rare exception might be a case where a particularly egregious act has resulted in only a small amount of economic damages. The case at bar is not a "small amount" case because the economic damages were substantial—$50,000. The controlling Supreme Court authority therefore implies a punitive damages ceiling in this case of, at most, $450,000 (nine times the compensatory damages)—not anywhere near the $5,000,000 (100 times the compensatory damages) that was awarded by the jury. Finally, under the third guidepost, the $300,000 statutory limitation on punitive damages in Title VII cases has been held to be an appropriate benchmark for reviewing § 1981 damage awards, even though that statutory limitation does not apply directly to § 1981 cases. Based on these considerations, the amount of punitive damages should be reduced to a figure somewhere between $300,000 and $450,000. The case is remanded to the district court for a determination of punitive damages falling within that range. Judgment for ARCO (D) as to this issue. [Affirmed in part, vacated in part, and remanded.]

ANALYSIS

Bains LLC (P) d/b/a as Flying B (P) had argued that the huge corporate assets of Arco Prod. Co. (D) justified a higher award than might be justified for a defendant less able to pay it, since a punitive damages award is supposed to sting so as to deter a defendant's reprehensible conduct. Although juries have traditionally been permitted to consider a defendant's assets in determining an award that will carry the right degree of sting, as this case illustrates, there are limits to basing a punitive damages award on a defendant's assets, since the wealth of a defendant cannot justify an otherwise unconstitutional punitive damages award and cannot make up for the failure of other factors, such as reprehensibility, to constrain significantly an award that purports to punish a defendant's conduct.

Quicknotes

DUE PROCESS The constitutional mandate requiring the courts to protect and enforce individuals' rights and liberties consistent with prevailing principles of fairness and justice and prohibiting the federal and state governments from such activities that deprive its citizens of life, liberty, or property interest.

NOMINAL DAMAGES A small sum awarded to a plaintiff in order to recognize that he or she sustained an injury that is either slight or incapable of being established.

PUNITIVE DAMAGES Damages exceeding the actual injury suffered for the purposes of punishment of the defendant, deterrence of the wrongful behavior, or comfort to the plaintiff. Also called "exemplary damages."

CHAPTER 9

Basic Assumptions: Mistake, Impracticability, and Frustration

Quick Reference Rules of Law

PAGE

1. *Stees v. Leonard.* If one binds oneself by a positive, express contract to do an act in itself possible, one must perform unless prevented by act of God, the law, or the other party to the contract and will not be excused by hardship, unforeseen hindrance, or difficulty short of absolute impossibility. *267*

2. *Renner v. Kehl.* Mutual mistake of fact is a basis for rescission. *268*

3. *Sumerel v. Goodyear Tire & Rubber Co.* (1) An offer is not made where communications do not invite acceptance and on their face are "too good to be true." (2) Where a party to a contract has made a unilateral mistake, that party will be able to avoid the contract where the other party knew of or had reason to know of the mistake, and even if the other party did not know of or have reason to know of the mistake, enforcement of the contract would be oppressive to the mistaken party and relief from the contract would impose no substantial hardship on the other party. *269*

4. *Mineral Park Land Co. v. Howard.* A party is excused from performing under a contract where such performance is so much more expensive than contemplated that it would be impracticable to complete. *272*

5. *Taylor v. Caldwell.* In contracts in which the performance depends on the continued existence of a given person or thing, a condition is implied that the impossibility of performance arising from the perishing of the person or thing shall excuse the performance. *273*

6. *Transatlantic Financing Corporation v. United States.* When the issue of impossibility is raised, the court must construct a condition of performance based on changed circumstances involving the following: (1) a contingency, something unexpected, must have occurred, (2) the risk of unexpected occurrence must not have been allocated either by agreement or custom, and (3) occurrence of the contingency must have rendered performance commercially impracticable. *274*

7. *Canadian Industrial Alcohol Co. v. Dunbar Molasses Co.* If the promisor is in some respects responsible for the event that makes performance of its promise impossible and takes no steps to alleviate the impossibility, its duty of performance is not excused. *276*

8. *Eastern Air Lines, Inc. v. Gulf Oil Corporation.* A requirements contract entered in good faith is not void for want of mutuality. *277*

9. *Krell v. Henry.* Where the object of one of the parties is the basis upon which both parties contract, the duties of performance are constructively conditioned upon the attainment of that object. *278*

10. *Swift Canadian Co. v. Banet.* Assuming a party is ready to perform, he is not obligated to perform in vain where the other party has given notice of refusal to accept performance. *279*

11. *Chase Precast Corp. v. John J. Paonessa Co.* A defendant may rely on frustration of purpose as a defense to a breach of contract claim if the risk of the occurrence of the frustrating event is not allocated by the contract to the defendant. *280*

12. *Northern Indiana Public Service Co. v. Carbon County Coal Co.* A party cannot avoid performance of a contract on the basis of impracticability or impossibility where the contract specifically shifts the risk of such to that party. *281*

13. *Young v. City of Chicopee.* There is an implied condition that a thing upon which work is to be done shall continue to exist, and if it is destroyed without fault, the owner is liable for the value of the work done. 282

14. *In re Hitz Restaurant Group.* A force majeure clause excuses contractual performance only in proportion to the degree to which a triggering event prevents such performance. 283

Stees v. Leonard

Property owner (P) v. Builder (D)

Minn. Sup. Ct., 20 Minn. 494, 20 Gil. 448 (1874)

NATURE OF CASE: Appeal from plaintiff's judgment in action for damages for breach of a construction contract.

FACT SUMMARY: Stees (P) alleged that Leonard (D) had breached a contract to build a structure on a St. Paul lot when the structure collapsed upon reaching three stories, as did a subsequent structure upon a second attempt. Leonard (D) claimed subsoil conditions were aggravated by quicksand, making it impossible for the land to support a structure.

RULE OF LAW

If one binds oneself by a positive, express contract to do an act in itself possible, one must perform unless prevented by act of God, the law, or the other party to the contract and will not be excused by hardship, unforeseen hindrance, or difficulty short of absolute impossibility.

FACTS: Stees (P) sought damages for Leonard's (D) failure to erect a structure as contracted on a lot owned by Stees (P) in St. Paul. Two attempts were made to build the building, but both times when the building reached the height of three stories it collapsed. Leonard (D) claimed that the soil under the foundation was quicksand and was incapable of supporting a structure whenever water flowed in. Leonard (D) had fulfilled Stees's (P) specifications for construction of the foundation. Stees (P) had judgment for $5,214.80 plus interest ($3,745.80 paid during progress of construction, $1,000 damages for loss of use of the lot, and $469 damage to an adjacent structure of Stees [P] injured by the collapse).

ISSUE: If one binds oneself by a positive, express contract to do an act in itself possible, must one perform unless prevented by act of God, the law, or the other party to the contract and not be excused by hardship, unforeseen hindrance, or difficulty short of absolute impossibility?

HOLDING AND DECISION: (Young, J.) Yes. When one has bound oneself to a contract, one must perform unless prevented by act of God, law, or other party to the contract. Performance will not be excused by hardship, unforeseen hindrance, or difficulty short of absolute impossibility. The apparent hardship is attributable to the contractor himself who has accepted an absolute as opposed to a qualified liability. The law enforces the contract only as the party has made it. Cases have held that latent defects in the soil and unexpected impediments must fall on the contractor, as a party must do what he agreed to do. Leonard (D) contracted to "erect and complete a building" and was required to do so even if it required going beyond Stees's (P) specifications. Affirmed.

ANALYSIS

Early cases as illustrated here held that if the building is destroyed or rendered less valuable because of defective plans and specifications supplied by the owner, then the builder, by accepting the owner's plans, promised to produce the structure called for and accepted the risks attendant upon using the owner's specifications. It was thought that the owner relied upon the technical knowledge of the builder. The modern cases have held that where the owner has hired professionals who have prepared the plans and specifications, the owner has warranted the plans to be adequate unless the builder has reason to know of inadequacy or unless the parties have contracted otherwise. The parties can allocate risks by agreement. Note that the rules for contracts to repair or alter existing structures are different than the rules for the construction of new buildings. Also, Restatement, Restitution, § 9 is authority for avoiding a construction contract made without sufficient information about soil conditions on the ground of mutual mistake.

Quicknotes

LATENT DEFECT A defect that cannot be discovered upon ordinary examination.

Renner v. Kehl

Purchaser (P) v. Seller (D)

Ariz. Sup. Ct., 150 Ariz. 94, 722 P.2d 262 (1986)

NATURE OF CASE: Action for rescission.

FACT SUMMARY: Renner (P) sought to rescind a contract entered with Kehl (D) for the purchase of land when several test wells failed to produce sufficient water to cultivate jojoba.

RULE OF LAW

Mutual mistake of fact is a basis for rescission.

FACTS: The Kehls and the Moyles (D) decided to sell their interest in undeveloped land. Renner (P) agreed to pay $100 an acre for the leases for the purpose of cultivating jojoba. Renner (P) abandoned the project when test wells failed to produce water of a sufficient quality for cultivating jojoba. The trial court directed the sellers to reimburse the purchasers and the court of appeals affirmed.

ISSUE: Is mutual mistake of fact a basis for rescission?

HOLDING AND DECISION: (Gordon, V.C.J.) Yes. Mutual mistake of fact is a basis for rescission. A contract may be rescinded where such mistake of material fact constitutes an essential part and condition of the contract. Here, the basis of the contract was for the purchaser to cultivate jojoba; thus, the belief that adequate water supplies existed was a basic assumption of the bargain. Upon finding that such belief was erroneous, the contract was voidable and the respondents were entitled to rescission. However, absent proof of breach for fraud or misrepresentation, a party who rescinds a contract may not recover consequential damages. This means that Renner (P) may not recover the costs of developing the land in the form of consequential damages, but he is entitled to restitution of the down payment and any amount to which the land was enhanced. Kehl (D) is entitled to fair rental value of the property. Affirmed in part, reversed in part, and remanded.

ANALYSIS

If a party rescinds a contract on the basis of mutual mistake, the proper measure of damages is restitution for any benefit conferred through either part performance or reliance. Such recoveries are intended to avoid unjust enrichment and are not intended to be compensatory. In determining proper restitution, the rescinding party must also return any value received.

Quicknotes

CONSEQUENTIAL DAMAGES Monetary compensation that may be recovered in order to compensate for injuries or losses sustained as a result of damages that are not the direct or foreseeable result of the act of a party, but that nevertheless are the consequence of such act and that must be specifically pled and demonstrated.

MISTAKE OF FACT An unintentional mistake in knowing or recalling a fact without the will to deceive.

RESCISSION The canceling of an agreement and the return of the parties to their positions prior to the formation of the contract.

RESTITUTION The return or restoration of some thing to its rightful owner to prevent unjust enrichment.

Sumerel v. Goodyear Tire & Rubber Co.

Consumer (P) v. Rubber products manufacturer (D)

Colo. Ct. App., 232 P.3d 128 (2009)

NATURE OF CASE: Appeal from judgment to enforce a purported settlement agreement.

FACT SUMMARY: Goodyear Tire & Rubber Co. (Goodyear) (D), which had been adjudged liable to various consumers (P) for various damages, contended that, in an attempt to come to agreement on the prejudgment interest owed on a portion of the damages, an email and erroneous charts that Goodyear's (D) counsel sent to the consumers' (P) counsel—which contained a $550,000 windfall for the consumers (P)—did not constitute an offer capable of acceptance because it did not invite acceptance and was, on its face, too good to be true. Goodyear (D) also contended that even if an offer had been made, any agreement based on it would be unenforceable under the doctrine of unilateral mistake.

RULE OF LAW

(1) An offer is not made where communications do not invite acceptance and on their face are "too good to be true."

(2) Where a party to a contract has made a unilateral mistake, that party will be able to avoid the contract where the other party knew of or had reason to know of the mistake, and even if the other party did not know of or have reason to know of the mistake, enforcement of the contract would be oppressive to the mistaken party and relief from the contract would impose no substantial hardship on the other party.

FACTS: In a products liability action brought by consumers (P) against Goodyear Tire & Rubber Co. (Goodyear) (D), a jury awarded the consumers (P) approximately $1.3 million against Goodyear (D), including repair and replacement costs, diminution in value damages, and "other costs and losses." In addition, the jury found that Goodyear (D) was responsible for 36 percent of such "other costs and losses" suffered by two consumers (P) and 48 percent of those incurred by two other consumers (P). Goodyear (D) was ordered to pay prejudgment interest on these various damages and, at some point in the proceedings, counsel for Goodyear (D) and counsel for the consumers (P) entered discussions as to the proper accrual dates for prejudgment interest on "other costs and losses." Goodyear's (D) lead attorney, Thomasch, discussed with the consumers' (P) lead attorney, Maywhort, a potential compromise on the applicable accrual dates. Thomasch proposed certain accrual dates and advised Maywhort of the amount of prejudgment interest that would result from using these proposed dates. Thomasch's calculation of these amounts took into account the jury's 36 percent and 48 percent allocations of fault, and Thomasch expressly conveyed that fact to Maywhort. Following up on the discussion between Thomasch and Maywhort, co-counsel for the consumers (P), Gray, called Brooks, co-counsel for Goodyear (D). Although the parties came to agreement on the applicable accrual dates with little difficulty, they had trouble getting their calculations of prejudgment interest based on these dates to match. Brooks advised Gray that his calculations showed a total amount owed by Goodyear (D) of approximately $2.7 million. At some point within the following few days, Gray responded that this amount appeared to be larger than his own estimates by "about six figures," but did not elaborate. Brooks then called Gray to speculate about the discrepancy, but without Gray's calculations, Brooks could not be sure whether he had, in fact, resolved the discrepancy. A few days later, believing that he may have discovered the source of the discrepancy, Brooks sent Gray an e-mail, stating, "Here are our charts providing the numers [sic] that Goodyear believes are appropriate.... Please review these, then let's discuss." Attached to this e-mail were charts that reflected Goodyear's (D) then existing calculations as to the total amounts due to each consumer (P). When Maywhort reviewed the charts, he realized that Goodyear's (D) calculations had failed to reduce the damages for "other costs and losses" according to the jury's finding that Goodyear (D) was liable for only 36 percent of the some of the consumers' (P) and 48 percent of the other consumers' (P) "other costs and losses." This was in contrast to other categories of damages set forth in Goodyear's (D) charts, in which Goodyear (D) had correctly applied the jury's fault allocations. This error resulted in an overstatement of the damages due by more than $550,000. Maywhort, however, did not call this error to Brooks's attention, or to the attention of any other Goodyear (D) counsel. Instead, he and Gray took the position that Goodyear (D) had intended this result, notwithstanding that the parties were not negotiating the amounts due but rather were attempting to determine why there was a discrepancy in their mathematical calculations. Ultimately, no consumer representative called Brooks to discuss his charts, as Brooks had requested. Rather, Maywhort, who had not been directly involved in the more recent discussions regarding the calculations, left a voicemail message for Thomasch, who also had not been directly involved, stating that the consumers (P) accepted Goodyear's (D)

Continued on next page.

"offer." Maywhort then followed his voicemail with a fax confirming the acceptance of that purported "offer." Notably, neither Maywhort nor Gray informed Brooks of this "acceptance," nor was Brooks copied on Maywhort's fax to Thomasch. Thereafter, Brooks prepared a form of satisfaction of judgment that he sent to Gray, with a notation that the document was a draft for discussion purposes only. That same day, before anyone had signed the satisfaction of judgment, Brooks realized the error in his earlier calculations. He immediately called the error to Gray's attention and sent Gray corrected versions of the charts and a revised satisfaction of judgment with corrected numbers. Instead of acknowledging the error and signing the satisfaction, counsel for the consumers (P) insisted that Goodyear (D) adhere to the parties' alleged agreement, which would have resulted in the consumers (P) receiving over $550,000 more than what was due them. When Goodyear (D) refused to do so, the consumer (P) filed a motion to enforce the purported "settlement agreement," which the trial court granted. Goodyear (D) paid the amounts that the parties agreed were due and owing, and appealed, contending that it had not made an offer that could have been accepted, and that even if it had, the resulting agreement was not enforceable. The state's intermediate court of appeals granted review.

ISSUE:

(1) Is an offer made where communications do not invite acceptance and on their face are "too good to be true"?

(2) Where a party to a contract has made a unilateral mistake, will that party be able to avoid the contract where the other party knew of or had reason to know of the mistake, and even if the other party did not know of or have reason to know of the mistake, enforcement of the contract would be oppressive to the mistaken party and relief from the contract would impose no substantial hardship on the other party?

HOLDING AND DECISION: (Gabriel, J.)

(1) No. An offer is not made where communications do not invite acceptance and on their face are "too good to be true." Goodyear Tire & Rubber Co.'s (Goodyear's) (D) e-mail and attached erroneous charts, sent by Brooks, did not constitute an offer that was properly capable of acceptance. The parties were not negotiating dollar amounts but were merely attempting to resolve a discrepancy in their mathematical computations. Thus, Brooks's e-mail used qualifying and indefinite language, noting that the calculations were what "Goodyear believes are appropriate." This indefinite language alone is an indication of a lack of a definite offer. In addition, Brooks's e-mail did not solicit an acceptance but rather solicited a return call—it ended with: "Please review these, then let's discuss." Thus, the email could not justify the consumers' (P) counsel in understanding that their assent was invited and would conclude a bargain. Based on these factors alone, there was no offer. In this case, this conclusion is bolstered by the rule that "an offeree may not snap up an offer that is on its face manifestly too good to be true." If a purported offer is "too good to be true," the offeree should know that an offer was not intended. The facts here present just such a case. Liability had been adjudged and apportioned, the parties agreed on the accrual dates, and all that was left to be done was a simple mathematical calculation. When the consumers' (P) counsel received Brooks's charts, they immediately recognized that the calculations assumed that Goodyear (D) was 100 percent liable for the "other costs and losses," rather than the 36 percent and 48 percent allocation of fault that the jury had found, resulting in an error in their clients' favor of over $550,000. Therefore, Brooks's e-mail and erroneous charts raised a presumption of error because they were inconsistent with (1) the jury's award; (2) Thomasch's prior discussion with Maywhort, in which Thomasch specifically pointed out that the calculations that he had provided were based on the percentages of fault that the jury had allocated to Goodyear (D); and (3) other calculations in the same charts, in which Goodyear (D) consistently used the jury's allocations of fault. At a minimum, these obvious inconsistencies gave rise to a duty on the part of the consumers' (P) counsel to inquire before attempting to accept the purported "offer." Without such an inquiry, there was no offer capable of acceptance. Reversed as to this issue.

(2) Yes. Where a party to a contract has made a unilateral mistake, that party will be able to avoid the contract where the other party knew of or had reason to know of the mistake, and even if the other party did not know of or have reason to know of the mistake, enforcement of the contract would be oppressive to the mistaken party and relief from the contract would impose no substantial hardship on the other party. Here, even if Brooks's email and charts constituted an offer, Goodyear (D) could avoid any agreement based on that offer. The principles regarding unilateral mistake are well established and almost universally followed. Where the offeror has acted in good faith and where the offeree knew of the mistake before accepting the offer, it would contravene fundamental principles of fairness to allow the offeree to take advantage of offeror's mistake and gain a windfall. The Restatement permits the mistaken party to avoid the contract where that party did not bear the risk of mistake. However, it is unusual for a party to

Continued on next page.

bear the risk of a mistake that the other party had reason to know of. Here, Goodyear's (D) calculations were in error, and it is undisputed that the consumers (P) knew or had reason to know of the error. Enforcement of the purported agreement would be oppressive to Goodyear (D) and unconscionable, because the consumers (P) would be exploiting Goodyear's (D) mistake to gain a windfall of over $550,000 more than the jury awarded to them, and relief from such an agreement would pose no substantial hardship on the consumers (P), since they would receive the amount to which they were entitled. Finally, Goodyear (D) did not bear the risk of mistake here. Goodyear (D) acted in good faith, and the evidence does not show Brooks chose to charge ahead in conscious ignorance, believing that his limited knowledge was sufficient. Instead, his email clearly shows that he was continuing to try to resolve the discrepancy and was seeking further discussion with Gray. Ultimately, this phase of the litigation should have never arisen. As soon as the consumers' (P) counsel recognized Brooks's (D) error, they should have immediately called Brooks, identified the discrepancy, and concluded the matter without further delay—thus sparing both parties the substantial expense of this needless litigation. Reversed as to this issue. Reversed and remanded for the sole purpose of allowing the parties to file a satisfaction of judgment for the amounts already paid by Goodyear (D).

ANALYSIS

Under Restatement (Second) of Contracts § 154, "[a] party bears the risk of a mistake when (a) the risk is allocated to him by agreement of the parties, or (b) he is aware, at the time the contract is made, that he has only limited knowledge with respect to the facts to which the mistake relates but treats his limited knowledge as sufficient, or (c) the risk is allocated to him by the court on the ground that it is reasonable in the circumstances to do so." Here, the consumers (P) argued that Goodyear Tire & Rubber Co. (D) bore the risk of mistake under subsection (b), contending that Brooks chose to charge ahead in conscious ignorance, believing that his limited knowledge was sufficient, but the court rejected this argument as unsupported by the record.

Quicknotes

OFFER A proposed promise to undertake performance of an action, or to refrain from acting, that is to become binding upon acceptance by the offeree.

Mineral Park Land Co. v. Howard

Builder (D) v. Landowner (P)

Cal. Sup. Ct., 172 Cal. 289, 156 P. 458 (1916)

NATURE OF CASE: Appeal from award of damages for breach of contract.

FACT SUMMARY: Mineral Park Land Co. (D) contended it was not bound to remove gravel from Howard's (P) land that would be commercially impracticable to haul away.

RULE OF LAW

A party is excused from performing under a contract where such performance is so much more expensive than contemplated that it would be impracticable to complete.

FACTS: Mineral Park Land Co. (Mineral Park) (D) agreed to obtain its gravel requirements for building a bridge from Howard's (P) land and to pay for it at 5 cents per yard. It hauled away all the gravel above the water level but refused to go below that because to do so would cost 10 to 12 times the usual cost of hauling gravel. Howard (P) sued to require Mineral Park (D) to perform fully. The trial court held that because it was merely commercially disadvantageous to remove the gravel, and not physically impossible, Mineral Park (D) was bound to perform and had breached the contract. Mineral Park (D) appealed, contending it was excused from performing due to impracticability.

ISSUE: May a party be excused from performing under a contract on the basis of impracticability?

HOLDING AND DECISION: (Sloss, J.) Yes. A party may be excused from performing under a contract where such performance has become impracticable because its cost would greatly exceed that contemplated. In this case, although it would have been physically possible to remove gravel below the water level, for practical purposes no further gravel was available due to the severe increased cost. Therefore, Mineral Park Land Co. (D) must be excused from further performance due to the nonexistence of the contractual subject matter for practical purposes. Affirmed as modified.

ANALYSIS

With this case, California led the way toward relaxation of the strict common-law rule that required virtual physical impossibility to excuse performance. Today, modern courts equate extreme impracticability with impossibility, and this was the approach adopted in the First Restatement in § 454. Uniform Commercial Code § 2-615 defines "impracticable" as including impossibility, and the Restatement (Second) adopts a similar approach.

Taylor v. Caldwell

Lessee (P) v. Music hall owner (D)

K.B., 3 B. & S. 826, 122 Eng. Rep. 309 (1863)

NATURE OF CASE: Action for damages for breach of a contract for letting of premises.

FACT SUMMARY: Taylor (P) contracted to let Caldwell's (D) hall and gardens for four fetes and concerts, for four days, for £100 per day. Taylor (P) expended money in preparation and for advertising, but Caldwell (D) could not perform when the hall burned down without his fault.

RULE OF LAW

In contracts in which the performance depends on the continued existence of a given person or thing, a condition is implied that the impossibility of performance arising from the perishing of the person or thing shall excuse the performance.

FACTS: By written agreement, Caldwell (D) agreed to let the Surrey Gardens and Musical Hall at Newington, Surrey, for four days for giving four "Grand Concerts" and "Day and Night Fetes." Taylor (P) was to pay £100 at the end of each day. Before any concerts were held, the hall was completely destroyed by fire without any fault of either of the parties. Taylor (P) alleged that the fire and destruction of the hall was a breach and that it resulted in his losing large sums in preparation and advertising for the concerts and fetes.

ISSUE: In contracts in which the performance depends on the continued existence of a given person or thing, is a condition implied that the impossibility of performance arising from the perishing of the person or thing shall excuse the performance?

HOLDING AND DECISION: (Lord Blackburn, J.) Yes. In contracts in which the performance depends on the continued existence of a given person or thing, a condition is implied that the impossibility of performance arising from the perishing of the person or thing shall excuse the performance. Caldwell (D) was excused from performance. First, the agreement was not a lease but a contract to "let." Second, the entertainments that were planned could not be made without the existence of the hall. Ordinarily, when there is a positive contract to do something that is not unlawful, the contractor must perform or pay damages for not doing it even if an unforeseen accident makes performance unduly burdensome or even impossible. This is so when the contract is absolute and positive and not subject to either express or implied conditions and that if it appears that the parties must have known from the beginning that the contract could not be fulfilled unless a particular, specified thing continued to exist and there is no express or implied warranty that the thing shall exist, the contract is not positive and absolute. It is subject to the implied condition that the parties shall be excused in case, before breach, performance becomes impossible from the perishing of the thing without fault of the contractor. This appears to be within the intention of the parties when they enter into a contract. The excuse from the contract's performance is implied in law because from the nature of the contract it is apparent it was made on the basis of the continued existence of the particular, specified thing. Judgment for the defendants.

ANALYSIS

It was important for Lord Blackburn not to find the agreement to be a lease; otherwise, the decision would come within direct conflict of *Paradine v. Jane*, K.B., 82 Eng. Rep. 897 (1647), which held that a lease must be performed to the letter despite unforeseen hardship or good fortune. Next, performance is excused only if the destruction of the specified thing is without fault. Had Caldwell (D) been shown to be guilty of arson in the destruction of the hall, he would not have been excused. If there is impossibility of performance due to no one's fault, the one seeking to enforce performance takes the risk. It might be said that the court was actually apportioning the loss if the contract was, in effect, a joint venture with Taylor (P) paying Caldwell (D) £100 out of each day's admission fees to the concerts (Caldwell (D) was supplying the band). The view of this case is found in Uniform Commercial Code § 2-613, where for total destruction of the specified thing, the contract is avoided, or if the specified thing is goods that have so deteriorated as to no longer conform, the contract can be avoided or the goods can be accepted with an allowance for their lesser value. Note that there is not a satisfactory distinction between a contract to let and a lease.

Quicknotes

IMPOSSIBILITY A doctrine relieving the parties to a contract from liability for nonperformance of their duties thereunder if the subject matter of the contract ceases to exist, a person essential to the performance of the contract is deceased, or the service or goods contracted for have become illegal.

Transatlantic Financing Corporation v. United States

Wheat exporter (P) v. Federal government (D)

363 F.2d 312 (D.C. Cir. 1966)

NATURE OF CASE: Appeal from dismissal of action for unforeseen costs in execution of a contract for carriage.

FACT SUMMARY: Transatlantic Financing Corporation (Transatlantic) (P), under charter of the United States (D), contracted to ship a full cargo of wheat from Galveston, Texas, to Iran. Shipment was contemplated on Transatlantic's (P) *SS Christos* through the Suez Canal, but war broke out between Egypt and Israel, forcing the closure of the canal. The *SS Christos* had to steam an extra 3,000 miles around the Cape of Good Hope.

RULE OF LAW

When the issue of impossibility is raised, the court must construct a condition of performance based on changed circumstances involving the following: (1) a contingency, something unexpected, must have occurred, (2) the risk of unexpected occurrence must not have been allocated either by agreement or custom, and (3) occurrence of the contingency must have rendered performance commercially impracticable.

FACTS: Transatlantic Financing Corporation (Transatlantic) (P), under charter to the United States (D), contracted to carry a full cargo of wheat on its *SS Christos* from Galveston, Texas, to a safe port in Iran. On July 26, 1956, Egypt nationalized the Suez Canal. During the international crisis resulting from this, the parties contracted on October 2, 1956, for Transatlantic (P) to ship the wheat as described. The charter stated the termini of the voyage but not the route. The *SS Christos* sailed October 27, 1956, on a planned route through the Suez Canal. On October 29, 1956, war between Egypt and Israel broke out. On October 31, 1956, Great Britain and France invaded the Suez Canal Zone. On November 2, 1956, Egypt obstructed the canal with sunken vessels, closing it to traffic. Transatlantic (P) sought an agreement for additional compensation for a voyage around the Cape of Good Hope from a concededly unauthorized department of agriculture employee who advised Transatlantic (P) that it had to perform the charter according to its terms but could always file a claim. The *SS Christos* changed course for the Cape of Good Hope, arriving in Bandar Shapur, Iran, on December 30, 1956. The planned 10,000-mile voyage was increased by 3,000 miles. Transatlantic (P) sought the added expense of $43,972 over the $305,842 contract price. The district court dismissed the libel (an action in admiralty).

ISSUE: Was the contract legally impossible, that is, able to be done only at an excessive and unreasonable cost?

HOLDING AND DECISION: (Wright, J.) No. While it was reasonable to assume that when no route was mentioned in the charter, the usual and customary route (through the Suez Canal) would be taken. But just because this means of performance was impossible, the court must find whether the risk of the contingency (the closure of the canal) was allocated and, if not, whether performance by alternate routes was rendered impracticable. Allocation of risk of the contingency's occurrence may be expressed or implied in the agreement or found in the surrounding circumstances, including custom and usages of the trade. Nothing in the charter specified the Suez route or implied continued availability of that route for performance. Nothing in custom or trade usage, or in the surrounding circumstances, supported such a condition of performance. An implied expectation of the Suez route was hardly adequate proof of an allocation to the promises of the risk of closure. Circumstances instead seemed to place the risk on Transatlantic Financing Corporation (Transatlantic) (P), as the parties knew or should have known of the crisis. Freight rates were most likely affected by the increased risk of voyage in the Suez area. While one might not have foreseen that nationalization of the canal would have brought about a subsequent closure, the circumstances did indicate Transatlantic's (P) willingness to assume abnormal risks. That legitimately causes the court to judge impracticability of performance by alternative route in stricter terms. Impracticability did not appear as the goods could be shipped in the less temperate climate. The ship and crew were fit for the longer voyage, and Transatlantic (P) was no less able than the Government (D) to purchase insurance. In fact, the ship's operator would be more reasonably expected to cover the hazards of war. To justify relief there must be more of a variation between expected cost and the cost of performing by alternative means than was present here as the promisor can be presumed to have accepted greater than normal risk and impracticability is argued on the basis of expense alone. Affirmed.

ANALYSIS

In determining impossibility, the court will look first to see which party assumed the risk of unforeseen

Continued on next page.

circumstances. If that cannot be determined, then it looks to see whether performance was legally impossible. Legally impossible means impracticable, that is, at excessive and unreasonable cost. Knowledge of the crisis would tend to show assumption of the risk. The court, with respect to unreasonable cost, examined Transatlantic Financing Corporation's (Transatlantic's) (P) theory of relief. If the contract was impossible, it was a nullity from the start. Transatlantic (P) asked for quantum meruit, not for the total performance as it should have. The court believed that Transatlantic (P) wanted to avoid losing any of what appeared to be an advantageous contract price. The court would not place a burden on one party to preserve the other's profit. Note that when the court discussed foreseeability of the risk, that foreseeability is as much a fiction as implied conditions, and the parties might honestly have not foreseen the canal closure. Foreseeability is used as a tool in considering where the risk was to be allocated.

Quicknotes

CHANGE OF CONDITIONS A defense to a claim of ameliorative waste, based on the theory that a change in the surrounding area warranted the alterations to the property.

IMPOSSIBILITY A doctrine relieving the parties to a contract from liability for nonperformance of their duties thereunder if the subject matter of the contract ceases to exist, a person essential to the performance of the contract is deceased, or the service or goods contracted for have become illegal.

QUANTUM MERUIT Equitable doctrine allowing recovery for labor and materials provided by one party, even though no contract was entered into, in order to avoid unjust enrichment by the benefited party.

Canadian Industrial Alcohol Co. v. Dunbar Molasses Co.

Molasses purchaser (P) v. Molasses seller (D)

N.Y. Ct. App., 258 N.Y. 194, 179 N.E. 383 (1932)

NATURE OF CASE: Appeal from judgment for plaintiff in action for damages for breach of a contract for the sale of goods.

FACT SUMMARY: Canadian Industrial Alcohol Co. (P) contracted to buy Dunbar Molasses Co.'s (Dunbar) (D) usual allotment of refined blackstrap molasses, about 1,500,000 wine gallons, Dunbar (D) received from a sugar refinery. That year, Dunbar (D) received much less than the amount contracted, less than 500,000 gallons in all, and could not fulfill its contracted quantity.

RULE OF LAW

If the promisor is in some respects responsible for the event that makes performance of its promise impossible and takes no steps to alleviate the impossibility, its duty of performance is not excused.

FACTS: At the end of 1927, Canadian Industrial Alcohol Co. (Alcohol Co.) (P) contracted to buy from Dunbar Molasses Co. (Dunbar) (D) about 1,500,000 wine gallons of refined blackstrap molasses, about 60 percent sugar of the usual run from the National Sugar Refinery, Yonkers, New York. Delivery was to begin April 1, 1928, "to be spread out during the warm weather." The refinery that year produced far less than its capacity, less than a half-million gallons. Dunbar (D), which had no contract with the refinery, shipped its entire allotment, 344,083 gallons, to Alcohol Co. (P). Dunbar (D) did not attempt to enter into a contract that would have assured it would get a sufficient supply of molasses, nor did it inform Alcohol Co. (P) that it did not have such a contract. Alcohol Co. (P) sued for damages, but Dunbar (D) contended that its duty was conditioned by an implied term: the refinery's producing enough molasses to fill Alcohol Co.'s (P) order. Judgment was rendered for Alcohol Co (P), and the state's highest court granted review.

ISSUE: If the promisor is in some respects responsible for the event that makes performance of its promise impossible and takes no steps to alleviate the impossibility, is its duty of performance excused?

HOLDING AND DECISION: (Cardozo, C.J.) No. If the promisor is in some respects responsible for the event that makes performance of its promise impossible and takes no steps to alleviate the impossibility, its duty of performance is not excused. Performance here was not implicitly conditioned by the refinery's producing enough molasses to fill Canadian Industrial Alcohol Co.'s (P) order. The contract as read in the light of circumstances did not keep Dunbar Molasses Co.'s (Dunbar's) (D) duty within such narrow boundaries. Dunbar (D) never even attempted to get a contract with the refinery between the time of acceptance and the start of shipments. Accordingly, contributory fault is implied to Dunbar (D), which put its faith in the mere chance that the refinery's output would remain as in past years. Dunbar's (D) customer did not take that chance; only Dunbar (D) did. Affirmed.

ANALYSIS

There is no one rule for allowing the unforeseen risk, but the basis of all existing rules is the attempt to place the risk where the parties would have if they had foreseen it. If it is reasonably foreseeable, the promisor will have been deemed to have accepted it. Excuse of performance on grounds of impossibility involves, in the interests of justice, the creation of a condition. If the promisor is in some respects responsible for the event making performance impossible, that is, if the promisor is guilty of contributory fault, performance will not be excused. Had the refinery in this case been destroyed without the fault of Dunbar Molasses Co. (D), Dunbar (D) would have been excused from performance. The destruction of the refinery would not have been a risk assumed by the promisor, Dunbar (D). Even had Dunbar (D) made a contract with the refinery, it would still appear that Alcohol Co. (P) would have a cause of action and that Dunbar (D) would still not be excused, as Dunbar (D) would have a cause of action against the refinery. The refinery would then have been liable for Dunbar's (D) loss.

Quicknotes

BREACH OF CONTRACT Unlawful failure by a party to perform its obligations pursuant to contract.

DAMAGES Monetary compensation that may be awarded by the court to a party who has sustained injury or loss to his or her person, property, or rights due to another party's unlawful act, omission, or negligence.

IMPOSSIBILITY A doctrine relieving the parties to a contract from liability for nonperformance of their duties thereunder if the subject matter of the contract ceases to exist, a person essential to the performance of the contract is deceased, or the service or goods contracted for have become illegal.

Eastern Air Lines, Inc. v. Gulf Oil Corporation

Fuel purchaser (P) v. Supplier (D)

415 F. Supp. 429 (S.D. Fla. 1975)

NATURE OF CASE: Action for damages and specific performance for breach of contract.

FACT SUMMARY: Gulf Oil Corporation (D) contracted with Eastern Air Lines, Inc. (Eastern) (P) to supply Eastern's (P) fuel requirements.

RULE OF LAW

A requirements contract entered in good faith is not void for want of mutuality.

FACTS: Eastern Air Lines, Inc. (Eastern) (P) contracted with Gulf Oil Corporation (Gulf) (D) for the latter to supply the former's fuel needs on a long-term basis. Price increases were tied to an index of posted prices for a certain oil grade. In response to the fuel crisis of 1974, the federal government created a two-tier price regulation system, wherein prices were regulated up to a certain per-well output and left unregulated the output beyond the specified amount. Only regulated prices were posted, which had the effect of tying the cost of Eastern's (P) fuel to an amount much less than the going market value. Gulf (D) refused to continue performance, and Eastern (P) sued for damages and specific performance.

ISSUE: Is a requirements contract entered in good faith void for want of mutuality?

HOLDING AND DECISION: (King, J.) No. A requirements contract entered in good faith is not void for want of mutuality. At common law, requirements contracts, while at first thought to be invalid because the buyer had not obligated himself to purchase in a theoretical sense, gradually gained acceptance where the buyer had an ongoing business and could demonstrate a real need for the product in question. Now, the Uniform Commercial Code, in § 2-306, specifically authorizes requirements contracts, provided that the requirements are not grossly disproportionate to stated estimates made in good faith. Here, the amount of fuel is not in issue, and there is no evidence of any bad faith. For this reason, the contract is binding and enforceable. [The court awarded specific performance of the contract.]

ANALYSIS

A supplier can proceed against a buyer in a requirements contract. If, for instance, a buyer shuts down merely to avoid a high-priced requirements contract, the seller would be entitled to some form of relief. However, if the buyer were to shut down for normal business reasons, his requirements would legitimately cease, and the seller would have no cause of action.

Quicknotes

BREACH OF CONTRACT Unlawful failure by a party to perform its obligations pursuant to contract.

MUTUALITY Reciprocal actions of two parties; in a contract context, refers to mutual promises between two parties to perform an action in exchange for performance on the part of the other party.

REQUIREMENTS CONTRACT An agreement pursuant to which one party agrees to purchase all its required goods or services from the other party exclusively for a specified time period.

SPECIFIC PERFORMANCE An equitable remedy whereby the court requires the parties to perform their obligations pursuant to a contract.

Krell v. Henry

Flat owner (P) v. Coronation spectator (D)

K.B. Ct. App., 2 K.B. 740 (1903)

NATURE OF CASE: Action for damages for breach of a contract for a license for use.

FACT SUMMARY: Henry (D) paid a deposit of £25 to Krell (P) for the use of his apartment in Pall Mall, London, for the purpose of a viewing sight for King Edward VII's coronation procession. The King became ill, causing a delay of the coronation upon which Henry (D) refused to pay a £50 balance, for which Krell (P) sued.

RULE OF LAW

Where the object of one of the parties is the basis upon which both parties contract, the duties of performance are constructively conditioned upon the attainment of that object.

FACTS: In two letters of June 20, 1902, Henry (D) contracted through Krell's (P) agent, Bisgood, to use Krell's (P) flat in Pall Mall, London, to view the coronation procession of King Edward VII, which had been advertised to pass along Pall Mall. The contract made no mention of this purpose. The period of use of the flat was the daytime only of June 26 and 27, 1902, for £75, £25 paid in deposit with the £50 remainder due on June 24, 1902. Henry (D) became aware of the availability of Krell's (P) flat as an announcement to that effect had been made that was reiterated by Krell's (P) housekeeper when she showed Henry (D) the rooms. When the King became very ill, the coronation was delayed and Henry (D) refused to pay the £50 balance, for which Krell (P) brought suit.

ISSUE: Where the object of one of the parties is the basis upon which both parties contract, are the duties of performance constructively conditioned upon the attainment of that object?

HOLDING AND DECISION: (Lord Williams, J.) Yes. Where the object of one of the parties is the basis upon which both parties contract, the duties of performance are constructively conditioned upon the attainment of that object. It can be inferred from the surrounding circumstances that the rooms were taken for the purpose of viewing the processions, and that was the foundation of the contract. It was not a lease of the rooms—they could not be used at night—but a license for use for a particular purpose. With the defeat of the purpose of the contract, the performance is excused. Appeal dismissed.

ANALYSIS

This case is an extension of *Taylor v. Caldwell*, 122 Eng. Rep. 309 (K.B. 1863), and as in that case it was necessary to remove the roadblock of a lease in order to avoid a conflict with *Paradine v. Jane*, 82 Eng. Rep. 897 (K.B. 1647). The rule explained here is "frustration of purpose" or "commercial frustration." It has not been made clear whether this doctrine rests upon the failure of consideration or the allocation of the risks. While there is a frustration, performance is not impossible. No constructive condition of performance has failed as Krell (P) made no promise that the condition would occur. Rather, a constructive condition based upon the attainment of the purpose or object has arisen. Note that the frustration should be total or nearly total, though that is a matter of degree.

Quicknotes

CONSTRUCTIVE CONDITION A condition that is not expressly stated in or implied by the terms of an agreement but is imposed by law.

FRUSTRATION OF PURPOSE A doctrine relieving the parties to a contract from liability for nonperformance of their duties thereunder when the purpose of the agreement ceases to exist due to circumstances not subject to either party's control.

Swift Canadian Co. v. Banet

Pelt seller (P) v. Buyer (D)

224 F.2d 36 (3d Cir. 1955)

NATURE OF CASE: Appeal from summary judgment for the defense in action for damages for breach of a contract for the sale of goods.

FACT SUMMARY: After Banet (D) contracted to purchase lamb pelts from Swift Canadian Co. (P), the U.S. Bureau of Animal Industry, after partial shipment was made, issued stricter regulations for the importation of lamb pelts, and thus Banet (D) refused to accept further deliveries.

RULE OF LAW

Assuming a party is ready to perform, he is not obligated to perform in vain where the other party has given notice of refusal to accept performance.

FACTS: Banet (D) contracted to purchase lamb pelts from Swift Canadian Co. (Swift) (P), a Canadian corporation located in Toronto, Canada. Part of the order was shipped F.O.B. Toronto to Philadelphia. On March 12, 1952, Swift (P) notified Banet (D) of its readiness to ship the remainder from Toronto to Philadelphia. On or about that day, the U.S. Bureau of Animal Industry issued stricter regulations for importation of lamb pelts into the United States. For this reason, Banet (D) refused to accept further shipments. The parties agreed that the price of the pelts would be U.S. $3.80 each, F.O.B. Toronto, that neither party was to be liable for orders or acts of any government or governmental agency, and that as pelts were sold F.O.B. seller's plant title and risk of loss passed to Banet (D) when the pelts were loaded on cars at Swift's (P) plant. The trial court granted Banet's (D) motion for summary judgment, and Swift (P) appealed.

ISSUE: Assuming a party is ready to perform, is he obligated to perform in vain where the other party has given notice of refusal to accept performance?

HOLDING AND DECISION: (Goodrich, J.) No. Assuming a party is ready to perform, he is not obligated to perform in vain where the other party has given notice of refusal to accept performance. If Swift Canadian Co. (Swift) (P) fulfilled its obligation when it did deliver, it is clear that when it failed to load the pelts because Banet (D) had signified his refusal to accept them, Swift (P) can assert the same rights as if it had loaded them. Generally, when goods are sold F.O.B., free on board, pursuant to contract, the goods pass at the point where they are loaded. Though this is merely a presumption, nothing was shown to counteract that presumption. When Swift (P) made its delivery, it was to send a bill of lading through a Philadelphia bank, Banet's (D) location. The seller's (P) performance was fully complete when the goods were delivered F.O.B. Toronto. The risk of loss and possibility of profit if the market advanced moved to the buyer (D) at that point. Despite the fact the pelts could not be imported into the United States, they could be delivered to most anywhere else in the world. Reversed with instructions.

ANALYSIS

In this case the buyer was allocated the risk. The court looks to the purpose of the contract. Remember that in *Krell v. Henry*, 2 K.B. 740 (1903), the contract had one purpose: to view the coronation procession. Here, the purpose was to buy pelts and resell them for a profit in Philadelphia. The buyer, Banet (D), knew he would need insurance on the pelts during shipment. F.O.B. means that seller's responsibility terminates at the location specified, here Toronto. But if the purpose of F.O.B. is to allocate the risk, the rule of this case would not be in line with that as the court looks mainly to readiness and willingness to perform. If the court placed a responsibility on each party to be aware of its respective government's possible new regulations and to be held to them, then there is a stronger basis for the rule of the case.

Quicknotes

BILL OF LADING A receipt or other documentation given to a shipper by a carrier evidencing the contract to transport such goods and that the shipper possessed title to the goods shipped.

F.O.B. Stands for "free on board"; agreement between a seller and buyer pursuant to which the seller agrees to deliver the subject matter of the contract to a particular destination at his or her own expense and until which time he or she assumes all liability therefor.

SUMMARY JUDGMENT Judgment rendered by a court in response to a motion by one of the parties, claiming that the lack of a question of material fact in respect to an issue warrants disposition of the issue without consideration by the jury.

Chase Precast Corp. v. John J. Paonessa Co.

Barrier supplier (P) v. Contractor (D)

Mass. Sup. Jud. Ct., 409 Mass. 371, 566 N.E.2d 603 (1991)

NATURE OF CASE: Appeal from denial of damages for breach of contract.

FACT SUMMARY: When a highway reconstruction project was halted due to citizen protests, John J. Paonessa Co. (D), the contractor, canceled the contract with its supplier, Chase Precast Corp. (Chase) (P), after Chase (P) had already produced one-half of the concrete median barriers required by the project.

RULE OF LAW

A defendant may rely on frustration of purpose as a defense to a breach of contract claim if the risk of the occurrence of the frustrating event is not allocated by the contract to the defendant.

FACTS: In 1982, Massachusetts entered into two contracts with John J. Paonessa Co. (Paonessa) (D) to replace a highway grass median strip with precast concrete barriers. Paonessa (D) subsequently contracted with Chase Precast Corp. (Chase) (P) to supply the concrete median barriers. After Chase (P) had produced about one-half of the barriers, angry residents brought a halt to the project. On June 7, 1983, Paonessa (D) notified Chase (P) by letter to stop producing the barriers, which Chase (P) did as soon as it received the letter on June 8. Paonessa (D) paid Chase (P) for all the barriers it had produced at the contract price. Chase (P) then brought an action against Paonessa (D) to recover its anticipated profit on the barriers called for in the contract but not produced. The trial court ruled in favor of Paonessa (D) based on impossibility of performance. The appeals court affirmed but noted that the doctrine of frustration of purpose was a more accurate description of the basis of the trial judge's decision than the doctrine of impossibility. Chase (P) appealed.

ISSUE: May a defendant rely on frustration of purpose as a defense to a breach of contract claim if the risk of the occurrence of the frustrating event is not allocated by the contract to the defendant?

HOLDING AND DECISION: (Lynch, J.) Yes. A defendant may rely on frustration of purpose as a defense to a breach of contract claim if the risk of the occurrence of the frustrating event is not allocated by the contract to the defendant. Frustration of purpose is defined by the Restatement (Second) of Contracts § 265 (1981) as follows: "Where, after a contract is made, a party's principal purpose is substantially frustrated without his fault by the occurrence of an event the non-occurrence of which was a basic assumption on which the contract was made, his remaining duties to render performance are discharged, unless the language or the circumstances indicate the contrary." Since John J. Paonessa Co. (Paonessa) (D) was in no way responsible for the state's elimination of the median barriers from the project, whether it can rely on the defense of frustration turns on whether elimination of the barriers was a reasonably foreseeable risk allocated by the contracts to Paonessa (D). Because Chase Precast Corp. (Chase) (P) had supplied barriers to the state before, it was aware of the state's power to eliminate items from its contracts, paying only the contract unit price for items actually accepted. Chase (P) was also aware that lost profits were not an element of damage, giving further credence to the state's power to decrease quantities. But even if the parties were aware generally of the state's power to eliminate contract items, they did not contemplate the cancellation of a major portion of the project of such a widely used item as concrete median barriers and did not allocate the risk of such cancellation. Affirmed.

ANALYSIS

Note the difference between impossibility and frustration as defenses to a breach of contract. The supplier of goods or services who finds himself unable to perform will use the impossibility defense. The buyer of the goods and services will typically use the defense of frustration. This is because it is always possible for the buyer to fulfill his promise to pay, even if he is no longer in need of the service or product and will essentially gain nothing for his money. To further add to the confusion, the Restatement (Second) of Contracts employs the same four criteria for both frustration and impossibility.

Quicknotes

DOCTRINE OF IMPOSSIBILITY A doctrine relieving the parties to a contract from liability for nonperformance of their duties thereunder if the subject matter of the contract ceases to exist, a person essential to the performance of the contract is deceased, or the service or goods contracted for have become illegal.

FRUSTRATION OF PURPOSE A doctrine relieving the parties to a contract from liability for nonperformance of their duties thereunder when the purpose of the agreement ceases to exist due to circumstances not subject to either party's control.

Northern Indiana Public Service Co. v. Carbon County Coal Co.

Public power utility (P) v. Coal supplier (D)

799 F.2d 265 (7th Cir. 1986)

NATURE OF CASE: Appeal from award of damages for breach of contract.

FACT SUMMARY: Northern Indiana Public Service Co. (P) contended that it was excused from performance of its contract to purchase coal from Carbon County Coal Co. (D) because governmental restrictions rendered performance impossible or impracticable.

RULE OF LAW

A party cannot avoid performance of a contract on the basis of impracticability or impossibility where the contract specifically shifts the risk of such to that party.

FACTS: Northern Indiana Public Service Co. (NIPSCO) (P), a public power utility, contracted with Carbon County Coal Co. (Carbon County) (D) to purchase a set amount of coal over a period of time. The contract was not a requirements contract; it obligated NIPSCO (P) to purchase a set amount of coal over a 20-year period. Subsequently, the Public Service Commission ordered NIPSCO (P) to use good-faith efforts to purchase power from other utilities if such alternatives were more economical than producing it. If such was available, NIPSCO (P) could not pass on the increased costs of creating power to customers. NIPSCO (P) could in fact purchase power more economically and decided to refuse performance on the coal contracts. It sued for a declaration that the governmental restrictions rendered its performance impossible or impracticable. Carbon County (D) counterclaimed for breach and specific performance. A damage award for Carbon County (D) was appealed by NIPSCO (P), and a denial of specific performance was appealed by Carbon County (D).

ISSUE: Can a party avoid performance of a contract on the basis of impossibility or impracticability where the risk of such is allocated to it in the contract?

HOLDING AND DECISION: (Posner, J.) No. A party cannot avoid performance of a contract on the basis of impossibility or impracticability where the risk of such is allocated to it in the contract. The risk of impracticability was placed on Northern Indiana Public Service Co. (P) by the governmental orders. Also, the contract being a fixed price contract is an explicit assignment of the risk of market price decreases to the buyer. Thus, performance could not be avoided. Specific performance was unavailable because continued production would be uneconomical. Affirmed.

ANALYSIS

The court rejected Northern Indiana Public Service Co.'s (P) argument that a force majeure clause excused performance. That clause excused performance where a governmental act prevents utilization of the coal. The act in this case rendered use uneconomical but not illegal; thus, the court affirmed the trial court's refusal to instruct the jury on this issue.

Quicknotes

FORCE MAJEURE CLAUSE A provision in a contract that excuses both parties from their contractual obligations if performance becomes impossible or impractical as a result of extraordinary, catastrophic, unforeseen events.

PRELIMINARY INJUNCTION A judicial mandate issued to require or restrain a party from certain conduct; used to preserve a trial's subject matter or to prevent threatened injury.

UCC § 2-615 Provides that a delay in delivery or nondelivery by a seller is not a breach of seller's duty under a contract for sale if performance as agreed has been made impracticable by the occurrence of a contingency, the nonoccurrence of which was a basic assumption on which the contract was made.

Young v. City of Chicopee

Contractor (P) v. Municipality (D)

Mass. Sup. Jud. Ct., 186 Mass. 518, 72 N.E. 63 (1904)

NATURE OF CASE: Action for damages for breach of a repair contract.

FACT SUMMARY: Young (P) contracted with the City of Chicopee (D) to repair a bridge. After part of the work was done, the bridge was destroyed by fire without fault of either party. Young (P) sued for the value of the work done and for his lumber destroyed in the fire.

RULE OF LAW

There is an implied condition that a thing upon which work is to be done shall continue to exist, and if it is destroyed without fault, the owner is liable for the value of the work done.

FACTS: Young (P) contracted to repair a bridge belonging to City of Chicopee (Chicopee) (D). Young's (P) compensation was to be measured by the number of feet of new lumber wrought into the bridge. So that public travel would not be unnecessarily inconvenienced, the contract provided that at least one-half the materials were to be on the job before work could begin. Lumber, not yet being used, was spread about the bridge and upon the riverbank. The bridge was destroyed by fire without fault of the parties. Part of the yet unused lumber was destroyed. Chicopee (D) did not dispute its liability for the work done but refused liability for the destroyed unused lumber.

ISSUE: Is there an implied condition that a thing upon which work is to be done shall continue to exist, and if it is destroyed without fault, is the owner liable for the value of the work done?

HOLDING AND DECISION: (Hammond, J.) Yes. There is an implied condition that a thing upon which work is to be done shall continue to exist, and if it is destroyed without fault, the owner is liable for the value of the work done. While it was required to be on the job, title to the lumber remained in Young (P). City of Chicopee (Chicopee) (D) had no care or control over it. The purpose of the requirement for the lumber to be on the job was to ensure rapid progress of the work and not to affect the parties' rights to the lumber. The contract was entire as the total compensation was to be fixed by the amount of lumber wrought into the bridge. Chicopee's (D) liability is measured by the amount of the contract work done that, at the time of the destruction of the bridge, had become so identified with the bridge that it would have inured to Chicopee (D) as contemplated by the contract. However, Chicopee (D) will not be liable for the loss of the lumber owned by Young (P) at the time of the fire that had not yet been incorporated into the bridge. Reversed. Judgment for the plaintiff.

ANALYSIS

Note that repair contracts are treated differently than construction contracts. Under a construction contract, the contractor would not be compensated upon loss for destruction. Under a repair contract, the contractor is excused from further performance and is compensated for that which he or she has done. The continued existence of the structure being repaired is deemed to be a basic assumption of the parties. This same rule has been applied to subcontractors working under a general contractor when a building under construction is destroyed. Therefore, the lumber here that was destroyed had not yet been placed into the repair work. While there may have been a minor benefit to City of Chicopee (D) in that travelers were not inconvenienced, it was not enough to transfer title.

Quicknotes

IMPLIED CONDITION A condition that is not expressly stated in the terms of an agreement but that is inferred from the parties' conduct or the type of dealings involved.

In re Hitz Restaurant Group

[Parties not identified.]

Bankr. Ct., 616 B.R. 374 (Bankr. N.D. Ill. 2020)

NATURE OF CASE: Chapter 11 bankruptcy proceedings for post-petition payment of rent by debtor-in-possession.

FACT SUMMARY: After Hitz Restaurant Group (Hitz) filed for Chapter 11 bankruptcy protection as a debtor-in-possession, Kass Management Services (Kass), which had leased commercial premises to Hitz for a restaurant, sought post-petition rent payments from Hitz. Hitz contended that its obligation to pay any post-petition rent was excused by the lease's force majeure clause on the basis of an executive order issued by the state's governor addressing the Covid-19 pandemic.

RULE OF LAW

A force majeure clause excuses contractual performance only in proportion to the degree to which a triggering event prevents such performance.

FACTS: Hitz Restaurant Group (Hitz) leased commercial premises for use as a restaurant from Kass Management Services (Kass). Hitz failed to pay rent due on February 1, 2020, and then filed for Chapter 11 bankruptcy protection. Hitz then failed to make its March 1, 2020, rent payment, or any payments after that. Kass moved for an order for Hitz to make these payments. Hitz argued that its obligation to pay any post-petition rent was excused by the lease's force majeure clause, which provided in pertinent part: "Landlord and Tenant shall each be excused from performing its obligations or undertakings provided in this Lease, in the event, but only so long as the performance of any of its obligations are prevented or delayed, retarded or hindered by . . . laws, governmental action or inaction, orders of government. . . . Lack of money shall not be grounds for Force Majeure." Hitz argued that this provision was triggered on March 16, 2020, the effective date of an executive order issued by the state's governor addressing the Covid-19 pandemic. The executive order banned on-premises food or beverage consumption for certain businesses, including restaurants. However, the order permitted, and expressly encouraged, such businesses to sell food and beverages for delivery, curbside pickup, or carry-out. The order was extended several times and finally was set to expire on May 29, 2020. Hitz acknowledged that 25 percent of its restaurant's square footage, which encompassed its kitchen, could have been used for such purposes.

ISSUE: Does a force majeure clause excuse contractual performance only in proportion to the degree to which a triggering event prevents such performance?

HOLDING AND DECISION: (Cassling, J.) Yes. A force majeure clause excuses contractual performance only in proportion to the degree to which a triggering event prevents such performance. Because the March lease payment became fully due and payable on March 1, 2020, and the governor's executive order did not become effective until two weeks thereafter, the lease's force majeure clause does not excuse payment of the past-due March rent. However, the force majeure clause unambiguously applies, at least in part, to the rental payments that became due thereafter, because the executive order was both a government order and government action that, to some degree, prevented Hitz Restaurant Group (Hitz) from generating revenue. Because the executive order did not prohibit Hitz from performing carry-out, curbside pick-up, and delivery services, but, to the contrary, encouraged Hitz and other restaurants to perform those services, to the extent that Hitz could have continued to perform those services, its obligation to pay rent is not excused by the force majeure clause. Accordingly, Hitz's obligation to pay rent is reduced in proportion to its reduced ability to generate revenue as a result of the executive order. Because Hitz conceded that it could have used its kitchen, which occupied 25 percent of the restaurant premises, for purposes permitted under the executive order, Hitz owes at least 25 percent of the rental payments due for April, May, and June 2020. Monthly rental payments due thereafter are likely to increase as the government's shut-down restrictions are gradually lifted. In sum, Hitz still owes at least 25 percent of the rent amount to Management Services (Kass) even after application of the force majeure clause. If Hitz fails to pay these amounts, Kass will have "cause" under the Bankruptcy Code to lift the automatic stay because of Hitz's failure to adequately protect Kass's interest in the leasehold.

ANALYSIS

Force majeure clauses in contracts supersede the common-law doctrine of impossibility, and, as this case illustrates, determining whether a force majeure clause is triggered is a matter of contractual interpretation under state law. In *Hitz*, the court applied Illinois law, under which a force majeure clause will excuse only contractual performance if the triggering event cited by the nonperforming party was in fact the proximate cause of that party's nonperformance. The court in *Hitz*

Continued on next page.

concluded that the force majeure clause in the parties' lease was unambiguously triggered by the governor's executive order. First, the court found that the order unquestionably constituted both "governmental action" and issuance of an "order" as contemplated by the language of the force majeure clause. Second, the court determined that the order and its extensions unquestionably "hindered" Hitz's ability to perform by prohibiting Hitz from offering on-premises consumption of food and beverages. Finally, the court ruled that the order was unquestionably the proximate cause of Hitz's inability to pay rent, at least in part, because it prevented Hitz from operating normally and restricted its business to take-out, curbside pick-up, and delivery. Kass argued that because the executive order had not shut down the banking system and postal service, Hitz was able to write and send rental checks to Kass. The court rejected this argument as specious and lacking any basis in the language of the force majeure clause. The court also rejected Kass's argument that Hitz's failure to perform arose merely from a "lack of money," since Hitz did not assert that lack of money was the proximate cause of its failure to pay rent, but instead argued that the executive order shutting down all "on-premises" consumption of food and beverages in restaurants was the proximate cause of its inability to generate revenue and pay rent. Finally, the court rejected Kass's argument that Hitz could have obtained money to pay rent by applying for a Small Business Administration loan, as nothing in the language of the clause, the lease, or case law required Hitz to seek or obtain such a loan.

Quicknotes

CHAPTER 11 BANKRUPTCY A legal proceeding whereby a debtor, who is unable to pay his or her debts as they become due, is relieved of the obligation to pay his or her creditors through reorganization and payment from future income.

DEBTOR-IN-POSSESSION In a Chapter 11 proceeding, a debtor who retains control of assets or property pursuant to a plan of reorganization.

FORCE MAJEURE CLAUSE A provision in a contract that excuses both parties from their contractual obligations if performance becomes impossible or impractical as a result of extraordinary, catastrophic, unforeseen events.

PERFORMANCE The fulfillment of a contractual duty.

CHAPTER 10

Third Parties: Rights and Responsibilities

Quick Reference Rules of Law

		PAGE
1.	*Lawrence v. Fox.* A third party for whose benefit a contract is made may bring an action for its breach.	286
2.	*Seaver v. Ransom.* A niece for whose benefit a promise was made to her aunt may successfully bring an action for breach of that promise.	287
3.	*Murray v. ILG Technologies, LLC.* A third party cannot assert a breach of contract claim where the contract itself does not clearly and unambiguously identify the third party as an intended beneficiary under the contract.	288
4.	*Grigerik v. Sharpe.* The intent of both parties to a contract determines whether a third party has contract rights as a third-party beneficiary.	290
5.	*Sisney v. State.* One who benefits only incidentally from a public contract and who is not expressly intended to be benefited by the contract does not have standing to bring suit to challenge a breach of the contract that allegedly affects him directly.	291
6.	*Sisney v. Reisch.* Where a contract is made expressly for the benefit of a class of individuals, a member of that class has standing to enforce the agreement.	293
7.	*Macedonia Church v. Lancaster Hotel Limited Partnership.* Where the circumstances and context of the making of a proposed contract show that one of the parties would have assumed direct obligations to individual third parties, those third parties are intended beneficiaries of the proposed contract.	294
8.	*Sally Beauty Co. v. Nexxus Products Co.* The duty of performance under an exclusive distributorship may not be delegated to a competitor in the marketplace or to the wholly owned subsidiary of a competitor without the obligee's consent.	297
9.	*Kingston v. Markward & Karafilis, Inc.* Where the assignment of an indemnification agreement significantly increases the risk to the indemnitor, the assignment is void.	299
10.	*Bel-Ray Company v. Chemrite (Pty) Ltd.* Contractual provisions limiting or prohibiting assignments operate only to limit the parties' right to assign the contract, but not their power to do so, unless the parties manifest an intention to the contrary with specificity.	301
11.	*Delacy Investments, Inc. v. Thurman & Re/Max Real Estate Guide, Inc.* Under Uniform Commercial Code (UCC) § 9-404, a secured assignee is not entitled to payment of an account receivable where the assignor is not entitled to the account, but an account debtor is entitled to it, even where the account debtor has notice of a previously executed assignment agreement between the assignor and assignee.	302

Lawrence v. Fox

Third-party beneficiary (P) v. Promisor in breach (D)

N.Y. Ct. App., 20 N.Y. 268 (1859)

NATURE OF CASE: Appeal from judgment for third party in action to recover damages for breach of contract.

FACT SUMMARY: Fox (D) promised Holly for consideration that he would pay Holly's debt to Lawrence (P).

RULE OF LAW

A third party for whose benefit a contract is made may bring an action for its breach.

FACTS: Holly owed Lawrence (P) $300. Holly loaned $300 to Fox (D) in consideration of Fox's (D) promise to pay the same amount to Lawrence (P), thereby erasing Holly's debts to Lawrence (P). Fox (D) did not pay Lawrence (P), and Lawrence (P) brought this action for breach of Fox's (D) promise to Holly. The jury returned a verdict for Lawrence (P) in the amount of the loan plus interest, and Fox (D) appealed.

ISSUE: Is a third party precluded for want of privity of contract from maintaining an action on a contract made for his benefit?

HOLDING AND DECISION: (Gray, J.) No. In the case of a promise made to one for the benefit of another, he for whose benefit it is made may bring an action for its breach. This principle, which has been long applied in trust cases, is in fact a general principle of law. Affirmed.

CONCURRENCE: (Johnson, C.J.) The promise was made to Lawrence (P) through his agent. Lawrence (P) could have ratified the action when it came to his knowledge, although he had not been privy to the action.

DISSENT: (Comstock, J.) In general, there must be privity of contract. Here Lawrence (P) had nothing to do with the promise on which he brought the action. It was not made to him, nor did the consideration proceed from him. If Lawrence (P) can maintain the suit, it is because an anomaly has found its way into the law on this subject.

ANALYSIS

This is the leading case that started the general doctrine of "third-party beneficiaries." In the parlance of the original Restatement of Contracts, Lawrence (P) was a "creditor" beneficiary. Restatement (Second) of Contracts § 133 has eliminated the creditor/donee distinction that the original Restatement fostered and has lumped both under the label of "intended" beneficiary. Although the court in the present case went to some effort to discuss trusts and agency, ultimately the court allowed Lawrence (P) to recover because it was manifestly "just" that he should recover. Such has been the creation of many new legal doctrines. The dissenting justices were primarily worried about freedom of contract and the continuing ability of promisor and promisee to rescind or modify their contract. As the doctrine has developed, various rules have arisen to handle these situations.

Quicknotes

NONSUIT Judgment against a party who fails to make out a case.

PRIVITY Commonality of rights or interests between parties.

THIRD-PARTY BENEFICIARY A party who benefits from a promise made pursuant to a contract although the party is not a party to the agreement.

Seaver v. Ransom

Decedent's niece (P) v. Estate executor (D)

N.Y. Ct. App., 224 N.Y. 233, 120 N.E. 639 (1918)

NATURE OF CASE: Action by a third party to recover damages for breach of a contract.

FACT SUMMARY: Berman made a promise to his wife for the benefit of their niece, Seaver (P), who sued Berman's executor (D) for breach of that promise.

RULE OF LAW

A niece for whose benefit a promise was made to her aunt may successfully bring an action for breach of that promise.

FACTS: Mrs. Berman, on her deathbed, wished to leave some property to her niece, Seaver (P). Her husband induced his dying wife to sign a will leaving all property to him by promising that he would leave a certain amount in his own will to Seaver (P). Mr. Berman died without making such a provision for Seaver (P). Seaver (P) successfully brought suit against Ransom (D), as executor of Berman's estate, for Berman's breach of his promise to his dying wife, and Ransom (D) appealed.

ISSUE: Does a niece for whose benefit a promise was made to her aunt have an action for breach of that promise?

HOLDING AND DECISION: (Pound, J.) Yes. Although a general rule requires privity between a plaintiff and a defendant as necessary to the maintenance of an action on the contract, one of several exceptions to the rule is the case where a contract is made for the benefit of another member of the family. Here, Mrs. Berman was childless, and Seaver (P) was a beloved niece. However, the constraining power of conscience is not regulated by the degree of relationship alone. The dependent or faithful niece may have a stronger claim than the affluent or unworthy son. No sensible theory of moral obligation denies arbitrarily to the former what would be conceded to the latter. The reason for this "family" exception (and other exceptions) to the rule is that it is just and practical to permit the person for whose benefit a contract is made to enforce it against one whose duty it is to pay. The doctrine of *Lawrence v. Fox*, 20 N.Y. 2008 (1859), is progressive, not retrograde. Finally, in this particular case, the "equities" are with Seaver (P). Affirmed.

ANALYSIS

In this case, the court (as does the original Restatement of Contracts) uses the term "donee beneficiary" to describe Seaver (P). The Restatement (Second) of Contracts erases the creditor/donee distinction and labels both types of beneficiaries as "intended." Although the court here is very insistent on the close family relationship, subsequent New York cases have erased that requirement for donee beneficiaries as the doctrine governing third-party beneficiaries has expanded. These subsequent cases represent the now prevailing view in the country.

Quicknotes

DONEE BENEFICIARY A third party, not a party to a contract, but for whose benefit the contract is entered with the intention that the benefits derived therefrom be bestowed upon the person as a gift.

PRIVITY The commonality of rights or interests between parties.

RESIDUARY ESTATE That portion of the estate that remains after all of the estate has been distributed through the satisfaction of all claims.

RESIDUARY LEGATEE The recipient of the residuary estate of a testator.

TESTATOR One who executes a will.

Murray v. ILG Technologies, LLC

Bar exam taker (P) v. Bar admission software company (D)

378 F. Supp. 3d 1227 (S.D. Ga. 2019), *aff'd,* 798 Fed. Appx. 486 (11th Cir. 2020)

NATURE OF CASE: Motion for summary judgment in putative class action asserting several claims, including breach of contract.

FACT SUMMARY: Applicants (P) to the Georgia Bar who received failing bar exam scores as a result of a software glitch on the part of ILG Technologies, LLC (ILG) (D)—even though they actually passed the exam—asserted numerous claims against ILG (D) and its owner, Mr. Misman (D), including breach of contract. ILG (D) and Mr. Misman (D) moved for summary judgment, contending that the bar applicants (P) were neither in privity with ILG (D), nor were they third-party beneficiaries of ILG's (D) contract with the Georgia Office of Bar Admissions.

RULE OF LAW

A third party cannot assert a breach of contract claim where the contract itself does not clearly and unambiguously identify the third party as an intended beneficiary under the contract.

FACTS: ILG Technologies, LLC (ILG) (D), a software company owned by Mr. Misman (D), contracted to provide a turnkey system to the Georgia Office of Bar Admissions (OBA) to aid in the administration of the entire bar admission process. As a consequence of a glitch in ILG's (D) software, 90 applicants (P) who took the July 2015 and February 2016 Georgia bar exams were incorrectly assigned failing scores. In fact, these individuals had passed their respective exams. The applicants (P) were not parties to the contract (Contract) between ILG (D) and OBA, even though the software system was intended to efficiently and effectively communicate relevant data to bar applicants (P). Some of the applicants (P) brought a putative class action in federal district court on behalf of the 90 applicants (P) who incorrectly received failing scores, asserting numerous claims against ILG (D) and Mr. Misman (D), including breach of contract. The applicants (P) asserted that the applicants (P) were intended beneficiaries of the Contract. ILG (D) and Mr. Misman (D) moved for summary judgment, arguing that, because the applicants (P) were not parties to the Contract, they could not recover, and they also alleged that the applicants (P) failed as a matter of law to establish that they were third-party beneficiaries under the Contract, which did not contain language indicating that the applicants (P) were intended beneficiaries.

ISSUE: Can a third party assert a breach of contract claim where the contract itself does not clearly and unambiguously identify the third party as an intended beneficiary under the contract?

HOLDING AND DECISION: (Baker, J.) No. A third party cannot assert a breach of contract claim where the contract itself does not clearly and unambiguously identify the third party as an intended beneficiary under the contract. Generally, only parties to a contract may bring suit to enforce it. Here, it is undisputed that the applicants (P) are not parties to the Contract between ILG Technologies, LLC (ILG) (D), a software company owned by Misman (D), and the Georgia Office of Bar Admissions (OBA) and, thus, are not in contractual privity with ILG (D) and Mr. Misman (D). However, a statutory exception to the privity rule provides that the beneficiary of a contract made between other parties for the beneficiary's benefit may maintain an action against the promisor on the contract. Such a person, known as a third-party beneficiary, has standing to enforce a contract where the promisor agrees to the promisee to render some performance to a third person. To decide whether a contract was intended to benefit a third party, courts must look at the contract itself. Where the parties do not dispute which writing constitutes the operative contract and the terms of the contract are not ambiguous, the determination of third-party beneficiary status is a question of law. Here, there is no question as to the relevant contract, and neither party argues that the Contract's language is ambiguous. Thus, the court will look only to the Contract itself to determine whether the applicants (P) are third-party beneficiaries to the Contract between ILG (D) and Mr. Misman (D) and the OBA. A party's status as a third-party beneficiary depends upon the intention of the contracting parties to benefit the third party, and this intention is determined by a construction of the contract as a whole. Additionally, the parties' intent must be identifiable on the face of the contract, and a third party is entitled to enforce only those specific provisions of a contract of which that party is an intended beneficiary. Here, there is no express language in the Contract that can be construed as intending to benefit the applicants (P). The applicants (P) assert that the Contract's entire purpose was to benefit them. However, the Contract does not validate this assertion. Instead, the Contract unambiguously provides that it was intended to benefit the OBA. Any mention in the Contract of the "applicants" is made in the context of identifying how ILG's (D) software will assist the OBA in communicating with the applicants (P).

Continued on next page.

Therefore, because ILG (D) and Mr. Misman (D) and the OBA did not intend for the applicants (P) to be beneficiaries of the contractual provisions the applicants (P) allege were breached, the applicants (P) cannot sue to enforce those provisions as third-party beneficiaries. Merely because the applicants (P) could have benefited from the proper performance of the Contract and were indelibly harmed as a result of ILG's (D) alleged failure to properly perform its contractual duties does not alter this result. Also unavailing is the applicants' (P) argument that the "whole purpose" of the Contract was for the OBA to deliver accurate test results to applicants (P), as is the argument that the applicants (P) are akin to customers of the OBA, since customers, particularly customers of public entities, are often natural beneficiaries of a contract yet are not considered intended beneficiaries for purposes of contract enforcement. For these reasons, because the applicants (P) were indisputably not in privity of contract with ILG (D) or Misman (D), and because they were not intended beneficiaries of the contractual provisions that they seek to enforce, they cannot recover under a breach of contract theory as third-party beneficiaries. Accordingly, ILG's (D) and Mr. Misman's (D) motion for summary judgment is granted.

ANALYSIS

Where, as here, the terms of a contract are not ambiguous, a court is not permitted to use parol evidence to interpret the terms of the contract. However, even where it is permissible to use parol evidence to resolve contractual ambiguities, such evidence cannot confer third-party beneficiary status where the contract itself fails to do so. Accordingly, the court in this case declined to consider testimony from Mr. Misman's (D) deposition where it appeared he identified bar applicants (P) as beneficiaries to the Contract. However, even if the court could have considered this parol evidence, it would not have altered the result, since Mr. Misman (D) was merely explaining that bar applicants (P) benefitted from ILG Technologies, LLC's (D) software, not that they were intended beneficiaries under the Contract as required to receive third-party beneficiary status. This illustrates the basic principle that merely because someone benefits from a contract, he or she is not by that fact alone a third-party beneficiary under the contract in the absence of the contracting parties' intent that he or she be such beneficiary.

Quicknotes

BREACH OF CONTRACT Unlawful failure by a party to perform its obligations pursuant to contract.

INTENDED BENEFICIARY A third party who is the recipient of the benefit of a transaction undertaken by another.

PAROL EVIDENCE Evidence given verbally; extraneous evidence.

PRIVITY OF CONTRACT A relationship between the parties to a contract that is required in order to bring an action for breach.

PROMISEE The party to whom a promise is made.

PROMISOR The party who promises to render an obligation to another in the future.

SUMMARY JUDGMENT Judgment rendered by a court in response to a motion made by one of the parties, claiming that the lack of a question of material fact in respect to an issue warrants disposition of the issue without consideration by the jury.

THIRD-PARTY BENEFICIARY A party who benefits from a promise made pursuant to a contract although the party is not a party to the agreement.

Grigerik v. Sharpe

Buyer (P) v. Engineer (D)

Conn. Sup. Ct., 247 Conn. 293, 721 A.2d 526 (1998)

NATURE OF CASE: Negligence suit.

FACT SUMMARY: Grigerik (P) contracted to purchase property based on Sharpe's (D) site plans.

RULE OF LAW

The intent of both parties to a contract determines whether a third party has contract rights as a third-party beneficiary.

FACTS: Grigerik (P) contracted to purchase land from Lang, subject to the town's approval of the tract as a building lot. Lang contracted with an engineer, Sharpe (D), to prepare a site plan for drainage. The site plan was prepared, and the sale executed. When Grigerik (P) later applied for a building permit, it was denied. Grigerik (P) brought suit against Sharpe (D) alleging negligence and an entitlement as a third-party beneficiary. Judgment was entered for Grigerik (P), but it was reversed on appeal.

ISSUE: Does the intent of both parties to a contract determine whether a third party has contract rights as a third-party beneficiary?

HOLDING AND DECISION: (Borden, J.) Yes. The intent of both parties to a contract determines whether a third party has contract rights as a third-party beneficiary. The right to performance in a third-party beneficiary is determined both by the intention of the contracting parties and by the intention of one of the parties to benefit the third party. Grigerik (P) cannot prevail on the breach of contract claim since the jury specifically found that he failed to prove he was an intended beneficiary of the contact between Lang and Sharpe (D). Reversed and remanded.

ANALYSIS

Note that although the jury found that Grigerik (P) was a foreseeable beneficiary of the contract, the court states that foreseeability is a tort concept and not sufficient to sustain a claim of rights for a third-party beneficiary in a contract.

Quicknotes

FORESEEABILITY Reasonable expectation that an act or omission would occur.

THIRD-PARTY BENEFICIARY A party who benefits from a promise made pursuant to a contract although the party is not a party to the agreement.

Sisney v. State

Kosher-observant prisoner (P) v. State (D)

S.D. Sup. Ct., 754 N.W.2d 639 (2008)

NATURE OF CASE: Appeal from dismissal of action for breach of contract on grounds that the plaintiff lacked standing to bring the action as a third-party beneficiary.

FACT SUMMARY: Sisney (P), a kosher-observant prisoner, contended that he was a third-party beneficiary of a contract between the State (D) and CBM Inc. (D) pursuant to which CBM (D) provided food services to the State's (D) prisons, and contended that CBM (D) breached the contract by failing to provide him with a sufficiently caloric or kosher diet.

RULE OF LAW

One who benefits only incidentally from a public contract and who is not expressly intended to be benefited by the contract does not have standing to bring suit to challenge a breach of the contract that allegedly affects him directly.

FACTS: CBM, Inc. (D) provided food services to the State's (D) prisons pursuant to a contract. The contract specified the number of daily calories that each prisoner would get and that the meals provided would accommodate prisoners' religious beliefs. Sisney (P), a Jewish prisoner who was kosher-observant, claimed that the kosher diet CBM (D) provided to him did not meet the contract's calorie requirements and also did not meet the dictates of his religious beliefs. After filing the appropriate administrative grievances, Sisney (P) was informed by Weber (D), the state's director of prison operations, that no further action would be taken on his grievance. Sisney (P) then filed suit alleging the State (D), Weber (D), and CBM (D) had conspired to allow a breach of contract to his detriment because of his religious beliefs and that that this breach resulted in financial gain to the defendants. Sisney (P) asserted standing to sue on the grounds that he was a third-party beneficiary of the contract and that the breach of the contract directly affected him and his well-being. The trial court granted the defendants' motion to dismiss for failure to state a claim on the grounds that Sisney's (P) claims were barred by statutory immunity and a lack of standing to assert a breach of a public contract. The state's highest court granted review.

ISSUE: Does one who benefits only incidentally from a public contract and who is not expressly intended to be benefited by the contract have standing to bring suit to challenge a breach of the contract that allegedly affects him directly?

HOLDING AND DECISION: (Zinter, J.) No. One who benefits only incidentally from a public contract and who is not expressly intended to be benefited by the contract does not have standing to bring suit to challenge a breach of the contract that allegedly affects him directly. By statute in this state a contract made expressly for the benefit of a third person may be enforced by him at any time before the parties thereto rescind it. However, not everyone who receives a benefit from the contract is entitled to enforce it. For the third party to have standing to enforce the contract, at the time the contract was executed it must have been the contracting parties' intent to expressly benefit the third party more than just incidentally. This is especially true with government contracts and, absent plain and clear language of the contract to the contrary, a private third-party right of enforcement will not be inferred because of the potential burden that expanded liability would impose. Consequently, when a public contract is involved, private citizens—as well as inmates—are presumed not to be third-party beneficiaries. Because public contracts are intended to benefit everyone, the inmate's benefit is presumed to be only incidental to the contract. Here, there was no language in the contract expressly indicating that it was intended for Sisney's (P) direct benefit or enforcement. To the contrary, the contract was expressly for the State's (D) benefit. Whatever collective benefit inmates may have received was only incidental to that of the State (D). Sisney's (P) argument, that because the contract provided that CBM, Inc. (D) would describe the complaint resolution process in place for addressing complaints, he possessed a right of enforcement, is unpersuasive. That process, however, was a general institutional process provided to all inmates independently of the CBM (D) contract. Therefore, the contract's reference to that policy did not confer contractual third-party beneficiary status on Sisney (P) to enforce the contract. Affirmed.

ANALYSIS

As this case suggests, government contracts pose unique difficulties in the area of third-party beneficiary rights because, to some extent, every member of the public is directly or indirectly intended to benefit from such a contract. Thus, the presumption applied in this case, i.e., that private citizens are presumed not

Continued on next page.

to be third-party beneficiaries, operates, as a general rule, to insulate private parties who contract with the government from liability at the hands of the public. Restatement (Second) of Contracts § 302, which distinguishes between intended and incidental beneficiaries, supports this approach.

Quicknotes

STANDING The right to commence suit against another party because of a personal stake in the resolution of the controversy.

THIRD-PARTY BENEFICIARY A party who benefits from a promise made pursuant to a contract although the party is not a party to the agreement.

Sisney v. Reisch

Kosher-observant prisoner (P) v. State official (D)

S.D. Sup. Ct., 754 N.W.2d 813 (2008)

NATURE OF CASE: Appeal from dismissal of action for breach of a settlement agreement on grounds that the plaintiff lacked standing to bring the action as a third-party beneficiary.

FACT SUMMARY: Sisney (P), a kosher-observant prisoner, contended that he was a third-party beneficiary of a settlement agreement between the state's Department of Corrections (DOC) (D) and a former inmate, Heftel, and that the DOC (D) breached the agreement by failing to provide him with prepackaged, certified kosher meals.

RULE OF LAW

Where a contract is made expressly for the benefit of a class of individuals, a member of that class has standing to enforce the agreement.

FACTS: Heftel, a former inmate who was Jewish and kosher-observant, entered into a settlement agreement with the state's Department of Corrections (DOC), pursuant to which the DOC agreed to provide a kosher diet to all Jewish inmates who requested it, and that the kosher diet would include prepackaged meals that were certified kosher for noon and evening meals. Several years later, the provider of food services to the state's prisons quit serving prepackaged kosher meals and began serving a new kosher diet. Sisney (P), a current inmate who was also Jewish and kosher-observant, alleged that this change violated the Heftel agreement and his religious beliefs. Sisney (P) subsequently submitted a grievance through DOC administrative procedures. When this was denied, he brought suit against state prison officials (D), claiming they had breached the Heftel agreement. The trial court dismissed on several grounds, including the ground that the complaint failed to state a claim because it contained no factual assertions supporting an inference that it was the prison officials' (D) responsibility to carry out the Heftel agreement. However, the trial court did not reach Sisney's (P) argument that he had standing to bring his suit as a third-party beneficiary of the Heftel agreement. The state's highest court granted review.

ISSUE: Where a contract is made expressly for the benefit of a class of individuals, does a member of that class have standing to enforce the agreement?

HOLDING AND DECISION: (Zinter, J.) Yes. Where a contract is made expressly for the benefit of a class of individuals, a member of that class has standing to enforce the agreement. As a threshold matter, the settlement agreement's history and content give rise to the inference that the prison officials (D) had the responsibility to enforce the Heftel agreement. State statute provides that a contract made expressly for the benefit of a third person may be enforced by him at any time before the parties thereto rescind it. Standing to enforce an agreement as a third-party beneficiary may also be conferred upon a class of individuals. As with standing for individuals, the contract must clearly express the intent to benefit the identifiable class. Here, the Heftel agreement clearly expressed that the DOC agreed to provide a kosher diet to an identifiable class of which Sisney (P) was a member, i.e., "to all Jewish inmates who request it." The agreement also expressly reflected an intent to benefit all members of that class. The explicit contractual language reflected the signatories' intent to provide more than an incidental benefit: the contractual language raised the inference that the Heftel agreement was intended to expressly benefit all Jewish inmates who requested a kosher diet. Because Sisney (P) alleged that he was a member of that class, he sufficiently stated a claim that he was a third-party beneficiary with standing to enforce the Heftel agreement. Reversed and remanded.

ANALYSIS

The decision in *Reisch* is distinguishable from the same court's decision in *Sisney v. State*, 754 N.W.2d 639 (S.D. 2008), which rejected Sisney's (P) argument that he had standing to enforce a contract between the state and a contractor that provided food services for the state's prisons, because the contract in *Sisney v. State* was a public contract that did not expressly indicate it was made for the benefit of Sisney (P) or a class of individuals of which Sisney (P) was a member. The key difference was that in *Sisney v. Reisch*, the court found that the contract at issue, the Heftel agreement, had been made with the express intent of benefiting the class of which Sisney (P) was a member.

Quicknotes

STANDING The right to commence suit against another party because of a personal stake in the resolution of the controversy.

THIRD-PARTY BENEFICIARY A party who benefits from a promise made pursuant to a contract although the party is not a party to the agreement.

Macedonia Church v. Lancaster Hotel Limited Partnership

Church (P) v. Hotel owner (D)

560 F. Supp. 2d 175 (D. Conn. 2008)

NATURE OF CASE: Renewed motion to dismiss for lack of subject matter jurisdiction, on the basis of lack of standing, in action under 42 U.S.C. § 1981 asserting unlawful racial discrimination.

FACT SUMMARY: Members (P) of Macedonia Church (P), a predominantly African-American congregation, alleged that they were denied reservations for lodging at Lancaster Host, a hotel owned by Lancaster Hotel Limited Partnership (the owners) (D), on account of their race, in violation of 42 U.S.C. § 1981. The owners (D) contended that the individual members (P) lacked standing because they did not have rights under the proposed contractual relationship between Macedonia Church (P) and the Lancaster Host. The members (P) countered that they had standing because they were third-party beneficiaries under the proposed contract.

RULE OF LAW

Where the circumstances and context of the making of a proposed contract show that one of the parties would have assumed direct obligations to individual third parties, those third parties are intended beneficiaries of the proposed contract.

FACTS: A few members (P) of Macedonia Church (P), a predominantly African-American congregation, visited Lancaster Host, a hotel owned by Lancaster Hotel Limited Partnership (the owners) (D), and met with a Lancaster Host representative for the purpose of arranging a stay at Lancaster Host for around 40 of the congregation's members (P). After a brief tour, the group of members (P) and the representative made preliminary arrangements for reserving approximately 40 rooms for specified dates, and the representative stated that they would send an introductory letter containing information such as room availability, pricing, and arrival and departure dates. The group was also informed that a signed contract would be necessary to confirm any reservation. Based on this meeting, the congregation was informed that they would be staying at Lancaster Host, and a sign-up sheet was created. The congregation was also informed that participants in the trip would pay the church, which would then take care of the payment to Lancaster Host. The representative sent a document to one of the members (P) with whom the representative had met. The owners (D) characterized this document as promotional material, with confirmation of the details discussed but without specification of the number of rooms to be reserved. Macedonia Church (P) characterized the document as a written proposal. In any event, the congregation interpreted the document as having "locked in" reservations at Lancaster Host. Afterward, the church needed to change its plans slightly, and after communicating those changes, there was more back and forth between Macedonia Church (P) and Lancaster Host. Ultimately, Lancaster Host informed Macedonia Church (P) that there had been an error in the booking process, and that Lancaster Host did not have enough available rooms for the dates sought to be reserved by Macedonia Church (P). When Macedonia Church (P) learned that their "reservations" had been "cancelled," they enlisted the help of a Caucasian friend, who was able to make reservations for the same weekend for a similar group, and who received a contract for such reservations right away. After the Caucasian friend cancelled, Lancaster Host left messages for the friend stating that the friend's group would be welcome at Lancaster Host in the future and solicited them to come at any time. Such calls were not made to Macedonia Church (P). Based on these events, individual members (P) of the church brought suit in federal district court, alleging that they were denied the group accommodations by the owners (D) because of their race, in violation of 42 U.S.C. § 1981. Section 1981 provides that "[a]ll persons within the jurisdiction of the United States shall have the same right in every State and Territory to make and enforce contracts ... and to the full and equal benefit of all laws and proceedings for the security of persons and property as is enjoyed by white citizens." The phrase "make and enforce contracts" includes "the making, performance, modification, and termination of contracts, and the enjoyment of all benefits, privileges, terms, and conditions of the contractual relationship." To state a claim under § 1981, a plaintiff must establish that "(1) the plaintiff is a member of a racial minority; (2) [there is] an intent to discriminate on the basis of race by the defendant; and (3) the discrimination concerned one or more of the activities enumerated in the statute. . . ." After having made an initial motion to dismiss for lack of subject matter jurisdiction, the owners (D) renewed their motion to dismiss the complaint pursuant to lack of subject matter jurisdiction on the grounds that the individual members (P) lacked standing. The individual members (P) argued, inter alia, that they were intended third-party beneficiaries under the proposed contract between Macedonia Church (P) and the Lancaster Host. The district court considered the motion.

Continued on next page.

ISSUE: Where the circumstances and context of the making of a proposed contract show that one of the parties would have assumed direct obligations to individual third parties, are those third parties intended beneficiaries of the proposed contract?

HOLDING AND DECISION: (Thompson, J.) Yes. Where the circumstances and context of the making of a proposed contract show that one of the parties would have assumed direct obligations to individual third parties, those third parties are intended beneficiaries of the proposed contract. In *Domino's Pizza, Inc. v. McDonald,* 546 U.S. 470 (2006), the Supreme Court held that "Section 1981 offers relief when racial discrimination blocks the creation of a contractual relationship, as well as when racial discrimination impairs an existing contractual relationship, so long as the plaintiff has or would have rights under the existing or proposed contractual relationship." Merely because the individual members (P) would not have been parties to the contract does not mean that they would not have had any rights under the proposed contract between Macedonia Church (P) and the Lancaster Host. Although the Supreme Court did not decide whether third-party beneficiaries to a contract have sufficient rights under a contract to assert a § 1981 claim, the Court did not preclude that possibility, and several circuit courts have recognized that third-party beneficiaries to contracts have rights under § 1981. Whether individuals are intended third-party beneficiaries to a contract for purposes of a § 1981 claim is determined by state contract law. Here, state law provides that the test for determining whether a person has a right of action as a third-party beneficiary is whether the intent of the parties to the contract was that the promisor should assume a direct obligation to the third-party beneficiary. That intent is to be determined from the terms of the contract read in the light of the circumstances attending its making, including the motives and purposes of the parties. Although it is not necessary that there be express language in the contract creating a direct obligation to the claimed third-party beneficiary, such an obligation is created if the parties to the contract are so intended. Macedonia Church (P) attempted to reserve rooms at the Lancaster Host to provide the individual members (P) with lodging for a church-sponsored weekend retreat. Therefore, the proposed contract was an agreement pursuant to which the Lancaster Host would have assumed a direct obligation to individual members (P), i.e., the obligation to provide them with accommodations during the retreat. For these reasons, the individual members (P) would have been third-party beneficiaries of the proposed contract. Because the individual members (P) would have had specific contractual rights under the proposed contractual relationship between Macedonia Church (P) and the Lancaster Host, they have standing to bring suit as third-party beneficiaries. The owners argue that the individual members (P) cannot be considered third-party beneficiaries of the proposed contract because (1) there was no contract executed between Macedonia Church (P) and the Lancaster Host, and (2) the owners (D) never knew the identities of the individual members (P). Both arguments are unpersuasive. As to the first argument, an executed contract is not required in order for plaintiffs to bring a § 1981 claim. Section 1981 is designed to protect the right to make, as well as to enforce, contracts from impairment by racial discrimination. As the Supreme Court has stated, "[s]uch a contractual relationship need not already exist, because § 1981 protects the would-be contractor along with those who already have made contracts." *McDonald,* 546 U.S. at 476, 126 S. Ct. 1246. If a contract had to be executed before a plaintiff could bring a § 1981 claim, as the defendants contend, the entire purpose of § 1981 would be frustrated. As to the second argument, which effectively is that the individual members (P) were merely foreseeable or incidental beneficiaries, the individual members (P) were intended by the parties to be beneficiaries because the rooms were being reserved so the individual members (P), not some group of individuals to be identified at some point in the future, could occupy them during Macedonia Church's retreat. Thus, under the proposed contract, the Lancaster Host would have been obligated to provide accommodation to the individual members (P) for the weekend of the church's retreat. Here, when Macedonia Church (P) attempted to contract for accommodations with the Lancaster Host, it was apparent from the context that the individual members (P) would be given rooms at the hotel for their personal use during the retreat and thus benefit from the contract. There was no point in there being a contract otherwise. For these reasons, the owners' (D) renewed motion to dismiss the complaint for lack of subject matter jurisdiction is denied.

ANALYSIS

Restatement (Second) Contracts § 302 provides that unless otherwise agreed between the promisor and the promisee, a beneficiary of a promise is an intended beneficiary if recognition of a right to performance in the beneficiary is appropriate to effectuate the intention of the parties and either (a) the performance of the promise will satisfy an obligation of the promisee to pay money to the beneficiary; or (b) the circumstances indicate that the promisee intends to give the beneficiary the benefit of the promised performance. Under the Restatement, an incidental beneficiary is a beneficiary who is not an intended beneficiary. A rationale for not permitting "foreseeable" or "incidental" beneficiaries to claim third-party beneficiary status is to promote certainty in enforcing contracts by ensuring that each

Continued on next page.

contracting party knows the scope of its obligations under the contract. Thus, rooting the range of potential third parties in the intention of both parties, rather than in the intent of just one of the parties, is a way of minimizing the risk that a contracting party will be held liable to one whom that party neither knew, nor legitimately could be held to know, would ultimately be their contract obligee.

Quicknotes

INCIDENTAL BENEFICIARY A person for whom a trust is not specifically created and who has no right to assert an interest in the trust yet derives incidental benefits therefrom.

OBLIGEE Promisee; a party who is the recipient of a promise or obligation to perform.

PROMISEE The party to whom a promise is made.

PROMISOR The party who promises to render an obligation to another in the future.

SUBJECT MATTER JURISDICTION The authority of the court to hear and decide actions involving a particular type of issue or subject.

Sally Beauty Co. v. Nexxus Products Co.

Beauty products distributor (P) v. Product manufacturer (D)

801 F.2d 1001 (7th Cir. 1986)

NATURE OF CASE: Appeal from a grant of defendant's motion for summary judgment in an action for breach of contract.

FACT SUMMARY: After Sally Beauty Co. (P) acquired a company with which Nexxus Products Co. (Nexxus) (D) had an exclusive distribution agreement, Nexxus (D) refused to continue complying with the agreement, since Sally Beauty (P) was a wholly owned subsidiary of a Nexxus (D) competitor in the hair care market.

RULE OF LAW

The duty of performance under an exclusive distributorship may not be delegated to a competitor in the marketplace or to the wholly owned subsidiary of a competitor without the obligee's consent.

FACTS: Sally Beauty Co. (P) acquired Best Barber Beauty & Supply Company (Best), which had an exclusive "best efforts" agreement to distribute and promote Nexxus Products Co. (Nexxus) (D) hair care products in the Texas market, in a merger and acquisition. Because Sally Beauty (P) was a wholly owned subsidiary of Alberto-Culver, one of Nexxus's (D) competitors in the marketplace, Nexxus (D) refused to continue its agreement with Best. Sally Beauty (P) sued Nexxus (D) for breach of contract and violation of antitrust laws. Nexxus (D) moved for summary judgment on the breach of contract claim. The trial court granted the motion, finding that the contract was not simply an ordinary commercial contract, but one based upon a relationship of personal trust and confidence between the parties. Sally Beauty (P) appealed.

ISSUE: May the duty of performance under an exclusive distributorship be delegated to a competitor in the marketplace or to the wholly owned subsidiary of a competitor without the obligee's consent?

HOLDING AND DECISION: (Cudahy, J.) No. The duty of performance under an exclusive distributorship may not be delegated to a competitor in the marketplace or to the wholly owned subsidiary of a competitor without the obligee's consent. Nexxus Products Co. (Nexxus) (D) should not be required to accept the "best efforts" of Sally Beauty Co. (P) when those efforts are subject to the control of Alberto-Culver. It is entirely reasonable that Nexxus (D) conclude that this performance would be other than what it had bargained for. When performance of personal services is delegated, the duty is per se nondelegable. There is no inquiry into whether the delegation is as skilled or worthy of trust and confidence as the original obligor. The delegate was not bargained for, and the obligee need not consent to the substitution. Nexxus (D) has a substantial interest in not seeing this contract performed by Sally Beauty (P); thus, the contract was not assignable without Nexxus's (D) consent. Affirmed.

DISSENT: (Posner, J.) Sally Beauty Co. (P) distributes hair care supplies made by many different companies that appear to compete with Alberto-Culver as vigorously as Nexxus Products Co. (Nexxus) (D) does. At most, so far as the record shows, Nexxus (D) may have had grounds for "insecurity" regarding the performance by Sally Beauty (P) of its obligation to use its best efforts to promote Nexxus (D) products. Since this is the case, its remedy was not to cancel the contract but to demand assurances of due performance. No such demand was made.

ANALYSIS

The majority noted that if the assignee were only a partially owned subsidiary, there presumably would have to be fact-finding about the degree of control the competitor-parent had over the subsidiary's business decisions. While the court of appeals affirmed the decision of the district court, it did so on a different ground. The court found instead that Sally Beauty Co.'s (P) position as a wholly owned subsidiary of a competing company was sufficient to bar the delegation of Best Barber Beauty & Supply Company's duties under its agreement with Nexxus Products Co. (D).

Quicknotes

ASSIGNABLE Capable of being transferred or conveyed.

ASSIGNEE A party to whom another party assigns its interest or rights.

ASSIGNOR A party who assigns its interest or rights to another.

OBLIGEE Promisee; a party who is the recipient of a promise or obligation to perform.

OBLIGOR Promisor; a party who has promised or is obligated to perform.

Continued on next page.

SUBSIDIARY A company, a majority of whose shares are owned by another corporation and that is subject to that corporation's control.

SUMMARY JUDGMENT Judgment rendered by a court in response to a motion by one of the parties, claiming that the lack of a question of material fact in respect to an issue warrants disposition of the issue without consideration by the jury.

UCC § 2-210 A party may perform its duty through a delegate unless otherwise agreed or unless the other party has a substantial interest in having the original promisor perform or control the acts required by the contract.

Kingston v. Markward & Karafilis, Inc.

Administrator of decedent's estate (P) v. Contractor for decedent's employer (D)

Mich. Ct. App., 350 N.W.2d 842 (1984)

NATURE OF CASE: Appeal from jury verdict for plaintiff in action for damages arising from death of building owner's employee allegedly caused by negligence of contractor and/or subcontractor, involving cross-claim for indemnity by contractor against subcontractor.

FACT SUMMARY: Chrysler Corp., which had Kaufmann Construction Co. (Kaufmann) (D) build metal plate covers for one of its oil reservoirs, assigned the contract it had with Kaufmann (D) to another contractor, Markward & Karafilis, Inc. (Markward) (D). The contract contained an indemnification provision that indemnified Chrysler against property damage and personal injury related to Kaufmann's (D) work. After Charles Kingston, a Chrysler employee, died while replacing some of the metal covers, his estate's representative (P) obtained a $3 million judgment against Markward (D). Markward (D) then cross-claimed for indemnity against Kaufmann (D) on the basis of the assigned contract. Kaufmann (D) contended that the assignment of the indemnity clause was void because substituting Markward (D) as a party materially increased the risk that indemnification would be sought.

RULE OF LAW

Where the assignment of an indemnification agreement significantly increases the risk to the indemnitor, the assignment is void.

FACTS: Chrysler Corp., as part of the renovation of one of its plants, hired Kaufmann Construction Co. (Kaufmann) (D) as a contractor, and had Kaufmann (D) construct metal plates for an oil reservoir. The plates were constructed in 1969 and 1970. The contract between Chrysler and Kaufmann (D) included an indemnification provision that indemnified Chrysler against property damage and personal injury related to Kaufmann's (D) work. In March 1969, Chrysler and Markward & Karafilis, Inc. (Markward) (D), another general contractor, entered into an agreement for Markward (D) to construct an addition to the plant. The metal plates constructed by Kaufmann (D) were considered a substructure of the building. In April 1969, Chrysler assigned its contract with Kaufmann (D) to Markward (D). Kaufmann (D) did not object to the assignment. Kaufmann (D) completed its work on the plates in May 1969. In 1976, Charles Kingston, a Chrysler employee, died while replacing some of the plates, which had slipped and caused Kingston to fall into the reservoir. The representative (P) of Kingston's estate brought suit against Markward (D), which the representative (P) identified as the contractor, against Kaufmann (D), which the representative (P) identified as a subcontractor, and against other entities. Third-party complaints for common-law indemnity were filed against Chrysler by Markward (D) and Kaufmann (D). Markward (D) cross-claimed for indemnity against Kaufmann (D) on the basis of the assignment of the contract by Chrysler. Chrysler tendered its defense to the third-party complaint to Kaufmann (D), claiming that it had a right to indemnity under its contract with Kaufmann (D). The trial court instructed the jury that Markward (D) was entitled to indemnification by Kaufmann (D) pursuant to the assigned contract if the jury found that Kaufmann's (D) negligence had caused Kingston's death, or that both Markward's (D) and Kaufmann's (D) negligence had caused Kingston's death. The jury returned a verdict in the amount of $3 million in favor of the representative (P), jointly against Markward (D) and Kaufmann (D). On the cross-claim, the jury awarded total indemnity in favor of Markward (D), and Markward (D) and Kaufmann (D) were found to have no cause of action against Chrysler. Kaufmann (D) appealed, contending that the assignment of the indemnity clause was void because substituting Markward (D) as a party materially increased the risk that indemnification would be sought. The state's intermediate appellate court granted review.

ISSUE: Where the assignment of an indemnification agreement significantly increases the risk to the indemnitor, is the assignment void?

HOLDING AND DECISION: (Shepherd, J.) Yes. Where the assignment of an indemnification agreement significantly increases the risk to the indemnitor, the assignment is void. The Restatement (Second) of Contracts, § 317(2), provides that a contractual right can be assigned unless "(a) the substitution of a right of the assignee for the right of the assignor would materially change the duty of the obligor, or materially increase the burden or risk imposed on him by his contract, or materially impair his chance of obtaining return performance, or materially reduce its value to him. . . ." What constitutes "material increase" depends on the nature of the contract and the circumstances. Here, it is clear that an assignment of the indemnity provision would significantly increase the risk to Kaufmann Construction Co. (Kaufmann) (D). The substance of the indemnity provision indicates that it was intended to protect the owner (identified as Chrysler Corp.) from claims for accident and injury. Kaufmann (D) was protected from

Continued on next page.

the greatest foreseeable risk with regard to Chrysler, however, by workers' compensation laws that would render Chrysler liable in workers' compensation benefits to its employees for injuries suffered on the job. With regard to those claims, Chrysler could not be sued in tort by an injured employee. If the right to indemnification were assigned to Markward & Karafilis, Inc. (Markward) (D), however, the risk to Kaufmann (D) became significantly greater, since Chrysler's employees could then sue Markward (D), which in turn could seek indemnification from Kaufmann (D). Because the risk was significantly increased by the assignment, the assignment was void. The indemnity promise here was aleatory in nature. The obligation to provide indemnification was to arise only when the "owner" was subjected to a claim for injury or damage. By substituting Markward (D) as the owner, the circumstances upon which the clause would be used were greatly increased—that is, with Chrysler as indemnitee, exposure to claims by employees for Chrysler's negligence was nil and by third persons very slim; with Markward (D) as indemnitee, exposure encompassed almost every foreseeable situation. Because the assignment of the indemnity clause to Markward (D) was void, Markward's (D) claim that it was entitled to a directed verdict on the operation of the indemnity clause must fail. [Reverse in part, affirmed in part.]

ANALYSIS

In the authoritative treatise, *Contracts*, by Corbin, it is explained that a party to a contract cannot by assignment change in any material way the performance to be rendered by the other party. Although a party may, via assignment, substitute a new party as holder of the right, the assignor has no power to change the performance that the right requires. Moreover, if the obligor's duty is aleatory in nature, i.e., the obligor has promised to perform only upon the happening of some event that is not certain to occur and that is not within the control of either party, the element that may be described as hazard, chance, or risk, is of special importance, so that an assignment will be void if the obligor's risk is materially increased, that is, if the happening of the uncertain event is made more likely. The promisee cannot change the performance to be rendered, and, in the aleatory case, must not increase the risk that the performance will have to be rendered. An unjustified act increasing this risk discharges the obligor's duty altogether. Corbin provides as an example illustrating this principle the case of a surety being discharged if the creditor discharges the principal debtor or grants him a binding extension of time to pay the debt. These principles also explain why the holder of a fire insurance policy cannot effectively assign the policy rights to a purchaser of the insured property. The burning of that property is the uncertain event upon which the duty of the insurer depends; the risk of its occurrence must not be increased; and the transfer of the property could substantially and considerably increase such risk. Here, the assignment by Chrysler of the indemnity provision to Markward & Karafilis, Inc. (Markward) (D) increased the risk to Kaufmann Construction Co. (Kaufmann) (D) because of the greater likelihood of tort suits by Chrysler employees. Even though the court ruled that the assignment was void, Markward (D) and Kaufmann (D) nevertheless were jointly and severally liable for the jury verdict.

Quicknotes

ALEATORY Dependent on the occurrence of an uncertain or fortuitous event.

CROSS-CLAIM A claim asserted by a plaintiff or defendant to an action against a co-plaintiff or co-defendant, and not against an opposing party, arising out of the same transaction or occurrence as the subject matter of the action.

DIRECTED VERDICT A verdict ordered by the trial judge in a jury trial.

INDEMNIFICATION Reimbursement for losses sustained or security against anticipated loss or damages.

JOINT AND SEVERAL LIABILITY Liability amongst tortfeasors allowing the injured party to bring suit against any of the defendants, individually or collectively, and to recover from each up to the total amount of damages awarded.

WORKERS' COMPENSATION Fixed awards provided to employees for job-related injuries.

Bel-Ray Company v. Chemrite (Pty) Ltd.

Seller (P) v. Buyer (D)

181 F.3d 435 (3d Cir. 1999)

NATURE OF CASE: Breach of contract.

FACT SUMMARY: Bel-Rey Company (P) sued Lubritene (D) for breach of an agreement assigned to it by Chemrite (Pty) Ltd. (D)

RULE OF LAW

Contractual provisions limiting or prohibiting assignments operate only to limit the parties' right to assign the contract, but not their power to do so, unless the parties manifest an intention to the contrary with specificity.

FACTS: Bel-Ray Company (P), a New Jersey corporation, entered into agreements with a South African corporation, Chemrite (Pty) Ltd. (Chemrite) (D), for the distribution of its products in South Africa. Later, Lubritene (D) acquired Chemrite's (D) business, including rights under the agreements with Bel-Rey (P). Bel-Rey (P) brought suit against Lubritene (D), charging it with fraud and violation of the agreements. The district court granted Bel-Rey (P) an order to arbitrate and Lubritene (D) appealed.

ISSUE: Do contractual provisions limiting or prohibiting assignments operate only to limit the parties' right to assign the contract, but not their power to do so, unless the parties manifest an intention to the contrary with specificity?

HOLDING AND DECISION: (Stapleton, J.) Yes. Contractual provisions limiting or prohibiting assignments operate only to limit the parties' right to assign the contract, but not their power to do so, unless the parties manifest an intention to the contrary with specificity. None of the agreements here contain language specifically stating that an assignment without Bel-Rey Company's (P) written consent would be void or invalid. Such language is not requisitely clear to limit Chemrite (Pty) Ltd.'s (D) power to assign the agreements; thus, the order to compel Lubritene (D) to arbitrate is enforceable. Affirmed.

ANALYSIS

Under the Federal Arbitration Act, a court may compel arbitration only if the parties have entered into a written agreement to arbitrate that covers the particular dispute.

Quicknotes

ARBITRATION An alternative resolution process where a dispute is heard and decided by a neutral third party, rather than through legal proceedings.

ASSIGNMENT A transaction in which a party conveys his or her entire interest in property to another.

Delacy Investments, Inc. v. Thurman & Re/Max Real Estate Guide, Inc.

Commissions factoring company (P) v. Real estate brokerage firm (D)

Minn. Ct. App., 693 N.W.2d 479 (2005)

NATURE OF CASE: Appeal from summary judgment for defendant in action for payment of account receivable.

FACT SUMMARY: Delacy Investments, Inc. d/b/a Commission Express (CE) (P), a commissions-factoring company, contended that commissions generated by Thurman on the sale of real estate that Thurman had assigned to CE (P) belonged to CE (P) because Re/Max Real Estate Guide, Inc. (Re/Max) (D), the real estate broker through which Thurman generated the commissions on the basis of an independent-contractor agreement, was on notice of the previously executed assignment agreement between CE (P) and Thurman.

RULE OF LAW

Under Uniform Commercial Code (UCC) § 9-404, a secured assignee is not entitled to payment of an account receivable where the assignor is not entitled to the account, but an account debtor is entitled to it, even where the account debtor has notice of a previously executed assignment agreement between the assignor and assignee.

FACTS: Thurman, a real estate agent, entered into an agreement with Delacy Investments, Inc. d/b/a Commission Express (CE) (P), a commissions-factoring company, whereby he assigned his future commissions, or accounts receivable, to CE (P). CE (P) had a security interest in the accounts receivable and perfected this interest by filing a Uniform Commercial Code (UCC) financing statement with the state. Over a year later, Thurman entered a standard independent-contractor agreement with Re/Max Real Estate Guide, Inc. (Re/Max) (D), a real estate broker. Under the agreement with Re/Max (D), Thurman agreed to pay certain overhead expenses, and the agreement provided Thurman would be entitled to commissions only to the extent that they exceeded Thurman's past-due financial obligations to Re/Max (D). Thus, under the agreement with CE (P), Thurman was the assignee, CE (P) was the assignor, and Re/Max (D) was an "account debtor," meaning that Re/Max had the potential right to receive that which Thurman assigned to CE (P). A couple of months later, Re/Max (D) executed an acknowledgment of CE's (P) security interest in Thurman's account receivable from the sale of certain real estate. Accordingly, Re/Max (D) directed that the commission be paid directly to CE (P). Subsequently, Thurman and CE (P) entered an agreement whereby Thurman assigned to CE (P) $10,000 of a commission he anticipated earning on the sale of a different property. Less than a couple of months later, Re/Max (D) terminated Thurman for poor performance and other performance-related issues. At the time of his termination Thurman owed Re/Max (D) over $11,000. Consequently, Re/Max (D) refused to pay the assigned receivable to CE (P) and, as per the independent-contractor agreement, applied the commission to Thurman's balance. CE (P) brought suit for payment of $10,000 of Thurman's account receivable. The trial court granted summary judgment to Re/Max (D), finding that because Thurman was not entitled to the commission, neither was CE (P). The state's intermediate appellate court granted review.

ISSUE: Under Uniform Commercial Code (UCC) § 9-404, is a secured assignee entitled to payment of an account receivable where the assignor is not entitled to the account, but an account debtor is entitled to it, even where the account debtor has notice of a previously executed assignment agreement between the assignor and assignee?

HOLDING AND DECISION: (Halbrooks, J.) No. Under Uniform Commercial Code (UCC) § 9-404, a secured assignee is not entitled to payment of an account receivable where the assignor is not entitled to the account, but an account debtor is entitled to it, even where the account debtor has notice of a previously executed assignment agreement between the assignor and assignee. This is a case of first impression in this jurisdiction. However, under UCC § 9-404, an assignee's rights are subject to all terms of the agreement between the account debtor and the assignor. Therefore, so long as Thurman was not entitled to collect a commission while his fees were in arrears, Delacy Investments, Inc. d/b/a Commission Express (CE) (P) was not entitled to the commission because it did not have a greater right to the commission than Thurman did. Or, as the official comment to the UCC indicates, an assignee generally takes an assignment subject to the defenses and claims of an account debtor. Moreover, it makes no difference whether the defense or claim accrues before or after the account debtor is notified of the assignment. Thus, under UCC § 9-404(a)(1), the rights of CE (P) are subject to all the terms of the independent-contractor agreement between Thurman and Re/Max Real Estate Guide, Inc. (Re/Max) (D). This conclusion is supported by black-letter law that an assignee can take no greater rights than the assignor and cannot be in a better position than the assignor, and it is also supported by case law from other

Continued on next page.

jurisdictions. For all these reasons, CE (P) is bound by the independent-contractor agreement and is not entitled to the commission. Nonetheless, CE (P) contends that under UCC § 9-404(a)(2), Re/Max (D), as an account debtor, was not permitted to contract away the rights of Thurman as assignee after having received notice of the previously executed assignment agreement. Although CE (P) is correct in asserting that Re/Max (D) had notice of the agreement, a perfected security interest is generally effective against creditors except as otherwise provided in the UCC. UCC § 9-404(a)(1) provides otherwise, so UCC § 9-404(a)(2) is inapplicable here. UCC § 9-404(a)(1) makes it clear that CE's (P) rights "are subject to . . . all terms of the agreement between the account debtor and assignor." Therefore, the trial court did not err by granting summary judgment to Re/Max (D). Affirmed.

ANALYSIS

In keeping with the holding of this case, the Restatement (Second) of Contracts § 336, ct. b (1981) explains that an assignor can assign "only what he has" and "is subject to limitations imposed by the terms of that contract [creating the right] and to defenses which would have been available against the [account debtor] had there been no assignment."

Quicknotes

ASSIGNEE A party to whom another party assigns its interest or rights.

ASSIGNOR A party who assigns its interest or rights to another.

SUMMARY JUDGMENT A judgment rendered by a court in response to a motion made by one of the parties, claiming that the lack of a question of material fact in respect to an issue warrants disposition of the issue without consideration by the jury.

Glossary

Common Latin Words and Phrases Encountered in the Law

A FORTIORI: Because one fact exists or has been proven, therefore a second fact that is related to the first fact must also exist.

A PRIORI: From the cause to the effect. A term of logic used to denote that when one generally accepted truth is shown to be a cause, another particular effect must necessarily follow.

AB INITIO: From the beginning; a condition that has existed throughout, as in a marriage that was void ab initio.

ACTUS REUS: The wrongful act; in criminal law, such action as is sufficient to trigger criminal liability.

AD VALOREM: According to value; an ad valorem tax is imposed upon an item located within the taxing jurisdiction calculated by the value of such item.

AMICUS CURIAE: Friend of the court. Its most common usage takes the form of an amicus curiae brief, filed by a person who is not a party to an action but is nonetheless allowed to offer an argument supporting his or her legal interests.

ARGUENDO: In arguing. A statement, possibly hypothetical, made for the purpose of argument.

BILL QUIA TIMET: A bill to quiet title (establish ownership) to real property.

BONA FIDE: True, honest, or genuine. May refer to a person's legal position based on good faith or lacking notice of fraud (such as a bona fide purchaser for value) or to the authenticity of a particular document (such as a bona fide last will and testament).

CAUSA MORTIS: With approaching death in mind. A gift causa mortis is a gift given by a party who feels certain that death is imminent.

CAVEAT EMPTOR: Let the buyer beware. This maxim is reflected in the rule of law that a buyer purchases at his or her own risk because it is the buyer's responsibility to examine, judge, test, and otherwise inspect what he or she is buying.

CERTIORARI: A writ of review. Petitions for review of a case by the United States Supreme Court are most often done by means of a writ of certiorari.

CONTRA: On the other hand. Opposite. Contrary to.

CORAM NOBIS: Before us; a writ of error directed to the court that originally rendered the judgment.

CORAM VOBIS: Before you; a writ of error directed by an appellate court to a lower court to correct a factual error.

CORPUS DELICTI: The body of the crime; the requisite elements of a crime amounting to objective proof that a crime has been committed.

CUM TESTAMENTO ANNEXO, ADMINISTRATOR (ADMINISTRATOR C.T.A.): With will annexed; an administrator c.t.a. settles an estate pursuant to a will in which he or she is not appointed.

DE BONIS NON, ADMINISTRATOR (ADMINISTRATOR D.B.N.): Of goods not administered; an administrator d.b.n. settles a partially settled estate.

DE FACTO: In fact; in reality; actually. Existing in fact but not officially approved or engendered.

DE JURE: By right; lawful. Describes a condition that is legitimate "as a matter of law," in contrast to the term "de facto," which connotes something existing in fact but not legally sanctioned or authorized. For example, de facto segregation refers to segregation brought about by housing patterns, etc., whereas de jure segregation refers to segregation created by law.

DE MINIMUS: Of minimal importance; insignificant; a trifle; not worth bothering about.

DE NOVO: Anew; a second time; afresh. A trial de novo is a new trial held at the appellate level as if the case originated there and the trial at a lower level had not taken place.

DICTA: Generally used as an abbreviated form of obiter dicta, a term describing those portions of a judicial opinion incidental or not necessary to resolution of the specific question before the court. Such nonessential statements and remarks are not considered to be binding precedent.

DUCES TECUM: Refers to a particular type of writ or subpoena requesting a party or organization to produce certain documents in its possession.

EN BANC: Full bench. Where a court sits with all justices present rather than the usual quorum.

EX PARTE: For one side or one party only. An ex parte proceeding is one undertaken for the benefit of only one party, without notice to, or an appearance by, an adverse party.

EX POST FACTO: After the fact. An ex post facto law is a law that retroactively changes the consequences of a prior act.

EX REL.: Abbreviated form of the term "ex relatione," meaning upon relation or information. When the state brings an action in which it has no interest against an individual at the instigation of one who has a private interest in the matter.

FORUM NON CONVENIENS: Inconvenient forum. Although a court may have jurisdiction over the case, the action should be tried in a more conveniently located court, one to which parties and witnesses may more easily travel, for example.

GUARDIAN AD LITEM: A guardian appointed by the court to represent a minor or incompetent person in a legal action.

HABEAS CORPUS: You have the body. The modern writ of habeas corpus is a writ directing that a person (body) being detained (such as a prisoner) be brought before the court so that the legality of his or her detention can be judicially ascertained.

IN CAMERA: In private, in chambers. When a hearing is held before a judge in his or her chambers or when all spectators are excluded from the courtroom.

IN FORMA PAUPERIS: In the manner of a pauper. A party who proceeds in forma pauperis because of his or her poverty is one who is allowed to bring suit without liability for costs.

INFRA: Below, under. A word referring the reader to a later part of a book. (The opposite of supra.)

IN LOCO PARENTIS: In the place of a parent.

IN PARI DELICTO: Equally wrong; a court of equity will not grant requested relief to an applicant who is in pari delicto, or as much at fault in the transactions giving rise to the controversy as is the opponent of the applicant.

IN PARI MATERIA: On like subject matter or upon the same matter. Statutes relating to the same person or things are said to be in pari materia. It is a general rule of statutory construction that such statutes should be construed together, i.e., looked at as if they together constituted one law.

IN PERSONAM: Against the person. Jurisdiction over the person of an individual.

IN RE: In the matter of. Used to designate a proceeding involving an estate or other property.

IN REM: Signifies an action against the res, or thing. An action in rem is basically one that is taken directly against property, as distinguished from an action in personam, i.e., against the person.

INTER ALIA: Among other things. Used to show that the whole of a statement, pleading, list, statute, etc., has not been set forth in its entirety.

INTER PARTES: Between the parties. May refer to contracts, conveyances, or other transactions having legal significance.

INTER VIVOS: Between the living. An inter vivos gift is a gift made by a living grantor, as distinguished from bequests contained in a will, which pass upon the death of the testator.

IPSO FACTO: By the mere fact itself.

JUS: Law or the entire body of law.

LEX LOCI: The law of the place; the notion that the rights of parties to a legal proceeding are governed by the law of the place where those rights arose.

MALUM IN SE: Evil or wrong in and of itself; inherently wrong. Describes an act that is wrong by its very nature, as opposed to one which would not be wrong but for the fact that there is a specific legal prohibition against it (malum prohibitum).

MALUM PROHIBITUM: Wrong because prohibited, but not inherently evil. Describes something that is wrong because it is expressly forbidden by law but that is not in and of itself evil, e.g., speeding.

MANDAMUS: We command. A writ directing an official to take a certain action.

MENS REA: A guilty mind; a criminal intent. A term used to signify the mental state that accompanies a crime or other prohibited act. Some crimes require only a general mens rea (general intent to do the prohibited act), but others, like assault with intent to murder, require the existence of a specific mens rea.

MODUS OPERANDI: Method of operating; generally refers to the manner or style of a criminal in committing crimes, admissible in appropriate cases as evidence of the identity of a defendant.

NEXUS: A connection to.

NISI PRIUS: A court of first impression. A nisi prius court is one where issues of fact are tried before a judge or jury.

N.O.V. (NON OBSTANTE VEREDICTO): Notwithstanding the verdict. A judgment n.o.v. is a judgment given in favor of one party despite the fact that a verdict was returned in favor of the other party, the justification being that the verdict either had no reasonable support in fact or was contrary to law.

NUNC PRO TUNC: Now for then. This phrase refers to actions that may be taken and will then have full retroactive effect.

PENDENTE LITE: Pending the suit; pending litigation underway.

PER CAPITA: By head; beneficiaries of an estate, if they take in equal shares, take per capita.

PER CURIAM: By the court; signifies an opinion ostensibly written "by the whole court" and with no identified author.

PER SE: By itself, in itself; inherently.

PER STIRPES: By representation. Used primarily in the law of wills to describe the method of distribution where a person, generally because of death, is unable to take that which is left to him or her by the will of another, and therefore his or her heirs divide such property between them rather than take under the will individually.

PRIMA FACIE: On its face, at first sight. A prima facie case is one that is sufficient on its face, meaning that the evidence supporting it is adequate to establish the case until contradicted or overcome by other evidence.

PRO TANTO: For so much; as far as it goes. Often used in eminent domain cases when a property owner receives partial payment for his or her land without prejudice to his or her right to bring suit for the full amount he or she claims the land to be worth.

QUANTUM MERUIT: As much as the party deserves. Refers to recovery based on the doctrine of unjust enrichment in those cases in which a party has rendered valuable services or furnished materials that were accepted and enjoyed by another under circumstances that would reasonably notify the recipient that the rendering party expected to be paid. In essence, the law implies a contract to pay the reasonable value of the services or materials furnished.

QUASI: Almost like; as if; nearly. Essentially used to signify that one subject or thing is almost analogous to another but that material differences between them do exist. For example, a quasi-criminal proceeding is one that is not strictly criminal but shares enough of the same characteristics to require some of the same safeguards (e.g., procedural due process must be followed in a parole hearing).

QUID PRO QUO: Something for something. In contract law, the consideration, something of value, passed between the parties to render the contract binding.

RES GESTAE: Things done. In evidence law, this principle justifies the admission of a statement that would otherwise be hearsay when it is made so closely to the event in question as to be said to be a part of it, or with such spontaneity as not to have the possibility of falsehood.

RES IPSA LOQUITUR: The thing speaks for itself. This doctrine gives rise to a rebuttable presumption of negligence when the instrumentality causing the injury was within the exclusive control of the defendant, and the injury was one that does not normally occur unless a person has been negligent.

RES JUDICATA: A matter adjudged. Doctrine that provides that once a court of competent jurisdiction has rendered a final judgment or decree on the merits, that judgment or decree is conclusive upon the parties to the case and prevents them from engaging in any other litigation on the points and issues determined therein.

RESPONDEAT SUPERIOR: Let the master reply. This doctrine holds the master liable for the wrongful acts of his or her servant (or the principal for his or her agent) in those cases in which the servant (or agent) was acting within the scope of his or her authority at the time of the injury.

STARE DECISIS: To stand by or adhere to that which has been decided. The common-law doctrine of stare decisis attempts to give security and certainty to the law by following the policy that once a principle of law as applicable to a certain set of facts has been set forth in a decision, it forms a precedent that will subsequently be followed, even though a different decision might be made were it the first time the question had arisen. Of course, stare decisis is not an inviolable principle and is departed from in instances where there is good cause (e.g., considerations of public policy led the Supreme Court to disregard prior decisions sanctioning segregation).

SUPRA: Above. A word referring a reader to an earlier part of a book. (The opposite of infra.)

ULTRA VIRES: Beyond the power. This phrase is most commonly used to refer to actions taken by a corporation that are beyond the power or legal authority of the corporation.

Addendum of French Derivatives

CHATTEL: Tangible personal property.

CY PRES: Doctrine permitting courts to apply trust funds to purposes not expressed in the trust but necessary to carry out the settlor's intent.

IN PAIS: Not pursuant to legal proceedings.

PER AUTRE VIE: For another's life; during another's life. In property law, an estate may be granted that will terminate upon the death of someone other than the grantee.

PROFIT A PRENDRE: A license to remove minerals or other produce from land.

VOIR DIRE: Process of questioning jurors as to their predispositions about the case or parties to a proceeding in order to identify those jurors displaying bias or prejudice.